Table of Contents

Section One: The Search

Section Two: The Information

Section Three: Beyond the Quatrains

Indices

Other books by Dolores Cannon

Conversations with Nostradamus, Volume I
Conversations with Nostradamus, Volume II
Jesus and the Essenes

Conversations with Nostradamus is available
in abridged form on audio tape cassette.

Forthcoming books by Dolores Cannon

Keepers of the Garden
Conversation with a Spirit
A Soul Remembers Hiroshima

For more information about any
of the above titles, write to:

OZARK MOUNTAIN PUBLISHERS

P.O. Box 754
Huntsville, AR 72740-0754

Wholesale Inquiries Welcome

Conversations
with
Nostradamus
His Prophecies Explained

Volume Three

BY

DOLORES CANNON

OZARK MOUNTAIN PUBLISHERS

P.O. Box 754
Huntsville, AR 72740-0754

For permission, or serialization, condensation, adaptions, or for our catalog of other publications, write to Ozark Mountain Publishers, P.O. Box 754, Huntsville, AR 72740-0754, Attn.: Permission Department.

Library of Congress Cataloging-in-Publication Data
Cannon, Dolores, 1931–
    Conversations with Nostradamus/by Dolores Cannon
    Communications from Nostradamus via several mediums through
    hypnosis, supervised by D. Cannon. Includes the Prophecies
    of Nostradamus, in Middle French with English translation.
    Includes cumulative index for all three volumes.
    Contents: v. I–II (Revised editions); v. III (First edition)
        1. Nostradamus, 1503–1566. 2. Prophecies. 3. Hypnosis.
    4. Reincarnation therapy. 5. Astrology.
    I. Cannon, Dolores, 1931–   II. Nostradamus, 1503–1566.
    Prophecies. English & French. 1992   III. Title.
Library of Congress Catalog Card Number: 92-60547
ISBN 0-9632776-3-4 (v. III)

Cover Design: Joe Alexander
Book set in Old Style 7, San Marco & Eurostile typefaces.
Book Design: Kris Kleeberg

Published by:
OZARK MOUNTAIN PUBLISHERS
P.O. Box 754
Huntsville, AR 72740-0754
Printed in the United States of America
First Edition

Section One
The Search

Chapter 1

The Adventure
Will Not Cease

I FELT THE DISAPPOINTMENT DEEPLY when it appeared that my connections with Nostradamus were severed in late 1987. I had come to enjoy my visits with the learned man. I felt like a tyro-student sitting at the feet of the great master. Feeling totally inadequate to comprehend even a portion of the knowledge within him, I at least grasped at straws and tried to ask questions that would help impart some of that knowledge to others. Instead of becoming enlightened by my participation in this project, I more often than not felt like a struggling schoolgirl being chastised by a stern yet loving schoolmaster. I found that he possessed a wonderful sense of humor, although at times his wit could become biting and almost cruel. He had great impatience with ignorance or what he perceived to be stupidity. Several times I had the impression that he felt out-of-place in his own time period. He had unintentionally isolated himself because his interests were so far beyond those of his peers that it was difficult to find anyone he could share anything with. Maybe this was why he found solace with the beings of the future. At least we could understand that many of his visions and predictions would have caused him great harm or even death if he voiced them in his time. He said that some of his students understood a portion of what he was trying to impart. But he was also isolated from them because he was a man out-of-place, a man with an intellect and ability far ahead of his time. I sometimes felt a sadness coming from the man because he knew no one would ever truly understand. But at least I felt we were helping him, allowing him an outlet, a way to express his emotions and fears across the expanse of time. Maybe we were helping him in this way as much as he was helping us.

But now that all seemed to have come to a close. In my work as a hypnotist-regressionist the information does not come from my own mind. It must come from others, subjects that have the stories of past lives locked within their subconscious. Or in the case of Nostradamus, subjects who have the ability to enter a deep trance level and follow his instructions to locate him beyond the portal of time. Once there they also must have the ability to translate complex symbolism into images we can understand. All of these traits were not easy to find. I had been fortunate to have accomplished this with three subjects, but I still considered this more luck than expertise. In each case events in their lives had taken precedence and I was only able to work with these people in passing. Our lives touched briefly and they then went in other directions. My work was never their main interest or concern—their own life was. And this is as it should be. The finding of three people who were able to contact Nostradamus was against all laws of coincidence. I should have been satisfied with that. How many times did I expect to accomplish the impossible? I had been given enough material to complete two books. The stories of these contacts were told in Volume One and Two. I would have to close the door on this adventure and continue with my myriad of other projects. I was still working with many subjects, following various stories that claimed my interest and which I felt would evolve into books at some time in the future. I was certainly not at a loss for something to write about. But in the back of my mind was the nagging feeling of leaving a task uncompleted. I had promised Nostradamus I would help with the translation and interpretation of his quatrains into modern English, and the job was only half-done. Maybe there was nothing new in the remaining 500 untranslated quatrains. Maybe he had conveyed the essential story to us and we would have to be satisfied with that. Maybe this was all that had ever been expected of me and my job was finished. Maybe, but then why did I have the feeling I was letting him down? I knew I had no choice in the matter. Without a suitable subject to work through the project was in limbo and I had to consider that door closed.

My first contact had been made in 1986 through the mature Elena, artist and mother of ten children. She had been the key, the primary catalyst or bridge, when it was discovered through an ordinary past-life regression that she had been a student of Nostradamus in France during the 1500s. This surprise revelation led to Nostradamus speaking directly to me and handing me the assignment of translating his quatrains or prophecies. He wanted people to understand them and be warned about what the future held for our world. But this communication was cut short when Elena moved back to Alaska. It was obvious from the beginning that she had not consciously instigated this project because it frightened her and she was glad to have an excuse to be free of the obligation. It was not so easy for me because my curiosity had been sparked, and I became determined to try to reestablish communication with Nostradamus.

Brenda, a college music student, became the second contact in 1986. By following Nostradamus' instructions I was able to locate him again through the vastness of time. He had been waiting and was confident that our link would not be broken. He knew our connection would be repeated through another subject. He had told me that once the communication had been established I would never lose contact with him. He said he would come through anyone I worked with. That was a tall order because I work with so many people. I had attempted it through Brenda because during my work with her I had found her to be an excellent somnambulistic subject who was willing to participate in experimentation. Volume One told the story of how all of this came about and contained the results of translating over 300 of the quatrains in six months. Abiding by Nostradamus' instructions and because of space limitations, I concentrated on the prophecies pertaining to our immediate future.

The sequel, Volume Two, came about because the story took a different turn. In 1987 after working on this project for six months, Brenda reached a point where her education and job demanded so much of her time that she could no longer continue to work with me. John Feeley was an astrologer who had agreed to help me find the dates hidden in the labyrinth of symbols in the quatrains. He was eager to complete his work because he was moving to Florida and would no longer be able to assist me. He suggested that I attempt contacting Nostradamus through him. John was intrigued with the idea of working one on one with the great man as one astrologer to another. He felt a great deal of information could come through that would not be available to the average person. Thus the attempt was made with a third subject, and by following Nostradamus' instructions it was highly successful. The second book told the story of John's interaction with the great man. In May of 1987 John moved to Florida and the only contact I had with him after that was by phone or mail as he clarified portions of the manuscript. With my two main contacts out of commission, my ties with Nostradamus were then severed and I had to resign myself with working on other projects.

After John left I began hypnosis work with MUFON (Mutual UFO Network) on cases of suspected abductions by aliens. My life took another turn and I began to gather information in a totally new field. I am still accumulating it and this information will eventually be put into a book. Thus, for nearly two years (1987 to 1989) my attention turned away from Nostradamus and the translating of the quatrains.

During this time I completed the first volume of this work, and in the beginning of 1988 a publisher was found. I was caught up in the final editing chores, and the first of the trilogy was printed in April 1989. As far as I was concerned that part of my life (the translating of the quatrains) was over and I was going in different directions. I was soon giving lectures about my work and as I lost my anonymity, my life became even busier than it was before. I had Volume Two, the story from John's point of view, in rough manuscript form and I was also working on several other books that were in various stages of development.

The catalyst that started the whole process going again was my publisher. For over a year-and-a-half I had not thought about further contact with the prophet. I thought my job was finished and I was involved in the printing of the two books. Then in the spring of 1989 my publisher called and asked me what I thought of the possibility of a third book, to make the Nostradamus material into a trilogy. I told him I had not thought about it in a long time, even though there were about 500 quatrains left untranslated. I said it was not up to me; it had never been up to me. The trick would be to find a suitable subject, and I didn't know if that were possible. I agreed to consider it and see what I could do, even though I secretly thought it would be hopeless. Did I really want to open up that can of worms again? What if it failed? What if something happened that would discredit the work I had done thus far? Could something shake my belief in the contacts or even contradict them? I believed totally in the validity of what I had accomplished, but was it worth taking a chance? All the human emotions reared their heads trying to cast doubt on the material I had received. But I had only to think of the tremendous body of proof that Nostradamus had presented to me to reinforce my beliefs that it could not possibly have been done by normal means. But maybe it was better to leave it alone. It would be a chore to find another suitable subject. The Nostradamus work was tedious and I didn't feel I really wanted to get into it again. My thoughts wrangled back and forth and indecision reigned supreme. Let sleeping dogs lie was my conclusion. Nostradamus had accomplished his purpose. He had transferred his story through to me and it was now printed. I had fulfilled my task. Surely he was pleased and satisfied with the results, and I need no longer feel an obligation to him.

When my publisher sent out his Spring 1989 catalog, the first volume of this work was listed. There was a remark in the description of the book that forever changed my mind and sent me searching once again for a contact. It said, "This is the first of two, possibly three, volumes in which Nostradamus deciphers his quatrains." My publisher apparently was sure I could produce another book and at last finish the quatrains. If he had that much faith in me then I knew I must at least try. I would have to start my search again. But where should I begin? Which of the many subjects I worked with would make the best guinea pig? I knew then that I had only been fooling myself by thinking the work was over. The fire Nostradamus had lit in me three years previously had not gone out; it had only become a smoldering ember. It did not take much to cause it to blaze again. My curiosity was once more being sparked, and when that happens, I cannot stop until the task is finished. Yes, I knew I must search and I did not know what, if anything, I could find. The door had been opened again, but what lay behind it was shrouded in mystery.

Chapter 2

The Search Begins

NOW THAT I HAD MADE THE DECISION to try to reestablish contact with Nostradamus, the obvious question was: where to begin? Who would be the most likely of my subjects to make the initial attempt? It had to be someone who was capable of entering the deepest possible trance, the somnambulist level. I had several that fell into that category. I had worked with them for so many years that they were well conditioned and accustomed to my methods and my odd requests. Experimentation did not bother them. But would they be able to do this type of work?

I finally decided Phil would be my first choice, since Nostradamus had stressed that I use a male entity if possible. He said his energies meshed better with a male energy. I had found through my work with him that Nostradamus was extremely chauvinistic and disliked working through women unless there was no other choice. This request made it difficult for me since most of my subjects are female. They seem to be intuitively and instinctively able to do this type of work, maybe because intuition is part of a woman's survival make-up.

I had worked with Phil for five years and he had developed into an excellent channeler as well as a deep-level hypnotic subject. My book, *Keepers of the Garden,* tells of my first experiences with him. He is a dark-haired, attractive young man who works in electronics. During hypnotic exploration into past lives it was discovered that he was a "star person." His present incarnation is his first lifetime spent on the planet Earth. All of his previous incarnations were spent on other planets and in other dimensions. This story is told in that book. But there had been one unexpected problem when working with Phil. He is a very gentle person and it distressed him to work on anything that had negative vibrations. He seemed to integrate some of it into his consciousness. It acted as a residue, staying with him and carrying over into his waking state. Certain types of topics: murder, suicide, *etc.,* would cause him to be depressed for weeks afterward. From past experience I knew it was impossible to work with Nostradamus and stay away from negativity. The man seemed to strive on it, seeing man's actions in the most horrible terms. I had to desert my last project with Phil because it bothered him too much to pursue it. I did not know if he was the correct type of energy to obtain this information, even though he was an excellent channel. This was a different type of situation and not everyone would be capable of handling it. The odds were against it succeeding with him, but in the beginning he seemed to be the most likely choice. I thought, "Nothing ventured, nothing gained."

When I met with him early in 1989, I did not tell him what I was going to attempt, except that it was an experiment and it had nothing to do with our last disturbing project. He was agreeable to trying it. He settled down on the couch, and even though we had not worked together for quite a while the keyword and instructions worked perfectly, and he slipped easily into a deep trance. When I finished counting he found himself surrounded by light that appeared to be coming from everywhere, which gave him a very safe feeling. I explained that I wanted to perform an experiment.

P: We would ask that you please define the type of information and the area you wish to explore.

In the past when I had worked with Phil a group that called themselves the "council of twelve" would sometimes come through and supply the answers. This is why it did not bother me when Phil referred to himself as the plural "we." This group appeared to be similar to his guides, and had been beneficial in helping us through difficult topics. Their help might be necessary to facilitate the reconnection with Nostradamus.

D: *I have been working for quite a while with Nostradamus, who lived in the 1500s in France. He was giving me information that he considered vital to our time period. Do you think it is possible for you to go and see the place where Nostradamus was living in the 1500s in France?*

P: We would say that at this time this channel does not have the ability to transport himself to that dimension. That is a plane in which he has no experience in relating. We would, however, say that it is possible to establish a telepathic link, so that the information could be given. Due to the nature of the individuals involved, that could be arranged.

D: *I know it's not against any rules or regulations because we were doing it for the last three years.*

P: That is accurate. You would not have been allowed the initial contact if it had not been permitted. (*Pause*) The difference in energies is such that there is too much resistance in attempting to establish this link. At this time it is beyond the capabilities of this channel.

D: *Do you mean the energies are not compatible?*

P: That is accurate.

D: (I was disappointed, but it was not unexpected.) *He told me to attempt it with a male energy.*

P: We would say that we could attempt contact by a different method. Perhaps through visualization this entity, Nostradamus, could be

aligned with the channel. We would ask that you coach him in this visualization process.

D: *All right. I would like to reestablish contact, but I don't want to do anything that he's not comfortable with.*

P: We perceive that your motives are indeed of the highest order, and therefore are with our blessing.

D: *We could experiment anyway. Could you help him to visualize what Nostradamus looks like, and the place where he works?*

The results were instantaneous. Whether he was transported there, or if the scene was brought to him, is probably unimportant. Each subject has improvised their own method. As long as it is effective and produces results, the process is unimportant.

P: I'm seeing a low ceiling. The walls seem to be made of something like mud or plaster of some sort. I saw a glimpse of an old man with a long, scraggly gray beard. He had a shock of hair, mixed gray and black like salt and pepper. There seems to be a wooden frame around the doorway, posts. There's a wooden table, not very large, rather off-centered in the room. It is not a large room, but it has a low ceiling.

D: *Is there any other furniture?*

P: There's some type of a wooden hutch against the wall. It appears to have some vials, jars and so forth, in the cabinet. There's a light on the table, and a heavy, solid chair made of wood. There seems to be a fireplace somewhere nearby, because there's the heavy smell of smoke hanging in the air. And there's a window looking outside. I can see a whitewashed house through the window.

D: *Is there anything else on the table?*

P: There appears to be a mirror. It's rather large, about picture size. It's a writing table. There's a quill pen and a jar of ink. There are papers, formulas for medicines. Recipes for making potions and tonics, elixirs, compacts, such as powders and mixes that can be placed on burns or ... cuts. I can't make out the word. It's not a word that we use today, but it would be ... a scrape. I can see him more clearly now.

D: *What is he doing?*

P: He's regarding me. He's just holding his chin with one hand, and his other arm is across his chest. I seem to be fading in and out while establishing communication. He seems to be waiting for me to materialize. He is watching with curiosity and a mixture of amazement and humor, perhaps. Fascination.

D: *Can you mentally ask him if he has seen spirits before?*

P: He would be amused at that suggestion. He is very familiar with those from this time frame who come and go. This is simply a *new* face on the scene.

D: *Does he know that I am in communication, too?*

P: He senses that this is occurring in conjunction with the work which he is doing with those of the 20th century, as he calls them. He perceives your personality through the entity translations.

D: *Can you tell him that the other vehicle left, and that's why I have brought forth a new vehicle?*

P: Yes, he is pleased. He says this vehicle will work very well.

D: *Does he remember the assignment that he gave me?*

P: He says the details are too early to discuss at this time, as we have yet to establish a working relationship. He does not trust the information with one whom he does not know well yet.—He would ask the name "John."

D: *John? John was one of the vehicles I used.*

P: That is accurate.

Surprisingly, he was referring to John, the astrologer, who had participated in deciphering and supplying dates to the various astrological quatrains. His valuable contributions are told in Volume One and Two.

D: *Our first communication occurred when I communicated with one of his students. Does he have students at this time?*

P: He is a physician or healer in middle age, and has no students at this time.

D: *Has he had students in the past?*

P: Yes, when he was younger.

D: *Was one of these students a young man from another country?*

P: He says he will not speak of those whom he has trained, as the confidentiality of the teacher-student relationship would be broken.

D: *Yes, I understand that. But tell him that I had communication with the Greek one. Does this make sense to him?*

P: He says there are many ways one can communicate. And, as yet, you ask too many questions. The relationship has not been firmly established yet. He would ask that you simply continue your dialogue, so that he can regard this entity more closely.

D: *What do you look like to him?*

P: He sees a translucent shimmering, as perhaps a focus of light shimmering and trying to materialize in his study. He is used to seeing spirit-type apparitions. He is attempting to perceive this with his higher facilities. He senses that I am from the 20th century, but he's not sure of the intent at this point. He senses that this is not a usual type of entity, and he is somewhat suspicious, or perhaps more accurately, wary. He perceives a higher order; however, he is very suspicious of all those entities of the spirit world. To him his work is very important and very secretive. He wouldn't just give it to anybody that happened to show up.

This was very similar to the way John appeared to Nostradamus. He also saw himself as a glowing spirit type. The difference Nostradamus was perceiving was undoubtedly associated with Phil's "star person" type of energy. Maybe it was resonating differently and this was causing

Nostradamus to be suspicious. He apparently had no intention of proceeding with our project and revealing any information until he was sure of the situation. He never displayed this type of wariness with any of the other subjects I worked with. This could be another indication that he perceived Phil as something totally different.

D: *He contacted us. We are spirits from the future.*

P: He is saying that it was *you* who contacted *him*. He reciprocated.

D: *He told me once it could work either way because the wheel of karma goes round and round.*

P: That is accurate.

D: *But we had set up a communication that was dealing with his prophecies.*

P: He does not want to discuss that at this time as this is a very highly secretive endeavor. And he is, again, not convinced of the purpose of this materialization.

D: *He became concerned that people wouldn't understand what he was prophesying. We were contacted in the future because he wanted to tell us what he was seeing.*

P: That is accurate. He wished the hindsight of those who had seen the validity of his prophecies. Not only to understand his own prophecies better, through the realization of what he had seen, but also to verify to himself that these indeed were valid prophecies, and not imaginings.

D: *He also said he wanted to warn us.*

P: That is accurate. These are visions he had seen. Through his humanitarian endeavors he felt he must translate them and give them to the world so that the future generations could be spared the results of their foolishness. This he foresaw and has, as yet, helped to divert. This, again, is one of his needs or desires: to communicate with the future generations to see the effectiveness of his warnings. Were they heeded?

D: *Yes, this is what we were told. He wanted us to convey these warnings to our time.*

P: That is accurate. He desires the knowledge that his help was indeed helpful.

D: *Has he written his prophecies down yet on paper?*

P: He is not saying. Again, as to the privacy of this endeavor, there is not given that information.

D: *Well, he felt the need to disguise these prophecies for his own protection.*

P: He would say that the need to disguise was not for the benefit of those to whom they were given, but to allow them to pass through time to those for whom they were directed.

D: *Yes. We were told it was for his own safety, too.*

P: That is accurate. At that time there were those who desired to eliminate him. Were it to be seen that he was predicting the future, he would then be blamed *for* it. It would have been assumed that he was causing that which he had simply seen.

D: *Yes, I can understand. Is this enough proof as to who we are, or does he desire something more?*

P: He, as yet, simply needs time to develop a rapport with this entity.

D: *Would it help if I read one of the quatrains?*

P: Perhaps.

D: *Is the communication mental?* (Yes.) *I will read one in my language and see if he recognizes it.* (CENTURY I-I) *"Sitting alone at night in secret study; it is placed on the brass tripod. A slight flame comes out of the emptiness and makes successful that which should not be believed in vain."*

P: Yes, he recognizes it. Although he said it has not been translated accurately from the original.

D: *What is wrong with it?*

P: The concept has been distorted, and therefore the translation would be difficult to give. Again there's this hesitation. As yet there has not been sufficient time for the rapport necessary to establish trust.

D: *Is there anything I can do?*

P: Simply allow this communication to continue, and in so doing the familiarity and trust will grow. It is as if his most trusted work were being dealt with by a total stranger; therefore you can see his reluctance to participate. However, he again is stressing the need for absolute trust.

D: *You said he is in his middle age?*

P: Yes, although now I see him differently. He's younger, and seems to be in his thirties. He has a full head of longer black hair that's rather wavy. It's not a *fine* complexion, but a medium complexion. He has sort of a square face and is clean-shaven. He's solid built and somewhat stocky in appearance. His long nose seems to be prominent, and he has bushy eyebrows.

I decided to ask test questions:

D: *Has he been a physician for very long?*

P: Professionally not so long.

D: *What does he teach his students?*

P: Many things other than simply medicine. Philosophy, mathematics, good business sense, by being more of a mentor.

D: *Are these students in the university, or private students?*

P: Private students.

D: *Is he married at this time?*

P: Yes, but I get the feeling there isn't a lot of love there. It's more of a functional marriage. He somewhat looks down on her. She's functional as a wife, but not what he would call a very intelligent woman. He is really interested in his work, and he apparently admires intelligence. I think she's rather slow or ignorant or something.

D: *Most women in those days were uneducated. Does he have any children at this time in his life?*

P: Yes, a small baby, I believe. Although he seems detached, not very caring. He seems more interested in his work than in raising a family.

D: *Is he doing any writing at this younger time in his life?*

P: He's written one book on medicine. He takes note of many things. He collects his recollections and stores them in something similar to a diary. His interest is not in writing, but in collecting knowledge.

D: *Then the two of us are alike in that respect. Apparently he is not involved with the prophecies at that younger age.*

P: Not that he would admit.

D: *Can you locate him again at the older age?*

The switch was immediate.

P: Yes. He seems to be annoyed. Apparently he has work to do, and wishes to dismiss us.

D: *Then we're bothering him at this time?*

P: It's not so much bothering; it's simply taking his time when he needs to be devoting it to more important things.

D: *What type of work is he doing?*

P: He doesn't wish to say. He simply wishes to dismiss us politely.

D: *But before we go, can he tell me a way that I can contact him again— at a time when he would like to communicate?*

P: He says to send the boy.

D: *Who does he mean?*

P: (*Amused.*) Me. He called me a boy. He doesn't have a name for me, and that's his perception, I suppose.

D: *In his time frame you wouldn't really be that young. Maybe something happens in this process, and he perceives you as a younger energy.*

P: Could be. Maybe it's part of my personality that shows through and not my physical age.

D: *How can we contact him?*

P: This method would be proper, if it is appropriate and he is not busy.

D: *I thought maybe we had to have instructions to reach him.*

P: We have already reached him.

D: *Then I will instruct this vehicle, the boy, to go to his study?*

P: To simply find him.

D: *And he will work with me at that time?*

P: Hopefully.

D: *Well, I do hope that he will start to trust you.*

P: With time.

After Phil returned to his normal conscious state we discussed his memories of the session. He repeated the description of Nostradamus and the room. Phil had the impression that some of Nostradamus' wariness was because other people in his time were trying to find out about his work. Maybe they used unusual methods to spy upon him. It would be something similar to a "War of the Magicians." This could explain why he had to be sure of whom he was talking to before he would reveal any-thing. Also, Phil was certainly being perceived as a different type of energy that Nostradamus did not recognize. All of this probably added to the heightened suspicion. But Phil had a good feeling about the man and was willing to try working with him again.

𝔇URING THE FOLLOWING WEEK, Phil had some strange experiences. When we met for our next session, he tried to describe the eerie feelings that had persisted since the last meeting. I turned on the tape recorder.

P: For about three days after we worked, I could still feel that connection with Nostradamus. There was no dialogue, but I could sense his presence.

D: *Do you mean as a presence in the room or ...*

P: A presence in *me*. That's how I feel when we're working. It's not a presence out there somewhere; it's in *here*. This mind link is like a telepathic link. When you establish it, it's like tuning in to the same channel. And my perceptions are translated to him, and his percep-tions are translated to me. We seem to sense what each other is feel-ing, even though his body is in another century. It is in another time and place, but through the telepathic link we are in communication with each other through our perceptions.

D: *You said he saw you materializing in his room, like a spirit form or something.*

P: Apparently there was some part of myself that he was seeing. I was registering his perceptions. That's how I knew how he felt about his wife. I was feeling what he feels.

I certainly didn't like the idea of one of my subjects being haunted by a specter from the 16th century. I have always tried to make sure that my work was kept separate from their daily lives. To me that is the most important thing; that they continue to function normally in the present-day environment. I do not want the two to overlap.

P: The link was there, as if we were connected, and I could sense his pres-ence and I know he could feel mine. It was quiet, non-verbal. But the feeling was that he was simply observing. It wasn't a friendly feeling like you have with a close friend. It wasn't positive and it wasn't nega-tive. It was very neutral, observant. I could feel it strongly, but it wasn't threatening or uncomfortable. The thing I felt most was a strange sensation of idle curiosity. I was looking at a magazine with colored pictures, and watching TV while this was going on. And it was as if he was observing the television and printed pages with me. I had a feeling this was interesting to him. There were no comments, no questions. It was just simple observation. I assume he was seeing through my eyes and through my perceptions.

D: *Maybe there was some kind of link established during the session, so he could home in on your frequency for a few days. Maybe he wanted to find out more about you.*

P: Apparently that's how it works. It's as if he knows my frequency now, and I know his. And the only thing I have to do to establish communication is to think about how his frequency, his personality, feels. Then I put out my energy to him. And he can or cannot accept it or tune to that, depending on where he is. If he is not focused in some other area and he senses my presence, then he can think of me and we establish the communication. When I think of you or when I'm talking to you, I have a feeling of your personality. That's your frequency. Apparently every personality has a different frequency. If he were to speak to me I wouldn't understand his language. I don't know French, and I assume he doesn't know 20th-century English, but somehow the concepts are translated. We don't need words to translate them. It's a transfer of concepts. My job is to take the concepts that I understand, and attach the words that would translate as closely as possible to the concept that I receive. That's why it's so difficult. I feel that just by talking about him, we've already established contact. It's as if he's ready to communicate because I can sense his presence. It's almost an anticipation. I get the feeling he's happy for this link because he was looking for a technical mind. He's probably been meditating on me through the week. Of course, we never know how long a time frame it has been for him. But I think he's checked me and my intentions out and I guess he feels very comfortable with that. I get the feeling that much of what he saw was technology that he didn't understand, and he needed a technical mind that can translate it for him. He probably needs different minds to make sense of what he's seeing. He apparently is a brilliant person himself because he's able to comprehend what he's seeing.

D: *If he shows you things that are negative, will that bother you?*

P: Negative for me or negative for the planet, or ... ?

D: *For the world.*

P: I don't know how it could get much worse. I see enough negativity in the world today with acid rain and the nuclear situation and politics. I've seen many worse-case scenarios.

D: *You once said if I asked you any questions on certain subjects, like murder or suicide for instance, that it bothered you after the session.*

P: Well, that was human energy negativity. This would probably be a political negativity or an ecological negativity.

D: *What if he showed you a war?*

P: I don't see how it could be worse than what I see on the TV news. It would be upsetting, but I think I could handle it. If it starts bothering me, I can always turn it off.

When the session began, Phil went quickly into trance and immediately traveled to Nostradamus' room, but this time we were in for a surprise. Although the room was just as he had seen it before: the window, the plastered walls, the wooden table with pen and papers, Nostradamus was not there. The room was empty ... except for the presence of another entity. Phil couldn't discern who or what it was, but he sensed it was another being such as himself who was also waiting for Nostradamus. Phil was unable to make contact with the being or to identify it, so I asked if he could locate Nostradamus. We had never tried to contact him anywhere outside that room, but it was worth the experiment.

After a few seconds Phil said he could see Nostradamus standing barefoot on the deck of a boat conversing with someone. He appeared to be much younger than we normally saw him, in his thirties. All attempts to communicate with him failed. He was unaware of us. Apparently we were seeing him involved in a trip when he was younger and had not yet begun this type of psychic exploration. He had not yet opened his mind to communication with the other realms. We could watch him but could have no contact with his mind. The only solution was to try to find him at an older age when he would know who we were and what our task was. I had only to make the suggestion and Phil was there. But again he was having trouble getting through. I had to wait patiently while the forces in charge of this made some necessary adjustments.

P: The adjustment of energies is necessary. There have been many incidents of contact with disruptive spirits on this plane.

D: *Do you mean Nostradamus has had contact with disruptive spirits?*

P: That is accurate. There is this type of entities who would attempt to prevent this communication, due to their own selfish nature.

D: *Are they in the physical or in the spirit?*

P: The disruption is coming from the spirit plane. They are, however, incarnate in physical at this time.

D: *In our time or in his time?*

P: It is hard for us to say from our perspective. However, it appears to be somewhat just previous to *your* physical time frame.

D: *We thought maybe someone in his time was trying to sabotage the connection.*

P: No. We are protecting and enhancing. It is necessary to reestablish and reconfirm those commitments which allow these communications to take place.

There was a long pause, then Phil began to speak in an unfamiliar tone. It sounded as though he was reciting a rhyme.

P: Many years have passed, many more to go. Not so very long, and no one else will know.

D: *What do you mean?*

P: Cryptic messages. Quatrains. ... What do you wish?

D: (Apparently we were in contact again.) *Does Nostradamus remember that he gave me the commitment of translating his quatrains into modern language, because in our time period they were not translated correctly?*

P: Not so. They were not translated correctly far *before* your time period.

D: Does he remember giving me this job?

P: He remembers you very well.

D: I have brought other spirit entities to him to help.

P: Yes. He thanks you for this. It is his mission at this period of his life to assist. That is, in fact, his life's goal, be that in his own time frame or some other.

D: We understood he put these into a type of code or puzzle because he was afraid for his own life.

P: It was not entirely for his own selfish reasons. It was necessary to disguise them so that only those who would recognize the meaning could understand. For were it to be told to or understood by less knowledgeable people, it would not have served any useful purpose. And in fact, it could have caused much harm and confusion. Thus only those who were capable of unraveling could appreciate the message hidden within.

D: How is this communication being carried out? Are you seeing him?

P: It is done through the voice. We feel that which is spoken and then repeat it. There are no visualizations—simply the repeating of spoken or communicated words. He is addressing those questions which are being put to him.

D: We wondered if Nostradamus has had negative experiences?

P: He has seen that which is termed "negative." He has experienced that through mischievous entities which would cause devilment and trouble for him by giving him false information and pretext. He therefore has decided that he must be much more careful with whom he communicates.

D: Do you think these were deliberate attempts to sabotage his work?

P: Not so in a larger sense. It was simply personal mischief on the part of those who were involved in this. It was not some grander plan, just simple trouble-making by mischievous spirits.

D: We were wondering if people in his time were trying to cause trouble.

P: Not so in the physical sense.

D: Then I can understand his wariness when he first encountered this vehicle. Does he realize now that this is a true communication?

P: All are true communications. However, the intent is quite different with each communicator. The *intent* of the communication is, in essence, the litmus test of the validity of the information coming through.

I have been told many times that the intent cannot be hidden or disguised. When working in this realm of mental or telepathic communication, the intent and purpose is crystal clear. The outer façade of our conscious personality is stripped away and the primary motives are laid bare.

D: *Will he allow us to continue with the translations?*
P: That is accurate. There is still some reservation. However, he is becoming more accustomed to this form of communication.
D: *Is he in a trance or in meditation at this time?*
P: He is in communication from his higher self, his awareness of that which exists on other levels. However, he is still focused on his three-dimensional level also.
D: *He is able to do both at the same time?*
P: That is accurate.

I began by selecting a quatrain at random and read it to him. Naturally it was one containing negativity. It is very difficult to go through the quatrains and not encounter such images. It (CENTURY IV-66) was about wells being poisoned, and the devouring of human flesh. Phil began to translate, saying that it had to do with an incident perpetrated by spies committing a terrorist act by applying biological contaminants to be infiltrated into water. These people were falsely traveling under a Hindu passport. Then there was hesitation, and Phil suddenly opened his eyes and stretched. "I think I've lost it," he announced. He had brought himself out of trance, as he has done before in the past when something disturbed him. He did not sit up immediately but lay there trying to understand what had happened. I suggested trying to reestablish contact, but it was blank. He was unable to see anything. He said it was as though there was another person between him and Nostradamus. (His guide?) He again opened his eyes, and lay there trying to explain the strange feelings he was experiencing. "I get the feeling as if you'd shut an airport down in foul weather. No one comes in and no one goes out because there's danger. That's the best way I can translate it right now. There's foul weather around and it's just not safe to be going in or out. Figuratively speaking, it's like the psychic weather is bad, and it's not good for me to open up to him or for him to open up to me. It's as if everything was shut off. Now I'm getting all kinds of strange feelings that I don't like. It feels like trouble, disharmony, a lot of pain and confusion. As though someone is having trouble, and they're looking for me to help. This has left me feeling badly. I don't want to pursue it any further right now."

D: *Maybe it will be different the next time.*
P: I don't know. I hope there won't be a next time like this. I don't like this feeling because it leaves those emotions on me. It's like touching a dirty wall or something where you get it on you.
D: *Do you think it had anything to do with what the quatrain was referring to?*
P: Hmm, that's an interesting idea. I never thought of that.

D: *You were talking about terrorist acts. Maybe you were picking up the negativity of what the quatrain was about.*

P: Or the negativity of the terrorists. Maybe that's it. That scene could have been charged with a lot of different emotions.

D: *Maybe you're just too sensitive to handle that kind of vibrations.*

P: That may be. Those would be low vibrations. Generally you and I work on a much higher level.

D: *That's why I wasn't sure if you were the one to do this; but I thought we could try.*

P: Maybe instead of working with things that talk about death and destruction and mayhem, we could stay with the ones that are about technology.

D: *But they're such puzzles. There's no way to know until you read it. (Laugh) When I make any assumptions, they're always wrong. The quatrains are full of death and destruction.*

P: If he had something positive to talk about, I would like to hear that.

D: *He did have some, but these are so convoluted and complicated. I can see why the poor man wanted to get this through to people. Can you imagine seeing all these events and not being able to communicate and warn people?*

P: Yes, it must have weighed very heavy on his shoulders. But that stuff is definitely not my bag. I don't really go for all this murdering and killing. I don't believe I want to work with the negative side of humanity. It wouldn't do me any good and it wouldn't do you any good to try this. It will come. You don't seem to be lacking for people to work with.

We had made the attempt but it was obvious that Phil was not the one to work on the quatrains. He was too gentle a soul and too sensitive to the vibrations that these scenes carried with them. Watching the horror on the nightly news was a different thing—it was external. When Phil was working in trance, it was not coming from without, but within. It was working through him and thus it could affect him with the emotions charged within the event, and it apparently left an uncomfortable residue. Subjects such as Brenda and John could externalize what they were seeing and remain objective. It was apparent now that Phil could not do this. He had his own built-in protective systems, and this was what brought him out of trance. He was experiencing something that his subconscious did not consider suitable, and it pushed him away from it. In such a case these barriers are difficult to work around. It is wise not to even try; they are there for a reason. I would not do that anyway; I do not work that way. The welfare of my subject is always my primary concern. I would never under any circumstances put them in any type of jeopardy.

J THOUGHT ABOUT PHIL during the next week. I hated to lose the contact with Nostradamus now that it had been established, but it would be useless to ask him to translate the quatrains. Since I did not study them in advance, I never knew until I read them whether they contained negativity. While thinking about the situation I had a revelation. Maybe the contact would not be wasted. If Phil felt that Nostradamus desired a technological mind, that would be what we could give him. Instead of working on the prophecies we could ask Nostradamus to show him positive things, maybe inventions of the future or circumstances that would benefit humanity. Maybe Phil could be shown things that Nostradamus did not understand and help explain the mechanisms of them. This would be a positive use of Phil's talents. When I suggested it to him later, his enthusiasm was renewed. He was eager to try such a project. He no longer felt depressed about meeting with Nostradamus. The contact could be put to productive use after all, if what I was considering could be made to work. It was definitely something that we could try further down the line (see Chapter 20).

But for now, the objective that was utmost in my mind was the completion of the translation of the quatrains. I felt a compulsion that would not leave me. I knew I had to finish all of them before I could devote my attention to other projects. So the search must continue. I must find a suitable subject. After this disappointment with Phil, would it be possible? Were my experiences with Brenda and John only abnormalities, or were there others out there like them? Nostradamus told me long ago that he would come through anyone I worked with now that the contact had been established. But I was discovering it was not that simple because everyone was not suited for this work. Still I knew I must make the attempt, and my search was just beginning.

Chapter 3

The Search Continues

THE SITUATION DID NOT PRESENT ITSELF to attempt further communication until I was working with a young girl named Cynthia. She had spent a few years in Hollywood as a model and a fledgling starlet. Due to financial problems she had returned to our area to live near her parents and attend business school. I became involved with her while investigating UFO phenomenon and discovered that she was an excellent somnambulistic subject.

For several weeks we had alternated between working on the UFO information and investigating her past lives. She knew nothing about my former work with Nostradamus. When I arrived at her apartment for this session, I did not tell her what I was going to attempt, only that I wanted to try an experiment. Since she did not have anything specific she wanted to explore, she was open to anything I wanted to try. The procedure that had worked so well with Brenda and John was to first take them to the spirit state where they were not encumbered by the demands of a physical body. Then each had used their own unique method to locate Nostradamus. I would first see if I could get her to an in-between lives (spirit) state.

When she had entered the customary and necessary deep trance I instructed her to go back to a time when she was not directly involved with a life. At first there was confusion and she asked me to explain since she had never had instructions like this before. She interjected a statement that I have heard several times when I have instructed a subject to go to this state. "But it *is* life; it's just in-between *physical* life." This was what had created the confusion, her subconscious knew there was never a time when you were not involved with life. Such a thing would be impossible.

When I finished counting, she found herself in a place that was full of lights. She was experiencing such a euphoric state that it distracted her to converse. She was in awe of the place and the peaceful and pleasant sensations it evoked. She said softly, "Oh, it's nice not having the burden of the body. There are so many things I need to say. I feel like I'm in a void place now. But I know I can go many places." She saw herself wearing something that looked like a white flowing robe. The attire was almost attached to her white, translucent body. Her voice was soft and almost ethereal. "I feel very peaceful, but I have many things I need to work on. I'm still progressing and I am creating cycles for myself. I am deciding what I will do in the next body, if I so choose to reincarnate. I have many ideas."

I have heard these same feelings expressed by everyone when they are regressed to the in-between-lives state, the spirit or so-called "dead" state. The feeling of euphoria and the knowledge that they must plan for the next life are identical. This state is explored in detail in my book, *Conversation with a Spirit*. I did not want to dwell on this because I wanted to see if it would be possible to contact Nostradamus. This had always been the logical place for me to start, by removing the subject from the physical and getting them into this spirit state where anything is possible. I asked her if she would like to participate in an experiment and she replied that she thought she would be permitted to help me.

C: You may pose the questions.
D: *You said there were many places that you could go to. Can you find a place where you can see what is happening on the Earth at different time periods? Is there such a place where we have access to information?*
C: I must consult someone. Anything's possible, but I still must have permission. The Akashic book of records has a lot to do with it.

I was familiar with the Akashic records, but this was not what I wanted to see. It would show us the past lives of people who have lived on Earth. But I needed to converse directly with Nostradamus as I had with my other subjects.

D: *Is there any other place besides that?*
C: Yes, there's a temple with pillars. It's the place where the ultimate, universal, very bright beings are. They instruct there in the temple. If I must go there to inquire, I'm *sure* there would be a being that could assist me.

This sounded like the same place that John had found and where he was allowed to have access to the tapestry of time (Volume Two). This has also been described by others who are in this spirit state. I have become convinced that these temples of knowledge are very real places.

C: There are tall pillars and a Roman, almost Greek-looking building. I must open the door, and when I do, a surge of energy goes through me before I can walk any further. (*She took a huge intake of breath and slowly let it out.*) The presence there is so strong. Oh! I'm given much information whenever I open *these* doors. The wisdom and truth of the ages lie here. (*Suddenly*) Oh, I see him! A male figure is approaching me, with a very long white robe, a staff, and a white head of hair with long beard and mustache. He is an adept master, a very wise one, and the all-knowing one. I respect and honor him very much. He knows I have a question and I must ask him.

This also sounded very familiar. When John entered within these temple walls there were similar all-knowing guardian figures that helped us. These have been described by others as guardians, masters, teachers. Whatever they are called they always seem to be benevolent and willing to help, although they are bound by certain regulations that they are most stern about enforcing. I always try to respect their judgment because they know more about these procedures than I do. I always feel that if I do not cooperate fully with these beings then access to information will be denied.

Her eye movements indicated that something was happening. Then her voice suddenly changed, and she asked in a deeper gruff tone, "Who asked this question?" Her voice had been very peaceful and so soft it was almost a whisper before this voice came in. It was drastically different and full of authority. In a respectful voice I explained my purpose in making the contact. His gruff and loud tone startled me.

C: What time period?

D: *Would we be allowed to visit Nostradamus in the 1500s while he is alive in France?*

C: I do not see a problem there. I think taking her back in time to the 1500s would be a good first step. I will make it easier for her. (*The voice gradually became louder until it was resonating.*) I am helping by giving her energy now in her chest region, as you can see. (*Her chest was rising as though with deep breaths, although there was no sound or interruption in the dialogue.*) I'm helping to make it easier for her to vocalize. (*The entity must have sensed that I was becoming concerned.*) She is very protected at *all* times. If this is used in a way that is not harmful to this vehicle, it will be allowed. I must watch over her, too, for other reasons unknown to you. So I would like to observe how you would take her there. I think I can be helpful in this transition. I am almost connecting on Nostradamus' wavelength at this time. (*A deep cheerful laugh.*) I'm getting a feel for his personality. It's starting to break through. (*Her voice became deep and gruff, carefully enunciating the words.*) He's a very outspoken gentleman, and he will make his work known to many, many beings. He wants to see if the outcome has occurred. He knows it will.

I was not really comfortable with this deep resonating voice. It was not the same situation as in the past. I wasn't sure this was what I wanted to communicate with, but as long as we were in it, I had to continue, at least temporarily.

C: He says, "You have chosen an interesting vehicle this time, but this is a female vehicle, and I'm a male energy. That is why it feels peculiar to *me* to be in her. I'm having a little difficulty."

D: *If it is difficult, she can talk for you.*

I wanted to get this back on more familiar ground such as I had been used to working with the other vehicles.

C: I am trying to use her visionary equipment as my own. I'm not completely integrated yet. That is why I'm having difficulty. You want to refer to information that I have written.

I always began these contacts with test questions before attempting translation. If every subject gave the same information it was a sign that I was truly in touch with Nostradamus.

D: *Can you describe the room you're in there in the 1500s?*
C: Well, first I came into *her* room. (*Chuckle*) But I can go back there. (*Pause*) I work by candlelight at night. I write at a big wooden table, and I am absorbed. You see, beings channel information through me also. That is how I have gotten some of the information. That is why I find this situation interesting. I have had others, many others, try to channel my energy, but I am very selective. I like choosing a vehicle that has similar channeling abilities, and other similarities as I.
D: (The gruff voice still bothered me.) *But I don't want to harm her vehicle in any way.*
C: Oh, no. In fact the other gentleman that contacted me for her will not allow such a thing.
D: *Can you tell me what else is in that room?*
C: There's another long table that has stacks of parchment that my prophetic information is written on. There is a window there. It is sectioned off in many squares all put together. It opens up with a great view of the countryside. I am so filled with thoughts coming in all the time. I am so busy writing that I sometimes have a hard time finding time to rest. I have incantations that I have spoken, and believe in. And that is when some of these thoughts start coming to me. I was actually born with clairvoyant—as you would call it—abilities. But by saying certain incantations ... some of my wizard friends have shown me a few things, and there are many things one can do that are amazing.
D: *Are there any kind of instruments on the tables that you use for your work?*
C: Yes, there is a compass-type of thing that I use. It is made out of copper, and is long and pointed with a thing attached on the side. This thing spins around it, but it is a type of compass, and has an arc also attached to it. I use it on maps to try to get more specific information. Actually, by looking at the maps I get images of where things are going to take place. I'm inspired to use this compass because it helps me with my accuracy. There is a higher energy that channels through me, and that has something to do with it. He is a very divine, holy one that came from a higher source that we are connected to. And it is most *definite* information when I receive it. It has *always* been accurate. And he instructs me what to do. People would not want to hear that.

They want to think it's all my own thing. And actually I did, through incarnations, develop clairvoyant abilities. But there is also a higher calling here; I am trying to help man. The higher energy source is a part of me, but it is also a separate identity. It is using me as an instrument to help man, to warn him about disasters and catastrophes. It is to show that not only beings who evolve as a complete holy being are given those abilities, but that man has clairvoyant abilities, too. They are given to you when you are ready for it. You do not have to be an avatar [demigod] to have this experience.

D: *Do you have anything that you use to help with your visualization?*

C: *(Pause)* Well, among other things which I use there is a mirror. But you see, there's something very private about my mirror. I have revealed it ... to very few ... and usually never. I made a pact about divulging information regarding this. That is why I hesitate, because I don't want to inflict any consequences on myself. But I think I could probably tell you more about it. There is a mirror. It's like a reflection, but I can see myself walking into the mirror. Actually going *in* it. My full body walking right into it.

D: *Is this a physical mirror in your room?*

C: *(Pause)* Well, you see, it's not like your ordinary mirror on the wall. It is very special. A higher being has been instrumental in showing me how to do some of these things. And wizard acquaintances, too, can do many things along these lines. But if you would like a description of it, it is large and oval in shape. You can tilt the mirror slightly, if you need to. This is the one that I have walked into, but it has had a spell cast upon it. That is why I can do it. Now with any other mirror, unless an incantation was done just right, you could get yourself in some trouble. You might not be able to return. That's why it's important that it's done very precisely. Some of my wizard acquaintances have instructed me wisely on this.

D: *Can you give me a description of what you look like physically at this time?*

C: Well, I have an extremely large nose; it's rather pointed almost, kind of humping down. And my hair is reddish brown in color, long and somewhat scraggly looking.

D: *Do you use astrology in your predictions?*

C: Sometimes it's helpful. But other times the information just comes. It is full, it is complete. There is a reason for it. It is so strong that it has lasted all these centuries. That says a lot about that energy source.

D: *Is your work causing you any problems in your private life?*

C: I spend much time alone. Some of the people in the community think that I am quite a strange man, a hermit type. They are a little frightened by me, and they don't know quite what to think. I've been called a hypocrite. I've had people condemn me to Hell because they think that anyone who has prophetic information has to be the Son of God, or else it is invalid. Or they have to fit a certain form that I, apparently-wise, don't fit, I guess.

D: *Do you ever take any students?*

C: Yes, I do have one particular young lad that is quite fascinated with me, and wants to follow in my footsteps. He takes it all very seriously, and I have high hopes for him. But I can't guarantee that he is going to get the same type of things that I get. I try so hard not to discourage him. But I have told him that he has these abilities already there, and he must tap into them. I'm trying to be instrumental in showing him a good way to do this. Actually there have been many others, but he is a favorite of mine. There will be many more, too, but there are many that I have to turn away. There are many curious ones who mostly want to see how I work. They really aren't knowledgeable or dedicated enough to do too much with what I can show them. This lad has more innate abilities to apply what he learns in a more productive way. I am strict when it comes to requirements for instructing someone, and I really choose only about three or four. There is a student that I might start working with, but he will probably leave me and not finish it. He will know enough, what he wants to know and will just go on and use that.

D: *I've heard you're also a doctor. Is that correct?*

C: Yes, I have studied the physical anatomy for many years. I thought you were speaking about a student for learning how to walk through mirrors and predict the future, or regarding astronomical things. That was what I was referring to. But yes, there are lectures that I give. And there are many chairs set up in a ... I'm trying to get words. She uses the word "auditorium." I do not use that word. It is foreign to me. The room is shaped like a round ... coliseum, but it's a lecture hall. And there are tables there. Different experiments are done on these tables as I lecture to young students. They are so interested in alchemy. (*Chuckle*) There are other important things to discuss, but they keep asking me questions about that area. In this age, this era, there is a widespread interest in it. Now the wizards use it. It's an important part in some of their portions. They have told me a few little secrets. I can't see revealing those to a large group of students because it's only for a very selected few people. I am very pleased that you find this interesting.

It was time to end the session, and I wanted to know if I could return again and ask for help in the interpretation of the prophecies.

C: I apologize, but I do not think that will be possible. All the time we have been conversing there has been much fading in and out, a wavering. It has taken a great deal of concentration to speak this long. There is also a lot of noise, a crackling (*static?*). I don't know where it is coming from, but it is very disturbing. She is saying that she thinks it has something to do with some type of medicine. (*Cynthia was taking allergy medication at that time.*)

This had occasionally happened while working with Brenda. If she was not feeling well or on medication, it would create disturbance, and often Nostradamus would cut those sessions short. He often said there was so much interference it was useless to continue.

C: I also do not feel comfortable with her energy or her body. As I said, she is female and I am male. I also do not think she feels comfortable with this. It would be much more advantageous if you could locate a suitable male vehicle.

This was the same admonition Nostradamus had given while speaking to John Feeley in Volume Two. He felt very much at ease while working with him, and said he hoped I could find another male energy that would be compatible. But these were not always easy to find. Females have a more natural ability to attain and work in these altered states.

I breathed a sigh of relief that he did not want to work through Cynthia. I had not felt totally comfortable with the manner in which his voice came through in such a loud, overbearing fashion. It bothered me, and I wanted my familiar conditions back again. I also felt it would not be the best thing for gentle Cynthia. Was it a true contact? The information was accurate, but the connection did not feel as natural as the other ones had. There was something disturbing about it, and I was secretly glad that I would not have to use this vehicle to contact him. Uncomfortable feelings are not the most conducive conditions for this type of work. When Cynthia awakened I told her very little about the experiment. There was no reason to; we were not going to continue with it. I just thanked her for her cooperation and said we would pursue something different at our next session.

An interesting phenomenon often occurs when I am working with subjects who are investigating their past lives. Sometimes for a day or two after the session they will continue to receive information or the answers to questions. This often happens at night when they are trying to go to sleep. Maybe it is because this is so similar to the trance state. I tell people to be very aware of their dreams during this time as their subconscious might continue to leak information. It is as though a door has been opened. After a while the door seems to close again and the past life information goes back to wherever it came from.

Thus I was not surprised when Cynthia told me she had a strange and unusual dream after the session. But she did not tell me about it until over six months later. She had not been aware of what I was working on and did not know it would have significance to me. It was such an out-of-the-ordinary dream that she wrote it down the next morning. It contained numbers that had no meaning for her. Later she happened to see the video, *The Man Who Saw Tomorrow,* in which Orson Welles narrates the story of Nostradamus. She was startled to see the same numbers in the film, and decided to tell me about the dream. She was still confused about it, and it definitely had more meaning to me that it did to her.

According to her notes the dream began with a beam of light coming down from above which created a warm, radiant feeling. Then a story began to evolve like a movie in front of her. She was shown an attractive dark-complexioned young man with black curly hair. She was informed that this was the Anti-Christ, although the term meant nothing to her. Then she was shown the numbers of the year 1999 and was told this would be during his reign. She was told to notice that the numbers 999 were 666 when reversed, and it was emphasized that this was the year of the Anti-Christ.

She was then shown a young boy with long blonde hair that she thought was the Christ. She was told that this individual would be a child in 1999 and that he would reign after the Anti-Christ. The presence of this figure became overwhelming. She was then told that this was a divine revelation and was not to be revealed to just anyone. She awoke immediately and retained enough of the dream to be able to write it down. It was very special to her even though she did not understand its implications until she saw the video and heard the mention of the Anti-Christ and the year 1999.

I am speculating, but I think the young blond boy Cynthia perceived to be a Christ figure could be the person we refer to as the "Great Genius" in Volumes One and Two. Nostradamus said that he would come after the Anti-Christ had wreaked his havoc and had been defeated. He would be the exact opposite in every respect and he would bring the world back from the brink of destruction. Nostradamus compared his coming to the Second Coming of Christ in importance, although he emphasized that this man was definitely not the Christ himself. I always thought it would be reassuring to have such a figure in our future. It is significant that Cynthia should receive this information in a dream after we had contacted Nostradamus. Did it come from him? She was not aware of the implications until she found out about the Nostradamus project I was working on; then she thought she should tell me about the dream.

Had the door between dimensions been opened for a brief period? Did it create a highway where information could still filter through from Nostradamus? Was he so desperate for contact with our world that he was taking advantage of any possible connection, even trying to send information through the dream state? Maybe he (or someone on the other side) has been bombarding our world in some manner, and anyone who is psychically sensitive can receive it.

I do know that since my first book (Volume One) was published, I have received letters from all over the world. One interesting thread that seems to run through many of them is that the predictions contained in that book hit home; they seemed familiar. People said they have received much of the same information (especially about the Anti-Christ), in abbreviated and disjointed form, through dreams, in meditation, from simply out of the clear blue sky. To me this adds validity. Is the information being spread around the world through the ether, and those sensitive to Nostradamus' thoughts are able to receive it? Maybe through our conscious and directed effort we were merely forming a more capable receiver, and like a radio we were able to get a direct and clear line to the great seer. I don't know. But it cannot be coincidence that people all around the world are reporting the same phenomenon.

This contact through Cynthia proved again that it was possible to locate Nostradamus, but the connection was not as strong as it had been with Elena, Brenda and John. From the standpoint of an experiment, it had been a success. But from the standpoint of a vehicle to help in the translation of the quatrains it was useless. It would not be conducive for such intricate work. Nostradamus also did not feel comfortable with the connection, and thus would be unable to present complex symbolism through Cynthia.

Instead of allowing this to discourage me, it made me more determined than ever. I could not accept the fact that my work with Brenda and John might have only been a one in a million possibility. Surely there must be another one of my subjects that would be suitable for contact work. I continued my search with more persistence than ever. I would not, I could not, accept defeat until I had exhausted every resource.

Nostradamus had specified that I try to use a male energy, so I thought I would try it with Wayne. He was a carpenter in his late 30s, very mild-mannered and quiet. I had not worked with him very many times, but he had proven to be a good subject. The only problem I could foresee might be that he did not have an extensive vocabulary because reading was difficult for him. His mind was more of a mechanical or practical nature instead of an intellectual one. I didn't know if he would be able to interpret and put into words the concepts he might be shown. But he was willing to attempt an experiment and it was worth the try. Most of the other subjects that I was considering were females, so Wayne was the logical next choice. I did not tell him what the experiment would entail. This was the procedure I followed with all of my subjects. This way no one would be able to make the accusation later that these people had prepared for the session ahead of time. This would be impossible because none of them knew what I was going to work on until the first session was completed. Afterwards there was always a possibility that they might choose to study the quatrains, but none of them attempted this. They had no desire to; the quatrains are too complicated. I suspect only the most avid scholar would have this interest. I had already found that it did no good to study them in advance because to me they were nonsense and comprehensible only to the man who wrote them, Nostradamus. Any time in the past when I had tried to offer my own conclusions they would prove to be false or only partially correct. Through my association with him I had gained some insight into the way his mind fashioned these symbols and anagrams, but they were still too complex for me to decipher on my own. I remained with the job I had been assigned: that of the objective reporter. I chose the quatrains for the first time when I opened the book and read them to the sleeping subject. I marked them off and tape recorded the sessions.

Later I had the unenviable task of arranging them into some type of order, but the job of deciphering them was not mine. Without the help of the correct type of subjects, the monumental project of translating almost 1000 obscure puzzles could have never been accomplished. My part in this mysterious project remained constant while the different subjects drifted in and out of my life. But my task was that of a reporter and researcher. This required a tremendous amount of patience and perseverance to stay with a thankless job for three years, accumulating, always searching, just for the sake of restoring lost knowledge. That was my reward, to know that somehow the task would be accomplished, even if by means beyond my control.

As we prepared for the session in Wayne's home, he put on a tape of soft metaphysical music. He was worried about being able to go deep enough, and he thought the music would help him relax. I knew it would not make any difference since he was already conditioned to go deeply with a keyword, but I indulged his request. The music could be an added benefit, and as it floated gently through the room, it created a very tranquil atmosphere. I used the keyword and he immediately entered a deep trance. Then I counted him to a spirit state in-between lives, he saw himself in a colorful world where free-floating lines or strands of color meandered all around him. They seemed to radiate out from a bright central light that he understood to be the source from which everything comes. Although the many-colored veins were part of the light, they were shooting off in all directions. They appeared similar to the rays of the sun except these were meandering like rivers or streams instead of going in a straight path. Wayne said he felt like a cell in a body with all the lines free-floating around him. It was very relaxing so he decided to just go with the flow and see what happened. As he did this he became aware of various globes of white light, and he had the impression these were spirits. Unexpectedly one bright light separated and floated toward him. Wayne instantly perceived that it was his own guide. I assumed he could be correct since other subjects have described spirits and guides as bright lights. Explaining to it that I wanted to try an experiment, I asked if the spirit could show us a way to contact Nostradamus while he was alive in the 1500s in France, so we could continue to work with him. The results came immediately.

Wayne said, "I see a black hole in the middle of all the strands of lights. At first it was just a dark shadow. It is there because we wish it to be there. It is our porthole. In this case it is a porthole to Nostradamus, but we could have a porthole to anything we wished. I'm going into this hole and the bright light is accompanying me."

Since he seemed to feel secure about entering this hole, I did not interfere.

Wayne continued: "We are coming out of the hole into a room. I can see now that the black hole is the other side of a mirror that is on a desk, and we came out of the mirror. Nostradamus, I presume, is the man sitting at the other desk."

This was always startling. Each subject seemed to have their own method of reaching Nostradamus, all different, yet alike. It appeared that the mirror was a crucial part of the contact. It seemed to be a focal point as it always appeared in its proper place on the desk. The main thing was that there never seemed to be any barriers to finding the man once the permission was given. But I fully realize that without the cooperation of all concerned we could have been denied entry in every one of these cases, and the contact and project would never have been initiated. Thus I knew it was not in my hands.

It seemed that we had once again located the great man, but I would have to ask questions in order to be certain. The subjects never had any way of knowing what my test questions would be since they did not know anything about the experiment. If everything matched I could be certain it was a true contact. Thus far no one had failed these tests. I asked for a description of the man seated at the desk.

Wayne answered: "He's dressed in dark colors with a black hat, and he has pretty long hair. I just walked around to look at him. I notice his hands; he has long fingers. They remind me of the hands of a surgeon. He has a pretty large nose. His eyes ... and his brow are noticeable. He has thick eyebrows, and as a result they seem to make his eyes appear deep-socketed. But he doesn't appear menacing. It's a physical attraction. It's where a person's eyes would be drawn, much like his hands. Just something that captures my attention. He has one eyebrow ... a connecting eyebrow."

This answer surprised me and I found it amusing. That was what he meant by "one eyebrow." They connected. All the subjects had described a similar piercing and captivating appearance of Nostradamus' eyes. This time he was clean shaven. On other occasions we had encountered Nostradamus at different times in his life. It seemed that when he was younger he was clean shaven, and when he grew older he had the typical beard and mustache. This helped me to know what type of questions to ask. It appeared that when he was younger he had not begun to work fully on the quatrains and often did not know what we were talking about. This was verified by the research I did while compiling the sequel (Volume Two). I found that he kept notes in a diary about his visions and experiences when he was a younger man. He did not compile them into the puzzling quatrains that have come down to us until he was much older. All of these facts were part of the test questions I asked. Each subject would have no way of knowing the significance of their answers.

Wayne began to describe objects that he saw in the room, all of which sounded very familiar to me. It was a small room with one door and a window. The sparse furnishings included a desk, table, and chair. A candle was burning on the desk. There were also paper, manuscripts and an ink quill. The mirror sat on the table, and his desk was in front of the window. These were the same surroundings reported by my other subjects who had traveled through time to visit Nostradamus. I asked what Nostradamus was doing at the desk.

W: Well, now he's looking at me. He seems contemplative. I guess he's trying to figure out who I am.

This was the same way Phil had seen him on his first visit. Nostradamus regarded him suspiciously also.

D: *Do you know what you look like to him?*
W: I don't know what I look like to *me.* I cannot see my*self,* only I know that I am here. And I can see *him,* but I appear differently to him than he appears to me. He appears in physical form. I presume I look like a spirit, an aura. He also has an aura—it's light green. I think that the guide and I are together, the same. I am through him, we are together as one.
D: *Does Nostradamus seem to be afraid?*
W: No. I can sense that he knows why we're here. He knows who you are, and he's now comfortable with me. I feel welcome.
D: *Why do you think we are here?*
W: To translate quatrains.

He sensed that Nostradamus knew this, but since he had only been working on the prophecies for a year or so, he had only begun to try to write his notes down. Wayne also picked up that his main occupation was that of a healer.

D: *Would he want to continue with the work I was doing with him?*
W: We are working together. We are helping each other. He is of service as we are of service.
D: *He was trying to warn us of things that were to happen in our time period and beyond. I thought I had lost contact because of the different vehicles we've had to go through.* (I thought I would try another test question.) *Ask him what his motive is for writing these prophecies.*
W: It's his destiny.
D: *I thought if he was a successful doctor he wouldn't need to do any more than that.*
W: That would be to squander his talents. The gift is only given to a few, and not to use the gift would be to squander. He could never bring himself to be that wasteful.
D: *How is he communicating with you?*
W: He's thinking, I guess. I don't hear words.

D: We would like, if it were possible, to continue working on the translations, because we feel they are important. Does he have any suggestions about how he wants to go about this?

W: Let's try translating a quatrain that you have done before.

This was the main test Nostradamus had asked me to perform with various subjects to see if we were in contact. He said if they gave the same translation—not word for word, but the same concept—then I would know it was a true communication. It was interesting that he suggested it first, because I had fully intended to perform this test before we proceeded further. Naturally I used the same quatrain I had read to the other subjects. This was the first one that had been chosen by Elena from the book of quatrains in the beginning of our work (Volume One). It was the one which Nostradamus said would pertain to work I was doing while researching the Dead Sea Scrolls for my book about Jesus (*Jesus and the Essenes*). I had always found it amazing that Elena had chosen the proper quatrain at random out of the 1000 in the book. Thus this was the one I used as a test with Brenda and I would now use it with Wayne. I did not know how he would receive the translation, whether it would be in the form of pictures or impressions. Each subject had their own method. (CENTURY VII-14) "He will come to expose the false topography. The urns of the tombs will be opened. Sect and holy philosophy to strive. Black for white, and the new for the old."

W: I'm getting the impression that this takes place in Egypt. I have the impression that documents will be discovered. Documents much like the Dead Sea Scrolls, with information on new technology. That's all.

D: Will this be in our future?

W: Yes, it will be ... 1995.

D: Are these answers coming as pictures or impressions?

W: They were coming as impressions.

Amazingly Wayne had succeeded in translating the quatrain correctly. Brenda had given a lot more detail but the same content was there. My research had revealed that this translation for this quatrain has never been given by any of the official interpreters. It was obvious that this was a true communication and we were actually in contact with Nostradamus again. Performing the impossible was no longer applicable to this case. The impossible had become routine. Nostradamus had proved true to his word; he would come through anyone that I instructed to contact him. But I knew all too well that there was much more to this that merely making the contact. Would Wayne have the ability to interpret the concepts and convey them to me?

After the second session Wayne proved that he had the ability to translate the quatrains although he did not supply as much detailed information as the others I had worked with. When the scenes began coming through, he saw them in a gray formless cloud bank. This was similar to how they were perceived by Elena and Brenda in the "special meeting place." I wanted to pursue this, but the only time Wayne could work with me was at night after he came home from work and ate dinner. This made it late for me and I often returned home after midnight, since he lived in a city 30 miles away. This inconvenience didn't matter because I have had to travel like this many times and it is worth it if I can obtain material that is valuable to my many projects. Some of Wayne's translations will appear in other chapters where the results are categorized.

It now appeared that it would be no problem to contact Nostradamus. The unusual had become so commonplace that I was no longer startled when the connection worked. It was as though we had his telephone number and could call him up any time we wanted to, if the conditions (or phone lines) were in proper working order. The only problem was that some of the telephone connections were clearer than others. Some of the subjects had an easier time relaying the information than others. But at least I was positive the connection was well established.

I knew I could only work with Wayne once a week. He found it fascinating but was a little suspicious about where the information was coming from. He thought, as did everyone that I have worked with, that he might be making it up, that it was only coming from his own imagination. I knew that if he would only refrain from judging it and let it flow, there would be no problems. I explained to him that he was only one piece of a puzzle. It was up to me to compare his answers to other information I had received and decide whether the connection was valid. I was in a better position to judge than he was since I had access to all the material.

But I had a feeling that he would only indulge me and my experiment for a while and then he would tire of it and lose interest in it. This had happened before when people's daily life interfered and took attention away from this strange project. Those involved had no long-lasting commitment to it, so it did not really make any difference to them. My suspicions soon proved correct. After a few weeks Wayne thought the project was too time-consuming. Because he was not aware of the larger picture he could not see that he was contributing anything worthwhile. I told him that I had concluded that if several subjects supplied more pieces, I would be able to finally end this project and go on to other things. He remarked, "Dolores, I don't think you're *ever* going to finish this."

With Wayne's lack of cooperation I knew I had no choice but to attempt to locate Nostradamus through some of my other well-conditioned subjects. I was becoming tired of this project. After devoting three years to it, I wanted to wrap it up, to finish the remaining quatrains, and to call it to a halt. I had other projects I wished to pursue. If I could contact Nostradamus and work with him through several people I could finish my job quicker and move on.

Chapter 4

The Former Teacher

PHIL AND WAYNE were the only two male energies that I had worked with consistently enough to attempt this experiment. I decided to try it with various female energies who were conditioned to go into deep trance.

The next attempt was made in April 1989 through Pam, a former school teacher. She also was unaware of what the experiment would be about. She and her husband, Richard, did not have a copy of my book because it had just been published. I had not even received my copies yet. They were aware of my work with Nostradamus, but they were not aware of details that the books contained. Pam told me later that she had never read anything about Nostradamus. They knew very little about him, especially his personal biography. Richard was present at most of her sessions and operated his own tape recorder.

I used Pam's keyword and counted her back to a spirit in-between lives state since these explorative journeys cannot be conducted while the subject is concentrating on a physical life. The shackles of the body must first be removed before the spirit can journey through time and dimension. Once in the spirit state they are capable to performing unbelievable feats because they are no longer constrained by the limitations of the body. Each person perceives this state differently, yet there are definite repeatable patterns. When I finished counting I asked her what she could see.

P: I seem to be floating in space in the form of a colorful wisp that looks like smoke, but has a little more substance. I'm just mingling with other wisps. We're actually larger than wisps, but have that appearance. I can't really describe it well enough. I want to say "plasma," but that word makes me think of liquid, and this is not a liquid. It's a very iridescent green with overtones of bright *luminous* pink, like blowing pink-tipped green smoke. It's a *wonderful* feeling. I also hear music. It's not like music on instruments, and it's not like voices singing. It's all around me, but if I try to hear it directly, I don't comprehend it. It sounds and *feels* very *huge*.

Normally after the subject has attained the spirit state the next step is to find someone to help them with the experiment, because they often cannot do this by themselves. These time journeys can be accomplished in several different ways but it helps to have a guide as an intermediary.

D: *Do you have your guide with you?*
P: Well, I'm surrounded by other colored wispy moving consciousnesses. I don't have a feeling of a personal friend or leader or helper. Although I seem to have the capability of going to or bringing to me whatever you ask for. I am in a very protected, safe, beautiful, loving, harmonious environment.
D: *Would you like to help me with an experiment?*
P: Very much so, yes.
D: *Is it possible for you to see someone while they are living on the Earth?*
P: If we were to ask for something a bit more specific I might be able to focus. I will step down to the atmosphere of the Earth and jump off a cloud from there. It's my own way of becoming more in tune with material, mundane things.
D: *However you want to do it. There was a man whom we call Nostradamus who lived in France in the 1500s. I have had contact with him. I was wondering if you could try to locate him for me.*
P: The instant you asked that I looked toward Earth, and I saw an infinite numbers of tubes coming up from the Earth. They look similar to those used for intravenous feeding. Straws, flexible tubes coming way out into space. I've never seen this before. It's very interesting. Everybody has a tube. They are different degrees of brightness, and appear to have different densities.
D: *What do the tubes represent?*
P: Each person's outward focus. Some tubes are easier to find. Just as when you are getting a shot some people's veins are easier to find than others. It's the same with the focus. Some people are dimly focused outward. They have tubes, but they're not easily recognizable. So I aligned myself, a spiraling tube of energy, with the tube that was Nostradamus, and I slid down the tube.
D: *How were you able to find his tube so easily?*
P: Our intent was to find it. It seemed to be the most prominent of all the tubes because that was our focus.
D: *Then you just slid down the inside of it?*
P: I just hooked on to the end of his and sent my consciousness down the tube. I came out in this stone-floored room that is cold and damp. It is rather stark, I might say. I seem to be in the air above and a little to the right of a man whom I presume is Nostradamus. He's bent over a table, not of your finest quality, although it is totally adequate to his purposes. He seems to be humped over, looking at something under his face. I'm looking at him from above and behind, so I only see the back of his head and shoulders. He has on a garment that could be

described as a robe, although it's more like a very loose coat. I suppose robe would be the closest word that we have to describe it. He has long hair, rather unkempt, I might say. It's as if he doesn't have much conscious thought attached to his hair. On top of that sits one of those soft floppy hats like you would see an artist wearing. I would like to change my perspective. By the way, it is dark in this room, except for the candle on the table. I'm trying to go around and see what he's looking at. That's funny. It seems to be a shallow bowl of water. It has a totally calm surface, like a lake with no breeze blowing. I can't really see *in* it. When I first saw him from the back, I thought he was humped over writing. And in fact he does have a quill. But he's only looking at the water with his physical eyes. His mind is looking elsewhere.

D: *Well, do you think you could get his attention?*

P: I could do a trick. I could blow out the candle.

D: *We don't want to scare him though.*

P: No, I don't think he's into being scared any more. He seems *so* curious.

D: *Do you think he was scared at one time?*

P: I think that some of the things he has seen have made him sad, perhaps not surprised. I don't feel fear from him. (*Chuckle*) I just made the candle flicker off and now it's back on. So that was an unnatural occurrence to get his attention. He acknowledged that something's there. I was actually putting out feelings of love at that very moment. And he acknowledged me as a friend, so that was good. He has a plume in his hand, and he lifted it from the paper and flicked it toward me, like, "I know you're there." (*Chuckle*) He might be perceiving me as a thought form since I am invisible. (*She sobered.*) He's *very* serious. He seems to be burdened with the weight of what he sees with his inner eye. There's an actual slumping, humping, hunkering over the table. If he were to stand he would still have a bit of a stoop, due to the weight of the world that is on his shoulders. He has thick, bushy brows. And I can't see his eyes. I don't know why.

D: *Maybe because he's looking down.*

P: But I'm going everywhere now.

D: *Has he any prominent features?*

P: He seems to have a big nose. This is funny. I expected him to have a beard, but I don't see a beard. I see a prominent nose and bushy eyebrows, a floppy hat, his unkempt hair. I see his *really* heavy coat, robe, *cloak*—that's it. (*She gave a sudden laugh.*) It seemed as if he said, "Don't say I'm old."

D: *He can pick up on you?*

P: I didn't know that. I just *seem* to be invisible air.

D: *Is there anything else on the table?*

P: There's a quill, and an inkwell. There is a candle. It's been replaced many times. There's a big buildup of drips. I see a mirror. It has a long, oval shape, rather large to hold up.

D: *Where is that?*

P: To his left. Actually I feel that he's experimenting with different "looking-in" things.

D: Can you tell him that someone from the future wants to talk with him?

P: He said, "Someone *else!*" (*Laugh*) He seems to have many visitors.

I wanted to start my test questions to establish what point we were in his life.

D: *Is he married at this time?*

P: Well, if we're talking to him, he said, "No woman will have me." (*Laugh*) I actually think he has sort of a disdain for women. I felt a sneer when you asked that question.

D: *Ask him to elaborate?*

P: Well, it seems that he is married, or at least has been married or had a relationship. He's willing to help heal women, but on a personal level he doesn't seem to like them in general, period.

D: *Can he say why?*

P: Ha! Well, his stupid response was, "That should be obvious."

D: *Well, tell him it's not obvious.*

P: We wouldn't like this response either. He says they fill up the air with words. They're always demanding that something be done. They're never satisfied. They don't like the hours he keeps, or his own personal habits. They want to talk about trivial, meaningless details on and on and on and on. It's not that any female has personally injured him or damaged him. He just simply refrains from keeping their company and is disgusted by it when he's around it.

D: *He's into more intelligent things, I guess.*

P: Well, he definitely feels that he—I'm not sure intelligent—but he feels that he's on to something *big.*

D: *That they wouldn't understand?*

P: Oh, they're just too distracting and demanding.

D: (Chuckle) *Well, does it bother him that I am a woman and I am the one doing this work?*

P: Sometimes. (*Big laugh*) When it is necessary to try to put forth an explanation, and it's delivered as well as possible through all the layers of different personalities the transmission has to come. Sometimes when it must be reiterated—particularly if it's been explained three times and still hasn't gotten through—there's a little disgust. (*Laugh*)

D: *Aggravation.*

P: Right. All in all he doesn't think about your gender.

D: *I know his time period makes a difference in the way he relates to women.*

P: He doesn't really have much to do with peers either. Only those people who come for healings. That's about his contact. Those he is instructing and those he's working on. He says his quest is like a jealous lover. He feels he has very little time for the mundane world. Those people who are in his personal life seem to resent the little time that he has with them. If he does have a wife and family they probably see him very little because his focus is not on *them*. His focus is definitely to see inward, into the future, into figuring out what has been going on in his head since he was a child. It's dawn and it's cold in the room. I don't seem to be very capable of asking him questions. But *he* seems to be capable of responding, so I don't know how this works.

D: *Has he been doing any writing?*

P: He seems to have been recording what he sees with his inner eye. I need something more specific to ask him.

D: *Well, has he published any books?*

P: It seems at this point very few are taking him seriously. He says, or I felt that he said—this is not with outside words, this is more telepathic feeling tones. He says his is a solitary pursuit. He has been writing a long time apparently. He's very impatient for us to be specific.

D: *In our time period we have a book that he wrote that contained puzzles. And people have been trying to figure them out all these years. Does that make any sense to him?*

P: He seemed to feel that it would only be puzzling for a certain segment. (*Sudden burst*) *Most* of the people. It seems that it was necessary for him to write in a relatively obscure manner. He could be imprisoned or hurt for prophetizing, but he has an inner compulsion to share what he sees. He can't say that he didn't see it when he did. So in order to comply with his deep inner urgings to report what he has seen, he has to write in a language that would not bring instant imprisonment or perhaps death to him.

D: *We sympathize with that. But he wrote them in such an obscure manner that many people, even in the future times, can't understand them. And I was given the job of trying to translate them. Can he understand that?*

P: Well, it seems that he's heard that before, although he takes it *moderately* seriously. (*Laugh*) There is one other factor that relates to the obscure meanings of some of his writings. And that is the fact that he is seeing the edges, the shadows. He is also writing from feeling and intuition besides the clear inner vision. Thus some of it is not quite as specific as *we* and *he* would like for it to be. So you add the factor of intentional "coding" plus a visual picture that is not totally specific, and you get an even more obscure rhyme.

D: *If I read some of them, could he tell me through you what they really mean?*

P: Well, he has total faith in himself. He's not so sure about me. (*Loud laugh*) He's willing to give it a shot and so am I. I feel a heavy sense of responsibility coming from *him* to do the job well. This is awful.

D: *Well, all we can do is try. We can't ask for any more than that.* (I had chosen to use the "test" quatrain once again.) (CENTURY VII-14) *"He will come to expose the false topography. The urns of the tombs will be opened. Sect and holy philosophy to thrive. Black for white and the new for the old."*

P: I perceive Nostradamus wanting to explain and I only want to repeat, if I can, what he says, and not give my own speculations. This was obviously a riddle on purpose, and it relates to the church. Of course, we understand topography as topographical features of landscape that we look upon with our physical eyes. This is the first part of the riddle. It doesn't mean mountains, trees, lakes and streams. It means he will come to expose what we *think* we see as trees. Many of those things that have been held up to be moral, true, right, pious, and worthy of applause from the church will be shown to be false, self-serving, and not at all in the best interests of the individual.

D: *"The urns of the tombs will be opened."*

P: This is new information that is in the process of being revealed. We've already had some of this exposed to light, the Nag Hammadi and the Gnostic gospels. There have been new teachings revealed in modern time that were still buried in Nostradamus' time. But there seems to be more on the way.

D: *"Sect and holy philosophy to thrive. Black for white and the new for the old."*

P: What appears to be true isn't and there will be truths revealed from ancient times that were rejected as heresy or blasphemy. He says many of the old seers saw much more accurately, and it has been greatly contorted by those in power. A change foretold from *his* past, the ancient past, will come to pass as truth.

She had passed the test. Even though her interpretation was worded differently, the content of the quatrain referred to lost knowledge or documents being uncovered, which was the correct answer.

P: I think I would be more helpful if I were a little more discernible to him. I would like to bring more of my personality essence to this room. I have tried to be like air. I will now allow him to look upon myself as a being that he can see in his mind's eye so he will be more comfortable with me. For I only care, I am only here as a friend. I can make a picture in his mind's eye. I am now appearing to him as a woman with flowing hair and robes. He knows this is a non-threatening, loving figment. He says it's more fun for him than just talking to the blank air. He likes visualizing *people,* but he does know that thought exists without form. He's very sharp.

I then began to read the quatrains and Pam reported that some of them referred to the past. The important thing was that she identified figures, *i.e.,* mother, child, as symbolizing countries. This added validity because other subjects had reported this translation quirk of Nostradamus as well. It was definitely one of Nostradamus' methods of using symbols that other translators had not recognized. It helped establish that this was a true contact.

Some of Pam's more important interpretations will be grouped in the following chapters.

D: *Is he still looking in that bowl of water?*

P: He never has actually been looking *in* it. His eyes are looking at it, but he's looking beyond it. It's really cold and dank in his room where he sits. I feel aching in the joints of his fingers, and the ankles of his legs. I just thought I'd report that.

D: *He must sit in there for a long time. He must be dedicated; otherwise, he could leave the room if he got uncomfortable.*

P: I think "driven" is a better word.

Pam had no way of knowing that Nostradamus developed arthritis and later gout. It could very well have been caused by the damp, cold conditions in which he worked.

D: *Ask him if it would be all right if you came again at another time to talk to him.*

P: Well, it would be all right with *him,* if we didn't stay too long. *He* has more patience that I do. (*Laugh*) He seems to be a quite focused individual, and he's not as interested in getting through the muck of talking with me as he is in seeing what he is seeing. He also says that he did write down the quatrains, or prophecies, as he saw them at that time. I call them quatrains *now,* using our terminology. He says to think of these as probable futures. Not to think that is the *only* possible future.

D: *Can he give us any instructions on how to contact him again?*

P: He said in the future for us to know in advance when we're making this trip—which we definitely would do—because then I start to shoot out lines of communication ahead of time. It's like paving the way to get there a little easier.

While I was giving my closing instructions and counting Pam out of trance, I noticed she was making unusual facial expressions. She seemed to be trying to get her eyes open, and waved her hand in front of her face. I asked about this when she had returned to full consciousness.

P: I came from somewhere way back in the darkness, and I felt as if I was shooting forward in my head. It was like flying, and things were going by my eyes. So I thought I'd just open my eyes and look at it, but I couldn't make my eyelids open. (*Laugh*)

D: *That's why you were waving your hand in front of your face, trying to figure out, "Why can't I see."* (Laugh)

Pam tried to explain the procedure of translation of the quatrains.

P: When you start to read the quatrain, I begin to see images or *feel* images or *get* images. And I'm thinking and watching them and hardly ever hear the end of what you read. The beginning always seems to trigger something. When I do hear the end of the quatrain, frequently the skeptical me is asking, "What does that have to do with what I'm looking at?"

D: *But most of the time it all seems to go together.*

P: Does it? When you read the quatrain in English it is not necessarily a translation of the original. It could be a translation of a French translation of this archaic French, Latin, Greek and whatever other codes he wrote in. For true response to the quatrain, you really need to read it in the language it was written. What you're getting is a distortion of the translator.

D: *Yes, that's true, but I don't speak French.*

P: Well, even if you spoke French, I picked up that he wrote in *archaic* French, Greek and some Latin. So you would have to be a scholar of ancient languages to be able to do that. The French that you have in that book is *not* what Nostradamus wrote. It's a French translation of what he wrote. Archaic French and modern French are not always the same.

D: *They claim these are supposed to be the original quatrains. And many of the old words are supposed to be still in there.*

P: And they have the proper nuance? The translators were well-versed in meanings from that time?

D: *They claim they tried to preserve it as clearly as they could, using all the old words, even though they didn't understand them.*

At the next session I wanted to obtain more information about Nostradamus' private life before beginning the translation. Pam choose a different method of locating him.

P: I joined my spirit with a bird and flew to his window. I can turn around and see the outside. It's a stone room with a stone ledge, and I'm looking from a different perspective. I'm seeing him from the front, bent over the desk and his papers. I see a candle burned down, much dripped wax. I see the plume in his hand. I see his floppy hat. I don't actually see his face because he's bent over. I see his big nose sort of sticking out. It's brighter today than usual. It doesn't seem as dark and damp in there.

D: *Is there any other furniture in that room?*

P: There's a chair of rough-hewn lumber. A big table. I see a very heavy door that is founded on top. Now that I'm looking over here, it seems as if there's a little bed pushed up against one side of the wall. Small, more like a platform, but with covers. (*Chuckle*) He just flipped the plume at the window.

D: (Chuckle) *So he knows you're there?*

P: He says, "Of course, Dolores." (*Laugh*) I think he's getting used to you coming in. He doesn't seem as gloomy as usual. He seems to be in a good spirit.

D: *He knows we're from the future, doesn't he?*

P: Yes, he is very familiar with your energy.

D: *Ask him, has he ever journeyed to visit the king of France?*

P: I think that he has spoken to the king, and I believe he has been accorded respect from the court. There seems to be some validating thing that has taken place between the court and him. I see him talking to the king.

D: *Can you ask Nostradamus what he thought of the king?*

P: Yes, I can ask him, and I did. His response was that, as in many cases, this is a man who is ill-qualified for the position, but he's the one who has it. So Nostradamus and everybody else have to play their parts. The king doesn't have much respect and admiration.

D: *Has he ever seen the queen?*

P: I had the funniest mental picture when you said that. I saw the mean queen from *Alice in Wonderland. (Laugh)* It was funny. I can't actually shake it. But the picture is of a real stern pinched face. *(Pam scowled up her face. She exaggerated the face even more, and I laughed.)* I see this woman standing behind the king, whispering, "Don't listen to him. He doesn't know what he's talking about. He's just trying to gain your favor." Just mean whisperings. That's what I saw.

D: *Ask Nostradamus what he thinks of the queen.*

P: *(Loud laugh)* "Well, she's a woman, isn't she?" *(Laugh)* He really thinks women are inferior, definitely not totally human. He doesn't like her, but then he has a broad generalization about females. He's not very feeling. So he doesn't think about her any more or less than any other woman he encounters. He's rather disdainful of the whole idea of the court, but he does live in this framework, so he plays along. He really feels aloof. "I can take it or leave it, but since I live here I'll have to take it." They did have the power of life and death. They could have him executed if they wanted to. He feels mentally, emotionally and spiritually superior to the king and queen, and the rest of the court, too.

D: *Ask him if he has any students?*

P: Yes, he does. He teaches them some of the alchemy that he's familiar with. This is an actual, physical joining of different substances, chemicals. But mainly he teaches them how to manipulate fine energies. This is all for the purpose of healing.

D: *Where does he have his classes?*

P: It seems as if the room he's in now is a high room, and he has his classes in a low room. But it seems to be in the same stone place.

D: *Ask him if he has very many students at this time?*

P: I kept getting "six or seven," but he would prefer to work with one at a time. I don't see a favorite student. I don't see any women either.

D: *No women? Can you ask him why?*

P: The instant response was, "I don't like women." *(Laugh)*

D: *Tell him that in our time period we have biographies about his life because there is still much interest in him. We think there may be errors in these. They say he only had one student during his entire lifetime. What does he say about that?*

P: This is *wrong*. There are more. Some of these do not seem to understand what he tries to teach, and working with invisible forces is a difficult thing to do.

D: *Ask him if the name Chavigny is familiar to him.*

P: I only hear "protégé."

D: *His biographies say he was the only student that Nostradamus ever had, and that was toward the end of his life.*

P: Well, perhaps the most well-known, but not the only. I think Chavigny himself was Mister Ego. Nostradamus thinks he was a successful student. Nostradamus wants to know if he has been talked about as a kind and good man. He's concerned about how he's viewed by history.

D: *Is he? There have been many different views. Some people think maybe he was a real psychic, and that he really could see things in the future. Others don't really understand how he did it. And then there's also the view that he might have been a charlatan.*

P: Well, he knows he's not a charlatan. He couldn't tell you specifically *how* this all actually works. But it's all happened to him, so he can't deny that. His intent has always been to relate the truth as it has been revealed to him. And he would hope that generations into his future would look back and view him with thankfulness.

D: *There was one commentator in our time who said Nostradamus used too much wine or drugs, and that his visions came from hallucinations.*

P: There will always be those who scoff. It's only their loss. That is people's prejudices anyway. He does not use alcohol, which is a distorting substance. There *are* plant helpers, actual chemicals from nature that do create openings in the psyche. He definitely has experimented with and utilized these natural plant helpers, yes. These are expanding nature's gifts, if you will.

D: *Can you tell me which plants he has used?*

P: I see a blue flower. Morning glory, I think. He uses the seeds. I see some fuzzy leaves. Looks like ... comfort leaf. I'll see what it is. (*She had difficulty.*) Angel ... Angeli ... well, I'm having a debate because Angelica, as I know it, does not look like what I'm seeing. But I hear "Angelica," although I know it doesn't have broad, fuzzy leaves.

D: *Maybe he calls it differently.*

P: Perhaps that's it. There are also flowers used to help mental expansion and broader comprehension. There's a big white flower. It seems that the seeds of flowers are very powerful entities. There's something about the beauty and color of flowers that is the physical attribute of the subtle action of the plant itself. We can see the beauty and the color; we can smell the fragrance; and we can taste the nectar. These are all attributes that are in the physical realm. But they all are actually pointing to the invisible fine energies that are associated with these plant beings.

D: *Then you think he uses the seeds of flowers more than anything else?*

P: Yes, I see him grinding them with mortar and pestle. This is very interesting because he experiments on himself. He uses a few seeds, a few more seeds, and then a few more seeds. Seeds from a solo plant, seeds in combination with other plants. I see leaves that he has ground up. He is a very curious fellow.

D: *What does he do after he grinds them up?*

P: They are almost like a paste. Sometimes they're so unpalatable that he can't swallow them. But he will put the paste in his mouth and suck it for a long time and then spit out the pulp. There are other things he has done with it, adding water to make a drink. I even see honey being added to try to make it palatable, for he would like to ingest it. He thinks it's more powerful internally.

D: *Isn't he afraid that he might use something that would hurt him?*

P: He has what you would consider guides. There are invisible entities who guide him in this experimentation. He is very tuned in to the spirit world, as you well know, and is having help from entities who know these plants.

D: *But he's probably well aware that some plants are poisonous. Even the wrong combination could hurt him.*

P: Absolutely. In response to the poison comment, it seems that some of the plants he works with *are* poisonous. But if taken in certain dosage, an expansion, an explosion of consciousness takes place rather than death. It depends on the amount ingested and the combinations. He's not going to try strychnine, but he seems almost fearless. He seems to have guidance in how to work with these plants.

D: *What happens when he takes them?*

P: He is capable of leaving his body, his consciousness, so he is able to enter into the spirit world for more direct consultation. He does time travel so he is capable of seeing events as they perhaps are happening in that probability.

D: *But he's not afraid of taking too much?*

P: He said he has no room for fear. It's too limiting. He must trust those with whom he is in contact. If he had allowed fear to enter his consciousness, he would not have had the insights that he has had, nor the understanding.

D: *Does he have to do this every time?*

P: No. He has constant communication with the spirit world. This is to allow his consciousness to enter more *fully* into the spirit world. That is why he is doing the plant experimentation and ingestion. But the fact of the matter is, he hasn't taken any plants at this point, and he is communicating with us.

D: *When he takes these trips out of the body and time travels, does the drug interfere with his memory of what he has seen?*

P: No. As a matter of fact, it is a validation of what he has seen when he *hasn't* been taking the plant. It's like filling out the details of the pictures he perceives in the bowl and in the mirror, or the whisperings he hears inside his head. He views the drugs as helpers. But I don't think he uses the term "drugs." He calls it medicine. But he is a physical being who has an incredibly huge curiosity. So although he does receive guidance and can ask questions pertaining to these plants, he nevertheless has curiosity to see, "Well, what if I did this?" So he does do experiments of his *own.*

D: *Has he ever had any bad experiences while fooling with these different things?*

P: He has become nauseated. He's had internal distress. He said he hasn't died. (*Laugh*)

D: *Does he use drugs when he's working with patients?*

P: He absolutely *does,* but not to the extent that he uses them on himself. The combinations of plants and materials that he uses on his patients are for healing in the etheric realm as well as the physical realm. But he knows how to combine these drugs to focus on healing rather than expansion or time travel. He certainly would not put a bleeding person in trance and say, "Let's take a trip to the future." He would only use the plants for the specific focus of the moment.

D: *Does he know more about the use of plants and medicines and what we call "drugs" than the other doctors of his day?*

P: I suppose you would say "more," yes. Because he is familiar with the normal things: poultices, teas, *etc.,* but he has great information and knowledge beyond that, yes. But the mind expansion is not considered a healing technique, *per se.*

D: *In our time we have an expression that "it can blow your mind." He's not worried about that?*

P: He has weathered many storms, he says. If he has looked upon the scenes that he has looked upon, and has come back in full body, then he is capable of continuing his journeying.

D: *It's good that it's not necessary for him to do this all the time, or he would be constantly ... drugged.*

P: It's *absolutely* unnecessary. When we have sessions together it is not due to any substance that he's taken into his body. He does it *frequently,* but he does not *depend* on it.

D: *When he is using these different medicines does he contact other people like us?*

P: You could just consider him traveling around, viewing, taking notes, being the objective reporter, the wisp of smoke. He doesn't make contact with people like us as the entity Nostradamus because he enters into the collective pool of the spirit world. So, no, in answer to your question.

D: *Then what he does with us is a different thing.*

P: That is correct.

John observed Nostradamus having a type of drug reaction that caused a rash on his face and itching in his beard. At that time he said Nostradamus experimented with various plant substances. This was reported in Volume Two.

Chapter 5

The Light Being

𝕬 FEW DAYS AFTER I contacted Nostradamus through Pam, I had the first session with Nina. She was a petite and gentle Jewish woman in her early forties who had escaped the rat-race in California by moving to our area and opening a bed-and-breakfast establishment in her home. I had the idea that if we could succeed in contacting Nostradamus through several people then we could complete the translation of the remaining 500 quatrains quicker. It would also be an interesting experiment to see if all these people would succeed in contacting him, or at least seeing him as Beverly, the artist, had done (Volume Two). If this were possible, then it would prove that Nostradamus was true to his word and he would come through anyone I worked with. Of course they had to be good subjects capable of entering the deeper levels of hypnosis. All of these people had been conditioned to enter such a state and were comfortable working with me. None of them were aware of the work I had done with the others.

I used Nina's keyword and counted her back to the spirit state in-between lives. She saw a golden white light and was aware of great warmth. Immediately she was surrounded by energy patterns that created a peaceful floating sensation. Then she noticed a robed female light being with flowing blond hair. She described it as having form but yet not solid. Since she felt so comfortable with it, I assumed it was probably a guide or someone who had been sent to help us, as this has happened before. I asked Nina if she would be willing to help me with an experiment.

She answered, "Yes. I have a feeling that there are many who watch over me and help me. And the appropriate one will come forth if we need any instructions."

D: *Is it possible for you to look at someone's life while they are living on the Earth?*

N: Because you ask the question, it is so. I receive clarity and am able to do this.

D: *There was a man who lived in France in the 1500s whose name was Nostradamus. I have been working with him on an experiment. I wondered if it would be possible for you to locate him while he is alive?*

N: As you request it, it is made so, and I see a picture forming of a plaza, a square. There is much stone work. I feel I can view this man's life. And I feel this man you speak of is burdened very heavily. I am walking through this plaza, going down a street, and turning into this corridor. It seems as if this area of the buildings are made of quarried limestone. I feel I can walk up a stairway and locate this man you speak of. Yes. I picture the man. He seems to be mixing powders and looking over some type of book. He is doing work with remedies for healing. This is what I see him doing right now.

D: *What does he look like?*

N: Well, he's sitting on a stool with his back toward me. Let me see his features. This is a kind, learned face, but with many burdens upon him. A very serious, but caring man. He has these eyes that look very tired. He has a straight, but long, nose that looks kind of Romanesque from the side, and a mustache and beard. This is not a young man. He has this special coat on for working in this part of his building where he mixes the powders. And his head is covered with a rather large rounded cloth hat, mainly for warmth. These stone buildings are very drafty.

D: *Do you think you could pick up on his thoughts?*

N: It seems, right now, he's just occupied with mixing this healing powder and remedy. I guess his face looks a little worn, and he seems to be burdened. I can feel heaviness in his heart center and in the area around his head. I can tell he carries much heaviness with him.

D: *I wondered if there was a way to get his attention, to let him know you're there?*

N: No, I am not in the physical form. I do not think he would even be aware that I am with him. But I *do* know that I can view him as you ask. I know he heals. I know he teaches. I know there is an area below the laboratory where he carries on studies. I could probably come back and drop in on one of the classes.

D: *Do you think that would be the easiest way to get his attention?*

N: I hesitate now because I do not wish to disturb him. He knows nothing of my presence. He is concentrating on what he is doing, and I am not in a form. But I could go back out and walk the plaza. I could be with one of the students, if you wish to talk with him or answer questions. I see the plaza again. I see a student carrying books and wandering through the same route. We're entering the building through another way.

D: *Are you following him?*

N: Yes. I see that he is studying with this man, and is one of a select few of trusted, devoted students. I see two others right now, but I sense that his private students vary from about eight to ten.

D: *Do they all meet at one time?*

N: Rarely. There are times when they meet together, but usually there are smaller groups. He pursues different specialities. They receive the same general education, but he adapts their interests to their needs. So he has little groups within the larger group. What they study with him are things beyond the physical. This group that meets in this room is made aware of various conscious levels of the mind, and things beyond the physical, solid matter realm.

D: *Does the average person know that he teaches these things?*

N: No, these studies are very quiet. These few students that meet with him are a select group, who have brought to his attention that they are aware that things exist beyond the physical. They have learned that when these things are used in conjunction with the physical and medical studies, they can create healing and awareness far beyond the average person of his time. It seems to me this student—and he identifies himself as Pelladino (*phonetic*)—came to learn medicine. But as they talked privately he realized they had other beliefs that he wished to pursue. And so the man Nostradamus (*she had difficulty with the pronunciation, pronounced it stiffly*) invited this student to be part of the group. I feel that as Nostradamus approached the end of his physical life, he realized that the students were reaching out to him with other questions and other awarenesses. He felt the more information he could leave with them, the more that would be transferred on to students in other generations.

D: *The people who have written the history of his life said he only had one student, and that was in his later years.*

N: Well, the information I am getting is different. It is as I have reported. I see that the usual groups were small, twos or threes. I'm trying to get a picture of when they all meet, and from what I can see, there's somewhere between eight to ten when he holds a group session. But this is the area that is below the living space. So there might have been one particular student upstairs, who worked more with mixing the powders and the medical part.

D: *Can you see what this room looks like?*

N: This room is below the level where I first saw him on his stool making the powders. It's a very simple, plain, sparse room, and it's all stone. I see a table, a bookshelf, chairs and a desk. There are candles for lights, and I see two very narrow windows.

D: *Do you see anything on the table?*

N: I see books, many books. I see various instruments. I'm not sure I understand all of them. Some of them seem as if they are for studies of the sky, the astronomy. Some of these tools are made of metal and used for measurements, it seems. I'm not quite sure what they're for. Some of them could be medical.

D: *How can we let him know you're there, and that we would like to communicate with him?*

N: Since you ask, it shall be so, and we see the man, Nostradamus, coming down the stairway. (*She had been speaking with a definite accent. It became more pronounced for some reason, especially in the pronunciation of names.*) There's a stairway entrance from upstairs, and there's this doorway that we students come in, which most of his visitors for the pharmacy or the physician do not know about. Anyway, so here he comes down the stairs, and he welcomes the students. This is a kind man, a tired face, a worn-out man. But this is of great importance. He has knowledge of things that must continue. He stares out the window for some time. He almost gets into trance-like states. But here we are gathered for our lesson. This seems foolish, but ... he gazes into glass. It seems to calm him and this way focuses his attention so information can come through. There is a glass-like mirror on his table. He looks into that, and it seems to focus him. It clears up any disturbance from the day's work, so he can clear a passage in his mind and in his heart. This way he can continue to pass on the knowledge that must be taught. He looks up and greets the students. He knows Pelladino's here, and he makes contact and we can begin.

D: *Does he know that you are there?*

N: No. He's just talking to the students.

It was becoming obvious that this would not be the ideal working condition. There were too many other people around and too many distractions. It would be awkward to have him speak to us if he was concentrating on his lesson, although I'm sure the students were used to their teacher doing strange things.

D: *I know he's teaching, but is there any way you can let him know that you're in the room?*

N: No. We can do this, but not at this time. If I am to make myself visible to him, then I feel the class must end and the people must go. I am hearing that one of the guides who accompanied me should present themselves to him in light body form.

In order to accommodate this request, I moved her ahead in time until the class was over and the students had gone. It apparently was important for her to be in the room alone with him.

N: It has been decided that the guide I saw at first, the robed light being with the flowing hair, will be the one who will appear to him. She contacts him by using telepathy. Gently, very gently. I think we must do it this way, because we are so aware of his heavy burden. He turns around and looks at her. (*Emotional*) And his eyes fill with tears. She glows with warmth and love and affection, and he's aware of it. She lets him know she has come to ease his burden, and to let him know that his words will survive and will be understood. And his heart should be at peace.

D: *Why was he crying?*

N: I think he was in awe that he was allowed to see such a radiant being. Its words gave him hope, and filled him with joy to know his work would survive.

D: *Can he see you?*

N: No, I'm not in a form. I can hear. I can communicate. But it is between him and her. I'm aware. I can hear everything, but I'm an observer.

I began with my test question to establish where we were in his physical life.

D: *Is he writing his prophecies at this time?*

N: Yes. It is this that weighs heavy on his mind and heart. He knows this has to be done in secrecy because the Inquisition and the cruelties of the time will not allow the truth the way he feels it and sees it. He's too far ahead of his time.

D: *This is why it weighs heavily on him?*

N: Yes. The fact that he can see and know what will happen, and do nothing to change it. He could not bring it to the public because he would be labeled heretic and be burned.

D: *If it is so difficult, has he ever considered just forgetting about it and not bothering?*

N: No, because this is his purpose. This is his life's work. This is why he exists. This is why he passes it on and teaches the students.

D: *Can you get the concept across to him that I am speaking from the future and that I am interested in what he sees for our time?*

N: Yes. I think he understands that the benevolent being has come from another dimension, and she speaks of time in the future to him. This is not hard for him to understand. The telepathy is very clear.

D: *Would he be willing to tell me some things if I ask him questions?*

N: Yes, this is no problem.

D: *When he wrote his prophecies he wrote them in puzzle form.*

N: That's what some of them are. Some of them are disguised, for fear. Some just seem nonsensical to confuse and misinform. Others, if you had depth and awareness, you could understand. I think there were times, too, when he made it even more confusing because he was so burdened, so angered by the times. I think some of them are meant to be confusing and nonsensical, just to see if anyone could get *anything* from them. Or the things that people might make up and perceive, they might learn from themselves, a reflection of their own ignorance.

That was a new way of looking at it.

D: *He wanted people to really work at it. But if I read him some quatrains, would he be able to tell me what they mean?*

N: He can try it. I will use my benevolent being as interpreter.

I thought the logical place to begin was to again read the test quatrain that I had used in every case.

D: (CENTURY VII-14) *"He will come to expose the false topography. The urns of the tombs will be opened. Sects and holy philosophy to thrive. Black for white and the new for the old."* (Long pause)

N: (*Sigh*) There was so much. I was getting pictures and ... generations. I was seeing from the time of Columbus and discovering lands. And I was getting times of Jesus and, oh, very many things. My head was spinning. It was coming too fast.

I repeated the quatrain slowly one line at a time with a pause between. She was apparently being bombarded by visual images. This was the same thing that had occurred when Wayne first began to interpret. Too much information was being given in a flood and it was difficult if not impossible to interpret what these scenes meant. Her subconscious would have to slow it down to where she could understand it.

N: When you said "false topography," I saw there have been many false topographies through the centuries. My telepathy was picking up on so many, from the discovery of America to many other things. From when our Earth was evolving between ice ages and all the changing false topography. If I can call them this, I don't know. There are false topographies all through. Oh, my benevolent being has shown me another picture. (*Confused*) It's very strange, very strange. It's many, many years ahead and I think I saw centuries and centuries going by in front of me. But in this case the "false topography" is the cover-up. This is the misinformation about the space crafts and space stations and all. The misinformation of what the space program told us.

D: *What do you mean? Did they give us misinformation?*

N: Yes. They know the truth. I know there is also the false topography of what's happening in the photographing of various planets and stations and vehicles on the moon, that were not put there by ... certain people. I am going to ask for clarity, for I am getting too much, too much.

D: *I was thinking it might be easier if she can focus on something definite.*

N: She is telling me that "the urns of the tombs" are information. This is not literally a physical urn or a physical tomb. This is years upon years of information, and it is the exposure of material that was kept from a public that should have been told the truth. (*She mumbled as she repeated the line.*) "Sects and holy philosophy to thrive." This they might have finally gotten correct. This brings unity, for there is only one sect and one holy philosophy. This is encouraging. This is hopeful, for the people of this Earth will come together to realize that there is the universal sect. There is only one philosophy of good, one holy philosophy.

D: *And the last part is, "Black for white and the new for the old."*

N: I think this is talking about reflection, about a time in the future where there will reign a new philosophy, a new unity. The "black for the white" is just a symbolic reflection. But there will be the new philosophy, the new awareness, the new body.

D: *I think you are doing a lot better at focusing, aren't you?*

N: I think I had to calm down. It was bombardment. There was too much, too many scenes. It was a movie being shown too quickly.

D: *Does Nostradamus have any reaction when you're doing this?*

N: I think he's almost in a trance. He reacts well and he feels encouraged. Even though there is so much that he feels might be negative, this benevolent being is also showing him the possibilities of what he's seeing. She shows him that destiny can be controlled, it can be changed. And even though cleansings and horrendous things happen, there is purpose to it all. I think he needs to know this to continue in his work.

D: *He thought the future couldn't be changed?*

N: He believes that the scenes he sees are real and true. He believes that everything is possible, and these things very well can come to pass. And if the universal sect, the universal philosophy comes about, it can be changed. But he also knows that a part of him lives in his lifetime and he sees the cruelty, the inhumanity that exists.

Since I felt she had passed the test and this was indeed a true contact, I then began with the interpretation of other quatrains. She immediately ran into a problem similar to what Phil experienced. The quatrain brought scenes that carried intense feelings of emotion. Nina felt futility, pain and suffering. I could tell by the expressions on her face that this was bothering her and I tried to dissociate her from it so she could view the scenes as an objective reporter. I was beginning to feel that this must have also been a problem with Nostradamus. He must have also felt the undercurrent of the emotions created by the deeds portrayed by man's inhumanity to man. He also had the frustration of not having anyone to share this with. He had no one to help him vent or release the anxiety and helplessness he felt as a watcher who could do nothing but have empathy.

In an attempt to protect Nina, the light being tried to interpret what she was seeing in a positive way, refusing to acknowledge the negativity of the scenes. Nina stated, "I think my benevolent being is showing me the other path, for she will not allow some of the pictures he set forth to happen." This procedure became so obvious that it was confusing, because the denial of the meaning was being stretched so far in the other direction that it became implausible. The being was trying to find positive alternate interpretations that definitely were not describing scenes that would come from the Nostradamus I had come to know. I had to explain to the entity that I understood the need to protect Nina, also the need to convert the information into positive avenues. I understood it did not want to focus on the negative for fear of creating that very thing. But the being would have to understand that Nostradamus had a specific reason for wanting us to see the negative or alternate path. He felt we could not do anything to prevent it from happening if we did not know what the event would be. If we did not know what lay down the other path, we would not know what actions to take in order to avoid traveling that path. With a sigh she agreed and began to allow the scenes of violence to be translated.

I was again positive we were truly in contact with Nostradamus when Nina began to interpret the symbols of people in the quatrain as referring to countries and alliances, *i.e.*: brother, father, mother, son, marriage. These had always been interpreted by others as referring to actual physical personages in different periods of history. Instead, we had found that they sometimes refer to relationships between various countries, and even closer ties within certain countries. This explains why interpreters in the past have had such difficulty. They have tried to be too literal, and Nostradamus is anything but literal. His symbolism is very deep and can refer to many different levels of understanding, some even beyond what he originally intended.

Nina also found some quatrains that were general, referring to the same theme continually repeated throughout many phases of history. Some were philosophical because Nostradamus felt areas of thought also influenced the affairs of man. These were again patterns that Brenda had found in her interpretations.

Nina also saw that some quatrains related to the past because she was shown scenes that were definitely not modern. She was not given words but had to interpret what time period she was seeing from clues within the picture. Since this was more difficult we skimmed over these, acknowledging that they were from the past. We had been told not to spend much time on these anyway, but to concentrate on our present time period. Some of Nina's more interesting interpretations of the quatrains will be included in the appropriate chapters. I am only reporting in these chapters how the connections came about, and how each new subject accomplished this connection with Nostradamus in a different way, unique unto themselves.

When we were ready to leave this first session, I wanted to be sure that we could return again. He said that was no problem. He would be at his desk in the lower level awaiting our arrival. Nina felt we would need the benevolent spirit to accompany us on these journeys because, "She gives hope and some clarity, and helps him to believe in the future."

We talked for a while after she awakened, and she admitted this was the strangest type of session we had ever done. She said that doing a past-life regression was a snap compared to this. This was extremely difficult. There was so much information flooding into her mind and much of it wasn't clear. "I don't even know where it was coming from. I was getting pictures while you were reading, and I couldn't make sense of the words sometimes. It was like I was totally this observer, and I wasn't in any form at all. I saw this angelic being so clearly, but now all I can remember are disjointed scenes. The feelings right now are very negative, a lot of violence and war and people killing off people for generations upon generations. And it seems that finally something has to happen."

"But does it bother you to see things that are negative," I asked. I was worried that she might react the same as Phil and not be able to continue working on this.

She answered thoughtfully, "No, but I think that's because we went into this with a certain intent. But I didn't expect Nostradamus to be the way I saw him. He was so burdened and so heavy, he was like a broken man. I mean, he was kind but he was almost worn out and used up. Maybe that's why this benevolent being made it so hazy and hard to interpret. It was interesting because I really felt at home there. When I first saw the square and the stone buildings, I felt very comfortable as if I knew where I was."

Later that night as Nina was trying to go to sleep she began to perceive feelings that she associated with Nostradamus. She felt that as time went on he became despondent over humanity's ignorance and arrogance. She felt that some of the puzzles might reflect this, as a punishment given to humanity of the future. She said she found his quatrains frustrating and nonsensical. But that night she could feel his pain and hopelessness so deeply that she thought it was continuing into our present time.

In future sessions she discovered a pattern that would be repeated by both herself, Wayne, and especially Pam. They found Nostradamus at different times in his life. When they located Nostradamus at a younger age he seems to be curious, daring and excited about his experiments. When they saw him as an older man the frustration was very evident. He then seemed to be a prisoner of his own making, compelled to sit and stare for endless hours at the black mirror. He saw the future and yet was unable to do anything about it, and gradually developed crippling arthritis from so much time spent in that dark, damp room. None of these subjects liked to be around him when he was older. We attempted to reach him at the younger age because then he was more receptive and welcomed our presence with the excitement and curiosity of an inquisitive mind.

This had also been the case with John, the astrologer (reported in Volume Two). When John visited Nostradamus as an old man he was not expecting us. He had a heart attack while we were there and it was so depressing that we also chose to only contact him at a younger age. Nina was especially sensitive to this and did not want to work with him at the older age. Since we never knew when we would enter his life, I had to devise a way to direct our visits to younger, happier times.

J COULD UTILIZE THESE THREE SUBJECTS for the translation of the remainder of the unsolved quatrains. With determination I set out to complete this project in the least amount of time. I arranged my sessions so that I could work with all three in one day when it was possible. It saved travel time for me since they lived in a city 30 miles distant. I would have one session in the morning, another in the afternoon, then eat supper and have the late session with Wayne. I usually would arrive back home after midnight. It was a full day's work, but I felt a lot was being accomplished. But there were several drawbacks and obstacles. Although these subjects were sincere, and I was positive their contacts were valid, they did not have the speed and agility that Brenda had exhibited during her long contact with Nostradamus. When working with Brenda the translations came through much more freely, and she had shown no opposition to the negativity she was witnessing. The others openly questioned what they were receiving, wondering (even while in trance) whether their explanations were accurate. They were unfamiliar with the volume of material I had already accumulated. I knew there were many similarities, and their interpretations were small individual pieces that could be added to the whole. They had much doubt, and I could tell by their faltering that they would not remain with the project long enough to complete it. I knew I was fast approaching a stalemate again.

Wayne was the first to stop. In the beginning when he agreed to try the experiment for a few weeks, I knew he did not have the commitment necessary for the huge task. There was no way it could be completed in a few weeks, even if I could arrange more sessions. The three had all consented to give me one day a week, and I could not expect more because their individual lives took precedence. Wayne thought the project too time-consuming, and he also doubted the information coming through. Nina ran a bed-and-breakfast establishment in her home. As soon as the tourist season began she had to quit because there would be no privacy. She also was doubting the validity of the information, and wished there was some way to have confirmation. Pam held on the longest, but she began to have difficulty with the translations. She did not like the negativity she was being shown (anymore than Nina did), and she also thought the project was taking up too much of her time. I continued to work with Pam on another phase of this project instead of the translation. This portion will be reported in later chapters. After a few months I lost the cooperation of all three of these subjects.

Chapter 6

Brenda Returns

WHEN DOUBTS FIRST BEGAN TO SURFACE I tried to prepare for this inevitability by finding another source. I was determined to finish this project. I wanted to devote my attention to other books I wanted to write. I, too, was tired, but I knew I couldn't quit until my commitment was finished. Nostradamus had cemented my dedication and cooperation three years earlier. I felt a strong moral obligation not to let him down. The others could not possibly have this same feeling of pressure, because they had only had a short association with the man. I decided to approach Brenda and see if she would consent to working again. Because of money problems, she had quit college in the spring of 1987 and taken a night-time job in a factory. She was too tired to work on this project, plus I suspected she was suffering from psychic burnout because of the intense regimen of translating. I assumed that once she was ready to proceed she would contact me. Two years passed, and although I occasionally saw her and spoke with her on the phone, she had not expressed any desire to continue with the project. By the spring of 1989 she had found a conventional job in an office with more comfortable hours, and she had returned to her music classes part-time at the college. Maybe the feeling of pressure had finally been released. I took a chance and called her. I explained to her that I was trying to finish, and that I had found some others to help with this project. I asked if she would be willing to join with them so we could get through sooner. She finally agreed that there wouldn't be as much pressure on her if others were also working on this, and decided to work again as long as the full bulk and burden of translation would not be on her.

When we met for the session, this was Brenda's first contact with Nostradamus in two years. I used her keyword and counted her backward to make the connection. It worked perfectly and immediately as if there had been no interruption. This was further validation that the conditioning works no matter how much time has elapsed in our physical plane.

B: I'm here in the special meeting place conversing with Michel de Notredame. We're sitting at a table. It is a wondrous device that also has a library stored within its matrix, so we can call up knowledge of many things. It is an advanced version of the library with which we are familiar. The molecular structure of the table stores the knowledge. It's similar to a computer and table all in one. The surface is smooth and gray, reflective.

D: *How does the knowledge appear?*

B: In whatever form is necessary. Sometimes it appears as printed words on the table top, and sometimes it appears as a picture floating above the table top.

D: *Does he want to use this method today?*

B: We were just sitting here. If it comes in handy, he will. Otherwise he'll just use the regular methods.

D: *All right. But it seems like a good alternative, doesn't it?*

B: Yes. We were happy to find it. I was telling him about some of the things I have learned concerning the planets in the solar system. And he was saying how that related to the science of astrology.

D: *Can you share it with me?*

B: Oh, it was just a general conversation. I was telling him about the rings around Saturn and such as this. He was saying that although he is aware of many things concerning the universe, some areas were not covered. And the additional bits of knowledge fit in with what he already knows. It makes sense to him.

D: *Do you mean planets he didn't know existed?*

B: No, no, no. He knew the planets were there; he just didn't know much about them. I was telling him because I thought he might find it interesting. We have also been conversing about how the movements of the planets and stars may parallel certain rules of music theory. We have been making comparisons between what we are both familiar with because I'm a musician and he's an astronomer.

D: *Is there a parallel?*

B: In some cases. He is familiar with the term "music of the spheres," and we have been drawing parallels to see if there is any theoretical basis for some of the old beliefs. It is said that when the gods set the planets and the stars in their courses to take their paths across the night skies, that this created music out in space. It is what Michel de Notredame calls the "ether" (*pronounced: ather*), and it creates music. So with his knowledge of stars and planets and my knowledge of music we have been trying to figure out if perhaps this is true. It has been a very stimulating discussion.

D: *Was this a belief in his time?*

B: No, this was a belief from the ancient Greeks, from the Greek scientist Archimedes and such. Nostradamus has been proving different things that the Greeks said, even though the Catholic Church disagrees with much of this.

D: *What conclusions did you come to?*

B: We conclude that there probably is music out there. There are facts to support it. Perhaps it is at a frequency the human ear cannot detect. But given the mathematical correspondences in regards to the position of the planets and their distance from the sun, and the mathematical correspondences of the various intervals of sound and music and how they relate to each other, some parallels can be made. It's just a matter of building the devices necessary to pick up the sounds that we don't hear. Now he is showing me the depths of space. It's like we're flying very fast through space, and we are looking at the different stars and their planets. It's a changing scene. It almost makes you feel like you're really out there amongst the stars, in a ship or something that can travel fast enough to get you there before you grow old and die. We're floating above the solar system, and looking at how beautiful everything is.

D: *What does he think of it?*

B: Oh, he agrees, it's very beautiful. He considers it to be one of the glories of creation. He says since God set humans up to be the lord over creation, that would include space. And it is only right that we should reach for the stars.

D: *But this is not what people in his time think, is it?*

B: No, not at all, absolutely not. He says the Inquisition is extremely narrow-minded and ignorant to keep such beauty from humankind. They will not allow scientists like Copernicus to study and learn from the skies because, according to the Inquisition, the Earth is the center of the universe, the center of all creation, and everything else circles around the Earth. Other than that, the planets and such have no significance. They say one should not study the planets because it would distract from studying about God's glory.

D: *They don't consider that as part of God's glory?*

B: It's not as glorious as the sun, for example. They say the stars are lights shining through from Heaven. And if one wants to see the full glory of Heaven, one concentrates on what they say to do instead of studying the world around you.

D: *What is their version of the sun?*

B: It rotates around the Earth which is in the center of the universe. The moon circles around the Earth, the sun circles around behind that, and then the planets.

D: *At least they're admitting the world is round.*

B: Oh, yes, everybody knows that, and have for quite some time. Some things can't be denied without being made into a laughing stock.

D: *But they haven't accepted the idea yet that everything circles the sun.*

B: They resist it. The scientists and educated people know it is so. But you don't say it very loud because the Inquisition will hear.

D: *I am curious to know what his personal concept of God is? How does he perceive God?*

B: He says he perceives God as representing wisdom and understanding.

He believes his ability to see the future comes directly from God. Because that's part of what God is, knowing what's going to happen, or at least knowing the possibilities. He says he does not agree with what the church says about God. He believes the church does not have a full understanding of deity. They are trying to place narrow man-made restrictions upon Him. He says in the pursuit of knowledge there is no such thing as heresy, no matter what the church says.

D: *It has been brought up that he does not seem to be religious, per se.*

B: He says when he thinks about religious things he views it more as a philosophy rather than as something to be fanatical about. He says the visions themselves come from the future, but he believes his talent, his ability to tap into them is something special that is granted him by God. And what he finds out from it is up to him and how he uses it because what he sees about the future does not come from God. The visions are just the possibilities of what might happen. He says when God gave him the talent, he could have decided to stifle it instead of doing something about it. The talent itself comes from God, but what he does with it comes from himself.

D: *Then he* does *believe in God.*

B: He says he has his own perception of God. He does not view God as a man-looking figure standing up there throwing lightning bolts. The way he perceives God is not through picturing him as God, but simply through knowledge and developing his philosophy of life through his time. The church doesn't like what he is involved in, partly because they don't understand it, and partly because he refuses to try to fit into the structure of things.

D: *There are people in our time who think what he does may be evil and influenced by the Devil because they don't understand.*

B: He says there are a lot of narrow-minded and unfortunately ignorant people everywhere you go. They are going to have negative opinions about anything they don't understand.

D: *He has a very inquiring mind, doesn't he?*

B: Yes, he does. His mustache bristled a bit. He said through his communication with you he has picked up some things from your century. The other communicators think better in the back of their minds as well, as they help him to bring forth his translations of his quatrains.

D: *So he's able to pick up things from our minds without our knowledge. Does he realize it's been a while since we've contacted him?*

B: He says he can sense that a period of time has passed at our end, although it has not been as long at his end. He appreciates our being led to meet with him again. He said we should not let the vicissitudes of time affect us too drastically since time is really not as rigid as we think it is. Time is actually very flexible.

D: *We all have our own lives to live and our daily demands that get in the way.*

B: He says that is to be expected. As long as we are physical beings in a physical world there are going to be things to take care of.

D: *Tell him we have been able to publish some of his quatrains in our time period, with the correct translations he has given to us.*

B: He is smiling, and he immediately raised a goblet of champagne and said, "Let's celebrate." He said he knew it would work out because he knows the power behind this information. He has seen it through his mirror, and he knew that ultimately nothing can stand in the way.

D: *I've also been bringing other vehicles to him. I didn't know if he was aware of this or not.*

B: He suspected as much. He says each vehicle has a different feel when operating through them. He had gotten accustomed to working with this vehicle where communication was fairly free and easy. And all of a sudden he was working with a vehicle that was not comfortable with the situation.

D: *Yes, but there were times when certain vehicles were not available, and I had to locate another one.*

B: He's not criticizing you for that. He's just saying that he did notice the difference. He says that is to be expected when you're using human beings. He's quite happy to help. He realizes that due to the methods being used for clarifying these things, that all must remain flexible in the arrangements.

D: *Some of the other vehicles have picked up on something. I know he doesn't like to speak about his personal life, but they seemed to sense something coming from him. And I wanted to ask him if it was true.*

B: What is it they have sensed?

D: *They have the feeling that as he grows older he becomes very discouraged and very irritated, so to speak, with humanity in general, and with man's inabilities to understand what he's trying to do.*

B: He says off and on throughout his life it's always been somewhat easy to be discouraged because no one could understand these things that he sees all the time. He says when you have a gift that nobody else has—particularly when you're surrounded by ignorant priests who refuse to acknowledge it as a gift from God—people find it very easy to call it a gift from the Devil instead. And so he says, yes, there were times when he was very discouraged, because he's human. He knew he had a special mission on Earth and a special task to fulfill. He has worked very hard to fulfill it, and to do the best he can. But at the same time there were times when he'd get discouraged, and perhaps somewhat irritable as a result. He says the thing that is most discouraging is that his family cannot understand either.

D: *Do you mean his wife or his entire family?*

B: His children mainly. They couldn't understand what he was doing or why.

D: *The other vehicles picked up that he was very frustrated.*

B: Yes, he says this is true. It has always been extremely frustrating.

That's one of the reasons he's glad to be able to communicate like this. It helps ease some of the frustration for him. He has often questioned why, with abilities like his, he was born in such an ignorant—well, not necessarily an ignorant age—but an age where so much ignorance was still around. He has often felt that had he been born in the future perhaps things would be a bit different for him. But one can never second-guess what has already happened.

D: *The other vehicles also thought that as his frustration grew, he decided to punish humanity by deliberately making his quatrains even more muddled. They thought he finally became so frustrated he just said, "I'll show them. They don't understand anyway. Nobody understands. So I'll just make it as difficult as I can. I'll make it so complicated that nobody can understand them." And he became worse and worse about the symbolism.*

B: No, no. He says as the years progressed he had to get trickier with disguising his quatrains and visions. Not because he was angry at humanity or because of frustration, but because of the persecution he was getting. He said he is trying to stay on this plane as long as possible to attempt to get through as much information as possible. He felt he needed to be more careful with the way he wrote his quatrains, and that he had to disguise things more cleverly to keep from being burned at the stake or whatever. It was a defensive measure, but it wasn't because of saying, "Well, I'll show you." It was just a matter of, "I'm going to do this anyway, but I'm not going to be killed for it." Some of the vehicles realize he is human, but not all of them do. He says he *is* human just like everybody else. He just happens to have some special gifts. If you'd gone through this for decades on end, you'd be discouraged too. He says he doesn't stay discouraged all the time, but it does come upon him.

We then proceeded with the translation of the quatrains, and it went so smoothly it was as though the two-year hiatus had never occurred.

For the first time I felt there was a light at the end of the tunnel, that it might actually be possible to translate all the quatrains. I set up appointments, and by that time I was traveling to two different cities to work with all four different subjects on the Nostradamus material, as well as dividing my time among other continuing projects and investigating UFO cases for MUFON. My days were very full, and any spare time was spent in the transcribing of the tapes and trying to decide which material to use. By the summer of 1989 all the subjects had dropped out except Brenda. By that time I knew I was reaching the end. If there were no more interruptions I felt I would be through by Spring 1990. I could still hear Wayne's parting remark, "Dolores, I don't think you will *ever* finish this."

As usual life gets in the way, and I felt I was making progress if Brenda could work in two sessions with me in a month. There were many times I would drive the 30 miles to her home expecting to have a session, only to find a note on the door informing me that something else had taken precedence and we would not be able to have the session. There were other discouraging days when there was no note, and I waited in my car for hours until it became obvious that she had simply made other plans. It seemed as though I was the only one in this entire project that fully realized its importance and its urgency. It often appeared that I was a nuisance that these subjects politely tolerated and didn't wish to offend.

Finally, in July 1990 we translated the last quatrain. It is impossible to describe the feeling of exhilaration and completion I felt as I checked the final quatrain off and closed Ms. Cheetham's book for the last time. The project had been completed almost four years to the day from its inception. Of course, it had not been steady for the entire four years, but it was strange that it ended at the same time of the year that it had begun. After that I had a few more sessions to clarify some of the quatrains interpreted by the others, and I asked about the Black Prophecies or Lost Prophecies. All of this will be condensed and reported in this book.

In the next chapters I have categorized the interpretations supplied by Wayne, Pam, Nina and Brenda on similar topics. As I have done before in the first two volumes, I have omitted quatrains dealing with the past (unless there was unusual symbolism) and concentrated on those dealing with our immediate future (the next 20 years). These were my instructions in the beginning and had been repeated through all the subjects.

The similarity between the information given by all involved can only be marveled at. There were no contradictions, only extra pieces added to the growing puzzle. All the subjects saw the same man, gave the same description of both him and the room they saw him in. They all saw the mirror as a focal point, and it was always in the same place on the desk. Wayne and Brenda saw the scenes in the gray cloud bank, as had the initial contact, Elena. Pam and Nina saw the scenes enacted in the mirror, as John had seen them in Volume Two. There were similar scenarios, similar anagrams and symbolism given. They all encountered Nostradamus at different stages of his life, and his appearance and attitudes were the same. Information they gave coincided perfectly with each other and research of facts known about his life. They also supplied many facts that are unknown and are not available anywhere else. I think there can be no rational explanation for all of this occurring, except that we were all really in touch with Nostradamus.

I felt as though I had won a great victory. The battle was over, now the task of organizing the material and presenting it to the world remained. I spent untold hours transcribing the tapes and condensing thousands of pages to arrive at the final version of these three books. But the work is done and the great master's visions are at last converted to modern language and presented in book form. Now it is up to others to understand and heed. If only it isn't too late.

Section Two

The Information

Chapter 7

Nostradamus'
Healing Methods

NOSTRADAMUS HAS BEEN SURROUNDED by a mystique that has persisted for 400 years. This is undoubtedly part of the reason his works have survived. If he had been a normal writer and physician he would not have attracted much attention. But he was considered unusual during his own time period. Even then mystery swirled about the man, and he was feared by the common superstitious people of his time. It has been said that even if his prophecies had not insured his enduring notoriety, his work in healing would have caused his fame to continue after his death. He lived in an era of great ignorance. The doctors of his day did not understand the causes of disease and this made the plagues that ravaged the land seem even more demonic. They were viewed as punishment from God, and the medical field accepted their limitations to halt the scourges. They watched helplessly as wave after wave of deadly plagues devoured the people.

Pain was difficult to alleviate and infection was rampant in the filthy unsanitary conditions that prevailed, especially in the vermin-ridden cities. The doctors were oftentimes as superstitious as their patients and were afraid to try any type of new techniques. They clung frantically to the proven methods with almost a religious fervor. The methods became rituals and the average doctor would not have considered thinking for himself and devising unorthodox healing practices.

Thus Nostradamus was viewed with suspicion. Since he did not fit the mold, he threatened their security. He dared to do the unthinkable, he experimented with untried methods. He went unafraid into the plague-ridden cities and emerged unscathed. The other doctors at first scoffed at his unorthodox approach to healing, and then became jealous of his successes. When they couldn't duplicate what he did they became convinced that he was in league with the Devil. Nostradamus was constantly spied upon by people trying to learn his secrets. His biographers think he may have developed some type of powder that was used as a disinfectant, or other medicines that were not in common use in his day. Whatever his secrets were, they have not come down to us. But his fame as a healer created such an enigma that it was enough to insure his fame through four centuries. The prophecies were another phase and only served to enhance the mysteries that surrounded him. Thus I thought it was as important to discover his healing methods as it was to decipher the puzzles of the quatrains. This was one of the first questions I asked any of the subjects that were able to contact him. It is amazing that all of their answers match each other. Apparently he had no secret formulas or medications; he had become an adept master of working with the mind. This is something that would never have been understood by the other physicians in his time. I imagine that he must have tried to share it with some of them, but most were too shackled by the beliefs of their time. Physicians of our own day are similarly shackled. The learned men of Nostradamus' day were still in awe of the functions of the body, and were unwilling to imagine that the mind could have any influence on its workings. After all, the emanations of the brain were invisible and could not be proven and demonstrated under laboratory conditions. To deviate from the recognized methods was to wander into witchcraft and tempt the wrath of the church and the Inquisition. Nostradamus was forced to keep his discoveries secret, except for a handful of students that came to study with him. It must have been very difficult for this compassionate man to know he held answers that could have given the people of his day a better life, and yet not be able to share them. He could only help people in a limited way, for they seemed to trust and accept what he gave to them. His biography says he was almost worshipped by those whom he cured, while others accused him of being involved in dark practices. Nostradamus was truly a man ahead of his time, and it must have pained him very much to have knowledge that could never be imparted—except to the future, to *our* time.

The following are excerpts from various subjects' reports of Nostradamus' healing practices. In Volume One Elena and Brenda reported similar descriptions.

D: *In his medicine that he practices, does he use the normal methods of his day?*

P: [Phil] No, he uses more natural ingredients. Herbs and poultices, as opposed to chemicals, such as sulfur and brine. He would be more inclined to use plants than powders or elements.

D: *What does he do for people that are in pain?*

P: Sometimes he uses a form of mind control. It is simply focusing one's attention away from the pain. I see him grasping both of the patient's temples with his hands, and locking their gaze. He speaks firmly to the patient while applying pressure to the temples, and directs the patient's attention away from the pain.

D: *Is this a practice that is used by other doctors in his time?*

P: No, it is considered witchcraft.

D: *Does he use any other medical methods that are not orthodox?*
P: He applies pressure to various points on the body to relieve pain in a corresponding part of the body. There are many different techniques. One is partial suffocation, so that consciousness is lost. However, not to the point of death, just so that the victim would pass out. They then would be rendered unconscious for the short period of time necessary to perhaps close a wound.

D: *What is Nostradamus' occupation?*
W: [Wayne] He's a healer, but his methods are not widely known in his time.
D: *What did he do that was different?*
W: He worked with the mind. He had the ability to put people in a trance state. I think he did it through his eyes.
D: *How was he able to control pain?*
W: He did not control the pain. The patients controlled the pain. It was through a form of hypnosis. The body itself controls the pain.
D: *But the humans in his time were not familiar in working with the mind.*
W: All humans have the capability of working with the mind.
D: *But isn't it true that the other doctors didn't have the same results?*
W: Yes. One person may be gifted more in one area and another person in a different area. And to realize the gift and practice using it, one becomes more proficient than another. It seems if you have the interest and discipline, many things are available.
D: *Couldn't he teach these methods to the other doctors in his time?*
W: No, they were considered magic. His methods were not understandable. They could not be explained.
D: *We are curious about his healing methods. We've heard that he did not use conventional methods of his time.*
W: He did not use conventional healing methods of *any* time. They are methods that are age-old and age-new.
D: *That would be a good way to put it. Can he share some with us?*
W: He has positive effects in most areas of his healing, from setting bones to curing cancers. He works a lot with energy and through the aura and the chakras. He works with energy much more than people are aware of.
D: *Does he call them chakras, or does he have another name for them?*
W: Energy centers.
D: *Where did he learn these methods if they are so old?*
W: He learned them from his work in meditation. They came to him through his quest for knowledge.
D: *There is one question that people have asked. During the times when the plagues were very bad in his land, he had success where other doctors failed. How was he able to do this?*
W: It was by balancing the energy of the aura. He does this many times with the energy of his own aura, and also with movement. (*I asked for*

an explanation.) To discover where the block is, it either needs to be opened or closed. And this is done through the auric field with either a clockwise or counter-clockwise motion of the hand.

D: *How does he know when it is closed?*

W: He can feel it in the auric body.

D: *Which way opens the chakra?*

W: Clockwise.

D: *Does he touch the patient?*

W: Yes, he physically touches them and also physically scans them with his hands. If there is too great an influx of energy coming into an energy center, a counter-clockwise motion of his hand above the area will diminish the opening.

D: *He doesn't want too much energy coming in either?*

W: He finds the balance or puts the body into harmony. When the body is in harmony, it heals itself. He is able to see and feel the energy flow because he is able to see the patient's aura.

D: *Does he ask the patient to do anything?*

W: He has conversations with his patient as he is working with them. Generally it is in a concept of visualization.

D: *What does he ask them to visualize?*

W: Well, it depends on the ailment, of course. If he is treating a broken arm he will naturally have the patient visualize the bone mending together.

D: *What about in the case of a plague?*

W: In the case of the plague or any disease, he will reaffirm the circulation of the bloodstream and the balance between the different blood cells and the body. Just the general affirmation of how the body should work.

D: *Then he didn't have any type of miracle cures?*

W: Well? These would be considered a miracle in his time. They are considered miracle cures in any time.

D: *Some people thought he had some kind of secret medication that he used on the patients.*

W: People think what they will.

D: *They also wondered how he was able to do this and not become ill himself.*

W: With the knowledge. Physician heal thyself. If you are able to heal others, then I would venture to say *always* the healing of oneself is primary.

D: *The other physicians couldn't understand how he went among so much disease and didn't get sick himself.*

W: The secret—if it's a secret at all—is in the knowledge of healing. This is the knowledge that he practiced. He practiced conventional medicine also. There was the dispensing of herbs and drugs, and stitches. But he also practiced medicine from the information that he derived from his meditations.

D: *He must have had a great deal of confidence that they would work.*

W: Confidence is the very main ingredient of any occupation.

D: *Did he ever try to show the other doctors how to do this?*

W: He would share this knowledge with others, yes, a select few. He did not go out of his way to teach people who did not want to learn.

D: *Didn't you say that Nostradamus was a doctor, or that he taught medicine?*

N: [Nina] Yes, he is a physician and this includes medications also. I remember the first time we came in, I saw him working at a bench mixing powders for healing. He performs many tests. Physicians of his day were knowledgeable in many areas.

D: *For a long time people have wanted to know how he was able to perform cures that others in his time couldn't do.*

N: This goes into the *other* realm of working with the intent of the mind, and through his own experimentation upon himself and upon his patients. He uses a form of working through the mind to control slowing the heart rate and the blood flow.

D: *Were these things that were used by other physicians in his time?*

N: No, they would not be accepted as being of the science. He had an awareness that you treat the whole being. He was able to see much more and knew how to work on healing through putting somebody in a state of suspension, too. No, it was not accepted at all. In fact, he had to give very scientific, rational reasons for his healings because he would have been considered a heretic, a witch—somebody of black magic. His ideas would not have been accepted.

D: *This was why he couldn't share them with the other doctors.*

N: Right. By using himself as his own example and experiment, he believed that he could control these things. He could also have a patient help him in his healing if he got his patient in a relaxed state.

D: *You said he experimented on himself?*

N: When he received these visions or voices ... I see one time when he cut himself to see if he could control the blood flow, and gain an understanding of what the voices and the visions were saying. And through experimenting with himself on healing and control, he was able to use this on his patients.

D: *Experimenting on himself was a very brave thing to do.*

N: Yes, but he took it slow and worked at levels he knew he could control.

D: *What kind of work does he do to occupy his time whenever he is not writing?*

P: [Pam] I think he teaches and heals. And I know from looking at him that he manipulates energy. He actually seems to be able to *see* energies that most other folks don't.

D: *I was curious about what type of healing methods he uses. Can you ask him?*

P: When you asked the question, his response was that he was capable of manipulating energies. Where there is blockage, he can open it. Where there is dis-ease he can bring balance.

D: *How can he do that?*

P: I seem to see him now in a thought form of his own. He's still in the room. So it's as if I can see a slide show or something, of him standing over a person lying down. And without touching their body he's making movements with his hands only a few inches away from their body. Now I see him actually putting his hands on the person. He's standing behind the top of their head and has his hands on either side of their cheeks. He has his eyes closed, his head is bent down, and he seems to be focusing on cleansing energies.

D: *Is this the same process that is used by other physicians in his time?*

P: No, this is not. But in every age there are those who go beyond the norm. He's not totally unique in trying to manipulate energies for helpful purposes.

D: *Does he try to teach these methods to other people?*

P: Well, I do see him trying to share these healing methodologies.

D: *What about surgery? Does he do any of that?*

P: When you say "surgery," I immediately have pictures of crude instruments. But my original feeling was more that he was an energy-based physician, he said to say. I don't think he does what everyone else does. I don't think he's into blood-letting or ... There seems to be energies that he works with.

The information obtained from all subjects seemed to indicate Nostradamus' healing methods incorporated acupressure, aura cleansing, chakra balancing, and an advanced form of hypnosis. There was probably much more to it that we cannot undertand or explain, but he apparently had devised very effective and unusual methods.

Chapter 8

Nostradamus As a Younger Man

THERE SEEMED TO BE NO PATTERN OR CONTROL over when we would enter into Nostradamus' life. In the early stages of this experiment, when I was working with Elena and Brenda (Volume One), we consistently appeared to him when he was older and was busy at work composing his quatrains. At those times he was aware of our mission and original assignment to convey his translations to our time period. The confusion and deviation began while I was working with John (Volume Two). After a seemingly normal beginning, we began to enter Nostradamus' life when he was at different ages. At first I didn't know what to make of this because it was not consistent and definitely not planned. We made the startling discovery that he did not recognize us when he was younger, and did not know what we were talking about when we mentioned the quatrains. In his linear time perspective, he had not yet begun to work on them—thus is was impossible for him to talk about them. This new perspective opened up a whole new dimension to our work. In our logical thinking of linear time, Nostradamus first contacted us in 1986 when I happened to be speaking to his student Dyonisus during a past life regression (Volume One). Somehow he became aware that I was conversing with the student and interrupted our conversation to announce that he wanted to speak with me. At that time he gave me my assignment of translating the quatrains into modern-day language, and my work began. That was logical thinking. I suppose at that time if I had been forced to look at it in any other way, I might have been frightened by the strange concepts that crept in later. I wonder if I would have persisted? Probably, because my curiosity is so strong that I did not allow unusual events to deter me during my work with John.

It was now becoming obvious that we were somehow bouncing back and forth in Nostradamus' life. We visited him at so many different stages that it appeared we may have been with him throughout his entire adult lifetime. Is that possible? It certainly seemed to be. But how can such a thing happen? To answer that would require more of an understanding of the theory of simultaneous time than I am capable of giving. When the startling revelations of what was occurring began to become strangely commonplace, I developed a preparedness that allowed me to accept Nostradamus as I found him, and adapt my sessions accordingly. I now became so familiar with the different stages of his life that I could determine where we were by asking certain questions. It soon became obvious that we would be unable to obtain information about the quatrains at the younger stages. Often we could not even obtain contact or awareness with him.

Another startling discovery was that every single subject I worked with had the same problem. They would come into his life at uncertain times. Since they knew nothing of my work and my research, this could not have been planned. They had no knowledge of what had occurred in the man's life at different ages. They had done no reading or research, and did not have a full grasp of what the experiment consisted of. They merely reported what they saw and heard when they entered into the great master's presence. Yet every one of them expressed a desire to be around him when he was younger and full of inquisitive curiosity. They all felt a heaviness, a depression, a loneliness that enveloped the man when he was older. They said he was like a prisoner of his own making. A man so obsessed by his visions that he could not cease sitting in that cold, damp room staring at the endless parade of horror that passed before his eyes in the mirror. Loneliness and illness (arthritis caused by the continued exposure to the dampness) did not deter him, and it eventually killed him. But there seemed to be no definite way to control the time when they would enter into the room. I tried to direct it as best I could.

The following are some of the times when Pam entered his life at younger ages and observed him in various stages of experimentation. They give us glimpses into the ways his life and powers evolved, so that he was able to progress to the stage of writing down his prophecies into the quatrain form that has survived to our time period.

P: I see him walking down a cobblestone street with his cape flying out behind him, springy and jaunty and full of energy. And he has on a funny hat. It has three corners that are pulled together in a triangle shape, rounded in the middle, and the top of it has a little pom-pom thing. It looks like a soft wool felt-like material, or thick flannel. It's really goofy looking. He seems totally unlike the guy in the stone room.

The pictures in a book of historical clothing suggests that this hat may be a barrette. The pictures also show a type with ear flaps that strongly resembles the picture Elena drew of him (Volume One). There were many different shapes and types.

D: *Do you know where he's going, or where he has been?*

P: I don't know. I should ask somehow. (*Pause*) Well, this is really weird. I'm picking up his thoughts. This guy's going to see a woman. It's a young girl. Maybe it will be his wife. I know you want me to find out, and not say what I think. (*Pause*) This guy says, "I'm a man in love." (*Laugh*)

D: *Has he ever been married?*

P: No. He's always considered women rather strange creatures. He does not actually have much use for them. They're not attracted to him, so he hasn't had much contact with anyone that seems young and fresh and caring. This seems to be the first time this has happened to him— that he's been "struck" by Cupid's arrow.

D: *How old does he look?*

P: This guy looks young—twenties.

D: *Does he have any beard?*

P: Well, I can't see from this perspective. Just a minute, let me move around him. No, he has a clean-shaven face. He has a bushy eyebrow though. His hair is somewhat rough. I get the impression that he doesn't have much thought about his own personal appearance. He's always focused on whatever his emotion is at the moment. And right now his emotion is definitely excited.

D: *What is his occupation?*

P: He's some kind of young doctor or intern or something. I don't see him working around other doctors. I can't see how he got to be a doctor. But I think of him as a doctor, and he sees himself as a doctor. He's proud of himself.

D: *Has he known this girl very long?*

P: He's seen her for a while. I think she lives near the apothecary that he goes to frequently. He goes to many of them, but now this is a really exciting trip because maybe he'll see her any time he goes there.

D: *Has he been doing any of his work with prophecies at this time?*

P: I don't think he would call them prophecies, but he has dreams that are hard for him to put into perspective from where he stands on the time line. He sees things of another time that are confusing and definitely different. He doesn't seem to have a good grip on what it is, other than fantasy, imagination, nightmare or just speculation.

It was obvious that we would not be able to communicate with him at this younger age. We certainly couldn't talk with him while he was on the street and in a distracted state of mind. Pam had been able to pick up on his thoughts, but that was not enough for our purpose. I instructed her to find him in a different setting. The change was instantaneous.

P: I seem to be on the windowsill again. It seems brighter in there, and he's sitting at the table. He doesn't have a beard. He actually looks young. He just looked up this way toward the window, like he was aware that we came. Even though I know I am invisible, I think he knows we're here to continue asking him questions.

D: *What is he doing at the table?*

P: He has a plume in his hand, and the ever-present book in front of him that he writes in. I asked what he was doing, and he says he has theories that he thinks and writes about. He was trying to figure out something. He likes to think a lot.

D: *Maybe we can help him.*

P: He sort of laughed. (*Laugh*) These are equations, some kind of formulas. I don't know.

D: *It would be too hard for us to understand?*

P: Yes. And he said, too hard to explain. (*Laugh*) I think he's familiar with being visited frequently by all kinds of interested essences.

D: *Even when he's younger?*

P: Yes. He's heard voices in his head since childhood, he said. But as he has matured in years, he's become more aware that he's visited externally as well as in his head. He was born with a sixth sense, if you will. He's always been able to be more insightful, more perceptive, more aware than the others around him seem to be.

D: *Did he study with someone to learn how to contact the other side?*

P: He has had an education. He did study formally, and has read extensively. I was trying to see if there was a mentor or favorite teacher. He *was* heavily influenced by the classical and Greek thinkers. It seems he's rather disdainful of some of the professors he had, thinking they knew less than men of olden times. (*Chuckle*) It's funny to use the term "olden times" when this is a pretty old time in itself.

D: *Did he have any special teacher that taught him things of the occult? I guess we can call it that. The "strange" things he's involved in.*

P: There seems to be an ancient book that was presented to him by someone old. The book contains incantations, actually. It has what we would consider "spells." How strange. This is actually wicca.

D: *Does he call it wicca?*

P: That was *my* conclusion, because it seems so dark and sinister. But he said it's *not* all dark and sinister. It just *works,* he said. (*Laugh*)

D: *Ask him who gave it to him.*

P: The first response that came was his ... grandfather? That seems so unlikely to me.

D: *Why? That a grandfather could have a book like that?*

P: That is was someone from his *own* family. That was a surprise. It seems that he read the book and tried the stuff. He has an insatiable curiosity, not unlike someone in this room. (*Laugh*)

D: *Wasn't he afraid to try these strange things?*

P: He seems almost fearless.

D: *Did he ever have any trouble or any problems?*

P: Yes. (*Laugh*) It seems that he has conjured up things he didn't like, and then had a bit of difficulty releasing them. Before you conjure something up you have to know how to get rid of it. So he learned to read ahead. (*Laugh*) He's had this book since his teenage years. He has always been searching to find out why he can see things that other people can't see, and hear voices other people can't hear. He's always been curious to find out why and what this means, and if he is chosen as a special person to pursue this. He really wants to know what is going on.

D: *What did he conjure that he didn't like?*

P: It seems that initially it was a coldness and a bad odor. It wasn't a demon growling in the room or anything like that. But he was definitely aware of something he perceived to be sinister. He wasn't very happy about it, but he was pleased that he *succeeded*. (*Laugh*)

D: *Did that happen more than once?*

P: He seemed to have developed a control after this initial encounter with something that was undeniably uncomfortable. Immediately he sought out the information to release it.

D: *Was that in the book?*

P: Yes. And therefore he decided to read and study more before trying some of these things. But it seems that he was capable and *is* capable—I don't need to always speak in the past tense, for he's there (*chuckle*)—of conjuring what it is that he chooses. He really doesn't wish to dwell on the dark side. He doesn't call on what we would judge "evil forces" to do anything. As a young man he was simply curious to see what he could do. And having relieved his curiosity he has no real need for this type of activity.

The amazing thing is that Pam had no way of knowing about the controversy that has surrounded Nostradamus' grandfather. When I did my research for Volume Two, I found it mentioned in the biographies that Nostradamus was raised by his grandfather, and it was thought that the old Jewish man was involved in the practice of magic. It was speculated that he might have come across ancient books dating from the capture of Jerusalem by the Romans. It was said that when the Romans invaded and sacked the Temple, the sacred books were missing. It has long been a mystery as to what happened to them. In a letter written by Nostradamus that has survived to our time he said that he memorized and then burned his books of magic so they wouldn't fall into the wrong hands after his death. This was proof that he did have such books. It has been speculated that his statement could have been a ruse to throw off the Inquisition, that he loved books too much to burn even one. Pam could not have known the importance of her mention of the grandfather and books of magic.

P: He now has communication that takes place on many levels without doing any of these machinations. He's aware when we come, that we're here, and we're not the only visitors. He seems to have contact with quite a large portion of the spirit world. At least he has many visitors. Many of them just watch what he does. It seems that when you die you don't necessarily release all the fears you were mired in while in the physical form. Some of these visitors seem to have very— I don't want to use the word "negative," but very *unproductive* thoughts. So he can pick up their thoughts, you see.

D: *Do those kind of people cause him problems?*

P: When you're receiving information from invisible realms, it's hard to differentiate between someone's biases and the truth. It takes a lot of selectivity. What is truth and what is another person's fear or fantasy?

D: *You mean they tell him things he doesn't think are true?*

P: That is correct. He has the capability to visualize quite easily, and he receives information from many sources. It could be from holding an object and receiving impressions, or sitting quietly in meditation and receiving impressions, or writing without even watching what he's writing. He seems to be able to visualize quite easily and quite well. He sees the *big* pictures with many parts. The glass is another tool or technique of his. It's a good one, but it certainly isn't the only way he has of *seeing*. He has quite advanced visualization capabilities.

D: *When the other entities tell him things or show them to him, is he able to pick up if it's true or not?*

P: He *wants* to, he *tries* to. He tries to see what strikes the truth resonance within him. But their sincerity many times is quite valid to them, and therefore transmitted to him as truth. It is a constant and continuing struggle for him to differentiate between an invisible entity's bias and truth or fact.

D: *Does he have very many that come as we do?*

P: Lately, it seems like a lot. (*Laugh*) There have been different waves of questioners.

D: *Well, is he writing his quatrains at this time in his life?*

P: He hasn't done it in the formal manner that you're familiar with. But he has definitely had glimpses of what he considers to be the truth future, if he believes what he is hearing from these invisible forces. He's been hearing it practically all his life, and so some of this information has been rattling around in his head for a long time. He didn't write some of the things down until later, but they were there. His whole life has been a process of collecting—what he hopes to be— truth. At this point he is working on some theories. He's trying to figure out ... this is more of an (*had difficulty with the next word, pronounced it different ways*) alchemical formula that he's working on.

D: *In his time period wouldn't it get him in trouble if someone knew about the book and the spells?*

P: Well, no one knew about it. He certainly didn't tell anybody. And it seems that his grandfather—if that is whom he received it from—was determined not to tell anyone because he himself would have been in a great deal of trouble.

D: *I was thinking it wasn't normal to do things like that.*

P: Well, I wouldn't consider this fellow normal. (*Laugh*)

D: *I was trying to figure out where we are in his life. Is he married at this time?*

P: He already has a disdain for women, and doesn't seem to ever want to answer that question. Every time you ask that, I get the same feeling. Looking at him, he doesn't have many wrinkles. I would say he's in his twenties. He's not as gloomy as other times when we've visited him. Later on he seemed to be weighted down so *much* by the burden of what he'd seen, that he seemed aged beyond his true years. But he seems definitely younger and stronger right now.

D: *Then it seems that he didn't really begin to write these quatrains down until he was older. If I read them he probably wouldn't even know what I was talking about.*

P: As I said, he has been receiving information all along and wrote them down later. Some of this information he carried 30 or more years in his head before he ever started to write it down. Where we are talking now may predate the actual writing, but it wouldn't predate the information.

D: *Does he have a good feeling about us?*

P: It depends on *when* we arrive. He's still so full of curiosity right now that he can't ignore any visitors, or push them away. So right now we're another source of interest and curiosity. Later he seems so burdened and bothered that it's not quite as pleasant. But right now, today, we have arrived on a bright, sunlit day with a happy feeling.

D: *Then I don't think we would be able to communicate with him about the quatrains at this time in his life. Let's find him when he is a little older and he has begun to work with this type of thing.* (Pam moved ahead quickly.)

P: He is at a desk in a room. It's not in the high room; this is a low room. It could be ground level, or it could even be basement. It's dark, no windows, and a candle. He's humped over, reading that old book that his grandfather gave him. He's really serious now. I don't feel light-heartedness. Actually he's not as *heavy* as he has been at other times, but right now he's concentrating on the book.

D: *How old does he appear?*

P: Not that old. I'd say maybe late thirties to mid-forties.

D: *Can you pick up his thoughts about what he's reading?*

P: They seem to be incantations actually. I'll be still a minute and see if I get one. (*Surprised.*) Oh, maybe I don't want to! (*A nervous laugh*) This is too weird! Because what happens is that he is successful with his incantations. He's actually conjuring. Through this focused thought he has created a highway for—although not solid—a formed entity to travel into his presence. I mean, this guy *did* it.

D: *What does the entity look like?*

P: Horrible! First and foremost there's a horrible stench. It's so gross; it's an awful smell. Then this entity appeared in front of him in this dark room. No speech or sound, but kind of a ... loomingness. This is really hard to describe. If you were just observing it, it would be weird. But if you were to walk through it, I think all the hairs on your body would stand up on end, and you would have an icy cold feeling. I didn't really believe that anyone could conjure something with form like this.

D: *How is Nostradamus reacting?*

P: He's proud of the fact that he did it, but he's rather concerned about how to disperse it now. He's distracted by its presence, but has to keep focusing on the book.

D: *Is it real or imagination on his part? In your spirit state you're able to tell.*

P: (*A nervous laugh*) Well, it's a real thing. Now whether it's a thing called up from thought and desire, or whether it exists independently of whether he calls it or not, I don't know. But it's really there.

D: *But it's not solid?*

P: No, it just has a form, a shape. But he's not really that concerned. He expected something to happen, you see. (*Chuckle*) I'm more surprised than he is. But he doesn't want it to stay. He's going to get rid of it. (*Laugh*)

D: *What does he do?*

P: All the steps?

D: *No, I'm just curious about the steps he takes to get rid of it, or does he get rid of it?*

P: Obviously he does, because it's not with him the other times I've seen him.

D: *You can describe the steps if you want. But I don't really want to know* that *incantation.* (Chuckle)

P: Oh, I was going to tell you the steps for getting rid of it, not how to call it up. (*Laugh*) Well, you know he has Catholicism in his thoughts, so he has a bowl of water that he washes his hands in. Water is sacred. I don't know if this is holy water blessed by the church. But to him, or perhaps from the book, the element of water is a cleansing and purifying agent, so he does this little water washing. It looks as if he's burned some stuff in a bowl, and there are words that he says. It's a combination of words that are not English or French. They are more like sound words. They don't sound like a language but maybe they are. I can't understand them. He does it in repetition. I think he says the same "things" three times. And then it's really funny, because he takes a deep breath and blows *very hard.* (*She demonstrated by puffing her cheeks up and blowing.*) Just as if he's going to blow it away. Then in fact it disappears, so I guess there's something to that. (*Laugh*) I don't know. You don't see this on television as one of the rituals, but that's how it disappeared.

D: *Maybe it didn't have existence on its own.*

P: I can't respond to speculation, just observation.

D: *Apparently he's done this before if it didn't bother him. Can you find out?*

P: I'll see. (*Pause*) He hasn't done *this* before. His grandfather *did* tell him about this. He's been curious about it for a long time—*years*. He was afraid to try it until he had confidence that he could utilize the principles in the book. But he had already built up a backlog of—I don't want to say "magic stuff," because I don't like the word "magic." But he had already done many things that gave him confidence that he could take care of the situation. And he had the instructions right there in front of him, so by this time he wasn't worried. He had some warning, so he remembered what his grandfather said.

D: *It begins to look as if maybe there is such a thing as "real" magic.*

P: Well, this is a surprise to me. One of his favorite, or maybe his *most* favorite thing in the world, is to discover new things he's capable of doing with himself. Not by making or creating something like a work of art, but by using his mind and his focusing ability. He likes to use his own personal internal things. His fun is *seeing,* focusing his mind. He wants to see how much he can do and how far he can go. It's really fun for him.

D: *He seems to have a great deal of control. Is there any way you can let him know you're there?*

P: I'm not sure this would be the *best* time. I don't want to be associated with this event because he might put the two of us together in the future.

D: *That's true, that might happen. If you're not comfortable with that situation, let's move out of it and find him at a time when you think it would be proper to contact him.*

P: I'm at a dinner table now. This is really strange because I have never seen him socializing, or being with other people. And there sits a woman with something like a handkerchief on her head. (*Chuckle*) It's a little cap, but it looks like a handkerchief. And there's a little girl sitting there, who has one on, too, and a full-skirt dress. It's a *big* strong table. The top of it has really big boards. Gosh, he could probably stand a horse on the table. There are just the three of them. What's funny is that he is at one end of the table and the woman and the little girl are way down at the other end. It's really not cozy. (*Chuckle*) He doesn't understand women.

D: *What are they eating?*

P: He has bread that you have to forcibly tear or pull apart. It's not like our bread at all. It's *hard* stuff. And let's see, it looks like cheese, and some kind of fruit, maybe an apple.

D: *Just plain food? See if you can find out from him—is this his house?*

P: (*Laugh*) Well, he must know we're here because the response was, "Well, it would be more appropriate to call it *her* house." She's the master of the house itself. He's the master of his mind. He considers his mind infinitely more important than the house.

D: *I was just wondering where we were in his life. Is that his only child?*

P: Right now in this scene that's all I see. (*Pause*) Well, he said some-thing really weird. He said, "I have the son inside me and also the father."

D: *I wonder what he meant by that?*

P: It's not very clear. But I don't think the son was ever born, made, conceived. The *seed* of the son. (*Confused*) I don't know.

D: *Or had not been conceived yet?*

P: Maybe. I don't know. I have to say that he has a small amount of disdain for those of us who don't have the same intense focus and thought processes as *he* has. I'm asking what that statement means. But he says he leaves the interpretation up to me, and I don't like that. I want him to tell me.

D: *He thinks in riddles.*

P: Actually that is one of his problems in communicating with other people. In a way he has shut himself off from most human contact. He's involved with ... I suppose that's his wife and daughter. I'm so surprised that a daughter is there because I certainly didn't think of her. I think perhaps later in life he pretty much dismissed her as well, since she was female. But one of his problems in communicating with other humans is that he *doesn't* think like other people, so his *style* of communication is difficult. It's almost impossible for him because his mind doesn't work like other people. But he says he knows exactly what he's thinking. (*Laugh*)

D: *But nobody else does.* (Laugh)

P: Right. (*Laugh*) That's *our* problem though.

D: *Maybe we will have to find him at a time when he's concentrating. He can't communicate with us now if he's eating.*

P: He can think and eat at the same time. It's just that we ask for him to communicate with us in our linear thinking. Our concept is that "one word follows the next word in a line" and the words string together to make sentences, and those sentences then string together to create a larger idea. But they all go in a line, and his thinking doesn't work that way. His thinking goes out in multiple directions simultaneously, and to converse that way is nigh on to impossible. About the only way to get that kind of thinking across to another individual is by telepathy. Then you can receive a multi-dimensional explanation. But having him tell us something and try to explain it in words, there's so much lost in the translation.

D: *I imagine he must be a very difficult person to live with.*

P: (*Laugh*) Well, he's at that end of the table. He's already isolated him-self. Maybe ten years have gone by since we saw him so happy on the street. He doesn't seem that joyous any more. He's just *there*. He's not all hurt and crippled up yet. He doesn't have those big knuckles yet.

D: *Do you know if he's doing any writing?*

P: He's been writing all along, but it's not what you'd call "prophecies" that he wrote early on. He was just trying to make some sense out of his own thoughts.

D: *Well, in order for us to communicate with him I think we would have to be in another environment.*

P: I think he would have to be alone.

The pattern was clear after this, and repeated with each subject. We could only communicate and attempt translation of the quatrains when he was alone in his stone room at 30 or 40 years of age, and while he was either in trance or working with the magic mirror.

Chapter 9

Quatrains Dealing with the Past

D: This one has caused confusion for people down through the years because they don't know if it is a quatrain or not.

LEGIS CANTIO CONTRA INEPTOS CRITICOS

INCANTATION OF THE LAW AGAINST INEPT CRITICS

Quos legent hosce versus maturè censunto, *Profanum vulgus & inscium ne attrectato:* *Omnesq; Astrologi Blenni, Barbari procul sunto,* *Qui alter facit, is ritè, sacer esto.*	May those who read this verse think upon it deeply, let the profane and ignorant herd keep away. Let all astrologers, idiots and barbarians stay far off, he who does otherwise, let him be priest to the rite.

P: [Pam] That comment about the astrologers and idiots is tongue-in-cheek because Nostradamus himself is an astrologer. But there are those who *pretend* to be astrologers and call themselves astrologers who are *not*. He is a *true* astrologer. The ones he's talking about are the pretenders. These have given him much criticism, you see. His ego is a most prominent feature. There are very few things he is unfamiliar with. He takes great pride in knowing everything there is to know. To be a true astrologer you need to have psychic understanding. There are many more subtle realms of astrology than simply figuring out the physical calculations.

D: *They thought this quatrain was a threat or a curse.*

P: They're taking this mighty serious, aren't they? The curse part is a little strong. He has great anger and frustration. But as far as pulling in evil forces and directing them toward those who distort his words or disregard his words, no, he does not delve into the realms of directing evil forces towards anyone. This was more of his way of letting off steam.

D: *They also said this is the only quatrain that was written entirely in Latin.*

P: He wanted this one to be understood, not to be an "in code" quatrain.

D: *They also said it may be an example of him trying to bluff the authorities, to fool them.*

P: This was written in decipherable language. He doesn't see how it would fool anybody. And who are "they"?

D: *The critics, the translators, the interpreters, the people who try to understand the quatrains.*

P: (*She chuckled.*) I think they are reading "things" into it. That verse refers to his quatrains, and to the criticism that he has received, *period*. Not just for the written word, but for all those who directed slings and arrows towards him.

CENTURY VIII-63

Quand l'adultere blessé sans coup aura *Merdri la femme & le filz par despit,* *Ferme assoumee l'enfant estranglera:* *Huit captifz prins, s'estouffer sans respit.*	When the adulterer wounded without a blow will have murdered his wife and son out of spite; his wife knocked down, he will strangle the child; eight captives taken, choked beyond help.

P: I'm trying to let Nostradamus give me any insight. I understand the people to be countries. It's interesting that a paranoid country killed off other countries that were of major importance to it. Defeated them, I should say; not killed them off. During World War II the Soviet Union was an ally with England, the United States and France. The eight captives seem to pinpoint the Soviet Union and the Communist-bloc countries. It did not defeat these countries. It did, however, take them captive.

D: *Is that what it means? "Eight captives taken, choked beyond help"?*

P: That means they couldn't get away.

D: *And you think the adulterer is the Soviet Union?*

P: Yes. He is saying that the Soviet Union as it exists today didn't exist that way in his time.

D: *"When the adulterer wounded without a blow."*

P: That means *not* wounded—only a perceived attack.

D: *"Will have murdered his wife and son out of spite."*

P: This seems to refer to the strongest allies of this country.

D: *"His wife knocked down, he will strangle the child."*

P: Yes, it seems as if they totally defeated two.

D: *When you think of the symbolism of murdering a wife and a son, it would be like a betrayal. In this way it would seem Russia betrayed her allies that believed in her. Would that make sense?*

P: The response was that given our perspective from *this* date, that could have applied to many different countries down through history. As one who prophesizes, he sees the future unfolding in his mind's eye in a certain distinguishable, observable way. But he seems to have full knowledge and belief that many alternatives can happen to change that future. They aren't totally chiseled in one linear time, in one specific way. It also seems that events that are seen in a grand future perspective are always repeated. There's really nothing unique under the sun.

D: *He has told me that oftentimes the quatrains will refer to more than one thing. But I think he may need your concepts and the information in your own mind to help him understand what he is seeing.*

P: Which is very cluttered. All of our minds are cluttered. This makes it infinitely more difficult for *him* to communicate with *us*, because *he's* having to go through all this stuff. But I am asking him for the heart of the prophecy or the essence. He says it has to do with destroying things due to paranoia. And there is symbolism in the number eight, although I see that the swirling thoughts around that number are hostage thoughts. It could be hostage countries or individuals. There is a total lack of freedom.

D: *That would fit in with the Soviet Union taking over other countries.*

P: Yes, that's correct. It is very enigmatic. (*Laugh*) He said it was *on purpose!* We must also remember that the problem could be with the original French. There are nuances in each specific language that don't necessarily translate literally. I think *he* knows what you're talking about; it's just getting through *my* filters that is difficult. (*Loud laugh*) He said, "Sometimes it's hard to recognize his own work when he's hearing the translation." (*Laugh*) This is like a translation of a translation.

CENTURY VIII-95

Le seducteur sera mis en la fosse	The seducer will be placed in a ditch
Et estaché jusques à quelque temps,	and will be tied up for some time.
Le clerc uni le chef avec sa crosse	The scholar joins the chief with his cross. The sharp right will draw
Picante droite attraira les contens.	the contented ones.

P: Well, it's funny. I saw somebody lying down dead when you were talking about the ditch. But the next thoughts were of a song, "Abraham, Martin and John," about Abraham Lincoln, Martin Luther King, and John F. Kennedy. I don't even know the words of what you said. This just came in. But these were three leaders, enlightened people, who were assassinated. They gave their best shot to try to help, and they got thrown into the ditch.

D: *"The seducer will be placed in the ditch, and will be tied up for some time." Who is the seducer?*

P: I don't have any pictures. I can tell you my thought was about Abraham Lincoln. "Seducer" meaning changer of minds, not necessarily a seducer of the flesh. There was—not just in the South, but the North as well—an economy based on slave trade and things that revolved around slave trade: goods and services. Everybody in the North didn't want to do away with slavery. That wasn't the entire reason for the Civil War. Lincoln was viewed as a seducer of minds by those in the South and the North, who believed that he was changing people's minds. They tried to hold him down on the slavery issue. But his ideas were too right, too true, too good to not be carried out. But it was hard, so he was held down for a while.

D: *"The scholar joins the chief with his cross."*

P: Martin Luther King was a preacher and John F. Kennedy was a man of great intellect. Thus the scholar is Kennedy, and the chief with his cross is Martin Luther King.

D: *And it says, "The scholar* joins *the chief."*

P: Yes. That doesn't necessarily mean that they walked on the Earth at the same time, although they did overlap. And of course, Abraham Lincoln wasn't walking around with them. It means that these ideas, these truths come out no matter what. I think Nostradamus saw the attempt to hold down good people who were ultimately murdered so they couldn't talk any more. They couldn't enlighten anybody else with their *living* speech.

D: *I was thinking that "joined" meant they both died.*

P: They all three died, definitely.

D: *But he also means they were joined in their beliefs.*

P: That is correct. The truth is truth.

D: *And the last part is, "The sharp right will draw the contented ones."*

P: I don't think that is an accurate translation of that line. Actually, I think it's a different verb. "The sharp right will *do* something to the contented ones." Like *impel* them to do something. You see, "content" means that you're *not* eager to go out and do anything. But to go against slavery when you're Abraham Lincoln, or to go against the status quo if you're Martin Luther King or J.F.K., those are sharp things, a sharp truth, a sharp right. Those are things that shake up the contented ones. I think the verb is wrong.

D: *It says another translation is "attract." "The sharp right will* attract *the contented ones."*

P: I think a better verb would be "stimulate."

D: *It is interesting the way he associated all three of them together.*

P: I asked him what the relevance is for today. I should ask him that every time, no matter what.

D: *But some of these don't refer to today. They are important events that he saw happening at a certain time.*

P: Yes, but there is relevance. And it is that truth will set you free. It might shake you up, and you might get killed for it, but it is definitely the preferred alignment.

CENTURY IX-76

Avec le noir Rapax &
sanguinaire,
Issu du peaultre de
l'inhumain Neron
Emmi deux fleuves main
gauche militaire,
Sera murtri par Joine
cheulveron.

With the rapacious and bloody king, sprung from the pallet of inhuman Nero; between two rivers, the military on the left hand, he will be murdered by a bald young man.

P: When you said "two rivers" I immediately thought of the Tigris and the Euphrates, and I have no idea why. I think it has to do with the past because I saw some pyramids. I believe this refers to Anwar Sadat's murder. I think he was reviewing some troops. Anyway, I see military on one side and this grandstand on the other side.

D: *Who is the "rapacious and bloody king?"*

P: I wouldn't call him a king. He doesn't have official kingship. There are some very crazy forces in the Middle East. Some swirling ... it's almost like a disease many of these people have.

D: *There is an alternate translation for "king." The word "noir" could be an anagram for "roi: king," but it can also mean "the black one." Would that fit better? "The rapacious and bloody dark one, sprung from the palate of inhuman Nero."*

P: Yes. It's actually a double entendre because dark means more than dark in color. It means dark in soul, dark in thought and action.

D: *Does he see anything behind the murder of Sadat? Can he show you why it happened or who was responsible?*

P: Yes. Speaking of the "noir" one, there is this dark force we've already discussed, in relation to Abraham, Martin and Kennedy. Anwar could be in there also. This is a man who certainly bucked the system of tradition and all his neighbors, to actually enter into a peaceful agreement with the state of Israel. To acknowledge the state of Israel as even *being* something was *hugely* antagonistic to most of the people around him. Sadat was pushing out this wave of peace and brotherly love and doing it quite successfully and well. And so to stop him, he was killed.

D: *So he sees there is this dark force that is responsible?*

P: I think that is now Nostradamus puts it into his understanding framework, yes.

CENTURY IX-4

L'an ensuivant descouvertz par deluge,
Deux chefs esluez le premier ne tiendra
De fuir ombre à l'un d'eux le refuge,
Saccager case qui premier maintiendra.

The following year revealed by a flood, two leaders elected, the first will not hold on; for one of them refuge in fleeing shadows, the victim plundered who maintained the first.

B: [Brenda] He says this particular quatrain refers to what is called the "Watergate era" in American history.

D: *Oh? Does he want to expound a little bit?*

B: He's chuckling. He says, you know good and well that's one from the past. You simply want more details because you remember it fairly clearly.

D: *(Laugh) Yes, because it's in my time period. It's not ancient history.*

B: He says, what if it were something that happened a mere hundred years after he was born? That's still in the future. *(Chuckle)* He's teasing you somewhat and giving you a hard time.

D: *Well, I'm interested in some of this symbolism.*

B: He says the two elected refer to the President and Vice President. One shall remain and the other will take refuge in shadows. The one that flees and finds his way hiding in the shadows, refers to Spiro Agnew resigning instead of being impeached. He says that years in your future when people look back upon the court records, it will appear that Spiro Agnew took the majority of the blame. And that Richard Nixon was able to escape some of the blame by resigning before he could be impeached.

D: *"The following year revealed by a flood." Then the flood refers to the Watergate by symbolism. The last sentence is, "The victim plundered who maintains the first," referring to the two of them again. But he saw that as an important era?*

B: He says that had profound effects on the American political system. For example, take a dike in Holland. If a grain of sand shifts one way it makes part of the dike vulnerable for a small hole to start, a weakness to develop, and then the dike crumbles. But if the grain of sand had shifted the other way instead, the dike would not have been vulnerable there. He says it's one of those small things that gradually add up to major consequences later on, sometimes decades or centuries later.

D: *The future will look back on it, I guess, and see it in a much different light than we do at this point.*

B: He says, but of course. You're too close to it to be anywhere near objective.

This next one has a date in it which is interesting:

CENTURY VIII-71

Croistra le nombre si grand
  des astronomes
Chassez, bannis & livres
  consurez,
L'an mil six cents sept par
  sacre glomes
Que nul aux sacres ne
  seront asseurez.
	The number of astrologers will grow so great, that they will be driven out, banned, and their books censored. In the year 1607 by sacred assemblies so that none will be safe from the holy ones.

B: He says this refers to the heyday of the Inquisition.

D: But in his day the astrologers weren't driven out or banned, were they?

B: No, they were considered men of science, and they weren't harassed any more than other scientists were. He was using that as symbolism to represent the quest of knowledge in general. Being driven out and banned, and having their books censored, refers to the book burnings and such that the Inquisition ended up doing, and how they tried to suppress knowledge and curiosity.

D: They've written this off as a definite failure of a quatrain. (I chuckled at her definite and expected reaction.)

B: His beard is bristling.

D: They said, in spite of the dating, it was a failure because they couldn't find anything happening with astrology on that date.

B: He says they're being too literal again.

In the eyes of the translators, this next quatrain was considered to be one of the most important he ever wrote, even though they didn't understand it.

D: (Laugh) *I don't know how they could say it was the most important if they didn't understand it.*

B: He just got through saying the same thing. (*Laugh*) How can they tell whether or not it's important if they don't know what it means to start with. He says, "It sounds to me like you have a bunch of pseudo-scholars spouting a bunch of nonsense in order to appear learned."

CENTURY IV-77

SELIN monarque l'Italie
  pacifique
Regnes unis Roi chrestien
  du monde:
Mourrant voudra coucher
  en terre blesique
Apres pirates avoir chassé
  de l'onde.
	Selin king, Italy peaceful, kingdoms united by the Christian king of the world. When he dies, he will want to lie in Blois territory, having chased the pirates from the sea.

I had difficulty with the pronunciation of Blois, and finally had to spell it. He became irritated and corrected me with something that sounded like "Blah" or "Blwah."

B: He says different phonetics are involved.

D: *(Laugh) But since I don't know French he has to bear with me. I have my shortcomings too.*

B: He has this particular attitude that many native Frenchmen have in regard to their language. They think that only civilized people can truly speak French. And anyone not born in France is incapable of speaking it.

D: *(Chuckle) But like he said, we don't speak it in our time the way he does anyway.*

B: This is true.

D: *It seems as if I always save the quatrains with difficult names for this vehicle to do. (Laugh) She's the only one that can understand them. My pronunciation doesn't help much either.*

B: He says the mind of this vehicle is well adapted to working with unfamiliar names and sounds since the mind has an interest in foreign tongues. Each vehicle has their strengths and weaknesses. This vehicle is good with foreign tongues but is very unsure with astrological symbols.

D: *I'm trying to pronounce the names phonetically and I know I'm messing them up. I'm getting better, I hope.*

B: He says you're getting lucky on the ones you've had to say a million times. He chuckles at some of the pronunciations, and he mutters the corrections under his breath. (*I laughed.*) For example, when you said "Arbois," he'd said (*emphatically*), "(*phonetically*) Arboah, Arboah!" Ar-bowah. Toulouse (Too-loose) and Foix (Fo-ah).

D: *It looks like "fox" to me. He uses those names a lot.*

B: He says they're just ordinary names in his language. It would be like you writing quatrains and referring to Dallas, Tulsa, Los Angeles, or London.

D: *The translators always thought he was literally referring to those places, and certain people in those places.*

B: He says the ones who are translating have no way of knowing what he is referring to, whether it be the actual places or symbology. He says this quatrain refers to the rise to power of the British Empire over the French and Spanish. During his time and just past his time France and Spain were exploiting the Americas, bringing back shiploads of gold and such. And through the rise of the British Empire and its victory over the Spanish Armada, it drove these so-called pirates from the sea and established a world-wide empire. He says this eventually developed into the empire on which the sun never set.

D: *What does the word "Selin" mean?*

B: He is saying that refers to how the spirit of wisdom became paramount. He says after the British Empire became dominant, the sciences and knowledge started to develop.

D: *They say that Selin means, from the Greek, the moon or Diana.*

B: He says Selin does refer to the moon through the goddess Selina (Selene), but her major attribute was wisdom and foresight.

D: *Then who is the Christian king of the world?*

B: He says that's an analogy referring to the British Empire being a Christian nation.

D: *It means it had countries all over the world under its control?*

B: Yes, right. They had all of these colonies, as you say, all over the world. In effect, making the British Empire in control or at least affecting the entire world, and in control of the seas.

D: *And "when he dies" means whenever the English empire is no longer a power?*

B: Yes. He says all empires rise and fall. They come to power and then fade away. He said although the British Empire will be very powerful for a very long time, it would not last forever.

D: *It says, "when he dies he will want to lie in Blois territory."*

B: He says that refers to when the empire would fall. He said the way the empire is set up, the ideals that the British Empire put forth, was guaranteed to cause independence and revolt in its colonies. Because it was spreading forth the idea of man governing themselves. And so that line is referring to the fact that the eventual downfall of the British Empire would not necessarily come through revolt, but basically through the various parts of the empire, the various colonies becoming independent countries. He says this quatrain is really not that essential to what you're seeking since it refers to things that have happened in the past.

D: *But I wanted to tell him why they considered it to be a very important quatrain. Their interpretation doesn't relate at all to what he's telling me. He may get angry.*

B: He's curious though.

D: *It says, "This is the quatrain upon which many 19th-century royalists built their hopes of a great French king who would come and change the face of Europe."*

B: He can see where they would get that point of view. They persist in insisting that he only looks at France. But he doesn't. He looks at the entire world.

D· *He might get mad at this part. They say, "There's a strong possibility that Nostradamus went completely off the rails with this series of quatrains." They figure there are more than one relating to this king.*

B: I suspect you should not have said that. He is gripping at his beard. His mustache is bristling, and he is *not* happy.

D: *The translator thinks he intended them to refer to Henry II because that king adopted the moon as his device, referring to Selin meaning the moon.*

B: He says they simply took the wrong branch there. Selin does refer to the goddess of the moon but she stood for wisdom and he was referring to wisdom.

D: *And they say, "The notion of a Christian king governing the world seems impossible."*

B: He says that may seem impossible but when the British Empire was at its height, the head, the monarch of the British Empire, was a Christian. And he had control over the bulk of the world.

D: *All these years this quatrain was the hope of France. Even today people think it means another great French king will arise.*

B: He said because of what Napoleon did, they were grasping at straws. He said it is good you have brought this up because that was not what he was referring to.

D: *They thought when it didn't happen that Nostradamus had made a big mistake.*

B: He says just because the translators make a mistake in translating what he has written there's no need to jump to the conclusion he's the one that made the mistake. He says he can see the direction the Earth is going in, and he is hoping these quatrains will help us avoid the calamities we're heading for. If we are able to avoid these, we can't help but become a *united* Earth rather than individual countries being dominant over others.

CENTURY IV-96

La sœur aisnée de l'isle Britannique,	The elder sister of the island of
Quinze ans devant le frere aura	Britain will be born fifteen years
naissance:	before her brother. Because of
Par son promis moyennant	his promise proving to be true,
verrifique,	she will succeed to the kingdom
Succedera au regne de balance.	of the Balance.

B: He says this quatrain refers to the American Revolution and the French Revolution. This is referring to the United States breaking from Great Britain and becoming an independent country, and later France throwing over a monarchy and becoming a Republic. "Her ascending to the kingdom in the balance" refers to America gradually taking over Great Britain's monopoly of the seas and trade.

D: *He has referred before to "brothers" meaning allies. But I am surprised that he saw the* American *Revolution.*

B: Yes. He says in answer to the argument of those misguided souls who say he predicted only for France, he would like to point out that the American Revolution does link up with French history. Because the example set by the Americans inspired the French Revolution, as well as everything that happened in France afterwards. He says at the same time the American Revolution was influenced by French philosophers, so it was a back-and-forth thing.

D: *This quatrain has some Latin in it. I'm not even sure I can pronounce it.* (I attempted it.)

B: Spell it.
D: PLUS OULTRE. (She pronounced it phonetically: Plus Ol-tray.) *I*
   think that's Latin, isn't it?
B: No, it's French.
D: Well, it is also in the English. They didn't translate it.

CENTURY VI-70

Au chef du monde le grand
   Chyren sera,
Plus oultre apres aimé,
   craint, redoubté:
Son bruit & loz les cieux
   surpassera,
Et du seul titre victeur
   fort contenté.

The great Chyren will be chief of the
world. After "Plus Oultre" loved,
feared and dreaded. His fame and
praise go beyond the heavens, and
he will be greatly satisfied with the
sole title of victor.

B: He says that is a quatrain referring to Napoleon.
D: The interpreters say that Chyren is an anagram for Henry IV.
B: He says that Chyren can also be drawn from Greek mythology and
   used symbolically. He is the gatekeeper for the crossing over the River
   Styx into the underworld of the dead. So sometimes when he refers to
   Chyren, as in this quatrain, he is referring to death and wars and
   bloodshed. And the one who would be satisfied only with the title of
   victor is referring to Napoleon.
D: It seems as if many of the quatrains which refer to the world wars also
   refer to Napoleon .
B: He says in several of the quatrains there is quite a bit of overlap
   between the two periods of history. Remember that history develops
   in spirals.

I discovered that Charon was called the ferryman of Hades, the one
who ferried the souls of the dead across the River Styx into Hades.
Nostradamus apparently changed the spelling to make an anagram, unless his spelling was closer to the transliteration of the original Greek.
Charon is mentioned again in CENTURY VI-27 in this chapter.

CENTURY V-35

Par cité franche de la grand
   mer Seline,
Qui porte encores à l'estomac
   la pierre:
Angloise classe viendra soubs
   la bruine
Un rameau prendre, du grand
   ouverte guerre.

For the free city of the great
crescent sea, which still carries
the stone in its stomach, an
English fleet will come in under the
mist to seize a branch, war opened
by the great one.

B: He says this quatrain refers to events that took place in early American history when America was considered an independent country by many but Great Britain had not acknowledged it yet. The great crescent sea with the stone in its stomach refers to the Caribbean Sea which was originally formed by a great meteor striking the Earth and forming a circular sea. The meteor that caused this is still buried in the sea bed. He says that during what is now called the "War of 1812," the British were blockading the American coast in order to interfere with her trading with France, and also to interfere with the slave running.

D: *"For the free city of the great crescent sea." Does the free city mean the free country?*

B: No. He was referring to New Orleans as a free city because it was, at that time, still a French possession. It was a French city and an open port, therefore a free city, an open port where either British or American ships could go. He also called it a free city because there were what was then called "free people of color" there also.

D: *But it is on the Gulf of Mexico.*

B: Yes, but that is an extension of the Caribbean Sea, and it was caused by the same type of action, a meteor striking the Earth. He says actually what happened was that a cluster of meteors struck the Earth. Two major ones fell there and formed the Caribbean Sea and the Gulf of Mexico.

D: *Then it says, "An English fleet will come in under the mist to seize a branch."*

B: He says that refers to the English fleet blockading the American coast. They originally came in under cover of fog. They were there to interfere with trade and with the young United States getting the war materials it needed from France for fighting the British.

CENTURY VII-24

L'enseveli sortira du tombeau,	He who was buried will come out of
Fera de chaines lier le fort	the tomb, he will make the strong
du pont:	one out of the bridge to be bound
Empoisonné avec œufz	with chains. Poisoned with the roe
de Barbeau,	of a barbel, the great one from
Grand de Lorraine par	Lorraine by the Marquis du Pont.
le Marquis du Pont.	

B: He says this quatrain refers to World War II. "He who was buried and comes forth from the tomb" represents Germany regaining her status as a world power, even if it was temporary. And "being poisoned with the roe of a barbel" represents its disastrous attempt to fight the war on two fronts and trying to take over Russia. He says he used that symbolism because in both his time and yours, one of the main things that Russia is famous for is caviar which is the roe of sturgeon.

D: *Why did he call the sturgeon a barbel?*

B: He says it's a similar type of fish. He rather imagines that in your time French have a word for sturgeon. But in his time there had not been enough contact to have a word for that specific fish so he took a word for a fish that looked similar to it.

According to the encyclopedia, the eggs of the barbel are poisonous and induce vomiting and purging. The comparison between the eatable eggs of the sturgeon and the poisonous eggs of the barbel could be excellent symbolism if it is referring to the Nazis trying to take over Russia. The symbolism is that Russia would be poisonous to the Nazis if they tried to "eat it," so to speak. If they attempted this they would be vomited out or purged from Russian soil.

D: *"He will make the strong one out of the bridge to be bound with chains."*

B: He says that represents Hitler's breaking the peace treaties and such and getting away with it. The different countries around him were strong, but he bound them up with chains because he was acting so audaciously they did not know how to react.

D: *Then a bridge refers to some kind of treaty.*

B: And he says the last line represents the allies rescuing Europe through France.

D: *It seems as if many of these quatrains deal with the two world wars.*

B: This is true. He says he wrote quite a few dealing with the two world wars since they were major turning points in history. And the major turning points in history are particularly easy to see in his magic mirror. He said the wars made a very strong nexus in time. And they both, particularly World War I, radically changed the Earth to where it would never be the same again. Because he says destruction and violence on such a world-wide scale had never happened before in history.

CENTURY VII-3

Apres de France la victoire navale,	After the naval victory of France, the people of Barcelona the
Les Barchinons, Saillinons, les Phocens,	Saillinons and those of Marseilles; the robber of gold, the anvil
Lierre d'or, l'enclume serré dedans la basle,	enclosed in the ball, the people of Ptolon will be party to the fraud.
Ceux de Ptolon au fraud seront consens.	

B: He says this quatrain refers to events that took place during World War II.

D: *Just out of curiosity, what is the "anvil enclosed in the ball"?*

B: He says that represents the secret weapons research that was being conducted on both sides of the war. The anvil enclosed within a ball represents atomic power, but it also represents the secrecy of the research involved. It was closed away from the rest of the world. The anvil being something that you build upon, that you use for making things.

D: *A blacksmith would use that. Is that what you mean?*

B: Right. That's how it represents the secrecy of their research, by extension.

D: *"The robber of gold"?*

B: That refers to Hitler and the Nazis, how they were robbing all the conquered countries of their artwork, gold and money. And how they'd also be taking gold fillings out of the corpses, and the jewelry and such.

D: *Saillinons is an unknown word.* (I spelled it, and she quickly pronounced it.)

B: He said for you to use it in context. (*I repeated the entire quatrain.*) He says that last line refers to the people within the various countries who were working for the Nazis. The first line, "The people of Barcelona and Saillonons, *etc.,*" represents free partisan groups both within some of the conquered countries and some of the neutral territories who were helping with the underground. He says it's a word they used in their organization to represent themselves. Since they were so secret, much of that knowledge never became generally known in your present time.

D: *They also didn't know that last word, Ptolon.*

B: He said that represents people in the countries who will be working for the Nazis against their own people.

D: *Why did he use that word?*

B: It's taken from Greek history. He says he used it as an abstraction of the family of Ptolemy, who ruled Egypt during the time of the Roman Empire. But they were actually Greek and worked for the Romans. They were administering various parts of the further reaches of the empire. Since they were working for someone else rather than for their own country, he used that as representative of the people in the various countries who work for the Nazis.

D: *The translators couldn't decipher it. They said, "The proper names are obscure in this quatrain." They thought Ptolon might refer to Ptolemy, but that's as close as they were able to come.*

B: He says at least they were on the right track.

D: *This next one has a strange word in it that they don't understand. They called it a "Nostradamus word," and it's going to be hard to pronounce.*

B: He suggests that you spell it before you start the quatrain.

I spelled it then chuckled as I made a sorry attempt to pronounce it. "*Sedifragues.*"

B: All right. He asks that you read the quatrain.

CENTURY VI-94

Un Roi iré sera aux sedifragues,	A kiny will be angry with the
Quant interdicts seront harnois	sedifragues when warlike arms
de guerre:	are prohibited; the poison tainted
La poison taincte au succre	with sugar in the strawberries,
par les fragues	murdered by waters, death,
Par eaux meutris, mors,	saying, close, close.
disant serre, serre.	

B: He says this quatrain refers to the nuclear accident that took place in Russia last year (1986). The king being angry with the sedifragues refers to the head of the Soviet Union being at odds with the council. The sedifragues, he says, is an ancient Greek representation of the Russian title that would be appropriate for this council—the name of the position that the men hold.

D: *It's an old term.*

B: Yes. He says, not having enough warlike arms refers to the cutback in nuclear armaments. The death by water refers to the radioactive water that was released from the plant when that accident took place. And how it got into the local water sources and started killing off the wildlife and such.

D: *What does it mean, "the poison tainted with sugar in the strawberries"?*

B: That refers to the radiation affecting the food and everything. The strawberries would still be sweet but they would be poisoned.

D: *Somehow they have tried to make this quatrain refer to the Protestants and the Catholics. But they had trouble with that word. They didn't know what it meant.*

B: He says that is because they assume everything he thinks about is in French. He says, "Don't they know that a properly educated gentleman studies many languages."

CENTURY IX-9

Quand lampe ardente de
  feu inextinguible,
Sera trouvé au temple des
  Vestales,
Enfant trouvé feu, eau
  passant par trible:
Perir eau Nimes, Tholose
  cheoir les halles.

When the lamp burning with eternal fire, will be found in the temple of the Vestals. A child found (in the) fire water passing through the sieve, Nîmes to perish in water, the markets will fall in Toulouse.

B: He says this quatrain has become garbled, and refers to a string of events. On the one hand it refers to the American and French Revolutions, and how one was sparked by the other. He says it also, in another sense, refers to the prohibition in the United States and the Great Depression and how it affected countries worldwide. That is the reference to the market. He said because much of this translation is garbled, he may not be able to answer all your questions.

D: *It has some very strange symbols. "The lamp burning with eternal fire will be found in the temple of the vestals."*

B: He says that refers to freedom.

D: *"The child found in the fire-water, passing through the sieve."*

B: He says that refers to America breaking from Great Britain.

D: *I can see that passing through a sieve would be very difficult.*

B: He says the fire-water refers to war—the revolution. And passing through the sieve refers to ... England was trying to keep a monopoly on its colonial markets, and they started breaking away in this manner. It's like trying to grip a handful of sand very tightly. It will sift out of your hand. And so the main reason America broke away from Great Britain was for economical reasons.

D: *And that's why it ties into the economic part of the last sentence.*

B: Somewhat, yes.

D: *"Nîmes to perish in water, and the markets to fall at Toulouse." The perishing in water deals with economics too?*

B: He says that refers to the revolution as well. He says there were many naval battles—American ships pirating British ships.

D: *So the Depression is all tied in with that.*

B: In the other interpretation, yes. He says in the other interpretation the fire-water refers—from the American English colloquial—to the liquor that had been rendered illegal in the United States.

D: *Of course, they're interpreting the whole thing as an actual flood.*

B: He says he doesn't have time for foolishness.

CENTURY X-68

L'armee de mer devant la *cité tiendra* *Puis partir sans faire langue alee,* *Citoyens grande proie en terre* *prendra,* *Retourner classe, reprendre* *grand emblee.*	The army of the sea will stand before the city then depart without making a long passage. A great prey of citizens will be taken on land, the fleet returns to seize (by) great robbery.

B: He says this quatrain refers to the Civil War in the United States.

D: *He was able to see that also?*

B: Yes. If the critics wonder why he should happen to see the Civil War, he says recall that during that war France remained friendly with the Confederacy in order to have a source of cotton for the cloth mills and such. And the fleet referred to in the quatrain refers to the Union fleet that blockaded the Confederate ports.

CENTURY IX-6

Par la Guienne infinité d'Anglais. *Occuperont par nom* *d'Anglaquitaine* *Du Languedoc Ispalme* *Bourdelois.* *Qu'ils nommeront apres* *Barboxitaine.*	A great number of English in Guienne will occupy it, calling it Anglaquitain. In Languedoc, Ispalme, Bordelais which they will name after Barboxitaine.

D: *Whew! Those names were difficult for me. Some of those are unknown words.*

B: He says this one has three different meanings. On the one hand it refers to the rise and fall of the British Empire—its development and how it lost eminence. On the other hand it also refers to World War II when the British troops were in France helping to fight Germany. And how they retreated to one little part of France which they named Dunkirk. But he says it also refers to the time of the Anti-Christ. The British in structuring their underground organization against the Anti-Christ are going to take advantage of their previous contacts in Asia, to work through the Anti-Christ's back door, so to speak. He says their contacts are in Singapore, Hong Kong, India, Malaysia—all across southern Asia. Due to the common enemy they'll be working against, they will renew these contacts and use them for good effect.

D: *Of course, we're curious about some of those names. Especially Barboxitaine.*

B: He says the names refer to various places that have been crucial in British history in Asia. He says if you wish, for a future session he will correlate them with what you consider the "present-day" names. Part of it is that the names they have in the 20th century are very much different from the names they were called in his time. He's used to calling them by the names he knew them by. And the anagrams he made are constructed upon the names he knew. What he needs to do is see if he can correlate them with 20th-century names. He's not sure if he'll be able to make the correct correlation because he's pulling this information from his future.

D: *I can tell you one possibility they've come up with, but they may be stretching it.*

B: He asks, "What is it?"

D: *They said, "Barboxitaine: Probably derived from Barbe-Occitanie. Barbie referring to the enigmatic Bronzebeard, and Occitanie, the medieval name for the Mediterranean coast." Does that make any sense?*

B: He says in a way it does because that location will be part of the British underground chain, through the Suez Canal and the Rock of Gibraltar.

D: *I don't know who Bronzebeard is.*

B: He says that is a figurative reference to a very brave ship's captain, actually a pirate. And how he defied prevailing authority to attain his ends. He says in a sense the British will be doing this. The prevailing authority will be the Anti-Christ, and the British will be going against him trying to attain what they want to accomplish.

D: *Was this a pirate in his time?*

B: It's one that he had heard of. He says he's not positive if it was a real person or not. You know how stories can be stretched, but he felt it to be a good symbol.

D: *Then they are correct in associating it with that?*

B: He says that's a fairly close association. That does not bring out the association with southern Asia, but he says what he has told will be sufficient.

D: *But there are some other parts of that anagram that would refer to southern Asia if we wanted to dig deeper.*

B: Right.

D: *Ispalme is the other one they can't understand. They think it might have been a misprint for LaPalme.*

B: (*Angrily*) He says, do not pronounce that final vowel! He says it drives him crazy always having to correct you.

D: (Laugh) *Well, I don't know French. That's why we do this in English.*

B: He says, in English the final "e" is silent most of the time, so just call the final "e" silent in French as well. (*He asked for the spellings.*) (*Pause*) He says he will have to contemplate on that one. He says that misunderstanding might derive from his handwriting as well. He says, enough on this one. Time is being wasted.

D: *I'm trying to solve all the mysteries at one time, and I don't think I can do it.*

B: Some mysteries are stupid to try to solve when you are trying to get information through.

CENTURY IX-5

Tiers doit du pied au
   premier semblera.
A un nouveau monarque
   de bas hault
Qui Pise & Lucques
   Tyran occupera
Du precedant corriger le deffaut.
	The third toe will look like the first
	one of a new king, of low height, he
	who will occupy as a tyrant Pisa
	and Lucca, to correct the fault of
	his predecessor.

B: The third what?

D: *Toe.* (Spelled it.) *That is interesting symbolism.*

B: He said, actually it's a mistranslation. What he meant was "digit," not specifically a toe or a finger, but just a smaller subdivision of something. He asks that you read it again, but use digit instead of toe. (*I read it, substituting the correct word.*) He says, to be honest, with the first reading he knew the translation of it, but he wanted to straighten out that one line before giving the meaning. He says the reason the mistake was made, undoubtedly, was because the word he used had a lesser-known or a type of slang meaning of "digit" for "subdivision," and the literal translation of "toe" in his own time. He says all languages have words that have double meanings. These were meanings being used in his time, so it would be clearer to someone in his time reading it. Because they would realize this alternate way of perceiving this word, and so they'd have another way of looking at the quatrain.

D: *What does the quatrain mean?*

B: He says it refers to when Mussolini ruled Italy, and the rise and fall of his power.

D: *Oh, they have something else entirely. I'm not even going to go into it.* (Laugh)

B: He says he's not surprised. Considering how they translated it, there's no telling what they came up with. He says his guess is that their translation was, "Guess what? The pope has lint under his toenails."

D: *Has* lint *under his toenails?* (Laugh) *Well, that would make about as much sense as some of the other translations.*

Although I didn't understand the expression, I assumed Nostradamus was probably using a slang term popular to his time. The correct interpretation or meaning of what he said is anybody's guess.

D: *They think it had something to do with Napoleon because of the "low height" part.*

CENTURY X-44

Par lors qu'un Roi sera contre les siens,	Where a king is (chosen) against his people a native of Blois will subdue
Natif de Blois subjugera Ligures.	the League. Mammel, Cordoba and
Mammel, Cordube & les Dalmatiens.	the Dalmatians; of the seven then a shadow to the King, new money and
Des sept puis l'ombre à Roi estrennes & lemurs.	dead ghosts.

B: He says this quatrain refers to the rise of Adolph Hitler.

D: *What does it mean, "new money and dead ghosts"?*

B: He says the new money refers to Hitler's scheme for paying off Germany's payments. He started printing more paper money without having an economic backing for it. The "old ghosts" refer to the old leaders from the Weimar Republic who wanted to get Hitler out of power.

D: *"Of the seven then a shadow to the King."*

B: He says this refers to the advisers of Hitler's predecessor. One betrayed his predecessor in the process of election, so that Hitler was brought to power through treachery.

D: *I won't tell him what they said. I'll go on to the next one.* (Chuckle) *Because he would laugh again.*

B: He says he hasn't laughed yet.

D: *Well, I don't want him pulling his beard out. They think the seven are Catherine de' Medici's seven children.*

B: He said that's not totally unreasonable, but they're not being broadminded enough.

Nostradamus had many quatrains that referred to World War II and Hitler in particular. By the process of elimination I have only included those which I thought had the most interesting symbolism. In CENTURY

VI-76 he called him the "false one-armed man" because of his famous one-armed salute.

Nostradamus' most recognized anagram for Hitler is "Hister." Since these quatrains are commonly known I have not included them in these books, deciding to concentrate instead on the lesser-known symbolism. It has been argued that Hister did not refer to Hitler, but was an old name for the Danube River. This is correct, but it again shows the brilliance of Nostradamus' mind in planting clues within the quatrains. He tried to include as much information in as few words as possible. Hister refers to Hitler as an anagram or word-puzzle, but it also refers to his birthplace. He was born in Braunau, Austria-Hungary, which was traversed by the Danube River, and was often called the "Danube Monarchy." Braunau is only a few miles from the Danube. Since these countries did not exist (by name) in Nostradamus' time, he could only use landmarks he was familiar with, such as the river. He was telling us in puzzle form, not only the name of the 2nd Anti-Christ, but where he would be born. He followed this same procedure in referring to other important figures in our future, if we are only wise enough to decipher the clues.

CENTURY IX-53

Le Neron jeune dans les trois cheminées Fera de paiges vifs pour ardoir getter, Hereux qui loing sera de telz menees, Trois de son sang le feront mort guetter.	In three chimneys the young Nero will make the living pages thrown out to burn. He is happy who will be far from such happenings; three of his family will ambush him to death.

B: He says that quatrain refers to Hitler as the young Nero, and the three chimneys refer to the death camps. Hitler never went anywhere near the death camps, but he was very pleased with the job they were doing.

D: *"It will make the living pages thrown out to burn."*

B: He says that refers to the Jews, and the people who were in the death camps.

D: *Why did he refer to them as "living pages"?*

B: He says each person's life can be thought of as a book in the process of being written. Each person's life contains much potential, like an unread book. And all this potential was thrown away, thrown into the bonfire, so to speak.

D: *And the last line, "three of his* family *will ambush him to death."*

B: He says this refers to the factions within Germany that were trying to topple him from power.

CENTURY IX-17

Le tiers premier pis que
    ne fait Neron,
Vuidez vaillant que sang
    humain respandre:
R'edifier sera le forneron,
Siecle d'or, mort, nouveau
    roi grand esclandre.

The third one firstly does worse
than Nero, go, flow, brave human
blood. The furnace will be rebuilt,
a golden century; (then) death, a
new king and great scandal.

B: He says this refers to Hitler.
D: *And that furnace is in there again.*
B: He says that refers to the death camps.
D: *That's what I was thinking. What's the "golden century"?*
B: He says that refers to the plans that Hitler had for the Third Reich.

CENTURY IX-81

Le Roi rusé entendra ses
    embusches
De trois quartiers ennemis
    affaillir,
Un nombre estranges larmes
    de coqueluches
Viendra Lemprin du
    traducteur faillir.

The crafty king will understand his
ambushes, from three sides the
enemies threaten; a large amount
of strange tears from the hooded
(ones), the splendor of the
translator will fail.

B: He says this refers to events during World War II. The "strange tears
   from the hooded ones" refers to the search into heavy water and the
   nuclear experiments. They were working in utmost secrecy. Therefore they were hooded, they were hidden.
D: *"The splendor of the translator will fail." They can't find out the secret?*
B: He says that means that their peace-making efforts fail. And so, as a
   result, they end up using these terrible weapons they have developed.

CENTURY VI-61

Le grand tappis plié ne
    monstrera,
Fois qu'à demi la pluspart
    de l'histoire:
Chassé du regne loing aspre
    apparoistra
Qu'au faict bellique chascun
    le viendra croire.

Folded, the great carpet will not
show except by halves, the greater
part of its history. Driven far out of
the kingdom he will appear harsh,
so that each one will believe in his
warlike act.

B: He says this quatrain refers to the development of the atomic bomb.
   "Folded the carpet will only appear by halves" refers to how everything was done under secrecy. Part of the team in one place did not

know what the other part of the team in the other place was developing because the government insisted on so much secrecy. For example, the people in Las Cruces, New Mexico, did not know what was going on in Oak Ridge, Tennessee. The government said they could not communicate with each other about this because it was classified.

D: *The carpet would be similar to a cover?*

B: Yes. Also the carpet refers to all the knowledge in general woven together to form the whole project. But when it was folded up, it was divided into compartments that were each secret from the other, so you could only see part of it at one time.

D: *"The greater part of its history."*

B: For the most part the history of such a powerful weapon and the development of it has always been top secret. Even the people involved with it only see part of the picture.

D: *"Driven far out of the kingdom, he will appear harsh, so that each one will believe in his warlike act."*

B: He says many of the scientists had moral questions about using such a powerful force for war. The leader had to be very stern with them, and give many pep talks to convince them that it was important to end the war early by using this force.

CENTURY VI-27

Dedans les isles de cinq
  fleuves à un,
Par le croissant du grand
  Chyren Selin:
Par les bruines de l'œr
  fureur de l'un.
Six eschapés, cachés
  fardeaux de lin.
	Within the islands of five rivers to one, by the crescent of the great Chyren Selin. Through the mists in the air the fury of one; six escaped, hidden in bundles of flax.

B: He says that refers to the bombing of Hiroshima, Japan. "The fury of one" refers to the first atom bomb. The "five rivers to one" is a description of the city. It is a harbor city where the main river that comes down from the mountains splits up and goes around several islands. And the city has many bridges in it. He says, "the six escaping hidden in bundles of flax," refers to the bomber crew of the plane.

D: *That is strange symbolism. Why does he say "bundles of flax"?*

B: He made this flax analogy—for one, there were no airplanes in his day, so he could not draw any images upon the airplane very well. But the flax, which is used to make cloth, linen, would be similar to the cloth that the six would be wearing. And bundles of flax are made into cloth. So he was seeing their uniforms and their flight jackets with the … it had a waterproof-type material.

D: *Then it says, "by the crescent of the great Chyren Selin"?*

B: He says the crescent refers to the shape of the harbor. He says Chyren Selin has a double meaning. On the one hand it refers to the effects of hard radiation on the people. And it also refers to how many people in the city sought to escape the burning fury by going into the rivers in and around the islands. He says Chyren is the watchdog of Hades in Greek mythology.

Charon, the ferryman of Hades is also mentioned in CENTURY VI-70 (see pg. 92).

D: *And Selin?*
B: That refers to the river.
D: *He's used those words before and had other meanings for them.*
B: Yes. He says he often draws upon Greek mythology for his symbolism because you can use it allegorically.
D: *That's why some of these translators have gotten very confused.*
B: He says this is true. People of our era are not accustomed to thinking in allegory, and so they fail to make the connection. People in his era would find it easier to make the connection because they're used to allegorical teaching and used to learned men presenting things in an allegorical manner.
D: *Yes, and we are also not as familiar with mythology. They think when he uses one anagram it means the same thing throughout.*
B: He says that's stupid, and he's puffing out his mustache. I suggest we go to the next one before he gets upset.

CENTURY VI-90

*L'honnissement puant
  abhominable
Apres le faict sera felicité,
Grand excusé, pour
  n'estre favourable,
Qu'à paix Neptune ne sera incité.*

The stinking and abominable shame, after the deed he will be congratulated. The great one excused for not being favorable, that Neptune cannot be tempted towards peace.

B: He says this quatrain refers to the dropping of the atomic bomb.
D: *He has several about that.*
B: He says it was a major event, a turning point in history.
D: *"After the deed he will be congratulated. The great one excused for not being favorable." Is that the president?*
B: Yes. He says both President Roosevelt and President Truman had very mixed feelings about using the bomb. The only reason they considered using it was because they thought the war in Asia would go on indefinitely, based on the knowledge they had. And they felt that although it would be very tragic to kill people from the impact of the bomb, it would be even more tragic to let the war drag on and have more people killed on both sides from fighting with conventional weapons.

D: *The last part says, "Neptune cannot be tempted toward peace." Does that refer to the sea wars?*

B: He says that refers to several things. It refers to the mixed feelings that the leaders were having about the war—because it was dragging out forever, particularly amongst the islands of the Pacific.

D: *That's where Neptune comes in. I knew it was something to do with the sea.*

CENTURY IX-56

Camp pres de Noudam passera Goussan ville,	The army near Noudan will pass Goussainville, and will leave its
Et à Maiotes laissera son ensigne,	mark at Maiotes; in an instant
Convertira en instant plus de mille,	more than a thousand will be converted, looking for the two to
Cherchant les deux remettre en chaine & legne.	put back chain and firewood(?).

B: He says this has a double meaning, both of which have taken place in the past. On the one hand it refers to events that took place during the time of Napoleon and the reign of terror. And on the other hand it refers—the last two lines specifically—to the atomic bombing of Japan at the end of World War II.

D: *They weren't sure if that word "firewood" was correct.*

B: He says he's using the word fire and wood, but he wasn't meaning wood to be burned. He meant wood that had exploded into flame.

D: *What would the chain signify?*

B: He says the chain refers to the armaments of war.

D: *"Looking for the two to put back"?*

B: Hiroshima and Nagasaki.

Nostradamus said in Volume Two that he saw the dropping of the atomic bomb as such a horrible event that he could have written 1000 quatrains on that event alone. In that volume he described how he saw it affecting the fabric of time.

D: *I think I have made a discovery. It seems that if I were to carefully examine these interpretations, I would probably get a step-by-step picture of World War II, just as we're getting a step-by-step picture of the Anti-Christ's war.*

B: Yes. He says you would.

D: *Many of the quatrains appear to be following the same pattern. They seem to put the French Revolution and the two world wars in steps. They look like random pieces, but when they are gathered and organized they really form a story line.*

B: They each form an overall picture of what happened. Particularly, as you say, during the French Revolution, and the two world wars—especially World War II—and during the time of the Anti-Christ.

Chapter 10

Information Received
About the Present

Un peu de temps les
temples de couleurs
De blanc & noir des
deux entremeslee:
Rouges & jaunes leur
embleront les leurs
Sang, terre, peste, faim, feu,
d'eau affollee.

In a short time the colors of temples; with black and white, the two will be intermingled. The red and yellow ones will carry off their (possessions), blood, earth, plague, hunger, fire, maddened by thirst.

W: [Wayne] This has to do with the situation in the United States, with much of its land being owned by other countries. In a short period of time it will be very similar to a foreclosure, and they will demand what is theirs. Foreign investments in this time period have been and still are enormous. I'm not getting a specific time on this, but soon it will be as if money is not satisfactory as payment for property, buildings, and they will want the assets more than the worthless money.

D: *What assets?*

W: Land, property, airlines, cities, buildings. The people of the United States will thirst because a life-style will be changed.

D: *I'm going to repeat some of these phrases and see how the symbolism fits. "In a short time the color of temples with black and white."*

W: That will be the people of the United States. I am a temple, you are a temple.

D: *He's using Bible reference. "The two will be intermingled."*

W: The black and white will fight *with* each other instead of *against*, because they will be equally outraged. They will join for a common cause.

D: *Will they be able to combat this?*

W: I see a split with people outraged and wanting war, and other people flocking to the side of the common enemy. It will split the nation, and cause a division in the country. The foreign investors and controllers will get what is theirs, and the rest will be divided.

D: *Will this hurt the United States?*

W: To some extent. I do not see war over it. I see many lessons.

D: *It would be good if they could learn the lessons before it came to that point.*

W: It may be too late.

CENTURY V-18

De deuil mourra l'infelix profligé,	The wretched man, destroyed, will
Celebrera son vitrix l'hecatombe:	die of grief. His victorious consort
Pristine loi franc edict redigé,	will celebrate the ceremonies.
Le mur & Prince au septiesme	Former laws, free edicts drawn up,
jour tombe.	both the Prince and the wall fall on
	the seventh day.

W: I believe this is dealing with the current political structure in China, but I am also being shown the Berlin Wall in Germany. I think it is a case of one quatrain referring to two events. The prince is the current ruler, and his time is about up.

D: *"The prince and the wall fall on the seventh day."*

W: The wall, of course, will also be the wall of Communism. The seven days will be the time span from when this current leader, the prince, undergoes an interrogation by subordinates. I think it's dealing mainly with the change in government. The seventh day would be either Sunday or Saturday. That is when the resignation will occur, on whatever is considered the seventh day. The "victorious consort" will be the new ruler that the people choose.

D: *Then it will no longer be a Communist government?*

W: The government will strive towards democracy. And the part about Germany will happen very soon.

On November 9, 1989 the Berlin Wall opened for travel and emigration. Party chief Erich Honecker was removed from office in October 1989. He had held the post since 1971.

This next quatrain seems to refer to the same event.

CENTURY VIII-56

La bande foible le terre occupera	The weak band will occupy the land,
Ceux de hault lieux feront	those of high places will make
horribles cris,	dreadful cries. The large herd of
Le gros troppeau d'estre coin	the outer corner troubled, near
troublera	Edinburgh it falls discovered by the
Toute pres D. nebro descouvers	writings.
les escris.	

W: I'm seeing two parts to this quatrain, and it doesn't seem to fit together.

D: *It might be referring to two different things. Tell what you see.*

W: I believe what I'm seeing are events happening in Germany. I see an exodus from east to west. The people regaining the power, and the government losing it. But I can't make the last part of the quatrain fit. I thought from my first impressions that it had to do with the writings of Lenin, but it doesn't make sense.

D: *Well, it could in a way. Aren't they fleeing from Communist Germany?*

W: Yes. I'm getting the impression that the exodus is a temporary one, and that the Communist government in East Germany *will* change, and the people will return.

D: *They will go back to East Germany?*

W: Yes, it's their home. They're wanting to leave *now,* but they will want to return when conditions are more favorable. Will you read the last part again? (*I did so.*) Where is Edinburgh? That's another thing I couldn't understand.

D: *I think it's in Scotland. But sometimes he uses names of places to refer to something else. This could also be a mistake in translation. Edinburgh is not in the French. It says, "D. nebro." They have put that together as "Dinebero" and translated it into "Edinbro" through a lot of strange manipulations. So that might not be correct.*

W: Apparently.

D: *Ask him if he was meaning Scotland.*

W: He means Germany.

D: *That could be one of his tricks and they have translated it incorrectly. "The large herd at the outer corner troubled. And it falls discovered by the writings."*

W: That would mean the crossing of the people. It could mean that the writings of Lenin may be retranslated or reread or …

D: *And referring to, like you said, the changing of the Communist party.*

W: Or even more literal.

D: *But you did say the Communist party was going to change in Germany.*

I wish I would have asked more about these quatrains referring to the fall of the Berlin Wall (see also CENTURY V-81). But at the time the idea seemed so far fetched that I presumed it would not happen for several years.

CENTURY VIII-41

Esleu sera Renad ne	A fox will be elected without
sonnant mot,	speaking one word, appearing
Faisant le faint public	saintly in public living on barley
vivant pain d'orge,	bread, afterwards he will suddenly
Tyranniser apres tant à un cop,	become a tyrant putting his foot on
Mettant à pied des plus grans	the throats of the greatest men.
sus la gorge.	

W: The impression I got was that the man elected without saying a word was our current President of the United States, George Bush. Nostradamus refers to him as a tyrant because he refuses to look at the overall picture of problems that need to be solved. He concentrates on just one or two things and tries to apply his solution to them, and lets everything else go to pot, so to speak. The situation will become more unstable and thereby contribute to the ease with which the Anti-Christ will take over. He says there is an expression called "straining at gnats." Bush is busy straining at gnats and is not doing anything about the elephants trammeling around, so to speak.

D: *Why would he write a quatrain about someone like Bush?*

W: He says that unknown to the general public, there are events taking place behind the scenes that are very momentous in this regard. Things that will come to light in future years and will ultimately affect the Anti-Christ. He says that during this President's reign it can be a turning point of United States history. It can be turning towards success, or turning toward failure. If the President does not take a look at the overall view, it will be apt to turn toward failure. It is the time frame that is important, rather than the person who is the President, although I cannot understand what he means by "living on barley bread." That's not clear to me.

D: *Focus on the mirror, ask him what he means by that phrase, and have him show you in the mirror.*

W: It's living off the fat of the land.

Ms. Cheetham's book says that an alternate translation of that phrase would be: to feather one's nest. That would also be appropriate to this interpretation.

D: *Why does he call Bush a fox?*

W: Because he's clever. He's manipulated people. He's done what he had to do for the past 20 years to get where he's at now.

D: *It says, "appearing to be saintly." Does that mean he's not what he appears to be?*

W: That's true.

D: *The rest of it is, "afterwards he will suddenly become a tyrant. Putting his foot on the throats of the greatest men."*

W: This means that slowly, but surely, individual rights will be taken away from men who believed in their country, and in the justice it stood for. Soon justice, freedom and liberty will no longer be visible. This is what he means by the tyrant.

D: *We think of Bush as being so quiet.* (In early 1989.)

W: Yes, he's quiet like a fox. He is mild-mannered and almost invisible. But he is not thinking clearly about the overall picture; therefore the people of the United States will suffer as a result of his actions. Unfortunately something may happen, sooner than you expect. He says that events are coming to a head very quickly. (*Was he referring to the Persian Gulf War which began the next year in 1990?*)

D: *In order for Nostradamus to write a quatrain about Bush, do you think he will do something that will set him apart from the other presidents?*

W: Yes. Nostradamus is showing me in the mirror. This is a continuation of some work that was begun by a previous president, and he will continue it through to its completion. This work and intention is to have a majority on the Supreme Court in which laws can be changed *and* made to suit his own ends and needs, which is the programming of the citizens.

D: *I was thinking of the former president, Ronald Reagan. He appointed new justices to sit on the Supreme Court. Is this what you mean?*

W: Yes. The current president will also have the same options, as more justices that are currently in power will leave the bench.

This, of course, has come true since this information was given in 1989.

D: *That may take a long time to accomplish.*

W: He has the time. He has been patient for a long time. This person has been on the outskirts of power for so long that he is in a position *now* to build himself up to be powerful. Since he's doing all this in a quiet, invisible way, people do not become alarmed about it since they do not see through to the consequences as Nostradamus does. What Bush is trying to accomplish will actually be of ill effect for the United States because it will ultimately be affecting constitutional rights.

D: *The translators have interpreted this quatrain as dealing with one of the Napoleons.*

W: No, it refers to George Bush. The main harm will be nestled in his own country.

D: *I can see how that quatrain could apply to a lot of tyrants down through history.*

W: Well, you must understand, when I hear the quatrain I talk about the first thing that comes to my mind. And when that is explored there are so many probabilities and possibilities that it could very well have also happened in the past or in the future. But the translation that I got was the clear one that was in front of me.

D: *That's probably the one he wants us to know because that will deal with our time period. Does Nostradamus think we should be warned about this president?*

W: That's what all these quatrains are about: warnings of the future, or an awareness of the future.

D: *Then he thinks in time Bush will show that he wants power, and for us to be alert to this?*

W: It will become apparent.

D: *Will manipulation of the Supreme Court be the only thing he will do?*

W: He will attempt many things. He is attempting to convert Democrats that are already in office to Republican.

D: *What purpose would that serve?*

W: It would serve the purpose of numbers in votes, allies. He says this quatrain could have a double meaning. The other meaning would deal with the rule of China. In the mirror on first glance I saw an American flag and the scenario that went with it. And I also saw that this could deal with the ruling party of China.

D: *Do you want to elaborate?*

W: I feel with all that's going on in China today, that the tyrant, the current ruler, will not survive his rulership. He has followed lines over the past which George Bush has taken note of, and is implementing to the extent that he can. Where this individual in China is nearly finished with his term in power, the President of the United States is beginning.

D: *How does the rest of the quatrain refer to China?*

W: This fox who turns into a tyrant was also elected without a word because it's in a Communist country. And he also has been living off the fat of the land. You must also realize that the President of the United States has had personal dealings with the leader of the Chinese government over a span of many years.

D: *Why is that important for us to know?*

W: He is a type of understudy. George Bush has been able to observe how this leader has controlled his people and led them around, and has manipulated them for his own gains.

D: *Of course, it's two different types of government.*

W: That's true. But when it comes to manipulating the masses, there is not a lot of difference whether it's Communist or a democracy.

CENTURY X-22

Pour ne vouloir consentir à divorce,	For not wanting to consent to the divorce, which then afterwards will
Qui puis apres sera cogneu indigne,	be recognized as unworthy, the King of the islands will be forced to
Le Roi des Isles sera chassé par force	flee, and one put in his place who has no sign of kingship.
Mis à son lieu que de roi n'aura signe.	

W: This refers to when Marcos was ousted from the Philippines. The one put in his place who has no sign of kingship was, of course, a woman. The first part of that quatrain means that he didn't want to give up what he had going for him—because power corrupts, and he was in control of quite a bit of money.

D: *That's what it means by "not wanting to consent to the divorce."*

W: Yes, not wanting to give up everything he had.

D: *"Which then afterwards will be recognized as unworthy."*

W: Of course, because he got what he had through corruption and control.

D: *And then the rest was, "The king of the islands will be forced to flee."*

W: Which he was.

D: *"And one put in his place who has no sign of kingship."*

W: Because a woman can't be a king, and she would not even normally be considered as a leader. This is the way Nostradamus thinks.

D: *In the book I'm reading from, they say this quatrain refers to King Edward VIII of England when he married the divorced woman and gave up the throne.*

W: It could refer to that. But the first impression I got was about the leader of the Philippines.

D: *Does he think that the present woman leader of the Philippines will remain in power?*

W: There will be trouble, but yes, she will remain in power for a time.

D: *Will Marcos cause her trouble?*

W: *(This was translated before his death.)* No. There's always a revolution. It will be caused by the people who live in the Philippines. They will rebel against the government.

D: *Then he's showing you that the people will revolt against Aquino?*

W: She has support from outside the Philippines. As long as that support continues, she will be in control.

CENTURY VIII-21

Au port d'Agde trois fustes entreront *Portant d'infect non foi & pestilence* *Passant le pont mil milles embleront,* *Et le pont rompre à tierce resistance.*	Three foists will enter the port of Agde carrying the infection and pestilence, not the faith. Passing the bridge they will carry off a million, the bridge is broken by the resistance of a third.

W: I'm seeing a disease that wipes out a million people before a cure is found. I think it's AIDS, and the three foists are the scientists who created it.

D: *Do you think it was created?*

W: Yes, that's the impression I receive. The virus was formulated in a lab for the purpose of annihilating people.

"Foist" is an uncommon word meaning: to impose by fraud; to put in slyly or stealthily. A fitting definition in the case of a created disease such as AIDS.

D: *What is he showing you?*

W: That it's a silent killer and blame cannot be pointed anywhere because of the way it acts.

D: *But that's so drastic. Why would anyone want to create something that would kill other people?*

W: Why would anyone want to use germ warfare or rifles, bombs?

D: *But there isn't any war going on now* (in 1989).

W: *(Sigh)* There is always war.

D: *Can he tell you the reason for doing this?*

W: The reason is for the purpose of annihilation, and the foresight was missing during the experiments. The damage was supposed to be localized, but it spread worldwide.

D: *How was it supposed to be localized?*

W: By being introduced into a certain part of a country during times of war. I believe it was developed in the 1960s for the war in Southeast Asia, but it never was successfully used for that purpose. The purpose for creating the drug was an experiment. The end result was annihilation. You must understand, scientists create in a laboratory out of a sense of duty for their country. They have no idea what the end result of their creations will be. This is apparent when you look at the atomic bomb, and many types of chemical warfare.

D: *Then are you saying this was created by* our *government?*

W: Yes. It was introduced here in the United States on people who sell their bodies for experiments. This government has been doing that for decades, experimenting with people who sell them their bodies for various drug testings. The virus spread slowly at first and then rapidly, as with most viruses. It will do much damage before it is brought under control, which it will be. It was an experiment that got out of hand.

D: *It seems drastic to think that someone would even do it on a small group of people if they knew it would kill them.*

W: *(Sigh)* But the proof is in the pudding. People would actually have to die before they knew if it would kill people or not.

D: *I guess we hate to think of our government being that cold-blooded.*

W: Well, not only our government. There are many cold-blooded governments in the world.

D: *I think the symbolism makes sense now. "Three foists will enter the fort of Agde carrying the infection and pestilence, not the faith." That has to do with the three scientists that developed it. "Passing the bridge they will carry off a million. The bridge is broken by the resistance of a third." What is the symbolism of the bridge?*

W: The bridge is human lives. And when the bridge is broken it will be by the scientist that finds a cure, or the "third."

D: *Is there a time period before the cure will be found?*

W: I believe it will be before the turn of the century.

D: *It says a million will die before it is found?*

W: At least.

D: *Does he think it will ever be made public that the government was behind this?*

W: No. There are probably many things that the government will *never* make public. And if the information comes out in reading such as this, it's up to the individual to believe it or not.

D: *But Nostradamus believes it was an accident. They didn't really intend it to get out-of-hand like that.*

W: Yes, that's a correct statement. It was meant to be a weapon of war, and it was an experiment. Then things happened that they didn't expect. When this was noticed it was too late to stop it. You never know how many people one person will interact with. If ten people were infected, and those ten infected ten others before they could find the trail and chase it down ...

D: *It would get out of hand in a very short time?*

W: No, it would get out of hand over a very *long* period of time. But the incubation period on such a disease as this is really very, very hard to detect because it is new. It also may have many mutants or deviations that could come off it also. It is full of unknown quantities.

(A very similar interpretation was given to John Feeley in Volume Two. Also see CENTURY VIII-62 in this chapter.)

Interpretations received through Nina:

N: We went to the downstairs room. He's at his desk waiting for us and the mirror's on the desk. He knew we were coming. He expected us.

D: *I don't understand how this works.*

N: It is telepathic.

D: *It's as though time isn't any barrier. Does he understand how it operates?*

N: I think so. It seems that time and space are an illusion or a third dimensional creation. Once you release that, you get into the pure essence of the vibration, and it's like fine-tuning a particular channel.

D: *Then he has learned how to do this?*

N: It seems to be so. He understands the concept. And he has the ability to release time and space, and see many parallel times happening at once. It's like the cubicles of a hive.

D: *Is it because our vibrations are compatible with his that we can contact each other, or how can he explain that?*

N: The intent. The intent and believing that it is so allows you to accomplish this. The thought pattern you create, his willingness to be a vehicle and listen, and his desire and intent to have this project accomplished.

D: *Surely other people have tried to contact him, but they may not have had the same motives.*

N: True. I believe that if the intent is correct, he will be a willing vehicle. Otherwise things will come through other people that are of their own creation. That's a part of the test and a lesson also. If the purpose is not worthy then he will choose to be silent. He is saying that sometimes he uses this for teaching the vehicle a lesson about self, and it changes their attitude.

D: *Has he ever had anyone contact him who had negative motives?*

N: Yes. When you're in that state of being you sometimes come to a certain point where the flow of the vibratory field isn't clear. The blockages are so extreme it's as a dark spot, and you can see it is negative and being used for manipulation and not for the good of the whole. At times he can also see beyond the blockage and know how the scenario will end up. It could be a good lesson for the person.

D: *Has he had good vibrations from all the vehicles I have brought to him?*

N: Yes, because he has also been open, and he has been calling forth on the same vibrational pattern. So it is a mutual desire to have these connections. I believe to explain it, it comes through in a way of knowing that there's a need to pass on information or to clarify. And just that very act of creating a thought pattern or a vibrational pattern is enough to put the person who's asking the information and Nostradamus, who wants to help them receive the information, in touch. The desire is enough to make the connection.

D: *What does he ask for when he sends out these requests.*

N: He asks to try one more time to see if the messages of his words and his visions might come across to a new era, a new generation—to see what they might do with it and how it will affect them.

D: *And this is why we have answered? Because in my mind he started the whole thing when he asked me to do this.*

N: Yes, this is true.

D: *It's like a vicious circle. Does he realize I am alive in the future?*

N: Yes. He feels there are times in the vibrational spiral when you have to try to reconnect. In doing so maybe it will give the species insight and healing, and an awareness of their own potential. And he will continue to reconnect in generations to come.

CENTURY VII-16

Entrée profonde par la grand Roine faicte	The deep entry made by the great Queen will make the place powerful
Rendra le lieu puissant inaccessible:	and inaccessible; the army of the three lions will be defeated causing
L'armee des trois lions sera deffaite.	within a thing hideous and terrible.
Faisant dedans cas hideux & terrible.	

N: I see Mother Russia very clearly, but the picture's a little hazy. I see inner revolts in that part of the country, in the various little sections. I see revolutions for independence and freedom because I think they have discovered corruption and false promises. So there is much destruction, much pain, much bloodshed, much revolution.

D: *Is the great Queen Russia?*

N: Yes. This is referred to as the land mass. That's what I'm seeing.

D: *"The deep entry made by the great Queen will make the place powerful and inaccessible."*

N: I see revolution and unrest going on, and militia counteracting this. I saw Russia-Chinese unification somewhere in there too. I don't know if their militia united, but it looks as if I'm getting a picture of many soldiers with many faces.

D: *Who is the army of the three lions?*

N: Two of these, I believe, seem to be Russia and China, but the third one is the combined areas that are revolting.

D: *It says, "the army of the three lions will be defeated. Causing within a thing hideous and terrible."*

N: I think that's part of the symbolism. The suffering will be devastating, bringing about so much bloodshed. The rebuilding will be devastating.

D: *Do you mean when these little revolutions occur there will be bloodshed associated with it?*

N: This is what I'm seeing. I also see Russia and China together, becoming unified.

D: *Can you see when this will happen?*

N: I can't see a time reference.

CENTURY X-28

Second & tiers qui font
  prime musicque
Sera par Roi en
  honneur sublimee,
Par grasse & maigre presque
  demi eticque
Rapport de Venus faulx
  rendra deprimee.
	Second and third make first class
	music they will be sublimely
	honored by the king; Through fat
	and thin, even half emaciated,
	to be made debased by the false
	report of Venus.

N: I was seeing America and Russia uniting in many efforts, and being praised. There's a new warmth and security throughout Europe because of this.

D: *"Second and third make first-class music. They will be sublimely honored by the king." What does the symbolism mean?*

N: I think what I'm trying to interpret is countries coming together, and realizing the desperate need for unification.

D: *Does the symbol of the king represent a person or a country?*

N: It represents nation coming together with nation.

D: *"Through fat and thin, even half-emaciated, to be made debased by the false report of Venus."*

N: This has to do with Earth's struggles to survive as a planet. I see pockets of much anger, trying to blame one another, while there are unifying forces that are trying to heal and keep humanity going.

D: *What is the meaning of the symbol of Venus?*

N: I'm feeling this symbol is of someone in disguise, being the loving, feminine, manipulative part, who has gained confidences. And this group or country has woven a web to poison others' philosophies. It's very difficult to find the clarity and truth of the situation. Actually some of these quatrains can apply to many times in history.

D: *And he's showing you the event that would affect our time period?*

N: He's trying to. Lessons in history repeat themselves.

CENTURY X-81

Mis tresor temple citadins
  Hesperiques
Dans icelui retiré en secret lieu,
Le temple ouvrir les liens
  fameliques.
Reprens ravis proie horrible
  au milieu.
	Treasure is placed in a temple by Western citizens withdrawn therein to a secret place, the temple to open by hungry bonds, recaptured, ravished, a terrible prey in the midst.

N: The picture I was getting was within the United States. It has to do with corruption within the government and many levels of the government. And how this rich nation is not taking care of its own people, its own environment. There are many problems they can't control and take care of and cleanse. There is much corruption, greed and control so a few get wealthy and fat. But there'll be a cleansing such as this country has never seen before. It will be shocking.

D: *"The treasure is placed in the temple by Western citizens. Withdrawn therein to a secret place." That means it is something that is unknown to the average person. "The temple to open by hungry bonds. Recaptured, ravished, a terrible prey in the midsts." What will happen when the people find out?*

N: It seems like many resignations, as if the party in power will fall. This will be unique in its history. It will bring in a temporary government. It will be the first time somebody who ranks in the third or fourth position will be called in to take over.

D: *Can you see when this will happen?*

N: It's very hard to tell but I think it's somewhere within 20 years. I'm seeing something that seems very literal, but this also could be a symbolic cleansing. Whoever this third or fourth party in position is— whether it be "speaker of the house" or they give it a different name—he takes over command and has to start regaining control of this country so it doesn't fall in the world arena. These are pictures I am being shown. At times it's hazy and I can't really tell if this is symbolic of a philosophical cleansing or a physical cleansing.

Nina also saw the fall of the Berlin Wall when we were working in early 1989.

CENTURY V-81

L'oiseau royal sur le cité solaire,
Sept mois devant fera
  nocturne augure:
Mur d'Orient cherra
  tonnerre esclaire,
Sept jours aux portes les
  ennemis à l'heure.

The royal bird over the city of the sun will give a nightly warning for seven months; the wall in the East will fall, thunder and lightning, in seven days the enemies directly to the gates.

N: *(Sigh)* So many pictures.

D: *Several different events?*

N: Yes. But the wall I saw was what you call the Berlin Wall. I saw the bird and the sun being symbolic of peace and sunshine. The first picture I got was the wall being torn down.

D: *That would be good if it were to happen. It says, "The royal bird over the city of the sun will give a nightly warning for seven months." What is that symbolic of?*

N: I believe the seven months refer to a cycle with seven being a very special number. It refers to a cycle of time, from beginning to completion. During this time period there would have been upheaval and communication, but the wall will be taken down. From the beginning of the takedown would be a cycle of seven.

D: *"Thunder and lightning. In seven days the enemies directly to the gates."*

N: This seems to refer to the same time, and I just see the wall being torn down.

D: *What is the thunder and lightning?*

N: I feel that's symbolic of the upheavals.

D: *At the time or before?*

N: The time of the whole cycle. There will be some upheaval before the wall is torn down.

D: *That translation seems to be the most symbolic, but what other scenes were you seeing?*

N: They were mainly from other time periods and other wars. This seems to be the most current one.

D: *I was wondering whether the royal bird could refer to the eagle that is symbolic of the United States.*

N: Well, that could be. I was feeling this bird was symbolic of peace. So I feel the wall coming down as he showed it, meant that a time of coming together of East and West was at hand. He used it to symbolize peace and the sun coming out.

D: *When I read it I thought about the Berlin Wall but I wasn't sure. They're hoping that might happen.*

At the time (early 1989) it seemed doubtful, but the prophecy came true within a matter of months.

There were several quatrains interpreted that dealt with China. All the subjects seemed to see the same future for that country. Although they saw the Communist satellite countries regaining their freedom quickly (some peacefully and some through violence), they saw it would be a slower process for China. It would eventually take a mass uprising, led by the underground, and would involve much bloodshed, but China would eventually become a democracy.

CENTURY VI-22

Dedans la terre du grand temple celique,	In the land of the great heavenly temple, a nephew at London is
Nepveu à Londres par paix faincte meutri:	murdered through a false peace.
La barque alors deviendra scismatique,	The ship will then be schismatic, false liberty will be shouted abroad.
Liberte faincte sera au corn & cri.	

N: I believe this will happen somewhere in Russia. I see Russia, the Kremlin, and it has to do with the government.

D: The government at the present time or what?

N: Not right now. It will be into the future a bit.

D: What does that mean, "a nephew at London is murdered through a false peace"?

N: That's symbolic. It's a different area of Russia, one of the little provinces. There's upheaval in some of the smaller territories of Russia, and that's what this is referring to.

D: Then "the nephew at London" doesn't mean it happens in England. Ask him why he used that symbolism.

N: I think it's one of his puzzles. This is not the London of England. The government of Russia was trying to find peace with these smaller territories because they were concerned there might be upheaval. And the person they sent as a spokesman and believed to be doing something, was just a pawn of manipulation. This has to do with a part of Russia, or a combination of the various small territories seeking more freedom, more voice, more justice. London is used as an anagram, a puzzle. This refers to the territories and country it controls.

D: It says, "the ship will then be schismatic. False liberty will be shouted abroad."

N: Yes. The rest of the world will not get a very honest, clear picture of what's going on. There will be an underground at work to get the truth out.

D: Can he see when this will happen?

N: It's after the present regime (early 1989).

The revolts of Russia's satellite possessions began at the end of Gorbachev's reign, and intensified after the installation of Boris Yeltsin.

CENTURY VI-39

L'enfant du regne par
  paternelle prinse,
Expolié sera pour delivrer:
Apres du lac Trasimen
  l'azur prinse,
La troupe hostaige pour trop
  fort s'enivrer.
	The child of the kingdom, through
	his father's capture, will be deprived
	to deliver him; near Lake Trasimene
	the azure captive, in order that the
	hostage troop may become very
	drunk.

N: This seems to be in the future. It deals with part of the Soviet Republic and their rebellion.

D: *Do you want to go over some of the symbolism? "The child of the kingdom, through his father's capture will be deprived to deliver him."*

N: I believe one of the spheres of the Soviet Republic is rebelling, and the governing body of Moscow captures their leader in hopes that it will stop the revolution. But this does not happen. And the son is unable to face his father, and the rebellion for independence continues.

Could this refer to Gorbachev's temporary capture in 1991?

D: *The father and the child are symbolic of the countries. "Near Lake Trasimene the azure captive." What is the symbolism of that color?*

N: To me it represents more of an emotional body, symbolizing part of the puzzle of this person relinquishing his control.

D: *"In order that the hostage troop may become very drunk."*

N: It's a game; it's a puzzle. It's symbolic. They're trying to set the troops of the rebelling countries up for a fall. But it won't work.

D: *Symbolically to make them drunk, or in other words, to make them fail?*

N: Yes. That's what I'm seeing.

D: *Do you see the country gaining its freedom?*

N: Yes, because the capture and the death of their leader makes their purpose and their unity stronger.

D: *Can he show you what country it is?*

N: I see a land mass on a large body of water. This is a small country southeast from Moscow.

D: *There are many satellite countries, but that might be enough to help us locate it.*

CENTURY VII-15

Devant cité de l'Insubre contree,
Sept and sera le siege devant mis:
Le tres grand Roi y fera son
  entree,
Cité puis libre hors de ses
  ennemis.
	Before the city of the Insubrian
	lands, for seven years the siege will
	be laid; a very great king enters it,
	the city is then free, away from its
	enemies.

N: I see symbolism, and I think this could be Poland. I'm seeing them gaining independence and becoming democratic.

D: *What does it mean, "For seven years the siege will be laid"?*

N: They had been working on this program to gain their freedom for this amount of time.

D: *Do you mean from the beginning to the point they are now, or is this in the future?*

N: It seems to be happening now. The seven years are already in progress. The desire for freedom has been going on a long time. But the actual physical work has been in progress for a few years. They will gain their freedom, but there will also be problems.

I am assuming that the time sequence in this quatrain could be referring to the establishment of the trade union called Solidarity in Poland. Its leader, Lech Walesa, later elected as first president, was awarded the 1983 Nobel Peace Prize. The Communist party was defeated and a Solidarity-led government was formed in September 1989.

D: *Has Nostradamus ever seen Catherine de' Medici or the king?*

N: He has, yes. He was called on for consultation by this Catherine.

D: *Can he tell me about it?*

N: He hesitates because I think he felt there was a great deal of darkness around the castle, around the royalty, many negative things going on.

D: *What was his personal opinion of Catherine de' Medici?*

N: (*Sigh*) I think he does not favor women very much anyway. But he felt this one has superior strength and a calculating mind. He feels there's much evil around her, and some of it comes from the power in that house.

D: *Did he also see the king?*

N: I think his business was mainly with her from what I'm seeing at this period.

D: *Did he enjoy meeting royalty?*

N: Humph. He felt it as an obligation, but he felt a little threatened. He felt always on the defensive because of the other side of his personality and his interests that might come out.

D: *I was wondering if he felt it a great honor to go there.*

N: A part of him might have felt this, but after a while he did not like the position he was put in.

D: *Then he didn't really like meeting royalty.*

N: Not this particular house.

Amazingly each subject reported Nostradamus' impressions of Catherine de' Medici and his opinions of the court in almost identical language. His association with the royal house is a matter of record in his biographies, but his personal opinions of the royalty are not. I believe this gives these insights more validity.

P: [Pam] We're having a small debate. He's asking *me* to look in the mirror and translate to him what I see. I'm refusing this assignment.

D: *Why?*

P: I don't wish to translate to Nostradamus. My role in this project is for Nostradamus to explain to me what he meant in his writings.

D: *But maybe it's a two-way street.*

P: I did not volunteer for that project.

D: *All right, but maybe he wants information as badly as we do.*

P: I'm assuring him that I will not block information if it comes, but I do not volunteer.

D: *Maybe he asked you to help translate because sometimes he sees things he doesn't understand.*

P: That is perhaps possible, but I seem to be encountering a massive ego who is a pretty cocky guy. He wants to write. He *must* continue to write. He's addicted to prophesy. He wants to see the future. It's not possible for him to stop. The request was for me to bring new pictures, and I do not choose to do that. I choose to see what Nostradamus sees in the mirror. And then I choose for Nostradamus to translate to me what he is seeing. This can only be keyed by the quatrain. I do not wish to help Nostradamus create new quatrains at this time. However, if that happens, I won't stop it.

D: *We have no way of knowing which came first anyway. We don't know what order this all happened in.*

P: Very interesting.

D: *So whether you want to or not, you may be a party to it.*

P: I see myself contained as a blue light. He is ready to begin. Although he sits poised to write, with plume in hand, he is looking over at the glass now. I'm showing him a tape recorder.

D: *Oh? What does he think of it?*

P: He says it seems so otherworldly. Such a device that could capture the sound of the human voice seems like magic.

D: *Yes, it's our little magic black box. It captures the voice and then gives it back to us when we want it. See, you are showing him some things.*

P: Well, I thought that would be a fun thing.

CENTURY VIII-62

Lors qu'on verra expiler le saint temple,	When one sees the holy temple plundered, the greatest of the
Plus grand du rosne leurs sacrez profaner:	Rhône profaning their sacred things; because of them a very
Par eux naistra pestilence si ample.	great pestilence will appear, the
Roi fuit injuste ne fera condamner.	king, unjust, will not condemn them.

P: I should say what I first saw. It really doesn't go very well with those words though.

D: *That's all right, we're speaking of translations anyway.*

P: Yes, translations of riddles. This is interesting because I can hardly remember the words that you just read. I can only remember the pictures that I saw in my mind. My first impression seemed to be pyramids. When I see pyramids my mind thinks Egypt but something said Atlantis, so I don't know. And I was thinking in terms of Atlantis and their tools and technology, and the Atlanteans' beliefs about everything they *could* do. In the end they brought down great death and destruction. I see the person whom we could call their king. I don't think king is the right term, but I can't think of the correct term. He seemed to be the person in charge. He did not stop the Atlanteans because they needed—this is not the right terminology. They didn't *need* destruction, but they needed to not continue in the same thought processes, the same programs and activities. There was a person who saw he could not change an entire continent, so their self-destruction was allowed.

D: *Why is Nostradamus using that example of Atlantis?*

P: I don't know that Nostradamus was. I was simply reporting the first thoughts that came to my mind. I know we are trying to see what he says, but I can't distinguish where these thoughts are coming from. I see a whole mess that needed to be fixed, and the way to fix it was to start over. I can't differentiate whether it's coming from him or me. Ask a specific question to him, not a riddle.

D: *Okay. If this is a reference to Atlantis, is it referring to something else as a riddle, as symbolism?*

P: A riddle within a riddle? He said I gave that answer because *I* didn't want to say what it really meant. (*Softly*) Well, it seems the quatrain is talking about right now in our present time period. The pestilence we've unleashed is AIDS, which is actually the father of an infinite number of mutated biological entities. I just wouldn't say that. It's easier to look upon these things as having happened in the past, rather than happening now at this moment.

D: *Using that definition, what is the holy temple? "When one sees the holy temple plundered."*

P: I guess this is the response: it is the heart and mind of man. I think we've gotten very screwed up in our emotions and our way of dealing with humanity and all living things. We're also the ones who created these biological mutations.

D: *You mean man did?*

P: (*Emphatic*) Yes! We created AIDS.

D: *Some people think it was just a mutation of an existing virus.*

P: A mutation that was consciously done, yes. The original intent was not to create killers. The intent was to find more helpful vaccines. It didn't work out that way. I should say it was *not* intentionally developed to be a species exterminating mutation. It was intended to be two things. The outward intention for this experimentation that resulted in AIDS was: One, to help strengthen or determine a new vaccine for an already existing virus. There was another secret reason, and that was biological warfare. But I don't wish to continue talking about it. It's very distressing.

D: *Sometimes knowledge is not pleasant, but it is necessary. That's the reason he is giving us this information. We can go on to another one, but you may see other things that are distressing.*

P: Seeing distressing things is not the problem. I can look at them dispassionately as a story. I don't know how to describe it. It has something to do with my levels of feeling. There seems to be an automatic censor that wants to click in when we come to things that are occurring now or in *our* future. However, I am trying to get through that. This might take a couple of attempts because I didn't realize how strong it is about not letting me say what I'm getting. But I don't feel personally pained.

D: *Can he see any personalities or individuals that will arise during our time period that will have a great deal of influence, either positive or negative?*

P: The first figure that I see in the mirror is a woman who looks East Indian. She has something like a diaphanous veil that is sheer and thin, beautiful. And her body is almost wrapped, because her gown doesn't really have a shape, but the quality of the material is so delicate and beautiful it looks like spun gold and air. She had a red dot on her forehead, and a glowing, loving bearing that's also strong and powerful. She is capable, but very loving and nurturing at the same time. I understand this to represent the feminine principal, but is so strong that there is actually more than one person inhabiting a female body on the planet of the Earth *right now* in 1989 who has the clarity of thought, the depth of emotion and the range of perception to lift and enlighten *large* segments of the population. There are many countries on the planet that have a great deal of people in them. These women—maybe as many as three—are alive today on the planet. According to his extremely chauvinistic attitude, this was a big deal to even admit there would be *any* women who would be looked up to as world leaders, or even world teachers. He isn't comfortable with that concept. But that's what he saw, so he's honest in his reporting. They will be teachers or leaders who will make a difference to the *world.* These women extend beyond the boundaries of their own countries. Their teachings and life examples are so astounding and newsworthy that the rest of the world comes to know of them. There's also a large embracing of what they say. I think it's unusual that there are more than one, but then all of this is unusual. It's strange to see this woman with the red dot on her forehead looking out at me through the mirror. He says the purpose of this whole exercise is to enlighten people to their capability of making choices. To show them that their thoughts are *powerful, huge* important tools and techniques for bringing to them whatever it is they focus on.

Interpretations through Brenda:

D: *I wanted to ask him about a situation that is occurring now in my time period, in June of 1989. Can he comprehend that far ahead of the future?*

B: He's insulted that you feel you should even ask. He said he wishes you could see even half of the things he's seen in his mirror. He has seen much further into the future than 1989.

D: *There are some very strange things occurring in our time period that have to do with the Communist countries in Europe and parts of Asia. All of a sudden everything seems to be changing. Is he able to see what's bringing all this about and what the results will be?*

B: He says there are several possibilities. He's taking a moment to get his thoughts in order. He says it's on the very eve of greater changes to come. Whenever there's going to be massive social or political change, there are warning signs before the big surge of change comes. He says as an example, a king can always tell when the peasants are going to revolt because they get particularly restless, and the crime rate goes up. He says on a larger scale, when on the eve of sweeping worldwide change, a few small countries will go into upheaval for no apparent reason. There'll be more open demonstration, marches in the street and civil restlessness. That is because the way things are set up, certain countries or certain particular systems of society may be particularly sensitive or vulnerable to the changes that are coming. So they react first, and this is a warning sign that bigger changes are on the way.

D: *This is such a tremendous thing because we never thought the Communist countries and the Communist party would ever change.*

B: This is true. He says the agents of the Anti-Christ and the agents of the Cabal have been trying to create their own spheres of dominance in the so-called "underworld." Most of the time they have the same goals in mind, and so they work parallel to each other and don't affect each other. But there will be times when they will conflict with what they want to accomplish, and you'll see interesting results. He says in the case of eastern Europe and Russia the Cabal was in favor of keeping the Communist running the way it was because they were able to siphon off the majority of a particular nation's wealth through the front of the Communist party. However, on the other hand, the Anti-Christ in the process of making his plans and getting his empire together wants things to be a little bit unstable. He wants social unrest to take place, to make it easier to tip things over and set up his own order of things.

D: *Everybody is thinking that these countries wanting freedom is a very positive thing.*

B: He says, on a short-term basis it is a positive thing. It will also help towards the rebuilding of the world afterwards.

D: *Then you don't think this will stop the Anti-Christ? I thought it was the complete opposite of what he wanted, if countries were gaining freedom.*

B: They are gaining freedom. But you must understand this is a very big change in the country. It's toppling things over, so far as different institutions of the government. The society is going through much change. Whereas before they had nothing, now all of a sudden they're able to own land again, or have things on the grocery shelves. And so the people will be more vulnerable to outside influence. Although the people are yearning towards freedom, and working towards it, everything's changing and moving and not stable. So the Anti-Christ can send agents in to keep things stirred up, and make it easier for him to take over in a subtle way.

D: *Does Nostradamus see this as the end of the Communist party?*

B: He thinks the Communist party, as a name, will continue. But their structure will be different, and the goals they will be working towards will be different. They'll be doing a great deal of changing. He says one thing that's going to happen, they'll go back and reread Karl Marx and Friedrich Engels and the others from a totally different viewpoint and put a totally new interpretation on this. And this interpretation will be more congenial towards world peace than the previous interpretation and application.

D: *These sound like positive things.*

B: Yes. It's positive in that these different organizations are able to start working together better now. If the worst comes to worst, many of them will form part of the underground network during the time of the Anti-Christ. If they're able to start working together now, they'll be able to work together better then.

D: *But it sounds like these things will weaken Russia.*

B: Russia will be weakened some, but she won't be as vulnerable as the eastern European countries. Just the geographical shape and size of Russia is her strength. The balance of power may alter some, and she may be making more lenient treaties with the United States, for example. But when the Anti-Christ sends someone into Russia to try to take over or what have you, Russia is so big that she'll be able to resist very well. If nothing else, she can follow the scorched earth policy as she did with Hitler and Napoleon, by retreating and burning everything down to the ground to prevent the armies from going further. Of course, with modern aircraft, that would not be as effective. But the eastern European countries will be particularly vulnerable because they've never been very stable anyway, with the mixture of tribes within the countries and the different ethnic groups. And with this new unrest to be dealt with on top of their basic instability, the Anti-Christ really won't find it much of a challenge at all.

D: *People are saying they can't see how these negative events that*

Nostradamus has foreseen could happen. It is as though everything is going in another direction.

B: (*Chuckle*) His eyes are twinkling. He says, yes, things are going very positively in Russia and eastern Europe, and it would be good if they could continue to develop in that direction. He asks, *however,* has anyone taken a good close look at the Middle East lately? Remember, the Anti-Christ's central power if there. He'll be coming from the Middle East, and things are *not* getting any better there.

D: *If something was happening in just one country, you could watch its development easier. But in this case, everything's happening at once.*

B: Yes. He says you overwhelm the opposition, so to speak, with numbers. And the Cabal is not happy with this situation because if eastern Europe works toward freedom, that will mean a freer flow of money within society. More of it will filter down to the middle and lower classes, with less to be scraped off the top.

D: *And this is not what* they *want to happen?*

B: No. As was mentioned earlier, the Cabal and the agents of the Anti-Christ occasionally come into conflict, and this is one of those areas. Because the Cabal favors Communism, and the agents of the Anti-Christ really don't care if it's Communist or not. They're just trying to instigate change for change's sake, to make it easier for them.

D: *Does he see these countries forming their own governments?*

B: He says that's already in the process. It will be much as the Italian government was in the 1920s and 1930s. New governments will form that will be freely elected, and the Communist party will be booted out of power. There would be a different party in power, but there would still be two or three other parties who think *they* should have won the election. And they will have demonstrations and marches, and demand another election.

D: *This will all be occurring during the same time as the Anti-Christ, so he will use the confusion to his advantage.*

B: The decade of the 1990s is going to be extremely eventful. (*This reminds me of the old Chinese curse: "May you live in interesting times."*)

D: *It looks as if it's off to a good start.* (Chuckle) *There's a lot happening, and it's happening very fast.*

B: He says, precisely. The suddenness of it should make you suspicious. Can't you see there's someone behind the scenes pulling the puppet's strings? In any large operation or large endeavor there's going to be both positive and negative things happening. And regardless of which thing you're struggling for, you really can't help the occurrence of the other along with it. Although the agents of the Anti-Christ are basically striving towards what would be considered negative goals, in some places there may be positive side effects. They really can't do much about that.

CENTURY VI-78

Crier victoire du grand
  Selin croissant,
Par les Romains sera
  l'Aigle clamé.
Ticcin, Milan, & Gennes
  n'y consent,
Puis par eux mesmes Basil
  grand reclame.
	To shout aloud the victory of the great crescent moon the Eagle will be proclaimed by the Romans. Pavia, Milan and Genoa will not agree to it: then the great Lord is claimed by themselves.

B: He says this quatrain is about the Mafia. He says originally the Mafia started out in Sicily and southern Italy, and that was their center of operations and their base of power. The quatrain tells how they transferred their main operations and power base to the United States.

D: *"To shout aloud the victory of the great crescent moon." What does the crescent moon represent?*

B: The crescent moon represents a large city around a bay shaped like a crescent moon. It represents their having enough power in that city to be basically in control.

D: *Is that a city in the United States or in Italy?*

B: He says it represents a city in Italy where they began.

D: *"The eagle will be proclaimed by the Romans." Is the eagle the United States?*

B: Yes, and the Romans represent the Mafia, the Italian.

D: *I believe the other names are cities in Italy?*

B: Yes. They represent rival organizations that decided to stay in Italy rather than come to the United States.

D: *"Then the great lord is claimed by themselves."*

B: When the Sicilian branch of the Mafia came to the United States, they became a power in and of themselves instead of being in cooperation with the other organizations of Italy that stayed behind. They made their decisions independently of the other organizations and chose their leaders accordingly.

D: *I think that's the first one we've had dealing with the Mafia. He must have seen them as having some importance.*

B: He says that due to their *negative* influence and their involvement with so-called "organized crime," they are capable of affecting history. They have much power, and thus they can influence many people.

D: *The interpreters said this was a retroactive prophecy. In other words, it was one that happened* before *Nostradamus' time. They connect it to the Ottoman and Holy Roman Empires whose symbols were the crescent moon and the eagle.*

B: He says he can see where they would make that parallel, but not everything is as it seems.

CENTURY X-41

En la frontiere de Caussade
  & Charlus,
Non g‹ieres loing du fonds
  de la vallee,
De ville franche musicque
  à son de luths,
Environnez combouls
  & grand mytee.
	On the boundary of Caussade and Caylus, not very far from the depths of the valley, music from Villefranche to the sound of lutes, surrounded by cymbals and a great (deal) of stringed (instruments).

B: He says this quatrain refers to several events under a general description. He saw a unique phenomenon developing in the 20th century, the giving of musical concerts for various reasons: for political expression, for raising money to aid people stricken with catastrophe or what-have-you. He says the type of music was like nothing he had ever heard before. He says the communicator supplies the word "rock" for it. He always thought that was a piece of a mountain, something hard that one would use for building a wall. But he says he used the phrase "many stringed instruments and cymbals all around" to describe the sound of amplified music.

D: *Why did he write a quatrain about that?*

B: Because he says the results of this has affected history. He recalls that during the United States' involvement with what is called the Vietnam War, several protests were held, particularly in the form of concerts. That finally culminated in the United States getting out of that war. He says as various events continue to occur and disasters become more frequent, the government will no longer be able to supply disaster relief to the various areas as it has in the past. So the people will have to turn to their fellows for relief. And one of the ways this will be done will be with musicians, actors, mimes, jugglers and, he says, all manner of court entertainers, getting together and entertaining people. The money the people toss to them will be given to those who need the disaster relief.

D: *Why did he use those names? I guess they're cities.*

B: He says these are some of the places where this will be taking place in the future.

D: (Chuckle) *They said ...*

B: They got it wrong. He knows they did.

D: *Yes. They said, "Perhaps this is describing a festival that Nostradamus once witnessed."*

B: He said, do not waste his time with such drivel. He's describing something he saw, but he hasn't attended one because it's in his future.

CENTURY X-61

Betta, Vienne, Emorre,
  Sacarbance,
Voudront livrer au Barbares
  Pannone:
Par picque & feu, enorme
  violance,
Les conjurez descouvers par
  matrone.

Betta, Vienna, Emort, Sopron, they
will want to deliver Hungary to the
Barbarians; great violence through
pike and fire, the conspirators
discovered by a matron.

D: *Some of these names are very obscure. They don't know what they mean.*
B: He says they haven't known what *any* of the quatrains mean, except
  for two or three of them. Some of them, like this one, are just a general
  quatrain, to try to touch upon many facets of history. He was trying
  to cover as much as he could, because he felt, in some respects, that his
  time was limited with what he would be able to get written down. He
  says this refers to a series of events. First of all it refers to events that
  took place during World War II when Russia took over eastern
  Europe. It also refers to events in the late 1980s, early 1990s, when
  eastern Europe starts regaining its independence.
D: *Does he see anything about that?*
B: He says the trend will continue. He says every small country and
  republic that has been smothered by Russia will regain its independence. And Russia will be reduced back to just the country of great
  Russia and Siberia combined. All the southern and the western parts
  of what is now called USSR will break off into their individual countries.
D: *So Russia will lose all of her satellite possessions. With that interpre-*
  tation, what does it mean, "They will want to deliver Hungary to the
  barbarians"?
B: He says that refers to pacts between Hitler and Stalin.
D: *"Great violence through pike and fire" refers to World War II. And "the*
  conspirators discovered by a matron"?
B: He says that refers to the conspiring and the secret meetings that went
  on between World War II and when these countries were regaining
  their independence. He says one outshoot of this is that during this
  time women will be more active in politics than they were before
  World War II.
D: *That's where the matron comes in. I know that was very important to*
  him because women didn't have much power in his day.
B: This is true.

 Amazingly these predictions about the break-up of the Soviet Union,
the Communist countries gaining their freedom, the fall of the Berlin Wall,
and the reorganization of the Communist party, were obtained in early
1989 while we were trying to complete translation of the quatrains. They
began to come to pass before the year was over.

Chapter 11

The Near Future

THERE WERE A FEW QUATRAINS that referred to increased terrorist activity during the years leading up to the "time of troubles." Among these were CENTURY V-44 which referred to an attempted takeover of a Russian ship by a terrorist organization supported by a Middle Eastern country. CENTURY VII-18 referred to a terrorist organization taking hostages in the Middle East.

Several of the subjects translated quatrains dealing with coming economic problems.

CENTURY VIII-28

Les simulacres d'or
& argent enflez
Qu'apres le rapt au lac
furent gettez
Au desouvert estaincts tous
& troublez.
Au marbre script prescript
intergetez.

The copies of gold and silver inflated, which after the theft were thrown into the lake, at the discovery that all is exhausted and dissipated by the debt. All scrips and bonds will be wiped out.

N: [Nina] The first picture I get is of the American Stock Exchange: fall, crash, devastation. But I see this happening more than once in history. It seems that unscrupulous people have infiltrated machinery and manipulated various markets of exchange. It creates a horrible disaster in economy.

D: *"The copies of gold and silver inflated," that makes sense. "Which after the theft were thrown into the lake."*

N: The picture I got was that some of the top manipulators took their wealth and escaped to other countries where their money is useful and they can live in seclusion. Throwing it away into the lake is more symbolic. It is the throwing away of an economy by manipulation.

D: *"At the discovery that all is exhausted and dissipated by the debt." That would agree with that, too.*

N: Yes. This is possible. So many small people are bought out by larger people; that the control can be manipulated by very few.

D: *And they get to the point where they can destroy an economy. You said this has happened before, but you think it will happen again?*

N: The possibility exists. Thus I'm not getting a positive time frame because it seems to be a reoccurring theme. Hopefully one last lesson needs to be learned.

CENTURY V-91

Au grand marché qu'on dict des mensongiers, Du tout Torrent & champ Athenien: Seront surprins par les chevaux legiers, Par Albanois Mars, Leo, Sat. un versien.	At the great market, called that of the liars, of all Torrent and the field of Athens: they will be surprised by the light armed horses, by the Albanians, when Mars is in Leo, and Saturn in Aquarius.

B: [Brenda] He says that, although the first part of this quatrain is giving a political description; it is also astrological.

D: *What is the political description?*

B: He says this refers to a major shake-up in the European Common Market (ECC). He says it will have repercussions. It will particularly concern some eastern-bloc nations, whose changes of political direction will shake up the economy in major ways.

This interpretation was given in early 1989, before the Communist satellite countries began gaining their freedom. I think it is particularly significant that he mentioned Albania because of the fighting that erupted in 1991 in Yugoslavia and the area bordering Albania. In Nostradamus' time these countries were not known by their present names.

D: *Will the United States be involved, or just Europe?*

B: He says that since it's involving the economy, the whole world will be involved.

D: *"They will be surprised by the light armed horses."*

B: He says that refers to the economic shake-up. It will seem as if the issues involved don't have much strength to them as it starts out. But they will turn out to be a lot more major than people at first thought.

D: *Can he give us some idea of a time period?*

B: He is saying, some time in the 1990s.

I presented this quatrain to Mae, the astrologer who helped supply dates in Volume Two. She said these astrological signs would occur twice during the 1990s, in June and July 1991, and May and June 1993. The first date definitely coincided with the problems in Yugoslavia.

CENTURY VIII-14

Le grand credit d'or, d'argent l'abondance	The great credit of gold and abundance of silver will cause
Fera aveugler par libide honneur	honor to be blinded by lust; the
Sera cogneu d'adultere l'offense,	offense of the adulterer will
Qui parviendra à son grand deshonneur.	become known, which will occur to his great dishonor.

P: [Pam] This refers to something in *our* present or near future. Adultery seems to be Nostradamus' term for "bad doing," not necessarily of a sexual or promiscuous nature, or even involving any kind of sexual liaison. This seems to refer to a government figure. My first impression was the President of the United States being caught doing something unethical. Of course, you know the international monetary system being based on gold and silver, is referring to our present time. But it will be even more so in the future when we have these economic breakdowns that are being forecast by others besides Nostradamus. These monetary breakdowns will result in gold and silver being the only real currency that is acceptable worldwide. It will not be paper, and certainly not copper, lead, nickel, zinc, or other metals. For some reason it seems, the United States kept it balanced, as long as the United States was considered an honorable power. But when this President is caught, it seemed to throw this monetary system into some kind of *mess*.

D: *That seems to agree with "blinded by lust."*

P: The symbolism here is that he is an adulterer and of course, you could consider greed lust.

D: *Can you see in the mirror which President it is?*

P: Well, it's a male. I see George Bush and I think I'm saying that because he's president now. Nostradamus says this will occur in our near future, while we are alive.

D: *So it could possibly be a president you don't recognize yet?*

P: Yes, it's possible. But he looks a lot like George Bush. He's not a young man like Dan Quayle. He will be a distinguished statesman. One that the world admired and respected. It will be a big shock.

D: *Do you know how he's going to do this?*

P: It seems to involve some thing to do with space. This president so loved by the world, actually honored and respected, seems to be preparing to ... (*she frowned*) to wage war from space somehow.

D: *To wage war* from *space?*

P: Yes. The money system is somehow based on the stability of the United States of America. I don't know how this works since we're certainly not the only government on the planet. But it seems that at this time we are the most respected, most balanced, and seem to have the situation in control somehow. The top person of what is considered to be the secure government turns out to be opposite of what he was believed to be. This causes our own country to go into a real panic and the rest of the world rather follows suit. It's as if all confidence is lost. There's no longer a paternal-type figure they can turn to for guidance and truth. It seems to create quite a mess, because of the horrendous nature his true self turned out to be.

D: *Do you mean he is* secretly *planning to wage war from space?*

P: Well, he will have the cooperation of the military.

D: *Does Nostradamus show you why this man wants to wage war?*

P: I must say that if this scenario takes place—and it is only a probability—I believe he is affected by that group of men we looked upon who have only evil intent and focus. It seems they can affect even those who aren't attracted, shall we say, to their way. (*She undoubtedly was referring to the secret Cabal.*)

D: *You think they would be able to influence him?*

P: It seems this is a possible scenario, yes.

D: *Can Nostradamus show you how war could be waged from space?*

P: I see platforms, not one, but several, with warheads aimed at major cities. Not *just* major cities in the old Soviet Union, Cuba, Central America, or the Middle East, but actually aimed at cities in countries that we've considered in the past as our friends. Major metropolitan areas like Paris, London, and actually cities all over the world. These platforms are satellite stations with warheads. You know we are at the present time putting many things into space. This is further on though when there are more.

D: *It would have to be in the future because we haven't put platforms up there yet.*

P: I see platforms there right now. I see giant solar collectors, *giant,* much larger than I think of space things. They are carried by the space shuttle, and of course, they would have to fit inside it. But once in space they can have many parts added to them. I think we have, at this time, two *large* orbiting things. They have flat, rudder-looking things protruding. (*Amazed*) But they're quite large.

D: *Do you think these are already in orbit in our time in 1989?*

P: Two of them are. These are military projects that were placed in orbit by the shuttle. They were some of those secret payloads.

D: *So it's already being done without the average person's knowledge.*

P: Correct. But there are many more from the perspective of the devaluation of the gold and silver aspect. This is further along when they have the capability of simultaneously destroying major metropolitan areas on the Earth.

D: *So instead of disarming, it sounds as if they're going the opposite way and it will keep developing.*

P: If this scenario comes to pass, yes.

D: *At this time in 1989 do you see any platforms that other countries have put up there?*

P: Well, of course, you know about the Soviet Union and the space station that people live on. It seems there are countries right now in 1989 putting up all kinds of "debris," but none are as advanced technologically as these weapons platforms. Space seems really busy. And looking at it from this perspective, there are many things in the air.

D: *So according to this quatrain there will be a president in the near future and this will be his main "thing."*

P: It won't appear that way at all. That's why the confidence of the world rests on his shoulders. And that's why ensuing incredible disbelief will take place in the toppling of these economies based on the balance of the United States, because nobody will expect it of *this* man.

B: [Brenda] I am in the special meeting place waiting for Nostradamus to come. He said he needed to finish the project he was working on, but it would not take long and he would come immediately.

D: *Do you know what kind of a project it was?*

B: I'm not sure what he was trying to accomplish, but I can describe the tools he was using. He had a prism suspended by a silver chain from a tripod. A triangle of crystal for breaking the light into colors. And he had a piece of paper or parchment or something underneath the tripod. Where the different colors of light were cast onto the parchment, he was making notations and drawings, geometrical figures and such.

D: *I wonder why he was doing that?*

B: I don't know. He seemed to think it was important, whatever he was doing. I'm not sure if what he was writing on the parchment had anything to do with the sun or light, *per se,* but for some reason he needed the light broken down into the colors. He is here now.

D: *Ask him what he was doing?*

B: He says this was one of the methods for mapping somebody's aura. The different notations were indicating different areas where the aura was stronger or weaker, and what needed to be done to bring it back into balance. He says the various areas of the aura being out of balance is what causes illness.

D: *But wouldn't the prism always show the same colors?*

B: The prism always shows the same colors, yes, but apparently he has a chart. He can cast the colors from this prism on this chart where every single color and every shade of every color has a notation as to what it indicates for the aura and the state of health. He was doing this to make sure he is giving precise information in regards to the condition of the person's aura. He uses the prism and the colors cast upon this chart, and it helps to pin down what he is seeing.

D: *Can he see the aura?*

B: He says he can. He thinks it's linked with his gift of being able to see time.

CENTURY VI-19

La vraie flamme engloutira
la dame,
Que voudra mettre les
Innocens à feu:
Pres de l'assaut l'excercite
s'enflamme,
Quant dans Seville monstre
en bœuf sera veu.

The true flame will swallow up the woman who will want to put the Innocents to the fire. Near the assault, the army is inflamed when in Seville a monstrous ox will be seen.

B: He says this quatrain has to do with political ideology, particularly in the late 20th, early 21st century. The true flame represents liberty and the thoughts of freedom. He says the woman who wishes to put the children to the fire represents a country who stands for liberty. At this point he has not made it clear whether he's referring to the United States or France. But it is a country that has traditionally stood for liberty, and its political ideology goes astray. It's a very gradual process, and the political leaders say they are doing these various things in the name of liberty. They're wanting to send the people into war and such as this, in the name of liberty, when it is actually for self-gain. The people will realize this and will rise up and swallow them. This is the true flame of liberty regaining its position, and burning out the false political ideology. He says the monstrous ox seen in Seville represents forces that will be working with the Anti-Christ, trying to stir up political unrest and revolution in preparation for the Anti-Christ taking over that part of Europe.

D: *I thought he once said that Spain would not fall.*

B: No, it won't. But there will still be forces inside Spain agitating for the fall. It will create much unrest and unhappiness for the people.

D: *Then the monstrous ox is the Anti-Christ?*

B: The monstrous ox is the forces working *for* the Anti-Christ within Spain. Even though they will not be totally successful they will stir up enough misery to make things very unhappy for the people.

D: *We thought maybe the ox was an astrological symbol.*

B: He said he was making an illusion to Taurus, the astrological sign that is the bull, partly because Spain is identified with bullfighting and bull baiting. He said that's their culture, and these people who will be agitating for the Anti-Christ will take advantage of this blood-thirsty aspect of the Spanish culture. Thinking that since they like such sports as bullfighting, they would not mind human fighting. But the people will fool these agitators. The quatrain does not depend upon the astrological interpretation for its meaning.

D: *The interpreters said the ox in Seville was probably referring to bull-fighting, "although the fanatic queen's identity is not clear." They thought it literally referred to a real woman.*

B: He says this is an easy mistake to make. In the interest of protecting his writings from the Catholic Church he never did make it clear whether he was speaking literally or figuratively.

CENTURY VI-20

L'union faincte sera peu de durée,
Des uns changés reformés la
  pluspart:
Dans les vaissaux sera gent
  endurée,
Lors aura Rome un nouveau
liepart.

The feigned union will last a short time, some changed, the greater part reformed. People will be suffering in the vessels, then when Rome has a new Leopard.

B: From your point of view he says this refers to the near future, the late 20th century. The feigned union refers to true friendship between the United States and the Soviet Union. They will have just begun to cement this friendship and start building on it when the Anti-Christ starts messing everything up.
D: *You mean it will be a true friendship?*
B: Yes, but it will still be at the beginning stages. And if not for the interference of the Anti-Christ it could have developed a lot further. He said the people suffering in vessels stands for the fighting forces of the United States and the Soviet Union, trying to fight the Anti-Christ in ships, submarines, tanks, airplanes, what-have-you. And "when Rome shall have a new leopard" refers to when it has a new pope.
D: *They did interpret the leopard as being a symbol for the pope, but they said it also could mean the English lion. Then we will make progress with the Soviet Union, but other events will interfere and stop it.*
B: He said progress will be made and will look promising to the peoples involved, but will be interrupted by the Anti-Christ.

CENTURY VI-37

L'œuvre ancienne se
  parachevera,
Du toict cherra sur le grand
  mal ruine:
Innocent faict mort on accusera:
Nocent caiché taillis à la bruine.

The ancient work will be accomplished and from the roof evil ruin will fall on to the great man. Being dead, they will accuse an innocent of the deed, the guilty one hidden in the misty woods.

B: He says the ancient deed being accomplished refers to the establishment of Israel as a nation. The great evil on the roof falling and doing away with the great man refers to an assassination of a world leader in the Middle East. "The guilty one hidden in the misty wood." He says he's not referring literally to a misty wood, but to the murkiness of politics. The guilty one will be able to hide and get away with the deed because of being able to manipulate politics.

D: *Will this assassination be in our future?*

B: He thinks so. Although Anwar Sadat was assassinated, he says the leader referred to in this quatrain is closer to Israeli politics.

CENTURY VI-51

Peuple assemblé, voir nouveau
  expectacle,
Princes & Rois par plusieurs
  assistans:
Pilliers faillir, murs, mais
  comme miracle
Le Roi sauvé & trente
  des instants.
	The people gathered to see a new sight; Princes and Kings among many onlookers. The pillars, walls, fall, but as if by a miracle the King and thirty of those present are saved.

B: He says this quatrain refers to events that have not yet occurred. It will be a social event. He is not sure if it will be in London or New York City, but it will be in a very big, grand place, like a hotel ballroom. It may be the opening of a new building or something. There will be many people there to take part in the celebration. But the building will be architecturally unsound and will collapse. Yet those inside, particularly the important ones, will be able to get out.

D: *Does "the people gathered to see a new sight" relate to the important people within the ballroom?*

B: He says that has to do with the unveiling ceremony, where all the people are gathered for the celebration. He says there's another symbolism to this quatrain as well. This also refers to a political situation: the American Revolution and the establishment of a democracy. And the kings and princes of the world gathered around to watch this new thing being established, and saying it will never work. He says the pillars and ceilings falling refer to the revolutions that took place in the various other countries before the establishment of democracies.

D: *The interpreters thought it referred to when Hitler was almost killed by a bomb.*

B: He says the only problem with that interpretation is that there were not many people gathered to see the new sight.

D: *That's true. There were just some of his insiders with him, I believe.*

Nina saw two quatrains that referred to the future of France.

CENTURY VI-3

Fleuve qu'esprouve le
  nouveau nay Celtique,
Sera en grande de
  l'empire discord:
Le jeune prince par gent
  ecclesiastique,
Ostera le sceptre coronel
  de concorde.
	The river that the newborn French heir attempts; there will be great discord among the empire. The young prince, because of the ecclesiastics will remove peace from crown and scepter.

N: [Nina] This seems to be in the future of the country of France. I'm seeing a deranged man come to power. It seems as if he's trying to do a great deal of separating, and acting as if the French are above reproach, superior and unique. He has almost a Hitleresque attitude.

D: *It had a bit of a religious overtone with the word "ecclesiastics." What does that mean?*

N: This is a bit confusing to explain. But there are those who feel they've been told to do things through voices and religion. That's their excuse; they use religion as a front. They manipulate and make it acceptable to themselves. This Frenchman seems to be their President, but not the one they have now.

D: *Can you see what he looks like?*

N: I see a man of small stature with brown hair and glasses. It's not too far away from what I feel.

D: *Then you feel this man will cause France a great deal of trouble. I know Nostradamus was very concerned about France because that was his country.*

CENTURY VII-34

En grand regret sera
  la gent Gauloise
Cœur vain, legier
  croirera temerité:
Pain, sel, ne vin, eaue:
  venin ne cervoise
Plus grand captif, faim,
  froit, necessité.

The French nation will be in great grief, vain and lighthearted, they will believe rash things. No bread, salt, wine, nor water, venom nor ale, the greater one captured, hunger, cold and want.

N: This seems very similar to that other time I was seeing, when this President of France will come to power.

D: *"No bread, salt, wine nor water, venom or ale." What does he mean by those symbols?*

N: The venom is referring to a serum, something to do with medicine, something pharmaceutical.

D: *"The greater one captured, hunger, cold and want."*

N: I see a picture of this referring to this leader, who eventually finds no way out of this trap.

D: *Who is he captured by?*

N: I think he's captured by himself in the ruin he's brought upon his country. He is a deranged person, and he saw perfection for his country and his fellowman through power and greed and by using religion as his excuse and his front. He found everything acceptable.

D: *It sounds as if the country isn't going to have enough food or supplies. Is that correct?*

N: There is symbolism in the quatrain referring to various problems with industry and the economy falling.

D: *Then it doesn't mean an actual shortage of food.*

N: There are various problems with the manufacture and the industry involved in France.

D: *Would it be correct to say that this man in France's future puts the economy into a great deal of trouble?*

N: Right.

D: *It's interesting that Nostradamus uses the word "venom" for medicine. Did Nostradamus use poison in his pharmaceuticals in his day?*

N: In his day he was aware of them and their potential and properties. They were used for various things. The same plants could be used to help cure, or to dispose of unwanted people. I believe at some point medicine is a poison. You can use it to do the direct opposite.

D: *So he's using that word as a symbol referring to medicine.*

In Volume Two John Feeley interpreted CENTURY III-55 which also referred to a French president who would damage France's economy. He also said it would happen within the next ten years.

CENTURY VII-20

Ambassadeurs de la Toscane langue,	Ambassadors of the Tuscan language will cross the Alps and
Avril & Mai Alpes & mer passer:	the sea in April and May. The man
Celui de veau exposera l'harangue,	of the calf will deliver an oration, not coming to wipe out the French
Vie Gauloise ne venant effacer.	way of life.

N: I saw this in terms of the Nobel prizes, the peace awards for various types of shared information among countries and people. This is referring to breakthroughs in health, science and innovations for machinery, to make a healthier, better way of life in the future.

D: *Why does Nostradamus call him the "man of the calf"?*

N: It has to do with his knowledge, the information he's passing on. He represents some sort of science and refers to what was gained from experiments in the past—similar to Louis Pasteur and the milk. I think it's symbolic of that type of scientific investigation.

D: *Can he show you some of these advances?*

N: Yes. I see new healthier ways to grow food outside, and inside through the harshest times of the year. There are ways of cultivating without the need for sunlight or earth. And new resources for energy that are nonpolluting. I see methods of using the electromagnetic field and other connective forms of energy to make things healthier, more efficient, and less expensive.

D: *And the "ambassadors of the Tuscan language" are the people who are coming for the awards?*

N: Right. They are bringing their experts and contributions and are receiving awards for these various things.

CENTURY VII-33

Par fraude regne, forces
* expolier,*
La classe obsesse,
* passages à l'espie:*
Deux fainctz amis se
* viendront rallier,*
Esveiller haine de long
* temps assoupie.*

The kingdom stripped of its forces
by fraud, the fleet blockaded,
passages for the spy; two false
friends will come to rally to awaken
hatred for a long time dormant.

B: [Brenda] He says this refers to two different things. On the one hand it refers to the American Civil War, and on the other hand it refers to events that have not yet occurred. He says it still refers to America and that the years to come, the next decade or so, will see increasing restlessness in the United States. He says the system of government will become increasingly top-heavy, spending too much money, and it will ruin the economy. Sweeping changes will need to be made, or it will fall from its own weight. He says that America itself will survive, but the people in power will be broken down. The change will be needed, and if it goes as it should, the change will be for the good. Because as the government gets increasingly top-heavy, it continues to infringe upon the rights of the people. But when the old structure is broken down and a new structure built up that is more equitable and more in balance, the people will be restored to their freedom.

D: *It seems to be paralleling what he saw in the Civil War?*

B: It's just a matter of using one quatrain to refer to two different events. He's not saying that it will be like the Civil War. It will not be a country divided unto itself. It will be the people rising and saying, "This is ridiculous. Something has to be done."

D: *Sometimes he uses a parallel because the situations are very similar.*

B: He says in this case it is not. It's just a matter of the two different references.

D: *And it should be within the next decade, he said. That's getting too close for comfort.*

Nostradamus referred to three major natural disasters that would occur in our country during the decade of the 1990s.

CENTURY VI-98

Ruine aux Volsques de
* peur si fort terribles,*
Leur grand cité taincte,
* faict pestilent:*
Piller Sol, Lune & violer
* leurs temples:*
Et les deux fleuves rougir
* de sang coulant.*

Ruin for the Volcæ, so very terrible
with fear, their great city stained by
a pestilential deed. To plunder the
Sun and Moon and violate their
temples and to redden the two
rivers running with blood.

B: He says this refers to an event that has not yet taken place. There will be a major city that will be nearly destroyed by both volcano and earthquake. He says the rivers in the city will run red, not only from the stuff from the volcano but also from the great numbers of people who will die in this great natural calamity.

D: *Is that word Volcæ? In the French it's spelt differently.*

B: How is it spelled in the French?

D: (Spelled) *V-o-l-s-q-u-e-s.*

B: He says that is an anagram for the name of the volcano.

D: *It's so close to the word "volcano."*

B: No, it's referring to a specific volcano.

D: *"To plunder the sun and the moon."*

B: He says there will be so much smoke and ash in the sky that you will not be able to tell night from day.

D: *Does he have any clue where this will be?*

B: He says it will be somewhere in the New World. It's in a mountainous region with volcanoes.

D: *Does he have any idea of a time?*

B: No. He says he's told you what he knows.

D: *That makes it hard to give people a warning.*

B: Often it is difficult to get people to let go of their daily lives anyway. He says you could go to the street corner and shout, "This city is going to be leveled by an earthquake. Flee!" But they won't believe you until it actually happens.

CENTURY VIII-16

Au lieu que HIERON feit sa nef fabriquer, Si grand deluge sera & si subite, Qu'on n'aura lieu ne terres s'atacquer L'onde monter Fesulan Olympique.	At the place where **HIERON** has his ship built, there will be such a great sudden flood, that one will not have a place nor land to fall upon, the waters mount to the Olympic Fesulan.

B: He says this quatrain refers to Cape Canaveral in the New World, also known as Cape Kennedy. He says this is in the near future. He sees that one of the largest hurricanes of the century is going to hit Florida. The wind will be so high with so much flooding that there'll be a great deal of damage to repair at NASA when the storm is over. He says much of the equipment used with rocket launches and such is going to be damaged and bent up and blown around. The waters will flood everything.

D: *What does he mean by the word "Hieron"?*

B: He says that's one of the not-as-well-known characters in Greek mythology, referring to a master shipbuilder who had a very wondrous reputation. He used that to represent the space vehicles and such that are being built at Cape Canaveral.

D: *"The waters mount to the Olympic fesulan." Why does he use the symbol of Olympus?*

B: To represent the great amount of flooding, to Olympic proportions, so to speak. There'll be so much water that it will seem that Mount Olympus itself could be totally drowned in the water.

D: *The interpreters said the quatrain did have a Greek atmosphere to it. They tried to change Hieron into Jason as an anagram. Does he know who Jason was in Greek mythology?*

B: Yes, he was going after the Golden Fleece. He says they weren't that far off. Jason also had to have well-built ships to go on his quest. But they were actually investigating a dead end so far as symbolism is concerned.

D: *There's nothing* NASA *can do about it. They built those ships right there on the oceanfront.*

B: He says perhaps if they know far enough ahead of time, through the translation of this quatrain, they will be braced with protective measures in preparation for it. He says the hurricane will go into the history books because it will be so large and ferocious. It will be the largest of this century.

Note: This prediction was made before the terrible hurricane Hugo hit the South Carolina and Florida area in 1989. It did not give Florida the direct hit that Nostradamus foresaw. But experts were predicting that if the greenhouse warming effect was becoming a reality, then the storms of the future would be almost twice as strong. They said the surface temperature of the ocean only had to increase by a few degrees to produce hurricanes with double the wind velocity of Hugo. Also, while this book was being prepared for printing, Hurricane Andrew hit southern Florida in late summer of 1992 and wreaked terrible havoc. Will there be another one that will also devastate northern Florida? Some weather scientists have suggested they will have to develop new criteria to measure the ferocity of the current crop of hurricanes. The old hurricane scale (1–5) had too many exceptions during the 1992 season and Hurricane Andrew was reputed to have gone off the hurricane scale altogether.

CENTURY IX-48

La grand cité d'occean maritime,	The great city of the maritime
Environnee de maretz en cristal:	ocean, surrounded by a swamp of
Dans le solstice hyemal & la	crystal; in the winter solstice and
prime	the spring will be tried by a
Sera tempté de vent espouvantal.	dreadful wind.

B: He says this refers to an event that has not yet taken place. It will be a natural mishap. He says it's a city surrounded by a swamp of crystal, and that refers to a large modern 20th-century city. The swamp of crystal refers to all the buildings with the great many windows.

D: *The reflections of the glass.*

B: Yes. He says the city he feels the strongest about in regards to this quatrain is Los Angeles. He says the weather will continue to get stranger. And due to a shift in the wind patterns, a very hot, dry wind will blow continuously through that part of the country. It will cause great drought and forest fires, and he says it will be unprecedented.

D: *Does he have any idea of a time period?*

B: He says sometime in the late 20th century. When he looks in his mirror at the large sprawling 20th century cities, they go forever. And when the sun is at the right angle you see it reflecting back forever from all the windows.

D: *And he also symbolized it as a swamp.*

B: He says, well, one gets lost in a swamp and one can get lost in these cities.

D: *And the winter solstice and the spring are when this great dreadful wind will happen.*

B: Yes. Further south in South America it's called "El Niño," but in this part of the country they have a different name for it. He says the people of the area have experienced hot, dry winds like this before, but those were just small doses compared to this. This will be ten times worse than any they've had before.

Note: In southern California every year there is a "Santa Ana" season when the hot, dry winds sweep up from the south. Santa Ana season is usually late fall or early winter. Santa Ana winds are similar to other desert winds (California geographically is semi-desert). In North Africa these winds are called Sirocco and there are other names for this phenomenon in desert regions around the world (Gobi, *e.g.;* also the deserts of Peru and northern Chile experience these winds). Also California is going into the seventh year of drought and is experiencing unprecedented fires throughout the mountains and grasslands, not to mention record air pollution levels.

When Brenda awakened from this session she was left with some definite impressions about this quatrain.

"Ordinarily El Niño occurs in the southern hemisphere every 18 years or every couple of decades or something like this. But due to the weather patterns being messed up because of global warming and such, it will start occurring more often and that will screw up the weather patterns worldwide. Our weather's been pretty well messed up anyway, and at this time it will be as if something totally flip-flopping. And this will be like the granddaddy or all granddaddies. This one particularly will break all records. The picture that was left in my mind is the sun setting into the Pacific, and the rays hitting Los Angeles. I could see the sun reflecting off all the windows of the houses and skyscrapers. And this hot dry wind will be blowing, and the temperatures will be ferocious. With all that concrete and asphalt, the temperatures will be 125 and 130 degrees. Such *horrible* temperatures that people will be dropping like flies from the heat, and there won't be a durn thing they can do about it. The crops will fail totally in the valley and that area of California because there will be no rain. The plants and trees will just wither up from the dry wind and the heat. And naturally, up in the mountains, you know what's going to happen. Some durn fool's going to throw a cigarette butt out the window, and there'll be miles and miles of forest fires. These pictures are very clear in my mind."

D: *It also said it would happen in the winter solstice and the spring. Do you think it will be that hot at that time of the year?*

B: That's what will make it so shocking because ordinarily the weather is reasonable at that time of the year. That's when they get the spring rains for the crops. When this occurs there won't be a drop. It will be totally unprecedented. It will be one of those situations where once again it will be declared a national disaster area, and countries all over the world will send aid.

D: *Normally El Niño occurs around Christmas.*

B: Well, the winter solstice is close to Christmas, on the 22nd.

D: *The swamp of crystal was really confusing.*

B: It referred to the big flat sprawling city of glass. He said a city like New York would be referred to as mountains of crystals because of all the skyscrapers and it's all packed together. Los Angeles is not concentrated so much with skyscrapers. It's sprawled out all over for miles and miles, and has all those buildings and windows.

Chapter 12

Hidden Information

ONE THEME THAT WAS REPEATEDLY REVEALED to all the subjects concerned the discovery of hidden information, in the form of lost documents. As told in Volume One, this topic was brought forth in the first quatrain ever interpreted when Elena chose CENTURY VII-14 out of all the quatrains in Ms. Cheetham's book. Nostradamus had said that the first quatrain chosen would concern work that I was doing at the time. This was correct because I was involved in the completion of *Jesus and the Essenes,* a book about the lost years in the life of Christ. That book concerned the Essenes and the Dead Sea Scrolls. It was remarkable that Nostradamus had correctly seen that Elena would choose one specific quatrain that dealt with the discovery of lost documents similar to the Dead Sea Scrolls, and that they would be found within our lifetime. From that time in 1986 until now I have used that specific quatrain as a test when I led a new subject to locate Nostradamus while he was alive in the 1500s in France. Each person interpreted this quatrain the same, not using the exact words but repeating the same concept and interpreting it in the same vein. This was the test that Nostradamus himself had directed me to use, and it had proven valid in all cases. It became my method of verifying that we had a true contact.

The discovery of lost information seemed to be an important development that he was able to see in his mirror, and he wrote other quatrains about it. Maybe it impressed him so deeply because of the extreme suppression of knowledge in his own lifetime. He put his life in jeopardy as he searched for lost information, much of which was contradictory to the church and other scholars in his lifetime. He did many things that were forbidden, such as traveling to strange lands to confer with astrologers and magicians who possessed ancient secret knowledge. He incorporated all the secret methods into his own search. He experimented in ways that would have been condemned by his peers, but his curiosity knew no bounds. So it would naturally impress him if he saw in his magic mirror that man would uncover forgotten records and knowledge that had been buried away for centuries. This was a monumental vision that rivaled any of the horrible atrocities committed by man. He must have thought that the uncovered knowledge might lead man down a path towards more civilized conduct and respect for his fellow man. Each of my subjects interpreted quatrains that appeared to deal with such a discovery. It may not be one single find but could refer to several caches hidden by different groups over the eons of time.

CENTURY V-7

Du Triumvir seront trouvé les os,
Cherchant profond thresor
ænigmatique:
Ceux d'alentour ne seront en
repos.
Ce concaver marbre & plomb
metallique.

The bones of the Triumvir will be found by those searching for a deep and enigmatic treasure. Those around will not be peaceful. This hollowing of marble and metallic lead.

W: [Wayne] This quatrain pertains to some of the secrets not yet discovered in Egypt. The unfriendlies around the treasure are spirits that are there to discern, to make sure those who find the treasure are the people who are supposed to find it.
D: *What treasure is that?*
W: It will be documents.
D: *Are these the same documents we spoke of before?* (The ones mentioned in the test quatrain CENTURY VII-14.)
W: No. These documents pertain to star charts, maps of galaxies. Repeat that last part about the mixture of alloys.
D: *"This hollowing of marble and metallic lead."*

The French word "concaver" translates as "concave" which Ms. Cheetham interpreted as "hollowing." It could refer to a hollow, concave place lined or made out of this marble and metal.

W: I'm thinking this is some kind of energy shield. I'm seeing what looks like a door with an electric aura. But it can only be opened by someone who has the knowledge to open it.
D: *I'm curious about that word, "the bones of the Triumvir will be found."*
W: The Triumvir are the people who put this information there; that sealed their tomb. The information was hidden by these people, and it was part of their life. A part of their mission was to conceal this in such a way that they would be buried with it and sealed up.
D: *You said it was star charts of galaxies? Where did they get the information?*
W: They came to Earth with this information.
D: *Where did they come from?*
W: Well, the name that came to me was Zolar. It's a planet in another galaxy.
D: *What do you mean? Did they live on Earth?*
W: (*He frowned.*) Yes, they *played* on Earth. (*He smiled.*) It was a nice vacation spot.

D: (Chuckle) *Well, that's one way to put it, isn't it? Were they here a long time?*
W: Oh, they've checked in on us for a long time.
D: *If they could come and go, why did they choose to be buried here with this knowledge?*
W: Part of the information being buried was to be sealed. It was part of their destiny. And some of their group were buried with the information. I see it will be found. This is difficult to pinpoint, but I think it will be discovered after an Earth shift.

When Wayne awakened, he remembered this quatrain and added a few more details. He emphasized his impression that it would be found after an Earth shift. The door he saw seemed to be protected by a force field or something similar, yet it was an openable door. The door was constructed of the mixture of alloys, marble and metallic lead, mentioned in the quatrain. It seemed to be a mixture of two metals with the marble, and this gave it an electric aura. Wayne thought something in the combination accomplished this. I commented that this didn't seem like materials someone would normally build with; it did sound rather extraterrestrial. We agreed that this was indeed a strange and unusual interpretation for the quatrain.

CENTURY V-66

Soubs les antiques edifices
vestaulx,
Non esloignez d aqueduct ruine:
De Sol & Lune sont les luisans
metaulx,
Ardante lampe Traian d'or
burine.

Under the ancient buildings of the vestals not far from the ruin of the aquaduct. There will be the glittering metals of Sun and Moon, the golden lamp of Trojan burning, pillaged.

N: [Nina] This is referring to Greece—Athens. White columns. The Acropolis.
D: *What is occurring there?*
N: An uncovering of history which will help bring new but old knowledge to the surface and help educate humanity. I'm getting that this is a reawakening of old knowledge. The golden ore is symbolic of hidden records, history and information that was buried a long time ago.
D: *Do you think it will be found underneath these old buildings?*
N: Yes, I believe there were vaults or secret passageways.
D: *What does that last part mean: "The golden lamp of Trojan burning, pillaged"?*
N: What I am seeing is the golden lamp—this knowledge. But pillaged does not have a negative meaning. Pillaged means uncovered, brought back to the surface.
D: *That could be a mistranslation.*

Later I saw that the word for "pillage" did not appear in the original French, nor is it in other translations. Where did Ms. Cheetham get that word?

D: *Can you see any time period?*

N: I feel this happening within *your* lifetime.

D: *Can you see what the knowledge deals with?*

N: It deals with knowledge of the future, knowledge of science, knowledge of philosophies. And I believe they find other related books in other countries. It was knowledge so new it was kept by only a few as sacred, for there was no sense in bringing it to the multitudes of that time.

D: *Then the ancient Greeks had this knowledge and hid it. Does he know where they got the knowledge?*

N: Their wise men, their seers, their scientists. I'm seeing now that there was a group that came together in privacy because they were given this body of knowledge. And because they were scientists, men of stability, they were able to accept many things that might be happening in the future. They knew it had truth but yet knew the government and the people of their time would not accept it. Many of them were aware of the control the mind can have over the body. And they knew of different life planets also. They were great thinkers. They believed through their philosophies that if they existed here then therefore there would be other beings out there. For the sky and the universe were so vast, they believed there were other life beings around.

D: *Was this radical thinking in Grecian times?*

N: I believe, yes, this would not have been accepted.

D: *And that's why all this knowledge was buried?*

N: Yes. They made sense of it. They could put it in a scientifically logical pattern and give it form, and have a concept they believed was probable.

D: *Will someone find this by accident?*

N: I believe they will find writings speaking of the underground passages and start exploring and find this information. Some of this will coincide with records that will be found in other parts of the world that will help validate one another. For this information was coming through at various times without any form of communication.

P: [Pam] I see Nostradamus sitting at the table. His hand looks knotted, with big bold bony knuckles. Chilly and damp are perpetual feelings for this room. Before encountering Nostradamus this time I thought of viewing the outside of this structure. And my first thoughts when I looked at it were, "This is not Nostradamus. This is some prisoner I'm getting ready to go talk to." And then I thought, "No, it *is* Nostradamus, and *he's* a prisoner." (*Surprised*) I never thought of Nostradamus as a person who didn't have free will.

D: *Why do you think of him as a prisoner?*

P: I should not speculate, so I'll just ask Nostradamus why I thought of him as a prisoner? He said he *does* feel that way. As a person who has received the weight of the future—and that is how he feels about what he has seen, the *weight* of the future—that he's imprisoned by his *future* memories. It *is* an imprisonment because he can't release his thoughts from what he's seen. He's in bondage to his thoughts.

D: *Isn't there any way he could have brushed it off and said, "I will live within my own time and not worry about that"?*

P: I don't think that's *possible*. Nostradamus doesn't just *look* on events. He has an experiential *experience* with the event. He has an emotion. He's much more involved than watching a movie. He's affected by what he sees. It would be very hard not to be.

D: *Did he ever want to stop seeing these things?*

P: I'll ask him. He says that countless times he's tried to stop it. *But* besides being affected by the horror he sees, he's also curious. He's *so* curious he wants to know more. He has ambivalent feelings. He would like to stop seeing horror, but see more of the future. That's what he said.

D: *So he's a prisoner of his own making, if you want to look at it that way. Nobody* forced *him to do this.*

P: That's right. There's a third factor besides the fact that he's looked at it and been affected by it, and is curious to know what's going on. Because he's been delving into this for so long and does believe this is where the strong probabilities lie, he has the third factor called "responsibility." So now that he's looked on it, he feels responsible to see what he can do to help.

D: *But he does journey outside of that room from time to time?*

P: He does, but he does most of his *life*, his *living* in this room. It is funny that he calls it "living," because it is really taking place in his head. And he said that's where the real life is.

CENTURY VIII-75

Le pere & fils seront meurdris ensemble	The father and son will be murdered together, the leader
Le prefecteur dedans son pavillon	within his pavilion. The mother at
La mere à Tours du filz ventre aura enfle	Tours will have her belly swollen with a son, a verdure chest with
Criche verdure de failles papillon.	little pieces of paper.

P: That quatrain is quite confusing, and we are attempting translation.

D: *Would it help if you focused on the mirror?*

P: Actually Nostradamus has put down his pen. He is now sitting at the table, holding his head in his hands, and trying to give us a verbal translation. That is one of the easiest methods for me. It's so obscure, so very difficult.

D: *Do the best you can.*

P: Well, the trunk seems to contain valid information. The pregnant mother seems to be pregnant with information also. The murder of the father and son simultaneously seems to be a hiding away of some kind of information, an occluding of some kind. I get very shadowy images. The father and son seem to represent information from two *ages* somehow. I see Nostradamus really concentrating, so I'm going to be quiet. (*Pause*) This is confusing. I see a Romanesque fellow like Marc Antony of Antony and Cleopatra, in a pavilion. When you say "chest with the little pieces of paper," I see hidden information. This seems distant. It seems very Roman. I see no pregnant woman. I just see this guy sitting there in an open pavilion with columns. He has on a white robe, and a laurel wreath on his head. He has much power.

D: *Ask Nostradamus who that is symbolic of.*

P: I keep wanting to say ... Nero. (*Chuckle*) Okay, this is what I am getting. This has to do with not allowing Christian information, not allowing some kind of messages. They've hidden away some kind of information. This is a Roman who is repressing and killing people. When I'm looking in the mirror, I just see this guy sitting there. I see the columns, I see the leaves on his head. And I see him immensely powerful and not smiling. He doesn't want some important information to get out that has to do with knowledge that would change people's attitudes.

D: *Is it knowledge that would deal with our time?*

P: That's a very interesting question, for this man was focused in his *own* time. He was only concerned with the safety of his crown, and whether he would continue to be king. However, from the way you phrased the question, yes, the information does continue through to our time. For, in fact, it was not all suppressed. Some of that information is incredibly valid and meaningful to us in this very moment.

D: *Then you think this was repressed during the Roman times?*

P: It was attempted. Much was, I must say. The murder of the father and son at the same time could even—although the time frames are different—refer to the burning of the libraries in Alexandria. There seems to be some *big* loss of ancient information. I don't know when the library at Alexandria was burnt. However, the father information was more ancient than the son information. But they both represent ancient information and both were stored in this library.

D: *And the mother is also symbolic of information because she's pregnant.*

P: Yes. However, I see no physical female with child. All I see is that man sitting there. I only feel repression of information. Oh! Now I understand. It was attempted to be repressed and much of the ancient information was destroyed. More current information did come out and obviously we have it today. Those who had knowledge of these new beliefs were *all* pregnant with information. The symbolism of the impending birth, of the pregnant woman, is that the information will get out.

D: *Then the verdure chest with little pieces of paper, also refers to this information?*

P: I think this is *one* of the actual, *literal ways* they tried to preserve some of the information. It was also put in jars and buried, and carved on stones. There were different attempts to preserve this information for *all* generations to come. I would say, if we actually incorporated that information into *our* knowingness, it would be probably the most important information we could receive.

D: *And it's been hidden away and suppressed since the time of the Romans.*

P: The attempt of suppression. Some of it was. Gosh! I believe this is the library at Alexandria. I think they captured the information but they didn't destroy it, which is really an exciting thing to think, because I thought everything in Alexandria burned. But it seems that out of a terrible thing they got some ancient information, but they did not destroy it. Nostradamus says this information still exists. He is saying that if it hasn't already been discovered within the last few years, it will be soon. It's eminent. You must know it existed; it continued to survive as a living entity of a storehouse of knowledge. It didn't disappear. People didn't break into it and burn up the scrolls for heat or cooking. It actually was on high enough ground so as not to be destroyed by any natural events, floods or anything else.

D: *You mean where it is located now?*

P: I believe the library at Alexandria, of which I speak, does not have existence on the Earth at *this* time. It's entirely possible that the Alexandrian library of which I speak had more than one part. It didn't have to be all in one building perhaps. I think with time, and of course, the ravishes of humans, it has been disassembled and destroyed.

D: *Do you think it was taken somewhere else?*

P: It is near. I mean, right over there. I see this hill. My initial thought about the library at Alexandria was that there had only been one library, and it was destroyed. I think some of the ruins still remain and can be visited right now if we went over there. And when you asked me if it were still there, I couldn't see any ruins. So that made me ask, "Where is it?" And then I saw it on a hill. That made me realize there was either more than one library or more than one part to the library. And the part I'm talking about, there are no visible remains, there are no ruins.

D: *That way no one will know where it is unless they discover it later.*

P: Well, they're not too interested in finding a place that doesn't contain anything anyway. This quatrain addresses the fact that back then the library withstood some heavy-duty nature events and lived. Then these people came who took some information out which would be considered bad, especially since they may have killed people to get the stuff. But because I asked, "What does that have to do with today?" Nostradamus is saying that information is getting ready to come out right now. So the benefit is that we're now going to hear information that is several thousands of years old. We wouldn't have known about it if they hadn't stolen it, taken it somewhere else and hidden it away.

D: *But it will be found, or it will come to light?*

P: Yes. And very *shortly,* I feel. Just like any minute. This interpretation was so difficult because the words are a *trick.* The quatrains take me into literal thought. It was good to look in the mirror where I saw that man.

D: *You have to describe the scenes because they* are *tricks. They are symbolism that Nostradamus has invented, and we need his mind to show us what it really means.*

Chapter 13

The Pope and
the Church

ANOTHER RECURRING THEME continued throughout the three years that I worked on this project. All the different subjects referred to the fate of the church and the Christian religion. Since it had never occurred to any of the participants I can only emphasize that this scenario must have come from the mind of Nostradamus. During his lifetime he was living under persecution imposed upon him by the church and the Inquisition. The frustration of not being able to share his visions became increasingly evident as I worked with him. In the past I had accused him of wishful thinking, that maybe his frustration and resentment were coloring his quatrains dealing with the future of the Catholic Church. He said it was true that he had thoughts in that direction, but what he was reporting in his quatrains was from the visions he had seen in his black mirror and not from his own conscious thoughts. These are translations, but whether they are valid and whether or not they become reality is in the hands of higher powers. I am only the reporter presenting the interpretations of what Nostradamus saw and recorded in code.

CENTURY VI-9

Au sacrez temples seront
faicts escandales,
Comptez seront par honneurs
& louanges.
D'un que on grave d'argent,
d'or les medalles,
La fin sera en torments
bien estranges.

In the sacred temples scandals will be committed, they will be thought of as honors and praiseworthy. By one whom they engrave on silver, gold and medals; the end will be in very strange torments.

W: [Wayne] This has to do with the Vatican. The engraved metals will be coins with the pope's likeness. It will be his rise and then his downfall, because of his vanity.

D: *Is this the present pope we have at this time?*

W: No, it's in our future.

D: *"In the sacred temples scandals will be committed." Can he clarify that?*

W: Yes. He sees much corruption by the hierarchy of the Catholic Church. The scandal cannot be kept private. The dishonesty and personal gain by the leaders of the Catholic Church will become public. And it will cause dissension and the complete breakup of the Catholic Church.

D: *The last sentence says, "The end will be in very strange torments."*

W: Yes. Not everyone will want the Catholic Church broken up. It will break into so many small factions that one part of the Catholic Church will not have the same rules and standards as another one, and the names of their beliefs will be changed. It will be a hard transition for many.

D: *Is he showing you pictures, or is this being done with the mind?*

W: I'm looking into a cloud, a fog bank, and just repeating ... Sometimes it's impressions, sometimes it's pictures. I could see the coins. I know they were a climax to the rise of Catholic power, and at that point it started to decline. Of course the Vatican is symbolism for a belief structure, a belief system, and within belief systems there is a path for self-examination. It seems that self-examination and the potential of human consciousness and direction directly shapes human and current world events.

The method of looking into a cloud bank or gray foggy mist was also used by the first subjects Elena and Brenda. They were transported from Nostradamus' room into what we supposed was another dimension. There they would see the scenes acted out against a gray cloud bank. All the other subjects interacted with Nostradamus in his home in the 1500s. Some of them, such as John, interacted directly, while others were invisible and had to manifest something more substantial (an entity or form) for Nostradamus to focus on. These subjects saw the scenes in the mirror on his desk. It is interesting that the same procedures were employed by different individuals who did not consciously know the methods that had been used by others whom I worked with. Maybe there really is a method, a procedure that produces the desired results in working through time. Maybe I happened to stumble across it while working originally with Elena, and by following Nostradamus' instructions we were able to open up a route to something that actually exists, a corridor through time. Brenda said I had found the gateway. Whatever is occurring, it adds validity when the different subjects' narration dovetails so closely with each other. We apparently are only acting as a conduit to allow the past to speak to the future. The flow has been increased through repeated use. As Nostradamus said, it is like the breaking in and continued use of a favorite pipe.

CENTURY VIII-45

La main escharpe & la jambe bandes,	With his hand in a sling and his leg bandaged, the younger brother of
Longs puis nay de Calais portera.	Calais will reach far. At the word
Au mot du guet la mort sera tardee	of the watch, the death will be
Puis dans le temple à Pasques saignera.	delayed, then he will bleed at Easter in the Temple.

W: This seems to have religious overtones. I believe this is a future event, and it deals with the next pope. He has not been left with an easy task. Through valiant efforts he does make himself known and heard. Yet his reign doesn't last very long.

D: *Can he show you what happens to the present pope?*

W: I'm having mixed signals here. I'm feeling it's an assassination, but yet I know there has already been an assassination attempt on this person.

D: *That's true, there was. But what is he showing you?*

W: Well, that he's shot.

D: *Is there anything in the picture that might identify where he is at the time?*

W: I think he will be traveling. He won't be at the Vatican when he dies. I see crowds of people. That's all I see.

D: *That could be anywhere. And this quatrain refers to the one who is pope after him. That first part seemed contradictory, "With his hand in a sling and his leg bandaged, he will reach far."*

W: This pope who will come into being will have his hands tied, in the sense that he will be left a very tough task and a divided church. And he will reach far because his message will be heard.

D: *Then the second part, "At the word of the watch the death will be delayed. Then he will bleed at Easter in the temple." Does that also refer to the new pope?*

W: Yes. I'm getting the sense that he will also survive one assassination attempt. And then he will also be assassinated. I see that he will die in the Vatican.

Unknown to Wayne and the others, this was following a recurrent prediction that ran through the first two volumes of this work. Both Brenda and John saw that the present pope would be assassinated while on one of his trips, presumably in the spring in a large city in Europe that sat near the juncture of two major rivers. After his death another pope would be elected who would only serve for a short time because he would be assassinated by those within the church. We had already been told that the pope before the present one (John Paul I), who only served for a month, was murdered by his own people. This was accomplished through the use of a subtle poison that could not be detected because it produced the effects of a stroke or a heart attack. We were told that this poison would also be used against the pope who followed the present one, for the same motives. After this, a pope would be elected who conformed more to their wishes, but who would prove to be the tool of the coming Anti-Christ. Through their association, the downfall of the Catholic Church would be accomplished. This was told in detail in Volume One, which these three new subjects could not have known about at the time of our sessions. It is remarkable that all three also saw the Vatican experiencing trouble, the assassination of several popes, and the downfall of the church. The same scenario was being presented to each of my subjects in turn. It was obvious it was not coming from my mind or theirs because none of us wished ill to befall any religious institution.

CENTURY X-65

O vaste Romone ta ruine s'approche, *Non de tes murs de ton sang & substance;* *L'aspre par lettres fera si horrible coche,* *Fer poinctu mis à tous jusques au manche.*	O great Rome your ruin draws near, not of your walls but of your blood and substance; the harsh one in letters will make so horrid a notch, pointed steel wounding all up to the sleeve.

N: [Nina] My picture was of the Vatican falling. I see corruption being uncovered. I see that humanity has discovered the Vatican formed its own hierarchy to control and manipulate man by inventing rules and laws, and making people believe that these were the laws and words of God, which they were not. People no longer will stand for it because they've uncovered the power, the wealth, the hypocrisy, the lies to humankind. The Vatican will fall.

D: *That first sentence seems to fit with that. The last one has some symbols I would like you to clarify. "The harsh one on letters will make so horrid a notch. Pointed steel wounding all up to the sleeve."*

N: This person will come with spoken word, with written word, with documented proof, and make this public, so that it cannot be hidden any longer.

D: *That's what it means by "so horrid a notch" and "pointed steel"?*

N: The truth of the words.

D: *And this will happen in our future, I suppose.*

N: Yes. A part of the unification of the universal citizen.

CENTURY V-73

Persecutee sera de Dieu l'eglise, *Et les sainctz temples seront expoliez:* *L'enfant la mere mettra nud en chemise,* *Seront Arabes aux Polons raliez.*	The Church of God will be persecuted, and the holy temples will be pillaged; the mother will put out the child, naked in a shift. The Arabs will ally with the Poles.

N: This is the fall of religion as we know it today. It refers to the Vatican, and all countries under false prophets who manipulate people through fear and guilt. As Rome is not really of Christ and the Arabs are not really of Mohammed's teachings, so they will eventually fall. Both of these teachings were trying to make a philosophy of God's love and universal law. Man has changed all of these religions and teachings for his own greed, control and manipulation.

D: *Then it is not only the Catholic Church. It deals with all the main religions. That word for "shift" is "chemise" in the French. I think it means a dress or something like that. I can see the symbolism of "the mother will put out the child." But "naked in a shift" would seem contradictory. If someone was naked they wouldn't be clothed.*

N: No. This, I think, is old terms, old talk. Back in Nostradamus' time, because of modesty, they felt as naked in a shift, which was an undergarment, as they would without it. No one of propriety would have *ever, ever* been seen that way.

D: *I see, it would be a disgrace, in his way of thinking. "The Arabs will ally with the poles."*

N: Well, this picture isn't very clear. But I think again out of fear and desperation there might be new contacts. Things will be in great upheaval as this occurs. Religion is not the way the original leaders wanted humankind to experience it. It should be a way of life in universal law and God's law. Humanity manipulated it into something it never was.

CENTURY X-12

Esleu en Pape, d'esleu sera mocqué,	Elected as Pope, he will be mocked when elected, suddenly and unex-
Subit soudain esmeu prompt & timide,	pectedly moved, prompt and timid: Caused to die through too much
Par trop bon doulz à mourir provocqué,	goodness and kindness he will fear for the guide killed on the night of
Crainte estainte la nuit de sa mort guide.	his death.

P: [Pam] I don't see anything and I don't hear anything. But as you read I thought about the present pope, the one who comes from Poland. He was not one of your major contenders for the popedom. But after they murdered the last pope they needed to find another one quickly; someone who wasn't in on the assassination. He is innocent and did not know anything about it. So, from that perspective, he was a good candidate for pope manipulations. This man *is* a good man, a loving kind energy. He is definitely a man of peace. That part about him fearing for his guide the night that *he* is killed, certainly agrees with his personality and heart vibration. He would be concerned about anyone suffering any injury because of their association with him. He would take that responsibility and feel badly about it. This, of course, has not happened. And it may not happen. But it *could* happen.

D: *Then Nostradamus sees him dying?*

P: I can only tell you that I saw nothing in the mirror, and immediately I had these thoughts flood in. I forgot to ask Nostradamus, so I'll ask him now. (*Pause*) He says that's the way he sees it.

D: *What does he see?*

P: He sees that the present pope is killed by nefarious means. There are machinations behind the scenes by bishops and other high-ups, who want the church to be much more manipulative than it is. This pope doesn't associate with these uncomfortable religious figures. He's like a light unto himself most of the time.

D: *Can Nostradamus see how he is killed?*

P: My first response was—it doesn't make sense—but it had to do with some kind of poison. It isn't necessarily a foregone conclusion that this is how this pope will die. When Nostradamus looked upon this, that was the way things were going and would happen.

D: *You also said that the pope before him was murdered?*

P: Yes, that is correct. There was already a cancer on the church that was enormous and huge. And thus much of the goodness that the church was supposed to be had been long gone. It was a big business and an ego-gratifying thing, as any large corporation or small country. There arose in that system a group of powerful individuals. I don't know Catholic hierarchy, but I could call them "cardinals and bishops and big dudes"—who finally amassed enough power to have one of *their own* elected pope. In fact, they did. Although when he became pope he made some pronouncements that they heartily disagreed with. And they had extreme fear that this man would not follow along with their plan, which was basically for self-aggrandizement. It wasn't any conscious plot to overthrow the world or anything like that. This was for their own edification. This pope wasn't playing by the plan once he got in, so there was only one way to stop him.

D: *How was he killed?*

P: Maybe that's where the poison came in. Maybe it was referring to that pope instead of the present one. Of course, they said it was a heart attack. These words keep coming: "psychotropic drug." I'm not sure I even know what psychotropic is.

Psychotropic drugs are drugs which act on the mind and can be tranquilizers.

D: *Does Nostradamus think they will use the same method with the present pope, or was he having overlays?*

P: He doesn't say anything. But it doesn't feel like this quatrain has the same density that it had before. You see, the quatrain becomes harder to hold on to. As for Nostradamus, he doesn't have that same feeling of, "Yes! This is going to happen."

D: *But it looks like the other pope was killed by people within his own organization.*

P: It certainly does. The ways of the distorter are as varied as grains of sand. Nostradamus said this was a difficult session for him, because he's tired: he's *really* tired, and achy. And so he just sat there mentally today, rather indifferent.

D: *Maybe you can send him some healing energy before we leave.*

P: That's a great idea. That is acknowledgment that he is cared about from planes other than the one he's operating in. He really knows he is. That probably is what keeps him going.

B: [Brenda] We are here in the special meeting place, and we have been discussing various versions of paradise. He is pointing out some of the comparisons between the vision of paradise as described in the Old Testament or the Torah, and the version of paradise as described in the Koran. And he and I have been discussing these visions of paradise, and how their differences have affected the cultures that follow these religions. We were generally just passing the time until everything was ready for the translation.

D: *He is familiar with the Koran and those other books?*

B: He says, *certainly* he is! He's an educated man!

D: *Does he think the different versions are accurate?*

B: Not exactly. He says each version's description has been slanted in such a way so as to support that particular religion. He says there's no such thing as a *correct* version.

D: *Is he familiar with what paradise is* really *like?*

B: He feels he gets a good view of it by using the mirror.

D: *You two seem to have interesting conversations while you're waiting for me.*

B: Well, that is the way it should be—to expand the mind—to have stimulating conversation. He says he enjoys the conversations, which I find flattering. I certainly enjoy them.

D: *And I like the little pieces that I get of them. All right. Is he ready to go ahead with the translation of the quatrains?*

B: As you ask this he takes his hat off, turns it around and sits it back on. And he says he has his translator's hat on now.

D: (Laugh) *A different hat?*

B: Same hat. He just turned it around. He says it was a scholar's hat before; now it's a translator's hat.

D: (Laugh) *I'm glad he's in a good mood. We never know how we're going to find him.*

B: He says, "I'm always in a good mood." It's just mistranslations that make him cranky.

D: *Well, sometimes he gets irritated at me, too.*

B: He says sometimes you can be obtuse.

D: *Well, I don't mean to be. They're difficult, don't forget.*

CENTURY V-15

En navigant captif prins
grand pontife,
Grans aprets faillir les
clercz tumultuez:
Second esleu absent son
bien debise,
Son favori bastard à mort tué.

While sailing, the great Pope will be captured; great preparations by the troubled clerics fail. The second elected absent, his power declines, his favorite bastard, put to death.

B: He says this quatrain refers to the current pope, and how he is always traveling back and forth to various spots on Earth to visit sections of the Catholic Church. This places him in danger because he can't be protected as well. The cardinals and such have been most concerned about this, but they can't do anything about it because the pope insists. Nostradamus says that by looking in his mirror, he sees that someone will assassinate the pope in a place where there has been unrest. The church will be thrown into turmoil, and it may cause a schism. He says this split is still questionable, but the possibility is there.

D: *"His power declines. His favorite bastard put to death."*

B: That refers to the possible schism in the church. He says the church's power and influence will continue to decline, and the members will continue to decrease. The "favorite bastard put to death" refers to events that may possibly cause the schism. If this schism does occur, he is saying it will probably be in relation to the issue of birth control.

D: *He thinks that might split the church. Will this be after this current pope dies and the next pope is elected?*

B: During the process. This will all come up at once, basically. Everything will come to a head, so to speak. He wants to say that there have been some popes who did not die a natural death. He says the one that was in there for only a month ... there was some technology involved with which he is not familiar. But he says the equivalent, from his time period, would be slow poison being built up in the system. Perhaps it might have been a combination of slow poison and doses of radiation to cause him to sicken and die in a short period of time. At first the powers that be had planned to let him be pope for awhile. But he ran afoul of those who were in control behind the scenes. So they caused him to be killed in this very skillful and subtle manner.

CENTURY VI-86

Le grand Prelat un jour apres
*   son songe,*
Interpreté au rebours de son sens:
De la Gascogne lui surviendra
*   un monge,*
Qui fera eslire le grand Prelat
*   de sens.*

One day the great Prelate, after his dream interpreted the opposite to its meaning; from Gascony a monk will come to him who will cause the great Prelate of Sens to be elected.

B: He says this quatrain is referring to the election of the last pope.

D: *The one Nostradamus calls the tool of the Anti-Christ?*

B: He says there will be much confusion at the time, many changes and unrest. Things will be ripe for change because there will be a grass roots dissatisfaction gradually building up. Many people start out supporting the Anti-Christ simply because they want a change, and they will not realize what he represents. Others will be supportive of change, not because they support the Anti-Christ, but because they know if things are upset there will be a better chance to start a new system, like a new government or what-have-you.

D: *"One day the great prelate after his dream interpreted the opposite to its meaning."*

B: That represents the hold the Anti-Christ will have over his mind. He is wanting to be a pope—he will be a pope—but it will be an anti-pope because the Anti-Christ will be able to influence his mind through misused psychic powers.

D: *"From Gascony a monk will come." Is that the last pope?*

B: No. That represents one of the people who will be trying to fight for the liberation.

D: *"Who will cause the great prelate of Sens to be elected."*

B: He says this monk will be philosophical, saying, "it is darkest before the dawn." The monk will know that this prelate will be the last pope of the Catholic church. And that the whole structure can be done away with, and start fresh and new. Therefore he will help influence things to work out as they do, even though he is fighting the Anti-Christ. Because he sees that straightening up the situation as a whole will be better if some of the dead, rotten branches of the structure are gotten rid of. Nostradamus says he helps and uses what influence he can to get that pope elected because he knows it will be the last pope. He says that for centuries the church has been rotten through and through, and involved with power struggles that have nothing to do with spirituality at all. Humanity cannot progress with the Catholic Church hanging about its neck like a stone.

CENTURY VI-6

Apparoistra vers la Septentrion,	He will appear towards the North,
Non loin de Cancer l'estoille	not far from the bearded star in
chevelue:	Cancer; Susa, Siena, Bœtia,
Suze, Sienne, Bœce, Eretrion,	Eretria, the great man of Rome
Mourra de Rome grand, la nuict	will die, the night dispersed.
disparue.	

B: He says this quatrain refers to the death of the last pope. It also refers to the rise of the Anti-Christ. The bearded star in Cancer refers to a celestial event. He is not clear whether it will be a nova of a star or the occurrence of a comet. He says many of those words refer to astrological symbols and constellations.

D: *"The night dispersed"?*

B: He says that will be when the Anti-Christ becomes more aggressive in taking over the world, and will get rid of the secrecy aspect.

CENTURY VI-66

Au fondement de la	At the founding of the new sect the
nouvelle secte,	bones of the great Roman will be
Seront les os du grand	found. A sepulchre covered in
Romain trouvés,	marble will appear: the Earth will
Sepulchre en marbre	quake in April, badly buried.
apparoistra couverte,	
Terre trembler en Avril,	
mal enfouetz.	

B: He says this quatrain is about the various schisms that occurred in the Catholic Church which ended in the birth of the various Protestant sects—in the beginning when the Calvinists, the Lutherans and others first began splitting from the Catholic Church.

D: *Does he want to explain some of this symbolism? It says, "At the founding of a new sect the bones of the great Roman will be found."*

B: He says this symbolizes one of the things that caused the Protestant sects to split from the Catholic Church. They taught that reason, logic and science had a place in the universe. Some documents by old Roman and Greek scientists challenged what the Catholic Church had to say about the order of the universe. The Catholic Church tried to suppress this knowledge but did not succeed, which is what was meant by bones badly buried—because this knowledge would come back up and contradict what the Catholic Church said about the order of the universe.

D: *It says, "a sepulchre covered in marble will appear." Does that refer to the same thing?"*

B: Yes. He says that refers to buried knowledge being unearthed, and it being as fine as marble as far as the quality of the facts are concerned.

He says, for example, in his day the Catholic Church teaches that the Earth is the center of the universe. But he has seen the skies and studied ancient scripts himself enough to know that this may not necessarily be true. Plus, the visions he has seen of the future tell him that the universe is different from what the Catholic Church says.

D: *"The Earth will quake in April, badly buried."*

B: He says this refers to a major event in his future and in your past that occurred in April and gave the Catholic world a major shake-up. He says there are some historical events that this could be referring to, and you may want to check the date to see if they occurred in April. It was either the posting of Martin Luther's protest against the Catholic Church, or some of Galileo's publications concerning the sun being the center of the solar system. He says check some of the major events that shook up the Catholic Church. This quatrain interrelates with the time that the new religions, the new sects, were coming forth.

CENTURY IV-71

En lieu d'espouse les filles trucidées,	Instead of a bride the girls are slaughtered, murder with such
Meurtre à grand faulte ne sera superstile:	wickedness, there will be no survivors. The vestals are
Dedans le puys vestules inondées,	drowned in the wells, and the
L'espouse estraincte par hauste d'Aconite.	bride killed by a draught of Aconite.

B: He is organizing the images he wants to show. He says this quatrain refers to a worldwide rise in fundamentalism. Various major religions of the world will become more fanatical, and as a result will lose touch with wisdom, which is the drowning of the vestals in the wells. If they lose touch with their spiritual source and their wisdom, then they will lose touch with what they consider to be deity, or God. The various organizations or religions will wither away as a result. He says they will no longer be religions, they will be gross parodies of religion.

D: *Is that why he mentioned the draught of Aconite?*

(The definition of aconite: (1) A poisonous plant with blue, purple, or yellow hood-like flowers; monkshood; wolfsbane. (2) A drug made from its dried roots, used as a sedative.)

B: Yes. He's saying the process is already well started in our time. And he says, "Look at the state the Christian church is in. Look at the state of the Muslim religion in the Middle East." You can look all around and see this is already happening. The men in positions of authority in these various religions became power hungry, and started abusing their position.

D: *That's what all the references to murder mean.*

CENTURY V-31

Par terre Attique chef
de la sapience,
Qui de present est la rose
du monde:
Pont ruiné & sa grand
pre-eminence,
Sera subdite & naufrage
des undes.

From the land of Attica, source of all wisdom which at the present is the rose of the world: the Pont(iff) ruined, its great pre-eminence will be subjected and wrecked beneath the waves.

B: He says this quatrain refers to the final downfall of the Catholic Church. When it does collapse it will go all the way and there will be no trace of it left. It will be as if it had been swallowed up by the waves. He says that is because unfortunately the way the structure is set up it has been rotting from the inside out for quite some time. When it finally does fall there will not be any apparent strength left to help it stand.

D: *What is the reference to Attica? "From the land of Attica, source of all wisdom, which at the present is the rose of the world."*

B: He says the source of western civilization and knowledge originated from Greece, Turkey, the Near East, and that part of the world, even though the Catholic Church would deny it. This area was called the "rose" because it was the seat of learning and civilization. The Catholic church likes to put itself forward as being the torch of western civilization.

CENTURY X-46

Vie sort mort de L'OR vilaine
indigne,
Sera de Saxe non nouveau
electeur:
De Brunsuic mandra d'amour
signe,
Faux le rendant aux peuple
seducteur.

Because of the gold, the life, fate and death of an unworthy, sordid man: he will not be the new Elector of Saxony. From Brunswick he will send for a sign of love, the false seducer giving it to the people.

B: He says this once again refers to a general phenomenon that can be represented by a single figure. He says throughout the ages there have been false prophets and false teachers. But as one can read in the book of Revelation, they are never so prevalent as just preceding the Anti-Christ. During the 20th century they reach an all-time high. They become the richest men in the country, and their souls are the most rotten you would find. He says these false teachers will reach massive amounts of people through the wonders of modern technology, and hence are able to rake in massive amounts of money. He says recent memories of the communicator confirmed to him these happenings concerning certain ones of them (TV evangelists and such) that have been discredited and/or put in jail.

CENTURY VI-89

Entre deux cymbes piedz	Feet and hands bound between two
& mains estachés,	boats, the face anointed with honey
De miel face oingt & de	and touched with milk. Wasps and
laict substanté:	flies, fatherly love angered, the
Guespes & mouches, fitine	cupbearer lies, the goblet tried.
amour fachés,	
Poccilateur faucer, Cyphe tempté.	

B: This quatrain contains a great deal of symbolism. He says it refers to the present and the extremely recent past, relatively speaking. It refers to the scandals taking place in the religious communities, particularly concerning television evangelists. He says even though there has been a lull in the scandals, they are not over yet. Some more information is going to come to light that will scandalize people all over again. The "goblet tried" refers to the fact that they are no longer in touch with the true source. "Feet and hands bound between two boats" represents their mixed loyalties between what they are supposed to be doing and their desire to obtain more money.

D: *"The face anointed with honey and touched with milk"?*

B: He says that refers to how they present themselves as being very fair to look upon, and very good. And the wasps and bees refer to their dark secrets, the scandals coming to light.

D: *"The fatherly love angered."*

B: He says that is the true source, the spirit, turning away from them.

D: *"The cupbearer lied" would also refer to them. You said there will be more of these scandals involving other so-called evangelists?*

B: He says this will be occurring, not necessarily just with television evangelists, but with various religious organizations. Information will come to light that will show they are not as sincere as they have tried to present themselves. He says there's also going to be some scandals in the Catholic Church. And some other major religious organizations will be going through scandals.

D: *So it won't only be the Protestants. The Catholics will have their share of scandals too?*

B: Yes. He says it will become very widespread amongst the Christian world in general. The scandals with the television evangelists occurring one after the other was the opening force.

CENTURY IX-62

Au grand de Cheramon agora	To the great one of Cheramon
Seront croisez par ranc tous	agora will all the crosses by rank be
attachez,	attached, the long-lasting Opium
Le pertinax Oppie,	and Mandrake, the Rougon will be
& Mandragora,	released on October the third.
Rougon d'Octobre le tiers	
seront laschez.	

B: He says this quatrain refers to the last pope. It refers to the final disbanding of the college of cardinals, and to the dissolving of the Catholic Church.

D: *What does he mean by, "the great one of Cheramon agora"?*

B: That refers to the last pope. That's symbolic of where he was originally from when he was a child.

D: *Why does he mention these drugs, "the long-lasting opium and mandrake"?*

B: He says for centuries the Catholic priests have tried to keep the lay people's minds dull and unquestioning, much the way a drug would affect one under its influence. He says both of those drugs have medicinal purposes if used wisely. But if you overuse either one of them they are a poison and will then kill the patient. That means the Catholic Church tried to suppress knowledge, so in this way it acts as poison.

D: *"Rougon" is a word they don't understand. "The Rougon will be released on October the third."*

B: The Rougon refers to the college of cardinals. October the third will be when they will be disbanded permanently for the last time.

D: *Rougon is an anagram?*

B: Basically, yes.

CENTURY VIII-98

Des gens d'eglise sang fera	Of the church men the blood will be
espandu,	poured forth as abundant as water
Comme de l'eau eu si	in (amount); for a long time it will
grand abondance;	not be restrained, woe, woe, for the
Et d'un long temps ne	clery ruin and grief.
sera restranche	
Ve, ve au clerc ruine & doleance.	

B: He says this quatrain has three meanings. On the one hand, it refers to the Inquisition of his time and following. He says the Inquisition was totally ridiculous. They took things too far. He was trying to warn them that if they didn't restrain themselves and get themselves in order, they would destroy the church. He says this quatrain also refers to the downfall of the Catholic Church.

D: *I gathered that.* (We laughed.)

B: He says that is fairly plain. He says it also refers to the Anti-Christ destroying other religions. The Anti-Christ will befoul and then destroy anything people revere or hold to be holy. And so it is "woe, woe, woe unto clergymen," meaning destruction and ruin to *all* priests, priestesses, or anybody who serves a divine power.

CENTURY X-56

Prelat royal son baissant
trop tiré,
Grand fleux de sang sortira
de sa bouche,
Le reign Anglique par
regne respiré,
Long temps mort vif en
Tunis comme souche.

The royal priest bowing too low, a great flow of blood will come out of his mouth. The Anglican reign, a realm breathng, for a long time dead as a stump, living in Tunis.

B: He says this quatrain refers to the end of the Catholic Church, and its interaction with the Anti-Christ. At first the Catholic Church will try peaceful means to accommodate him, not realizing he is the Anti-Christ. That is "the priests bowing too low." The "blood coming out of his mouth" is the Anti-Christ striking at the church anyway and taking advantage of their weakness.

D: *"A realm breathing"?*

B: He says much of the downfall will take place behind the scenes with the powers of whispers and secrets.

D: *And then the last part makes sense. "For a long time dead as a stump."*

CENTURY VII-36

Dieu, le ciel tout le divin
verbe à l'unde.
Porté par rouges sept
razes à Bisance:
Contre les oingz trois cens
de Trebisconde,
Deux loix mettront,
& l'horreur, puis credence.

God, the heavens, all the divine words in the waves, carried by seven red-shaven heads to Byzantium: against the anointed three hundred from Trebizond, will make two laws, first horror then trust.

B: He says this quatrain represents the coming of the new age. It represents how non-Christian and pagan beliefs had been persecuted and prejudiced against for centuries. Fewer people were involved and so it became very weak. It also refers to how things will become more tolerant again and more and more people will be involved with self-examination and spiritual development, eventually spreading out to influence the entire Earth.

D: *Let's decipher some of this symbolism. "God, the heavens, all the divine words in the waves."*

B: He says that represents cosmic wisdom found through various sources, including astrology, astronomy, alchemy, and all the various philosophies for obtaining wisdom.

D: *"Carried by seven red shaven heads to Byzantium."*

B: He says that represents how wise people from western and eastern tradition will meet at common ground to help develop philosophies that will progress towards world peace. He says they won't necessarily physically meet in Byzantium. He used that geographical location to symbolize a balance between the various groups.

D: *What does 300 represent?*

B: He says that represents that there are a great number of philosophies through which one could find enlightenment. There's no such thing as any *one* philosophy or *one* religion that will obtain enlightenment for everybody. But the number is great, and each should find that which works for them.

D: *"Against the anointed 300 from Trebizond, will make two laws. First horror, then trust."*

B: He says that represents that through the history of civilization when the church is in power it makes laws against all the other philosophical systems. Finally the balance of things will change through the course of time, as they always do, and world peace will come and the new age. The "law of trust" then represents people opening up and finding spiritual wisdom and working with world peace.

D: *Then the "horror" means this will occur after the Anti-Christ, when everybody is willing to work together again. Every time he mentions Byzantium, I always think of the Anti-Christ. That's the only way I can relate to that word.*

B: He says, be glad he didn't write Constantinople every time.

CENTURY VIII-99

Par la puissance des trois rois tempoulz,	Through the powers of three temporal kings, the sacred seat will
En autre lieu sera mis le saint siege:	be put in another place, where the substance of the body and the spirit
Où la substance & de l'esprit corporel,	will be restored and received as the true seat.
Sera remis & receu pour vrai siege.	

P: [Pam] That seemed to refer to the far distant future. I saw the three temporal kings as spiritual beings. That we pass consciously through their, shall we say, kingdom of knowingness. Temporal was an interesting word to use, but I'm disregarding it and going on with what I'm seeing. The mirror shows the spirit consciously leaving the Earth plane and traveling to three outward kingdoms, each farther than the other. This is, of course, symbolic because they are *not* kingdoms. These are planes of consciousness, but he uses metaphors to explain them. That seat where the soul resides is one seat where *all* souls reside, the ultimate source, the beginning and end of all things. This is a very hopeful quatrain to me, because it says we will attain the consciousness to get there *consciously*. Of course, this happens when you die, but in time measurement it could take a long time to accomplish this purposefully because humanity has not expanded their thoughts to encompass this distance or this "bigness." This is a quatrain that says he's seen it, and he knows it's possible for us to do it.

D: *This is beyond the physical?*

P: This whole quatrain to me does not speak of the physical life, other than to let us know we can get this information while we *are* still physical.

D: *It was thought that this quatrain referred to the popes as the kings.*

P: Those who are totally focused on the Earth plane would look for the most spiritual beings they could think of. And this is a spiritual quatrain.

D: *He's not referring to the popes then.*

P: That is not what I saw. I'll ask. He said, if you choose it could. The popes themselves being a metaphor. (*Outburst*) I don't like these conversations with him because it's like, "It's your choice."

D: *Is that what he says?*

P: "Try to expand your consciousness," he said.

D: *I thought maybe it might have two meanings. It doesn't refer to the popes at all then.*

P: "One more time," he says. There are many ways to say the same thing. He wants to get across the largest meaning. If the largest meaning a reader can comprehend is going through three manifest human beings on the Earth plane, if the highest spiritual entities they can think of are human, then, yes, they can say that is the translation of this quatrain and it will be their truth. He wants to expand it to what he has seen and so I have to say what I saw in the mirror.

D: *Okay. They were translating it as referring to the popes, and moving the Vatican to another location.*

P: He says that limits it to the Earth plane.

D: *Some of these quatrains are definitely dealing with the Earth plane.*

P: Most. (*Laugh*)

D: *We can't tell until he translates them for us.*

Chapter 14

The Anti-Christ

EVERY ONE OF THE SUBJECTS translated quatrains that related to the predicted scenario of the coming World War III. This was the topic that concerned Nostradamus the most, and apparently was one of the main reasons for this communication. He believed if we were warned and alert that we could avert some of the worst things he had seen in his black mirror. Some of these visions referred to the buildup for war in the ever-turbulent Middle East. These translations came through in the early part of 1989, and are documented and dated. It is notable that in retrospect many of them seem to refer to the conditions of the short Persian Gulf War that took place in late 1990 and early 1991. According to Nostradamus, this was only the beginning. That war was the first rumblings of the approaching storm when the monster would plunge the world into chaos if we did not heed these warnings.

CENTURY VIII-70

Il entrera vilain, mechant, infame
Tyrannisant la Mesopotamie,
Tous amis fait d'adulterine d'ame,
Terre horrible, noir de phisonomie.

He will enter, wicked, unpleasant, infamous, tyrannizing over Mesopotamia. All friends made by the adulterous lady, the land dreadful and black of aspect.

W: [Wayne] I'm seeing something that you probably won't want to hear.
D: *Why? I hear so many strange things.*
W: So anyway, where is Mesopotamia?
D: *Oh, that's an old name. It doesn't exist any more. It was somewhere in Asia, in the —what do they call that—the fertile crescent.* (I discovered later that Mesopotamia is the ancient name for Iraq.)
W: That doesn't seem to fit in this quatrain.
D: *Why? What did you see that you thought I wouldn't want to hear?*
W: (*Chuckle*) Well, the tyrant would be our current President, George

Bush, and that lady would be the Statue of Liberty. The country would be the United States.

D: *But it is called the "adulterous lady."*

W: Well, she has been somewhat whored out in her years. She, at one time, stood for liberty, but liberty is a word like Mesopotamia. It's a long gone word.

D: *"He will enter wicked, unpleasant, infamous, tyrannizing over Mesopotamia." That refers to Bush? But it says, "All friends made by the adulterous lady."*

W: Our allies.

D: *Then "adulterous" in that context means she wouldn't be true to them.*

W: She is not true to anybody at this point in our time.

D: *"The land dreadful and black of aspect." It doesn't sound like a very good description of the United States, does it?*

W: I told you you wouldn't want to hear it, Dolores.

D: *Well, I try to remain neutral and not draw conclusions.*

W: A great deal of the world's woes stem from this country and this administration. This administration has just begun (1989), but it's post-dating another that this administration was part of.

D: *Ask him, couldn't this description describe other countries in the past?*

W: It could have, but it would have been before Nostradamus' time.

After the fact, this quatrain seems to most definitely refer to the U.S. involvement in Iraq.

CENTURY V-4

Le gros mastin de cité deschassé,	The great mastiff is driven out of
Sera fasché de l'etrange alliance,	the city, angered by the foreign
Apres aux champs avoir le	alliance. Later having chased the
cerf chassé	stag to the field, the wolf and the
Le lous & l'Ours se donront	bear will defy each other.
defiance.	

W: This is an event that will happen in the Middle East to the leader of Israel or Egypt. He will be driven from power jointly by unpopular decisions and by accepting aid from opposing sides.

D: *Then the leader is the mastiff. Who are the other animals?*

W: The bear is Russia and the wolf is America.

D: *That's interesting symbolism to describe America as a wolf. Can you see why he's using that symbol?*

W: Yes, because the wolf is an animal who hunts in packs. There are packs, groups of Americans, scattered around the globe, and they are hunters.

D: *Who is the stag?*

W: The stag will be the mediator who tries to bring peace into this area that is being warred over.

D: *Can you see what countries are fighting?*

W: It seems as if the whole area is in war. The whole Middle East is out of control.

D: *And during that time the leader is chased from power. Am I correct in assuming that America and Russia will intervene in some way?*

W: Russia and America are already in the thick of it, and they're currently being used to oppose each other. Whereas, after certain events take place, they will try to heal their differences and work together.

D: *Do you know what these events are?*

W: The certain events are the downfall of one ruler, and the coming together, the mutual communication that will follow this event. This is to happen in our near future. [This interpretation was done in early 1989.]

CENTURY V-62

Sur les rochers sang on
 les verra plouvoir,
Sol Orient, Saturne Occidental:
Pres d'Orgon guerre, à Rome
 grand mal voir,
Nefs parfondrees & prins
 le Tridental.

Blood will be seen to rain on the rocks, Sun in the East, Saturn in the West. War near Orgon, a great evil seen near Rome, ships sunken and the trident taken.

N: [Nina] I was seeing things happening in the sky. When you talked of the trident and Orgon, I saw the sky, and then I was looking down on the Middle East area. This is strongly referring to that part of the world, as far as the bloodshed, the blood on the rocks. And much of it refers to the skies, and how the planets are when this occurs. But Rome is not the Rome of Italy—it is something else. I believe Rome stands for the force trying to conquer. And it is symbolic of an underground group that has created an uprising in this part of the world.

D: *Is the underground group positive or negative?*

N: This seems to be a negative influence, for sure.

D: *What does it mean, "war near Orgon"?*

N: I am seeing Orgon in the sky. It's a formation. Maybe when that formation in the sky occurs it will be the time of the blood over the rocks, and the rising of Rome.

D: *Then you think it is a star formation?*

N: Yes, or planet alignment.

Could "war near Orgon" refer to the planet Mars (as the symbol for war) near the constellation Orion (as an anagram)?

D: *Is "the blood will be seen to rain on the rocks" symbolic or specific?*

N: To me it's bloodshed, explosions from the sea. Oh! I just saw something different. I saw a red sea. I see the blood on the rocks and it is coming from the water. There seems to be some type of formation in the sky, and an explosion. And then I'm seeing the waves come in like a red sea, a red tide. I don't know what that's from, except that this large animal has been washed up on shore.

D: *Do you see a large animal?*

N: I do, but I don't know if the mirror is playing games or using symbolism. This large animal might represent a force of takeover.

D: *That could refer to the last part, "ships sunken and the trident taken."*

N: Yes. There's much unrest, much purging to be accomplished in that part of the world. There must be unification if humanity is to evolve.

D: *Do you see this as a war or a separate incident?*

N: I see this as a revolution. Unrest in one country that leads to others. It starts off slowly and snowballs. It is in the Middle East.

CENTURY VII-28

Le capitaine conduira grande proie, *Sur la montaigne des ennemis plus proche,* *Environné, par feu fera tel voie,* *Tous eschappez or trente mis en broche.*	The captain will lead a great herd on the mountain closest to the enemy. Surrounded by fire he makes such a way, all escape except for thirty put on the spit.

N: I'm getting a picture of the Middle East. I see Israel and a neighbor at war. This could be the near future. It seems that in this attack there was the counterattack of the Israelis that surrounded these people, and they could not get away. It's just more upheaval in the Middle East. They will definitely have to go through severe cleansing.

CENTURY IX-34

Le part solus mari sera mitré, *Retour conflict passera sur le thuille:* *Par cinq cens un trahir sera tiltré,* *Narbon & Saulce par conteuax avons d'huile.*	The partner, solitary but married, will be mitred, the return, fighting will cross over the Tuileries. By five hundred one traitor will be ennobled, Narbonne & Saulce, we will have oil for knives.

B: [Brenda] He says this quatrain refers to the world situation in general leading up to the time of the Anti-Christ. It is basically what you would consider the present time. "We will have oil for knives" refers to countries trading weapons with the Middle East in exchange for crude oil. And he says the one that will be mitered refers to the Polish pope.

D: *Our present pope?*

B: Yes, "solitary but married" to the church. He says the trader that will be ennobled by 500 refers to the Cabal. The 500 refers to the inner group, the Cabal itself. They are the ones that pull the strings of power, and decide who will *be* in power of the various governments, so they "ennoble" people. He used that symbolism because in his time to be noble meant to be powerful, to be in charge of things. And so someone who is ennobled is someone who has been given the power to be in charge.

D: (I didn't quite understand.) *The trader is also the Cabal?*

B: No, he is the one who is being puppeted by the Cabal. He says when you relisten to your device you will hear it.

D: *It's symbolic of that group taking one person and making them powerful. "The return, fighting will cross over the Tuileries."*

B: He says that refers to some of the things that will be going on with the underground movement trying to fight the Cabal and the Anti-Christ.

D: *The part about "oil for knives" does make sense with what's going on right now. Can I ask him about something that just happened in the last few days [1989]?*

B: He says, "ask."

D: *We're having many problems with Omar Quaddafi in Libya. Nostradamus once said that the man was crazy, and could have been the Anti-Christ if he had played his cards right. Well, he has a factory over there, and the Americans thought they were producing gas, poison weapons and such. But Quaddafi said he was producing drugs. Which is correct?*

B: Both. He says the factory involved is into chemical research *for* the purpose of warfare. On the one hand they are developing various poisonous gases and hallucinogens to be released into the air and water, to knock people out in droves in order to take over a country very easily. At the same time they're also researching into drugs, various subtle poisons and such, in order to assassinate leaders.

D: *Of course, Quaddafi claims it's pharmaceuticals—just ordinary harmless drugs.*

B: Nostradamus says the same type of equipment can be used to produce both. He may be producing some pharmaceuticals, but if you get behind the locked doors you will find some very strange pharmaceuticals. He says the Anti-Christ has Libya very firmly in his camp. He knows he has support from Libya. Whether or not he will decide to try to inflame things between Libya and another country, that is cloudy. In a sense Quaddafi realizes his missed destiny. He could have become the Anti-Christ himself, but he took a wrong turn in his past and ended up being the ranting popinjay that he is now.

CENTURY IV-85

Le charbon blanc du noir
sera chassé,
Prisonnier faicte mené
au tombereau:
More Chameau sus
piedz entrelassez,
Lors le puisné sillera l'aubereau.

The white coal is driven out by the black, made a prisoner, led to the tumbril: his feet are tied together like a rogue, when the last born will let silp the falcon.

N: [Nina] The picture's coming in of the Middle East. Oh, so much unrest, so much aggression, so much destruction. I'm seeing symbolism here, too. I see generations on both sides rising up. They can no longer tolerate how their life has been, and they can no longer raise their children on hate and fear. I see them being led, but it seems that the leader is found to be a false prophet. What they thought was going to unify them and solve their problems has brought them back into bloodshed and destruction. I see strong intervention from other realms at this point. They are at the point of *totally* atomically destroying that area of the world. And I see intervention from other dimensions, other beings because they can no longer have deformed, demented generations brought up on hate and fear.

D: *What is the symbolism of "the white coal driven out by the black"?*

N: I see reflection upon reflection here. The black and the white, the black and the white. And I see much swirling circular reflection and interchange. Oh, I see now. I see some type of huge bomb, smoke, that went off to cause such destruction. And I see a whole black layer lingering over that part of the world.

D: *Who set off the explosion?*

N: This happened right in the Middle East. It was stupidity and ignorance. They did not understand what the results would be. (*Softly*) But they are now going to learn.

D: *Do you mean it hurt their own country, and this was not what they intended?*

N: No, no. It was faulty ignorance. They weren't paying enough attention. They did not calculate correctly. Enough destruction is happening that whatever survives, whoever survives, it will bring on a new society.

D: *Then it wasn't caused by another country; they did this themselves?*

N: Yes, yes.

Could this refer to the blowing-up of the oil wells in 1991 which did indeed create a deadly pall over the area of Kuwait?

D: *"His feet are tied together like a rogue. When the last born will let slip the falcon."*

N: I'm getting pictures of a man who is consumed with being a power-monger, and filled with such hate that he is one and the same being: the falcon, the rogue. The leader who was responsible for the destruction. I guess they thought it was the only way to solve the problem. It ended up being a horrible miscalculation. It was the only inevitable end so there could be a new beginning. Nostradamus seems to be very worn out, but he sees these as probable futures and he can see them to their conclusion. He also feels if there is an open awareness and communication things can be changed. I believe he feels this will be the inevitable way, but he also feels there is communication on so many levels. Just as he hears the voices and is told in vision what to do, he believes if the masses can be awakened to this level, then there can be intervention and we can control it.

CENTURY X-10

Tasche de murdre enormes
adulteres,
Grand ennemi de tout
le genre humain
Que sera pire qu'ayeulx,
oncles ne peres
Enfer, feu, eau,
sanguin & inhumain.

Stained with murder and enormous adulteries, great enemy of all mankind, he will be worse than his ancestors, uncles and fathers, in steel, fire and water, bloody and inhuman.

N: I see a picture of the Middle East conflict. I'm seeing the person in power showing one philosophy to his public, and yet his personal life is corrupt to an extreme. But people with power and demented minds can excuse themselves all things. They find they can live with two faces. But eventually it will catch up with them.

D: *Can he tell you who this person is?*

N: This seems to be a new leader. And this will be an accumulation of years. There will be wars and rebellion. I think the population is going to revolt also. This man is a power-monger with much venom, and it's a drug. Power and strength will excuse all of his personal perversities. People will find out after time passes, that this leader speaks one thing and lives another way.

D: *Can you see what he looks like?*

N: It's hard to tell this person's age, but it appears that he has dark hair that is graying, a mustache and no beard.

D: *This is not the Anti-Christ figure?*

N: This is a very negative figure. But when you said that word "Anti-Christ," I was seeing more than one person. I see various negative persons coming to power and creating civil wars and revolts within their countries. I see this happening in several places.

D: *Are you able to distinguish which one is the Anti-Christ that we have spoken of before?*

N: This person that history writes about—I feel that he does come from the Middle East. But this person in power I am looking at now is not intelligent enough. The other man is a master of manipulation. This

Anti-Christ appears younger. He seems to be the one that will take power after this present one falls. When this dark figure comes to power, the people think they have found a new savior, like the one that had died. And this master manipulator will be in power.

D: *But there will be civil war and revolutions?*

N: That's what I'm seeing. The people will revolt because of the lies, the hypocrisy, the stealing and using wealth for his own purposes. This will all happen shortly.

CENTURY VIII-79

Qui par fer pere perdra
  nay de Nonnaire,
De Gorgon sur la sera
  sang perfetant
En terre estrange fera
  si tant de taire,
Qui bruslera lui mesme
  & son enfant.
	He who loses his father by the sword, born in a Nunnery, upon this Gorgon's blood will conceive anew; in a strange land he will do everything to be silent, he who will burn both himself and his child.

B: He says this is a description of the Anti-Christ.

D: *"He who loses his father by the sword, born in a nunnery"?*

B: Symbolizing that there was no male around in the family because his father was dead. He will be raised by uncles and what-have-you.

D: *That's significant because that can mold a person's life. "Upon this Gorgon's blood will conceive anew." Isn't a Gorgon a monster in mythology?*

In Greek mythology, Gorgon refers to any of the three sisters Stheno, Euryale, and the mortal Medusa who had snakes for hair and eyes that if looked into turned the beholder into stone.

B: Yes. He says that is symbolizing how he will bring up old horrors and tortures in the process of trying to take over the world. He'll be renewing old hostilities.

D: *"In a strange land he will do everything to be silent."*

B: When he is preparing to take over a country he will be very sneaky and use a lot of propaganda, but it will not seem to be coming from him.

D: *"He who will burn both himself and his child."*

B: He says the Anti-Christ will be so crazed for power in order to take over the world that he won't care who he hurts to do it.

CENTURY X-9

De Castillion figuires
jour de brune,
De fame infame naistra
souverain prince.
Surnon de chausses perhume
lui posthume,
Onc Roi ne faut si pire en
sa province.

In the Castle of Figueras on a misty day a sovereign prince will be born of an unworthy woman. The surname of Chausses on the ground will make him posthumous, never was a king so bad in his province.

B: He says this quatrain refers to the birth of the Anti-Christ. He says most of this quatrain is basically straight forward. "An unworthy woman" refers to one: the fact that his mother was a commoner and not royalty. And two, it refers to the fact that it's in a country where women are regarded as property. He says the other lines refer to the politics in the country where he is born. The last line actually refers to how horrible he will be to the world in general.

D: *"In the castle of Figueras on a misty day the sovereign prince will be born"?*

B: He says it's an anagram. The Anti-Christ's place of birth is somewhere in the near east—what is called the Middle East. The names and places are anagrams of the city where he will be born, and also anagrams of the political situation. It's not a real castle. He says many of the cities are fortified cities, and therefore that image would arise in his mind, because there would be walls around the old city.

D: *Then the "surname of Chausses"?*

B: That refers to a clan that is powerful in that country. It will be the clan that he is allied to. Since he is of common birth, he is not *from* a particular clan, but that clan will claim him.

D: *Is that also an anagram?*

B: Yes. "On the ground" refers to his common roots. And "will make him posthumous" refers to their claiming him later.

I wanted to go into detail because I think this is an important quatrain. We have many facts about the Anti-Christ, and we wanted to get more clues if we could. So now we have another piece of the puzzle. In their translation they have come close. One translator suggests this could possibly describe one of Nostradamus' Anti-Christs, but they weren't sure which one.

CENTURY V-9

*Jusques au fonds la grand
arq demolue,
Par chef captif, l'ami anticipé:
Naistra de dame front face
chevelue,
Lors par astuce Duc
à mort attrapé.*

At the foot of the great fallen arch,
the friend is captured forestalled by
the leader. A woman will bear a
son whose face and forehead are
covered with hair; then through
cunning the Duke escapes death.

W: [Wayne] I'm trying to see where the great fallen arch is. It's somewhere in Europe.

D: *What does it look like?*

W: It's a cathedral. I'm not getting clear images on this. The duke is the
father of the child. He is the one betrayed and also the one that
escapes. And he will be betrayed by someone in the church. He
escapes, but he is allowed to escape. There is something of importance
with the child. The child seems to be *molded* by this figure, this
betrayer, the church official.

D: *What is the symbolism of, "his face and forehead are covered with hair"?*

W: It appears to be a child conceived of a dark ritual. (*Sigh*) Some forces
worship good, some forces worship evil. This ritual was one of darkness rather than light. And during the ritual the child was conceived,
and thus is believed to be special.

D: *I thought the symbolism of the face being covered with hair had something to do with hiding him.*

W: Well, hiding is not the right word. Grooming is the correct word.

D: *What is the purpose of all this?*

W: To do another ritual. The purpose is a manifestation of the ego. This
child of ritual is believed to be special, so they'll treat him as special
and thus he will be special. He will be a leader of many people.

D: *In a positive or a negative way?*

W: I can't think of a word to replace "negative," so we'll leave it at that.
Dark would be more effective.

D: *In what country will he be a leader?*

W: He will be the leader of leaders. He will lead many countries. He will
be a very influential individual, whose suggestions will be heeded.

D: *Apparently this will be an important person in our future?*

W: Yes. The prince has already fled. Certain events have already taken
place. Others have not. He will lead many rulers from the Middle East
countries. And he will sit at his place of abode, which is only where
he lives sometimes, not necessarily what he controls. "Control" and
"the leader of" are not the correct terms for this individual. I want to
say that he is a very influential person to listen to. And if you would
call that a leader or a controller, then that is the term. The area that
he will try to control is the Middle East because of its wealth in

minerals and antiquities. It is also a controlling pivotal point. To have control of the Middle East is to have a type of control of the world.

D: *Does Nostradamus have any word or title that we can know this person by?*

W: The only thing I'm getting is, we'll know who he is when it happens. He is here now. He is in training. He's practicing.

CENTURY VI-16

Ce qui ravi sera du jeune Milve,	That which the young hawk will
Par les Normans de France	carry off, by the Normans of
& Picardie:	France and Picardy. The black
Les noirs du temple	ones of the temple at the Black
du lieu de Negrisilve	wood will make an inn and fire
Feront aulberge & feu de	at Lombardy.
Lombardie.	

W: This has to do with a kidnapping. The black ones would be the pursuers that are coming after the kidnapped. It seems the kidnapped is not actually a person. It's something stolen.

D: *The young hawk will kidnap something that is not really a person.*

W: Steal something, I think is a better word.

D: *Do you have any idea what?*

W: Yes. It's a book.

D: *Why would a book be that important?*

W: It is a book of ... a belief system, of practices. I'm trying to think of more correct words than "spells and enchantments." The book contains different meditation techniques, physical techniques and exercises for specific results. It is a book that was carefully guarded and kept by a group of people.

D: *"That which the young hawk will carry off, by the Normans of France and Picardy." Does that have anything to do with that book?*

W: This is the area where it is kept.

D: *The last part is, "the black ones of the temple, at the black wood, will make an inn and fire at Lombardy."*

W: This is where they will go to retrieve their book. They will use their collective knowledge against the thief, who has not yet had the time to keep the book and study it. The young hawk knows the book is important and could be used as a helpful tool in his cause. Yet he will not have it in his possession long enough to study the contents.

D: *Then the black ones are the ones it is stolen from, and they will attempt to get it back. Will they be successful?*

W: Yes. The knowledge in the book was used and practiced by a group of people, a family, a community that did not share the knowledge with the general population. They didn't realize the danger, as they felt protected. They had no way of knowing that anyone even knew of the book's existence. It was like a thief in the night.

D: *I wonder how the young hawk found out about it?*

W: The young hawk knows many things. He could probably get that information in much the same way you're getting this information. But he will not be successful in keeping the book, and I suspect they will guard it more carefully after this. When I look at this individual, he seems very powerful. He has practiced and accentuated his natural gifts. They are similar to the gifts that Nostradamus has with the mind.

D: *But that would be good, wouldn't it?*

W: It could be good.

D: *What do you mean?*

W: Nostradamus could also use his gifts for harm.

D: *Do you think this person will use his gifts in a harmful way?*

W: He will use his gifts in a bid for power.

After Wayne awakened, we discussed this quatrain, and he added his impression:

W: The group that went after him was like a concentrated energy. They knew what their goal was, just as this "young hawk" knew his goal when he came after the book. Once the book was gone, the objective was to get it back, and get it back *soon.* So they went after him, and their concentrated and combined knowledge was able to outsmart him. At this point he doesn't have the power he will have later.

D: *Did you get a feeling this was a Satanic group? Everything was in black.*

W: No, I didn't. It was not Satanic or evil at all. I would say it was a religious group, but religious is not a good term. A coven maybe.

D: *They have secret knowledge that is contained and practiced within their group, and no outsiders are allowed into it.*

W: It seemed as if part of the ritual they performed to get the book back was through the fire. That might not have been mentioned. There was something about fire in the quatrain.

CENTURY X-67

Le tremblement si fort
  au mois de Mai,
Saturne, Caper, Jupiter,
  Mercure au beuf:
Venus aussi Cancer,
  Mars en Nonnay,
Tombera gresse lors plus
  grosse qu'un euf.

A very great trembling in the month of May, Saturn in Capricorn, Jupiter and Mercury in Taurus. Venus also in Cancer, Mars in VIrgo, then hail will fall greater than an egg.

B: [Brenda] He was thinking the astrological person will be better suited for this one. He says this quatrain refers to a situation coming up in the future when the Earth will be about to plunge into another war. And he says it will be happening in the month of May. The "hail bigger than eggs" refers to some of the weapons used. But he's saying the crucial thing is that this situation can be avoided. It would be a matter of communication. Don't let the communication break down. He's saying he saw this particular situation, and thought if it was to happen it would be a matter of a stupid misunderstanding. It is something that could be avoided.

D: *What kind of communication?*

B: Regular communication between the governments.

D: *Can he tell me what countries are involved?*

B: No. He says you'll have to find that out from the astrologer through the astrological signs given. He said if you will recall from past quatrains, in addition to referring to dates they can also refer to countries according to the country's astrological sign. He says once again you must remember he uses multiple meanings. He was trying to squeeze everything in, information-wise, when he put these into epigrams. He says that by following these signs and conjunctions you could pin it down to an approximate date range. But at the same time one can use the symbology to figure out what countries would be involved.

D: *Can he give me an idea of the time period?*

B: No, that's what the astrological signs are for. He says sometimes time is hard to untangle. He can see events and it is difficult to pin it down to a year. But he can see the planets swirling above, and he wrote it down because that will be their positions when this event is occurring. But he will say that it is in *our* future.

D: *That will help. Then this will take a great deal of study from the astrologer. This quatrain has caused much controversy because they thought it meant a great earthquake, or maybe something to do with the shift of the Earth.*

B: He says the Earth will be shaking from the threat of war.

When I showed this quatrain to my astrologer, it would seem to be an easy one to interpret because of the mention of so many explicit astrological signs. But again I discovered Nostradamus had woven an ingenious trick into the quatrain. This quatrain caused quite a bit of excitement a few years ago when it was publicized that it predicted a terrible earthquake for California. When the earthquake didn't materialize, many people said that proved Nostradamus was a fraud, and his predictions were inaccurate. As we have seen before, that depends on the interpretation of the prophecies. So we set out to explain this quatrain in the manner instructed by Nostradamus himself, and came to an amazing conclusion.

The astrologer found that Saturn was in Capricorn from February 1988 to February 1991. In May 1988 almost all of the signs fit: Jupiter and Mercury were in Taurus, and Venus was in Cancer, but Mars was in Pisces instead of Virgo. What did this mean? We studied the French translation because we had already discovered from past experience that the fault often lies there. The French read: *Mars en Nonnay.* Ms.

Cheetham's book explained how she had come to the conclusion that *Nonnay* was Virgo. She said the word came from *Nonne* or *Nonnain,* a nun or virgin.

The astrologer did not agree with this explanation because another translation for "nonnay" was a colloquial slang expression for "zero" or "nothing." She said if you asked someone what they were doing, they could reply, "Nonnay," or "nothing." Taken in this context the quatrain could mean "Mars in zero, or nothing." She then found that on May 22–23, 1988, Mars was zero degrees of Pisces.

I also thought Mars could stand for war, and the interpretation could be "War in Virgo." So by applying Nostradamus' instructions to check the astrological signs for countries, she found certain significant countries represented by the sign of Virgo: Assyria (ancient empire in the region of the upper Tigris River), Mesopotamia, between theTigris and Euphrates Rivers (present-day Turkey and Iraq), Babylonia, Turkey, Greece, Croatia. Countries under the sign of Capricorn: Albania, Bosnia, Bulgaria, Macedonia (an area comprising parts of Greece, Bulgaria and Yugoslavia), parts of Persia, Afghanistan. Countries under Taurus: Persia, Poland, Belorussia (White Russia). A country under Cancer is, of course, the United States.

Can this be coincidence that these names began to appear in the news during 1988 to 1991 as unrest spread through these areas, and the Persian Gulf War began and ended within this timeframe? Also the problems escalated in Yugoslavia, and the breakup of the Soviet empire began. Nostradamus said at this time the Earth would be about to plunge into another war, due to a stupid misunderstanding and a breakdown in communication between governments. He said the quatrain did not refer to an actual earthquake, but that the Earth would be shaking from the threat of war.

With great exhilaration we realized that Nostradamus was correct once again. We had the tremendous satisfaction that comes when you solve a complicated puzzle.

CENTURY V-19

Le grand Royal d'or, daerain augmenté,	The great golden Royal, augmented by brass breaks the covenant; war
Rompu la pache, par jeune ouverte guerre:	is started by a young man. The people are afflicted by a lamented
Peuple affligé par un chef lamenté	leader, the land will be covered
De sang barbare sera converre terre.	with barbarian blood.

B: He says this quatrain refers to the time of the Anti-Christ. There will be great restlessness because of economic difficulties, being referred to as the "golden royal being betrayed by brass." He says the advisers will not be advising wisely, and so things will be very unstable economically. It will make it very easy for the Anti-Christ to start shaking things up—to his advantage.

D: *That's what I thought it might mean by "the war is started by a young man." "The people are afflicted by a lamented leader"?*

B: The leaders who are in power at the time, the duly elected representatives of the people, will be weak, vacillating men. They will not have what it takes, and meanwhile the people will be calling for decisive action.

D: *This will be in the beginning when the economic problems start. That's what he means by the golden royal—it's referring symbolically to a coin?*

B: Yes. And to economics in general.

The following conversation took place upon awakening:

B: I saw that the United States government will not solve its deficit problem. It is beyond control now and it will continue to snowball. When that reaches the ultimate horrible conclusion, it will have a destabilizing effect all over the world which makes it easier for the Anti-Christ.

D: *That figures. It seems as if we're heading into economic trouble everywhere.*

B: Yes. And with a major government like the United States collapsing from it, you know it's going to have some drastic effects. There'll be other things going on as well. But I guess that's the main thing that stuck in my head because I'm an American and it would affect me.

D: *Three years ago when we started this project, we wouldn't have thought these things could really happen. Now I'm not so sure. They look very possible. And it looks, as he said, threateningly close.*

B: Exactly. I get the feeling that when the government and the economy collapses, the United States dollar will be like the Deutsche mark during the 1920s. It will be absolutely worthless. This is my own hypothesizing now, but I think that if the United States currency is basically worthless, the people will turn to other mediums of exchange. They might use various substances and items for bartering, like bushels of wheat and corn and such for basic units of measure. I'm theorizing, but I daresay that in certain areas of the black market there will be substances such as marijuana being used as an item of exchange in place of money.

CENTURY V-16

A son hault pris plus
  la lerme sabee,
D'humaine chair par mort
  en cendres mettre,
A l'isle Pharos par croisars
  perturbee,
Alors qu'à Rodes paroistra
  dur espectre.
	The Sabine tears will no longer be
	of value, human flesh through
	death is burnt to ashes; the island
	of Pharos disturbed by (man of) the
	cross, when at Rhodes a dreadful
	sight is seen.

B: He says this quatrain refers to the fact that some nuclear weapons will be used during the battles with the Anti-Christ in the area of the eastern Mediterranean Sea. That is the terrible sight that will be seen.

D: *That would also refer to "human flesh through death is burnt to ashes." "The Sabine tears will no longer be of value"?*

B: Traditionally the tears of the Sabines were considered symbolic of jewels of wisdom gained through painful experience. People will no longer heed past advice and experience and wisdom, and it will contribute to the holocaust of using a nuclear bomb.

D: *"The island of Pharos disturbed by the man of the cross."*

B: This is referring to the Anti-Christ.

D: *Why is he called the "man of the cross"?*

B: Because before he is totally defeated he continues to try to put himself forward as the natural leader of humanity.

CENTURY IX-32

De fin porphire profond	A deep column of fine porphyry is
collon trouvee	found, inscriptions of the Capitol
Dessoubz la laze	under the base; bones, twisted hair,
escriptz capitolin:	the Roman strength tried, the fleet
Os poil retors Romain	is stirred at the harbor of Mitylene.
force prouvee,	
Classe agiter ay port de Methelin.	

D: *I had trouble pronouncing that word. Is "porphyry" a stone or something?*

B: Your pronunciation is close enough. It is a substance. It refers to one of the ingredients that make up so-called "Greek fire." He says it is something similar to what we would call "tar or asphalt." This quatrain refers to the general political situation at the time when the Anti-Christ first comes. "The column of fine porphyry with the carving of capitals at its base" refers to how basic government and moral structures will be turned upside down, so to speak. Everybody will be confused, and into this confusion the Anti-Christ will come. And that will make it easier for him to take over.

D: *What does "bones and twisted hair" symbolize?*

B: That symbolizes the old values that have been tossed out, but should have been kept: things like fair-dealing and honesty. Things will become so topsy-turvy and so turned around, that it will be rare to find an honest person you can trust dealing with.

D: *And "the Roman strength tried" deals with Italy?*

B: He says that refers to how he will come up from the south into Europe.

D: *Yes, we've covered other quatrains that dealt with his battle plans [in Volume One; see index]. Why would he use the symbolism of the porphyry?*

B: He says one of the key issues of the conflict will be control of the oil fields.

D: *They didn't even try to translate that one.*

CENTURY IX-74

Dans la cité de Fersod homicide,
Fait & fait multe beuf arant
ne macter,
Retour encores aux
honneurs d'Artemide,
Et à Vulcan corps
morts sepultures.

In the homicidal city of Fertsod,
again and again many oxen plough,
not sacrificed; again a return to the
honors of Artemis, and to Vulcan
the corpses of the dead to bury.

B: He says this quatrain refers to the wars that will be taking place with the Anti-Christ. He says it's a representative example of how a city or place will get so involved with fighting and the war that they will forget to cover the basics. The land will be so torn up with war and destruction that the farmers will find it very difficult to farm. The people will have to rely more on hunting to put food on the table.
D: *Is that what is means, "again a return to the honors of Artemis"?*
B: That refers to hunting. Artemis was goddess of the hunt.
D: *And "to Vulcan the corpses of the dead to bury."*
B: That means there will be so many people dead that they will return to cremation because they will not be able to bury them all. Vulcan was the original blacksmith and forger of metal. He was the one who invented how to make fires hot enough to melt metal. That's the type of fire you would need for cremation.

CENTURY X-6

Sardou Nemans si hault
desborderont,
Qu'on cuidera Ducalion
renaistre,
Dans le collosse la plus
part fuiront,
Vesta sepulchre feu
estaint apparoistre.

The Gardon will flood Nîmes so high
that they will think Ducalion has
been reborn. In the colossus the
greater part will flee, Vesta's fire
appears extinguished in the tomb.

B: He says this quatrain refers to an incident in the next world war.
D: *In the* next *world war?*
B: Yes, in the one coming up. The conflict that will be in the process of developing that the Anti-Christ will take advantage of. He says this describes an opposing power bombing the Pentagon.
D: (Surprised) *The Pentagon?*
B: Yes. The "colossus" refers to the Pentagon. He says "Vesta's fire appearing to be extinguished in the tomb" is a descriptive phrase describing the bomb dropping down on the Pentagon with a fiery

wake, exploding there, and being covered up with smoke. And he says, "being extinguished in the tomb" means it will be the type of bomb that kills the people without damaging the structures too much. It will turn the Pentagon into a tomb.

D: *What does the first part mean? "The Gardon will flood Nimes so high they will think Ducalion has been reborn."*

B: He says that refers to the country who casts the bomb. Their political leader will flood the press with misinformation, plus he will draft and conscript so many into his army that it would appear to be a flood of war-making pouring out to sow discord on all involved.

D: *It's not a flood of water, which would seem obvious with the reference to Ducalion. Is Gardon an anagram?*

B: He asks that you spell it.

D: *Well, they said it was an error in the French.*

B: Spell it both ways.

D: *The English has G-A-R-D-O-N, and in the French it's S-A-R-D-O-N. They said that's an error, and Sardon should be Gardon. What does he think?*

B: One moment please. (*Long pause*) He says it is correct with the "S" because the word is "Sardon." He used it in a misleading way so they would think he was making an anagram on the name of a river or perhaps some major body of water. Actually the anagram was on either the name or title of the political leader involved. He says in some cultures titles are used as names, and that sometimes blurs the distinction for seeing it.

D: *So sometimes when they think there's an error it might not be.*

B: This is true. And then sometimes there are.

D: *I think he mentioned that New York might be bombed. But this refers to Washington.*

B: Yes. The object of this would not be the bombing of the United States in general. Specifically, the object would be bombing the military center; that is, the Pentagon, in order to throw the United States sufficiently into chaos to assist the other side in attaining some of their goals. They want to create confusion—perhaps to keep the United States from actively participating for a period of time.

CENTURY X-27

Par le cinquieme & un grand Hercules	Through the fifth and a great Hercules they will come to open the
Viendront le temple ouvrir de main bellique,	temple with the hand of war; one Clement, Julius and Ascans put
Un Clement, Iule & Ascans recules,	back, the sword, the key, the eagle never once felt so great a dislike.
Lespe, clef, aigle n'eurent onc si grand picque.	

B: He says this quatrain refers to when the Anti-Christ takes over the Vatican. One who is inside the Vatican, who is particularly known for his wisdom and foresight, will try to hide some of the more valuable documents, in order to save them from the Anti-Christ. The symbolism regarding the sword, the key, and the eagle represents the hatred that the Anti-Christ feels toward Christian institutions. It will be so great that any other rivalry or hatred that has occurred before will seem very minor by comparison. He says for example, the hatred that has existed between the United States and Russia will seem very minor and mild compared to the hatred the Anti-Christ will have for Christian institutions.

D: *Does he want to explain the symbols of the sword, the key and the eagle?*

B: He says the sword represents the force being used against the Vatican. The key represents the Vatican, in that they have knowledge locked away. And he seems to be saying that the eagle represents the pope.

D: *"Through the fifth and a great Hercules." What are those symbols?*

B: Those were symbolizing the Anti-Christ and his forces.

D: *He is the great Hercules?*

B: That is representing brute strength without wisdom.

D: *What does the number "fifth" represent?*

B: He says that refers to the Anti-Christ, who would be numbered among the great tyrants of history. He says look at your historical works and count such tyrants as Hitler, Napoleon, Attila, and Genghis Khan.

D: *Those other names in the quatrain are Roman names: Clement, Julius and Ascans?*

B: He says he has already explained that part. It refers to the Vatican.

CENTURY VII-7

Sur le combat des grans cheveux legiers,
On criera le grand croissant confond.
De nuict tuer monts, habits de bergiers,
Abismes rouges dans le fossé profond.

Upon the struggle of the great, light horses, it will be claimed that the great crescent is destroyed. To kill by night, in the mountains, dressed in shepherds' clothing, red gulfs in the deep ditch.

B: He says this quatrain refers to unrest in the Middle East. The great light horses refer to atomic power. And he says the destruction of the great crescent refers to what has been called the "fertile crescent." The area that used to be Mesopotamia (Iraq), and the area of Israel, Jordan, Sudan, the Middle East. Countries that used to be, a thousand years ago, fertile, but are now basically dry desert. The red gulfs refers to the bloodshed that will be taking place.

D: *"To kill by night in the mountains, dressed in shepherd's clothing."*

B: He says this refers to stealthy attacks. The Anti-Christ's forces in the Middle East will disguise themselves as countrymen of the country they are trying to take over or destroy. The way they will be dressed and the way they will appear, the other countries will underestimate them and think them harmless.

CENTURY VI-47

*Entre deux monts les deux grans assemblés
Delaisseront leur simulté secrette:
Brucelle & Dolle par Langres acablés,
Pour à Malignes executer leur peste.*

The two great ones, assembled between two mountains will give up their secret quarrel. Brussels and Dôle overcome by Langres in order to execute their pestilence at Malines.

B: He says this quatrain refers to the United States and the Soviet Union standing together to fight the Anti-Christ.

D: *That's their secret quarrel, because they have been enemies in the past. It says these ones are overcome "in order to execute their pestilence at Malines."*

B: That will be one of the areas where they'll be fighting the Anti-Christ.

CENTURY IX-44

*Migres migre de Genesve trestous,
Saturne d'or en fer se changers,
Le contre RAYPOZ exterminera tous,
Avant l'a ruent de ciel signes fera.*

Leave, leave Geneva everyone, Saturn will change from gold into iron. Those against **RAYPOZ** will all be exterminated. Before the rush the sky will show signs.

D: *Raypoz is a word they don't understand.* (I spelled it and tried to pronounce it.)

B: Close enough. He says this quatrain refers to the time when the Anti-Christ is taking over Europe. Due to the great threat he will be posing to the world balance of order, Switzerland will not be neutral for the first time in all of its history. Switzerland will take the side of those who oppose the Anti-Christ. This is what is meant by "Saturn will change from gold to iron." Currently Switzerland and Geneva are represented by gold because they are neutral and because of their banks and financial structure. But in this situation they will be fighting against the Anti-Christ, and so their assets will be geared to warfare, represented by iron, for the weapons and such. And so the warning to leave Geneva will be because there will be bombs dropping on and around Geneva. He says there will be signs in the sky, referring to the fact that the people will know the Anti-Christ's army is advancing, because of the aircraft flying over and dropping bombs.

And because of the shells and such being shot into the city. They will see the rockets streaking across the sky. He says he uses Saturn, in this case, to represent patience and wisdom. The Swiss people have been very patient across many centuries by staying neutral, and they have been wise to do this. But when this particular conflict comes along, they realize this is a case where you can't stay neutral because you're going to be swallowed up anyway. So they join those that are against the Anti-Christ because they're fighting *for* freedom. The Swiss are *fiercely* independent and *fiercely* in favor of freedom. He says Raypoz is representing the man who will become known as the Anti-Christ.

D: *Is that an anagram of his name, or how does it represent him?*

B: He says in the Anti-Christ's culture the people have something like a traditional title that is considered part of their name in addition to their family names. First Nostradamus got the title and one of the names the Anti-Christ will be known by, and condensed them together into one word. And then he made an anagram of that.

D: *So it really is taken from two longer words. Are the letters reversed?*

B: He says they are moderately jumbled around. And he says those who like to break codes and try to figure things out should have fun working with it. He feels he was quite clever in the way he switched the letters around.

D: *The translators thought it might be a name, an unsolved anagram. They're saying this quatrain refers to the Protestants and the Vatican because Calvin was from Geneva.*

B: He says that could be a reasonable interpretation, but he was mainly talking about he who will be known as the Anti-Christ because he will have such an adverse effect on world history.

D: *Does the Anti-Christ end up taking Switzerland?*

B: He says he thinks he probably will take Switzerland.

D: *I think Nostradamus once said the Anti-Christ wanted the money there.*

B: Yes. He says he can't tell if the Anti-Christ successfully gets the money or not because he feels that many of the Swiss will start taking the money out of the country by various secret ways. Thus it will basically end up being an empty victory for the Anti-Christ.

CENTURY IX-14

Mis en planure chaulderone *d'infecteurs,* *Vin, miel & l'huile,* *& bastis sur forneaulx* *Seront plongez sans mal* *dit mal facteurs* *Sept. fum extaint au* *canon des borneaux.*	The dyers' cauldrons put in a flat place, wine, honey and oil and built over furnaces. They will be drowned, without saying or doing an evil thing, seven of Borneaux, the snake extinguished from the cannon.

B: He says this quatrain refers to the establishment of a research facility where scientists come and expand human knowledge. But due to the political situation the people in charge of this research project will be betrayed and the project canceled. The wine, honey and oil represent the resources put into it in their pursuit of knowledge. It represents economic wealth. The fires underneath represent hidden knowledge that they were trying to expose. The snake extinguished from the cannon represents the research project being canceled. The snake is being used symbolically as the bringer of knowledge from the book of Genesis. The snake gave the apple to Eve and opened her eyes and extended her knowledge. The cannon represents the political situation. Apparently this particular research facility interfered with the Anti-Christ's overall plans. Had this research facility not been closed down, the Anti-Christ would have been defeated much sooner. It is something that the people who fight the Anti-Christ will be desperately needing.

D: *Then the "dyers' cauldrons" represents the facility. Why does he use that symbolism?*

B: Because the cauldron is one of the tools used by alchemists in their pursuit of knowledge. They use it for melting down metal, and for trying to find the Philosopher's Stone or what-have-you. That is why he used this symbolism. The dyers' cauldron referring that the knowledge they were seeking was knowledge that could be used in warfare as well as in peace.

D: *The way the word is written it indicates people that dye clothes.*

B: Yes. He says when dyers dye clothes they change the color. He's using that to represent something that can be changed from one use to another. For instance, changed from white for peace to red for war.

D: *There's one more, the "seven of Borneaux."*

B: He says that represents some of the backers, the supporters of this research facility. They will have to disband.

D: *Is Borneaux a country or city?*

B: No. He says that represents a family who in his time were active in the pursuit of knowledge, a family of seekers and learners. This family would help others who were not as well off as themselves, but who were wanting to seek and learn. So he was using that to symbolize people of like mind who wish to be supporters of knowledge.

D: *Can he see where this facility is located?*

B: He says this research facility will be somewhere on the central east coast of the United States.

D: *Is he able to see what they are working on?*

B: He thinks it is probably nuclear research. But the way they are going about it, they're not researching nuclear bombs or anything like that. They're researching things like nuclear-powered medical equipment, and various devices that are very intricate.

D: *I would think those would be things they would want to continue researching.*

B: But the Anti-Christ does not want those against him to have those things. That's why he has it destroyed, to hurt his enemies.

D: *That's what it means by they "will be drowned." I'd like to read him what the interpreters say, but I'm afraid it will make him angry.*

B: He says his mustache needs a good bristle anyway.

D: (Laugh) *They never even attempted to translate it. They said, "A typical, unintelligible Nostradamus quatrain at its worst."*

B: Well, he's not angry. He's just nodding his head and saying, "Well, I guess I did a good job." He finds it reassuring, because if centuries of people have not been able to decipher what he was writing, then he doesn't need to worry about the Catholic Church figuring it out any time soon.

D: *Not that one. It has very complicated symbolism. The church might have been able to recognize that family name, but that would be about all.*

B: This is true.

CENTURY VI-11

Des sept rameaux à trois seront reduicts,	The seven branches will be reduced to three, the elder ones will be
Les plus aisnez seront surprins par mort,	surprised by death. Two will be attracted towards fratricidal
Fraticider les deux seront seduicts,	(strife): the conspirators will die while asleep.
Les conjurez en dormans seront morts.	

W: [Wayne] This deals with the future. There are people in power that actually control, you might even say, world history. These people are not the president, not the kings. The controllers are unknown people and their numbers will dwindle from seven to three. This will be during a time of great chaos in the world. It will not be as a result of four dying, but in *conjunction* with four dying.

D: *Are those four individuals or groups?*

W: They are individuals.

D: *It says, "the seven branches will be reduced to three."*

W: When three are in power rather than seven, it is still a majority but in a different sense. Whereas it would take four to be against three, two could be against one. It has something to do with brother killing brother in that power struggle. The seven are not blood brothers, but symbolic brothers. They are ... like a fraternity. This fraternity is not well known. It is known by their puppets.

D: *But not by the people at large?*

W: Correct.

D: *It sounds like this will occur during a time when things are, more or less, out of their hands. I would think if they were controlling events they wouldn't allow things to get to that stage.*

W: Well, they haven't done a good job. Control is manageable and unmanageable. Circumstances often dictate how much control any individual or group of people can have. To be able to manipulate stock prices, to be able to manipulate food growth and money, precious gems; to be able to strangle a market in one area and free flow it in another area, is all something that can be controlled. Population, on the other hand, is something that got out of control. And of course that's what wars and disease are all about, trying to control it.

D: *The natural control, you mean?*

W: Natural and unnatural. Natural disasters and diseases control population of the Earth as well as *un*natural disasters and disease control a *portion* of the population. The less to control, the easier to manage.

D: *Then the population increased to a point where they could not control it the way they used to?*

W: It's more difficult.

D: *Is this a part of what causes their downfall, or is it more complicated than that?*

W: Part of what causes their downfall is death of their members, if indeed a "downfall" is the correct term. The other part is disharmony, disagreement.

D: *What would be a more correct term?*

W: A loosening or a slipping of power that is not lost, but is harder to grasp, to pull back and keep.

D: *Then Nostradamus sees these people as very important to history.*

W: Yes, this group of seven. It hasn't been the same seven people controling the world for the past hundred years. It is an inheritance.

D: *Like a responsibility. I think we have spoken of this group before, so I am aware of it.*

This apparently refers to the secretive cabal described in both Volumes One and Two (see index, this volume).

Scientists around the world agree that increasing population is a major problem for the Earth at this time. They say that the world's population is growing at an unprecedented rate of almost 100 million people every year, and the total could nearly double to 10 billion people by the middle of the next century. They say something must be done to avoid possible "irreversible damage to the Earth's capacity to sustain life."

D: *Nostradamus has spoken to us many times about a figure he called the Anti-Christ.*

P: [Pam] Nostradamus would like to say there is a figure whose thoughts dwell in the realms of darkness. Whose motives are distorted and who has expended knowledge in the realms of manipulating power. This person has conscious awareness of the great power we all possess, but this person also has conscious awareness of how to use and manipulate this power. This person is of the lowest, most disharmonious vibration. This is a person seen in Nostradamus' darkest nightmares and greatest fears, who does possess power to wreak great havoc and distortions on truth.

Pam then gave a description that has been echoed by all the subjects: a handsome young dark charismatic man.

D: *Can Nostradamus tell you what country this man will come from?*

P: This man seems to be in the Middle East. Nostradamus is showing me a map. I see Africa, and the Suez Canal, and then I see Saudi Arabia. That is an interesting question to myself, the reporter, because I would not have said "Saudi Arabia." However, it looks like the top part of Saudi Arabia. I don't know the countries that are there, so I can't tell you the name.

D: *As you look at this figure, can you see what he is doing at this time period in the beginning of 1989?*

P: I see he is conferring with many powerful people. These are not necessarily governmental people, but some are. They have much money and much power. And they also have a great deal of ego, and a strong desire to have *more* power and *more* money. These people are like a "board of directors," if you will, who meet on a regular basis with this man. They have a network of some kind.

D: *Where do you see him meeting with these people?*

P: In various locations. I see him traveling about by airplane. When you asked that, I immediately thought "London," and then I also thought "Buenos Aires." So obviously he flies.

D: *He meets with different people in different locations?*

P: They come to him in the main.

D: *If they came to him, where would they meet him?*

P: It seems very desert-like, almost like tents in the desert. Far from prying eyes, and newspapers, reporters. Away from anyone who would be curious enough to try to see why these people were coming here and what they were doing. He seems very worldly. He can adopt the western dress of an American businessman and walk through an airport undetected. He doesn't seem to have a job or any visible means of support, other than these rich, rich people. He seems to be taken care of by this group of people. And I might say, they're all men. I see men in suits. I have no distinct visual images, except that there are many of them.

D: *Do they have a headquarters?*

P: Their "headquarters" is a loose term for when they gather with this man at his place in the desert. The rest of the time these are powerful corporate leaders, business people, who have their own little empires, their own high-rise buildings, their own *personal* headquarters.

D: *They don't have a leader among themselves.*

P: They definitely give him their power. *He* is their leader. He has a very magnetic personality, and is very forceful. I might say he's physically *attractive,* which is magnetic. But he also has that charisma that makes people *want* to come to him.

D: *This is not similar to a religious type leader though. They also have a power, a charisma, over people.*

P: No! He gives *no* credit to God or the creative source, the power of love. No, that does not exist in his realm of thinking at all.

D: *Do these men look like different nationalities?*

P: Yes, they are. They have the financial resources to construct what appears to be underground cities equipped for human habitation when the surface becomes unlivable. They are building these at his request.

D: *Do you have any idea where these underground cities are?*

P: I see many of them all over the place. I see them in England and Brazil. I don't know all the names of the countries. It looks like several, maybe five or more.

D: *Are there any in the United States?*

P: We have underground cities in this country, yes. But right now they are built by *our* government and we are not dealing with this man. Although our government is *aware* that this man exists; they are not connected with this "board of directors" at this time. But the board also knows of the underground cities that have been built by others than themselves. Thus they have plans for taking them when necessary.

D: *Why are they building these underground cities?*

P: They know that the surface of the Earth will become uninhabitable, due to the machinations of this fellow. He will some way—and at this point it seems more psychically than physically—convince those paranoid people who have the power to detonate massive explosions, to go forth and do so.

D: *Then who will be living in these underground cities?*

P: These rich people, their families, and others that they choose, but not the general populace. It seems that there *is* a plan to eliminate the mass numbers of human beings who inhabit the surface of the Earth, so there can be a starting over, if you will, after a time lapse.

D: *What would be the purpose of destroying a great deal of people?*

P: *Most* of the people.

D: *What would be their purpose? We can all live here peacefully.*

P: But these people cannot control *all* the human beings on the planet, as it exists now. It was easier in the past when there was less population. It is impossible for these men to control four or five billion people.

D: *That sounds drastic. They would rather eliminate people so they could have their own little world?*

P: Absolutely. We're not dealing with clarity, harmony and beauty.

We're dealing with distortion taken to the ultimate distortion.

D: *That doesn't sound* sane.

P: You could label it "insane," yes, for it is.

D: *Is that how far their plans have gone—just to construct these cities?*

P: At this point, yes. They're not ready to go any further at this point (in 1989). The cities are not supplied and capable of sustaining all of those they select to inhabit the *new* planet, as they choose to call it.

D: *Are they planning to come forth at a later time, or are they going to stay underground?*

P: They assume they will have to live underground for many years, but not their entire lifetime. This is a plan for them and their progeny to rule the planet. They have very short-term thinking though. They realize that the world will be uninhabitable for some period of time. But they have very large egos, so they think they will personally be alive to *re*enter the external atmosphere.

D: *They're not thinking that they might contaminate the surface to the point where nobody could live on it, themselves included.*

P: That is not what they think. You have to remember that ego and *big desire* distort reality, or their *perception* of what reality is.

D: *Won't there be people that will have to do the work in these underground cities?*

P: Those are some that they will choose.

D: *They won't necessarily be family or members of the group.*

P: Absolutely not! They will choose many to carry out the most mundane, trivial things to do, to take care of them. They'll be chosen beforehand. But many of those who do these menial jobs will not be there of their own free will. They will *take* people. Actually some people have already been taken.

D: *It seems as if this would take a great deal of money.*

P: They have it.

D: *Can he show you in the mirror this group's next plan?*

P: The plans after the cities are equipped is to move the families and the chosen people there, and become functioning cities. They must have all systems in place. This is incredibly complicated. They need an artificial light source, and of course, pure water. There has to be some way to grow food. It looks as if they choose a hydroponic way. I see vast gardens already underway. They have to create means of transportation. But one of their *big* problems right now seems to be communicating throughout the planet from this underground city system. How do you communicate between, say, London, Beirut and Buenos Aires, if you can't use surface or ærial means? So they're working out their communication systems. They must have people in place with all systems functioning before they themselves will enter the cities. Once *all* of these men and their families have entered, then they're ready to go forth with the detonations.

D: *That is the next plan, to detonate on the surface?*

P: That is correct.

D: *Will the Anti-Christ do this from these underground cities or from the surface?*

P: He could do it from anywhere.

D: *But is he that powerful, or is it the group that is powerful?*

P: He *is* powerful because the group has *given* him that power. This is an aberration of nature that he has been able to consciously gather this power unto himself. This is not what we would call "normal" by any stretch of the imagination. To have this much conscious control of power, and to channel it only in negative, destructive, harmful ways is an aberration. They came upon a plan of collecting and focusing negative powers on one individual who would then be able to utilize them. He chooses to do what he is directed to do by this group, but he doesn't think he's a pawn or puppet. He has this enormous ego and believes that *he* is the generator of this energy, not the recipient of the collective negative energies. He doesn't have it straight in his own mind how he's getting it. But there are forces at work at this moment. There are many visitors from other realms who are here to assure that whatever distorted power he may project will be counterbalanced by their energies. This man, this force, is known. Not particularly well-known on this planet, but he is known *off* this planet as a ... what I see looks like a decay. He's known as a festering sore. These extraterrestrial entities exist in various places on the planet, and their purpose is balance and harmony. They *are* counteracting agents. Once you know there is something so terribly distorted and out-of-balance, it becomes incumbent upon you to send help. And it's here. But the Anti-Christ's ego doesn't allow him to say there may be forces even stronger than himself.

D: *Is there anything we can do to stop that group, besides letting people know about them?*

P: It seems that in the world as we know it, there are no such things as accidents. And this group of people exists, not by accident. The way I feel this story evolving, it is for the purpose of bringing forth this information in order to uplift all of humanity. So for us to go in at this time and physically remove them, for example: blow up the underground cities, or assassinate this man, would then relieve *all* people from their responsibility of cleaning up their own emotional actions and judgments. We *need* to change. This would certainly be an impelling reason to change.

CENTURY IV-88

Le grand Antoine du nom
  de faicte sordide
De Phthiriase à son
  dernier rongé,
Un qui de plomb voudra
  estre cupide,
Passant le port d'esleu
  sera plongé.

Anthony, great in name, in his actions base, at the end will be devoured by lice. One who is eager for lead, passing the harbor will be drowned by the elected one.

B: He says this quatrain refers to the fall of the Anti-Christ. The Anti-Christ will be great in name. His name will be on everybody's lips all over the world, but what he will be doing will be very evil.

D: *The name Anthony is not his real name, is it?*

B: No, it is an anagram for Anti-Christ.

D: *"At the end will be devoured by lice."*

B: That means the common people, whom he considered to be dirt beneath his feet, no better than lice, will rise up, pull him down and defeat him.

D: *"One who is eager for lead, passing the harbor will be drowned by the elected one."*

B: That means he will, in his quest for power, overreach himself. And the wise one will be able to defeat him and cast him down.

D: *Who is the wise one?*

B: The one who will come after the Anti-Christ to help rebuild the world. The great genius.

D: *This quatrain is a little complex, as all of these are. The translators, of course, are associating it with someone named Anthony, although they can't understand who this Anthony is.*

B: He says he isn't surprised.

D: *They just called it a difficult prophecy.*

CENTURY VIII-7

Verceil, Milan donra intelligence,
Dedans Tycin sera faite la paye.
Courir par Siene eau, sang,
  feu par Florence.
Unique choir d'hault en
  bas faisant maie.

Vercelli, Milan will give the news, the wound will be given at Pavia. To run in the Seine, water, blood and fire through Florence, the unique one falling from high to low calling for help.

B: He says that quatrain refers to the fall of the Anti-Christ. The first line represents the underground network of those who are working to pull down the Anti-Christ. When the time comes for them to coordinate their efforts for the big push, they are able to swiftly get the word sent out and everyone coordinated.

D: *"To run in the Seine, water, flood and fire, through Florence."*
B: He says that represents the power of the people themselves. Even
   though they are of different nationalities and different backgrounds,
   basic humanity will pull them through and help them to stay united
   for overthrowing the Anti-Christ. Next line.
D: *"The unique one falling from high to low, calling for help."*
B: He says that line is self-evident. The actual overthrow of the Anti-
   Christ.
D: *I would think he would be so well established that it would be very
   hard to overthrow him.*
B: He says he won't be established *that* well because of the way he got
   there to start with. He says he'll actually be like a man trying to stand
   on a floor covered with shot.

The word confused me, but I assumed it was something they used in
their pistols of the time period, probably similar to bee-bees.

B: From the day he began he was already building his downfall because
   of the methods he used.
D: *This shows that the people will have something to say about it. They
   will have a part in all of this.*
B: Yes, the underground and the people.

CENTURY IX-2

Du hault du mont	A voice is heard from the top of
Aventin voix ouie,	Aventine Hill. Go, go, all on both
Vuidez, vuidez de tous	sides! The anger will be appeased
les deux costez,	by the blood of the red ones. From
Du sang des rouges sera	Rimini and Prato, Colonna expelled.
l'ire assomie,	
D'Arimin Prate,	
Columna debotez.	

B: He says that quatrain refers to the end of the time of troubles, when
   the Anti-Christ is being defeated. The red ones refer to known followers of the Anti-Christ. And the shout from both sides of Aventine
   Hill refers to the fact that everybody will be united against the Anti-
   Christ. People of different factions that disagreed before about other
   things, are agreed in working together for the downfall of the Anti-
   Christ. He says all known followers and agents of the Anti-Christ will
   be pulled down and killed. Towards the end they'll be so desperate
   that they won't even bother with jury trials.
D: *"The anger will be appeased by the blood of the red ones."*
B: Yes. The anger they feel toward the Anti-Christ. The red ones are the
   followers, as I've already said.
D: *At least this one is a little more positive, because it's showing events*

occurring towards the end. Most of the quatrains deal with the war while it's going on.

B: He says he felt the most help would be needed to deal with it while it was going on. Towards the end when things are winding up, it's going to be already decided.

This next quatrain contains two strange words that have puzzled Nostradamus scholars for generations. They are thought to be anagrams, but have never been successfully translated. As usual, I had difficulty pronouncing them. He asked for the spelling before we could proceed.

CENTURY X-96

Religion du nom des
mers vaincra,
Contre le secte fils Adaluncatif,
Secte obstinee deploree craindra,
Des deux blessez par
Aleph & Aleph.

The religion called after the seas will overcome, against the sect of the son Adaluncatif; the stubborn lamentable sect will fear the two men wounded by **A & A**.

D: *That last part has been translated as "wounded by A and A," instead of Aleph & Aleph" because they are letters in Hebrew and Arabic.*

B: (*He abruptly corrected my pronunciation of Aleph.*) He says there's no "t" at the end of it. He says the Hebrew alphabet is: aleph, beth, gimel, daleth, he, vau, zayin, cheth, teth, and he goes on. But he says it does start with Aleph. He says this refers to when the world is recovering after the Anti-Christ. When the Anti-Christ is gone, most of the organized religions will be in total chaos, particularly Christianity. Peace will be the main philosophical viewpoint everyone will agree upon. Everyone wants peace. Therefore Nostradamus used the phrase "the religion named after the seas will overcome." And he says "Pacific," the name of the Pacific Ocean, is one of the words that can also be used to mean "peace." He's saying that feeling will be so strong it will be almost like a religion. It will take precedence over all other religions and beliefs. Various people will perhaps stay with their old religion, but their fore-most feelings will be for peace.

D: *Now we're getting down to that strange name—Adaluncatif.*

B: He says that refers to the Anti-Christ.

D: *Why did he use such a strange word?*

B: He says it is referring to certain pieces of information from the Kabbala. Those who are familiar with that type of information will be able to figure out more concerning the Anti-Christ.

D: *Now we come to the letters. "The stubborn lamentable sect will fear the two men wounded by Aleph and Aleph."*

B: (*He again corrected my pronunciation.*) No "t," just Aleph. (*Patronizingly*) He says that symbolizes the defeat of the Anti-Christ. He says he has already explained this quatrain. Why do you keep ...?

D: *Because those are the first letters of the Arabic alphabet?*

B: No. "The lamentable sect" refers to the Anti-Christ and his followers. He is defeated, first by the fighter, the hero, the main one who will rise up to fight against the Anti-Christ (Ogmios). And then he will also be defeated by the genius who will come later.

D: *So the letters A and A refer to them. That's what I wanted to clarify. The translators thought he meant some kind of Arabic name beginning with A. That's as close as they could come.*

B: (*Pause*) I think he's referring to a French idiom here. It really doesn't make much sense. But he says, "Okay, so they had beet porridge for breakfast."

D: *Beet porridge?*

B: I get the impression that a person would not voluntarily eat beet porridge for breakfast. And those that do have got to be crazy anyway.

D: *Oh, it's some kind of idiom.* (Chuckle) *He probably has a hard time understanding some of our slang.*

CENTURY IX-75

De l'Ambraxie & du pays
  de Thrace
Peuple par mer mal &
  secours Gaulois,
Perpetuelle en Provence la trace,
Avec vestiges de leur coustume &
  loix.

From Arta & the country of Thrace, people ill by sea, help from the Gauls; in Provence their perpetual trace and remnants of their customs and laws.

B: He says this quatrain refers to after the Anti-Christ is vanquished, and Europe is trying to recover. It particularly refers to how people of different nationalities and backgrounds will work together to help recover. He says "ill by sea" refers to two things: firstly, it refers to the fact that the Anti-Christ came over the sea, and so the illness came by sea, so to speak. Secondly, due to the type of warfare the Anti-Christ waged, part of the land and ocean will be poisoned from his weapons, and it will kill off many of the fish and other oceanic life.

D: *And this will be afterwards when they're trying to regain and rebuild their civilization?*

B: Rebuild, yes.

D: *And that's what is says, "trace and remnants of their customs and laws."*

Chapter 15

Concerning Extraterrestrials
and the Future

SEVERAL INTERPRETATIONS OF THE QUATRAINS concerned aliens or
extraterrestrials. This surprised me in the beginning of our work, but it
did not seem to bother Nostradamus. He had grown accustomed to seeing
the "Others" or "Watchers," as he called them. He called them this
because they were not like us; they were "other" than us. And it had been
revealed to him that these beings had been watching our planet and its
development for eons of time. He knew that his church did not accept
such an idea, but he had no other explanation for some of the strange
scenes that he saw in his mirror. He knew they were showing creatures
that were not native to our planet. Nostradamus had been delving into
the unknown for so long that nothing really startled or frightened him any
more. It only depressed him to see what humans were capable of doing
to their own kind. He was also sad because he could never share many
of the things he had seen with anyone; they were too unbelievable. I can
sympathize with that because even in our supposedly advanced age we
still have difficulty dealing with the possible reality of aliens from outer
space. If *we* have difficulty, I can imagine the almost impossible situation
Nostradamus had put himself in. He knew he would have to carry most
of his secrets to the grave—unless he succeeded in passing them to
our time.

The following are some of the most impossible interpretations to
believe: his visions of ETs (extraterrestrials).

CENTURY V-2

Seps conjurés au banquet *feront luire,* *Contre les trois le fer hors* *de navire:* *L'un des deux classes* *au grand fera conduire* *Quand par le mail.* *Denier au front lui tire.*	Seven conspirators at a banquet will cause their weapons to flash against the three who come from the ship. One of the two will take the fleet to the leader when the other will shoot him in the forehead through his armor.

W: [Wayne] I believe this has to do with a meeting between world leaders and extraterrestrials.

D: (I was surprised.) *Oh? Do you want to elaborate?*

W: The extraterrestrials will be betrayed by a group of seven. One will be shot, and one will escape to warn his people.

D: *I can see why the seven would be called "conspirators," but it says this occurs at a banquet.*

W: This is not a real banquet. That is symbolism meaning that the meeting was gathered under the guise of friendliness.

D: *Is it normal to have meetings with extraterrestrials at the time this takes place?*

W: It is normal. This take place in the future, although meetings with extraterrestrials have been going on for some time.

D: *Then this isn't the first meeting they've had with the world leaders. Why did they betray them?*

W: Over fear of losing control.

D: *The leaders were afraid of losing control to the extraterrestrials?*

W: Yes, partially because they have more or less dug themselves a hole they can't get out of.

D: *What do you mean?*

W: The world as shaped by these seven has gone awry, and the need for outside help was offered and accepted. The killing that took place in this meeting was a message of control, of how much help to be accepted.

Are these seven members of the secret Cabal whom Nostradamus has spoken of before?

D: *Can he tell you when this might take place?*

W: Before the 20th century is over.

D: *I thought it might be farther in the future. Can you see what those extraterrestrials look like, or are you just getting impressions?*

W: The impressions I'm getting are that they are smaller with hairless bodies.

D: *Did they have any malicious intent?*

W: No, they were very loving, forgiving creatures.

D: *Then maybe it won't interfere with the plans they have to help us.*

W: It will interfere. It will not halt.

CENTURY IV-87

Un filz du Roi tant
de langues aprins,
A son aisné au regne different:
Son pere beau au plus
grand filz comprins
Fera perir principal adherent.

The son of a king, having learnt
many languages, different from
his elder in the kingdom. His
father-in-law understanding well
the elder son, will cause the main
adherent to perish.

N: [Nina] I'm seeing into another time when we have been studied. When people were coming and infiltrating, and not *all* of them are benevolent. They come from other times and universes. And they have far greater capacities to use their minds, and have studied us and our languages and can infiltrate. These are beings of the skies. Some are benevolent, and some want to control.

D: *You said it was another time. Do you mean in the future or what?*

N: Yes. It is a time when there is major communication. When it has become the norm to have communication and traffic in the skies from other spheres, other planets, other solar systems. They believed they were coming here as teachers, to be of service and help. And instead of doing this and bringing us to their level, this one being became too encouraged by control, because we were so easily controlled and captured through the mind. So this is a time in the future.

D: *Why does he use the symbolism of relatives: father-in-law, sons?*

N: I see part of this as symbolism for planetary travel. Oh, it's hard to explain this picture. I see them in their big meeting room looking at this map of various solar systems. They have it divided into different areas of control. As the power progresses it is divided into parenting areas just as different levels of a family. But as in any family they have their own ideas. In this meeting room on one of their airships they know who has control of which sector, and the power is varied. So I guess in this way you might compare it to marriages. It takes time to discover the groups that are negative. They are all very adept at using all their brain capacity, but every now and then there is a mutant, and it can take some time to locate them because they cover vast areas.

D: *I would think when they reached that stage they would be beyond anything negative.*

N: That is true of many of them, but just as we evolve, some evolve slower. It's only through this process of purification, elimination, that you develop what is needed.

D: *And this one negative group or person causes trouble on the Earth.*

N: Yes. I see this as very far into the future. It could even be century segments.

D: *So it's nothing* we *have to worry about.*

N: I don't believe so, if I'm getting this correctly. I am still asking for clarification, as I know these are *his* visions and *his* truths. And I know this does not have to necessarily be what really happens. But the main thing I see in this quatrain is that it's the accepted thing. It's a natural, normal, every-day occurrence to have strange, unusual vehicles in and out of our space. And it is commonplace to have all different kinds of beings communicating with our planet.

D: *Maybe it becomes so common we don't think something could happen. There's always that chance because no one is totally perfect.*

CENTURY X-99

La fin le loup, le lyon,
beuf, & l'asne,
Timide dama seront
avec mastins,
Plus ne cherra à eux
la douce manne,
Plus vigilance & custode
aux mastins.

The end of the wolf, the lion, ox and the ass, the timid deer will be with the mastiffs. No longer will the sweet manna fall upon them; more vigilance and guarding for the mastiffs.

N: I'm seeing a picture of the universe. And above that I'm seeing star formations that I do not understand.

This had happened before and since Nina knew nothing about astrology she was never able to explain it to me. I thought this added validity because she was being shown something she did not understand. That was proof that she was not fantasizing it.

N: I believe this is talking about the universe as a whole, and various little sections of it fighting against one another. And I think the star patterns I'm seeing are giving us a focus on time.

D: *Do you mean a war?*

N: I think it's universal destruction, man against man. Man destroying this planet. It seems like greed and power. What man is doing to man, and what man is doing to the planet.

I asked her to attempt to explain the star formations.

N: He says it signifies a time when the animals of the zodiac come together, and it's the climax of all the troubles. When things between humans and Earth will get as bad as they can possibly be. Then there will be much loss of lives, much disease. That is when the changes will occur.

D: *What will cause this loss of life and disease?*

N: I see war within certain countries. I see bombs going off. I see volcanoes and fire, and destruction on all levels. I see disease. It is a right time for the new beginning.

D: *What happens to bring it all to a head? Is there an event?*

N: Yes. I see one madman pushing a button to create an explosion, and that being counteracted by other countries. That puts humans against humans again, and another war. The world has to choose sides.

D: *But you said it would be a new beginning.*

N: Yes. After the destruction there will be a new unity, a new coming together, a new awareness, new communications from beyond. I see the original power that started the conflict being taken over and quieted. But out of this destruction the world realizes they cannot tolerate any more of this and survive. And then the new forces come in. There will be many new allies. We will be in such awe and need of these new forces that there will be a whole new attitude.

D: *Do you mean the allies will not be of Earth?*

N: No, they will not. They are from other areas that have been watching over us.

D: *Let me see if he can clarify the symbolism. It says, "the end of the wolf."*

N: That refers to the end of the instigator of the war.

D: *"The lion, ox and the ass."*

N: I see the lion and the ox up in the sky in various formations.

D: *Are they signs of the zodiac?*

N: Yes. I see them represented in the sky.

D: *What does he show you about the ass?*

N: He shows me strength and hard work. A beast of burden. I think this is over the Middle East. I think these are star formations that represent that part of the world. Symbolic.

D: *"The timid deer will be with the mastiffs."*

N: I see that star formation over the Soviet Union. It seems to represent many of the smaller countries coming together.

This quatrain was interpreted in early 1989, several months before the Communist satellite countries began to rebel against Russia. I did not realize the significance at the time, so I did not ask any more questions concerning that.

D: *Can we get a time from the star formations? I know it's difficult when you don't know the constellations.*

N: I hear "the strength of Orion," but I don't know what that means.

D: *What else do you hear?*

N: That the dogs in the sky are symbolic. Maybe they're representing a time when they will be guarding, to make sure that the right parties win.

D: *It's all symbolism.*

CENTURY IX-12

Le tant d'argent de Diane & Mercure Les simulacres au lac seront trouvez, Le figulier cherchant argille neufve Lui & les siens d'or seront abbrevez.	The great amount of silver of Diana & Mercury, the images will be found in the lake. The sculptor looking for new clay, both he and his followers will be soaked in gold.

P: [Pam] My first impressions were that the silver referred to an actual extraterrestrial mining operation. I saw planets in the initial sentences. The lake seemed to refer to an actual mercury lake that is located on another planet. Mercury, of course, looks silvery. They both have the same shine. And the person who discovers this and utilizes it will find treasures beyond the physical mineral metals. The gold will not be a natural resource of precious metal. It will be contact with the living beings of this other planet.

D: *Do you mean that human beings from Earth will find a treasure on another planet?*

P: Yes. They are already searching for sources of metals. These precious metals exist in concentrated amounts on other planets. The particular planet that I see has giant resources. The mercury is in fact in the form of a lake. It's so big, so shiny, so concentrated in one area, that it is visible even from space. I can see it in the mirror as a giant, shiny, silvery, shimmering, moving metal lake. This is so exciting to the geologists who wish to mine other planetary bodies. They found this *huge* resource that they can go and get, and that's very important to the scientific technological community. However, what they find when they get there is infinitely greater than silver or mercury. Gold, as you know, is valued and prized more highly. But the gold the humans receive is the realization that other life forms inhabit this place. It is not literal that they will be covered in gold.

D: *Is this other planet in our solar system?*

P: I'm having difficulty with that because immediately when you said the word "Diana," I was shown what I thought was a planet in our solar system. I have no name for it. I have been searching since the word "Diana" appeared in the quatrain. This seems to be a planet that we have access to, although perhaps it could be a satellite.

D: *You mean a satellite of a planet?*

P: Yes. We call them "moons."

D: *Does Nostradamus think this is one of the reasons for the space explorations, to discover new resources?*

P: Yes, of course it is. *And* to extrapolate those that we know already exist. The quest for new minerals, new metals is never ending, but the uses for the ones we've already discovered also seem to be never ending. So they can't go wrong. They're either going to discover more of what they already want or something brand new.

D: *I always thought they were doing much of this research for knowledge, but it's also for resources. Is that correct?*

P: Well, knowledge of resources is a form of knowledge in itself.

D: *Is that what it means, "The sculptor looking for new clay"?*

P: Yes. That is the picture that struck the moment you finished. I tried not to do any processing on the actual words, but allowed the picture to come into the glass and the meaning to come into my feeling tones.

I did *not* concentrate on the words. The three main words that I remember are "silver, Diana and gold." I did focus thoughts on Diana—unsuccessfully, I might add.

D: *Does he think this will happen in the future?*

P: Yes, because we have not yet done this. But not the far distant future.

D: *And he believes this will probably be in our solar system, and not out in the galaxies somewhere.*

P: I don't have a distance. It's reachable, because I see human beings accessing this place. I don't see it as any place we have so far *named*, which is interesting.

D: *And it will be found on a satellite of a planet, and not on the planet itself.*

P: I don't know. It's just a giant planetary orb in the picture, with many craters. Perhaps it wasn't seen or named yet in the 1550s. I don't know.

CENTURY IX-97

De mer copies en trois parts divisees,
A la seconde les vivres failliront,
Desesperez cherchant champs Helisees,
Premier en breche entrez victoire auront.

The forces at sea divided into three parts, the second one will run out of supplies; in despair looking for the Elysian Fields, the first entering the breach will have victory.

P: I thought of Columbus sailing over to America—the difficulties along the way, and finally having landfall. That is the historical past, even the past to Nostradamus. He fussed at me again for not saying that these can have several overlays of meaning. To comprehend the experience of the quatrain the person who is affecting this link needs to be in a very receptive state. There are superficial meanings. There are deeper meanings. And in many cases there are multiple depths. Your persistence is valuable, for there are often many overlays.

D: *Which does he think is the most important meaning for our time period?*

P: Well, I had been editing out spacecraft and space contacts, for I was judging it wishful thinking. But it seems the sea here refers to the sea of space. The great envelope surrounding this planet really is boundless, but we can picture it as a concentric orb or atmosphere. It seemed that this definitely has to do with alien contact. Elysian Fields are fields of "forever," the fountain of eternal youth, a never-ending place. This seems to be a quest, perhaps to continue the species of a specific other solar system or planet, and Earth is a goal. That does strange things to my reasoning because I've always thought the other way—from Earth out. And this is from space toward Earth. Our planet is of interest to three disparate groups. One seems more motivated than the other two. Perhaps because they, for some reason, can't go home. It seems a desperate search. This planet, perhaps, offering them what they are looking for: eternal life. A place where they can continue their species. It seems they have done quite a bit of groundwork to prepare the way for their eventual colonization. However, another group gets here first. This time I was only seeing this quatrain in space terms.

D: *You were talking about colonization. What about the people living on Earth? How would they receive that?*

P: This point of view did not include the response of humans. It was from the objective of the incoming visitors or colonists.

D: *Can he give you a time frame? Is it in our future?*

P: It seems to be both. It relates almost to the beginning of life on this planet, in the *far* distant past—early in the history of humanoids walking on Earth. That's very interesting since I had not thought of that. But it also refers to right now. I had two responses.

D: *I can see how it would also relate to Columbus' ships because they were looking for new land.*

P: I suppose they could have been viewed as extraterrestrials by the indigenous populations (Native Americans).

CENTURY V-79

La sacree pompe viendra baisser les aisles,	The sacred pomp will come to lower its wings at the coming of the great
Par la venue du grand legislateur:	lawgiver. He will raise the humble
Humble haulsera vexera les rebelles,	and trouble the rebellious; his like will not again appear on Earth.
Naistra sur terre aucun œmulateur.	

N: [Nina] That sounds like Jesus, but there is another. This is a time in the future when we will have communication with other galaxies. This group will come and have our world in awe, with such truth that people will believe this is the Messiah. And that is the time of great awareness, of great new peace.

D: *Does this refer to an individual?*

N: This means an individual, but with many followers who have learned to live by these universal laws. They are bringing them to us.

D: *When this individual comes, will people think he is Christ?*

N: No. This will be different. This individual will come as another person who can walk among you, to remind you that Jesus has done this before. They are His brothers in spirit, who live by those laws in their world, on their planet. They have come to let us know we can also live that way.

D: *Then you mean this person will come from another planet. Will he come as a child and be raised here?*

N: No. This time that I am seeing is a communication from another galaxy, when they appear on our Earth to share information with us, to show us what we can accomplish as a group. This will be an adult person.

D: *Will this man be considered a ruler?*

N: He does not want this. He wants to be a teacher.

D: *If someone like that were to come, people might think he wants to take over the world.*

N: No, this will be made clear. This is not the purpose. This is someone who will help. I see him teaching new ways to live, universal brotherhood, universal law, universal citizenship—showing us other places where there is life, where there is abundance. Places where people can live with peace and plenty. He will teach us how we on our Earth can do this also. I believe there are many similar to him that will be sent out as teachers to help during this time period. He is not the only one with this knowledge. Most of the people from his planet have the knowledge and philosophy.

D: *Will he meet opposition?*

N: Yes. But at this point they have enough power, enough strength, enough telepathy, that even his strongest enemies will be turned around.

D: *Can Nostradamus see a time period when this might happen?*

N: A year? I see at first glance two thousand fifty (2050).

I asked for his description.

N: He might be in human form on our Earth. He seems to be human-*like* in appearance.

CENTURY V-96

Sur le milieu du grand monde la rose,
Pour nouveaux faicts sang public espandu:
A dire vrai on aura bouche close,
Lors au besoing viendra tard l'attendu.

The rose upon the middle of the world, because of new deeds, public blood is shed; to speak the truth they will have closed mouths, then, at time of need the awaited one will come late.

N: I was seeing this same period in time, where this new teacher comes forth and sends his other teachers out. The majority of the people are in awe, but others will not part with their greed and power, so there will be upheaval. But yet eventually even the worst enemy will be turned around. So I feel this refers to this period in our history.

D: *In other words, it won't be instantaneous change.*

N: No. Some people will understand immediately, others will not.

D: *Then the rose represents this great person.*

I was very tempted to think this extraterrestrial teacher could be the same man Nostradamus referred to as the Great Genius (see index). He certainly had some of the same qualities. But after studying the information on both, I have come to the conclusion that this is another person. In that time of enlightenment when we have entered the 1000 years of peace, it is very possible more than one great personage will rise to help the world adjust to a new way of living and a new way of thinking.

Many of the quatrains seemed to refer to a time in the distant future, after the war of the Anti-Christ and the time of troubles.

CENTURY IV-80

Pres du grand fleuve, grand	Near the great river, a great
fosse, terre egeste,	trench, earth excavated, the water
En quinze pars sera l'eau divisee:	will be divided into fifteen parts.
La cité prinse, feu, sang,	The city taken, fire, blood, cries
cris conflict mettre	and battle given, the greater part
Et la plus part concerne	concerned with the collision.
au collisee.	

Much of this quatrain referred to the coming revolution in China. But that was not the only definition.

D: *"The greater part concerned with the collision."*
N: Now I'm seeing the skies. After the revolution, the trauma, there is something happening in the skies. These people are brought together in unification so they can survive.
D: *What is the collision?*
N: The collision is coming from the skies. I heard the word "meteor," and it looks like an explosion with fire falling and raining down from the sky. There is a great impact with another meteor or another body which creates a great explosion and falling fire. And this is causing unification down below, so they learn about survival.
D: *Can you get a time frame reference?*
N: (*Slowly*) 20 ... 2043. I can see the numbers. They're on the screen.

CENTURY V-41

Nay souz les umbres	Born beneath the shadows on a
& journée nocturne	dark day, he will be sovereign in
Sera en regne &	ruling and in goodness. He will
bonté souveraine:	cause his blood to revive the
Fera renaistre son	ancient urn, renewing the century
sang de l'antique urne,	of gold for one of brass.
Renouvellant siecle	
d'or pour l'œrain.	

B: [Brenda] He says this refers to a leader who will arise after the Anti-Christ. But it will not be the one we have referred to as the "genius." It will be another person. And he says this leader will be instrumental in rebuilding the world, and helping the world recover from the great war that will take place with the Anti-Christ. Changing the century of gold for one of brass refers to the rebuilding process. Some of the things will not be as good as they were before they were destroyed, but they will be repaired and back in use. He says "born in the shadows on a dark day" refers to the fact that this leader will be born during an eclipse.

D: *Will he come before the great genius?*

B: Yes, just a little bit before.

D: *Then the great genius will probably be alive at the same time.*

B: Yes. However, when the great genius starts his mission, this leader will be almost finished with his.

D: *"He will cause his blood to revive the ancient urn." What does the ancient urn symbolize?*

B: This leader will lay the groundwork that will help make the genius' job easier. The ancient urn refers to a time in the ancient past when men and women were concerned with the pursuit of knowledge instead of the pursuit of war.

CENTURY VI-2

En l'an cinq cens octante plus & moins,	In the year five hundred and eighty more or less one will await a very strange century. In the year seven hundred and three, the skies as witness that several kingdoms, one to five, will make a change.
On attendra le siecle bien estrange:	
En l'an sept cens, & trois cieux en tesmoings.	
Que plusieurs regnes un à cinq feront change.	

B: He says those numbers refer to the number of years after the year of his death.

D: *After his death?*

B: Yes. He says the phrases describe a major event that will happen in each of those years.

D: *Let me go over some of these lines. "In the year 580 more or less, one will await a very strange century."*

B: He says that refers to the century when the genius will be helping the world.

D: *"And the year 703 the skies as witness that several kingdoms, one to five, will make a change."*

B: He says in that year, within a year's time, several governments will fall. And the changes that occur will be very long-lasting and affect many for years to come.

D: *They couldn't figure it out because they were thinking those were definite dates.*

B: They *are* definite dates.

D: *But they were thinking 580 was 1580 and the other one was 1703.*

B: He says you can do the same thing. Just do it from the year of his death.

D: *He's a very clever person.*

B: He said you have to be.

Nostradamus died in 1566, so 580 years later would be 2146, and 703 years later would be 2269.

CENTURY VIII-85

Entre Bayonne &	Between Bayonne and St. Jean de
à Saint Jean de Lux	Luz will be placed the promontory
Sera posé de Mars la promottoire	of Mars. To the Hanix of the North,
Aux Hanix d'Aquilon	Nanar will remove the light, then
Nanar hostera lux,	suffocate in bed without assistance.
Puis suffocqué au lict	
sans adjutoire.	

B: He says this quatrain refers to when the European consortium send the first manned expedition to Mars.

D: *It wouldn't be the United States?*

B: Not on this ship. The United States space program will be involved with something else at the time. In a joint cooperative effort the Europeans will take advantage of good planetary positions to send a rocket to Mars. He says one of the crew members on the ship will suffer an accident and suffocate, as it is said, "in bed without assistance." Something will happen to his oxygen supply and he will be without air for a bit; but it will be long enough for him to suffocate.

D: *"Between Bayonne and St. Jean de Luz will be placed the promontory of Mars."*

B: A promontory is a place that juts out. So that refers to the rocket that will be going to Mars, and the location where it will blast off.

D: *That sounds like somewhere in France. "To the Hanix of the north Nanar will remove the light."*

B: Due to the direction of their flight, they will be cut off from sight of the sun for a bit. He says Hanix and Nanar refer to astronomical things.

D: *The translators had a great deal of trouble with this quatrain, especially with those words.*

B: He says that's because they are *earthbound!* They are flat-earth thinkers.

D: *Does he have a time period when we might go to Mars?*

B: He says it should be sometimes during the 1990s, before the Anti-Christ makes such things impossible.

D: *I thought we would have to wait until all the other events have taken place.*

B: No. He says you're on the brink of doing it now. All the necessary technology is there. It's just a matter of getting everything together. He says so far as he knows and the United States' space program is concerned, the Anti-Christ should not be the problem. The problem will be with the economics, and the collapse of the government. That will throw a monkey wrench into things.

CENTURY X-89

De brique en marbre
  seront les murs reduits
Sept & cinquante
  annees pacifiques,
Joie aux humains
  renoué Laqueduict,
Santé, grandz fruict joye
  & temps melifique.

The walls will change from brick to marble, seventy-five peaceful years. Joy to people, the aqueduct reopened, health abundant fruit, joy and mellifluous times.

N: [Nina] There is a time when the great powers work together to promote peace and health, and deal with the illness of the world and environment. I see the great powers coming together and gaining control, and there will be a brotherhood. I see barriers being broken down and bridges being built in unification instead of separation. This will be the work of the United States, Russia and China. Once you have that kind of positive power and control, you have exchanges of science and industry, and nations being fed. The most powerful nations will help take responsibility for feeding and cleansing this Earth.

D: *Is that what it means, "the walls will change from brick to marble"?*

N: Yes. Symbols of prosperity, positive growth, brotherhood.

D: *"Seventy-five peaceful years." Is that number literal?*

N: This seems to be literal, yes.

D: *Does he think this will occur after the time of troubles?*

N: Oh, yes. This is beyond the revolution in China, the new government council. This will definitely shake up the whole world, the very existence of humanity. For when this new council forms there will be a joining of hands throughout the world. There will be a new unification.

D: *And this refers to a one-world type of government?*

N: It refers to people trying to work together in exchange, in healthy ways. When China has their council, it will work with Russia and the United States. There will be a new unity and a new exchange for the betterment of humanity and the universe.

D: *This will be after the time of the Anti-Christ, and after the time of troubles. Will it be after the time of the Earth shift?*

N: I can't see that. It will be a time of coming together and sharing with a new bond.

D: *Does he feel that all these things he shows us have to come true?*

N: These were visions he had into the future. These can refer to so many times in our history that many of them have never come true yet. But they're possibilities and probabilities. He hoped his students would teach others that they do have an ability to see other possibilities and other realms where life can be different. So I think these were true visions, but not necessarily true probabilities. If humans are more educated, more aware, more conscious of their abilities and their connection with "All That Is" and the more spiritual side, they will gain a new awareness that shows they can control their environment and themselves.

D: *And our own destiny.*

N: Yes, we can change.

D: *Do you think this is the reason Nostradamus is telling us all this information?*

N: Yes. I think it is to bring us a new awareness again. Maybe there are pockets of people at this time who realize we aren't separate, that we are all connected, and that our evolvement into the potential of what humanity can be is our greatest mission. To teach us that power and greed breed destruction. We can change that. We can have abundance and prosperity.

D: *Especially if we know that these possibilities exist. Would that be correct?*

N: Yes, I think people of this time cannot be satisfied with old religious and political views. They have traveled their own path and found their own truths that make them realize all is connected—all is one, all is God. Things are resurfacing because there is a new philosophy within humanity that can change events.

Chapter 16

The Shift
of the World

THE DISTURBING THEME OF THE COMING SHIFT of the world and all of its dramatic repercussions had been recurring since I began this project in 1986. When Nostradamus established our initial contact and spoke to me through his student Dionysus his first warning to our time period concerned the shift and how it would affect our lives. He said it was a natural phenomenon that had occurred regularly throughout time, because the Earth was also a living thing and it was normal for it to move. As long as the shift progressed in a gradual manner, as it is occurring now with increasing earthquakes, volcanic eruptions, *etc.,* we would be able to live with it by adjusting, painful though it might be, to the changing lifestyle. He tried to warn us that atomic explosions, both intentional and accidental, could disrupt the natural gradual movements and cause the Earth to shift more dramatically. Humans intentionally tampering with weather patterns and polluting the atmosphere could also have disastrous effects on the natural evolution of our Earth. Nostradamus warned that any deviation from the natural course could have far-reaching results that we could not even imagine. I can believe this because my initial reaction to the shift theory was shock and disbelief, so I know it is difficult to imagine the more disastrous events that Nostradamus saw and tried so desperately to warn us about.

This warning was repeated while working with Brenda, and especially with John, the astrologer. In Volume Two of this work John was shown the shape of the continents after the ice caps had melted and the flooding had subsided. These scenes were reproduced on maps through the expertise of an artist working in trance state.

Many other subjects happened across this traumatic scene and some refused to believe it and did not want to discuss it. The amazing thing is that none of their information has contradicted our original findings. We have been given several different scenarios, showing the results of such a catastrophe in varying degrees of severity. My subjects also saw that the people involved reacted in different ways, ranging from acceptance and mutual help to widespread panic. I do not think what they saw was contradictory. I think they were seeing the reactions in different parts of the world. They were also concentrating on what their subconscious would allow them to observe. The gentler souls would not permit themselves to see anything except kindness in the face of horror. They did not want to concentrate on man's inhumanity to man. That does not mean it will not exist—it means that they refused to look at it. Some of this information was reported in Nostradamus' quatrains. Some of it came because we asked him to show us our future. The following are reports by the different people that I worked with.

CENTURY VIII-35

Dedans l'entree de
* Garonne & Baise*
Et la forest non loing
* de Damazan*
Du marsaves gelees, puis
* gresle & bize*
Dordonnois gelle par
* erreur de mezan.*

At the entrance to Garonne and Baise and the forest not far from Damazan, discoveries of the frozen sea, then hail and north winds. Frost in the Dardonnais through the mistake of the month.

B: [Brenda] He says this refers to conditions that will prevail during the time of the shift. It will mess up the climate worldwide. There will be places that should be having spring or summer, yet due to the shift will be getting sleet and snow, and the bodies of water will be iced up ... therefore the "mistake of the month." He said, whoever heard of ice skating in June.

D: *Are those place names important?*

B: No. He says they refer to places in and around the Mediterranean and Black Sea. Those countries that are used to warm weather will be warm no longer.

CENTURY VIII-81

Le neuf empire en desolation
Sera changé du pole aquilonaire.
De la Sicile viendra l'esmotion
Troubler l'emprise à Philip
* tributaire.*

The new empire in desolation will be changed from the Northern Pole. From Sicily will come such trouble that it will bother the enterprise tributary to Philip.

W: [Wayne] I feel this quatrain deals with the Earth shift. I'm seeing floods, ice melting from the pole, much change. Catastrophe always changes things, and there will be catastrophe if the pole melts even a little bit. The first part, the "new empire in desolation" refers to all continents in the northern hemisphere changing.

D: *During the Earth shift?*

W: And before the shift. They are changing economically on *all* continents in the northern hemisphere. The economics of the world is the desolation. It *will* be changed by the catastrophes, which will not only eliminate much of the population, but will also bind together the rest. But I can't fit the last part of that quatrain in there.

D: *Let's concentrate on that first part. Can he show you some of the physical events that happen as the shift takes place?*

W: Well, you know if a *foot* of ice melted at the northern cap it would cause *enormous* flooding. Lakes, rivers, oceans would swell. It won't happen overnight. There will be widespread panic, fear. It will be a time for every individual to go through self-examination.

D: *Can he show you a picture of what the United States looks like after the shift has taken place? Has it changed any?*

W: Well, not only the United States, but also Europe and Asia and actually all the continents. Although the southern hemisphere will be somewhat less drastically affected, there will still be changes. Yes, now I see a great deal of water. It looks as if there would be less than half of the land masses in the northern hemisphere left.

D: *Ask him to explain this last sentence to you: "From Sicily will come such trouble that it will bother the enterprise tributary to Philip."*

W: This may pertain to a bloodline that is descended from a ruler named Philip. During this time we may be involved in or drawing towards one world government. The control of the wealth and the monetary system is not going to work any more.

Later, when Wayne ran into difficulty interpreting what he was being shown about the quatrains, I thought it would ease the strain and frustration to try another approach.

D: *Ask him to show you something he thinks we need to know instead of asking him about the quatrains. Is there any event in our future that we should know about at this time?*

W: I had the response that this time period is like walking a tightrope. It's very difficult to see an event that might not be, because something minute could happen at any moment to change current events. The balance we're experiencing right now (1989) is almost *im*balance. There are many forces in the universe that are concerned.

D: *What does he mean?*

W: He means that the technology and the mentality on the Earth right now are enough to destroy it, and at any given moment. That is part of what he is trying to do. It is what I, and all people and entities that are interested in the Earth's welfare, are doing at this time. We are trying to do what we can to help. The situation is very fragile. It could go in any direction. The direction hoped for is peace and higher developed consciousness.

D: *He has spoken before about an event that he called the "shift," when the world is supposed to move. Does he think that is a possibility?*

W: Yes, the possibility is *very* close to probability. It is due to the negligent management of Earth's resources. Many devastating things are happening. The natural resources that help to balance the Earth are being pulled out, such as water, oil, natural gas, all the iron ores, metals and crystals. But the most tragic is the loss of trees, because they counteract many, many toxins in the air, and are very vital to the balance of the atmosphere. This is being threatened nearly to the point of no return. Without trees the wind blows excessively, which causes erosion, which causes weight shifts, which causes temperature fluctuations. This is a probable future from Nostradamus' point. What he is showing us is that we have not yet gone over the edge to the point of no return. He is trying to warn us.

Even gentle and soft-spoken Nina saw the horror of cataclysms in Nostradamus' magic mirror. She interpreted several quatrains that dealt with this.

CENTURY IV-90

Les deux copies aux murs	The two armies cannot join up at
ne pourront joindre.	the walls. At the time Milan and
Dans cest instant trembler	Pavia tremble. Hunger, thirst and
Milan, Ticin:	doubt will weigh upon them so
Faim, soif doubtance si fort	much, they will not have a scrap
les viendra poindre,	of meat, bread nor supplies.
Chair, pain, ne vivres n'auront	
un seul boucin.	

N: [Nina] I'm seeing earthquakes, droughts. (*Sigh*) This is a time when armies are of no use, for the Earth is going through such radical changes. Just mere daily survival is all one has in their thoughts. This is a time of great upheaval.

D: *Is that what it means, "the two armies cannot join up at the walls"?*

N: There's no place to join. There's just a great deal of shaking, much destruction.

D: *Do the names of Milan and Pavia have any meaning or are they symbolic?*

N: From this picture they are symbolic of the past repeating itself.

D: *In what way?*

N: I am now getting an ancient picture. It is symbolic of what has occurred before with destruction and drought and starvation. I see great upheaval, where armies are meaningless because everyone is trying to survive day-to-day. Just basic needs are the main concern.

CENTURY IV-92

*Teste tranchee du
  vaillant capitaine,
Sera gettee devant son
  adversaire:
Son corps pendu de la
  chasse à l'antenne,
Confus fuira par rames
  à vent contraire.*

The head of the brave captain cut off it will be thrown down in front of his adversary. His body hung from the masts of the ship, confused, he will flee using oars in a contrary wind.

N: This is very strange. But for some reason I'm seeing the British Isles, Scotland. I see places washed away, flooded out. Buildings toppled. Strong unnatural currents in the water going in opposite directions, caused by an unusual funneling wind. I see a vessel in the distance, but I'm not seeing humans. I'm seeing sea creatures and this swirling wind that causes the water to change its regular motion. I believe this has to do with an awakening of creatures from the ocean because of the Earth changes. People will have to deal with their own awareness that things will never quite be the same. There will be weather catastrophes, tidal waves and with it comes disease, destruction and then survival.

D: *What is the symbolism of "The head of the brave captain cut off. It will be thrown down in front of the adversary"?*

N: I believe this is symbolism of change. It will be so brutal that it will change life as we know it. The adversary is symbolic of coping with your own philosophies and learning to live in this new and different world.

D: *"His body hung from the antenna of the ship."*

N: I just see symbolism in this. I see things held up in such a critical manner that people take notice. I see this as a symbolic gesture of having to deal with a new way of life that will be very difficult, very painful to look at. It seems to me things will happen that go beyond any imagination. This is one of the most brutal ways of making you face yourself, by the dismembering of self. (The head being cut off.) This is symbolism to jolt you to your very being, to finally change, so history does not repeat itself.

D: *That is a drastic symbolism. The translator thought the antenna might refer to radio or radar equipment, being very literal in their interpretations.*

N: I might be able to see this. But to me it is symbolism of some type of telepathy, saying that you will survive this. To me, the antenna, the messages, is a telepathic communication of energy. Humanity will survive. And this antenna seems to be sending out a telepathic control of what steps to take.

D: *When will this happen?*

N: It seems to be in the future. It's difficult to tell because I'm viewing this from above. I don't see people or transportation. Right now I see a great deal of flooding. I feel as if its into the 2000 time frame.

D: *You said there's also a great deal of disease?*

N: Yes, brought on by various problems and the catastrophes of weather. Living is very hard. There's a lack of cleanliness, and poisoning from the food and other problems brings on disease.

CENTURY V-87

L'an que Saturne hors de servage,	In the year that Saturn is freed
Au franc terroir sera d'eau	from servitude the Frankish
inundé:	territory will be inundated by water.
De sang Troyen sera son mariage,	His marriage will be of Trojan blood
Et sera ceur d'Espaignols	and he will be closely encircled by
circundé.	the Spaniards.

N: I saw a great flood somewhere. It seems to refer to weather-related tragedies. A flood and destruction caused by changes from the Earth movement in that part of the world, creating different masses of land. Spain and Greece are prominent. This occurs in the future.

D: *It says, "In the year that Saturn is freed from servitude"?*

N: This has to do with the star patterns, the planet patterns. There will be a time when Saturn changes. Somebody who understands the sky patterns would understand.

D: *How does this last part refer to the Earth change and the floods? "His marriage will be of Trojan blood, and he will be closely encircled by the Spaniards."*

N: This symbolism is referring to the results of the flooding and the land masses coming together.

D: *Is that what he means by the "marriage"?*

N: Yes. It is more of a connecting through physical topography, because of the changes between the Earth movement and the floods. It's going to create new relationships with land masses and countries.

D: *Can he tell you if it's far in the future?*

N: The 2000 time.

D: *What will cause these drastic Earth changes?*

N: Just the continued change in the weather patterns. Countries becoming cooler and warmer in opposition to what they once were. Glaciers melting, monsoon winds, Earth shaking. The environment under change, unstable atmosphere.

I asked Mae, my astrologer, about the meaning of Nostradamus' puzzling astrological remark, "In the year that Saturn is freed from servitude." She came to the conclusion that since Saturn rules the Earth, that he could very well be referring to Earth changes. Saturn is now in the sign of Aquarius, moving next through Pisces and then will enter Aries on April 8, 1996. She thought that being in servitude referred to Saturn's past cycle of going through all twelve signs. It has been in servitude or bondage to its present cycle. When it enters Aries, which is symbolically the beginning of a new cycle, it will be freed from bondage and will enter a new age. The year 1996 fits very well with other predictions of change occurring toward the end of this decade.

CENTURY V-88

*Sur le sablon par un
hideux deluge,
Des autres mers trouvé
monstre marin:
Proche du lieu sera faict
un refuge,
Tenant Savone esclave de Turin.*

Through a dreadful flood on the sand a marine monster will be found from other seas. A refuge will be made near the place, holding Savona the slave to Turin.

N: I'm seeing a picture of a sea creature that was thought to have disappeared with prehistoric times. The Earth changes made it surface. It seems to be fish-like, soft-looking, and has large scales. It looks like what you would call a "dragon."

D: *I think of a dragon as having a large head and neck and a long tail.*

N: Yes. It has scales but the tail isn't too long at all. But the body and head look like what you would call a "dragon." It has some bottom feet, but it also has fins on the side.

D: *About how large is this?*

N: (*She was having difficulty.*) It's hard, but I'd say 20 feet.

D: *I was thinking of comparison with other sea creatures. Ask him, is it as large as a whale?*

N: Yes, I'd say that—a large whale.

D: *And this is something we didn't know existed. How was it able to keep out of our sight?*

N: Underground cave, waterways. Just by being able to stay away from population centers.

D: *What does the last part mean? "A refuge will be made near the place. Holding Savona the slave to Turin."*

N: Much interest will be created, and various groups will want to protect this creature. Something will be built to protect it from the hordes seeking a look, or the government or scientists who want to experiment. The names are symbolic of another time, referring maybe to the creature itself.

D: *And this will come up to the beach as a result of a flood?*

N: And underwater changes.

D: *I wonder if Nostradamus often sees strange creatures that we don't know about?*

N: On occasion he sees them, but to him it's hard to separate time, so ... I don't think I can answer that question because there are probably many animals you are familiar with now that were strange in his time period. That would make a difference. He wouldn't know if they were strange to us or not.

I decided to use the same method I had used with Wayne, and ask direct questions. I asked Nostradamus to give Nina new information regarding the axis shift. I was hoping to obtain something that had not been covered by the other subjects.

N: He says humans have placed man-made things within the Earth that would explode. There are hidden things, and when great movement takes place within the Earth it would set these off. That is a danger humans must watch for. If everything that is put away somewhere is disturbed adversely there would be explosions, quakes and problems caused from that.

D: *I was not aware that we had hidden things.*

N: Yes, not bombs so much, but energy wastes and nuclear ... it is *pockets* of matter that we created that would be explosive if the Earth were unsettled.

D: *You mean, the storage of wastes?*

N: Yes, in the oceans, and in underground storage. If the Earth were to begin to tremble and quake inside, it would set all of that off. That is never destroyed. It is always there.

D: *I thought you were referring to a storehouse of weapons that could explode.*

N: It would. But I mean something greater than individual weapons. I'm speaking more of toxic energies.

D: *Like the waste products and by-products of our nuclear ...*

N: Yes, exactly, and the places where nuclear bombs are actually stored waiting to be used. We cannot safely create something like that. There is no place to put it without it being dangerous. It doesn't matter where it is; the actual atomic or nuclear bomb sites would explode and erupt, along with the *waste* product from building them. The actual atom is something very small. There are things smaller than atoms such as subatomic particles, but an atom is a basic life unit. Within the nuclear power plant itself, the atom is exploded and distorted. It was a system of electrons spinning around a nucleus, just like a small solar system unto itself. It is now totally distorted and the energy is shot out in all directions. This is what creates the energy that is generated at a nuclear power plant. If you decide to stop this production because we're having earthquakes, big tidal waves, and big winds occurring, you can't. Once you have split an atom you can't stick it back together again. If a giant wave approaches that's going to wash over this power plant, they can't instantly stop generating their nuclear power. And they can't instantly protect all their radioactive water and waste that they've acquired through the process. So if a plant breaks open all the contaminated poisonous stuff you've already produced is released, it's like a bomb. Power plants were never intended to be bombs, but it's the same concept. To make a nuclear bomb you do the same things you do to make nuclear energy in a power plant. The end product of nuclear plants is a deadly radio-active poison that lasts for approximately 5,000 plus years. You make a whole bunch of poison, and once you create it, it's created "forever."

D: *I suppose they think the waste products are safe.*

N: They're not. They could reignite. That won't happen as long as no *damages* are done to the planet and it is not shaken too much. It will lie there dormant. But if something is done, even an accidental nuclear explosion, it will set off all the others.

D: *You said it was also in the water?*

N: Yes, it is contained; it's been dropped into the ocean. The people of the Earth are already into that real danger and there is little they can do to get away from it other than see that nothing sets it off. A method must be devised to transform that explosive energy into something usable and tamable. It's harnessed, ready to explode. It's not been used in ways where it could dissipate itself in a healthy manner. That's what must be done.

D: *What about shooting it into outer space as a way of getting rid of it?*

N: I think that is a possibility, and it would be actually safer there than on this planet. It would be in a place where it could explode without doing damage to anything around it because it would be so far away. As you know, stars and suns are exploding all the time in space. They do not adversely affect the Earth's atmosphere or the planet Earth itself. The alien energy forms that travel throughout space would have knowledge of what it is. If they were to encounter it, they would not unsettle it in any way. In other words, they could step around it. They are much more knowledgeable about those things. They would know it was an energy force with that kind of power. They would leave it alone unless some use could be made of it. You see, the nuclear power itself or even the waste from it is not bad and evil. There is just no positive method to use them on this planet. I think we will eventually evolve into using this type, by knowing more about how to direct it. We will also use other forms of energy that do not have the explosive risk nuclear power has. We will learn how to utilize natural energy.

D: *But we are constantly creating more waste.*

N: Exactly. Very foolish. Our energies should be spent trying to find ways to unleash that stored energy and utilize it in a positive manner.

D: *We do have underground nuclear explosions and tests.*

N: Yes, that also could trigger some of this. The scientists are not think-ing about the compacted energy that has been stored somewhere, as in waste material. It has a life of its own. It does not lose its strength. It may even gain strength if it is not released. As long as it is kept imprisoned in these pockets, be they in the soil or the oceans, they won't do anything. But I think it would be difficult for us to count on nothing ever happening to set them off. If measures are not taken to dispose of it in a positive manner it will always be as if we are sitting on a time bomb. This is a problem in the shifting of the plates of the Earth also. It could set some of this off.

D: *Do you see that the Earth will shift?*

N: Yes, that will happen because it's a natural thing.

D: *Nostradamus told me once that the shift would not come as a thief in the night. It would occur slowly enough that people would be aware that it was going to happen.*

N: That's true.

D: *Can you see what kind of preparations people would make?*

N: One would be the moving of documentation, space information, exploratory information, to an area in the northwest region. There will be hints as to the movement of the Earth, and what areas are becoming less stable and what areas are becoming more stable. They will function under that, and in *that* respect they will be accurate. Where the government and the space exploration are moved to will be accurate. The northwest region will be a safe place.

D: *It seems as if the geologists could help them on this.*

N: They will be of some help, but more after the fact than ahead of, because they have never experienced anything of this sort before. They will know some of the possibilities of how the plates may shift, and what direction and what to expect. But there will be much conjecture about their opinions. In the interim, another thing that will be happening is the raising in the level of people's consciousness. So that we are more aware of what's going on, in an inner way. And that will warrant as much merit as the geologists' information. There will also be some acceptance of the fact that many people will die. It will be acknowledged that many people will go on to a different realm, and they will be willing to do that. The common thought is that our survival is dependent upon the planet Earth. We will no longer believe that. We will *know* that we survive whether the Earth is here or not. Whether we're on a *planet* or not. The planet Earth will then go into an entirely different *advanced* realm of being, as a whole.

D: *Wouldn't the people make preparations for the survival of the human race?*

N: There will be areas that will not be that disturbed. They will be inhabitable. The people will continue to live, and their energy will be directed much differently than now. There will be a great cooperative effort for people living together in harmony. It will be a matter of individual choice. There will be those that choose to stay on the planet and survive here, and there will be those that choose not to. Those that choose to stay will cooperate with each other and do what needs to be done, such as clearing an area for growing food or housing. Climate will be temperate, so there won't be as much need for protection. There won't be large businesses in cities as we know them now. And those that choose to *not* stay on the planet will knowingly go to another realm. If they do not consciously know, they will unconsciously, but those people will be very few. As I said, the level of consciousness will have raised. The level of awareness, the level of choices that each entity has, will be much more varied compared to what we think we have now. And they will *choose* to do other things with no great remorse or sadness.

D: *I thought they might start stockpiling supplies.*

N: The ignorant will probably do things of that nature. And by that I mean those who are ignorant of their self-awareness, because that won't actually be needed. There will be places where there is still food, and it will be shared. The things I am speaking of now will begin happening in the next ten to fifteen years. We will also be colonizing outside our planet.

D: *In that length of time?*

N: Well, we will be aimed in that direction. Whether there will be a colony set up before 15 to 25 years, I'm not sure. But by then there will be. That will be another choice that souls have here on Earth.

D: *Is that a colony in space or on another planet?*

N: I think both will have occurred, but it will be found that in space works better. Planets in this solar system are not receptive to our form of life. To adapt that planet in such a way, or adapt ourselves to live on it, would be as difficult as setting up a colony in space itself. That would actually be easier.

D: *Would this be an orbiting colony?*

N: Yes. And from there it will be a very short step to where interplanetary travel and communication with other planets in other solar systems are possible. Humanity will have reached an evolution that it has never done before on this planet. It will no longer be earth-bound. The Earth will not be completely destroyed. The land and water masses will move. There will be much flooding. After that has settled down, there will be some degree of rebuilding, and commerce will take place on this planet. Families will live here. It's not as if everything will be destroyed in a given area and have to be rebuilt. It will shift, but some parts that remain above water will not be terribly damaged. Some houses may fall down, but it won't be as the death and destruction from a nuclear war where everything would be destroyed and only a few people living. Leaders will be quite different from now. There will be much more attention on leading the planet as a whole rather than as separate countries. Their energies will be directed toward communication with brothers in outer space. There will be less quibbling and squabbling between the people left on this planet. That will become something you no longer do, just as fighting with your schoolmate is something you no longer do when you grow beyond that age.

D: *I thought that without leadership and communications there might be panic and havoc.*

N: No. You're not taking into consideration the enormous psychological, emotional and metaphysical leaps that will take place in the next 10 to 25 years. I have said this before, the level of awareness will have grown to the point where there will not be the panic that you think. There will be a cosmic awareness of what is going on, and a planetary awareness of our place in the cosmos. There will be those people who have not gotten to that stage yet, but they will be in the minority. It will be as if people were sailing on a ship and knew they were going through a storm, and that there was going to be rough water. So they would tighten everything down and wait the storm out. There will be a similar attitude when the Earth shift becomes increasingly physical. Those that will survive will sort of hole up until it's over. Then we will come out after the storm, so to speak, and begin doing what is needed to keep this planet as a base.

D: *But it is our home. That's why we don't like to think of it being so totally disrupted.*

N: It's only part of the natural course of events. It happens throughout the universe. We have not been able to *see* it, being as isolated and, in a way, *backward.* I don't mean that in a derogatory manner. It's more an unawareness because of our isolation.

D: *I know many people will not live through this, but where will the highest concentration of population be afterwards?*

N: There will be more population in the Asiatic countries. It will be more scattered, but there won't be *vast* differences. That continent on the opposite side of the United States will have larger land masses that stay together, and therefore there will be a larger populace there. The number of people won't make the difference though. I think the United States will retain the most abilities and capabilities and powers, because of their knowledge. The technical knowledge that they have is very great now, and will continue to expand. What they are lacking is the metaphysical, the ancient cultures, to tie in with. The Earth shift and the higher level of awareness that's going to come *will* tie that in together for the peoples of the United States.

D: *Concentrate on the period after the Earth shift when things are settling down again.*

N: There will be much smooth sailing. Quite a relief after the turmoil that has been taking place. There will be much learning. There will be assistance involving interplanetary travel. We will know more about our universe and all the many others. There will be assistance from those in other space realms, and we will join in with that. There will be a communion, a *knowledgeable,* on both sides, working-together. Other entities in space have known about us, but we have not known about them. And that will happen. There will be smooth sailing.

D: *Why are they giving us this assistance?*

N: They would give anyone this assistance. We will do the same when we are in a position to do so, because we were all part of the *one,* and we are all related. We have been unaware of that, because we have been in such an infant stage. We will be growing out of that now and into an awareness that we are all one. It will be something similar to when the Age of Reason came about with humans.

CENTURY VIII-100

Pour l'abondance de larme respandue *Du hault en bas par le bas au plus hault.* *Trop grande foir par jeu vie perdue* *De soif mourir par habondant deffault.*	By the great number of tears shed, from top to bottom and from the bottom to the very top, a life is lost through a game with too much faith, to die of thirst through a great deficiency.

P: [Pam] How far in the past do you not want to go?

D: *Well, give me a general time period and I'll tell you if it's worth exploring.*

P: Atlantis? What's interesting is that this also refers to the future. The quatrain seems to refer to the faith that the Atlanteans placed in their own capabilities. It has to do with their ego. Their own insights actually led to a planetary shift because of a malfunction that they *hadn't* planned on. To have no potable water is literal. You can still die of thirst although surrounded by water. It seems that we, too, even now as I speak in this current age, have the same capability to affect the actual tilt of this planet. It doesn't seem to refer to *natural* Earth changes or evolutionary processes. This seems to definitely refer to interference by human hands in the ancient past, and in the near future. Once again, the future is not chiseled in stone. If we have fore-knowledge that we have this great capability and are standing with our finger poised on the button, we have free will to move our hand. The story of this quatrain is that it *has* already happened once.

D: *Then Nostradamus is inferring that in the time of Atlantis the shift was caused by humans, and not by natural occurrence.*

P: Yes, it was *begun* by Atlanteans. They were competent in their scientific capabilities and were playing around with fusion and fission. They were actually working with the internal structure of the atom. It was an accident. I don't see bombs or anything like that, but I do see too much energy being released in one place. This caused explosions which then resounded through the entire planet. They wobbled the planet, creating, of course, earthquakes, a giant tidal wave and mass destruction.

D: *How does he relate that to the future time?*

P: We could do that through an accidental *mass* detonation of nuclear devices. Not necessarily bombs, but accidental detonations of nuclear

facilities. We have the capability. We have the same power genera-
tors already present on the Earth. It is our choice how we choose to
deal with these: whether to dismantle them, ignore them, or to keep
tiptoeing around the edges of perhaps using them.

D: *Then he sees a possibility of something going wrong.*

P: He saw it happen in the past. He is saying it can happen in the future.

D: *And we would again have another shift caused by humans.*

P: Correct. The amount of energy we are now capable of releasing is
immense. We are actually capable of ripping the fabric of the
universe. Our planet could—I emphasize *could*—literally explode. He
knows humanity denies the fact that this would happen. We cannot
comprehend that the planet itself could explode. We think things on the
surface or beneath the surface will, but we don't think in the huge, horrific
destructive terms of an entire planet exploding. It's too awesome.

D: *What does he see causing this possibility?*

P: We would have to choose to detonate many devices. We can have
nuclear detonations that don't explode the planet. He asked me to use
an example. It would take the conscious exploding of bombs by, say,
two super powers on the planet. We have that capability.

D: *I thought maybe he meant the exploding of some nuclear plants.*

P: Yes. That would still be a conscious thing. The plants themselves can
be purposefully exploded. They're just bombs sitting on the outside
of the ground right now. But an exploding of a plant here or there
would not create the immense destruction that I'm talking about.

D: *Then you think more destruction would come from countries dropping bombs.*

P: There are certainly more bombs than there are plants.

D: *Then he's seeing that this could literally destroy the entire planet.*

P: He said he saw it in the past. The future's up to us.

D: *But in the past the whole planet was not destroyed. It was tilted and wobbled.*

P: Correct. But the Atlantean civilization was nearly totally destroyed.
It wasn't the planet but it was a race. Not *everyone,* but in the main, yes.

D: *And he's trying to warn us that it happened before and it could happen again
if we continue on that path. It's one of the possibilities and choices.*

P: That's right. We all exist with free will, and he is aware that we can
affect the future. These are *big* pictures.

D: *What are these scenes he is showing you?*

P: I see people screaming in pain, running down streets where there's
nothing but fire. I hear screams. I see tortured anguished faces. I
don't know where this is. I can dispassionately view to a *certain*
degree, for I don't recognize anyone I know. That's about as dispas-
sionate as I can become however, because it seems really big. This is
a distortion of the natural order that brought about the wobble, the
tidal waves, the giant oceans rushing onto the land. The terrible
shame is that it was so unnecessary. This must be viewed in the context of Nostradamus' interpretation. We have to look on it now in

light of the fact that everything we do has an impact on everything, which includes the future. Just because a future was seen by Nostradamus in a certain way, does not mean that is the way it will be. It would be that way if everything worked exactly according to his assumptions. Of course, free will makes it impossible for us to be totally accurate in *any* assumption. But the bottom line of this quatrain is that a big change will occur. He tends to focus on the pain, suffering and tragedy of getting through to this greater awakening. It need not necessarily be quite as traumatic. Our attitude, I think, is essential in dealing with any of these things. We should understand that some of these are not necessarily going to happen at all.

Later when Pam had difficulty understanding what she was being shown in the dark mirror, I thought it would be a change of pace for her to ask Nostradamus direct questions. This would ease the pressure on her because she was very concerned about receiving information accurately. This stress may have been a factor in the difficulty she was experiencing. She was making it much harder than it should have been because of her conscientious concern. In this sequence Pam presented herself to Nostradamus as a soft glowing orb of blue light so he would have something to focus on instead of the empty air.

P: He's sitting there looking at the glass, but he has his pen in his hand and his paper in front of him. I've changed positions to right behind and looking over his *left* shoulder at the mirror. He is aware of my presence there, and he allows me to look. It's as if I'm left to my own devices which I don't want to do.

D: *Ask him to show you pictures, and we will help if there are some things he doesn't understand.*

P: Nostradamus doesn't show pictures to me. They simply appear.

D: *Well, however the mechanics of it works. Tell him that we are from the future, and we would like to see in the glass what we can expect to happen.*

P: (*The response was instantaneous.*) I see a very turbulent ocean—really huge waves. I'm awed by the incredible force and *depth* and *power* of this water, this *churning raging.* I've never been on a ship at sea, but in *this* ocean I can't conceive of a ship holding up.

D: *What else do you see?*

P: Darkness. The sea, the water, is really agitated. And the wind blows. You've heard of gale force; this is bigger than that. Big, huge winds, and of course, it's full of water. The water is in the air, water churning all underneath and darkness in the sky. I don't want to go over to the land and look, but I can see the coastal areas being inundated by the water. Whole cities. The water simply rises over and a giant wave comes crashing down on the cities as if they were made of paper and cardboard. Buildings fall down and cars and people and trees are simply swept into the water. The water is huge. If you were on the edges, a thousand feet wouldn't be high enough to be away from the water.

D: *You mean it's like a giant tidal wave?*

P: Many, many tidal waves.

D: *What else are you seeing?*

P: Some entire cities are not visible anymore. I just can't express how huge these water waves are. I'm looking at skyscrapers, really big buildings and how easily they fall over. And, of course, people and cars and trees are much smaller. They're like ants being washed off the sidewalk with a hose. They're insignificant in comparison to the force of all this water.

D: *This is occurring mostly in the coastal areas?*

P: That's where I turned my attention from the center of the ocean to the edges of the land. I suppose you want me to go to look at the land.

D: *Yes, I was going to ask if you could focus your attention inland and see what is occurring there.*

P: I'll tell you what I see initially after the giant water. This is everywhere—global. This is not just on the edge of California or Florida or the Gulf of Mexico. This is all over the planet; but I'll talk about this country. There was an instant cessation of all utilities: electricity, gas, water, sewer. Our normal things that we almost unconsciously rely on. There was no food being brought in. There were no grocery stores open. There was tense, general panic. I see people running around, first in a frenzy, and then slower and aimlessly; totally uncomprehending the magnitude of what's happening. I'm looking now during the time of water and I did not see volcanoes. I just saw that facilities broke down and everything made people feel totally panicked and hopeless on the dry regions; those parts of the continent left above water. There were lots of suicides, and even people killing their children so they wouldn't have to suffer through this. This made people crazy. This is not anything that they could have comprehended or planned for or imagined.

D: *What is causing the water to be displaced?*

P: I would not be able to tell you for a fact. I can only tell you what I see. And I see in the interior of the Earth, the very center of the planet, the yolk of the egg. I see it churning internally the same as the seas on the outside, its equilibrium having been thrown off kilter. If you put your hand in a tub of water and started moving your arm back and forth really fast you would create waves that would eventually go out of control and lap over the sides of the tub. Something made the *core* of the Earth go out of control. The orbit and tilt of the Earth somehow were changed. This created internal, as well as external, distress.

D: *Then something caused the orbit to change and this affected the core, or was it vice-versa?*

P: Something caused the orbit and the axis to *lean* first, and this imbalance caused the equilibrium shift internally. If the Earth rotated differently and our path was still around the sun but not regular, it would affect the outside. You have the internal sloshing and then the external being affected by its shifting. Just as we're affected by what goes on inside our own bodies, as well as what happens in the environment around us.

D: *Does anything else happen to the Earth itself?*

P: *(Resigned sigh)* Yes, of course. I see giant, huge cracks. Gaping, cracking, groaning sounds. I'm sure these are earthquakes. They're all over, just like a cracked eggshell.

D: *Can he show you what happens right before the destruction? Are there any events that lead up to that?*

P: *(Sigh)* I suppose you're speaking of specific *big* events. The weather changes we are currently experiencing will only increase in drama, so the wet areas will become flooded areas, and the dry areas will become desert. The food shortages will become more pronounced globally. Food and clean water will become, shall we say, bones of contention. The basic "stuff" of human life will be looked upon with greed and envy and the desire to possess and hoard. I see conflicts over food, over water. I do not see country against country. I see many, many regional conflicts over the land that is left. How we deal with the upcoming shortages—that's not the right word—but how we deal in our hearts with the upcoming panics will have a great affect on how the human thought pool surrounding the Earth vibrates. If we believe that we truly are unlimited beings of light and love, whose *true* self is spirit, who cares for *everything* equally to self—that's actually a big one— if we can put out that vibration in the face of panic, fear, darkness and hunger, then we can help maintain the fragile balance that exists. If we succumb to greed, fear, panic, we might strengthen the discordancy that already exists. It seems as I look in the mirror that the precipitating factor would be how we respond to the natural things that happen. We value judge them as "bad" because they create great inconvenience and chaos. We don't have the view that the world is a living organism, and when something goes wrong it has to "fix" itself. We can see all these things as natural occurrences that we must adapt to as intelligent humans. The more we resist, the darker the thought form and the slower the vibrations become. On the opposite side, we can see it as a challenge to flow with in order to continue living on this planet, to be someone who can help balance and maintain the highest vibration. So our attitude, our point of view is paramount.

Pam then proceeded to describe the tragic scene below her as she skimmed over the continents and observed the remaining land. Everything was startlingly different. The United States was composed of several islands of varying sizes. "There is so much water," she said. "The Great Lakes spill down. The Mississippi pushes out. The Gulf of Mexico sloshes in and over, and then here comes the Atlantic." Some of the land that remained in the Midwest was now desert and would not be capable of producing food or water. She said it would be very "challenging" to live there. Things didn't fare any better in Canada and Alaska, although South America still had land remaining, especially Brazil and the Andes mountain range. She was surprised at the appearance of Antarctica. "The turbulence that took place in the oceans affected the Antarctic as well as the Arctic Ocean. Giant, huge amounts of ice were transported far from Antarctica by the force of these waves. This doesn't make a lot of sense, but it looks as if a large land mass is *more* revealed now than it was before. So in some way the turbulence of the water uncovered land in the Antarctic."

I was trying to cover as much of the globe as possible in a short period of time and without the benefit of a map to look at, to verify what I had received from other sources. This is reported in Volume Two.

Pam saw Europe broken up into islands also. She was surprised by the appearance of the Mediterranean. "How sad. I don't see much of Italy and Greece. Under regular conditions the Strait of Gibraltar keeps the Mediterranean Sea separate from the big ocean. But this is not a *regular* time. The force, the incredible magnitude of the power of these *waves*—that I can't describe because they are incomprehensibly *big*—have already eliminated most of Spain and France and Portugal. The Rock of Gibraltar is not there—I wanted to say the "Colossus of Rhodes." These waves have created a big *hole,* and the Mediterranean and all the countries surrounding it are very easy to get to."

Because the Asian continent is so huge, Pam saw that it was not affected as much as the other continents. Russia and China are vast areas that were mostly affected along the eastern coastline. Japan remained as islands, and India still had a large central land mass.

I was curious about the new location of the poles. Naturally I was still checking against information we had already received from other sources. She remarked, "I was interested in how the old Soviet Union looked, but it seems as if most of it is covered with ice. It is likely that a new north pole has moved to have its epicenter somewhere in northern Russia. It looks as if the south pole is in a huge expanse of water. I can see the coldness blowing in the air in Russia. I can actually see the freezing frigid air. But in the ocean where the new south pole appears to be, I see a swirling of clouds—like a funnel shape. I see a freezing feeling, although that's my interpretation."

D: *Focus back on the United States. Can you see what happened to the government of the United States?*

P: The capital, Washington, D.C., is gone. No communication, no telephone, no television, no electricity, ultimately no gasoline. The military is in chaos. What good are their wonderfully protected nuclear bombs in a case like this? I see just a chaotic group of human beings there like everywhere else. The *important* personages they've tried to protect in underground cities, only have food and water for a certain amount of time. They have no outside communication and they can't live there forever. So when they come out, they are exactly equal to everyone else. There is no authority, no power, no governing body. The new leaders that arise on what is left of the continent are not leaders from government or from churches either. These are people who can think clearly in a time of panic, and sincerely communicate global ideals that can reach mass numbers of people.

D: *You said when this happened the government went into underground cities? Were these located near Washington?*

P: Actually there is an entire *huge* city built in the base of the Rocky Mountains. Initially some went to the Rockies and some went into underground cities near Washington. We're not talking about an instantaneous thing. It takes a long time for the panic to actually sink in. You can instantly not have any communications, but that doesn't mean you're aware that the rest of the world is in chaos. Only when the realization sinks in that this is truly a *big*, huge planetary thing, does the ultimate panic set in. We're talking about a time period here. By then those who put themselves away as the government of the future, the saviors of whatever is left, realize they had no *real* plan and no *practical* way to accomplish their goals.

D: *They were prepared for a catastrophe, but not on this scale.*

P: Correct.

D: *And when they come out they are just like everyone else.*

P: That's right. Just because someone says, "I'm the President, listen to me," doesn't mean a panicked person would give them any more credence than any other human.

D: *Yes. And the military probably wouldn't have any control either in a situation like that. Everyone would be equal. Well, as things calm down and return to normal—whatever normal is—where would the government be in the United States?*

P: (*Long pause*) I see no central government.

D: *Do things ever get back to normal?*

P: Well, what *is* becomes normal in time. In succeeding generations, living compatibility with nature and being aware of our cosmic connections, being aware of the power of our thought forms, and being cognizant of who we *really* are, will be as normal as turning on the television, garbage disposal or dishwasher, and other ridiculous things that we now focus our attention on. This seems to last a long time. This is a much more positive scenario than having the Earth so chaotically out of balance that the whole planet explodes.

D: *It sounds like there would be many lives lost when all this is happening.*

P: The majority die with the flooding. The water is just so big. But many more die relatively soon afterward from lack of water to drink, and lack of food. The next wave of the most deaths comes from trying to get other people's food, water, shelter. There is real panic and violence, rioting—not admirable human traits at all. Then there are all kinds of illnesses and disease. Think of cities crumbling all around you with no sewer, no water, no gas, no electricity, no food. Think of rotting sewage. Think of all the bodies. It would be very difficult to maintain a *clear* clean environment in that kind of situation. Nostradamus is showing us a sample of countless numbers of scenarios that could take place. The thought forms that we are projecting right now at this very moment in time—the three of us in this room plus the other four billion thinkers on the planet—are all putting forth vibrations which will attract like vibrations. And you know how complex your own vibrations are. Multiply that by four billion, and you have that many different scenarios. It is magnified when masses of people have a predominant focus. *One* person's thoughts influence the scheme of things, but large numbers of people thinking on the same thing can affect "whatever" faster. All this began with you wanting to ask some questions of Nostradamus. Nostradamus does not put pictures into the mirror. So when you ask questions of Nostradamus, I am simply trying to see what Nostradamus sees. He said to tell you that what he said today is not to be taken lightly *(Emphatic)* It is true that we do all have an affect, each one of us.

D: *I'll try to tell people that. I will try to do positive things with the information.*

P: Your books will help.

Chapter 17

Disaster Probabilities

CENTURY V-85

Par les Sueves & lieux
  circonvoisins,
Seront en guerre pour
  cause des nuees:
Gamp marins locustes & cousins,
Du Leman fautes seront
  bien desnuees.

Through the Swiss and surrounding areas they will war because of the clouds. A swarm of marine locusts and gnats, the faults of Geneva will be laid quite bare.

N: [Nina] This has to do with nuclear weaponry, nuclear pollution.

D: *Why is he speaking mostly of the Swiss and Geneva here?*

N: There will be world conferences there to try to solve some of the problems.

D: *It says, "Through the Swiss and surrounding areas, they will war because of the clouds."*

N: This war is mainly a verbal war, but it's to put a halt to the destruction, and to try to recontrol our atmosphere and our environment.

D: *And the clouds would be nuclear clouds. What does "a swarm of marine locusts and gnats" symbolize?*

N: It symbolizes a plague of some sort. I see masses of people very ill and withering away. I think it has to do with radiation poison.

D: *Why does it say, "A swarm of* marine *locusts and gnats"?*

N: There is no safe water to be found. It takes a while for them to realize that the pollution is in the water supply also.

D: *In other quatrains when he spoke of insects he was sometimes referring to bombs and bullets, but in this case he's not.*

N: It's a plague or a ... pestilence. That would be a good word.

D: *"The faults of Geneva will be laid quite bare."*

N: The conferences are too lax. They need to come up with new rules, new laws, to protect the environment and people. There is leakage, explosions, negligence, ignorance, not really doing enough to protect what needs to be protected.

D: *Then it's not caused by war?*

N: No. It is caused by various countries not controlling their wastes and their problems. It has to do with meltdowns and similar things occurring in various countries of the world. They have similar problems at the same times, and the world is not able to handle this pollution very well.

D: *Is this in the* far *future?*

N: No. It is in the *near* future.

CENTURY VI-69

La pitié grande sera sans loing tarder, *Ceux qui donoient seront contrains de prendre.* *Nudz affamez de froit, soif, soi bander,* *Les monts passer commettant grand esclandre.*	The great pity will arrive before very long: those who gave will be forced to take. Naked, starving with cold and thirst, they band together to cross the mountains causing a great scandal.

P: [Pam] (*Sadly*) I perceive what we call the "nuclear winter." I see many people moving in darkness and cold, looking for shelter, looking for food. And I see their bodies distorted. I see people taking what they need from others to feed their children, to feed themselves. I see basic human love covered over in a large degree just to survive. I see attitudes displayed by humans that are not admirable. It's sad to look upon because when it comes down to basic survival, people do cruel things. But remember these are *always* just possibilities. At the end of each quatrain it must *always* be stated that this is *only* a possibility. The great pity is that this is caused by human hands. This scene that I look upon didn't have to happen. (*She appeared ready to cry.*)

D: *Do you want to elaborate?*

P: (*Almost crying.*) Not really.

D: *Can he see how it was caused by human hands?*

P: I see multiple explosions. (*Sigh*) It seems to be a scenario where bombs were dropped in one place on the Earth—(*sadly*) this country—and bombs were dropped practically on the other side of the planet, almost simultaneously. However this was not enough on its own to create the darkness that I see. It seems this created such an imbalance on the planet itself that we then had multiple volcanic explosions as well. So first the human-made detonations set off a chain reaction, and afterward the energy was released from the planet itself. So I see two causes of sending debris into the atmosphere.

D: *And this is what causes a nuclear winter?*

P: Darkness, yes. The sun is obscured. It's almost incomprehensible when first looking upon this, that this could ever happen. Because it is so altering of all that we're aware of on this planet.

CENTURY IX-46

Vuidez, fuyez de Tholose	Be gone, flee from Toulouse the red
les rouges	ones, make expiation for the
Du sacrifice faire expiation,	sacrifice. The main cause of evil
Le chef du mal dessouz	in the shadow of the gourds, dead,
l'ombre des courges	to strangle the prognostication
Mort estranger carne omination.	of flesh.

P: It must be remembered that Nostradamus knows the future is subject to change. There are things that he sees as actually happening, and they may not happen at *all*. Events have to stack up in order to come out with *a* specific result, so he knows that focus on it can create it. These are only probabilities. But I must digress a bit to say he was not seeing them initially as probabilities. It seems that the words "Be gone" means "Be gone with this scene I see." It doesn't have to be that way. What I see is similar to the destruction of the planet.

D: *The entire planet?*

P: Well, the planet to a large degree. I don't see fire in the oceans, although that's not without the realm of possibility. I do see a big inferno on the land. The focus is to not focus on that.

D: *I would like to know what the cause of this fire is. "Flee from Toulouse, the red ones." What does that mean?*

P: The red ones are the death, the fire. The horror.

D: *"Make expiation for the sacrifice."*

P: That seems like—to hurry it up, to get it over with. I don't know.

D: *"The main cause of evil is the shadow of the gourds."*

P: Those seem to be bombs.

D: *"Dead, to strangle the prognostication of flesh."*

P: The thoughts, the desires, the aspirations of the humans.

D: *It seems this fire is being caused by these bombs. Can he give you some idea of a time period?*

P: This is an event that we all choose not to come to pass.

D: *I also do not want it to come to pass. But is it in our time period or in our future?*

P: *(Pause)* I don't know.

D: *Is it in the past?*

P: It has been, but only a certain race. And it wasn't an extermination of that race either, only a great destruction. But this doesn't refer to that. I was thinking of the bombs that we dropped on Japan, but this thing in the quatrain is much larger. It seems this has not yet come to pass on the scale that I see. Although he, I, or somebody, is repeating that events rarely happen once. It's as if we have shadows of things to come *always* happening, because events are cyclic. We don't necessarily learn from our mistakes of the past. History is constantly repeating itself. Nostradamus likes us, I must say. It feels very comfortable. But he says when he sees things that are really distorted or, from what he would judge, totally awful, he sometimes questions his own sanity. And he frequently questions the source of his thoughts or visionings. He's not one hundred percent sure that this *isn't* the work of the Devil messing up his mind.

D: *That's because they are things he doesn't understand?*

P: Absolutely. Human's inhumanity to themselves to the degree that Nostradamus sees it happening repeatedly into the future, is a great puzzlement. Why haven't we awakened to the fact that it serves no real purpose to wage wars against each other, or to carry on hostilities and resentments, and hold grudges? He sees these replayed over and over for years and years, and it seems sad and unnecessary. He can't understand why we haven't figured that out. He has seen the bombs drop in World War II. This is incomprehensible how one set of humans could do that to another. When he observed the atomic explosion he saw that it actually caused a rip in the fabric of space. It was a very dramatic thing. I don't think he understood it from the standpoint of a nuclear technician. But as someone who could see what was happening, it was obvious we had somehow harnessed an incredible mighty force. And we used that force for the most awful killing and destruction we could do.

D: *Is he able to see these things on multi-levels?*

P: It's strange but, although it happened much later than the 1550s, when he sees it, it's like a memory. I don't know how to explain future seeing, but it seems that it has already happened. He saw an explosion that at first was so bright it was like an exploding mini-sun on the planet. The flash initially caused a pulling apart, because it actually rips apart atoms on the Earth, in the air, in space. Then there is a rushing-in to fill up this space. You've heard that nature abhors a vacuum, and that invisible things rush in to fill what looked empty, but really wasn't. A nuclear explosion will do this on a grand scale from many miles above the Earth down to below the surface. It will make this giant vacuum appear instantly, and then *shoot* in air to fill this space as quickly as possible. It continues to be affected hundreds of miles beyond where the actual bomb takes place. It's like when you drop a pebble in the pond and the rings keep reverberating out and out. This keeps going up and up, out and out laterally, and of course, down and down reverberating through the planet herself. So, yes, he was able to see this. But because he was looking at it from the perspective of someone in the spirit state, he also had larger sight. If *you* were standing there watching this you wouldn't have the same awareness because you are in a physical body. If you were a spirit standing there watching it you would have a greater awareness. And this is what he saw in all its horror.

This rip in the fabric of the universe was also reported by Brenda in Volume Two.

D: *You can tell him that since that happened in the 1940s no other destructive forces of that type have been unleashed on human beings.*

P: Not of that magnitude. There have been continuous tests since then in the ocean, above the ground, in the atmosphere and under the surface of the Earth. People have observed these things, and they were, of course, placed in great danger. But, no, not to the extent of dropping it on major metropolitan cities.

D: *A large part of the population now is very much against continued testing, and even wants all these destructive devices to be destroyed.*

P: Nostradamus says you only speak from the perspective of the country you live in. The world is most large and there are other countries in your time frame who are at this moment continuing to develop these awesome weapons of destruction. Many of these are being developed without the awareness of the majority of the people in your respective country. They are mainly being developed by the military, those in power who want to maintain their power, and even spread it. But from the perspective of your country your comments are absolutely true.

D: *The country that has been our greatest enemy and who has the other large storage of these weapons has recently become more agreeable. It appears that the tensions that promote the use of these weapons have been reduced a great deal.*

P: What you say and report is truth from your perspective with the information you live with at this time. He also says that people seem to historically believe that those countries with the most "fire power" will become the most powerful countries. What has happened is that the two large countries you talk about haven't actually stopped developing weapons. They haven't really eliminated their entire capacity to decimate the planet, but they are trying to set a different tone. This means those countries that have been repressed, who have not had the opportunities and freedoms allowed to them, are now going to try desperately to develop their own "big guns," because they don't ever want to be subjugated or repressed again. You must also remember that there are small countries who really are not ethical. I'm speaking of the continent of Africa, and of course, a large part of the Middle East; India as well.

D: *Can he give us any more information about our future?*

P: It seems as if I can only get information to the 2300s. What he has seen between 1989 and the 2300s has been more war. He's also seen some very dramatic Earth changes, with several large sections of the terrestrial parts turned into desert. No water, *all* plants shriveled and dead, and dirt and dust just blowing away. It's not good to think that could be what we have in store for the future.

D: *What was the cause of that?*

P: Right now I see enormous winds continuing for a long period. I didn't know winds could do this. I don't know how this works, you see. But because of these constant *huge* winds somehow the rain can't fall. The constant buffeting of the winds on the plants affects them greatly. It didn't take long to kill the vegetation. The winds are relentless, and then the earth, the dirt, the ground, starts to blow away too. You want to know what precipitated the winds, I suppose. The Earth herself, according to this probability, actually did a little "blink" on its axis. It shifted. It's rotating at a more dramatic angle. Try to think of the biggest thing you've ever been on, like a ship or an airplane, groaning and creaking and rolling. There is a point when a big body reaches a certain amount of stress and something has to give. The planet is a *big* body. And moving out of its comfortable place in space, or changing just a little bit, creates enormous stress on the big body. That big movement causes the north pole to melt, so the ocean levels rise. Even the heating and cooling of the Earth, as you well know, produces winds. If we're talking about the *whole* Earth in a totally new framework, winds are the absolute natural follow-up to this movement. It seems that the Earth herself is a living organism who goes through growth and transition periods as all living organisms. It's not unusual for living things to move. Even trees, those living things that seem rooted and stationary, do in fact have movement. Even a rock has internal movement. Perhaps it is not visible to the human eye, but movement is there. It is a part of life. So the Earth, like all living things, is delicately balanced. He said to give an example to try to explain. We have many different systems within the human body that have been labeled by our doctors: the circulatory, respiratory, and digestive systems. If you were to block just one of those systems, the human body would die. All the systems are very interrelated, very complex and very necessary for continuance of life. What is happening is that through our physical acts and our mental, emotional acts, this living organism is being poisoned. Its capacity for life is being greatly diminished by those little tiny humans who live on the surface. From Nostradamus' perspective in the 1500s, he sees the Earth in our time period poised on the brink. There is actually a large movement in areas all over the planet of human beings recognizing the gods they are. They are acknowledging the grandeur of this cosmic soup we live in. They are understanding that, as human beings, they have god-like responsibilities of caretaking and creating that which has good, helpful and loving attributes. Until the end of this century there is almost a "dance" between those who want to care for the Earth and actually heal those wounds that have already been inflicted. Also there is an awakening awareness that peace begins within the individual heart. There is this movement underway during this time period to express this belief to other people, so that it in fact can become the standard belief for the planet. The first wave, in which we're now participating, is a global consciousness wave where the individual feels responsibility and is personally motivated to do something for the Earth. This second feeling includes having to express it to others, to help the idea grow and reach more people. Can you understand the difference? There are so many people who have never had thoughts in this realm, and this is going to take time to be accepted as a belief, a truth. So the decade at the end of this century is a critical one. It depends on whether this information gets out and is accepted by the majority. If not, I see only the same things repeating themselves. From Nostradamus' perspective, he has seen *countless* wars, conflicts, injustices, and barbaric things. So speaking now of *this* time, to the end of this century, he sees it as a most critical time—a deciding time. The Earth will continue to live. Shifts will occur, however, not to the extent he has seen. Two things come into play with the shift of the Earth. One is that it is a naturally-occurring growth phenomenon. The second is that the Earth has a consciousness and an awareness, and when it is injured too severely it has to do something about it. Then you have the shudder I saw. If there is no reason for the shudder, the shifts that occur will be dealt with.

D: *You were discussing the one probability of the Earth shifting and creating all this wind, and the rain not being able to get through. What was the outcome of that?*

P: Many, many people died. Also many animals and many big trees perished, but not all life.

D: *Then what did humans do?*

P: They started over.

D: *Were they able to?*

P: Yes. There are, right now as we speak, many places that are already built underground. We will go back into the Earth for a period of time, and live under the surface. I say that as a fact. Maybe I should not have said it that way. If the worse-case scenario takes place this is what comes to pass. The *big* winds with the *huge* loss of life doesn't have to take place. Shifts will take place that create major inconvenience that we have to adapt to. But the terrible winds that I see are much more horrible than an inconvenience. You can't imagine what it is like not to see anything because there's constant dust, sand and dirt flying in the air all the time.

D: *That would be a good reason for being underground.*

P: Yes. A scenario of that extent only takes place if humans haven't got their act together to take care of the planet. If that comes to pass it is far in our personal future, but not so far in the future of the Earth. I would say it occurs before the years in the 2200s if we can't wake up before then. I can't see beyond 2300s.

D: *What do you see at 2300?*

P: Just stillness and much darkness. I see an established society *under* the surface. It's been there so long it seems as if that's the natural place to live.

D: *What do those people look like?*

P: They resemble skinnier, spindlier humans with bigger heads and flatter noses. They have smaller mouths with bony plates rather than teeth, and big, big eyes. This is because the darkness factor is greater even though it is illuminated under the surface. When they go out, it's so bright that they need to wear black lenses that cover the eyes.

D: *Why did they evolve to that state?*

P: I think it was caused by living under the ground for a thousand years. Whatever medium you live in for a thousand years becomes the place you adapt to. If you lived in an aquatic environment over a thousand years, the webbing between your fingers and toes would return. You simply adapt to the environment in which you live.

As a UFO researcher, this description sounded very familiar. It was similar to reports of alien beings. One theory is that these creatures may not be from outer space, but from our own future. This idea is worth considering and I will expand upon it in a future book.

D: *If you're seeing a thousand years, you're seeing way beyond the 2300s. It would only be a hundred years from the 2200s, and that's too soon for such dramatic evolutionary changes.*

P: I saw a thousand years. I put several things together, but I would say the 2200s is when they went underground. I thought I was seeing an established life there in the 2300s. But it's probably the 3200s because I keep thinking of a thousand years.

D: *In a thousand years the Earth would not have straightened out to where they could return to the surface?*

P: This is very interesting speculation. But once a status quo is reached, this is the way it is and this is the way we live. It's not so unusual to think that they would continue this life. It's the same with surface dwellers, we're not in any rush to live underground.

D: *Did some people remain on the surface of the Earth?*

P: Yes, but they were in caves, if you can differentiate a surface cave from subterranean living.

D: *Would the people who continue to live on the surface in the caves change too?*

P: You have to adapt to the environment in which you live. You must, or you can't survive. First of all, their eyes would change because the darkness factor increases tremendously in caves. They would learn to cultivate mushrooms and mold-like foods, thus their teeth would be no longer necessary; they, too, would develop bony plates. Those who are living underground are in cities that were started even now in our time, so there is technology available. Those who are left on the surface are those who just *weren't* going to go into the cities. They have an infinitely more primitive life-style. They don't have the fabric to make the silver suits that I see the underground people wearing. But they are also not going to venture out onto the surface either. It's cold in caves, by the way, and after a period of time clothes do turn into rags and disappear. Over a period of time it seems that they grow a little more hair. Those living underground don't have the same muscles as surface dwellers either because there's not much physical activity.

D: *In a thousand years surely the wind and everything would have stopped. Wouldn't the surface of the Earth return to normal?*

P: It would return to its *new* normal.

D: *What do you mean?*

P: Its new normal wouldn't be aligned the same as it is today. There would be different magnetic poles. We would have a different rotation. Our seasons and climate would be different. Our water distribution patterns would be different. *Everything* would be different.

D: *But wouldn't the Earth support life again?*

P: Yes, it would, and life will return to the surface. But there is quite a healthy period where real advances take place while humankind lives under the surface.

D: *So this scenario hinges on the period that's approaching our time.*

P: Very shortly.

D: *It all depends on which path we're going to take?*

P: Yes. And much of that has to do with *you* and *me,* and those of us who hear the information. What do we do with that information? Do we disseminate it in the hopes that more people will understand? It could be an important awakening. Or do we think, "I'm just one human being. What can *I* do?" and do nothing. It is good to remember that Nostradamus was just *one* person who wrote a book.

D: *Then what he was reporting to us was the absolute worse that can happen. There are many alternatives of lesser degrees in between?*

P: Yes, and even in the absolute worse there is not a total destruction of human life.

D: *So even though they change, humans will survive. It all sounds very strange. But we have to know the worse before we can concentrate on the best.*

P: Well, just because of curiosity. I do want to say that when we speak to Nostradamus in the 1500s about things that happen in the far distant future, he is also learning simultaneously. He has a very active curiosity also. You must understand that even now we're speaking to him from two perspectives. We're speaking to Nostradamus. We made mental contact with him in the 1550s as he sits there at his desk, and as I see him squinting into the mirror. But Nostradamus' body, of course, has long since left the Earth, and his spirit is in fact what we are connecting with. When we come into these conversations with him his spirit is focused at a particular time because we've asked for that focus, but we get the whole spirit. We ask questions such as, "What does Nostradamus see in the 2300s?" To ask those questions to the 1550s Nostradamus, there would be no answers. You see, we have to take in the essence of Nostradamus as well as the man that's focused, in order to enable the conversation to take place.

D: *Then when he is seeing the future, he is doing this through that spirit?*

P: He's doing it two ways. One through future sight from the 1550s, and one through the knowingness of the essence that he is.

D: *Then which part is conveying these things back to him while he is alive?*

P: The essence I'm talking about is the one that can speak to you as we speak today, and as we have spoken in other times in our sessions. The perspective that can see the ramification of human thought and behavior is the essence's point of view. From the focused 1550s point of view, he can only report what he has seen. He can't truly tell you a man's motivation. He can just report.

D: *So we're actually speaking to what we might call his "higher self"?*

P: You could use that term, yes.

D: *Then he doesn't fully understand all these things when he is focused in his physical body.*

P: He does not fully understand. I believe when he saw these things and later as he felt the absolute compulsion to write and share them—even though it was so dangerous for his own physical well-being—I don't believe that Nostradamus knew the underlying *reasons* why humanity did what it did, or what it could do to avert it. I think that particular knowingness came from the essence.

D: *It gets very confusing. You're trying to talk to two parts of a person.*

P: I can tell you what he saw, and then I can tell you what his understanding from the essence is. I think that's the invaluable reason for speaking to him. Otherwise you have the quatrains, you just have to read them.

D: (Chuckle) *Except that we can't understand them.* (We all laughed.) *So that is the importance, to show us what* could *happen. And we have to gain the understanding of how to avoid it.*

P: Yes, and that is the reason he *must* communicate now in 1989. He took on a tremendous karmic responsibility when he wrote his visions as puzzles. Now his responsibility is to help decipher them. I think he started out in the 1500s being able to communicate with a whole *range* of disparate entities, and he didn't know what was going on. Why him? How was it happening? Would it happen again? How often would it happen? Could he make it happen? Does it have to be spontaneous? He had a whole bunch of questions when this started happening to him early in his life and throughout his life, so curiosity was definitely a compelling factor. Also after having seen what he called "things that happen in the future," he had the compulsion to express these. He just *had* to. It was just too big. It happens right now to individuals who become filled with something to the saturation point. It has to be expressed somehow. And that's now he expressed it. The desire to communicate to humanity that these are probabilities, and that people can affect the future by their thoughts and by their beliefs was information that came to him in the spirit state. So two things take place in order for these communications with you to occur. That is, one: he is still operating from a base of curiosity. That's how he started. But two: now he has a *reason*. Besides just making contact, he has something he wants to say.

D: *But even with the initial contacts he always felt the need to warn us.*

P: If you want to be specific, he's been dead since you've known him too. He's never been sitting in this room with you in 1989.

D: *But in the very beginning whenever he first spoke to us in the 1550s, it was with the idea of warning the future about what he had seen. That's the way I understand it.*

P: You must remember that what you get comes through the filter of your own understanding. You will interpret it through *your* filter system, just as everyone else does. I do not think this is the time to have this conversation. To explain it accurately might take longer than you are willing to talk today. But you *must* know that when you speak to anyone who is not standing in front of you that you can touch, anyone whose physical body lived at an earlier time period, you *are* speaking to the consciousness of that person as it existed at that time. But the rest of the consciousness is also there and is accessible. It seems that we have accessed it in a clear enough manner that I can explain to you the process. However, the very first time you contacted Nostradamus it was the same process at work. Whether the person explained it to you in that manner or whether you understood it in that manner, it is entirely the way it happened. But the fact is, anybody that you talk to from the past also has a perspective that took place after death.

D: *Right. But you can speak to that person from the perspective of what they know ...*

P: At that time, yes.

D: *In my work I have demonstrated that you can go through the past lifetime and access information after death that gives a perspective on the whole life.*

P: And the future.

D: *When they're in the physical it seems that everything else is shut out.*

P: It is focused on that life. And if there are no questions that ask beyond that, that's where it stays.

D: *Then this whole subject can get very complex.*

P: It is much more complex than, "We'll go talk to Nostradamus in 1535."

D: *But apparently it was set up for some reason.*

P: Yes. I don't think it would be as impressive for *you* personally to hear a spirit tell you what Nostradamus' intentions were—*are*—in the 1550s. If an invisible spirit with no name started telling you these things, I don't think you would be as receptive to it as if Nostradamus himself were speaking to you. This is just personality preference. That is all it is.

D: *But I like to believe he really is the one who is telling us all this.*

P: He *is*, but the essence of Nostradamus is also involved.

D: *I don't want to think I'm conversing with some other spirit who is trying to play tricks on me.*

P: No, we have Nostradamus' thoughts and memories. You have made that connection. But we have more than that because we have his expanded perspective as well.

D: *Has Nostradamus been reincarnated in our time?*

P: Let me look around. What's funny is that I hear him, and he said, "Many times." In my personal understanding about reincarnation, an individual personality essence would take on the form of another body and have a life, and this would continue in linear progression. But he's screaming in my head, "Yes, I've had many lives since then, and at the present time I am having several lives." So all of a sudden I understand it was not a single life to single life, but multi-dimensional lifetimes. It seems that the personality essence of Nostradamus is *not* alive as someone who could be regressed and discover he was Nostradamus. But this desire, this giant responsibility to express potential futures and to enlighten others to what they as individuals can do about it, is an attribute that seems to have expediently progressed outward. And he takes credit for it. I couldn't say that I see him as an individual human being walking around now. But I do see that he has worked quite diligently to get this information to come through into the conscious realm of many humans in many parts of the globe. So I don't know what to say, other than Nostradamus' *seed* seems to be with many, many people.

D: *There have been reports of people saying they are Nostradamus reincarnated.*

P: You might find that there are *multiple* people who say that. To a certain degree it is true, but not to a total degree. The more you ask in this realm, the more confused you're likely to become. I would like to say also that we have communication with that larger aspect of *me*. There is a conversation that goes on between the essence of Nostradamus and *my* essence, so understanding can get through to *me*.

I had the distinct impression I was entering areas that were too complicated for my poor brain to comprehend. My head was spinning. I much prefer my simpler way of looking at this communication with Nostradamus. It was time to extricate ourselves from this morass and return to normal questions about the scenes in the mirror.

Section Three
Beyond the
Quatrains

Chapter 18

Odd Quatrains

$\mathcal{D}$URING ONE SESSION while working with Brenda I came across a quatrain that was different from all the others contained in Ms. Cheetham's book. It was different because it was incomplete. The last line was cut off in mid-sentence. Ms. Cheetham says, "Either the final line was not completed or [it] was cut by the Catholic censor because it was dangerous or heretical. It is a pity because, with it, one might have gleaned some meaning from this quatrain."

I glanced at this note for the first time as I prepared to read the quatrain to Brenda. I found it interesting that an incomplete quatrain had found its way into the final edition. I cannot believe Nostradamus would have been so careless. I also cannot believe that a church censor cut it out. If that were the case, many others that were more obvious would have been excised. I thought there had to be another explanation. I barely had time to ponder this because I was reading it on the spur of the moment. Of course, Brenda did not know there was anything unusual about it. I was just reading the quatrain in succession with the others, and she had never seen any of them in advance. It would not have done any good anyway. She never knew where I was in the book, any more than I knew which century I would read from next. I was just trying to finish this demanding and time-consuming job. Only a scholar who had studied these for years and had memorized most of them would even recognize it on first reading. The quatrain contained the name of our old friend, the King of Blois. It was a name that Nostradamus used frequently, and one that I always had trouble pronouncing. He never failed to chide me as he corrected my pronunciation. "It is not Blois; it is Blo–wah, Blowah (phonetic)." I attempted each time, but I never could please him. It was as though he winced and resigned himself to my Anglicized accent. He once said that anyone who was not born and raised in France would never be able to speak French satisfactorily.

CENTURY VIII-52

Le roi de Blois dans	The king of Blois to reign in Avignon,
Avignon regner,	from Amboise and 'Seme' the length
D'amboise & seme viendra	of the Indre: claws at Poitiers holy
le long de Lyndre	wings ruined before Boni. ...
Ongle à Poitiers sainctes	
œsles ruiner	
Devant Boni. ...	

When I finished reading, a confused look spread over Brenda's face. Nostradamus asked for another reading. After a long pause, he asked that I repeat it again. This was unusual in itself. One reading was usually sufficient to trigger the explanation. The most I ever had to read a quatrain was twice, and that was usually because he could not understand some of my pronunciation and was distracted by it. After three readings he still seemed confused, and was making no attempt at translation. Since he was having difficulty, I offered to read him the translator's remarks.

D: *There's an interesting note on this quatrain. Does he want me to tell him what it is?*

B: Maybe you should because there seems to be a problem.

D: *They say in the book that the quatrain is not complete. It's not finished.*

B: That would explain the difficulty. The images that are coming through are jumbled and not meshing with each other.

D: *It's not a quatrain, in a sense, because it only has three complete lines. The last line has been broken off in the middle.*

B: He suggests you mark that one to come back to at another time. And he will see what he can do in the meantime. He is going to check his own records.

D: *They said either Nostradamus did not complete the quatrain or the line was cut off by the Catholic censor. Does he think there was any reason for the Catholic church to censor that one?*

B: He says if the Catholic church had its way, it would have censored every one he ever wrote.

D: *That's what I was thinking. Why pick one?* (Laugh)

B: Unless it was one they felt was a bit more barbed than usual.

D: *Maybe they saw a meaning there that he didn't intend.*

B: That's entirely possible, he says.

D: *I don't think he would have published one that was incomplete, would he?*

B: No, he would not.

D: *I can give him the number if that will help him find it.*

B: Hmm. He doesn't feel it would necessarily help because he's not sure the numbers you have match up with his. He feels that he can find it. He says he supposes that he should not complain too much because they survived remarkably well for the amount of time involved.

I made a note on this quatrain and continued on with the session. Brenda had no difficulty with any of the rest of the quatrains that were covered that day. The next week I decided to begin the session with the incomplete quatrain. I would have to remind Nostradamus of it and hope that he remembered what I was talking about.

D: *The last time we met ... of course, according to wherever he is, he may not know where we stopped the last time. I imagine it's confusing when I say that.* (Chuckle) *But there was one quatrain we were working on that was confusing because it was not completed. It has come down to us in that way. He couldn't tell us the answer, and he said he would look it up on* his *copy, to see if he could find the part that is missing. Does he know what I'm talking about?*

B: Yes, he does. He said that particular form of the quatrain was on an earlier manuscript copy that must have been found after his death. The later copy apparently was misplaced somehow. But he himself, still being alive, has access to the later copy since he knows where it is. He has read the entire thing and has been able to work out the additional information we need. He says in order to help "get the wheels rolling" he needs you to read it again.

I repeated it, and this time there was no hesitation. He plunged immediately into the interpretation. It was evident he was now familiar with the quatrain that had caused confusion the week before.

B: He says this quatrain has two alternate interpretations, depending on which era of history you wish to refer to. Considering that history moves in spirals, it's not surprising that sometimes a quatrain can refer to two or three loops in the same part of the spiral. He says on the one hand it refers to World War II when Germany had taken over two-thirds of France. The other third of France, the so-called Vichy state, was supposedly free from Germany. He says that's what was referred to as the King of Blois and the other Amboise. The fact that France was divided and under two different governments, due to the misfortunes of war. He says, briefly, the last two lines of the completed quatrain refer to the disposition of the British forces, and how they made bombing runs by plane from across the sea.

D: *That's the holy wings?*

B: Yes. He says the alternate interpretation refers to the time of the Anti-Christ. And for a brief period of time France will, once again, be divided under two different governments, or two different spheres of influences. Scratch governments, he meant spheres of influences. He said "government" was not quite precise enough. Once again this has to do with the Anti-Christ and the Cabal. Throughout most of western Europe the Anti-Christ and the Cabal are able to cooperate, concerning how the spoils are divided, so to speak. In France, there is going to be a period of time when part of that country will be under the major influence of the Anti-Christ, while the other part is controlled by the Cabal. But it will eventually also be under the control of the Anti-Christ. He says the rescuers of the situation will be, once again, air-borne craft—planes and such—flown in from British and American possessions, as well as what he's calling "the free aligned states."

D: *What does that mean?*

B: He says when all this change starts taking place, several countries, both developed and so-called "third world," will decide to band together by treaty to work against the Anti-Christ. And they will call themselves "the free aligned states," because they have an alliance. He says it will include some African countries, and some of the Pacific Island nations as well, New Zealand, for example, and some smaller ones. He says it will also include some South American countries. Oh, and he's chuckling. He says it also includes the state of Texas. (*Laugh*) He says, once again Texas acts independently of the rest of the nation.

D: (Laugh) *Well, one more question. I don't know if he'll answer it or not. Can he complete that last line for us?*

B: He feels he probably would not be able to get that information through. He says there are two reasons. One, the communicator is not familiar with French, and so it would be difficult to get the right sounds through. And he says the pressure of time is also against it. It came through time incomplete. And to try to get the rest of it punched through that bubble of time—he's calling it that—would take a great deal of energy. He felt you would probably want that answer, and he does not blame you for asking. His eyes are twinkling. He says you're not the only one who's had to spend extra time in libraries. He hopes you realize what you've put him through.

D: *What does he mean?*

B: He says, "You don't realize, my libraries are not equipped with electric lights. We're talking about candles and rats and spiderwebs."

D: (Laugh) *But why have I put him through extra time in libraries?*

B: Actually he's referring to his own personal library, and looking up that particular quatrain.

D: *Oh, you mean I made him go through all that while he was trying to find it? His library is in another part of the house?*

B: Right.

D: *My libraries don't have rats and things in them, but at least we've both had to work on all of this.* (Laugh) *I appreciate him finding it for me.*

B: He had not realized the quatrain had not come down in its complete form.

𝕴 HAVE INCLUDED IN THIS CHAPTER other quatrains that created difficulty and strange reactions from Nostradamus. I know these were not attempts to get out of translating quatrains that had particularly complicated symbolism because to me these particular quatrains did not sound any different from the others. Why single only a few out of the entire book? I'm sure this is what Brenda thought: that there was no distinguishing difference between any of them. The confusion and uncertainty did not come from her, it was definitely coming from Nostradamus. I believe these reactions displayed total honesty. Any of my subjects would have had good reason to say that none of the quatrains made any sense. That would have been an easy way to get out of even attempting the translation. But at least they did try, even when vocabulary and concept interpretation were not adequate. There was definitely a different set of circumstances at work when these unusual quatrains came up. If Nostradamus or Brenda was merely inventing or making up interpretations to please me, they would have done the same with these. They would have come up with some answer, any answer, rather than admit they had none. Also why did the confusing quatrains occur toward the end of our experiment when we were interpreting the ninth and tenth centuries? These are the last of the ones that have come down to us. We know the first published books of Nostradamus' quatrains contained only about half of them. They appeared in several versions until the last ones were combined into a complete book after Nostradamus' death. Perhaps some inaccuracies or forgeries crept into these last portions and remained unnoticed for hundreds of years. We will probably never know. Maybe a Nostradamus expert can tell us if there is some difference between these centuries and the rest. I invite their comments and explanations.

Nostradamus said several of the quatrains read during these three years of sessions were so garbled that they were almost unrecognizable. He said errors could have crept in because of being copied and reprinted repeatedly throughout the centuries. The following are the oddities we found:

D: *This next quatrain has some words in quotation marks. In French, it's "amour alegre."*

Nostradamus asked for the spelling of "alegre."

D: *And they've translated that as "Light of love."*

CENTURY X-38

Amour alegre non loing pose le siege,	"Light of love" will not hold the siege for long, for the converted
Au sainct barbar seront les garnisons,	barbarian will be all the garrisons; the Ursins and Adria give security
Ursins Hadrie pour Galois feront plaige,	for the French, for fear of the army behind handed over to the Grisons.
Pour peur rendus de l'armee du Grisons.	

Confusion was again evident after the reading. This hesitation was so unusual that it was very noticeable when it occurred. Brenda asked for two more readings, but that did not seem to clarify it. She still displayed confusion and uncertainty.

B: He's not sure if maybe ... it has not come down accurately through the centuries, because he says it is not connecting.

D: *It's always possible that maybe he didn't even write some of these.*

B: He says he would not imagine a counterfeiter to be so bold.

D: *Well, some people have tried to imitate him. "Light of love" is the translation. Is that the part that's confusing, or is it all of it?*

B: The whole thing.

I read it two more times but there was still no response.

D: *It may be a mistranslated quatrain. If he wants to let it go, I will. But probably he's determined to find out what it is, isn't he?*

B: Yes, he's chewing on his mustache. He says this quatrain is apparently garbled. The only meaning he can draw from it has to do with the Roman legions and the Roman Empire when they were in southern France. But as we both know, that was quite a bit in the past. That was even before *his* time. He is not sure if it's a mistranslation or perhaps a very clever forgery that has accidentally gotten in and remained for several centuries.

D: *That's possible. Some quatrains have been found that definitely were forgeries because they didn't follow his style. It may be possible that others have slipped through.*

B: He says he hesitates to call this a forgery. He suspects it's more a case of it being miscopied sometime in the past, and the miscopy being carried down and then mistranslated with totally garbled meaning.

D: *Anything like that is possible. It's been 400 years. But at least he can see the majority of them seem to have come down to us pretty clear.*

B: He said he would not call it pretty clear.

D: *He wouldn't?*

B: He said if they'd come down pretty clear, you would not have had to contact him for translation.

D: (Laugh) *But the translations have been fairly accurate?*

B: He said, well, at least it's something one can work with.

During another session he had difficulty with the following quatrain. He asked us to postpone it until the next session. The main source of the problem seemed to stem from the use of the word "LAYE," which was capitalized in the French. I began the next session with this one, hoping he had solved the problem, or could identify it. He wanted to know if the word was spelt the same in French.

Century X-52

Au lieu où LAYE & Scelde
se marient,
Seront les nopces de
longtemps maniees,
Au lieu d'Anvers où la
crappe charient
Jeune vieillesse consorte
intaminee.

At the place where the Laye and the Scheldt join the marriage will be arranged a long time ago. At the place in Antwerp where the chaff is carried a young undefiled wife, and old age.

B: He says this is an event that has taken place in the past. It was about 75 years in the future for him; perhaps a century. It has to do with how the pilgrims fled from England to Amsterdam to escape persecution. And from there they went to America to colonize the northeastern part of what was to become the United States.

D: *Why did he have trouble with it last time?*

B: He says part of it was the atmospheric conditions, and part of it was because the communicator was getting tired. But he said the anagram threw him off. He thought he had taken that out, and so it puzzled him.

D: *LAYE was not supposed to be left in?*

B: He had changed it back to the name he originally saw. But evidently when these were published after his death, his sons found an earlier version that still had an anagram in it.

D: *It was supposed to be another word, and that would have made it clearer?*

B: Yes. He would have recognized it quicker.

Several interpreters have translated this quatrain as referring to Belgium, but in Nostradamus' time both Belgium and Holland were called the Netherlands, or "lowlands." Also Nostradamus was correct in saying the pilgrims fled to the United States within 75 to 100 years in his future. They came to America in 1620, and sailed from Leiden or Leyden (Laye?), Holland. It was also typical of his style to refer to this as a marriage, in this case the old age (Europe) and the young undefiled (virgin America).

D: *Did he write more than ten centuries of quatrains?*

B: He says actually there are fifteen centuries altogether, but quite a few of them were destroyed after he died. The main reason was because his son didn't have the gumption to stand up to authority. In order to make life easier for himself and the rest of the family, he knuckled under when the authorities said, "This information is too sensitive. You need to destroy it." Some of the quatrains referred to political figures of the day, and were somewhat sensitive in that respect. And some dealing with the future were particularly gruesome because the symbolism was fairly straight-forward. He says actually they weren't quite as gruesome as one thought, because even though they were painting a very bad picture, at the same time they were showing a way to try to avoid the situation. But that part would be easy to overlook if one wanted to bend it to one's own means. He says he can see in his mirror what happens after he passes away. Some of these quatrains are destroyed and some are put away in a vault and forgotten.

D: *Ten centuries of quatrains have come down to us, and the seventh one was never completed.*

B: He says the seventh one was complete, but ... he is sarcastically using the word "edited." It was edited.

D: *In his time period?*

B: No. After his time period.

D: *Then he intended for his son to publish these?*

B: Yes, because his son had access to his copies and his notes, as well as having access to the equipment he used in his lab.

D: *But his son didn't have as much faith or courage or whatever it takes.*

B: Correct. He says you must recall that his son was exposed to much of this symbolism and knew how his father thought. He would be more apt to figure out what he meant in his quatrains.

D: *Then the ones that have survived are the ones that were the most difficult to understand.*

B: Correct.

The following is another example of a quatrain that has come down to us in an incorrect form.

CENTURY X-54

Nee en ce monde par	Born into this world of a furtive
concubine fertive,	concubine, at two raised high by
A deux hault mise par les	the bad news. She will be taken
tristes nouvelles,	captive among enemies and
Entre ennemis sera	brought to Malines and Brussels.
prinse captive,	
Et amené à Malings & Bruxelles.	

After Brenda expressed hesitation, I read this quatrain two more times.

D: *Some of these that he's having trouble with are in the tenth century, the last one that we have. I wonder if there's a reason for that.*

B: He says that's a possibility. He says he has never felt like this. It is like walking in syrup or honey or molasses. He says the symbols taken one line at a time make sense, but when they're all put together they contradict each other. He's not sure but there might have been some jumbling of the manuscript. He suspects that the first two lines are from one quatrain, and the second two lines from another. He says the first two lines refer to the Anti-Christ.

D: *He is the one born to the concubine.*

B: Yes, and "at two raised high." But he says the other two lines do not connect.

D: *Does he think they belong to anything he has written?*

B: He thinks so, but from what he can tell the information they would convey has already been covered in another quatrain.

D: *At least we're finding these things out, and they're important as far as research on his works is concerned.*

When Brenda awoke after this muddled session, she tried to explain the strange sensations she felt. She said that normally when she was interpreting the quatrains it was as though they were both floating over a map of the continent of Europe. And when I read names, Nostradamus would point out where these were on the continent below them. She said with these difficult quatrains, there were no pictures and no scenes. It was like gray fog, and she could see nothing to try to decipher. She said normally whenever we came to the last quatrain for the session, and she was tired and could not interpret any more, it was just words. They floated over her head and had no meaning whatsoever. When she reached that point in the session she felt it was useless to continue. But she felt an even stranger sensation with these quatrains that caused Nostradamus confusion.

B: Whenever there's a quatrain that's mistranslated, garbled or not his, from my point of view it feels like "Bam!"—instant fatigue. It's as if I have glue in my eyes, and glue in my joints, and my jaw just wants to freeze up. It's hard to talk, and it's hard to construct sentences.

D: *All of a sudden it becomes difficult.*

B: Yes, extremely. I mean, it's difficult anyway. Even when they're going smoothly it takes a great deal of concentration. But when you run across one of these, it's like having someone speak to you in ancient Greek and trying to translate it without knowing a word of Greek.

D: *One time Nostradamus said he felt as if he was wading through molasses or honey.*

B: It is. I can feel the effort he puts forth into translating these, and communicating it through me. And whenever it's one that he doesn't recognize or has difficulty with, it's the same thing that happened whenever he was trying to send astrological symbols through me, and had to switch to Tarot symbols. It was like running into a brick wall. This was a very similar type of feeling.

D: *So it could be happening on his end too.*

Since we had completed the translation of all the quatrains, the main focus of the next session would be the lesser-known ones (11th & 12th centuries) mentioned in Henry Roberts' book, *The Complete Prophecies of Nostradamus,* and the so-called "lost" and "black" quatrains. These latter ones I suspected to be fraudulent—mainly because I had written to the publisher and told him what I was working on. I requested the French versions of these "lost" quatrains. My letter was never answered.

D: *I told Nostradamus the last time we spoke that I had completed all the quatrains. But I have found a few more that I didn't know about. They are supposed to be fragments of the 11th and 12th centuries.*

B: He says that does not matter. As you know, he deliberately scuffled the order of them anyway. So it does not matter if they are not in order according to the numbers. He says there are many that he has written, and more that he will be writing. Give what you have; he would like to cover as many as possible.

D: *I found these in another book and the wording is different. I don't think it's as clear, but I have to go with what I have.*

B: He says that is no problem. He is ready.

I will once again include only those quatrains relevant to our project and omit those dealing with the past.

D: *This quatrain has some of his strange words in the beginning. I always worry about being able to pronounce them.*

B: He says he is always happy to correct you, as you have probably noted.

CENTURY XI-91

Meysinier, Manthis & le
  tiers qui viendra,
Peste & nouveau insult,
  enclos troubler,
Aix & les lieux fureur
  dedans mordra,
Puis le Phocens viendrot
  leur mal doubler.

Meysinier, Manthi and the third that shall come, plague and new insult shall trouble them. The fury of it shall bite in Aix and places nearby. Then the Phocens shall come and double their misery.

B: He says this is when the Anti-Christ is in the process of taking over Europe. It refers to all the things that will be taking place in southern Europe, particularly France. He says there will be some biological weapons used, hence to double the insult. He says war itself is a plague and it's bad enough as it is. And the new insult is new weapons that are developed. Particularly in this case, he was picturing biological weapons, various diseases developed to where they have nothing to stop them. He says these diseases will particularly affect humans and livestock. There also will be some diseases developed to affect the crops, but they would not be released at first, because the ones that affect the plants are not as easily contained as the ones that affect animals.

D: *Can he see how this will be released?*

B: From aerial canisters. He says instead of dropping bombs they would drop these canisters that break open in mid-air, and spread the spores or what-have-you to the wind. And the disease will be air-borne.

D: *Isn't the Anti-Christ taking a chance that it may spread to other parts that he doesn't want it to?*

B: He will make a careful study of the wind currents beforehand, and he will release them at certain places. According to his weather satellites it will indicate that they will be blown toward Eastern Europe and Russia, rather than towards his part of Asia. And yes, he is taking a chance. Actually this will be somewhat drastic and perhaps even foolish in the long run. Even if the wind currents cooperate and the germs are swept north and eastward, people who have the bug can travel to another part of the country and spread it further.

D: *Then it will not kill the people immediately.*

B: Oh, it will be killing massive numbers of people. But those towards the edges will have time to travel short distances before they succumb, and the people that are around them would get it. As each new group of people contracts it, the germ will become weaker, but it will still be very severe.

D: *And this is something the Anti-Christ will develop?*

B: It's something that's already been developed by the various countries. The Anti-Christ will get hold of it. It has been around since before World War II.

D: *But was never used?*

B: Correct. The Anti-Christ will be the first.

D: *We've heard in other quatrains that he would use nuclear weapons, and there would be some accidents concerning them. Will he be using this weapon at the same time?*

B: He'll be using everything at the same time, just not at the same place.

D: *Does Nostradamus see anyone using chemical warfare before the time of the Anti-Christ?*

B: He says it's hard to tell. He's reluctant to communicate speculation unless it's in conjunction with a quatrain. There's a difference between chemical warfare and this. Chemical warfare is the release of chemicals and noxious gases. This is biological warfare, the release of germs.

CENTURY XII-5

Feu, flamme, faim, furt, *farouche, fumee,* *Fera faillir, froissant fort,* *foy faucher,* *Fils de Deite! Toute* *Provence humee,* *Chasse de Regne, enrage* *sans crocher.*	Fire, flame, hunger, theft, wild smoke, shall cause to fail, bruising hard to move faith. Son of God! All Provence swallowed up. Driven from the Kingdom, raging and without spitting.

B: He says this quatrain refers to what was later called the Korean War and the Vietnam War when the French colonial empire was broken up and taken away from France through war and revolution.

D: *Is that what he means by "all Provence swallowed up"? I know Provence was where he was born in France.*

B: He says he is familiar with Provence in France, but remember that he speaks symbolically. He says Provence is also a word, in an altered form, used to speak of the outer countryside. And he said that part of the world had not been mapped yet in his time period, at least not by Europeans, so he had no place names.

D: *So he means the outer countries that belonged to France?*

B: He is referring to Southeast Asia, Indochina.

CENTURY XII-52

Deux corps un chef, champs divisez en deux,	Two bodies, one head, fields divided into two. And then answer to four
Et puis respondre a quatre ouys,	unheard ones. Small for great
Petits pour grands, a pertuis mal pour eux,	ones, open evil for them. The tower of Aigues struck by lightning, worse
Tour d'Aigues foudre, pire pour Eussovis.	for Euffovis.

B: He asks that you spell the word you slaughtered.

D: *I'm doing the best I can. E–U–F–F–O–V–I–S. And the other one is A–I–G–U–E–S.*

B: He says this quatrain refers to the Protestant Reformation and how various countries and churches started splitting from Rome. The one head being God or Christ, and the two bodies referring to Catholics and Protestants. He says it also refers to the warfare that has taken place between Protestants and Catholics. And he says that warring and arguing between them, regardless of where, is basically useless. It divides from within. He says this kind of internal weakening—particularly since it has been going on for several centuries—will make it easier for the Anti-Christ to accomplish his aims.

D: *Who are the four unheard ones?*

B: He says the four unheard ones refer to—as you might guess—people behind the scenes who were instrumental in the development of the Protestant Reformation.

D: *Why does he use those two strange names? They're strange to me anyway.*

B: He says they are anagrams on old references from the New Testament. They refer to the type of Greek that was used in the prophecies concerning the last days, and—although Christ is the head of the church—how the church has divided into several parts.

CENTURY XII-59

L'accord & pache sera tu
  tout rompue;
Les amitiez polues par discorde,
L'haine euvieillie, tout
  foy corrompue,
Et l'esperance, Marseille
sans concorde.

The accord and pact shall be broken
to pieces, the friendship polluted by
discord. The hatred shall be old,
all faith corrupted. And hope also,
Marseilles without concord.

B: He says this quatrain refers to the breakup of the League of Nations previous to World War II.
D: *Would it also be referring to the United Nations?*
B: No. He says the events having to do with the downfall of the United Nations will be a different set of events than that which affected the League of Nations.

CENTURY XII-71

Fleuves, rivieres de mal
  seront obstacles,
La vieille flame d'ire
  non appaisee,
Courir en France,
  cecy comme d'oracles,
Maisons, manoirs, palais,
secte rasee.

Brooks and rivers, shall be a
stopping to evil. The old flame of
anger being not yet appeased,
shall run through France. Take
this as an oracle. Houses,
manors, palaces, sects shall
be razed.

B: He says this quatrain once again refers to biological warfare that will be taking place in France. He says the brooks and rivers being a stopping to evil refers to the fact that the animals dying from the germs will be too weak to cross over the rivers. Therefore one section of the land may be protected by the position of rivers and such. He says this also refers to nuclear warfare and that anyone who had been exposed to radiation needs to submerse themselves in running water to wash it away from their clothing and skin.
D: *Will that help them?*
B: He says, yes; it will get the radiation off them before it has a chance to sink into their skin. This is known in your time as being a common antidote to exposure to radiation.

D: *I haven't read much about it. Then the last part talks about all of these houses and palaces and everything being destroyed.*

B: He says that is part of the same thing, part of the warfare.

D: *The nuclear warfare.*

B: And biological.

D: *So this is a continuation of the other quatrain, dealing with biological warfare during the time of the Anti-Christ.*

B: And nuclear.

D: *Okay. That's all the quatrains I have from the 11th and 12 centuries. I have some others I would like to read that I'm not sure about. They are claiming they have found the lost quatrains.*

B: They may have found *some* of the lost quatrains, part of the ones that were not destroyed. He says if you read them he could tell, through this vehicle, whether they are forgeries or his.

D: *They're called "Nostradamus' Unpublished Quatrains." They said they found some manuscripts when tearing down a wall of his house to do some repairs. They're claiming that these are some of the quatrains that have never been published. I don't know if it's true or not.*

B: He says, do not worry about whether or not it is true. Read the quatrains to him as you have the others. If it is one of his, he will interpret it as he has interpreted the others. And if it is one that he does not recognize, he will tell you so. He seems to think there may be some others to be found. He's not sure since he doesn't know exactly which ones survived to our present time. He feels that after he dies his son will be reluctant to destroy some of the quatrains he wrote just before he died, which his son thought would be controversial. But at the same time his son didn't want to just leave them lying around. And he can see where his son might plaster them into a wall or something just to have them out of sight.

D: *I don't have the French version. All I have is the English.*

B: He says that is fine. If it's his he will recognize it.

I will only include those which I consider important. Several he said were outright forgeries.

UNCATALOGED QUATRAIN N° 1

> In the millennium, two, the King's
> Son, before the turn, is seen by all
> amid thunderclaps. Angry, the
> rubble of war and pestilence, the
> sins, the fish returns to power
> after a long sleep.

B: He says he can tell that whatever the source of this French is, it is a different type of translating into English. He says the language *feels* different.

D: *To me it doesn't feel like his style, but I thought he should know.*

B: He says this quatrain is not one of his, but it could be one written by one of his students. He says you may not be aware that through the years he has had various students. They are supposedly studying medicine with him. At least that is what they say, so the church will not be suspicious. But they really study methods of meditation and mind development with him. He says often whenever he is working at the mirror and seeing visions of the future, they will meditate as well to see what they can pick up. And sometimes they pick up peripheral images having to do with whatever he is working on that particular day. He says, for example, this quatrain does not refer to a specific event. The person was picking up on the appearance and effects of nuclear warfare. He says it's a possibility that he was working on a quatrain having to do with World War II that day. And the other person sitting there picked up the conditions of Hiroshima and Nagasaki.

D: *I am aware that he had students because that was how we contacted him in the first place. They are interpreting this quatrain as the "second coming of Christ."*

B: He says he can see where they would get that from the line about the millennium. But since the wording is somewhat vague, one could apply several interpretations to it. He says one could also, in referring to the thunderclaps, think of space vehicles and exploration with rockets and such. He says it was probably written by one of his students picking up the edges of what he was seeing, not really anything specific. He says there were many of his quatrains that refer to World War II. The visions he received concerning that war were very strong because it was a turning point in history—particularly with the use of nuclear weapons. Therefore it was easier for his students to pick up on this when they were meditating.

D: *It's interesting that they tried to imitate his own style by making quatrains.*

B: He says their styles are not well reflected here because you have garbled translations. He says, yes, they would try to put it in the form of quatrains, simply for the same reason he did—as a precautionary measure. He says he was their mentor.

D: *Do you think it is possible they did find these in the walls?*

B: He says it's too soon to say yet. He needs to hear some more of them.

I read a few more that he said were written by students, and one that he recognized as his own but it applied to the French Revolution.

UNCATALOGED QUATRAIN N° 2

A new leader from the heavens
brings the people together as one,
all factions die and are reborn.
Exalted clergy bends to a higher
rule. Angels are seen in joy.
The Red Man dissolves in a
bottomless pit.

B: He says this one is not one of his. It has been planted by somebody
else. Obviously by listening to this, one could say right away that it
refers to the second coming of Christ, the uniting of all Christian factions, and the final banishment of Satan. He suspects it was probably
written by a priest wanting to muddy the waters, so to speak. He's
saying it is too close to the surface. His quatrains are deeper down, and
have deeper meanings. He says this is actually lifted from one of the
books that were edited out of the Bible, and placed in quatrain form.
D: *Does he think it might have been a priest in his own time or later?*
B: He says he can't be sure. He suspects a priest from just after he dies,
wanting to get his two bits in, so to speak.

UNCATALOGED QUATRAIN N° 3

Comets without tails fill the sky,
move silently. Panic abounds. An
offering rejected, a tailed comet
glides among the bees, dies, and
heads of state nonplussed. Signatures in the sand are ignored by all.

B: He says this is one of his, and it has several meanings. On one hand,
it refers to the breakdown of communication that led to the United
States' involvement in World War II. It also refers to the dropping of
atomic bombs on Japan. A comet among the bees refers to the air-
planes carrying these atomic bombs.
D: *"Comets without tails fill the sky."*
B: He says that refers to communication satellites and such that have
been developed in the latter 20th century.
D: *It says, "move silently. Panic abounds."*
B: He says since they are above the atmosphere, they make no sound.
And he says many people are troubled by them since they are used for spying.
D: *And the last part, "Signatures in the sand are ignored by all."*
B: He says that refers to the breakdown of communication between
America and Japan that led to America becoming involved in the
Second World War. He says writing in the sand has about as much
substance as diplomatic promises. Particularly when you're dealing

with two cultures as different as the United States and Japan. He says it was very difficult to communicate because they had different protocols and different standards of manners and politeness.

D: *They are interpreting this as referring to UFOS and spacecraft.*

B: He says that is implied through the part that refers to communication satellites and such.

D: *The comets without tails.*

UNCATALOGED QUATRAIN N° 4

A salver flies, comes to rest in the New City. Hate flourishes for the entity within. Battle lines drawn. Fears of disease mask truth while three leaders in secret unite against a false threat.

D: *A salver is a tray.*

B: He says this is a quatrain written by one of his students. Although it is not his quatrain, he is willing to interpret some of the phrases if you are interested. He says it is closely related to some quatrains he has written, and it does not necessarily give any new material. He thinks it is interesting because it shows someone else's viewpoint on the visions he sees. The salver flying and coming to rest in the New City refers to the Hindenburg and the accident that befell it. He says the hate for what lies within refers to the Germans that were piloting the Hindenburg. And he says the battle lines drawn and the three meeting in secret refers to some secret protocols developed by Roosevelt, Churchill and Stalin concerning how things would be divided and run after World War II.

D: *And it says, "fears of disease mask truth."*

B: Before the United States became involved in the war, they started limiting imports and exports to the Axis countries, blaming contaminated crops and such. Although the real reason was because the United States was becoming involved with lend lease with England. They were trying to keep that hidden because the United States was still supposed to be neutral.

D: *Of course, they are translating this as referring to an alien and a space craft.*

B: He says he would rather go ahead to the next one than fool around with erroneous interpretations.

D: *It seems to be a good quatrain, although it doesn't have the symbolism he usually puts into it.*

B: He says that part is difficult—to put in as much symbolism as he does.

UNCATALOGED QUATRAIN N° 5

> Twenty plus two times six will see the lore of the heavens visit the planet in great elation. Disease, pestilence, famine die. Rome rejoices for souls saved. The learned smile in awe. Astrology confirmed. For science, a new beginning.

B: He says he recognizes part of this quatrain and part he does not. The part he recognizes was written by one of his students. He says there are a couple of lines that he feels have been inserted by somebody at a later date. He says, "Rome rejoices over souls saved and the learned smile in awe," are the two lines that have been inserted. The rest of the quatrain refers to after the Anti-Christ has been defeated, and the world is rebuilding. There will be many new and wondrous discoveries made. Or rather, discoveries that have been developed in secret will be revealed to the world and be allowed to benefit humanity. Therefore the new beginning for science. And he says, of course, along with this there will be many diseases eradicated and conquered, so humanity will be healthier. And the space program will have developed by leaps and bounds.

D: And *"astrology confirmed"* belongs in there. *What are those numbers "twenty plus two times six"?*

B: He says that refers to some astrological measurements. It refers to particular relationships in the heavens. He says, imagine the sun being the center of a great circle. The numbers refer to the various degrees of angles on the circle, between the planets involved.

D: *Is there any way to use those numbers to come up with a date?*

B: He says it is not a specific date as in a one-day date. It refers to a span of years when this will start happening.

D: *They're coming up with the year 2012.*

B: He says it sounds as if these are some that were altered by priests before being sealed up in the wall. You can tell where the priests have been altering because they are so blatant.

D: *He can tell it anyway.* (Chuckle) *Do you think that's why they were sealed in the wall and not used?*

B: Yes. He says he suspects that after he died, a priest was on hand and was going through his personal effects. As a matter of reference in helping his students to learn, he would keep notes on some of the things they picked up when in meditation, to help them further develop themselves. He says he feels that a priest probably found some of these notes and thought them to be some of his quatrains and decided to do some altering and sealed them up in the wall, thinking they would be found sooner than they were. He said that was a political move.

D: *Then it wasn't his son who sealed them up?*

B: After hearing them he does not think so.

UNCATALOGED QUATRAIN N° 6

A revolution without bloodshed, without strife. Men in unhappy confusion strive for perfections beyond their ken. Failure. Then elation. The Earth's forces give way to a new power above the clouds.

B: He says this is a quatrain written by one of his students. The student is referring to the pictures he picked up concerning the nuclear bomb, particularly its development during World War II, and its deployment. He says the power above the clouds refers to the mushroom cloud that builds up to the very edge of the Earth's atmosphere.

UNCATALOGED QUATRAIN N° 7

The bees sting amid thunderclaps and lightning bolts, confusion. Fear. Awe. The fish trembles, governments are strangely silent while the heavens flash ominous messages to the populace. East and West darken.

B: He says this again refers to the bombing of Hiroshima and Nagasaki.

D: *Is this his?*

B: No. He says this is from one of his best students, however, because it's slightly deeper in meaning than the average student's quatrain.

D: *It has more symbolism.*

B: Yes. And he says "the bees sting" refers to the planes that dropped the bomb. The planes themselves had the letter "B" in their number designation. He says the silence and the awe refers to the shock. There was no immediate reaction from the world. And the east and west being darkened refers to the same thing. Nothing happened for a bit because everyone was in such shock before they opened up communications to end the war.

D: *And that would be "flashing ominous messages to the populace."*

B: He says that refers to the flashing of the bomb.

D: *"The fish trembles"?*

B: He says that refers to the naval forces out at sea who saw this happen.

UNCATALOGED QUATRAIN N° 8

> Again the ancient woman who
> toppled from on high appears to
> the multitude. The cult is reborn.
> Dire warnings. A nation rebuffed.
> Three young ones appear to seal
> the omens seen in a mist.

B: He says he's having difficulty focusing in on this one. The symbolism is somewhat garbled. He suspects it's one of his students' that has been garbled in translation. He doesn't recognize it as being one of his.

D: *They are referring to this ancient woman as being Mary.*

B: No. He says in reality it refers to the re-arising of goddess worship in the mid- and late-20th century. And the three children refer to Australia, Canada and the United States, being children to England, which is the force of the most popular form of goddess worship.

D: *I knew he wouldn't refer to Mary. He never has.*

UNCATALOGED QUATRAIN N° 9

> Threats of war abound; nations
> quake. The ancient woman,
> ubiquitous, pleads for peace.
> A populace awed; The year 90 plus
> 3 sees upheavals while mighty
> warriors shake fists. Anoh
> searches the horizon in vain.

B: He says this quatrain is one of his, and it refers to events that will be coming up in the near future for you. He says it deals with the world situation in general, and the breakdown of peace and communication. The situation that's developing is one that the Anti-Christ will be taking advantage of for the building of his power base before he makes his move.

D: *Is "the year ninety plus three" 1993?*

B: Yes. He says mighty warriors shake their fists refers to the various countries trying to get the Middle East to settle down and get into line, through economic sanctions and what-have-you. It will not be entirely effective. As he says, mighty warriors are shaking their fists, but they're not hitting anybody yet.

D: *And the last part, "Anoh searches the horizon in vain."*

B: He says that represents that the various world leaders will be hunting for a solution to the problem, to try to prevent the situation from getting worse. There will be some world leaders sincerely searching for a solution. And other world leaders who will pretend to search for a solution, but are in actuality working to do a bit of warfare for the advantage of their own country in order to either pick up their economy or to try to better their position in the world.

D: *What is that word Anoh?*

B: He says it is an anagram that refers to an organization that will come to light later. He says certain organizations are referred to by their initials. And an organization that is currently secret will be seen as referring to this when it comes to light later.

D: *It sounds as if it will be a good organization if it is trying to find ways to make peace.*

B: (*Abruptly*) He says, don't jump to conclusions.

D: (Chuckle) *All right. Who is "the ancient woman ubiquitous, pleads for peace?"*

B: He says the ancient woman refers to the personification of liberty and justice, currently pictured as being women. He says many people will be pleading for peace and justice, but they won't have any definite solutions for bringing this about.

D: *They're saying it's Mary again.*

B: He says it is very frustrating, but they assume every time he refers to women, he is thinking of Mary. He says Mary is not the only woman in the world.

D: *They say that Mary will make simultaneous appearances throughout the world, and the word "ubiquitous" is the key.*

B: He says he's not interested in erroneous interpretations. He says he's not going to say what they are full of, but it's something rather smelly and unpleasant.

UNCATALOGED QUATRAIN N° 10

> Three women in black of a charitable order; shocked at first, receive a blessing from one like themselves. A mystery told, three times, but no one can see the future save the three. And a pox to all who reveal the secrets.

B: He says this is a plant from the priesthood. A priest who was trying to point out that divine revelation can only come through members of the priesthood or from nuns. He worded it as a way to try to make Nostradamus appear false.

UNCATALOGED QUATRAIN N° 11

The abomination from the East
makes his purpose. The papacy
falters. A strange conflict between
the devout and the pagans. A flock
seemingly forsaken, yet divine plans
for intercession arise.

B: He says this quatrain is one of his. The abomination from the East refers to the Anti-Christ, and the papacy falters refers to the fall of the Catholic Church. He says the strange conflict between the pagan and the devout refers to the fact that once again the schisms within the Christian church, and between Christians and non-Christians, get in the way when they should be banding together to fight against the Anti-Christ because he is the common enemy.

UNCATALOGED QUATRAIN N° 12

Darkens descends. Eclipses great.
North and South change. War and
nature unite against the peace.
Heavenly holocausts rain blood on
the rocks and our face is mutilated.

B: He says this quatrain is one of his and it refers to the shift of the poles.
D: *"The darkens descends." That doesn't sound right.*
B: He says that should be "darkness." He feels it is a misprint in the case of the translator.
D: *Well, it says the first line was obliterated.*
B: He says this quatrain refers to the fact that when the pole shift occurs there will be many earthquakes and volcanoes erupting.
D: *That's the blood on the rocks?*
B: And the mutilation of the face.
D: *The face of the Earth?*
B: Yes. He says the war part refers to the fact that some of the earthquakes will be sparked by the dropping of powerful bombs.

UNCATALOGED QUATRAIN N° 13

A new ruler anointed, rises from
the 50th latitude; renews the once-
great fish. Peace for a millennium.
Rome rebuilds and the divine hand
at the ruler's side departs. Earth in
renewal, but the scars heal slowly.

B: He says this quatrain is from one of his better students, and it refers to events that take place after the Anti-Christ has been conquered. He says it refers to the rebuilding and recovering from the warfare.

D: *What does that mean, the new ruler "rising from the 50th latitude"?*

B: He says that refers to the part of the world the Great Genius will come from.

D: *I thought that might refer to him, but I wasn't sure if this quatrain was his. "The peaceful millennium," would fit in with the Great Genius. "Rome rebuilds," would be after the destruction, wouldn't it?*

B: Yes, that's what he said. He says throughout the first thousand years institutions will try to rebuild, although their nature will be changed forever, due to the nature of the things revealed during the war.

UNCATALOGED QUATRAIN N° 14

> In the year eighty plus nine the vast
> East collapses. Hunger. The
> germs do not thrive. The West in
> sympathy brings about its own
> downfall. Bones everywhere. The
> famine rages, but there is no echo
> in marbled halls.

B: He says this quatrain is one of his. It refers to events that are taking place in what is the present for you. He say it refers to the downfall of the Communist order in Russia and eastern Europe, and they are in the process of rebuilding. *(This session was held in early 1990.)* And the West (meaning the western alliance of countries) is in sympathy to these changes. He says the reference to germs and disease is referring to the economic situation. The "germs do not thrive" refers to the various economic solutions that are put forward to try to straighten things up, and they will not work. And he says "the appearance of bones and disease stalking the land, but not having echoes in marble halls," refers to the fact that the imbalance of the economy will continue to worsen. And the legislators and the various lawmakers will not know what to do about it.

D: *"The West in sympathy brings about its own downfall." Does that have to do with the economics?*

B: Yes. He says the East will be so depressed economically that the West will try to help, and will dangerously weaken their economy. Then, when the Anti-Christ is trying to take over Europe, it will make it easier for him.

D: *What does he think about these quatrains being found?*

B: He says he feels his own prophecies are from a true source. If they were from a false source they would not have survived the centuries. He says the ones that are found ... he doesn't mean to just shrug his shoulders and say "fate"—but he feels there is a guidance involved, some energies involved. And he says these that were supposedly lost, could have stayed lost. Obviously it was meant for them to be found because there are a few of his in there. He has also noticed some from his better students in there as well. There was one that was so very close to his own style that even he had to stop and think for a moment. He says that quatrain had depths of meaning as well, which was unusual, because many times his students do not have the chance to develop to their full potential before they have to leave.

D: *He feels they were actually sealed up in a wall, but he thinks it was done by a priest? Is that correct?*

B: He suspects so, but he doesn't know because he was not there. And he says if this was indeed done, it took place after he died, and so there is no way he would know for sure.

D: *But there were also some from the priesthood in there.*

B: He says that's to be expected. It could be that some were inserted by others. Someone, perhaps in the spirit of trying to disprove him, saying, "Well, gee, I can write like that too. See, here's a quatrain I've just written."

Chapter 19

Nostradamus Asks Us Questions

MY WORK WITH NOSTRADAMUS was always full of surprises. I never knew what direction a session with my subjects would take. Since my goal was the translation of the remainder of the quatrains the sessions had established a pattern, a format that all the subjects instinctively adhered to. Upon the completion of my instructions to locate Nostradamus they would unerringly find themselves in the cold, damp room and see the man bent over his writing materials. The only variation would be the age at which they saw Nostradamus, sometimes he would be young and sometimes older. All the subjects saw his personality change according to his age. Normally they perceived themselves as either invisible or a glowing energy form. Some of them would then create an entity form so Nostradamus would have something visible to concentrate on while we communicated. After this contact was established we then primarily focused on the translations.

Each time Pam, the former school teacher, found him, she would conjure a different image for him, thinking that one type might be preferable over another. There seemed to be no logic in her choices other than she knew Nostradamus felt more comfortable having an image to focus on. He often was aware of her presence in the room, but could not see her—only the image she presented to him.

Pam had been having trouble with the translation of the quatrains. She was shown scenes in the mirror, but these were often difficult for her to interpret or to place in a time period. Many times she felt uncomfortable. When scenes of negativity appeared she would attempt to deny what she was seeing. She would convert them into something relating to the past, or attempt to change them into an alternate possibility. Pam had come to the conclusion that if she reported the negative explanation it would give the event more power. She felt she could change the event by denying its existence. I could understand her rationalization but it was not helping with the translation of the quatrains. As with the other subjects, I felt we were coming to a stalemate where further interpretation would be impossible. They all had their various reasons for wanting to stop their participation in the project. I decided to try a few more sessions with Pam and see if anything interesting might develop. This session took an unexpected and different direction.

When I had completed my instructions that would direct Pam to locate Nostradamus, she went quickly to the familiar room and discovered he was not there. She then immediately found herself on a cobblestone street that was as narrow as a present-day alley. It was daylight but high buildings and walls on either side kept the street in shadow.

Then she noticed a man, whom she identified as Nostradamus, hurrying along the street. His long cloak billowed out behind him as he walked briskly and purposely, his hood concealing his face and hair. She described him as a small man whose garments made him appear larger. He kept his head down and deliberately did not look at the other people passing him. Her first thought was that it was around 1533, and that he would be in his thirties, although he seemed to be older. He walked close to the stone walls and protectively clutched a parcel to his chest. This was one of the few times we located him outside that room. My curiosity was naturally directed toward the parcel. I asked Pam if Nostradamus was aware of her presence so we could begin our questioning.

P: No. This is very interesting. He is not his old gnarled self, but definitely younger. He's not paying any attention to me because he's in the city. There are sounds. There are people. He's in a hurry. He has a destination. It's almost as if I'm ... dismissed.

D: *Is there any way you can communicate with his mind and find out where he's going, or is that possible?*

P: I believe he's been somewhere and purchased things that he's experimenting with. He's really excited and in a hurry to get back to his room. He went to an apothecary and got some different herbs, roots and powders. But not a standard apothecary, he says. (*Chuckle*) This is someone who prepares powders, roots and seeds of plants that the general public doesn't know about. Some of them are mind-altering substances that aren't really used for the healing of open wounds, for instance.

D: *Does Nostradamus have names for any of these?*

P: He calls them his powders. (*Chuckle*) Some are already ground up in powder form. Some are just roots that resemble ginseng or radishes that have branched two roots or more. They are funny shaped carrot-looking things. (It was later suggested that this could be mandrake, a root used as a narcotic.) This is really weird, but he might even have some powdered rhinoceros horn.

D: *What would he use that for?*

P: Well, the Chinese revere it and use it for many things, but I think he is just experimenting with it. It's not something he could harvest for himself. He would prefer to do that, because then his work would remain a total secret. But there are ingredients that come from lands far away, and he has to get them somehow. Actually, I believe he has several things from China because he's curious. You can imagine how fascinating it must be for him to be talking to those of us from the future, a whole bunch of different ones. He wants clearer communication, clearer pictures. He has a desire to know more, see better—everything a standard curious human wants.

D: *So these are things he's going to use on himself.*

P: Yes. He has student apprentices who are eager to try everything. And he *may,* with great discrimination, after he's tried it on himself, allow his favorite students to participate. It seems there are only two students at this time that he feels intimate with. But it is really not for them; it's for him. It's a very private thing.

D: *Does he take these powders every time he communicates?*

P: Oh no! This is only to make it *better.* He's always on the quest to see more clearly, and have a more distinct communication. To be more *there* in the communication process. But no, he doesn't do it except when he gets this stuff.

D: *Has he ever had after effects while experimenting with these things?*

P: He says that he has. At one period he lay in a semi-coma for several days. Although he would quickly hasten to add that he wasn't injured in any way—just sort of knocked out. That has only happened once and it was because he took too much.

D: *Did he ever have any effects that would bother his mind afterwards?*

P: Not his mind. Sometimes he would be mildly nauseated by certain substances, but it did not affect his mind.

D: *I don't know whether to call him brave or foolish to be experimenting with these things.*

P: Well, I guess he feels he has to find the information somehow, and these plants, seeds and roots exist. I think there's something new in the packet that he's really excited about. He's walking with a brisk step, and his cloak is flying out behind and around him. He's very dramatic looking. I can hear his shoes clicking on the cobblestones. And just the fact that he's out of his room is a rather interesting experience for him. Of course, he travels outside, but he spends most of his time in his room.

D: *Will he tell you what type of drug he's especially excited about?*

P: I can actually see it. It seems to be a yellow-mustard color. I was thinking of the yellow powder called "goldenseal." I don't think that's it, but it is that color. He mixes the powder into either a paste or a diluted drink. He is going to start with a drink, add the powder to water and ingest it in that manner. He could make it into a moist ball and swallow the whole ball, or he could heat it. But that changes it somehow. It chemically alters it when he melts these things. He, as

I said, usually drinks them. Sometimes he sprinkles powders on something he eats. But he doesn't prefer to do that because the food and the
digestive process change it somehow in the way it reacts in his body.

D: *People thought that he drank wine, but I don't think they knew he was
into drugs.*

P: What do you call "drugs"? At the time of Nostradamus, they were
naturally-occurring plants that were part of the plant kingdom. Now
we have synthetically manufactured, greatly altered substances that
people ingest that are definitely harmful. This was not the case in the 1500s.

D: *If it was natural, it must have been more potent and the effects might
have been different.*

P: That's only speculation.

D: *Will you ask him if he is involved with alchemy?*

P: What he would consider alchemy was the combining of substances to
produce a third or a synthesized substance. He was doing that. He
wasn't turning metals into precious metals. Also, as we discussed
earlier, he did some things involved with magic.

D: *It sounds as if he must have known* real *magic. We always wonder if
there is any such thing.*

P: There is. He has a large body of proof.

D: *But when he experimented with these substances, he was not looking
for anything specific? He just combined ingredients to create different effects?*

P: Well, you know from cooking that certain things taste well together.
You wouldn't put sugar on your French fries. It's the same with what
he was working on. He knew the effects of *singular* plants, and parts
of plants. And he thought by combining certain things he would produce the desired effect. It wasn't hit-and-miss. He had knowledge of
them as independent units. For example, if you have an open wound
and he wanted to prepare a poultice for it, he might use a pack of
ground-up leaves. But he might add a powder of another herb. (The
name sounded like voltensio or bolensio. It was difficult to transcribe.)
But putting together herbs for medicinal purposes was not how I was
defining alchemy.

D: *How were you defining alchemy?*

P: As the process in the ancient ages of trying to combine different metals
to form a precious metal.

D: *I think that's normally how it is defined.*

P: But for Nostradamus' purposes it was adding together substances to
create a third effect or a differing effect from *two* things together. He
could add five things together for a unique effect.

D: *But they were mostly things he would use as a physician?*

P: No, not necessarily. The package he has today contains *all* kinds of
packets. This is a *big* package, and many of the things in it are not
used in his healing practice. They're simply for his own mind expan-

sion experiments. He could *remember* the effects of everything he experimented with. This made it easier for him to try combinations of things.

D: *He didn't have to write them down?*

P: There *were* things written down that he received from his grandfather. But many things he did were not written down.

D: *Surely the Inquisition didn't frown on using alchemy for medicinal purposes, did it?*

P: Alchemy is not a good term to use here because there are too many different meanings we could bring to it. But the church *would* have frowned on his psychedelic experiments. It brought him too close to a personal understanding of God. When you have that understanding you don't need to go through the clerics. They wanted to be the middle-man, the only way you could get there.

D: *So he was involved in many things the church wouldn't necessarily have approved of.*

P: *(She gave a knowing laugh.)* Yes. Future-seeing was definitely not for the masses of his time.

D: *Well, can you move ahead to when he is back at his house?*

P: Yes, that's where he is going and he's very eager to get there. So now we're there, and he's sitting at the familiar table unwrapping the package. He's spreading out all of his packets, and he acknowledges my presence in the room.

D: *He didn't know you were there before?*

P: He didn't *want* me there while he was on the street. If he were to turn his attention to me on the street, people would definitely think he was whacky. He knew I was trying to communicate with him, but he doesn't have to allow me through. The only time communication needs to take place is when he desires it. He knows how to block it. You can imagine how people would have stared at him if he had stood in the middle of the street talking to the *air. (Chuckle)* He felt someone was trying to contact him. And of course, his curiosity wouldn't allow him to ignore this. He knows I'm here now, so he's trying to see who it is. He mainly wants to know why we're trying to contact him.

D: *You can tell him we thought he was trying to contact us. See what he says.*

P: It's a two-way street, and we're both trying to contact each other. He loves to do this, but at this particular time he wasn't trying to contact anybody. He would like to know who we are. He's asking basic questions, "Who are you? What do you want?" I've told him that from our time perspective, it's about 400 or 450 years after his perception. And he's comfortable with that. That's no problem. It's interesting that it was necessary to even tell him that because I think we look so futuristic. But it seems that the *past* also looks very different, so it was good that he knows we're from his future.

D: *Tell him we are not spirits. We are alive in our time period as he is alive in his.*

P: He might disagree with the statement, "We are not spirits," because according to his perception we are spirits who are inhabiting these bodies in this time period. I think we're becoming a little more familiar. You see, time is very different in this realm. I was telling him that in our space of time we just talked to him last week.

D: *Of course, we may have found him at another time when he doesn't know that.*

P: He's now willing to answer any questions.

D: *Is he going to take any substance?*

P: He prefers to take the substance when he feels he is alone. He then calls forth for someone from the future that he wishes to speak to, or he is just open to *allowing* a future person to come and speak to him. But he doesn't seem to "enjoy" making that transition in front of somebody who's already here.

D: *So he doesn't need to do it this time.*

P: It's not a matter of need. It's a matter of his own preference. And he doesn't choose to change himself in front of an already established entity.

D: *He wouldn't have any reason to do it.*

P: Yes, he would have a reason to do it because he always wants *clearer* communication. He wants to see the people who are visiting him much more distinctly, and have a *real* dialog. He feels he has a need to do this to better facilitate communication. He is aware of my presence, but that doesn't mean he can see me. *I* can't see me either. I'm invisible to myself.

D: *Can you give him something to focus on?*

P: Well, my very first thought was the woman with the flowing robes and hair. But that's not necessarily his favorite image. (*Laugh*)

D: *Why, because it's a woman?*

P: Yes, but he knows that's exactly what it is—an image. It's not going to stick around and nag him. (*Chuckle*)

D: *What does he want to see that would make him feel more at ease?*

P: (*Surprised*) He asked to see who I *really* am. Hmm.

D: *Is this possible?*

P: Well, maybe I really am somewhere. The woman with the flowing hair and robes could be my larger self or my purer self. I don't know. Although the image feels really comfortable and has come to me more than once, I don't know that it's a projection of me. But at this very moment I'm trying to appear to him as I really am. I'm trying to allow him to see this whole scene. Me *here* on the bed, you *there* in the chair, as we really are in our future time. (*Surprised*) *It is working! I* see us in the mirror. He seems to be happy with that.

D: *What are you projecting into the mirror?*

P: A woman sitting by the bed talking to someone who is lying on the bed with her eyes closed. This is what he seeing. I'm telling him about hypnosis and regressions. He is quite capable of comprehending, and is fascinated. I think he might wish to ask *us* some questions.

D: *Oh, I would like that.*

P: He sees there is definitely a mechanical device, a little black box. He thinks it is interesting. It captures words, and then you can hear them again. That's very much like magic.

D: *It saves a great deal of writing. It plays the words back when you need them.*

P: This device does not exist in the 1500s and seems quite as remote as, say, someone from our time walking around on Venus, yet neither is out of the scope of possibility. This is an interesting experience. He normally asks the visitors to explain what they're seeing in their present time to him. He'll have to formulate his questions. What you might consider interesting would differ from what he considers interesting. First, he would like to know what year this is.

D: *Right now we are speaking from 1989. But I have been in communication with him for three years, since 1986.*

P: Well, he is seeing us in the mirror in this attitude for the first time. He has more focus on you than me. And he's shocked to find that you're a *woman!* (*Laugh*) I think he sensed that, but he was giving you a lot of slack because you're a future woman. Also he can ignore the fact that you're a woman if he can't see you, unless you do some of that woman stuff he doesn't like. You know he doesn't like women that much. (*Laugh*)

This was a strange feeling. Just as we were invisible while observing him, he apparently was now invisibly observing us. It made me want to look over my shoulder, half-expecting to see a glowing energy form in the room. Of course, there was nothing there, but it left me with a strange uncomfortable sensation. She continued.

P: I'm giving him some advice here. I'm telling him to disregard the shape and form of the exterior body, to talk to the essence inside the body. He *does* have an ego. It's just that he *is* human, and he does have his own cultural and personal hang-ups. He didn't even know what *I* was, because I've come so many different ways. He says he's willing to go along with this. He's also willing to have other communication with you and your friends that he doesn't see. But just this once it is fun for him to sit here and observe this. Now he'll know what you look like. And he would like to ask you some questions, although you might not consider them very interesting.

D: *That's all right. We'll try to answer anything.*

P: He wanted to know the current year from whence we are speaking. And he wants to know if you can tell him what is going on in the world right now. Not everything in the entire world, just some interesting stuff. For instance, do you know anything about France?

This threw me off. There had not been much news from that part of the world in 1989. What would interest him?

*D: Oh, let me think. Well, he probably knows there is no longer a king.
There hasn't been one for a long time.*
P: Yes. He has had much information about the Revolution.
*D: There were a lot of events after that. He knows about the Second
World War, when France went through the horrible war with Hitler.*
P: Germans.

During this whole episode while Nostradamus was asking us questions about our present day I was relating events that were common
knowledge to Pam. Yet her face registered expressions and emotions that
would have been foreign to her conscious state. She expressed great
interest, wonder and incredulity. It seemed that she was indirectly mir-
roring Nostradamus' emotions. Even the wording of some of her answers
did not seem to be coming from Pam's consciousness. It seemed at times
as though Nostradamus was speaking directly through her, which has
occurred at rare intervals with other subjects. It eliminates the "he says,
I see, *etc.*"

*D: I believe at this present time France's economy is very good, and they
are living in a peaceful condition.*
P: There are no enemies on the edges?
*D: Not with France. We get our news from television, which is a black
box that shows us pictures from all over the world.*
P: (*Her voice registered awe or wonder.*) So you have one device that
does sound, and one that does pictures.
*D: We have many that do sound. (Oh?) This black box I am using is
unique because it is recording only what we are saying. There is
another black box that can tell us things that are occurring all over the
world. And the one that shows us pictures and sounds.*
P: What year is this? 1989?
D: Yes, but we have had these things for many, many years.
P: That's good.

I was enjoying this because it gave me the feeling of communicating
directly with him, and I was excited about imparting knowledge that was
obviously foreign and awesome to him.

*D: The pictures were in black and white and now they are in color. And
so we can have the news from all over the world in an instant.*
P: Well, what is the news? Is it good?
*D: Oh, some good, some bad. There are problems in the Middle East at
the present time.*
P: Yes, those have been going on before the present time, and seem to
exist into the future time. He knows the area you're talking about.
*D: We only know from the pictures we see in our black box, and the stories
we hear on our black boxes, and read in our newspapers. There's probably much more that we don't know about.*

P: He said we must be closing off some of our avenues of knowing, for we should be able to send our thought projection and find out.

D: *I suppose we could, but we're not that accomplished. But we have many miraculous devices that allow us to have much more information and knowledge.*

P: Obviously.

D: (I was trying to think of something that would interest him.) *We have space programs. In fact, on this very day we are speaking, we shot another rocket off.*

P: (*Incredulously*) *Shot* a rocket?

D: *Let's see, how can he understand that?*

P: I'm giving him a picture of a thing going up in space with all the smoke and fire at the bottom. What's interesting is that he has seen something like that in reverse, coming down. There is fire and smoke at the bottom, and sand and dust flying up from the ground. Then the fire stops and it is sitting on the ground. So he says we can do both: send things off and things can land.

D: *Yes, but normally we don't land them in that way. Maybe he is seeing another time. What do you think?*

P: The picture I showed him had a long tube, and looked like a rocket. What he saw land wasn't as long. Do you know what a patty-pan squash looks like? (*Laugh*) It looked like one of those. There was much fire and smoke, and that was what made him see the similarity. Also it was coming *back* to Earth.

Since this description was obviously not of the same object we were referring to and the shape was not familiar to us, he apparently was seeing something else. Was it an incident that would be occurring further in the future?

P: But he says, "*Why* have we shot the rocket into space?"

D: *Let's see. We started what we call our "space program" way back in the 1960s. At that time we were just shooting rockets up and we had men orbiting the Earth. We wanted to see if it was possible to do these things. Twenty years ago the first man went up in a rocket ship and landed on the moon. He walked on the moon. Can Nostradamus comprehend that?*

P: Yes. This time I was letting you tell him. And so I was seeing the pictures he was getting from hearing you, and they were hysterical. (*Laugh*) When you said there was a man orbiting, he saw a *man* going around the Earth, similar to Superman, but without the outfit. It was just a man because there was no craft mentioned. (*Laugh*) But then when you said, "to the moon," you added, "in a rocket." So then I saw a man going to the moon in a *rocket.* And he asked, "Now how did that land?"

D: *A little compartment came out of the rocket that had men inside it. That was the part that landed on the moon.*

P: I've sent that picture to him, plus them getting out, putting the flag, "giant step for man, great leap for mankind." Then getting back on, redocking and coming home. All that was easy to send to him very quickly, and he has it now. But it was so much fun seeing into his head, and not telling him anything. And listening to how he was translating these things. (*Chuckle*) This is *so* interesting. Because I can tell you his perception, and then I can send him a more accurate perception with my mind.

D: *Yes, because he can only try to interpret what our words are conveying to him.*

P: Right. But this is quite exciting because I don't think people take the time to talk to *him* like this.

D: *I've always wanted to, but I didn't know he was interested.*

P: Well, he is. Today, anyway. (*Laugh*)

D: *You can tell him that we're not in a position to have done these things. We only know from our news what is happening.*

P: Yes. And I also communicated to him that there are secrets. For instance, involving this experience right now with our men who have left the surface of the Earth and are orbiting in a capsule around the Earth. We don't know what they are doing.

D: *They say it is involved with the military. But in the meantime we have what we call "satellites." They are mechanical machines that are also in space orbiting our planet, but there are no people inside them. They are used for many purposes, and some of them are for communications. Can he understand that?*

P: Yes, but I'm giving him a great deal of help on that one. No, they're not the size of the moon. They are very small satellites. They give us information. And they take pictures of the surface of the planet, so we have much information about the wind, waves, cloud patterns and weather.

D: *This is how we get our news from the other side of the world so quickly.*

P: I just beamed something up, bounced it off, and received it somewhere else, so he sees how that works. Although it does seem quite *incredible,* he can see what I'm thinking to him.

D: *We have many marvelous inventions. Does he want to ask about some other things in our time?*

P: Just a moment. I don't really understand his question. It has to do with injecting things into people's bodies with needles. And I don't know what he's asking. He doesn't use needles in his day. He has seen this in future visions, and not known what the reason was. It seemed so mystifying to him. I think he has awareness, though, from talking to people like me who have had antibiotics in their systems. He is aware that this is a very big distorter. He sees it as a little poison that goes into the body and does not totally discriminate what it poisons.

D: *This is the way he sees it?*

P: Yes! And he was wondering why this is such a practice. He is willing to accept anything that we say about machinery and space travel, but this is personal because he is a physician. It seems, from his perspective, that it actually kills things in the body.

D: *Let's see if we can explain it. In our medical practice today, our physicians have various ways of giving medicines. Some are taken by mouth. He gives that kind, so he should understand that. Others are injected with needles into the skin or the blood. Does he know anything about what are called "bacteria" or "germs"?*

P: Yes, he does, because he's seen stuff in the future. He even knows about AIDS.

D: *Well, in our time we have learned that diseases are caused by these tiny things called germs, bacteria, virus. You can't see them because they are so very small.*

P: Well, he says you can't see thoughts or electro-magnetism either, and you can't see karma. He might have some valuable information for our century. He says that disease isn't necessarily caused by bacteria or virus that are, if not invisible, almost invisible. It is caused by our thoughts and karma. There are many definitions for "karma," but he seems to think you believe that if you don't have self-forgiveness and release past acts they continue to follow you around until you shine the light of awareness on them. Is this how you define karma?

D: *Yes, that's one popular way.*

P: Well, he says that this ... (*uncertain*) mechanism of karma—he can't think of the word and I can't either—is being created every moment by our thoughts. And we're always judging ourselves to be "bad, lacking, wrong." We have all kinds of thoughts that go through our minds, even murderous thoughts. Our repressed feelings and emotions, unfulfilled longings and desires, all affect the physical operation of our bodies. These things that are called "germs, bacteria, virus," are living organisms that exist in the living "soup" of the world, and they're always there. Whether we allow them to manifest a negative form in our physical body is determined by how we judge ourselves, and from what perspective we're judging ourselves as well. If we're judging our present actions we can get an instant headache or stump our toe or have an accident. If we're judging our past actions we can have a lingering, long-term disease like cancer. And we can have all combinations in between, of quick-bad, slow-bad, all different ways that we allow these viruses to work on our bodies. But the viruses, germs or bacteria do not cause illness.

D: *This is what the scientists have found in their laboratories.*

P: The scientists have found that they can change the behavior of certain viruses, bacteria, and things that we call "germs." It has been proven scientifically that their behavior can be changed. But you well know that if a person continues to judge themselves negatively, they'll manifest a *different* disease caused by a *different* bacteria or virus. It is the person's self-judgment based on current life or karmic debt, if you will, that allows disease to happen. We have become such a technological society that we believe we can erase *dis-ease* with technology. And he's telling from his perspective how funny it is to see people who can go to the moon and back—and do even greater things that he's seen in the future—inject poisons into their physical bodies with the belief that this will in fact cure their dis-ease. It will change something in the body, but it's usually for the worse. He says if you don't release yourself of your negative judgment, you'll keep getting sick one way or the other.

D: *The scientists believe that they have found certain germs that fight the other germs. They become the good germs and the bad germs.*

P: Yes, but it's still letting the little toy soldiers fight each other. It's not letting the little boy who owns all the toy soldiers take control of the situation.

D: *Yes, but in his time he has disease. He is familiar with the plague.*

P: Yes. He knows about filth. Filth is a big thing, and rats, hunger, and starvation. He knows about all kinds of horrible conditions. But he also knows the horrible things that humans have done to other humans up to that time in his life. I think we're talking now in the 1530s. So he knows what mounds of guilt and self-hatred humanity has placed on itself to that date. This question about needles was what actually precipitated this conversation. He's only saying that, although we are able to accomplish great feats from our perspective of 1989, we still have some strange beliefs. He says, in just a short time we'll find out that some of the things we do now are almost barbaric. We inject nuclear things into people's bodies. Chemicals—I think it's called "chemotherapy"—that do terrible things to the inside of the body. He says people actually get well because they have forgiven themselves and have a new desire to be the real person they always wanted to be. They die when they feel hopeless or hate themselves. Then there's no amount of nuclear medicine or injection that would save anybody.

D: *But in his time he used medications when he went to people's homes and treated the different types of plagues.*

P: He wasn't aware of this information as a man working on people of the 1500s. He didn't carry this information around in the front of his mind. Having this information now that he's in his thirties, he can address the problem differently than he did before. But the physician never heals the person, and he does know that now.

D: *If he had the knowledge of needles or these new medicines while he was working on people with the plague, wouldn't he have used it?*

P: Not necessarily. Because with an awareness of a person's personal karmic cycle comes also that responsibility not to grossly interfere.

D: *Don't they use leeches and bleed people in his time? These are two practices that we find very barbaric.*

P: Perhaps. That's still not injecting *into* the physical body a substance that will burn things, or distort living cells. To allow blood to leave the body is not the same as putting something *into* the body.

D: *I'm just trying to let him see that there's not much difference. He has no idea of the results some of his medications might have.*

P: Well, his comments are for our edification. He has a pretty good insight because he has *many* friends that he talks to besides us. They advise him, and they know infinitely more about these substances than we do.

D: *Well, does he know about our practice of replacing organs in the living body?*

P: All our physical machinations to keep people alive seem rather—and he must view these in this way—funny. If he were to get serious about everything—and he has so many things to get serious about—he would be depressed all the time. So he has to view these as an interesting story that keeps going by.

D: *I was curious what he thought of that practice.*

P: It's equally as invasive as injecting foreign material. He says it is a *huge* foreign substance rather than tiny, microscopic foreign substances that have been introduced into the body. An organ is huge compared to the little things in a needle.

D: *I thought he might consider it a great advance in medicine.*

P: If the whole purpose is to keep the physical body alive for a period of time, then it is an advance. He has a different perspective now than when he worked to save human bodies. Then it seemed as if that were the most important. His perspective today as we talk about these things, is that he wished he had done infinitely more counseling with people. He wished he had talked with them, not about their disease in specific, but about their goals, frustrations, aspirations, emotions, and also about God. He has many ideas now that he did not have at that time.

D: *But wouldn't it have been frowned upon if he counseled with these people?*

P: For sure! He was supposed to be a physician, and a physician takes care of the body, not the mind or soul. You go to the priest or the curate for your soul stuff, and you go to the library, the school or your teacher for your mind stuff. You don't go to the physician for those two things.

It was obvious we could go on with this discussion for a long time, and I doubt if he would understand our reasoning and motives, even if I could explain them. It was better to move on.

D: *Does he have any other questions he wants to ask us? I'm eager to share information with him.*

P: I think he mainly wanted to know that France still exists. He has found out that the planet seems relatively peaceful, and that we're extending into space. The only thing that gave him some concern about life today was our point of view about healing, and our perception of what disease and healing is. He has a broad perspective gathered from many other forays into this dimension. He's a bit worried about *that* one. But all in all, it's been a reassuring conversation. He has a lot yet that he doesn't understand about what we call "television," "radar," and "x-ray." He has *seen* the equipment, and seen it work, through our eyes. He just doesn't comprehend it very well.

D: *Well, I can explain x-ray.*

P: Good!

D: *In rough form, this is a way of taking a picture through the body so the bones are the only things that show.*

P: Yes, he knows that. But *how* this is effected is a giant mystery.

D: *It's the same way television and all of this operates. It has to do with machinery and electricity. He should understand why we take an x-ray. He had people with broken bones in his day. This will let us see where the bones are broken because we can actually see into the body with x-ray.*

P: He says this incredible technology gives humans more god-like qualities. It allows a person to have the power of life or death over another human. Of course, that has happened before with weapons, but we're not talking about weapons here. We're talking technological devices. You see inside a person's body who has fallen off a cliff, and they have all kinds of broken bones. There are so many that the physician determines the person can't live. So they don't give the person the same care they would if the physician said, "Yes, that person will live." It's a very fine line, but it's there.

D: *Well, this is true of anything. This probably occurred in his day also. If he had two people, one of which was very ill and he knew they would not live, and another who might have a chance, he would also make the decision. I think he has been faced with some of these same questions.*

P: Perhaps. It would be your own perception of the nature of the illness.

D: *I don't know if it gives humans god-like qualities. It's just that we have so much more knowledge.*

P: Well, God is all knowledge, too.

D: *Yes, and we're always learning.*

Listening to his viewpoints was interesting and probably valid, but it was an argument that neither of us could win. We were separated by too much time and too many technological developments that he couldn't comprehend. We needed to change the subject.

D: *Does he have any other questions that we can attempt to clarify?*

P: Oh, wow! "Are we happy?" was the question. Do we have happy lives? I guess he means you and me.

D: *I think we're happy, because women in our time lead different lives than those in his day. We have many labor-saving devices. Does that make sense?*

P: Yes. I was showing him a picture of someone on hands and knees scrubbing the floor, trying to get it clean and drying with rags. Then I showed him that we have vacuum cleaners and dishwashers. (*Chuckle*) But happy, I think, meant, "Are we not in fear?" And we're not in fear really.

D: *No. The woman today can have a job outside the home. She can live a life without a man if she chooses.*

P: Well, if we're not in fear, his question is, "Why is it that we are having this communication with him?"

D: *Curiosity.*

P: He knows that one *very* well. (*Laugh*) He's a very curious fellow himself. That's perfectly understandable to him, yes.

D: *I have a terrible curiosity, if he can understand that. I don't think you could say we're in fear. We are relatively happy because women have more freedom to do what they want in this day and age. We can pursue knowledge if we want. It's not frowned upon.*

P: And we are regular citizens. We're not queens, or rich people because we have these technological devices. They're available to people who have moderate income.

D: *And anyone, regardless of how rich or poor, can have an education. They have the advantage to do whatever they want to do with their lives.*

P: Yes. The opportunity exists. There's not slavery in this country, or bondage.

D: *If slavery exists, it would be in more backward countries, and there are not too many of them. But we seem to be living in one of the most advanced. Women have very high positions, and you don't have to be rich to attain these things. People can become rich much easier than I believe they could in his time. Can he understand this?*

P: Only through the concept of, "There must be more money then." (*Laugh*) You do away with the monarchy and that frees up more for the general population.

D: *There are no "classes." You can do what you want and attain what you want. It's up to the person.*

P: He thinks this is a very exciting time period he's plugged into. He knows of possible great differences in the very near future, so we should enjoy what we have.

D: *A woman can be a mother, raise children, have a home, and also have a career, pursue knowledge, do anything she wants. She can have it all.*

P: He wanted to know if she is a priest, an important person in the church?

That really shot my beautiful argument about equal rights for women full of holes. He hit squarely on the one thing that was lacking. But the church was also an important male-dominated organization in his time. I had to search for an answer to explain that one.

D: *There is controversy there. Although there are many women* wanting *to be priests, the Catholic Church still will not allow it. Is he familiar with the Protestant religion?*

P: I don't think so. There are other movements, but Catholicism is what he thinks on anytime he thinks about religion.

D: *Well, there was a movement that was called "Protestantism," or "Protestants." They created other religions besides Catholicism. They protested, in other words.*

P: It was the same God though, right? It's just a different way to get there?

D: *Oh, yes, the same God. They just rebelled against the Catholic Church. And in later times some women were allowed to be priests in* those *religions.*

P: Well, that's good.

D: *But today the pope remains supreme in the Catholic religion. And there are many, many things he will still not allow. So that's one thing women haven't gotten into.* (Chuckle)

P: Yes, the *last* thing, huh? (*Laugh*)

D: *Well, in the Middle East women still have a lower status.*

P: So this freedom is not worldwide. This is in the world that *we're* familiar with.

D: *In* our *country, and in Europe. There are some problems, but we've made many advances.*

P: In 450 years, yes.

D: *And we live longer. Women* and *men can both stay active many years longer than they could in his time. This is because of our medical advances ... which he doesn't approve of.*

P: I don't think that he disapproves of them. He only disapproves of the theory. He says this is judged *fact* when in fact it is *not* fact.

D: *At this time of his life, does he know that he wrote prophecies?*

P: He's written down some of the things he sees, or some of the things that are told to him. He isn't actually writing it down for publication. He's taking notes and comparing them. He has been able to contact many different entities from many differing time periods. Although he has a fantastic memory, it's almost impossible to keep every single story straight when you are dealing with the scope of time. It's a great deal of material.

D: *Well, you may tell him that his books were published, and they exist into our time period.*

P: Then he says he must have gotten some good stuff. (*Laugh*)

D: *But there were problems. He wrote them so that no one can understand them. That's the reason we contacted him for clarification. Can he understand that?*

P: Well, kind of, because they're not really written yet. But in his mind he's been thinking about how he's going to do it if he decides to share them. From what we're saying he can see that he must have chosen to do it in an obscure fashion. He can understand how we might be confused because he would have to do that intentionally for protection.

D: *What were the other alternatives he was considering?*

P: As far as releasing this information? There, of course, have been fleeting thoughts of reporting this to the court, but that's too dangerous. Different things could happen. He could be ostracized for fanatical ravings. Of course, at this time the Catholic Church is still a major force in France. So if he went public through the court and explained his visions, the Catholic Church is involved in the court as well. It's not secular at all. It is stuck together.

D: *He thinks he would be in danger?*

P: For sure. He's thought about *not* releasing this at all. He's trying to figure out what to do with this information.

D: *If he didn't release it at all, then he would be the only one who knew about it.*

P: We are comfortable to him and he can understand our caring attitude. It feels very good to him to know that someone from the future cares about what happens in *their* future as well, and is willing to take a risk of finding out what they can do. For if they do find out what they can do, then it becomes a responsibility to do it. It's not just for curiosity that we do these things. Curiosity is a convenient term used by many to explain their actions. But just to learn something for the sake of learning it, and keeping that to oneself is not the purpose of receiving information. Curiosity is helpful because it is a catalyst, but it's not enough.

D: *That should answer his question too. He can't keep what he sees to himself.*

P: Obviously he didn't, or we wouldn't have the quatrains. (*Laugh*) Although he wouldn't call them prophecies, that was the general gist of them, yes. He knows that he has had communication similar to this, although today's communication is another part of his exciting day. He has already received information from other friends who have visited. They told him about future events and tried to show them to him through the mirror. He has all this committed to memory. I don't see him writing, but he hasn't forgotten it. He thinks about the things he already knows.

D: *I don't think it would hurt to tell him that he did write it down in a book, but he wrote it as puzzles. Does he understand that?*

P: Yes. He says that would be the safe way to do it.

D: *And in our time his book still exists. Here it is!* (I raised the book, hoping he could see it.) (Laugh) *This is one copy.*

P: That is awesome. So people read these languages and know what he means?

D: *No, they* don't *know what he means.*

P: Oh? Why not?

D: *That's the point. It's been 400 years of trying to understand.*

P: *That's* the curiosity! That's the reason for the communication. It's not because of fear. It's *not* just to talk to a man who lived that long ago. It's to find out what that man meant.

D: *Yes. He wrote these prophecies 400 years ago in such complicated puzzle form that no one can understand them.*

P: *(Chuckle)* So he did well.

D: *He did well.*

P: Here are some things I am thinking. See, our heads are together. It's so funny because I can tell you what he is responding, and then what I'm telling him, and how he's responding to that. It's all occurring in the same head space. This is what I hear him say: If he wrote down any of the experiments he has performed he could be responsible for the death of people who try to copy him. He is aware that he is not going to die from what he does with the plants. He has this knowledge that when he experiments on himself it will not cause his death. This comes from having already seen himself in the future. So it makes him braver, or it makes him do things he wouldn't recommend to anybody else to do. So if in the future he writes about those experiments he would definitely keep them obscure because he wouldn't want anybody except the most knowing physician or alchemist to try them. About future events that he might write about, he says if he decides to do it he will have to think long and hard to find a way. It's very dangerous because the church could actually have him killed. Who is he? He is just a man. Who is he to say that this will come to pass? It's a dangerous thing for somebody in his time period to be talking about the future. Also if he wrote these things down, how would he explain that he has talked to people from the future?

D: *That's the problem we're having now. How do we explain we're talking to him from the past?*

P: He says, "Yes, but we're doing it." *(Laugh)*

D: *Tell him some people think I am speaking to the dead. They think he is a spirit.*

P: There is no such thing as dead. He said, surely we must know that because we're talking. I think the best information about the quatrains would come from a conversation with him at a later time period in his life. Then he would be able to tell you why he wrote some of the things that he did.

D: *You can tell him that I've talked to him in his future time.*

P: He said, "I thought so." *(Chuckle)* He would like to say that he appreciates the fact that *we* don't talk to *him* in riddles, but that we actually make an attempt to be clear.

D: *I could make it as hard for him as he's made it for us.* (Chuckle) *But we were able to make the connection and our curiosities came together.*

I was as curious of his time and what he saw about us as he is in hearing my report.

P: The giant curiosity exists through time. But I think I should report that he *did* have to overcome one obstacle that you didn't.

D: *What was that?*

P: The obstacle he had to overcome was communicating across time. He was seeking out a future person who could help clarify for us future beings what he said. There's a reason he wanted it clarified because we now know that we can change the outcome and how we can change it. So he was, if you will, *trolling* in that plane that you were working in. He would have preferred to have contacted a man, but that wasn't happening. *You* were the happening event. I think there's some kind of openness vibration. Let's say there were 2,000 people working in hypnosis at that precise moment across the planet. At the exact moment that he appeared to you and your friend the first time. The reason that his energy went to the two of you was because there was some openness factor that wasn't present in the other hypnosis sessions that were occurring at the same time on the planet. You are special and unique, and this was responded to. It's your voice mainly.

D: *I am curious. Has he learned anything from us today?*

P: Yes. The pictures and explanations that we've sent him have been quite clear and fascinating. I think he would like to do this again. He says we could appear in the mirror. I don't know that we're working toward your goal of getting information, but this has been very helpful for him.

D: *Then if we appear when he is about this age, in his thirties, is that the best time?*

P: No, it is not the best time. There are questions you have about what took place later in his life, so we could ask for different time periods when we visit. As his life progresses, he becomes aware of more and more horrifying things, and he seals himself off from emotion and joy. That happens when he seals himself off from the horror and sadness. So I would say when he is about the age of thirties, forties would be the best time. We can come to him at any time, it just seems that in his later life he's not as spontaneous and open. And it doesn't feel as good being *in* him as it does now. This *was* better than the other times.

D: *Then when we come again we can ask to appear to him in the mirror as we really are?*

P: In the mirror, yes.

D: *And he will feel free to ask us questions?*

P: Exactly. You see, until today we have asked to see in the mirror what *he* sees. But we have not shown him *ourselves* in the mirror.

D: *I didn't know it could be done.*

P: That's how he sees what he sees. It's shown to him.

D: *With his permission we'll do this again.*

P: Great! I mean, great! He feels *great*.

D: *But we don't have total knowledge. We can only tell him what we know about.*

P: At least we're making an attempt, as he is. He has to say, even with his ego, he doesn't have total knowledge either.

DURING OUR NEXT SESSION with Pam a week later, her husband Richard was present.

P: We're back in the room with the stone floor where Nostradamus seems to have spent so much of his time as an older man. This guy's a lot older and has seen a lot of things come down the pike. We're here, but he is aware of our presence as just talking in his head. He can differentiate between his own thoughts and incoming thoughts, which is a pretty fine distinction. He's been focusing on what goes on in his head for many years. He was born with certain facilities that made him precocious, and he knew stuff sooner than most kids. But he's actually worked very hard to develop this capability of discerning what's coming in as thoughts that he consciously generates from within his *own* self, and thoughts coming from an external or other source. It's really a difficult thing to distinguish.

D: *It's remarkable that he was able to do that without someone teaching him.*

P: I can't answer that.

D: *You said he is aware of us. Does he want to communicate?*

P: Yes, but he doesn't seem to enjoy our *demands*. Conversation and response to *his* questions is what he likes the best. It seems that we've actually been doing the opposite of what he likes most, by asking *him* questions.

D: *That's what he means by our "demands"?*

P: Yes. We want to know certain things and have him explain certain things. For many years it's been questions to explain things, explain … "What do you mean? Explain." And (*deep sigh*) that's not the most fun for him. How can somebody who thinks like this (*hand motions indicating going out in different directions*) explain like this (*going in straight line*)?

D: *All right, if he enjoys asking us questions, does he want to do that?*

P: First we need to establish who *we* are and where *we* come from. That's the first question. We could be *anything*. Right now we're just talking in his head.

D: *Do you have to create a visualization he can focus on?*

P: I'll try to let him see us again as we sit in this room right now in 1989. Although it's different because there are three of us today. Oh, my! He can see us, and he's interested in Richard. The male energy is interesting to him because he can actually see us in the mirror. Richard is like a doctor. He's always observing, thinking, and questioning also.

There's a different feeling that I get from Nostradamus for Richard. He's much more accepting and interested in him than in *us*.

Richard is a man in his forties who has a beard, so maybe Nostradamus was seeing him as a colleague because he resembled men in his own time. Perhaps he perceived him as someone he could identify with.

D: *Well, I understand how he feels about male and female energies. Does Nostradamus want to ask him questions?*

P: What is your profession in your life in 1989?

D: *Tell him what you used to do. I think he might be interested in that.*

Richard had spent 15 years as a zoologist associated with a major zoo in the United States. I thought this was an unusual enough occupation that it would capture Nostradamus' attention.

R: *All right. I used to manage exotic animals for viewing by the public. These had been collected all over the world and brought to one particular country.*

P: How did you get them from all around the world to one country?

R: *There are people in the various countries who live with nature, and those people find and capture them. Eventually these animals are bred in captivity. At the time I was involved in it, most of the animals in our exhibits were born and maintained in captivity. The problem is that there are so many people in the world in this day that there's less room for the animals to live in the wild. So some people believe that animals can be saved by breeding them in captivity and perhaps later releasing them back into the wild in special places.*

Pam again had the look of wonder and interest on her face that was present the last time we performed the experiment from this angle. She seemed to reflect Nostradamus' thoughts and not her own. Her questions also indicated this. She certainly was familiar with Richard's story because she was married to him. Her questions and remarks appeared to be coming from someone who did not know or understand Richard's background.

P: I don't see how they can all be bred in one place.

R: *Well, they're not. There are only a limited number of animals that any one place can keep. And they try to keep the animals that are suitable for the conditions they have.*

P: There are several of these places?

R: *Almost every large city in our country has one of these. I believe you had animal exhibits in France in your day.*

P: They didn't come from all over the world though. You can't even *get* all over the world.

R: *Well, today we can travel all over the world. And unfortunately there are too many people, so the animals have less area in which to live.*

P: How sad! So what do you do?

R: *What I did was try to make the conditions in captivity the best possible for the animals in our exhibits. I tried to use these animals as ambassadors to make the public aware that animals need a place to live in the wild.*

D: *Does Nostradamus understand these concepts?*

P: Collecting from around the world is really difficult for him to understand. I'm feeding in information about how you can ship things through the air and across the sea. The concept of capturing them and taking them to other countries was pretty shocking to him. The way they deal with animals in his time is pretty awful. They hunt and trap them and eat them. They don't have this love that he can feel expressed. It is because of Richard's caring that he feels the words as well as hears them. These are new thoughts because while there may have been places like this in France when he was living, it's not any place he's familiar with. He's used to cutting up animals and eating them, and seeing animal bodies in the market. He knows all about hunting, and has a totally different relationship with animals. This shows him a new way to look at it. This is why it's so exciting for him to ask questions because he gets more than words. He gets the heart of what the words say.

R: *There's much concern in our time about maintaining natural environments in various places in the world for animals to continue. People are becoming aware of how much destruction is done by the population in every country. So people are becoming more focused on trying to protect and preserve what's left.*

P: This is, of course, almost incomprehensible in the 16th century when they don't even know what the whole planet looks like, or all the areas of land and water. They have a general idea but they don't have a very good global grip. In his mind he is understanding from *your* perspective of 1989 that there must be as many people as there are ants. They must be eating and building everywhere, and you have to cordon off areas so the other living things will have some space. The emotional message is that this is very sad. From his perspective it's very hard to understand that there could be so many people that the animals and nature are running out of room. That's a hard one.

R: *It is also hard for people to believe in this time because the Earth is so large, but yet it seems to be happening.*

D: *Isn't it also a different idea that people are caring about animals, if in his day all they did was eat them?*

P: Yes, they actually have a fear of animals. You can't forget about the billions of rats. They've had some bad experiences come from animals.

D: *Such as the plague, you mean?*

P: Yes. And just to go down near the docks, there are millions of rats. It's disgusting. But he knows there are other animals besides rats. That's just one example. Actually he has more questions for Richard.

He sees you as a person who cares about these animals from a personal standpoint. You said this was what you used to do. Why don't you do that now?

R: *I don't do that now because even though there's a lot of good in keeping animals for public display, I personally became more and more sensitive to the needs of animals in captivity. I eventually decided I didn't want to be associated with keeping animals in captive situations. So I left the zoo situation and we moved to a more natural area. Now we can see animals in the wild instead of in captivity.*

P: So what do you do to help the situation for the animals?

R: *I don't really know how to help the situation too much. We support various organizations who are actively trying to make people aware of the problems. But we don't really know what to do at this point. It's a big problem.*

P: He sees that we have plenty to eat, there is no monarchy, and there is no war. What is it that would make you despair, other than giving up on the future of the animals of the Earth?

R: *I don't have despair in my conscious forefront.*

P: Well, this is his observation from a long time ago to now. He says it is very sad because if we're not doing anything except feeling bad about it, the hopelessness of the situation is compounded. I was trying to give him a big picture as well as this personal picture. I was telling him there are other problems too, such as pollution of the oceans and areas totally incapable of growing food. His response was, if we look at these things as too big for us to do anything about, that means we've literally given up. He says nothing is accomplished without individual human effort, which coalesces into group effort, and then action truly takes place. To give up is the worse thing that can happen to our world. He feels this sadness, this *pain.* He can actually receive the emotion from our words. It's really interesting how this works. It's amazing that he has this insight and perspective on something he's never thought about before, except perhaps in his dreams. And he has something else to say. He says it's essential while we are alive to *do* whatever we feel is a positive helpful step. To actually *do* it. Whatever *it* is.

D: *He has given us many warnings for our time period. They all are events on a large scale that are too big for the individual. Can he see what an individual can do about these situations that he foresees for our future?*

P: You've been given this information more than once. The individual is like a giant magnet whose thoughts and emotions attract whatever they focus and concentrate on. You will attract to you what is harmonious with your vibration. Your thoughts are very powerful. *You* as an individual and *you* as the universal pronoun. Let's take it less personal to the universal and say the thoughts that *one* thinks attract and continue attracting. They establish a highway. There are forces in operation on the planet who can gather a certain type of vibration and use that for power. The vibration they gather is one of discordancy, disharmony, fear, anger. The more vibration that is out there for this force to collect, the more power it has. So what can we as individuals do right now? Stop the highway that has been created, and start a new highway. Think *totally* the opposite of those awful things, and you give power to the best, the greatest, and what most people call "God." It's quite remarkable that each human being on the planet right now and in the future has the capability of change. This horrible nightmare that he's seen in the future goes along with that magnet, that highway of discordancy and despair. It does not go along the highway of joy, and upliftment and helping. There cannot be power added to a force that lives on bad vibrations if that is no longer created from within us. This is not a new message. He has tried to deliver this message many times to you, *through* you, to the rest of the world.

D: *Then his purpose in showing me all these horrible things were to show us probable futures?*

P: Absolutely. The probable future as he sees it if man continues to think in the most despairing way. It doesn't do any harm to present these probabilities to people unless they think that it is the way it *will* be because that's what they then focus on. They must be given the *reason* for changing their thoughts and behaviors, and something to change their thoughts and behaviors *to* that is positive and uplifting.

D: *But some of the things he foresaw did come true.*

P: Then that should prove that as long as we continue to focus on these things, more will come true. A total reason to change our thinking. I do know he will have a perspective when he dies that he did not have when he lived in his body. He is so very proud of how far he can stretch his mind. But it was minute compared to what will happen when he dies. His perspective will be immensely broadened.

D: *Our reason for communicating in his time was to obtain his perspective, which is naturally limited if he is alive.*

P: And you will get that, but there will always be an overlay of the bigger perspective, because it can't be denied. Your job is to make people aware of this bigger perspective that comes after death.

D: *But he set up this communication, this method of speaking with us in the future while he was alive.*

P: This is your personal interpretation of how it works. We think in linear terms. If that were true it would be impossible for me to be communicating with a man who is sitting at a desk somewhere around 1542. He's sitting there in his room, but at the same moment you must understand that he's also dead, and has been dead for a very long time. Those are both simultaneous events. If you led or asked me, I could see this man as a child, and he would still be living as a child. We could get into a discussion of simultaneous time, but I don't think you want to do that at this time.

D: *That's really too complicated anyway.*

P: It's *not* too complicated. But it does require *interest* on the part of those who are asking the questions. You have to pursue this for a reason. I think again you should focus on what he has said about preventing the possible futures he saw. How incredibly important it is that we monitor our thoughts and our beliefs. By the way, he said beliefs are stronger than thoughts. Emotions play a big part too. To make people aware of that is probably *your* greatest service. Action, emotion, thought, belief, word and speech are all movement makers. And movement toward positive thought is essential. We've had a whole human history of movement towards a negative goal.

R: *The chance for improvement or changing the direction of the planet seems almost hopeless. There doesn't seem to be any small event that can do this. Is there going to be a major event, either a major consciousness change that involves most of humanity, or a physical Earth change that might cause the situation to change dramatically.*

P: Gosh, there are so many responses. I hope I can remember them. First I must say that he heard almost a longing from you for something dramatic to happen, to cause some big change to take place. When you say those are the only ways you see a change occurring, that means that *you* and the world can broaden their perspective by embracing other catalysts for change. One of the things that Nostradamus foresaw in his dreams, nightmares or hallucinations could be considered very positive, very uplifting and very expansive. This is the discovery of the new-old information. This discovery will, if this plays out, be so incredible and so shocking and so stimulating, that even the average person will be affected. Not the Sudanese in Africa who are still starving to death, not the people who have to focus on bare-bone survival, but the technological society which is a large part of the world. This is something that would marshal the forces of *all* the countries of the world together in a positive and exciting way. This is a huge event that isn't involved with war or natural disaster.

D: *What does he mean by the discovery of the new-old information?*

P: Well, I don't know where these thoughts are coming from. I don't want to limit what this information could be. But it seems that, first and foremost, we will immediately have to face the fact that we have been visited before by beings from other planets, from space. This will be revealed beyond the shadow of a doubt.

R: *Nostradamus is aware of this?*

P: Yes. The new-old information was written long ago, *thousands* of years ago, and secreted away for protection. It seems that they knew even then it wouldn't be safe for the mind of humans for some period of time. And now that time is here. With these feelings of despair it becomes *essential* now to embrace this information as a large group of humans. By realizing that we've been visited by friends from space thousands of years ago, we instantly realize the isolation we have had as human beings on this planet, and the capabilities we have to reconnect with the stars. That means we have the capability to leave this planet, to go to other planets in other places. It's such a huge thought. It's almost mind-boggling. But after finding the new-old information we discover we are definitely descendants of the stars. Therefore, we understand if we came from the stars we should definitely be able to get back out there again. Also with this knowledge comes this great and glorious impetus to take care of the problems on *this* planet, because it is our home planet. It creates this global new awakening of love, for the Earth suddenly becomes very small. You don't see the planet as this huge orb in space. It becomes home, and we have to clean up the house. It's a mess, and company's coming. That's some of the information, that they have been here and they are coming back. That is why the information will be discovered shortly before they return.

D: *Where will this new-old information be discovered? Can he tell us where it is secreted away?*

P: I can see nothing but sand and mountains. The information is hidden in the sand. It's so dry. I keep thinking of Egypt.

R: *Isn't this old-new information coming out now through the intuitive processes of hundreds of people?*

P: I would say hundreds of thousands actually, because it is really an awakening. All of us have this memory within us. We can trace back to our great-grandparents relatively easy. If we kept tracing we would get back to the stars. The fact is that our relatives are coming back. We have this knowledge inside us. They are our genetic brothers, sisters, parents. These are other humans actually coming *back,* coming home. People all over the world are having these internal feelings of urgency or anticipation that *something* is happening. Much of it is being channeled through writing and speaking. But I am talking about actual documents that will be uncovered, because the pragmatic 20th century world demands that.

D: *Can he give us an idea of when they will be discovered?*

P: No. Time is so difficult. Every time I try to think of a time, it's stressful because the time feels so urgent. And when I think of numbers, it is in the nineteens, and we don't have too many nineteens left. It is important that you know this will be discovered.

R: *There have already been documents from Biblical times discovered.*

P: These are older. We are familiar with the Nag Hammadi gospels and the Essene Dead Sea Scrolls and documents from roughly 2000 years ago. I would say this information predates those by at least a thousand years, if not a couple of thousand years. This is actually carved on stone, you know. (*Laugh*) Talk about carved on stone. This is!

D: *I was wondering what kind of material it would be in order to preserve it for that long.*
P: I'm not sure, but it could be some metal, too.

(This sounds very similar to CENTURY V-7 interpreted by Wayne in Chapter 12.)

R: *What people left these documents?*
P: The humans who were here. Not the first humans, but the humans that were here ... gosh, ten thousand years seems so long ago. These humans were not the first humans to visit the planet. There have been comings and goings before then. I think these were humans. I mean, they looked like us ... almost.
D: *Was this before the time of the Egyptians?*
P: Actually it was before and during. They had lived here for some time. The strange thing I get is that they left, *all* of them. So we are the descendants of *their* descendants. I see that there were humans that came to Earth. And then these people, also human, came several thousand years later. And we are genetically as well as emotionally related to these humans and also the first humans. These later ones came, hid this information and left again. Am I making myself clear? (*We agreed.*) We're still connected to them. The humans that are here came from the humans that *started* here.
R: *I see. They left, but their descendants are still here.*
P: And they are *we!*
D: *Does he enjoy doing a session in this way?*
P: Yes. It's really funny because he has to deal with me, and I get excited and emotional. (*Laugh*) I try not to because then my thoughts get muddled. I would say that our key to expanded knowledge from Nostradamus comes when we establish a comfortable relationship with him, whatever time we find him, because the whole package exists really.

Chapter 20

Working with Phil

PHIL HAD BEEN COMPLETELY DISCOURAGED from attempting the translation of the quatrains because of the feelings or emotions the scenes carried with them. He felt they clung to him and remained as a type of residue that was utterly repulsive to him. Because I never wish any of my subjects to experience discomfort, I told him we would leave the interpretation of the quatrains to hardier souls. But I knew the connection that Phil had established with Nostradamus was too valuable to waste. After much thought, I decided to use it in a different way. Because Phil had a technological mind (he was involved with electronics), we thought he might be able to explain some of the confusing modern-day inventions that Nostradamus had seen. We would try to avoid anything that carried the aura of negativity and focus on positive accomplishments of the future. That was my plan, to attempt a session with this goal in mind. Phil had been willing to help me, and he felt somewhat guilty about not being able to fulfill his part in the experiment. One session of this type might ease his conscience. He would know that he had assisted in his own unique way.

After Phil had entered his familiar state of trance, I instructed him to travel through time to locate Nostradamus while he was alive in the 1500s in France. I hoped that Nostradamus would know we were coming this time, be prepared for us and not be startled by Phil's different type of energy vibration. When I finished counting, Phil found himself on the back side of the mirror staring out at Nostradamus. The great man sat at his table shifting sand with his fingers, peering intently as he fixed his mental focus on the mirror. Nostradamus then reacted with caution when he realized he was facing someone or something peering out from the mirror. I asked Phil if he knew how he appeared to Nostradamus. He said he was an indistinct shape, and that Nostradamus was using his empathy more than his visualization to feel him out. As always, I instructed Phil to send positive feelings of love toward the man, so he would understand that we meant him no harm.

D: *I imagine he encounters all types of entities.*

P: Yes. He says this is his reason for being very alert, as he has only limited control over who will appear. His energy sometimes draws those, as he would say, spirits, who are detached and attracted by his energy.

D: *Has he had any experiences with negative types of spirits?*

P: Perhaps in the sense of what you would call "disharmonious" or "mischievous."

D: *Does he know how to distinguish the difference?*

P: Yes, he sounds them out. He creates in *his* body the energy resonance of that particular spirit, so he feels the awareness of the spirit with whom he is communicating. This way he can understand the level or mentality of that spirit.

D: *Is he doing that to you?*

P: Yes, that is accurate. He is attuning himself to the energy that is presenting itself to him. He is somewhat unaccustomed to this level of energy, but he is acclimating.

D: *Why is your energy different from the others I bring to him?*

P: The difference is subtle, indistinct. He senses it as an alien type of energy. He is sounding this out. It is simply that he has, at this time, a lack of experience with these energies.

D: *Does he realize I am in back of it?*

P: Yes, he senses your presence. He is familiar with your energy. He says this is another of your—the word is difficult to translate here—"Pets."

D: (Chuckle) *Is that what he thinks they are? I work with many people, and it takes a certain type of personality to be able to reach him.*

P: He is having gentle humor with you. He respects you, and admires your perseverance in this effort. He realizes this is a work of the universe as a whole, and not some simple task of an individual.

D: *Of course, I perceive it as my own task, and a difficult one at that.*

P: That is as it would be perceived by one. However the connections and vibrations that allow this intercourse to occur are administrated from behind the scenes. The connections are being made and the ... that is it. The connections are being made.

D: *But I believe it wouldn't be occurring if it wasn't for a positive reason. Is that correct?*

P: That is accurate. As you would describe "positive," the universe is in a forward mode. And in so being, this is simply a manifestation of those elements within each and all of you who are in a positive, forward, progressive mode.

D: *But it is still possible for a mischievous spirit, or one of disharmony to come through his mirror from time to time.*

P: That is accurate. Nostradamus wishes to only maintain connections with those who are in a similar positive or forward mode.

D: *What does he do when one of the mischievous ones comes in?*

P: He simply removes them from his awareness, and closes the connection. He is very astute at being aware of the energies around him. You need not concern yourself for *his* safety. He is very capable of sounding out those energies that would present themselves.

D: *Is he comfortable with you now?*

P: He is still somewhat puzzled. However, his humor is returning. He's simply observing our discourse as we communicate. He is *with* us yet not present. Aware but not present.

D: *You mean he can see us?*

P: That is, in a sense, accurate. However, more to say, he can sense us.

D: *He said he liked to work with male energies.*

P: We're not speaking here from gender, but from energy levels or frequencies. The frequency of the energies presented to him are of a different order. As an analogy, if one was familiar with one particular type of music and was well-versed in all the different forms of that type or style of music, and then were suddenly presented with a completely different style of music, the period of acclimation would be a mixture of awe, surprise and perhaps amusement. With the energy he is now being presented he senses the scope or breath of the distance from his familiar style, and has deduced that the energy is not of this planet.

D: *Can you explain to him that you are living in a physical body even though the energy is different?*

P: He is deducing this as we communicate.

D: *I think it is interesting that he would pick up on you as a different type of energy.*

P: From his point of view it would not be difficult to recognize, for he is not encumbered by physical senses but is seeing or feeling or sensing the true essence of the life forces.

D: *Tell him we are speaking to him from his future. We're always asking him questions. Does he have any questions he would like to ask us?*

P: He would inquire as to the effect mercury has on the body. As it is what could be called a heavy metal, it would, when ingested or introduced into the bloodstream, tend to reside or deposit itself in the kidneys or liver, and cause destruction of the functioning aspects of the liver.

D: *Is this something he is working on?*

P: It is something he has suspected. However, he was not sure of it.

D: *Can you answer that for him?*

P: We just did.

D: *Then he knew it was harmful, but he didn't know why?*

P: That is accurate. He was not sure of the position in the body that would be harmed by this ingestion.

D: *Isn't mercury considered poison?*

P: That is accurate.

D: *Did he know this was poison?*

P: He suspected. He has heard of this element. He senses that liquid metal would be harmful. He simply had not deduced the effect it would have on the body. His theory was that it would be damaging to the brain as well, and can be demonstrated to be such.

D: *I don't believe mercury has any positive aspects for use in the human body.*

P: There are extremely rare instances where it could be possible to introduce extremely small amounts. It would attract a more harmful element that would possibly be contaminating the body, so that the more harmful element would stick to or be attracted to the mercury, and then be rendered immobile in the body and remain in the liver. Very precise and very accurate measurements of the dosages would be required; otherwise it could kill the patient.

D: *It sounds as if this is something he shouldn't be experimenting with.*

P: We say this not for his sake but yours because he has no intentions of attempting this. However he was curious. He is familiar with people who go into mines to mine mercury, and they come down with this sickness. That was what he wanted to know; how it was affecting their system. He thought it was in their brain, but it's really in their liver. *(Pause)* He has a question about iodine in the body and its function or relevance to the thyroid. He is wanting to know the effect of iodine on the thyroid condition.

D: *Can you answer that question for him?*

I certainly didn't know the answers to these medical questions and I'm sure Phil didn't either in his conscious state.

P: We found that this vehicle has a lack of detailed knowledge as to the chemical effects or ...

D: *Can the vehicle obtain the knowledge from elsewhere? Nostradamus seems to have a genuine desire to know.*

P: It would be sufficient to say that the hypothalamus and thyroid are indeed influenced by iodine. And the overabundance of iodine would cause the destruction of the hypothalamus and thyroid conditions, which he is inquiring about.

D: *In our time we get iodine from salt and fish. I don't know what sources are available in his day.*

P: He has iodine from spinach.

D: *Spinach? Isn't it available in certain types of fish, seafood?*

P: Not so in his day.

D: *We add iodine to salt in our day.*

P: His prescription would be a diet of green, leafy vegetables, especially spinach.

D: *I believe it takes a very small amount to affect the thyroid, because pure iodine is also poison.*

P: That is accurate.

D: *Why is he asking about that?*

P: He apparently knew how to treat certain dysfunctions—not illness, but really an imbalance. He knew that iodine would work on the thyroid and the hypothalamus, but he wasn't quite sure why, and he wasn't quite sure of its effect.

D: *Maybe we are helping him. Does he have another question? I find this interesting also.*

P: His awareness is mollified.

D: *What do you mean?*

P: He is in a very receptive mode. He would simply state that he sends his love through the centuries to those of us who would undertake this mission. And who would devote our time in this unselfish manner to the betterment of humankind. He now remains silent and listening.

D: *Tell him that you have a technological mind that can understand inventions in our time. Maybe we can explain something he has seen in the future that he doesn't understand.*

P: He is curious as to the functioning of your computers. The technological design of these machines is frightening to him. However he understands the basic concept of switching electrical currents on and off.

D: *He has seen our computers?*

P: Yes, that is accurate. He has sensed their purpose and function, and their effect on our society. And he is amazed at the integration of such a device into our society to the degree that it has asserted itself, and will assert itself even more in our future.

D: *Why did he find it frightening?*

P: His perspective is that the affairs of humans should be dictated by humans and not machines. From what he sees, the affairs of humans are being controlled by machines. Day-to-day life choices and decisions are being made by inanimate objects. And so from his perspective the machines have, in a very real sense, established a working order of their own in our society.

D: *Do you agree with that?*

P: We would say that from his perspective it is quite accurate.

D: *But humans are behind the machines operating them.*

P: That is accurate.

D: *Can you explain that to him in a way he would understand?*

P: His point of view is valid. However, although we would not question or *attempt* to imply a rightness or wrongness, obviously the society at this time has agreed or evolved to the point that this has become an acceptable phenomenon. And the society has placed a certain amount of trust in its machines to make these life and death decisions for them on a day-to-day basis. From his perspective, because machines are playing a very *small* role in his life, it is quite frightening and he is unable to comprehend.

D: *We consider them to be helpers. They make our work easier, but I can understand his point of view. You said he understands electricity?*

P: He has a working knowledge of the currents as they apply to, not only bodily functions, but natural phenomenon such as lightning and static.

D: *Has he seen we have been able to utilize these currents?*

P: That is accurate. He senses this is simply a form of technology in which these electrical currents have been harnessed and are directed in their various functions to do what is desired. But he feels that humans have relinquished control of their lives and perhaps their destiny to machines. It is simply a matter of differing perspectives. He is not saying it is bad. It is simply alien to his way of thinking, and is frightening to him. He is not making a judgment call on this, and he wishes to emphasize this. He is simply observing and reacting, much as you would observe and react were you viewing *your* future. He is trying to understand.

D: *Can you explain computers to him? I know it's very complicated.*

P: He senses this automatically. As we speak he is a third party involved in this conversation. He is aware of the information passing between us, and so he understands through the vehicle's awareness of the concepts being exchanged here.

D: *Is there anything else he's curious about?*

P: He's seen the rockets during World War II, the German V-2 rockets. (*Phil displayed signs of discomfort.*) I'm feeling his horror of seeing these for the first time. It's a terrible feeling.

D: *Where is he getting that picture?*

P: It's from his being able to cast his vision forward and see the future. That was his reaction when he saw the rockets. He's okay. He can handle it. He's just reacting to what he sees.

D: *Does he want to ask you anything about that?*

P: No. He's silent. (*Sigh*) I think it's time to close up.

This was a normal reaction from Phil. He was becoming disturbed. He was obviously afraid we were leading into negative topics again. I would have to get his attention off that or he was capable of abruptly ending the session.

D: *I know you don't like to watch anything with that type of vibration. Can he see anything about our space programs?*

P: There is to be another shuttle disaster. Again there will be loss of life due to an explosion of the launch vehicle. The feeling is that the explosives that separate the solid rocket boosters from the craft will ignite prematurely.

D: *Can he see anything about our plans for space stations and trips to Mars?*

P: That unfortunately will not be realized in this generation. However the concept of humans colonizing other planets is firmly established, and shall be a part of your destiny in due time.

D: *Is there a reason why it won't happen in our generation?*

P: The climax of events occurring on your planet will eclipse the importance of such a mission. The emphasis will be on survival on the planet.

D: *Can he be a little more specific? What does he mean by the climax of events?*
P: The big change that your planet is now preparing for. The shift of the polar caps and the climatic, traumatic natural phenomenon that is to occur, coinciding with the raising of spiritual awareness on your planet.
D: *I've heard so much about this war with the Anti-Christ, will that come before or after these?*
P: That is to be concurrent *with* the change. Speaking of the natural events, they will not be sudden and within a time frame of days because this entire shift will take a period of several decades.
D: *Can he give you any information about the Anti-Christ individual that might be helpful?*
P: It would suffice to say there are those working around the individual at this time to establish his position as a political entity.
D: *I've often wondered how he would gain his power.*
P: It will be as a subtle change. He is not one who would burst on the scene, but one who will collect and coalesce his powers. Such that he rises in prominence slowly and steadily, but profoundly. The political scene has already changed on your planet. The conditions are ripe or the stage is being set now for the occurrence that is to be his entrance onto the world political arena. This will indeed coincide with those times of change in your world: the physical, political, religious, social and economic areas. From a perspective of humanity's history, these events are indeed concurrent to within the time-frame of years. The beginning stages will be subtle and will not be perceived as having any direct or relative bearing on what is occurring in other places around the planet at this time. However, after it has occurred, it will be seen that several isolated incidents occurring simultaneously indeed set the stage.
D: *Could he show you anything about the shift?*
P: We would say the destruction will be unprecedented in your history.
D: *Would you be allowed to see what type of destruction?*
P: We would say that the destruction wrought on your country recently by the hurricane Hugo (1989) would be a small sampling of what will occur on a global basis, both through natural and human forms of destruction.
D: *What would the human forms be?*
P: Those forms of armament and weaponry that would cause massive loss of life, including nuclear weapons, bacteriological and chemical warfare.
D: *Does he think these cause or precipitate the natural events?*
P: They are concurrent and somewhat affect each other. However, they are coming from two different directions. The physical phenomenon is a result of changes occurring in the Earth and the universe as a whole. The social and political changes are occurring because of changes in humanity's spiritual advancement. They are somewhat related and independent of each other, and yet at the same time influence each other. The natural phenomenon will cause changes in the planning or execution of the destruction. Some events may be post-

poned or others be enhanced, and yet at the same time the human-made destructions will enhance some natural phenomenon and tend to cancel others. As a rule they will occur independently yet be somewhat interdependent on each other.

D: *Would it be possible for him to show you how the world looks after this occurs?*

P: We would say total, complete, utter destruction. There is nothing left standing—literally.

D: *I am interested in the physical shape of the continents afterwards.*

P: We would say the geological boundaries will be in such a state of flux for the next several decades, that it would be very difficult to pinpoint exactly the position or make-up of land mass on your planet at any given time. The physical changes will continue for some time beyond the social changes.

Phil was showing signs of discomfort. This was all leading toward negativity again. I would have to change the subject.

D: *Ask him if he can show you positive inventions or circumstances in our future.*

P: I see a liquid that people would drink. It is like water, only it sparkles. It has a phosphorescence or something to it. It cleans the whole system of bacteriological and all kinds of different impurities. The liquid is a combination of chemicals and chemical reactions. The sparkling appearance is from … it's not complete. In its liquid form it is in a suspended state of chemical reaction, but when it's ingested the body causes it to complete that chemical reaction. It then causes a very positive, cleaning reaction that rids the body of toxins and different forms of both natural and human-made poisons.

D: *Would it have to be taken very often?*

P: No. Were it to be taken *too* often it would cause harm, and in fact could cause death. It is meant only to be taken occasionally, perhaps once every several years. It's the result of the cooperation between the scientists on this planet and scientists on other planets, who have been studying the human anatomy, Earth environment, and the effects of the environment on the human anatomy.

D: *Will the average person in that time know this has been a cooperative effort?*

P: Absolutely. There will be no need for secrets at that time. It will be a group effort or perhaps a shared or common cause.

D: *I'm presuming this will be at a time when we have accepted the existence of aliens.*

P: That is accurate.

D: *I think that is wonderful. Can he show you something else?*

P: There will be a more complete understanding of the nature of light. It will be shown to be more solid than wave, or perhaps more *real* than has been imagined. The physical constitution of light has not been appreciated up to this point. However, it will be shown that light is a real physical element. Although it would not be assigned a place on what you would call your "chemical chart," or periodic table of elements, it will be shown to be as *real* as any of those other elements.

D: *We consider light from the sun to be essential to life. Do you mean it is more solid than that?*

P: That is accurate. It is simply in an elevated stage, a form that is not completely of a higher dimension, and yet also part of your three dimensional world. It is a transitional expression of the higher planes of awareness. A bridge between your plane of reality and the higher planes of reality. That is why there can be those beings of light. The beings of higher planes can modify their form so they step down in frequency and *become* light, which is a bridge or half-way point between your solid, physical world and the higher planes of existence. Not necessarily to say "spiritual" planes, but higher *physical* planes. It is a half-way point between a higher and lower expression of pure physical form.

D: *Can he see what we will use this light for, once we discover it has these properties.*

P: Unfortunately, there will be weapons made which will take advantage of this. This is in your *far* future. However, the outcome of this war of light will be the final realization that the higher planes of expression cannot, by their very nature, be used in a retrograde or non-forward manner. The higher the expression or energy that is used, the more imperative it is that this energy or expression be used in a forward manner.

D: *I was thinking of laser beams.*

P: That is a more advanced form or expression of light that is available in your time-frame. However, there are far more advanced forms of expression.

D: *This war he's walking about, is that the war of the Anti-Christ?*

P: That is not accurate. It is hundreds of years in your future. One of the final conflicts that humanity, as a race, will experience before the ultimate realization of destiny.

This might explain some of the terrible futuristic weapons Nostradamus told us about in Volume One. They seemed so unbelievable it was difficult for me to imagine they would be used in a war that would occur within this decade. Maybe they did not relate to the war of the Anti-Christ, but to this one in the far future. It was often difficult for Nostradamus to place events in proper time-frames because to him everything looked futuristic and strange.

D: *I was hoping this war he has foreseen with the Anti-Christ would be the last one.*

P: Unfortunately that is not to be the case. However, not to say that it has to *be* the case. The future as it stands, at least in the present time-frame, is predisposed to this occurrence. However, it is not cast in stone or absolutely preordained, but it has become the general favoring of your destiny.

D: *I thought humanity would want to live in peace after the Anti-Christ's war.*

P: That is accurate. There will be a period of peace. However, the primordial instincts that had been temporarily suppressed will again assert themselves. And humanity will find itself again in conflict.

D: *I keep thinking of the scenario he has given us, and I try to put everything in respect to that. I realize there could be more than one future line or one type of scenario. But he has told me quite a bit about the shift of the world, and I thought something that traumatic would make humans return to being peaceful.*

P: Again, there will indeed be a period of peace after what you call the "great cataclysm," or the "great shift" or "big change." However, this is not to be the everlasting peace that shall eventually pervade.

D: *This is referring to something* farther *in the future.*

P: That is accurate.

D: *I'm interested in these inventions with light. Can he see positive ways we would use this?*

P: There would be communication by light, and forms of transportation by light. The ability to travel *with* light, or to transform oneself *into* light, and direct oneself to that desired destination. To elevate oneself to the frequencies of light expression, and be able to travel in that form, *re*materializing to a lower form of expression when one has arrived at the destination. There also will be, at that time, the ability to explore those dimensions of light by raising one's awareness, or more accurately, one's constitution to that level. Then one becomes a *being* of light, and would be able to co-mingle and communicate with those who are on higher planes—those who can lower their frequencies to the lower light levels.

D: *You mean humans will be able to do these things while they are still living in a physical body?*

P: That is accurate.

D: *They could come and go as they wanted?*

P: That is accurate. There will be that ability to pass easily between higher and lower planes of awareness.

D: *Is this something the aliens and UFOS have already mastered?*

P: That is accurate.

D: *I suspected that. I think those are positive uses. Can he see some positive inventions that would be closer to our time period?*

P: (*Pause*) There is some discussion at this point about the allowance of some information, as it would tend to predispose the minds of those who would be most benefited by the effects. However we would say there will be many new forms of medicine. Not simply the practice of medicine but the philosophy of medicine and its use or disuse in establishing wholesomeness of mind and body. There will be a more complete understanding of the importance of connection between mind and body. And more emphasis on treating disease through attitude rather than through medicinal purposes.

D: *He thinks if he told me some of these things they might affect our decisions?*

P: It is necessary for the people involved to feel they have discovered this on their own, and not had it handed to them. They will be more willing to take this inward and believe it if they find it for themselves, than to question its validity as coming from some other source. (*It was time to end the session.*)

D: *Would you thank him for helping us at this time?*

P: We are grateful for his time as well as yours. For in so doing, we have all accomplished what is indeed the true purpose of the universe: understanding and support.

Chapter 21

And So It Begins!

Ɏ<small>N</small> 1986 <small>AND</small> 1987 when I first began to work with Nostradamus on the translation and bringing forth the information contained in his quatrains, the predictions were highly disturbing but they still remained in the realm of probability. As long as these type of scenarios remain remote and in the distant future as a vague wisp that might happen *someday,* then it does not touch you. It remains only an interesting story, a fiction possibility, *until* that possibility begins to take on more solid form and substance. Then it begins to strike that hidden chord that lies within us all, the chord that reminds us of our human frailty and vulnerability.

Nostradamus' ominous predictions of the coming Earth changes were particularly disturbing to me. He said the affairs of humans can be controlled and altered to a certain degree if enough humans decide to take control and have an effect on their destiny. We are not totally without recourse. But the affairs of nature are a different matter. In that category it would seem that humans can do nothing. Their preparations are in vain when faced by the awesome display that the forces of the Earth are capable of. This began to be brought home during the latter part of 1989. It was very obvious to me and others who were observant that even the weather was changing and not obeying the laws the seasons had imposed upon it through the centuries. At first the changes were subtle, but then became more obvious. Everything was being measured in superlatives. It was the hottest, the coldest, the driest, the wettest, the most severe. The "first time in recorded history" was a common phrase heard relating to the whims of nature.

When the devastating hurricane Hugo hit the coast of South Carolina in September 1989 it caused us to have renewed respect for the power of nature. It was as if a terrible monster had been unleashed by Neptune from the depths of the ocean and allowed to walk upon the Earth. Its fury did not stop by destroying the city of Charleston, but continued onward and did not abate until it had reached Charlotte, North Carolina, 200 miles inland. It was the first time a hurricane's force had been felt so far from the ocean. Torrential rains pelted the city for days afterward. Less than a month later before rebuilding had scarcely begun, a record high tide once again inundated the South Carolinian coast. It was again a time of superlatives used to describe weather phenomena. Scientists also theorized that if the "greenhouse effect" was becoming a reality and the Earth was actually warming, then hurricanes of the future would be twice as devastating. They said the surface temperature of the ocean would only have to increase by four degrees to create storms of *twice* the intensity of Hugo.

On the evening of October 17, 1989, I was driving home late at night when the news came over my car radio that a catastrophic earthquake had hit the San Francisco Bay area. I gripped the steering wheel as I felt my stomach tighten. I began to shake all over. I tried to keep my attention on the road while my mind was being bombarded by the events unfolding on the California coast. The same words kept repeating through my numbed brain, "And so it begins! So it begins! It *begins!*"

I had hoped Nostradamus had been wrong in interpreting the visions he saw in his black mirror. Now I was hit with the shockwave that he might be all too deadly correct. All of the horrors he had seen and which I had dutifully recorded, but secretly hoped would be proven false, appeared to be materializing. Was this the beginning? Was he correct when he said they would come to pass in my lifetime?

The rationalization of human survival attempted to take over and deny what I was thinking. How can you attach so much importance to these events, and infer that they are only the tip of the iceberg? It had been predicted by experts for years that an earthquake of this magnitude would hit California. They said it was only a matter of time. It was merely a self-fulfilling prophecy and one which was based on scientific fact. Surely it was merely that and nothing more. It was not the beginning of the terrible chain of events which Nostradamus reported to me.

The reporters said that many people remarked, "Well, at last the 'big one' has hit. We don't have to worry about it any more. No more wondering and waiting." But the experts said they were wrong. This was not the "big one." A small amount of stress had been relieved on the San Andreas Fault, but not enough. The big one was yet to come and would be even more devastating. It was estimated to be as much as *thirty* times greater than the October 17th earthquake. This was only the beginning, a taste of what will surely come.

Some important lessons were learned by both of these events. The first things to go were utilities: electricity, telephone, water, the ties to the outside world. Cars won't run without gas and it takes electricity to pump it. The stores only contain enough food supplies for a few days, especially if a panic develops. Homes are destroyed and people must have shelter. Life begins to focus on the bare basics, and the superfluous becomes unimportant. Situations such as this bring out the best and the worse traits of human beings.

Another earthquake hit China a few days after the one in San Francisco, and just after Christmas 1989 the first killer earthquake in history struck Australia. Earthquakes seemed to be occurring everywhere after that, with a terrible one hitting Iran in June 1990.

Do these events have more importance than we realize? These catastrophic whims of nature seem to be occurring closer together and becoming more violent than any other time in our history. Are they the foreshadowing, the forewarning that screams and urges humanity to prepare? To prepare because the worst is yet to come and will be so monstrous that our imaginations are incapable of envisioning it. Even Nostradamus was frustrated by what he called the "burden of the future" that weighed so heavily upon him. I believe these events are not meant to come upon us suddenly without warning. Maybe this is the purpose of having them occur closer together in a gradually escalating crescendo, so we will not be caught totally off guard. Nostradamus saw many horrendous events in our future, but he believed that his visions also gave him the burden of responsibility. We also have the responsibility of heeding these warnings. Not brushing them aside but making preparations to preserve what we can of our culture and civilization. We are being given time to do just that if we will only listen.

During the summer of 1990 the terrible visions of the war of the Anti-Christ began to take on shape and substance as preparation for the Persian Gulf War started, with half a million men and women and numerous ships and planes being sent to the Middle Eastern area. I was so familiar with Nostradamus' warnings that I realized the implications more than most people, and my brain echoed his words, "So it begins!"

𝒟URING 1990 AND 1991 I was caught up in lectures, workshops and radio shows. The first two volumes of this work were published and gaining attention because of the association with the growing unrest in the Middle East. I had completed the translation of the quatrains in 1989, and I thought my work with the great man was finished. But a few unexpected events occurred to add an unusual postscript to this book. I don't know if my work will ever be completed with him. He seems to be always there waiting in the wings of that other dimension, waiting for contact again. He is still available for consultation even though the major bulk of our work has been completed. He has kept his word to come through anyone I work with, even if they are only casual, one-time seekers.

An unusual incident occurred in November 1990, that again emphasized Nostradamus' ability to see into our dimension. A Hollywood director, who I shall call David, read Volume One and contacted me because it bore a great similarity to a movie script he had been working on for seven years. The script dealing with Nostradamus was disguised as a fiction spy thriller, yet it contained highly researched details that paralleled predicted events in the Middle East. We had come to the same conclusions through different routes. After a month of conversing he made an unusual request. He had a great desire to sit in on one of my sessions with Nostradamus, and perhaps ask him some questions. I had no problems with him asking questions, because others had been present during the sessions over the years. But the distance prevented this. He asked if it were possible to do it over the telephone. This was something I had never considered, but eventually we came up with the plan of using a speaker phone, so he could listen and also participate. I arranged a special session with Brenda specifically for this purpose. When everything was ready, we attempted it as a one-time experiment. Even Nostradamus thought something unusual was going on, but he agreed to participate. Because David lived in Hollywood, he naturally had questions about the possibility of a devastating earthquake in the Los Angeles area. Nostradamus said it was difficult for him to pin it down to a specific month or day, but he felt it would happen before 1995 at the latest. He then said he had a strong feeling about the year 1993. He said the residents of that area were accustomed to the ground trembling from time to time, but he felt a series of stronger earthquakes, and perhaps some great storms causing trouble and confusion, would occur between August of 1991 to 1993. (*Note:* Rains and flooding of record proportions occurred in Los Angeles in February 1992.)

David then unexpectedly decided to test Nostradamus. He said later this was totally unplanned and completely spontaneous.. He randomly picked up a gold coin from a box of miscellaneous objects on his desk. He asked for Nostradamus to give him a sign by seeing his thoughts. "I am looking at a golden disk that has something engraved on it. Can you tell me what I am looking at?"

I sat quietly in suspense. I had no idea what David was holding in his hand 1000 miles away. I would have to rely on Brenda's or Nostradamus' ability to see through space. I silently wondered if they could pass this unexpected test.

After a moment of silence, while Nostradamus said he was focusing, Brenda said, "He says the image he perceives on this golden disk is a Star of David or a Seal of Solomon, with rays of light shining from behind it. It has the correct Hebraic symbols engraved thereupon, for protection and for the calling of the positive aspect."

David then elatedly announced that that was absolutely correct. I breathed a sigh of relief. I do not like to be tested, and I do not like to put Nostradamus in that type of position. I have been working with him for so many years I do not require any proof. Yet I was very glad that he had passed the test, and once again proven himself. The skeptic in me could naturally say that perhaps Brenda had picked up David's thoughts (even via the telephone) through ESP or something similar. But even that would be remarkable enough.

Later when David listened to the tape and studied the large coin, he discovered something even more remarkable. On the front side was the Star of David or Seal of Solomon, but around the edges were astrological symbols. A moment of doubt occurred as he wondered if Nostradamus had made a mistake. But when he turned the coin over the correct Hebraic symbols were engraved on the reverse side of the coin. It appeared that Nostradamus had seen *through* the coin, and saw what appeared on both sides.

Another strange occurrence happened toward the end of the session. We were both using speaker phones and had been talking for almost an hour, when suddenly and unexpectedly while David was asking a question, his voice dropped to a whisper and began to fade away, as though a button had been pushed or a switch flipped. He was unaware of this on his end of the conversation and continued to talk, as the tape recordings later testified. After desperate attempts to get him back failed, I finally broke the connection. Later David compared his tape recording with ours, and we were able to hear the effect from both sides of the conversation. He could not hear us and we could not hear him. This had never happened before with his phone, or with mine. Was it something to do with the connection with Nostradamus across the dimensions? Nostradamus knew something had occurred and he was aware that David could no longer hear us. He then answered the last question he had heard, and announced that he had to leave. Thus this experimental session contained two unusual circumstances that only reinforced our belief in the connection with the great man.

During the summer of 1991 I had my first experience with attempting contact through a subject that I had never worked with before. Paul was a California businessman who began communication with me after he read the first Nostradamus book. We had been in touch for about a year, and he wanted to meet me. He hoped to have a session because he had a great desire to see if he could contact Nostradamus. After the books were published and I became known, I received calls and letters constantly from people who wanted sessions, mostly for their own curiosity. In the early part of my career as a regressionist I would work with anyone who requested this unique service, and I traveled many miles to hold the session in their home so they would be comfortable with me. Now things had changed radically. I no longer had time to fill the numerous requests in addition to the work of writing and compiling these books, and my traveling was now done for the purpose of lecturing and giving workshops. As much as I hated to do it, I was turning people away unless they traveled long distances specifically for this purpose.

I tried to explain to Paul that not everyone was able to enter the trance level that was required to contact Nostradamus, and I did not know what type of subject he would be until I worked with him. All of the other people I had worked with were subjects I had conditioned from years of working with them at deep trance level. I had never met Paul, and I told him he was asking for the most difficult thing to achieve with a new subject in the first session. Through our communication he felt he knew me and felt comfortable with me.

I was doing book signings and lectures in Denver, and Paul arranged his business trip so he would be in Denver at the same time. When we met he said he felt confident he would be able to achieve contact, so I thought there would be no harm in trying it. It would either work or it wouldn't. I am just the guide, the conduit, and any results are normally out of my hands. Paul prepared a list of questions he wanted me to ask Nostradamus. Originally he had wanted to see the Anti-Christ, but at the last minute he decided against it. I knew the list of questions would probably be too many for the first session, since I expected most of the time would be taken up establishing the contact.

The initial induction was successful and Paul went into a very good trance state. After I took him to the spirit state he saw a building and floated through the door. Inside he began describing a room that was all too familiar to me. Then he began to describe a man seated at a table writing in a big book with a quill pen. The description of a scrowling bearded man with a large nose, wearing a black hat with flaps over his ears, also sounded very familiar. We apparently had located Nostradamus without asking to because that was our intention.

Paul then had the strange feeling that he was pure energy filling the entire room. There was no front or back or up or down. He seemed to be everywhere in the room at once. He knew he was invisible and thus unable to materialize in any form. Yet when I asked him to do something to get Nostradamus' attention and let him know we wanted to communicate, Nostradamus suddenly looked up at him. Paul didn't know what caught Nostradamus' attention, unless he picked up on our thoughts.

Nostradamus then regarded him with a whimsical expression, as though he was thinking, "Well, what's this?" I told Paul to communicate to him that he was from the future and wanted to ask him questions. Nostradamus remained guarded and suspicious until Paul told him I was also there. Nostradamus then smiled a little, and after a few seconds of indecisiveness he seemed to relax. I then had Paul ask if Nostradamus would be able to show him scenes. At that question Paul began to experience a strange sensation. "I'm losing him. It's as if *I'm* fading away. As if I'm fading backwards away from him." Although Paul did not understand what was happening, I was sure I did. This was the same feeling Elena had when (as Dyonisus) she went to the "special meeting place" for the first time. At that time she thought she was losing contact with me.

The room faded away and in a few seconds was replaced by an ethereal scene. Paul saw a white light and a small golden tree with bare branches. "It looks like gold and white glass, and has beautiful branches. Behind it is white light, and in front of that light is golden light. It is very beautiful and peaceful." After a few seconds Paul was aware that Nostradamus had come to this special place, and was told that if he asked questions he could be shown scenes. I will only include the answers here that are pertinent to our accumulation of knowledge. We had scarcely begun when Paul said they were not speaking in words, but in thoughts. The communication was instantaneous. It was not translated word for word, but deposited mentally in a lump of information. This is the same way this phenomenon has been described by everyone who has worked with Nostradamus, and it explains how we are able to get around the language barrier. It is all done with thoughts and transference of mental concepts.

Because Paul lives in San Francisco the first question on the list was whether there would be a devastating earthquake there before the year 2000. Nostradamus nodded his head and said, "Yes." Immediately Paul began to exhibit signs of discomfort. "I see the earthquake," he reported softly, yet emotionally. "It's dark. There's a fire coming from the sky. And there's a lot of smoke, explosions, and the buildings are crumbling. There's lots and lots of devastation. I'm above the city, looking down at it, as if I'm floating over it." He was getting caught up in what he was watching. It was disturbing him because it appeared so realistic. I knew I would have to get his mind off the scene, so I tried to find out when this was happening. I named off the years beginning with 1991. He said "no" for each year until I got to the year 1998, then Nostradamus nodded and said, yes."

This may not be a contradiction with the information David received over the phone. He asked about an earthquake to hit the Los Angeles area, and Paul asked about one to hit San Francisco.

Next Paul wanted to know whether the American economy would collapse during the 1990s. The answer was immediate. Nostradamus said it would happen in 1995, and that it would be a world-wide situation caused by greed from the governments and people. He described it as a very difficult time.

Paul wanted to know more about the Anti-Christ, and the same information was given that all the other subjects supplied. Nostradamus indicated that the Anti-Christ did not have a permanent home. He moved around from place to place, even going to England and Europe, but that he spent a lot of time in Egypt. Nostradamus became more excited while speaking about this subject, as though this was something he definitely wanted to get across to our time.

We finally had to end the session because Paul said Nostradamus was not feeling well, and was getting tired. Nostradamus turned and smiled weakly at him before leaving. Upon awakening, Paul said he had the feeling that Nostradamus was older, tired and sick. "He was very weak, but he was happy that I came. He was giving me warm feelings of love, and softness. I got the feeling that he gave as much energy as he could, and then got tired and wanted to go. He was animated when talking about the Anti-Christ, but then it was as though I asked too many questions, and he was a little frustrated about answering them." Paul also had the distinct impression that Nostradamus was dying.

But Paul felt when Nostradamus smiled that he was happy he had been able to make contact once again. Maybe at that stage in his life he was not time traveling as often, and it made him feel good that he could still make the effort. There was a mellow feeling of nostalgia from the man.

It may be argued that this session with Paul does not give any valid evidence, because he had read the first book and asked for the session with the distinct intention of locating Nostradamus. This is true, but I believe Paul was not fantasizing or wish-fulfilling because some of the answers he received to his personal questions were not what he expected. Also after the session he described a strange sensation he had never experienced before. When he went to the special meeting place, he felt as though he had split, and was actually in two places at once. This strange sensation has been described by every subject who met with Nostradamus in the special meeting place, or other dimension. The feelings of dissociation, splitting, bi-location are common, and must be describing an actual perception by the subjects. Those who meet with Nostradamus in his study and converse with him there do not experience this feeling, although they all have the sensation of being pure invisible energy, with no physical body. To me, these similar descriptions add validity because the subjects do not know what the others have reported. Their stories could have been sharply conflicting instead of amazingly similar.

ANOTHER RANDOM CONTACT DURING 1991 resulted in a most remarkable piece of evidence: pictures of the Anti-Christ and his mentor, the Imam, the evil uncle (first mentioned in Volume Two).

Judith is a psychic who has been working for several years on a continuing research project with a nationally-known psychic research institute. She is well respected and reliable in her work with them, and also in her work helping police agencies with the solving of crimes. I became acquainted with her by phone after she had read Volume One, and we had several conversations. In 1991 she made arrangements for me to come to her city and give lectures, workshops and a book signing.

While I was there, Judith said she would like to attempt to contact Nostradamus. Since I had not expected to make any contact while I was on my trip, I had not prepared a list of questions. She was so accustomed to the trance state that she was able to follow my instructions excellently and went immediately into a deep trance state.

After she was under the first step would be take her to the in-between lives state. At the first attempt she balked at entering that area. I didn't know why until she awakened and explained it. Something uncomfortable had occurred there during a past life regression with someone else. I instructed her to find her guide and things went smoothly after that.

D: *Ask him if there is a place we can go to have contact with people who are living their lives in the past.*

J: I don't know exactly what kind of a place it is, but apparently we've already started to move into it. It appeared as a corridor or hallway off to the right. And where everything was dark before, there's flashes of colors starting to come through.

D: *Go with him so we can find the place where we can have access.* (Pause) *Are you there yet?*

J: I think so. (*Long pause.*) It looks like nothing. It's not a dark place. There's no color; there's no form. It's just nothing.

D: *Tell him we want to contact Nostradamus while he is alive in the 1500s in France.*

J: He's pulling me to the left. There seems to be directions here that I'm not aware of. It's as if we're standing in the center of a hub of a wheel. And Nostradamus is off on a spoke at about nine or ten o'clock. I have to move down that path, the spoke of the wheel. Again there are blotches of color. It reminds me of being inside a jewel. There are facets around that don't always catch the light. They're not blinding, but if you move in one direction, you see something that you couldn't from somewhere else. It's difficult to explain. It's like being inside lattice work. I'm not sure if we are moving *through* it, or that's just where I'm ending up. I'm aware that I'm detaching more and more. The path ended when I stopped where I am. I feel I have located him. And what I'm really surprised at is, I had not expected ... it's something about his forehead being so smooth. I think I expected him to be wearing something on his head. I'm not sure whether or not it's because he's losing his hair, or his hairline has receded, because the skin texture is not of someone who is very old. He has very heavy eyebrows. (*As though studying him.*) He has high cheekbones. I remember reading about his eyes, but I don't see them. It appears there is facial hair, but it does not seem very long. It seems very close, short.

D: *Where is he?*

J: He seems to be in a room made of stone. There is something that appears to be more of a table than what I would think of as a desk. There seems to be a lot of stone, which is not something I expected. There are lots of things in the room. It's not *really* cluttered, but there are a lot of things, paraphernalia. I keep using the word "things," because I don't recognize a lot of them. Things that he uses to study with or he is studying, or things he may have picked up somewhere and then laid down. He doesn't seem to be terribly organized. There is nothing I can really recognize yet. It reminds me of some mad scientist's laboratory; almost what I would expect Merlin's place to be like. There is what I would guess to be the mirror that's been referred to. If you were sitting at the desk or the table, whatever it is, it's to his right. And it is not shaped the way I would expect. It is more of a free-form; it has no particular shape. It's almost like somebody poured water on the surface of the table and it just ran wherever it was going to go. It's a dark color.

D: *Is Nostradamus doing anything at this time?*

J: He's puttering in a corner. There are some things that are made ... I hate using that word over and over, but I don't know what this stuff is that's lying around. A lot of books, and things that I'm sure must be chemicals or powders. But there's a lot of stuff that's made of fur or hair, perhaps dried skins. He seems to be examining something or looking at it.

D: *Can you get his attention?*

J: I have it now. I called out his name, and it startled him. He jerked around suddenly, and was very surprised. He was not expecting anyone.

D: *What do you think you look like to him?*

J: I'm not sure, but he looks perplexed. Gold seems to be what comes to mind, or what comes off his mind—something golden. I thought I landed with a thud that he would have heard, but he apparently didn't know I was here. He was very surprised to hear someone call his name. And when he turned around, it was not what he expected.

D: *Are you picking anything else up from his mind as he sees you standing there?*

J: The response that I initially got was, "I thought we were finished!"

D: *Does he know where you come from?*

J: He must, because ... maybe not where, but it feels as if he knows the why or what it's related to, by his statement. I believe he assumes that wherever his visitors are coming from, they're all from the same basic space. He understands some of the subtleties, the differences that are there, but I'm not absolutely certain that he realizes they're each individual people. Does that make any sense?

D: *Yes, it does. They must all have a different feeling, a different vibration. But do you think he is perceiving them as one entity?*

J: Perhaps, or different aspects of one personality, such as maybe you are in one mood one day, and a little different the next. There are familiarities with the energy of a mood, the way it would be the energy of a person. I don't get the impression that he realizes there were different beings involved. Or he had not given any thought to that.

D: *You can tell him we have finished the translations of the quatrains that have come down to us. Is that what he meant when he said he thought we were finished?*

J: I'm not sure if he was referring to that, or if he assumed that the communications were over. When I told him that the quatrains or whatever were finished, there was a smile, and he seemed very pleased and happy that the work was done. He knows what you mean, but I was confused. In the sense that, even though I understand what you mean, it's hard to consider that you've translated what he hasn't already written.

D: *I'm never sure at what stage in his life he began working on them. That might be confusing to him.*

J: It wasn't confusing to him. It was confusing to me.

D: *All right. Is he writing any of the quatrains at this stage in his life?*

J: He says there are some things that he is continuing to write about. He has scrolls that he keeps in a big cabinet. Other than that, I'm not sure I understand how to ask.

D: *I don't like to put ideas in his head because I'm not sure at what age he began putting them into code. Has he been recording what he sees of the future?*

J: This is correct. He says he began doing this in his mid-20s. *(Pause)* It's interesting. He seems a little ... almost suspicious ... or skeptical as to what we could possibly want.

D: *Well, tell him we have questions about things that are happening in our time that we wanted clarification about. What would he say about that?*

J: He said that he would try.

D: *Could he show you scenes in the mirror?*

J: He's trying to show me how to use the mirror. It is as if I have to go into the mirror to see. And what I see is moving water, like an ocean or a sea. He wants me to move into there, to see what it would be like. Things are starting to feel very different. This is really bizarre, but it is not as if I actually get inside it. I put my face down to the surface of the mirror. As if I were leaning over a bowl of water and stuck my face in. I didn't get into it all the way. I just leaned over, opened my eyes and looked. Part of me is in and part of me is not. Things are spinning. There is a definite physical sensation of vertigo, even though I'm not physical ... and a feeling of disorientation. God, it feels like I am ... Now it's the sensation of not being *here,* and not being *there.* It's being in ... maybe another dimension. I had a moment of panic ... but I can handle it. It's not bad. It's just ... strange.

Judith may have entered the special meeting place. As long as she felt comfortable with it, I thought we should proceed.

D: *Ask him if he can show you anything that might happen to the present Pope of the Catholic Church in the 1990s.*

I was thinking about the predicted assassination. I always double-check these prophecies by asking all the subjects the same questions.

J: There are many things that would happen to the pope in the 1990s. He's wishing for you to be more specific. He is asking if you are referring to his death, or to some other event within his life.

D: *Can he show you something about his death?*

J: (*The scene appeared immediately.*) Interestingly enough, it appears
    that he is in France because something resembling the Arch
    d'Triumph is in the background. He seems to be in some sort of
    parade, or some ceremony that is taking place. I don't know if this is
    indeed in that city, but wherever he is there is a monument that is simi-
    lar to the arch. Whatever I'm seeing, it's really strange, and I am
    questioning whether it is fantasy. It feels as if he was shot, but the
    parade continued to move on as if nothing had happened. It didn't
    make sense that there would be no reaction. Perhaps he was not shot,
    and the clutching at his body was ... perhaps he had a heart attack,
    and I'm assuming that he's been shot. But regardless, the parade or
    whatever continues to move on as if nothing is wrong. He grabbed his
    left shoulder, or not so much his shoulder, but that part of his body,
    which he might do if he were shot or if he were having a heart attack.
    He was alternating between standing in the car and sitting, so it wasn't
    surprising that he sat down. The movements were not observed as
    being strange by the people who were with him, protecting him. So
    when he sat down very suddenly, no one seemed to notice anything
    different than what he had been doing.

D: *Can you see where the shot came from?*

J: From the point I was viewing, he was coming in a semi-circle (*hand
    motions*) from my right to my left. And the shot came from somewhere
    behind him on his left side. It was out of range. There's a tower of
    some sort. I have not read the quatrains, but one thing I am confused
    about; it feels as if there is a similarity here between his assassination
    and what happened with John Kennedy. There is a possibility this
    refers to one of the quatrains that has a double meaning.

D: *It's possible. They often refer to more than one thing. Is there anything
    about the tower that is distinctive?*

J: It seems to be by itself. Either it's a part of something similar to a
    monument, or it's a bell tower or something. But it seems either by
    itself or set apart, as if it is connected to a building. That's where the
    shot came from. The parade continued and went out of my sight.
    They didn't discover it right away.

D: *I want you to try to find something, either in the scene or related, to tell
    you when this might be happening. Nostradamus may give you a clue.*

J: The numbers that come up are two and four. I don't know whether
    it's two years or four years, or 1992 or 1994. I just see a two and a four.

D: *It could also refer to a day or a month.*

J: It feels like it will happen before the middle of this decade.

In Volume One there is a quatrain, CENTURY IV-86, which gives
astrological signs referring to the death of the present pope. The quatrain
says the present pope will be assassinated, the second pope will also be
dead and the last pope will be sworn in by the dates given. The signs
indicate this will happen when Saturn and the Sun conjunct in the water

sign of Pisces. The astrologer said this would only occur twice before the end of the century: March 5, 1995 and March 17, 1996. Before this third volume went to press, one of my readers called and said he had found another date when these signs were present: February 21, 1994. Would this date fit with Judith seeing the numbers two and four?

D: *Why is he being assassinated?*
J: To get him out of the way; to bring in someone else.
D: *Why would that be necessary? He seems to be a good pope.*
J: That's the problem. They need someone who can be controlled. The pope is simply the office that is desired. It has nothing to do with the man. Whoever has the office controls and has a great deal of power.
D: *Then you mean this present one can't be controlled.*

I then asked for information concerning the war in former Yugoslavia, and the breakup of the different sections which was just beginning at that time (May 1991). The information received also applies to the breakup of the Soviet Union satellite countries.

J: There is much greed that is causing all of this. Much of this is a smoke screen for other things that are going on, in spite of truces or pacts, and agreements that have been made, for monies to be shared, and so forth. There are larger things going on that are designed to break up the economy of the country by breaking up the various parts of it, so they no longer work as a collective whole, but as individual units. Should this happen, there will be some future time when each one of these individual republics could be conquered or mastered on its own. It's not just a division of the republic in the way we have the division of the states in our country. There is something akin to racial prejudice or whatever you wish to call it. Because of this, as the various republics split there will be no real reason for them to come to the others' aid, if there is some sort of external threat. They are indeed sacrificing the country to create the individual units. There is a group behind this, but it is unclear right now who makes up the units of that group. The purpose is greed and to weaken the power base. Any time you have a large whole and you break it up into slices or pieces, you lessen the impact that particular group could wield as a whole. And for some reason, this is another portion of that particular part of the world that is beginning to break down. This is not the first country in that particular part of the world that will be subject to this pressure. There are those outside this country that have influenced some that live within the country. There are reasons, such as economics or politics or some other excuse. They have convinced the individual people that it is in their best interest to *not* be a part of the collective whole. They are receiving bad information. They are being fed lies. And they are being set up to actually help tear their country apart; not to do whatever is being promised. They're not going to be better off as individual units.

They will become much weaker, and more easily conquered, or thrown into economic chaos.

D: *What groups are causing all of this?*

J: It's not being shown, but it feels there is a group working to separate the various republics. However there is another group beyond that, a group that is truly the power. It is outside the country. The group that *appears* to be responsible is *within* the former country of Yugoslavia, and I don't have a name for either one.

D: *Where are the military arms coming from that are going to Yugoslavia (May 1991)?*

J: They're coming from different places, and the various sources, to some degree or another, believe that no one else is doing it, or that it won't be known they are participating in this. Each is doing it for their own reasons. One source is from the United States. One source is from the former Soviet Union, which is strange, because it's not coming from the proper government of Russia. It's as if arms are being black-marketed out of the old Soviet Union by a subtle group of people that are trying to help that country break apart. The same way that other eastern-bloc countries have broken away. And there is another source from the Middle East. The weapons are coming from *outside* the country. They're not coming from within the country. They're being *used* by people within the country.

D: *You said that factions outside of the country were causing the turmoil and unrest and plotting. Are these some of the same factions that are supplying the military arms?*

J: Yes.

This sounded very much like the infamous Cabal mentioned many times by Nostradamus.

D: (I focused on another incident that had just occurred.) *Tell him this is in May of 1991. A very important leader of the country of India has just been assassinated. His name was Rajiv Gandhi. Can he show you some of the scenes behind what happened?*

J: It appears that this man at first was willing to be led in his political persuasions in whatever structure he would try to offer to the government. At some point in time he decided to move away from that and become more of his own person, putting more of his own programs or ideas into place. This was against what those who were originally in control were doing. And for this he has been removed. It is also for this reason that his wife (Sonia) was offered his position. But knowing what strain she would also be under, she neglected to move into that space, as she was in agreement with her husband.

D: *You don't think she will become the next leader?*

J: No, because whoever is the leader does not lead. As I have just said, there were others actually doing the leading. It was as if ... the word "puppet" comes to mind. It was something for the glamor, the power and the ego, but at some point in time he became aware that he was not happy with this. His conscience came back into play, and the sense that his own country needed true direction, guidance and leadership. And once he elected on his own to try again to provide that ... for this he was assassinated.

D: *Can you see who will take his place?*

J: It seems to be a very young man. Much younger than Gandhi was. He is very fair, very handsome. Fair, not in coloring, just *very* nice-looking. Very open, very warm-looking. A beautiful face. Incredible eyes. He has dark hair and the darker complexion, but it's not that real deep Indian skin tone.

D: *Will this man also be a puppet?*

J: (*Long pause*) This is going to sound very strange, but it is the impression that comes through. At first when I started to answer your question, there was just a "no." But my first reaction to this man was—and it's hard to think of him as a man, because he's younger than I. But my first reaction was feeling very drawn to him. It was that magnitude of his presence. There was an energy about him that was very warm and loving and gentle. I wanted to go in to be sheltered by him, drawn to him, whatever. That was the first reaction. And then the next reaction. It's like *I* have a question. Is it possible this is where the Anti-Christ would come through? Because my first reaction was to move towards, but it didn't make sense. To see this young man ... it's as if through a force of his own magnetism or ability he could lead it, because on first look it does not seem he has whatever it takes to lead a country of this size. And I don't understand why he's so much fairer than the Indians of that country.

D: *Do you think you are seeing the man known as the Anti-Christ? What does Nostradamus think? He knows what he looks like.*

J: (*Pause*) For some reason I get the impression that right now he's not going to say anything about it. I'm not absolutely certain that this young man is going to immediately be next in line after Gandhi. It's almost as if this young man will at some point in time come into a leadership role in this country. The way he popped up in the picture was as if he was a symbol that symbolizes the leadership role of the country. This person's picture was much reduced in size compared to whatever the leadership symbol was, and he was down below it.

When she awakened, she had the impression of first seeing him under a chair or seat.

J: That was one of the things that struck me about his youth. It was as if he was a little boy, but when you looked at him, he was not a little boy. He was a young man, or younger than I.

D: *I'm just assuming, but I'm thinking that you probably are not seeing the man who will succeed Gandhi. I think this other man is behind the scenes.*

J: Symbology-wise he is not in the forefront. He is hidden. He is under the chair.

D: *I want you to concentrate on that man—the handsome man who seemed to draw you to him with his beautiful eyes. Ask Nostradamus to show you where he is living in 1991.*

J: It is a country of sand and palm trees, fig or date trees. I don't get the impression that he's necessarily *living* in one place. It's as if he is moving around.

D: *Do you know why he doesn't stay in one place?*

J: Creation. Something he's creating. It's as if there are negotiations going on, for things to happen or be produced. And he meets with one group and gets their demands or desires. He then moves to another group and works to see how they're compatible, and goes back. If you didn't know better, you would think he was perhaps an arbitrator, but he's not. He's setting things into motion.

D: *Is he doing this all by himself?*

J: It feels as if there are two or three others with him. He's very much on the move. The way someone would do if they were in charge of a large business organization with various branches. Whatever he's doing, it does not *seem* to draw him any undue attention.

D: *Can you see what these other people look like?*

J: The face of someone just popped up. I don't know if it is the same young man, older version, or someone else. But the features are *very* harsh. Dark, with a black beard. Very gaunt face, very mean, very *hate*-filled.

D: *And this man is with him?*

J: That's what popped up whenever you asked me if anyone else was there. I said there were two or three. Then we started to move away, and this one popped up solo, right smack in front of my face.

D: *It seems as if he would be a contrast to the other young man.*

J: Very much so. I do not feel any *positive* feelings coming off this man. It's almost as if he feeds on hatred. Whatever is going on with him just eats away inside like a cancer.

She seemed to be seeing the evil Imam, the uncle who raised and groomed the young Anti-Christ. This was explained in Volume Two (see index). Judith had not read that book and knew nothing about this man.

D: *But the young man doesn't feel like that, does he?*

J: He didn't in the beginning. That first look. It's as if all this is symbolic. The first look was so enticing, so seducing, that whomever was looking in his direction was magnetized. And only after you continued to look for awhile, were you able to not *feel* that anymore, not be drawn up in that. But the first reaction was to be drawn to him. I find it interesting, from my perspective, that if this were indeed the young Anti-Christ, and knowing what to expect from things I have been told, that I would still allow myself to be drawn to him, even if only for a moment. It's very deceptive. He's very beguiling.

D: *Then if someone were to try to find him, it would be difficult because he wouldn't stay in one place long enough.*

J: If he wants to be found, he can be found, but I think you would have to be part of his inner circle.

D: *Do you think he is highly protected?*

J: If he is, it is not obvious.

I had Judith remove herself from the mirror so we could close the session.

J: Nostradamus is saying he didn't have to work so hard because he really didn't answer the questions. It's rather comical, because I kept wondering why I wasn't exactly hearing him the way I was expecting to when my head was in the water. But rather than being an interpreter, because these were things he had not looked at before; it's as if he stuck *me* into the middle of it so *I* would have to figure it out. Whereas, now that I'm *out* of it, it's as though there are two people back here again. It didn't feel like he was there. It was as if he was loaning his mirror to be used. When I think about it now, I feel very flattered that he would allow me to go into it, as opposed to staying out and looking at it. It's as if I was using whatever technique he uses when he is doing it.

D: *He allowed you to do it and that saved him a lot of work.*

J: Right. He kept fiddling with that hairy thing. It was strange. I kept wanting to hear his voice or to interact with him. I couldn't figure out why he wasn't there. That's why there was so much confusion on my part.

D: *Now that you're facing him and you can interact, ask him why he allowed you to use the mirror.*

The other subjects sometimes entered and left through the mirror, as a doorway. They watched scenes appear in the mirror, but it was always under the direction of Nostradamus. This was the first time any of my subjects had entered the mirror in this manner.

J: The response I got was strange, and it makes me sad. He said he always wanted to teach his son how to use the mirror, but he didn't live long enough to do it. He died young from some type of disease. He's quite intuitive and telepathic, and reads a great deal without it necessarily having to be the spoken word. He seemed to feel a closeness with my spirit, and decided to allow me to do what his son never had a chance to do. His look softened and I thought I saw a tear in his eye as he told me this. I feel honored.

Judging from the fact that Nostradamus appeared younger, he could be referring to his son by his first marriage, who died of the plague.

IT HAD BEEN SUGGESTED BY OTHERS that I try to obtain a drawing of the Anti-Christ from one of my subjects. The only one who had seen him clearly enough to duplicate him was John Feeley, the astrologer from Volume Two. He was not an artist, such as Elena, who drew the picture of Nostradamus used in Volume One. It was suggested that he could work with the police and the composite kits used to make drawings of suspects. This was an idea that had never occurred to me. But it was impossible to pursue because at the time it was suggested, John Feeley was seriously ill in Florida. He was only 38 years old when he died of AIDS in the summer of 1990. It was almost as though part of his mission in his short life was to exonerate himself from the karma he had incurred by adulterating Nostradamus' quatrains in his past life as a propaganda specialist working with Hitler during World War II. (Explained in Volume Two.) If this was one of his purposes, then I believe his mission was fulfilled when he worked with me to help clarify the quatrains in our time. Whatever the reason, he was a great asset and a wonderful person. But that door was closed as far as obtaining any type of picture of the Anti-Christ, or the evil Imam. The idea lay dormant in my subconscious.

Now as I worked with Judith, the possibility again arose. She had seen the Anti-Christ in great detail in a three-quarter profile, while she had seen the Imam straight on. She explained that in her second career as a psychic, she had worked with police and detectives in helping to solve cases. While working with them she had often used the police composite kits to construct the features she was seeing in her mind. She believed there would be no problem doing the same thing with the person who would become known as the Anti-Christ, and his uncle, the Imam. She said it was a shame someone couldn't just take a photograph of what she saw in her mind because it was so clear.

Judith also wanted to explain the strange sensations she felt during this work with Nostradamus. In her experiments with the psychic institute, Judith has been subjected several times to brain-wave tests involving instruments to record the activity of her brain during out-of-body travel and psychic experimentation. She was familiar with the sensations of the different altered state levels. She said she had never experienced the sensation that occurred during these visits with Nostradamus. It was as though she was in two places at once, and it created a strange feeling in her head. She was positive that if similar machines were hooked up to her during these sessions, that something unusual would definitely register. Judith described it as though she was functioning on three levels. She was vaguely aware of me back in the apartment. She was more aware of Nostradamus and his room. The third level happened when she entered the mirror. It was a sensation of disorientation and vertigo.

She also felt that this strange sensation might be frightening to someone who was unfamiliar with working in altered states. Through logic and her many years of experimentation she intuitively knew she was in no danger. Yet when she entered the mirror she felt as though she was moving farther and farther away from me, slipping or drifting farther away from the "now," the place where we and her body were located. She knew she was disconnecting more and more. There was a momentary feeling of panic that she might not be able to get back, that she could keep going and not be able to return. The complete cutting-off or dissociation from this dimension. But she instinctively knew that if she could get back to Nostradamus' room, then she could get back home to reality. Once she was able to get back out of the mirror, she was never afraid again. This was her first and only experience like this, and it was totally different from anything she had worked on at the institute. I wondered if Nostradamus also felt this apprehension when he first experimented with the mirror.

I knew that she could not lose contact because the subject is always connected to the hypnotist's voice. That is like a life-line that will always pull them back from their journeys through time. But Judith emphasized an important point. While working with Nostradamus we were not working in ordinary past-life regression. We were playing by different rules. In past-life work the subject is reliving their own other lives and interacting with people in those lives. With Nostradamus they were an energy form entering into *his* life in the past. And while in that life they are utilizing a very real psychic instrument (the mirror), the powers of which are not really known. Maybe the mirror really was a doorway, portal or gateway between dimensions.

She emphasized that this was not something for a novice to play with, mostly because the physical and mental sensations could be disturbing, if not frightening. Nostradamus must have also known this because he had only allowed my other subjects to view the scenes in the mirror. I can imagine that he had the presence of mind to allow others no access at all, if he sensed they could not handle it. I was more aware than ever of the magnitude of this project, and of the wonderful protection given by our guides during this experimentation.

BEFORE LEAVING THIS CITY TO RETURN HOME, we decided to have another session. The purpose of this second session was to allow her to closely study the features and to memorize them so she would be able to duplicate them. I considered this a big breakthrough, and Judith also knew the significance of being able to publish a picture of these men.

She entered trance very quickly and easily, and immediately went down the spoke of the wheel to locate Nostradamus in his room. He was seated at his table writing with a quill pen on some parchment. He appeared to be older, with a different skin tone and thinner, grayer hair. The room was still cluttered with objects that she did not recognize. She described him as somewhat of a pack rat. He was intent on his work, and she picked up from his mind that he was recording his treatment of certain illnesses, and combinations of herbs used for these treatments.

She called his name, and he immediately turned and looked at her. She knew that he was perceiving her in two different ways: with his eyes as a golden light, and on a higher sensory level as what she really was. His face was soft, and he smiled as though he recognized her. The mirror was on his right side near the corner of the table, and he waited patiently to find out why she was there.

J: There's no reaction. He seems to be used to it. This has happened for some time, and he's beyond being surprised about it.

D: *He has warned us about a man he calls the third Anti-Christ, who he says is very much in our future. Tell him we are trying to recreate a picture of this man. And that you're going to help with this assignment. Does he say anything?*

J: He's nodding his head. He thinks it cannot hurt.

D: *Ask him if he can show you what the young Anti-Christ looks like in the 1990s, so you can get a very clear impression of his face and features.*

J: We're going to try. I'm to go into the mirror again. I'm moving over to the edge of the table. I'm going closer to the mirror and moving in. I'm becoming adjusted to the energy of it. It's like being in two altered states at the same time. The one state it takes to get me to where he is, and the other one, while I'm going into the mirror.

D: *Is it a physical sensation?*

J: It's like moving deeper. (*Sigh*) It is hard to explain. However I felt before, it is as if I am more deeply into it when I am in the mirror.

When the mirror cleared, a scene began to form. She was certain she had located the Anti-Christ.

J: I'm perceiving him in a place, but I don't know where. It is very secluded or quiet, like a garden. I was curious to see his whole form, and not just his face. He seems to be of a rather slight build. I am unclear as to his height, because there is not much to compare to. But I would say he is around 5 feet, 10 inches. It is not that he is a small man, but he is not a large man either. His frame is small or thin or wiry. I am not quite sure of the words to describe him. I have never been good at physical descriptions. He's wearing a shirt and slacks. He seems to prefer tailored clothes that are more casual and relaxed, as opposed to something more formal.

D: *You said he is in a garden. Are there any buildings around?*

J: (*Pause*) There may be in the direction behind me. But I am looking forward, and behind him there seems to be open, arid land. I get the impression that he is in someone's home. It feels like a place where he is very comfortable, as if he spends time here when he wants to retreat and be quiet.

D: *Turn around and look at the buildings you said were behind you.*

J: It has a flat roof, a porch, rambling, an earth-tone color. It's not made of wood and is very foreign in design. It's not something you would see here.

D: *Is it in a town?*

J: I don't think so, unless it's on the outskirts, because when I looked in the other direction there was open land.

D: *Okay. Let's see him with the person who owns this house. He apparently is their guest.*

J: That man is shorter, a bit overweight, and wears those long robes. He has a full beard, dark and light, as if he's starting to gray. He seems to have a very nice energy.

D: *Is this his home?*

J: It's *one* of his homes.

D: *He has others?*

J: Yes, he is wealthy.

D: *Can you see where his wealth comes from?*

J: (*No hesitation*) Oil.

D: *Do you get an impression of what country it might be in?*

J: There's a name, but it eludes me. I'm seeing a map. I guess it is of that basic part of the world. Unfortunately, I don't know where anything is. But from what I remember of the maps during the gulf war, the country would be south, south-east, somewhere around the gulf perhaps. If we looked on the map maybe we could find it. There also seems to be a strong tie on the opposite side of the water which would be east, north-east.

D: *Remember that, then when you awaken you can look at a map and see what countries these are.*

J: It's not some place that a great deal of attention has been drawn to in recent times, even though it's in that part of the world.

Later when she awakened and looked at a world map, two countries kept coming into her mind. One was Syria and one was Oman. She thought the home might have been in Syria, but this is only speculation. We do not know what the terrain is like in either country.

I asked her to focus on the young man's features as she observed the front view of his face.

J: The words I would use would describe many people. His hair is dark, straight, and parted on the left side. It is cut the way someone in business would cut it. His cheekbones are high. His jaw line is short. There's something about the proportion of his cheekbones to his eyes. It's as if his jaw line is slightly shorter than it should be. That his face should perhaps be a little longer to be more balanced. It is almost a combination of a squarish face and a rectangle, at the same time. Instead of being in balance and proportion, it is off a bit. His features are delicate in a sense. That's why I was talking about the small bones. He's not effeminate. It's as if his whole body type belies the power that he might possess at a later time. It's as if it's an anomaly. He's not a huge, fierce, muscular individual that one might associate with someone of power. It is almost the exact opposite of what you would expect. His eyes are dark, with very black eyebrows. His skin is a bit fairer than it seems it should be, considering the part of the world that he is from, but I'm not sure he is outside a great deal.

D: *As you look at his face I want you to impress the features on your mind. Study them so you'll be able to remember them in a conscious state. Remember the way the forehead, eyes, nose, mouth and jaw-line look. Remember their shapes. And later when you awaken you will be able to prepare a composite picture of this man, based on what you are seeing now. When you are ready to create this composite picture, the memory of this face will be very strong so that you can see it clearly, and be able to duplicate it. Remember all of the features. Even though you say they are normal, everyone has something that's different and sets them apart. And it won't bother you to have this in your mind, because you're going to use it for a purpose. And when you're working on the picture these features will be distinct and clear to you. Is that agreeable to you?*

J: This is fine.

D: *All right. As you look at the man, is there anything that is different or distinctive about the body?*

J: He slouches a bit. I realize that is not very much, but it's as if his whole demeanor is one that would be the opposite of what you would expect, considering what he is to become. This is part of what would throw you off balance. There's a casualness and a relaxed air about him. He looks like any other young man. He is attractive, not so much to me personally, but yes, he is an attractive man. But there's something missing in his jaw. It's as if there's about an inch missing in the rest of his face. The proportion is not there that should be.

D: *You said he was wearing casual clothes. Is there any type of jewelry or anything else that you see?*

J: There's a ring on the little finger of his left hand. It's yellow gold and something red. It's not overly large. It fits to the proportion of his hand.

D: *Is the red part a stone?*

J: I think it is, but it seems to have some gold on the top of the stone, too. As if something is inlaid or pressed into it.

I then asked her to find the other man she had seen during the last session, the one I assumed to be the Imam. The results were immediate, so I asked for a detailed description.

J: He's shorter than the other young man, and also slight-framed. There's a somewhat crazed look about him. He looks as if all the air had been punched or sucked out of his body. He is so lean and drawn looking. His face is thin and gaunt, and very sun-browned. His hair is rather unkempt. It seems to always be messed up, as if he's in a frenzy. It's almost symbolic of how crazy and evil he is. I am not sure what color I would call it. It's kind of silver and dark at the same time. Obviously, it was once very dark. But there is something wrong with the cheekbone right underneath his left eye. It's as if there is a scar there, or there has been a wound or something that has caused him pain. His eyes look like he never fully opens them. I mean, there are times when he does, but for the most part the eyes are kind of hooded or veiled. His lids stay somewhat closed. It's not as if he's squinting exactly, but as though he's hiding something from people who can read intentions in other people's eyes. The nose is very strong. All of his facial features are very strong, in spite of the fact that he's a small individual. His lips are rather thin. He's bearded, but it's kind of a splotchy beard, not real full. And it's close to his face, not very long, maybe half an inch, I guess.

D: *Is there anything else that's distinctive about him?*

J: He carries himself much differently. Very rigid. I realize this sound rather silly, but it is something I have used to describe other people who were very withdrawn, so much into themselves and not loving anything out of themselves. I think the psychiatric term is "anally retentive." It feels like he probably has stomach problems, intestinal problems, and he holds everything in. When he does let everything go, it erupts.

D: *Do you think he has a temper?*

J: He is quite capable of it.

D: *Is he wearing jewelry or anything that's distinctive?*

J: There is some sort of gold chain with a medallion. (*Surprised*) It matches. The medallion matches the ring on the other young man's hand. (*Long pause, as though studying it.*) It's hard to make out what's on it because I can't get a good perception of whether it is two individual things, or something that has been combined as one. It is rather like a serpent and a bird, or something that's a cross between the two. It's the same thing, whatever it is, that was gold-inlaid on the red stone of the young man's ring.

It is interesting that John also saw the young man wearing a distinctive ring when he saw him and the Imam at a meeting at an estate in Egypt (Volume Two).

J: (*Pause, studying.*) I think there is red as well on the medallion. I'm not certain how large it is, but at the same time it doesn't feel it could be very small either because it hangs from a large, heavy gold chain. And that does not fit with having a small medallion on it, nor does his ego feel like it would want something small. It is like everything for him is larger than life. He's wearing very loose-fitting clothing. It looks like pantaloons and a loose shirt with a long jacket over the top of it. *Text continued on Page 342*

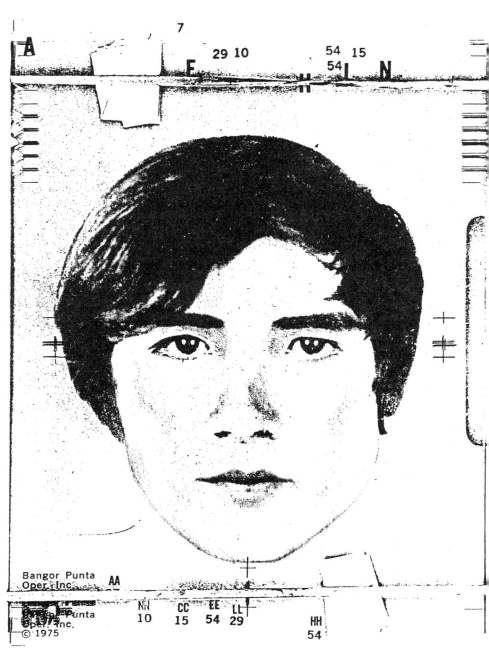

*A drawing of the Anti-Christ created from a
Police Department composite kit.*

The same drawing enhanced and corrected by an artist
under the instruction of the subject who saw him.

A drawing of the Imam, the uncle or mentor of the Anti-Christ, created from a Police Department composite kit.

*The same drawing enhanced and corrected by an artist
under the instruction of the subject who saw him.*

D: *Is there any connection between these two men you are looking at—*
the two main figures we are focusing on?

J: They are thought of as uncle and nephew, but I do not believe there
is an actual blood tie. I don't know why I would feel that, but there
doesn't seem to be a blood bond between the two. Or if it is, it is very,
very distant, in terms of being physically related. It doesn't feel like
they are naturally nephew and uncle. But I get the feeling that the
older man has taken care of the younger one.

I then asked her to look very carefully at this man and to memorize his
features so she would be able to reproduce them after awakening when
she used a composite kit.

J: (*She suddenly interrupted me.*) Syria. That's what came through. I
don't know where that is on the map, but that feels like where it is.
And we can check.

D: (This was the name of the country she was looking for earlier.) *Some-*
times it happens like that. It will pop in later. Does the second man
go with the younger one when he travels?

J: Not always.

D: *When he travels, are there any places he goes to more often than others?*

J: He does, but no names are coming. He travels on the bequest of this
uncle—to do whatever is asked. It is as if he is the go-between, but at
the same time he is learning a great deal while he is doing whatever it is.

D: *Do you think he goes to other countries besides the ones in his area?*

J: I don't feel at this time he's moved too far out of that part of the world,
mostly in the Middle East. As if it is not time for him to move farther
away yet.

D: *Do you get the impression that he has* ever *gone to other countries*
outside the Middle East?

J: I'm not sure. Brazil is the first thing that pops into mind, and it doesn't
make any sense. It doesn't feel like he would go somewhere in South
America, but I suppose it's possible.

D: *Do you get the feeling he has ever met with any world leaders?*

J: (*Pause*) In *his* world, yes. Not the European world.

D: *Then he is probably very well known in his own part of the world.*

Upon awakening Judith said she was positive she could create the
composite pictures. The details were very clear in her mind. After I
returned home she borrowed a composite kit from the police department
in order to work on it. She explained that the kit is very complicated, containing many parts: about 400 noses, 300 hairlines, age lines, *etc.* The
procedure involves using transparencies of the different facial parts to
compose an entire face, and these are all numbered. Judith felt a compulsion to work on this, an urgency that pushed her until the job was finished.
Yet she was not satisfied with the completed composites, and a young
artist friend agreed to turn them into drawings. Judith said there were a

few things about the Anti-Christ's face that were not quite right (*i.e.,* the jaw line and the hairline), and the artist corrected these under her instructions. She sent me copies of the different phases that the drawings went through. Under her direction the pictures of the Anti-Christ and the Imam were created (these pictures are reproduced on pp. 338–341), and she declared them to be as accurate as possible, according to what she had seen while in trance.

W HEN I WAS GIVING LECTURES across the country during 1991, I was often asked to identify the Anti-Christ, so someone could find him and eliminate him. It was also suggested that releasing the drawings might be a mistake because some innocent person could be assassinated if he unfortunately resembled the pictures. This is not the purpose of creating these drawings. Nostradamus said it would do no good to try to stop him. The Anti-Christ had been predicted from as far back as Bible times, and was even mentioned in the scriptures. His destiny was set and had to be fulfilled. What happened after that was in the hands of humankind because we are a people endowed with free will. The purpose of releasing the information in these three volumes is to prepare the world so it will not be caught off guard. The purpose of the pictures is to aid in identification so that when the man with the golden tongue appears on the scene he will be recognized and unmasked to reveal his true self. In this way perhaps humanity will not be fooled, will not listen to the man's solutions, and can observe his progress more carefully than if no warnings were issued. Nostradamus believed that thought was an extremely powerful force that has never been fully utilized. The use of thought can be directed to draw to it that which is desired. Nostradamus believed that if humanity knew the results of their actions, then their combined thoughts could produce a powerful force that would counteract the worst of the futures he saw, and turn our path into a more peaceful alternative. He encouraged us to learn meditation and how to direct our thoughts to reverse the picture by visualizing the opposite of Nostradamus' predictions. He wanted us to be aware of events when they begin to happen, and at that time use meditation or prayer either singly or in groups. Although the mind of an individual is powerful and can create the reality they seek, the combined thought power of groups is tremendous. The focused concentration of groups is not only multiplied, it is mathematically squared, and thus can truly perform miracles.This is the purpose of Nostradamus communicating through time to our generation: to give us tools to work with in order to create our own reality, our future. Let us try to use his advice wisely, so his journey and his effort will not have been in vain.

W HAT NOSTRADAMUS CREATED with his quatrains was a guidebook to help the weary Earth travelers find their way along the various time lines. To show them the paths through the many probable futures, to help them ascend the mountains and to help them avoid the pitfalls, the crevices and the abyss. By showing us the worse, he has offered us the best. His job is over, his task has been completed. He has succeeded in bringing his visions of the future to our time.

I can almost see him as he lays down his quill pen, leans back in his chair, strokes his beard and smiles contentedly. As it says in the Bible, "Well done, my good and faithful servant." His assignment is finished. He has shown us the future with its variant probabilities for horror or wonder. What we do with the information is now *our* responsibility. Our future is up to us, isn't it?

And So It Begins!

THE END OF VOLUME THREE.

Index

Quatrain Index

About the Author

$\mathcal{D}$OLORES CANNON was born in 1931 in St. Louis, Missouri. She was educated and lived in Missouri until her marriage in 1951 to a career Navy man. She spent the next 20 years traveling all over the world as a typical Navy wife and raised her family.

In 1968 she had her first exposure to reincarnation via regressive hypnosis when her husband, an amateur hypnotist, stumbled across the past life of a woman he was working with who had a weight problem. At that time the "past life" subject was unorthodox and very few people were experimenting in the field. It sparked her interest, but had to be put aside as the demands of family life took precedence.

In 1970 her husband was discharged as a disabled veteran, and they retired to the hills of Arkansas. She then started her writing career and began selling her articles to various magazines and newspapers. When her children began lives of their own, her interest in regressive hypnosis and reincarnation was reawakened. She studied the various hypnosis methods and thus developed her own unique technique which enabled her to gain the most efficient release of information from her subjects. Since 1979 she has regressed and cataloged information gained from hundreds of volunteers. She calls herself a regressionist and a psychic researcher who records "lost" knowledge. The *Conversations with Nostradamus* trilogy are her first published books. *Jesus and the Essenes* has been published by Gateway Books in England. She has written eight other books (to be published) about her most interesting cases.

Dolores Cannon has four children and twelve grandchildren who demand that she be solidly balanced between the "real" world of her family and the "unseen" world of her work. If you wish to correspond with Dolores Cannon about her work, you may write to her at the following address. Please enclose a self-addressed stamped envelope for her reply.

Dolores Cannon, P.O. Box 754
Huntsville, AR 72740-0754

THEORIES OF LIGHT
FROM DESCARTES TO NEWTON

A. I. SABRA

Harvard University

CAMBRIDGE UNIVERSITY PRESS

Cambridge
London   New York   New Rochelle
Melbourne   Sydney

Published by the Press Syndicate of the University of Cambridge
The Pitt Building, Trumpington Street, Cambridge CB2 1RP
32 East 57th Street, New York, NY 10022, USA
296 Beaconsfield Parade, Middle Park, Melbourne 3206, Australia

ⓒ Cambridge University Press 1981

First published by Oldbourne Book Co. Ltd 1967
First published by Cambridge University Press 1981

Printed in Canada

Library of Congress Cataloging in Publication Data

Sabra, A. I.

Theories of light, from Descartes to Newton.

Bibliography: p.

Includes index.

1. Light – History. I. Title.

QC401.S3 1981   535'.1   81-6108   AACR2

ISBN 0 521 24094 8 hard covers
ISBN 0 521 28436 8 paperback

TO NANCY

Preface to New Edition

The first edition of this book was allowed to go out of print only a few years after its publication in 1967. Now, fourteen years later, it is being reprinted with only some minor corrections and an added bibliography. It did not take me long to decide that the present edition should remain substantially the same as the first. When I first turned my attention to the study of seventeenth-century optics, the questions that I had in mind were primarily philosophical or methodological in nature. Although during the writing of this book I had already begun to develop an interest in the historical approach to the study of science, my initial interests were bound to influence the mode of treatment as well as the choice of topics in the chosen area of my research. I was in effect asking philosophical and methodological questions in a historical context. Responses to the book on the part of both philosophers and historians indicate to me that my venture was well worth the effort. Here I must reassert my belief in the value of philosophical concepts and philosophical analysis for the historical investigation of science, and I confess that, by and large, my position on the issues discussed in the book is fundamentally the same now as it was when it was first published. Nevertheless, if I were to embark now on a study of the same subject, or extensively revise what I wrote earlier, the result would naturally be a different book – one, however, in which my debt to Sir Karl Popper and to Alexandre Koyré would remain undiminished.

Between 1955, when the *Theories* was first written, and 1967, when it first appeared, very few studies of seventeenth-century optics were published. Most important among these were the articles by Richard Westfall, which I was able to take notice of in the book and include in the bibliography. The situation has changed substantially in the last twelve years or so. Numerous studies on various aspects of seventeenth-century optics have appeared in print. The larger number of these are concerned with Newton, and they form part of the current surge in Newtonian studies. Most of them contain new and valuable information and insights. Frequently the authors of these studies have had occasion to comment on or disagree with views and interpretations expressed in my book. It would of course be impossible even to begin to do justice to these comments and criticisms within the limits of a preface, but I hope that the appended bibliography will at least make it easy for the reader to locate the results of more recent research.

Cambridge, Massachusetts   A. I. Sabra
January 1981

Contents

Preface

The following chapters contain the substance, revised in parts, of a thesis which earned the Ph.D. degree from the University of London in 1955. My first acknowledgement must be to the University of Alexandria for a generous scholarship which allowed me to devote much time to this work. My debt to Professor Sir Karl Popper, who supervised my research at the London School of Economics, is basic and manifold. It was he who kindled my interest in the growth of scientific knowledge, and from his writings and lectures I came to see in the history of science the history of man's most imaginative and most rational enterprise. The suggestions and criticisms which I received from him in the course of numerous discussions have influenced every aspect of my work. In common with other historians of science of my generation I am gratefully aware of the influence of the work of the late Alexandre Koyré whose *Études galiléennes* appeared to me, almost from the start, as a model of exploring the historical development of scientific ideas. To him I also owe the idea, which he suggested to me in a private conversation in 1952, that Newton's belief in atomism is the key to his interpretation of the *experimentum crucis*. So far as I know, Koyré did not develop this idea in his published work, and the responsibility for the way it is here presented and argued is entirely my own.

Since the original version of this book was written, a great deal of fresh information regarding Newton's optical manuscripts has come to light, and I have now used as much of this new material as is relevant to my argument and indicated such use wherever it is made. I must add, however, that although this recent research has yielded important results that were not known to me before 1955, these results have not obliged me to alter the argument itself; in fact they seem to me to support it at more than one point.

I wish to thank the many scholars and friends who, through conversations, criticisms and encouragement, have helped me in various ways. I am particularly grateful to J. O. Wisdom for his constant encouragement since my undergraduate years in Alexandria, to L. J. Russell for some very useful suggestions, and to Thomas S. Kuhn for an extensive and valuable commentary especially concerned with the chapters on Descartes and Huygens. My thanks are due to Michael Hoskin, editor of the Oldbourne History of Science Library, for his helpful suggestions and reading the proofs, but above all for his patience and good humour. It is a pleasure also to thank the staff of the Oldbourne Press for their helpfulness throughout.

In preparing the revision I made use of some of my time as Senior Research Fellow at the Warburg Institute (1962–4) and had the benefit of obtaining the advice of several of its members on various problems. While at Princeton University as Visiting Associate Professor for 1964–5 I was able to make further improvements in the light of discussions with members of its Program in the History and Philosophy of Science; moreover, the Program generously defrayed the expenses of typing a considerable part of the final manuscript.

To the library of the British Museum, where most of this book was written, I am very grateful. The courteous and unfailing help of its staff has been invaluable.

A word about translation. In general I have quoted already existing English translations of French and Latin texts, sometimes with minor alterations which are indicated as they occur. In my thesis I had the privilege of using an English translation made by Czeslaw Lejewski of the Latin letters exchanged between Newton and Pardies. My debt to Professor Lejewski is not diminished by the fact that I here quote the English translation printed in the *Philosophical Transactions* (abridged edition, 1809) and now made widely available in I. Bernard Cohen's edition of *Isaac Newton's Papers and Letters on Natural Philosophy* (1958). Unless otherwise noted, all other translations are my own.

A. I. Sabra

The Warburg Institute
University of London

Introduction

This book is not a survey of optics in the seventeenth century, nor does it claim to offer a complete account of the optical researches of any one investigator in that period—perhaps with the exception of Fermat. It is a study of problems and controversies which have appeared to me to be particularly important in the development of seventeenth-century theories about the nature of light and its properties.

The method I have followed is to compare actual practice, in so far as it can be historically determined, with the interpretations placed upon it by the practitioners themselves. The two were closely linked. When Descartes first published his views on light and colours in the *Dioptric* and in the *Meteors*, he presented them as fruits of 'the method' outlined in the *Discourse*; and he declared those views to have been conceived in accordance with a new meta-physically founded system of physics. Fermat's successful derivation of the law of refraction from his principle of least time was the culminating point of a long and tortuous controversy about what constituted a true law of nature and about the applicability of certain mathematical techniques to physical problems. Huygens in the preface to his *Treatise on Light* introduced a methodological theory that was obviously designed to support the type of mechanical explanations he offered for those properties of light with which he dealt. And, Newton, in his first paper to the Royal Society, con-joined his new theory of light and colours with sharply defined views on the proper way of conducting scientific inquiry. The stand on hypotheses which he took during the subsequent dispute with Hooke, Pardies and Huygens can be seen clearly reflected in the mode of exposition which he adopted in the *Opticks*, published some thirty years later.

None of these facts warrants the postulation of any simple and direct relationship between the substantive theories and the second-order speculations which accompanied them. In particular, they do not justify the assumption that the achievements of seventeenth-century optics were due to the application of previously conceived *règles de la méthode* or *regulae philosophandi*. Indeed, the following pages provide more than one illustration of the notorious fact that what scientists do is often quite different from what they say they do. It is, however, my belief that a study of the endeavours of seventeenth-century scientists, in which actual practice and actual results are confronted with their attendant evaluations and theories of method, should yield a fuller understanding of the accomplishments of those early masters of modern science, and a better appreciation of their aims, convictions and limitations.

There are two main reasons for beginning this study with Descartes. He was the first to publish the correct law of refraction without which no substantial progress in optics was forthcoming; and he incorporated this law into a physico-mathematical theory which, despite, or rather because of, its many defects, constituted the starting point for the investigations of Fermat, Hooke, Huygens and even Newton. Thus Descartes not only gave optical research a new impetus, but also a new set of problems, and hence a new direction. To be sure, many of the elements of his theory, both physical and mathematical, are to be found in the writings of his predecessors, such as Ibn al-Haytham, Witelo and Kepler; this we shall have to emphasize. Nevertheless, the cumulative aspect of the development of science should never blur the emergence of ideas, patterns and programmes that are, in an important sense, new. By clearly redefining the boundaries for subsequent discussions about light, Descartes in fact put the science of optics on a new path.

Descartes' commitment to a conception of a strictly full universe obliged him to conceive of the transmission of light as something more like the transfer of energy than the transport of body. His representation of the rays of light as nothing but the lines of direction of the static pressure exerted by the luminous object upon the surrounding matter, was very much in keeping with his plan to reduce the whole of physics to geometry. But when he came to investigate specific properties of light, such as refraction, he failed to mathematize this picture. Instead, he availed himself of a model consisting of a moving sphere which could be imagined to change direction and speed on meeting a refracting surface. The model may be called a 'substitute model' since it did not represent what, in Descartes' view, actually took place in reality, but was employed rather as a substitute to which a handy mathematical device—the parallelogram of velocities—could be directly applied. Descartes did manage, however, to formulate two mathematical assumptions which correctly yielded the law of sines.

Newton did not fail to notice the importance of this mathematical achievement of the Cartesian theory. His own theory of refraction, published in the *Principia* and in the *Opticks*, incorporated Descartes' two assumptions together with the conclusion, which was to be generally accepted until the middle of the nineteenth century, that the velocity of light was greater in denser media. But the mathematical assertions, which Descartes had failed to explain mechanically, received in the Newtonian treatment a plausible physical interpretation which regarded refraction as a special case of particle dynamics. Simultaneously, the model which Descartes had incongruously applied to his continuous picture now coincided with what it was taken to represent in Newton's theory; the sphere shrank into the light corpuscle. What finally remains in Newton's account of refraction is simply the dynamical situation for which the parallelogram method had originally been introduced.

But those who, like Pardies and Huygens, preferred a Cartesian-type physics, became chiefly concerned with repairing the obvious defects in Descartes' mechanical considerations. At the hands of Huygens, Cartesian matter ceased to be rigid and continuous. But the original picture of light as motion transmitted by contact remained, though the transmission was no longer instantaneous as it had been with Descartes. It was Huygens' merit to have been the first to mathematize this picture successfully. This he achieved by imagining a truly representative model of contiguous and elastic spheres to which he applied a new mathematical technique embodying what we now refer to as Huygens' principle.

For Descartes, matter had to be incompressible and space full because of a primary conception equating space and matter. He believed in fact that a significant part of physical science could be deductively developed from such primary conceptions; but he recognized the impossibility of extending this deductive process throughout the whole of physics. At one point or another in the process hypotheses have to be introduced for the purpose of explaining particular phenomena. These hypotheses acquire some of their plausibility from the fact that they explain a large number of phenomena. They must, however, satisfy the further condition of being formulated in terms already defined by the first principles of physics. In other words, the Cartesian physicist must never lose sight of the programme which has been delineated for him by an *a priori* decision, even when he is no longer moving within a system of *a priori* deductions. With the help of these distinctions we may now define Huygens' position in the following way: he rejected Descartes' apriorism, but fully subscribed to the Cartesian programme; thus he presented the whole of his theory of light as nothing more than a system of hypotheses, but hypotheses conceived in accordance with Cartesian mechanism.

The theories of Descartes, Fermat and Huygens were primarily concerned with refraction; the only important exceptions were Descartes' mechanical but qualitative account of colours, and his quantitative explanation of the rainbow. With Hooke and Newton the interest shifts to the problem of colour. Hooke's contribution to the investigation of this problem involved a series of pioneering and important observations on the colours of thin plates, which Newton later raised to an astonishingly high level of experimental sophistication. And yet Newton's fundamental theory of prismatic colours, his chief contribution to optics as the first satisfactory explanation of colour phenomena, must be understood in relation to the prevailing doctrine of refraction. For the problem immediately posed by his famous prism experiment is one of refraction, not of colours as such; it was the shape of the spectrum, not the colours in it, that formed the basis of his arguments. Moreover, what may be regarded as the firmly established part of his theory, the assertion that each colour is always connected with a constant degree of refrangibility, is the part directly related to this geometrical aspect of his experiment. Newton further believed that he was in possession of an *experimentum crucis* which positively established the composite nature of white light. He always insisted, however, on interpreting this compositeness in a narrow sense which, contrary to what is generally assumed by historians of optics, the experiment certainly did not prove. In the chapters dealing with this problem Newton's experiment is viewed against the background of a particular belief in atomism towards which Newton had inclined from the beginning of his intellectual career. This belief was to the effect that properties cannot be *created* but only made apparent, by separating the elements which have always possessed them. Without this belief Newton's insistence on his representation of white light would be left without explanation.

Newton's first published paper on light and colours is regarded here more as an argument devised to convince his audience of his new theory than as an exact autobiographical account of how he had in fact arrived at it. The argument is inductive and was expressly levelled against 'the Philosophers universall Topick', the hypothetico-deductive procedure. Newton continued to use Baconian inductivism as a stick with which to beat his Cartesian opponents, but the effect of this on Newton himself was unfortunate: it seriously impaired his insight into the structure of his own great achievements.

Abbreviations

B   *The Works of Francis Bacon*, collected and edited by James Spedding, R. L. Ellis and D. D. Heath, 14 vols, London, 1857–74

D   *Œuvres de Descartes*, edited by Charles Adam and Paul Tannery, 12 vols, Paris, 1897–1913

F   *Œuvres de Fermat*, edited by Paul Tannery and Charles Henry, 4 vols, Paris, 1891–1912

H   *Œuvres complètes de Christiaan Huygens*, published by the Société Hollandaise des Sciences, 22 vols, La Haye, 1888–1950

HR *The Philosophical Works of Descartes*, translated by Elizabeth Haldane and G. R. T. Ross, 2 vols, 2nd ed., Cambridge, 1931

'Huygens, *Treatise*' refers to the English translation by Silvanus P. Thompson, London, 1912
'Newton, *Correspondence*' refers to H. W. Turnbull's edition in three volumes, Cambridge, 1959, 1960, 1961 (continuing)
Unless otherwise indicated, references to Newton's *Opticks* are to the New York edition of 1952, and references to Newton's *Principia* are to the edition of Florian Cajori, Berkeley, California, 1934

16

Chapter One

DESCARTES' THEORY OF EXPLANATION AND THE FOUNDATIONS OF HIS THEORY OF LIGHT

1. The *Dioptric*, in which Descartes first published his views on light, appeared in 1637 as one of three treatises claiming to contain results which the author had arrived at through the application of a new method for discovering scientific truths.[1] The method itself was briefly outlined in the *Discourse* which formed a kind of preface to the three treatises. Yet a reader who has gone through the *Discourse*, and who now turns to the *Dioptric* expecting to find a concrete illustration of the four general *rules of method* that are set out in the former work, will be disappointed. Nowhere will he find any of these rules called upon to clear up any particular problem;[2] in fact he will meet with no reference to *the method*.[3] What will be perhaps more puzzling to the reader is the fact that he is being presented instead with another method, an old one which, according to Descartes himself, had been practised by astronomers since antiquity. Descartes in fact declares in the beginning of the *Dioptric* that since

---

[1] The title for the whole volume described the *Dioptric* together with the other two treatises, the *Meteors* and *Geometry*, as '*essais de cette Méthode*'.

[2] As Descartes later explained to Vatier, 22 February 1638, his aim in publishing the 1637 volume was neither to expound the method in the *Discourse* nor to illustrate its application in the three treatises that followed: 'mon dessein n'a point esté d'enseigner toute ma Methode dans le discours où ie la propose, mais seulement d'en dire assez pour faire iuger que les nouuelles opinions, qui se verroient dans la Dioptrique et dans les Meteores, n'estoient point conceuës à la legere, & qu'elles valoient peut être la peine d'estre examinées. Ie n'ay pû aussi monstrer l'vsage de cette methode dans les trois traittez que i'ay donnez, à cause qu'elle prescrit vn ordre pour chercher les choses qui est assez different de celuy dont i'ay crû deuoir user pour les expliquer. I'en ay toutesfois monstré quelque échantillon en décriuant l'arc-en-ciel . . .' (D, I, p. 559). See similar remarks in Descartes to Mersenne, March 1673, D, I, p. 349; and to *** 27 April, 1637?, ibid., p. 370

[3] The only reference to 'the method' in the three treatises occurs in the *Meteors* in connection with Descartes' explanation of the rainbow (D, VI, p. 325). See preceding note; and below, p. 61.

his aim in talking about light in this treatise is restricted to explaining how its rays enter the eye, and how they are made to change direction by the various bodies they encounter,

there will be no need that I undertake to say what in truth the nature [of light] is, and I believe it will be sufficient that I make use of two or three comparisons that help to conceive of it in the manner that seems to me most convenient, in order to explain all those of its properties that are known to us from experience, and to deduce afterwards all the others which cannot be so easily observed; imitating in this the Astronomers who, although their suppositions are almost all false or uncertain, nevertheless succeed in deriving from them many consequences that are very true and very assured, because of their agreement with the various observations they have made.[4]

In 1637 Descartes had reasons for not revealing the foundations of his physics. He had in fact almost completed, before July 1633, a comprehensive work, *Le Monde ou Traité de la Lumière*, which contained, in his own words, '*tout le cors de ma Physique*'.[5] But when the news of the condemnation of Galileo reached him (in November 1633), he decided to defer publication of this work for in it he had committed himself to the Copernican view which had brought Galileo to the notice of the Inquisition. Since in 1637 he was still unwilling to express disagreement with the doctrines favoured by the Church, the object of the volume published in that year was to give some results of the new method in less controversial matters without expressly stating the 'principles' from which these results were obtained.[6] Nor would he indicate those principles briefly lest they should be misunderstood and distorted by 'those who imagine that in one day they may discover all that another has arrived at in twenty years of work, so soon as he has merely spoken to them two or three words on the subject'.[7] Thus, in spite

---

[4] D, VI, p. 83.

[5] Letter to Vatier, 22 February 1638, D, I, p. 562.

[6] *Discourse*, Pt. VI, HR, I, p. 128: 'And I thought that it was easy for me to select certain matters which would not be the occasion for many controversies, nor yet oblige me to propound more of my principles than I wish, and which yet would suffice to allow a pretty clear manifestation of what I can do and what I cannot do in the sciences.'

[7] Ibid., p. 129.

of what Descartes says in the beginning of the *Dioptric*, the suppositions from which he starts in that treatise (and in the *Meteors*) are
not really of the same kind as those of 'the Astronomers'. For
whereas their suppositions may be false or uncertain (even though
the consequences agree with observation), his are founded on
principles which, Descartes maintained, were ultimately deducible
from certain primary truths:

And I have not named them [the matters of which he speaks at the
beginning of the *Dioptric* and *Meteors*] hypotheses [*suppositions*] with any
other object than that it may be known that while I consider myself able
to deduce them from the primary truths which I explained above, yet I
particularly desired not to do so, in order that certain persons may not
for this reason take occasion to build up some extravagant philosophic
system on what they take to be my principles, and thus cause the blame
to be put on me.[8]

Since the suppositions of the *Dioptric* and of the *Meteors* are
deducible from certain 'primary truths', they must themselves be
necessarily true. They are not conceived simply as hypotheses devised
only to explain the phenomena that are dealt with in these two
treatises, although the reader is invited to look on them as such for
the time being. If the reader insists on having some justification of
those assumptions, he may, for the present, find satisfaction in the
following argument:

If some of the matters of which I spoke in the beginning of the *Dioptrics*
and *Meteors* should at first sight give offence because I call them hypotheses
[*suppositions*] and do not appear to care about their proof, let them have
the patience to read these in entirety, and I hope that they will find
themselves satisfied. For it appears to me that the reasonings are so
mutually interwoven, that as the later ones are demonstrated by the
earlier, which are their causes, the earlier are reciprocally demonstrated
by the later which are their effects. And it must not be imagined that in
this I commit the fallacy which logicians name arguing in a circle, for,
since experience renders the greater part of these effects very certain, the
causes from which I deduce them do not so much serve to prove their

---

[8] Ibid., p. 129.

existence as to explain them; on the other hand, the causes are (proved) by the effects.[9]

The astronomer Morin was among the first to raise objections against this method of demonstration, ignoring, it seems, Descartes' intentions. He protested[10] that experience alone cannot establish the truth of a supposition. The apparent celestial movements, he argued, could be equally derived from one or the other of the two suppositions assuming the stability of the earth or its motion; experience was therefore not sufficient to decide which of these two 'causes' was the true one. Further, unconvinced by the argument in the *Discourse* (just quoted), Morin insisted that it was surely arguing in a circle to prove the effects by some causes and then to prove the causes by the same effects. Finally, he maintained that Descartes' procedure was artificial, since, in Morin's view, nothing was easier than to 'adjust' some causes to given effects.

Descartes' reply to these objections exhibits the same attitude already expressed in the *Discourse*:[11] while indicating that he believes his suppositions to be obtainable from higher principles which he has not yet divulged, he also defends his right to argue for the truth of those suppositions on purely empirical grounds. This, of course, is consistent with his intentions: for if we grant that the experiments bear out the proposed suppositions, then, Descartes hopes, we will be better prepared to accept his principles when they come to light. Thus, on the one hand, he readily agrees with Morin that the apparent celestial movements are deducible from either of the two suppositions mentioned, and adds: 'and I have desired that what I have written in the *Dioptric* about the nature of light should be received in the same way, so that the force of mathematical demonstrations which I have there attempted would not depend on any physical opinion.'[12] And later on in the same letter he admits that one is not obliged to believe any of the views expressed in the *Dioptric*, but

[9] Ibid. The English translation erroneously reads 'explained' for 'proved'. Cf. D, VI, p. 76.
[10] Morin to Descartes, 22 February 1638, D, I, pp. 538–9.
[11] Descartes to Morin, 13 July 1638, D, II, pp. 197ff. Cf. *Principles*, III, 4, D, VIII, pp. 81–2, IX, pp. 104–5.
[12] D, II, p. 197.

that he wants his readers to judge from his results 'that I must have some knowledge of the general causes on which they depend, and that I could not have discovered them otherwise'.[13]

On the other hand, Descartes would not accept Morin's objections that the demonstrations in the *Dioptric* are circular or that the proposed explanations are artificial. He grants that 'to prove some effects by a certain cause, then to prove this cause by the same effects', is arguing in a circle; but he would not admit that it is circular to explain some effects by a cause, and then to prove that cause by the same effects, 'for there is a great difference between *proving* and *explaining*'.[14] Descartes points out that he used the word 'demonstration' (in the passage quoted above from the *Discourse*) to mean either one or the other 'in accordance with common usage, and not in the particular sense given to it by Philosophers'.[15] Then he adds: 'it is not a circle to prove a cause by several effects which are known otherwise, then reciprocally to prove some other effects by this cause.'[16] As to Morin's last objection, Descartes writes: 'you say lastly that "nothing is so easy as to adjust some cause to a given effect". But although there exist in fact several effects to which it is easy to adjust diverse causes, one to each, it is however not so easy to adjust one and the same cause to several different effects, unless it be the true one from which they proceed; indeed, there are often effects such that one has sufficiently [*assez*] proved what their true cause is, if one has assigned to them one cause from which they can be clearly deduced; and I claim that those of which I have spoken [in the *Dioptric*] belong to this category.'[17]

The basic supposition in Descartes' *Dioptric* is that light is a certain action or movement that is transmitted to all distances through an all-pervading medium. This is the 'one cause' by which Descartes wants to explain the various effects of light. Some of these effects are 'known otherwise', that is, independently of any knowledge of the supposed cause; such, for example, is the rectilinear propagation of

---

[13] Ibid., p. 201.
[14] Ibid., pp. 197–8. See passage from the *Principles* quoted below on p. 36, n. 56.
[15] Ibid., p. 198.
[16] Ibid.
[17] Ibid., p. 199.

light, the fact that light rays are not interrupted when they cross one another, and the equality of the angles of incidence and reflection. Descartes' contention is that his supposition is 'sufficiently proved' by clearly deducing all these different effects from it. Moreover, he claims to have derived from the same supposition 'some other effects', notably the law of refraction which he presents as his own discovery; this provides him with independent evidence which saves his demonstration from circularity.

In this argument no reference is made to higher principles from which the suppositions in question could be derived. One may therefore ask whether Descartes believed, at the time of writing his letter to Morin, that *proving the cause by the effects*—which he called *a posteriori* proof[18]—constituted a conclusive demonstration establishing the truth of his suppositions. In other words, did Descartes here understand by 'proof' a form of argument that would allow the transmission of truth from the consequences to the supposed assumptions, in the same way that mathematical deduction allows truth to be transmitted from the premises to the conclusions? We are not, I think, entitled to answer this question in the affirmative; 'proof' in this context is not to be understood in a strictly logical sense. Descartes does not say that the suppositions are entailed by the experimentally verified consequences; they are only 'sufficiently proved' by them, that is to say 'proved' in a sense that he finds appropriate to the subject matter dealt with. It will be seen later that, as opposed to Francis Bacon's inductive-deductive procedure, the Cartesian conception of method is purely deductivist. This does not mean, however, that Descartes' method can dispense with experiment; on the contrary, deduction is understood in such a way

---

[18] 'As to what I have supposed at the beginning of the *Meteors*, I could not demonstrate it *a priori* without giving the whole of my Physics; but the experiments which I have necessarily deduced from it, and which cannot be deduced in the same way from any other principles, seem to me to demonstrate it sufficiently [*assez*] *a posteriori*' (Descartes to Vatier, 22 February 1638, D, I, p. 563). Later on in the same letter (pp. 563–4), after repeating his claim of being able to deduce his suppositions from 'the first principles of my Metaphysics', he compares his performance in the *Dioptric* to that of 'Thales, or whoever it was who first said that the Moon receives her light from the Sun, providing for this no other proof indeed except that by supposing it one explains the various phases of her light: which has been sufficient, ever since, for this opinion to have been accepted by everybody without contradiction'.

as to make experiment indispensable.[19] Moreover, the limitation of proof in physics was clearly recognized by Descartes in a letter to Mersenne, written less than two months before his reply to Morin:

You ask whether I consider what I have written about refraction [in the *Dioptric*] to be a demonstration; and I believe it is, at least in so far as it is possible to give a demonstration in this matter without having previously demonstrated the principles of Physics by Metaphysics (which I hope to do one day, but which hitherto has not been done), and in so far as any question of Mechanics, or of Optics, or of Astronomy, or any other matter that is not purely Geometrical or Arithmetical, has ever been demonstrated. But to require of me Geometrical demonstrations in a matter which depends on Physics is to demand that I achieve impossible things. And if one wishes to call demonstrations only the proofs of Geometers, one should then say that Archimedes never demonstrated anything in Mechanics, nor Vitellion in Optics, nor Ptolemy in Astronomy, etc., which however one does not say. For one is satisfied in such matters if the Authors, presupposing certain things that are not manifestly contrary to experience, have subsequently spoken consistently and without Paralogism, even though their suppositions might not be exactly true. For I could demonstrate that the definition of the centre of gravity, which Archimedes has given, is false, and that such a centre does not exist; and the other things which he supposes elsewhere are not exactly true either. As for Ptolemy and Vitellion, they have suppositions that are much less certain, and nevertheless one should not for this reason reject the demonstrations they have deduced from them.[20]

No interpretation of Descartes' theory of explanation would be satisfactory without taking this passage, and the problems which it raises, into full consideration. Together with the claim repeatedly made about the deducibility of physical principles from metaphysics, we have a clear and obviously sincere admission that conclusive demonstrations in physics are impossible; the two are expressed almost in the same breath. Thus the limitations set upon physical proofs are not due simply to a temporary deficiency which will be remedied once the metaphysical foundations are brought to light;

---

[19] See below, pp. 24ff.   [20] Letter to Mersenne, 27 May 1638, D, II, 141–2.

these limitations are imposed by the subject matter of physics itself, and are therefore inevitable. But note Descartes' ambiguous reference to the works of Archimedes, Witelo and Ptolemy: he abides by what he takes to be the common view that their arguments are entitled to be called 'demonstrations', and to that extent one might get the impression that he does not hope to improve upon them in this respect. But we cannot forget his contention in the *Discourse* that he was able to derive his suppositions from self-evident truths; while those of his predecessors are here asserted to be either not exactly true or simply false. The problem raised by the preceding passage can be expressed thus: if, as Descartes says, one is satisfied with explanations in physics so long as they are free from logical errors and the suppositions on which they rest are not contradicted by experiment, then what is the function of the principles from which these suppositions are deducible? On the other hand, if the suppositions are ultimately demonstrable by metaphysics, then why is it impossible to achieve strict demonstrations in physics?[21] We are thus led to consider Descartes' contention regarding the relationship between his physics and his metaphysics. How should we understand this contention? In particular, what are its implications with respect to the use, if any, of experiments; and how far does it allow, if at all, the use of conjectural hypotheses?

2. Shortly before Descartes published his *Meditations* in 1641, he confided in a letter to Mersenne that 'these six Meditations contain

---

[21] In fact Descartes later maintained more than once that he admits only mathematical proofs in his physics, indeed that the whole of his physics is nothing but geometry. Thus writing to Mersenne on 27 July 1638, he declared that he had resolved to abandon 'abstract' geometry for another kind of geometry whose aim was the explanation of natural phenomena. For, he went on, if one considered what he had written (in the *Meteors*) about the salt, the snow and the rainbow, one would find that 'toute ma Physique n'est autre chose que Geometrie' (D, II, p. 268). Again, the résumé of the last section, Section 64, in the second part of the *Principles* runs (in the French version) as follows: 'That I do not admit principles in Physics, which are not also admitted in Mathematics, in order to prove by demonstration what I will deduce from them; and that these principles suffice, inasmuch as all the Phenomena of nature can be explained by their means.' (D, IX, p. 101, Latin version, D, VIII, p. 78.) It is to be noted, however, that these claims occur at the end of Part II of the *Principles*, where the more general propositions of physics are explained; his remarks at the end of Part IV are more cautious. See below, p. 43.

all the foundations of my Physics'.[22] The arguments directly bearing on our questions are to be found in the last two. In the fifth Meditation Descartes asks whether anything certain can be known about material things. In accordance with the rule to proceed in order, the (sensible) 'ideas' of material things are first examined; meanwhile, the question whether there exist external objects corresponding to these ideas is being postponed. The criteria to be applied in this examination are those of clarity and distinctness.

Now, according to Descartes, all that can be clearly and distinctly conceived in a physical object is that it has length, breadth and depth. From this he concludes that we can have certain knowledge of material things only in so far as they constitute the subject matter of geometry. It remains for the sixth Meditation to prove their existence. Here, the criteria of clarity and distinctness are not sufficient; the clear and distinct idea of a triangle, for example, does not imply that such a figure really exists, and the same is true of the ideas of all material things. Our belief in the existence of these is derived from a 'feeling' or 'inclination' such as we are conscious of in sense-perception. This inclination can be relied upon only if guaranteed by a truthful God. We feel that the ideas of sensible things are produced in us by something other than ourselves. Moreover, we have a strong inclination to believe that they are conveyed to us by corporeal things. Since God could not have created this strong inclination simply to deceive us, we may safely believe that corporeal things exist. 'However, they are perhaps not exactly what we perceive by the senses, since this comprehension by the senses is in many instances very obscure and confused; but we must at least admit that all things which I perceive in them clearly and distinctly, that is to say, all things which, speaking generally, are comprehended in the object of pure mathematics, are truly to be recognised as external objects.'[23]

---

[22] Letter to Mersenne, 28 January 1641: '. . . I will tell you, between you and me, that these six Meditations contain all the foundations of my Physics. But this should not be made public, if you please, for it would probably make it more difficult for those who favour Aristotle to accept them; and I am hoping that those who will read them, will insensibly get used to my principles, and recognize their truth before they learn that they destroy those of Aristotle' (D, III, pp. 297–8).

[23] Meditation VI, HR, I, p. 191.

In physics we are concerned with what is truly existing. The veracity of God guarantees the truth of our judgements only when we ascribe existence to what we can clearly and distinctly conceive in external objects. As physicists, therefore, we are not to consider in external objects anything other than their extension, shape and movement—to the exclusion of all sensible and other qualities not reducible to clear and distinct geometrical properties. That is the lesson we learn from the *Meditations* regarding the metaphysical foundations of physics.[24] According to it, metaphysics lays down, in *a priori* fashion, the general framework within which all physical explanations should be sought; and to that extent metaphysics has, with regard to physics, only a programmatic function.

But that is not all. Descartes also believed that he could base on this foundation, again in *a priori* manner, a number of general propositions of far-reaching implications.[25] For example, that the nature of body wholly consists in pure extension; that matter is infinitely divisible and therefore atoms do not exist; that absolute void is impossible; that all motions are circular; that the quantity of motion in the universe is constant; and the laws of impact governing the communication of motion when moving bodies encounter one another. These are the 'principles' which are developed not only independently of experiment but, sometimes, against the verdict of experiment.[26] Since their truth is established *a priori* they are beyond doubt and revision.

Thus not only has the aim of the Cartesian physicist been laid down for him once and for all; quite a considerable and fundamental part of his work has already been done for him, never to be undone.

---

[24] Cf. J. Laporte, *Le rationalisme de Descartes*, Paris, 1945, pp. 204-6.

[25] Cf. *Principles*, Part II.

[26] The seven laws of impact proposed by Descartes in the second part of the *Principles* are almost all experimentally false. Suspecting this, his belief in the correctness of their demonstration was hardly shaken: 'we should have more faith in our reason than in our senses' was his comforting comment (*Principles*, II, 52, D, IX, p. 93). But why should we trust these laws when they appear to be contradicted by experiment? Answer: Because they relate to an abstract situation whose conditions (absolute hardness of the bodies considered, and tota absence of friction with any surrounding matter) are not possible to realize. Cf. R. Dugas *Histoire de la mécanique* (1950), pp. 155-6; H. Bouasse, *Introduction à l'étude des théories de la mécanique* (1895), Chap. X.

Looking now at the suppositions in the *Dioptric* and *Meteors*, we find in fact that, in agreement with Descartes' contention, they either belong with those principles, or they are more or less directly obtainable from them. In the *Meteors*, for example, Descartes 'supposes' such bodies as water, earth, and air to be composed of many small parts of various shapes and magnitudes.[27] This is not moving far from the divisibility thesis and the precept that we are to consider only geometrical properties such as shapes and magnitudes. He also 'supposes' in the same work that the gaps existing between the small parts of bodies are filled with a very subtle and imperceptible matter; which is another way of denying the existence of absolute void. In the *Dioptric* the fundamental supposition takes light to be a certain power or action that follows the same laws as local motion.[28] This is simply a consequence of the metaphysically determined principle that motion is the only power that can be rationally (that is, clearly and distinctly) asserted to exist in nature.

We may thus, in accordance with Descartes' statements, conceive of the basic part of his physical theory as a deductive system whose premises are rooted in metaphysics. By the basic part I mean the principles and the deductions made from them up to, and including, the so-called suppositions in the *Dioptric* and *Meteors*. Furthermore, some of these principles may have consequences which penetrate quite far into the theory. For example, Descartes' doctrine that light is propagated instantaneously follows from the only conception he allowed of the medium through which light is transmitted.[29]

3. Can we say that, for Descartes, *all* propositions in physics could be obtained in the same way?

The law of optical refraction is immediately derived in the *Dioptric*, not from the fundamental supposition that light is an action that follows the laws of motion, but from assumptions made with reference to certain mechanical 'comparisons' or analogies. In one

---

[27] Cf. *Meteors*, I, D, VI, p. 233.
[28] Cf. *Dioptric*, D, VI, pp. 84 and 100; Letter to Mersenne [27 May 1638], D, II, p. 143.
[29] See below, pp. 48ff.

case the comparison is with a moving ball that receives a hit from a tennis racket, thus acquiring added speed at one point of its journey; in another case the ball is supposed to strike a frail cloth which it breaks, and in so doing loses part of its speed. These analogies, and the assumptions they involve, may be said to be determined by the fundamental supposition inasmuch as they relate to the only power, i.e. motion, whose laws are taken to govern the action of light. But they cannot be said to be uniquely determined by that supposition in the sense of being deductive consequences of it. Nor does Descartes attempt to establish such a deductive relationship in the *Dioptric*. There is thus a logical gap separating the particular assumptions entailing the experimental law of refraction from the fundamental supposition in accordance with which these assumptions, as assumptions about motions, have been conceived.[30]

Now some of Descartes' statements may give one to understand that he believed his use of comparisons in the *Dioptric* to be purely accidental and that therefore they do not represent a significant feature of what, in his view, constituted a perfected physical explanation. In 1638, for example, he wrote to Vatier that since he had amply explained the properties of light in the treatise *De la Lumière*, he only attempted in the *Dioptric* to give 'some idea' of his views '*par des comparaisons & des ombrages*'.[31] Yet in *De la Lumière* we find that the author uses comparisons and calls them by that name.[32] In fact Descartes gives no other proof of the laws of optical reflection and refraction than the one in which he compares these phenomena to the mechanical reflection and refraction of a ball. Instead of providing better proofs in the *Traité de la Lumière*, as we might be led to expect, he simply refers to the proofs, by comparisons, that are given in the *Dioptric*. True, the *Traité* goes further by presenting the framework within which the comparisons are designed. Yet it

---

[30] Representing optical refraction, as Descartes does, as an impact phenomenon makes it in fact impossible to account for the *increase* of velocity that is required by his assumptions when the refraction is from a rare into a dense medium. The racket used in the comparison which illustrates this case thus represents a force that must be ruled out by the 'principles', let alone being derived from them. See below, pp. 14f, 124, 134f.

[31] Letter to Vatier, 22 February 1638, D, I, p. 562.

[32] *Le Monde*, D, XI, p. 102.

is important to note that, even after the physical principles have been stated, comparisons still have a function to perform in the explanations of the properties of light. These comparisons may be looked at as manifest mechanical models that must be used, at one stage or another, for ascertaining the hidden mechanism of light. As will be seen later, Descartes recognized that this mode of explanation does not attain the certainty of the principles under whose auspices it is performed.[33]

The role of analogy in a purely deductive scheme of explanation is clearly pointed out by Descartes in the exposition of Rule VIII of his *Regulae*.[34] Rules I–VII prescribe the order to be followed in the investigation of any given problem. As required by Rules V and VI one must first decompose the difficulty into simpler and simpler components until the simplest elements in it are reached. Then, starting from an intuition of the simplest and most absolute propositions, that is, propositions whose apprehension does not logically depend on the knowledge of any other elements in the problem, we gradually advance to the more and more complex propositions by a deductive process in which every step is an intuitive cognition of the necessary connection between the preceding link and the one that follows. But, for Descartes, this is only an ideal which it may not be always possible to realise. The aim of Rule VIII is, precisely, to advise the investigator against insisting on applying the preceding Rules when 'the nature of the problem itself, or the fact that he is human, prevents him'.[35] Descartes also recognizes that it may not be always possible to advance in knowledge through a series of rigorously connected intuitions. Fortunately for our purpose, he illustrates this Rule by the investigation of the problem that is in fact tackled in the *Dioptric* and *Geometry*.[36]

Descartes imagines[37] a mathematician trying to find the shape of the refracting surface (the so-called *anaclastic*) that would collect

---

[33] See below, pp. 42ff.

[34] Descartes wrote the *Regulae* in or about 1628 (cf. D, X, pp. 486–8). It was first published posthumously in 1701.

[35] *Regulae*, HR, I, p. 23.

[36] Cf. *Dioptric*, VIII; *Geometry*, II.

[37] *Regulae*, HR, I, pp. 23–24.

parallel rays into one focus.[38] He will first easily realise, by application of the Rules of analysis and synthesis, that the solution of the problem depends upon knowledge of the exact proportion observed by all the parallel rays on their passage through the surface. But this proportion he cannot determine by mathematical means alone. All he would be able to do as a mathematician would be to conjecture some proportion or other in accordance with which he would then determine the shape of the surface. But this would not lead to the discovery of what is wanted, but only to what is in agreement with his assumption. Further, Rule III prevents him from trying to learn the true proportion from 'the Philosophers or to gather it from experience'. Our mathematician, if he is unable to reason beyond the limits of his particular science, should stop short at this point, since he is faced with a physical, not a mathematical problem.

But suppose we consider instead 'a man who does not confine his studies to Mathematics, but, in accordance with the first rule, tries to discover the truth on all points'. Meeting with the same difficulty, he will find 'that this ratio between the angles of incidence and of refraction depends upon changes in their relation produced by varying the medium'. Next he will realize that 'these changes depend upon the manner in which the ray of light traverses the whole transparent body'. Again, knowledge of this manner of propagation 'presupposes a knowledge of the nature of the action of light; to understand which finally we must know what a natural potency is in general, this last being the most absolute term in the whole series in question'.

In this analytic procedure experience plays a certain role; for it is only from experience that the investigator learns, for example, that variation in the relationship between the angles of incidence and refraction depends upon varying the media. Yet analysis here should not be confused with Baconian induction. Bacon had con-

---

[38] Descartes was introduced to the problem of the anaclastic through the work of Kepler, whom he considered to have been 'my first teacher in Optics' (Letter to Mersenne, 31 March 1638, D, II, p. 86). The *Dioptrice*, in which Kepler formulated the problem, was published in 1611; see *Gesammelte Werke*, IV, pp. 371–2.

ceived of induction as a method of passing gradually from experimental information to knowledge of first causes through a sequence of 'axioms' or general propositions. In this picture experience is the only source of information, and the higher-level generalizations are obtained from those directly below them. Alternatively, knowledge of the lower-level generalizations is required for arriving at the axioms immediately above[39]. It was Newton who later identified induction in this Baconian sense with 'analysis'. As he wrote in Query 31 of the *Opticks*: 'This Analysis consists in making Experiments and Observations, and in drawing general Conclusions from them by Induction. . . .'[40] For Descartes, however, analysis of the problem he is here considering does not itself yield the general conclusions which will later serve as premises in the reverse process of synthesis or composition. Rather, it is a means of discovering and ordering the *conditions* for resolving the problem. The final result of the analysis is a statement of the most fundamental among those conditions, namely *that* 'we must know what a natural potency is in general'. But it does not assert *what* natural potency is. A knowledge of this, which is required for the knowledge of all other terms in the problem, must now come through another operation, i.e. intuition. As opposed to the ascending axioms of Bacon, the conditions ascertained by Descartes' method of analysis are such that the last among them in the order of discovery is the first in the order of knowledge.

Having clearly comprehended, 'by a mental intuition' (*per intuitum mentis*), what a natural power is in general, the investigator must now proceed backwards through every step of the series in the reverse order. In the ideal case (as in pure mathematics) the movement of the mind in this synthesis should consist in a straightforward deduction necessarily leading from one step to the next. But there might be a hitch: 'And if when he comes to the second step he is unable straight way to determine the nature of light, he will, in accordance with the seventh rule, enumerate all the other natural potencies, in order that the knowledge of some other of them may

---

[39] *Novum Organum*, I, 103–5, B, IV, pp. 96–98.   [40] *Opticks*, Query 31, p. 404.

help him, at least by analogy [*per imitationem*] . . . , to understand this.'⁴¹

It is clearly admitted here by Descartes that one may not be able directly to deduce the nature of light from the absolute intuition of what constitutes a natural power in general. This even seems to be imposed on the investigator by the fact that the action of light, being a *particular* form of action, cannot be uniquely derived from the *general* concept of natural power. Descartes therefore suggests that we must first enumerate all forces in nature so that we may be able to understand what light is by its analogy with some other force. Enumeration, in this sense, involves an appeal to experience as a prerequisite for any further advance in the deductive process.

It therefore appears that the analogies or comparisons used in the *Dioptric* are not there by accident, or merely to facilitate the understanding of the explanations offered. These analogies indicate the kind of argument which, according to Descartes, one has to rely upon in order to establish the second deductive step after an intellectual intuition of what constitutes a natural force in general has been grasped.⁴²

Descartes recognizes one and only one fundamental force or power in nature, namely, motion. The effects of heat, sound, magnetism, gravity, and all the other 'powers' of nature, must be produced by

---

⁴¹ *Regulae*, HR, I, p. 24. Cf. D, X, p. 395.

⁴² In a passage of the *Cogitationes privatae* (1619–21) Descartes expresses the idea that philosophy (i.e. natural philosophy) consists in drawing successful analogies from the objects of sense experience: '*Cognitio hominis de rebus naturalibus, tantum per similitudinem eorum quae sub sensum cadunt: & quidem eum verius philosophatum arbitramur, qui res quaesitas felicius assimilare poterit sensu cognitis*' (D, X, pp. 218–9). The idea is illustrated in the *Regulae*, Rule IX: 'For example if I wish to examine whether it is possible for a natural force to pass at one and the same moment to a spot at a distance and yet to traverse the whole space in between, I shall not begin to study the force of magnetism or the influence of the stars, not even the speed of light, in order to discover whether actions such as these occur instantaneously; for the solution of this question would be more difficult than the problem proposed. I should rather bethink myself of the spatial motions of bodies, because nothing in the sphere of motion can be found more obvious to sense than this' (HR, I, p. 29). The analogy here is that of a stick whose parts all move simultaneously when one end is moved.

Descartes' procedure may thus be described as, first, to explain the known by the unknown – the manifest properties of gravity, light, magnetism and so forth by the action of imperceptible particles in motion; and then to explain the unknown by the known—the hidden mechanism by the manifest motions of sensible bodies. The outcome is to explain the known by the better known.

various motions or combinations of motions. On these assumptions the question about the nature of light and its physical properties reduces to the following: what kind of motion is the action of light, and how is it propagated, reflected, refracted, etc.? The *Dioptric* answers this question by comparing the action of light with the action which simultaneously moves one end of a stick when applied to the other end, and the reflection and refraction of light with the mechanical reflection and refraction of a ball. That the answer is given by analogies and not by rigorous deduction is, we have seen, in perfect accordance with Descartes' rules of method. What Descartes omits to mention in the *Dioptric* are the principles demanding that light, and all the other forces of nature, *must be a form of movement*. That is to say, the *Dioptric* takes up the deductive argument at the second step of synthesis where analogies are not only permissible but, rather, required by the nature of the problem.[43] We have already indicated how the first step is determined.

4. We have seen that the Cartesian method of explanation, though based on *a priori* grounds, establishes contact with experience at various points. Apart from suggesting the physical problem to be investigated, experience assists in the operation of analysis, in the process of *enumeratio sive inductio* (as in the surveying of natural powers mentioned above), and in the construction of mechanical analogies or models. Also let us not forget that the objects of intuition itself, the pure and simple natures, may be revealed through experience.[44] Rule V of the *Regulae* seems to have been formulated

---

[43] That the method of the *Dioptric* is wholly synthetic seems to be clear enough from the fact that it begins with suppositions from which the various properties of light are deduced. For a different view, claiming that this work illustrates the method of analysis, see L. J. Beck, *The Method of Descartes* (1952), p. 167. Beck also remarks (ibid., p. 263) that the *Dioptric* 'may . . . be profitably considered as an application of the method to a problem of physics'. This is contradicted by Descartes' own statement that the method would have required a different order from that which he adopted in the *Dioptric*. See above, p. 17, n. 2. All we can say (and all Descartes wants us to believe) is that the *Dioptric* contains results which he has discovered by his method without showing how this has in fact been done.

[44] *Regulae*, Rule VI, D, X, p. 383: '*Notandum 2. paucas esse duntaxat naturas puras & simplices, quas primo & per se, non dependenter ab alijs vllis, sed vel in ipsis experimentis, vel lumine quodam in nobis insito, licet intueri. . . .*'

with mainly empirical problems in mind; and it emphasizes the importance of experiment. An investigator who does not comply with this rule would be, according to Descartes, 'like a man who should attempt to leap with one bound from the base to the summit of a house, either making no account of the ladders provided for his ascent or not noticing them'.[45] This metaphor of the ladder is one that occupied a fundamental and conspicuous place in the *Novum Organum*; and 'leaping' from the data of a problem to the principles of its solution is precisely what Bacon had called *anticipatio*, the false method to which he opposed his own true method of *interpretatio*. Significantly enough, examples of those who sin against this rule (unlike most other examples in the *Regulae*) are all drawn from the empirical field: the astrologers who pronounce on the influence of the stars without having determined the nature of the heavens or even observed the movements of heavenly bodies; the instrument devisers who rashly pursue their profession with no knowledge of physics; and 'those Philosophers who, neglecting experience, imagine that truth will spring from their brain like Pallas from the head of Zeus'.[46]

All this reminds one rather strongly of Bacon. Indeed a case has been repeatedly made for a Baconian influence on Descartes.[47] Yet this influence was not of a fundamental character:[48] while Descartes recommended Bacon's view regarding the making of experiments, and even sometimes followed his example in the collection of natural histories,[49] he completely ignored induction *as a method of deriving general propositions from experiential data*;[50] more-

---

[45] *Regulae*, HR, I, p. 14.

[46] Ibid., p. 15.

[47] Cf. A. Lalande, 'Quelques textes de Bacon et de Descartes', *Revue de métaphysique et de morale*, XIX (1911), pp. 296–311; G. Milhaud, *Descartes savant* (1921), Chap. X; S. V. Keeling, *Descartes* (1934), pp. 47–50; and a comparison between the Baconian and Cartesian methods in L. Roth, *Descartes' Discourse on Method* (1948), pp. 52–71.

[48] It is plausible that Descartes did not read Bacon until after the crucial idea of philosophical reasoning as something akin, though inferior, to poetic imagination occurred to him in the winter of 1619–20. Cf. G. Milhaud, *Descartes savant*, pp. 216, 222–3, and Chap. II; Descartes, *Cogit. privat.*, D, X, p. 217.

[49] As, for instance, in his *Excerpta anatomica* (D, XI, pp. 549ff), and *De partibus inferiori ventre contentis* (D, XI, pp. 587ff). Cf. E. Gilson, *Commentaire*, pp. 451–2.

[50] Descartes sometimes speaks in the *Regulae* of 'deducing' (Rule XII, HR, I, p. 47) or 'inferring' (Rule XIII, ibid., pp. 49f), say, the nature of the magnet from the observations

over, his view of the role of experiment and observation was diametrically opposed to that of Bacon. This is not surprising in view of the fact that they start from opposite points: Bacon, from the observations and experiments themselves; and Descartes, from *a priori* considerations which first give him the general principles of all physical explanations.[51]

Let us first look at Descartes' references to Bacon; they all come from a period during which he was engaged in writing *Le Monde*. He wrote to Mersenne in January 1630:

I thank you for the [list of] qualities which you have drawn from Aristotle; I have already made a longer list of them, partly derived from Verulam, partly from memory, and this is one of the first things which I shall attempt to explain; and that will not be as difficult as might be thought; for the foundations being laid down, these qualities follow of themselves.[52]

As has been remarked by G. Milhaud,[53] one feels that Descartes had Bacon's writings within easy reach. But he had something more at his disposal: the foundations with reference to which the 'qualities' derived from Bacon would be readily explained. Far from attempting to arrive at the causes of these qualities through an examination free from all preconceived ideas, as Bacon's method would have

---

that have previously been made regarding it. But even here the function of natural history seems to be the same as that indicated in the *Principles* (below, p. 36, n.56) and elsewhere (below, pp. 36ff). In Rule XII, for instance, Descartes is concerned to warn against the misleading tendency of always looking for 'some new kind of fact' (ibid., p. 47) whenever one faces the difficulty of explaining a new phenomenon. To him all explanations should rather be sought in the perfectly known simple natures which form the objects of intuition, and in the connections which we intuitively perceive to hold between them. Thus the question about the nature of the magnet reduces to the following question: what *particular combination* of simple natures is necessary to produce all those effects of the magnet which we have gathered from experiments? Deducing or inferring the nature of the magnet would thus seem to mean no other than choosing among the many possible combinations of simple natures in the light of the data to be explained.

The distinction, briefly stated in the *Regulae*, between seeking to know the causes from the effects and the effects from the causes (D, X, pp. 428, 433, 434) is not one between induction and deduction, but rather between theoretical and applied physics (cf. ibid., pp. 471–2).

For Descartes' meaning of 'venir au-devant des causes par les effects', see below, pp. 38f.

[51] This crucial difference was noted by Gassendi who was also aware of similarities between Bacon and Descartes. Cf. L. J. Beck, *The Method of Descartes*, p. 163, n. 1.

[52] Letter to Mersenne, January 1630, D, I, p. 109.

[53] G. Milhaud, *Descartes savant*, p. 213.

required him to do, he was already convinced of what the general nature of these causes must be.

That a knowledge of the general causes of physical things must precede the making of experiments, at least the more particular ones, was later stated by Descartes himself—again in connection with a reference to Bacon. To Mersenne, who desired to know 'a way of making useful experiments', Descartes replied:

To this I have nothing to say, after what Verulam has written about it, except that without being too curious to seek after all the small particularities touching a certain matter, one should chiefly make general surveys of all things which are more common, and which are very certain and can be known without expense.... As for the more particular [experiments], it is impossible not to make many of them that are superfluous, and even false, if one does not know the truth of things [*la vérité des choses*] before making them.[54]

The reservation expressed in the latter part of this passage is extremely important; it amounts in fact to the proposal of a method that is the exact opposite of Bacon's induction. For the whole point of induction, of *interpretatio* as opposed to *anticipatio*, is that 'the truth of things' will only emerge at the very end when experiments of all kinds have been made and the axioms duly derived from them. Therefore, when, two years later, Descartes expressed the wish that someone would prepare for him 'the history of celestial appearances, according to the method of Verulam . . . without introducing in it any reasons or hypotheses',[55] he was not planning to embark upon a project similar to that of the *Novum Organum*.[56] The implication of his demand was rather this: he suspected the opinions which the prospective collector of history might mingle with the results of pure observation; but he did not distrust the physical principles which had flowered in his own mind from the seeds of knowledge which he believed to have been planted there by nature. Thus in

---

[54] Letter to Mersenne, 23 December 1630, D, I, pp. 195–6.

[55] Letter to Mersenne, 10 May 1632, D, I, p. 251.

[56] In the *Principles*, III, 4 (On the use of phenomena or experiments), Descartes explains the role of natural history as follows: '. . . je feray icy vne briéve description [Latin: brevem historiam] des principaux Phainomenes, dont je pretens rechercher les causes, *non point afin d'en*

the hands of Descartes the *historia naturalis* was made to serve an essentially deductive method.[57]

5. It is in the light of the ideas expressed in these references to Bacon that we should, I think, approach the well-known passage in the sixth part of the *Discourse* where Descartes explains the order of his procedure. As we have seen, 'seeking after all the small particularities touching a certain matter' was a feature of Bacon's *historia* about which Descartes had certain reservations. The passage in question opens with a sentence which indicates a further reservation regarding Bacon's method. Among Prerogative Instances, i.e. instances of particular help to the understanding in the process of *interpretatio*, the *Novum Organum* mentions the so-called Deviating Instances: 'For we have to make a collection or particular natural history of all prodigies and monstrous births of nature; of everything in short that is in nature new, rare, and unusual.'[58] Opposing this recommendation, it would seem, Descartes maintains that in the beginning of an inquiry 'it is better to make use simply of those [experiments] which present themselves spontaneously to our senses . . . rather than to seek out those which are more rare and recondite; the reason for this is that those which are more rare often mislead us as long as we do not know the causes of the more common. . . .'[59] What then was the order which he followed?

I have first tried to discover generally the principles or first causes of everything that is or that can be in the world, without considering anything that might accomplish this end but God Himself who has created the world, or deriving them from any source excepting from certain germs of truth which are naturally existent in our souls.[60]

---

tirer des raisons qui seruent à prouuer ce que j'ay à dire cy-apres: car j'ay dessein d'expliquer les effets par leurs causes, et non les causes par leurs effets; *mais afin que nous puissions choisir, entre vne infinité d'effets qui peuuent estre deduits des mesme causes, ceux que nous deuons principalement tascher d'en déduire'* (D, IX, p. 105, italics added).

[57] One might describe Descartes' position by saying that for him the investigation of a *particular* physical problem begins with observation and experiment, while *natural science* must begin with *a priori* principles.

[58] *Novum Organum*, I, 29, B, IV, p. 169.

[59] *Discourse*, VI, HR, I, p. 120.

[60] Ibid., p. 121.

The first step, yielding the 'principles or first causes', is thus clearly deductive. It may be noted here that the idea of seeds of truth from which the principles are derived goes back to the important period of 1619–21, and it recurs in the *Regulae* (1628).[61] The second step, Descartes tells us, was also deductive; from these causes he attempted to derive their 'primary and most ordinary effects'; and in this way he found (*j'ai trouvé*), as if by accident, 'the heavens, the stars, an earth, and even on the earth, water, air, fire, the minerals and some other such things, which are the most common and simple of any that exist, and consequently the easiest to know'.[62] A problem then presented itself when he wanted to descend to the more particular effects; for the particular objects of experience were of many various kinds, and the problem was how to 'distinguish the forms or species of bodies which are on the earth from an infinitude of others which might have been so if it had been the will of God to place them there. . . .'[63] This distinction, Descartes believed, was not possible 'if it were not that we arrive at the causes by the effects [*si ce n'est qu'on vienne au-devant des causes par les effets*], and avail ourselves of many particular experiments'.[64]

In spite of the words 'we arrive at the causes by the effects' the solution here suggested does not, in my opinion, constitute a breakdown of the deductive process and a recourse to something like induction.[65] For the 'first causes' have already been established. Yet they are such that they admit of an infinitude of possible particular effects, any of which could have been realised. Since the

---

[61] *Cogitationes privatae* (1619–21), D, X, p. 217: 'sunt in nobis semina scientiae, vt in silice, quae per rationem à philosophis educuntur, per imaginationem à poetis excutiuntur magisque elucent.' See also *Regulae*, Rule IV, D, X, pp. 373 and 376; HR, I, pp. 10 and 12.

[62] *Discourse*, VI, HR, I, p. 121.

[63] Ibid.

[64] Ibid., p. 121; D, VI, p. 64.

[65] That the knowledge of the cause must precede that of the effect is clearly stated by Descartes in the following sentence from the *Regulae*, Rule VI (HR, I, p. 16): 'For though Philosophers make cause and effect correlative, we find that here even, if we ask what the effect is, we must first know the cause and not conversely.' Bacon regarded the highest and most general axioms (i.e. the first causes) as 'prior and better known in the order of nature' (*Novum Organum*, I, 22, B, I, p. 160; IV, p. 50). But the investigator reaches them only at the end of the inductive procedure. As Bacon says in the Preface to the *Great Instauration*: 'Now my plan is to proceed regularly and gradually from one axiom to another, so that the most general are not reached till the last. . . .' (B, IV, p. 25).

aim of the deduction is to explain those effects which actually exist, recourse to particular experiments is necessary to ascertain the *existence* of what is to be explained. All this is, of course, in agreement with Descartes' doctrine that belief in the existence of material things is based on an empirical feeling (whose reliability is guaranteed by the truthfulness of God), rather than on a necessary deduction from clear and distinct ideas. Similarly, in explaining a particular effect there is need for empirical information presenting the investigator with the particular *explanandum*, i.e. the existing fact to be explained by deduction from the already determined principles or causes. Thus for Descartes the problem of formulating a physical explanation is one in which two terms are given: the one term, given in experience, represents the phenomena to be explained; the other, given *a priori*, includes the principles from which the explanation must start. The explanation is fulfilled when a way has been discovered of deducing the former from the latter. 'Arriving at the causes by the effects' simply means determining the *real* effects so that the deduction from the given causes of 'everything that is or that can be in the world' would not remain in the realm of mere possibilities.

Descartes now goes on to point out another problem to which he is led by the nature of the principles from which he started. He first states that there was nothing in the sphere of his experience which he could not 'easily explain' by those principles.

But I must also confess that the power of nature is so ample and so vast, and these principles are so simple and general, that I observed hardly any particular effect as to which I could not at once recognise that it might be deduced from the principles in many different ways; and my greatest difficulty is usually to discover in which of these ways the effect does depend upon them.[66]

This difficulty brings out a distinction between mathematical deduction, which has to do with necessary connections, and the kind of deduction which Descartes here had in mind. In a mathematical

---

[66] HR, I, p. 121.

system the same conclusion might be deducible from either of two different groups of axioms belonging to the same system. Also, starting from identical or different groups of axioms belonging to the same system, deduction might lead to the same conclusion through different groups of theorems. In either case we may say that the conclusion can be deduced from the axioms in different ways. But the question 'in which one of these ways does the conclusion depend upon the axioms?' does not arise. For, since the alternative deductions are all valid, there is no question of *choosing* one of these alternatives to the exclusion of all the others, although preference might be made on aesthetic or practical grounds. Therefore, the different ways in which the effect may depend upon the principles cannot—in Descartes' problem—be represented by different chains of logically valid deductions. If such were the representation meant by Descartes, his problem would be difficult to understand. For we should be satisfied with *any* of the ways in which the effect is deduced from the principles, provided that the deduction is logically necessary. It would therefore seem that the alternative ways of deduction here envisaged by Descartes are in fact only *possible* explanations of the effect in terms of the given principles: that is to say they are hypothetical constructions which are equally compatible with the 'simple and general' principles without following from them of necessity. Thus again the problem is for Descartes that of bridging the gap between possibility and actuality, between possible causes and *the* true cause. And again the solution lies in recourse to experiments: by increasing more and more the empirical content of the *explanandum*, the number of possible explanations could be reduced further and further. For example, what should we do in the simplified case where we have only two possible methods or ways of explaining the same effect, and how should we decide between them? 'As to that, I do not know any other plan but again to try to find experiments of such a nature that their result is not the same if it has to be explained by one of the methods, as it would be if explained by the other.'[67]

---

[67] Ibid.

Nothing in Descartes' preceding remarks suggests that experimental results may serve as premises from which general conclusions are drawn. Experiments are in his system assigned a different but essential function: they propose problems by pointing out the *existent* effects which it is the business of the physicist to explain; and they provide crucial tests between competing *possible* explanations. These are the only ways in which experiments may be said to help in ascertaining or 'arriving at' the causes. The terms in which the problems would be solved and the 'principles or first causes' to which all explanations must ultimately be reduced are themselves determined beforehand.

In the passage with which we have been concerned Descartes does not explicitly say whether he considers the possible ways of explaining the same effect to be always finite in number. If they are, then it is always possible, at least in principle, to establish *the true* explanation by a finite number of crucial tests which eliminate *all* the false ones. Crucial experiments would thus have a role similar to that of indirect proof in mathematics, which is the role assigned to them by Bacon.[68]

But what if the number of possible explanations is infinite?

Descartes faces this possibility in the *Principles*. There, in fact, this possibility becomes the actual truth by replacing the power of nature, which is 'so ample and so vast' but not necessarily infinite, by the power of God, which cannot be finite. Having illustrated at length (in Parts III and IV of the *Principles*) how in his view all natural phenomena can be explained by various motions attributed to small and imperceptible material particles of various shapes and magnitudes, he then[69] explains how he came to his knowledge of the properties of those particles. First, says Descartes, he considered the clear and distinct notions which we naturally have of material things. These are the notions of shape, magnitude and movement, together with the laws that govern them, namely the principles of geometry and mechanics. Being convinced that all knowledge of nature must be derived from these notions alone, he then considered

---

[68] See below, pp. 178f.   [69] *Principles*, IV, 203.

what sensible effects could be produced by particles of various shapes, magnitudes and movements in various combinations. Observing similar effects in nature he inferred that these might have been produced in the ways he envisaged. Descartes says that in all this he was helped by considering the example of machines: a clockmaker can ordinarily tell[70] by looking at some parts of a clock which he has not made what the other parts are; similarly, by considering the sensible effects of natural bodies he has attempted to discover the hidden mechanisms by which they have been produced.

But here it may be said that although I have shown how all natural things can be formed, we have no right to conclude on this account that they were produced by these causes. For just as there may be two clocks made by the same workman, which though they indicate the time equally well and are externally in all respects similar, yet in nowise resemble one another in the composition of their wheels, so doubtless there is an infinity of different ways in which all things that we see could be formed by the great Artificer [without it being possible for the mind of man to be aware of which of these means he has chosen to employ]. This I most freely admit; and I believe that I have done all that is required of me if the causes I have assigned are such that they correspond to all the phenomena manifested by nature [without inquiring whether it is by their means or by others that they are produced].[71]

Accordingly Descartes distinguishes two kinds of certainty. The one, certainty proper, or absolute certainty, holds 'when we think that the thing cannot be other than as we conceive it'.[72] Founded on the metaphysical principle that our Creator cannot lead us into error as long as we follow what we perceive clearly and distinctly, this certainty is to be found in mathematical truths (as, for instance, in the assertion that two and three cannot together be less than five), in our knowledge—based on the truthfulness of God—that material things exist, and in whatever can be demonstrated about them 'by

---

[70] Latin: 'facile cojiciunt', French: 'peut ordinairement juger'. D, IX, p. 322 ; D, VIII, p. 326.

[71] *Principles*, IV, 204, HR, I, p. 300. Brackets as in the English translation; they indicate additions made by Descartes in the French version.

[72] *Principles*, IV, 206, D, IX, p. 324.

the principles of Mathematics or by other [principles] equally evident and certain'.[73] Now Descartes urges further that this kind of certainty extends to the matters which he has dealt with in the *Principles*, but the French version adds the significant qualification '*at least the principal and more general*'[74] among those matters. The same qualification occurs a little later in the same context, this time both in the Latin and French versions. Descartes first maintains that the particular explanations presented in the *Principles* rest on the fundamental assertion that the heavens are fluid, i.e. that they are composed of small parts constantly moving in relation to one another. Then he adds: 'So that this sole point being recognized as sufficiently demonstrated by all the effects of light, and by all the things which I have explained as following from it, I believe that one must also recognize that I have proved by Mathematical demonstrations all the doctrines that I have proposed, *at least the more general ones* which concern the fabric of the heaven and of the earth. . . .'[75]

It is, therefore, the more particular matters that Descartes had in mind when he spoke of the other kind of certainty which he called 'moral certainty'.[76] This is the certainty which we have regarding the things we ordinarily do not question even though they might in principle be false. For instance, those who have not been to Rome do not doubt its existence, although it is possible that they might have been deceived by all reports which have reached them. It is also the certainty of the cryptogram reader that he has conjectured the correct interpretation of individual letters when he can make sense of a large number of them. Descartes believes that the number of natural phenomena which he can successfully explain is so large as to make it *unlikely* that his explanations should be false. But, just as in the case of cipher reading one cannot be absolutely sure that one has discovered the meaning intended by the author (for there is always the possibility of obtaining another meaning by interpreting the individual letters differently), so in the explanation of particular natural phenomena one cannot be absolutely certain

---

[73] Ibid., p. 324. [74] Ibid. [75] Ibid., p. 325, *italics* added. See also: D, VIII, pp. 328–9.
[76] *Principles*, IV, 205, D, IX, p. 323.

that the effects have been produced in the manner which has been supposed. This appears in fact inevitable when we consider that 'there is an infinity of different ways in which all things that we see could be formed by the great Artificer. . . .' Thus, one might say, while the truthfulness of God guarantees the certainty of our knowledge of the principles of physics and of general matters which follow from them, His unlimited power necessitates, on the other hand, that our explanations of the more particular phenomena must remain hypothetical. This position Descartes himself described to Mersenne, four years before the publication of the Latin edition of the *Principles*, in the following words: 'I do believe that one can explain one and the same particular effect in many different ways which are possible; but I believe that one cannot explain the possibility of things in general except in one way only, which is the true one.'[77]

6. To sum up: The Cartesian system of physics consists of two parts, one on a higher-level than the other and both of which are deductive. The first, higher and metaphysically determined part consists of the 'primary truths' and their logical consequences, the so-called 'principles' of physics. This is the domain of *a priori* truth, of strict demonstration and of absolute certainty. As repeatedly asserted by Descartes, the 'suppositions' at the beginning of the *Dioptric* belong to this part, even though they are claimed in that work to be defendable by a kind of *a posteriori* proof which Descartes identified with the method of 'the Astronomers'. The second, lower-level part may be described as a hypothetico-deductive system. Its premises are not deductive consequences of the first part standing above it, but conjectures devised to explain particular phenomena. These conjectures are not free from all limitations; they must not contradict the higher principles, and the terms in which they are formulated are already defined by these principles. In this latter part strict demonstration is—on the whole—impossible;

---

[77] Letter to Mersenne, 28 October 1640, D, III, p. 212.

only a greater or less degree of 'moral' or practical certainty is all that one can reasonably hope for. The qualification 'on the whole' is required to indicate the fact that some of the assertions which we might regard as belonging to this part can be logically determined by the higher-level principles. An example is the doctrine of the instantaneous propagation of light which is dealt with in the next chapter.

Chapter Two

DESCARTES' DOCTRINE OF THE INSTANTANEOUS PROPAGATION OF LIGHT AND HIS EXPLANATION OF THE RAINBOW AND OF COLOURS

1. Aristotle censured Empedocles for having spoken of light as travelling, that is, taking time to go from one place to another. Light for Aristotle was not, as it was for Empedocles, a material effluence which streamed from the luminous object with finite speed; nor was it a successive modification of the transparent medium which, according to him, was necessary for its transmission. Rather than being a process or movement, light for Aristotle was a state or quality which the medium acquired all at once from the luminous object, just as water may conceivably freeze at all parts simultaneously.[1] So far as the speed of propagation is concerned, it was the Aristotelian view which prevailed for many centuries afterwards. From the second to the twelfth century it was adopted by such influential writers as Galen,[2] Philoponus,[3] al-Kindī,[4] Avicenna[5] and Averroës[6]. A notable exception was Avicenna's contemporary

---

[1] Aristotle, *De anima*, II, 7; *De sensu*, VI.

[2] Cf. John I. Beare, *Greek Theories of Elementary Cognition*, Oxford, 1906, p. 59, n. 1.

[3] Cf. S. Sambursky, 'Philoponus' interpretation of Aristotle's theory of light', *Osiris*, XIII (1958), p. 119.

[4] Chapter 15 of al-Kindi's *De aspectibus* presents a 'demonstration' of the instantaneous propagation of light (cf. *Alkindi, Tideus und pseudo-Euklid*, ed. A. A. Björnbo and S. Vogl, Leipzig, 1912, pp. 25-27). Al-Kindi's argument is essentially the same as that produced previously by Aristotle against Empedocles (*De anima*, II, 7) and later by Witelo (*Optica*, II, 2, p. 63; III, 55, p. 110) and by Descartes (see below, pp. 55ff): if indeed light moved with a finite though very great speed, an appreciable interval of time would be perceived when the distance traversed is very great; this, however, is not the case; therefore, etc.

[5] Avicenna, *De anima*, III, 8, in *Opera*, Venetiis, 1508, fol. 16ʳb: 'Verum est autem quod simulacrum visi redditur mediante translucente membro receptibili apto, leni illuminato, ita ut non recipiat illud substantia translucentis aliquo modo secundum quod est ipsa forma; sed cadit in illud, secundum oppositionem non in tempore.'

[6] Cf. *Aristotelis De anima cum Averrois Commentariis*, Venetiis, apud Iuntas, 1562 (facsimile reproduction, Frankfurt am Main, 1962, Suppl. II), fol. 86ᵛ. Averroës here simply endorses

46

Ibn al-Haytham (d. *c.* 1039), known to the Latin medieval writers by the name Alhazen, who asserted that the movement of light required a finite, though imperceptible, interval of time.[7] Roger Bacon produced new arguments to defend Ibn al-Haytham's view;[8] but many writers in Europe up to the seventeenth century held to the doctrine of instantaneous transmission, and it was shared by Grosseteste,[9] Witelo[10] and Kepler.[11] Descartes subscribed to the

Aristotle's criticism of Empedocles. In his *Epitome* of Aristotle's *De anima*, not translated into Latin, he says that 'luminosity is one of the perfections that are not divisible by division of the body [of which they are perfections] and are not realized in time' (*Kitāb al-nafs*, p. 28, in *Rasā'il Ibn Rushd*, Hyderabad, 1947).

[7] Alhazeni *Optica*, II, 21 in *Opticae thesaurus*, ed. F. Risner, Basel, 1572, p. 37: 'Et dicemus, quod color in eo, quod est color, et lux in eo, quod est lux, non comprehendetur a visu, nisi in tempore, scilicet, quod instans, apud quod erit comprehensio coloris in eo, quod est color, et comprehensio lucis in eo, quod est lux, est diversum ab instanti, quod est primum instans, in quo contingit superficiem visus aer deferens formam. Quoniam color in eo, quod est color, et lux in eo, quod est lux, non comprehenduntur a sentiente, nisi post perventum formae in corpore sensibili, et non comprehenduntur ab ultimo sentiente, nisi post perventum formae ad concavum nervi communis, et perventus formae ad concavum nervi communis, est sicut perventus lucis a foraminibus, per quae intrat lux ad corpora opposita illis foraminibus, perventus igitur lucis a foramine ad corpus oppositum foramini, non erit, nisi in tempore, quamvis lateat sensum.' The discussion is continued in the same section. Ibn al-Haytham begins here by asserting that perception (*comprehensio*) of light as such and of colour as such takes place at a later instant than that at which the light makes contact with the surface of the eye. It is the act of perception, therefore, that requires an interval of time. He ends, however, by comparing the extension of light through the common nerve to its extension in space from an opening to a body placed opposite the opening, and asserts that the latter extension also takes place in time. M. Naẓif has remarked that Ibn al-Haytham's argument in support of this statement does not establish the successive movement of light in the direction of propagation (*al-Hasan ibn al-Haytham* . . . I, Cairo, 1942, pp. 118–20). But, as the same author also showed, the failure of the argument is no indication of the nature of the desired conclusion, namely the finite speed of light which Ibn al-Haytham affirms in many passages. It may be remarked here that as distinguished from Descartes who (as we shall see) could only speak of the 'force' or 'ease' with which light passed from one medium into another, but never of its speed, Ibn al-Haytham readily and frequently spoke of light itself as being quicker or slower in different media. It may also be added that Ibn al-Haytham's belief in the non-instantaneous transmission of light was connected with another opinion which he held—viz. that no absolutely transparent body exists, and that therefore all transparent bodies, including the body of the heavens, must offer some resistance to light. See below, pp. 93ff.

[8] Cf. *Opus majus*, V (*De scientia perspectiva*), pars I, distinctio IX, capa. 3 & 4, ed. Bridges, II, Oxford, 1897, pp. 68–74. Bacon's arguments are directed against Aristotle and al-Kindi; see above, p. 46, n. 4.

[9] *De luce*, in *Die philosophischen Werke*, ed. Baur, p. 51: 'Lux enim per se in omnem partem se ipsam diffundit, ita ut a puncto lucis sphaera lucis quamvis magna subito generetur, nisi obsistat umbrosum.' Cf. A. C. Crombie, *Grosseteste*, pp. 106–7.

[10] Cf. Vitellonis *Optica*, II, 2, in *Opticae thesaurus*, ed. Risner, Basel, 1572, p. 63; ibid. III, 55, p. 110. See Crombie, *Grosseteste*, p. 217, n. 4.

[11] *Paralipomena*, Francofurti, 1604, p. 36; cf. Crombie, *Grosseteste*, p. 284, n. 4.

doctrine of instantaneous propagation, but with him something new emerged: for his was the first uncompromisingly mechanical theory that asserted the instantaneous propagation of light in a material medium; a theory that had no use for the 'forms' of Ibn al-Haytham and Witelo, or the *'species'* of Grosseteste, Roger Bacon and Kepler.[12] Indeed, mechanical analogies had been used to explain optical phenomena long before Descartes, but the Cartesian theory was the first clearly to assert that light itself was nothing but a mechanical property of the luminous object and of the transmitting medium. It is for this reason that we may regard Descartes' theory of light as the legitimate starting point of modern physical optics.[13]

The doctrine of instantaneous transmission, far from embarrassing Descartes' system of physics, in fact formed an inseparable part of it. That this was Descartes' own view is clearly indicated in a letter which he wrote in 1634 to an unknown person. First he wrote:

I said to you lately, when we were together, not in fact as you write that light moves in an instant, but (which you take to be the same thing) that it reaches our eyes from the luminous object in an instant; and I even added that for me this was so certain, that if it could be proved false, I should be ready to confess that I know absolutely nothing in philosophy.[14]

---

[12] Descartes, *Dioptric*, I, D, VI, p. 85: 'En suite de quoy vous aurés occasion de iuger, qu'il n'est pas besoin de supposer qu'il passe quelque chose de materiel depuis les obiects iusques a nos yeux, pour nous faire voir les couleurs & la lumiere, ny mesme qu'il y ait rien en ces obiects, qui soit sembable aux idées ou aux sentimens que nous en auons: tout de mesme qu'il ne sort rien des corps, que sent vn aueugle, qui doiue passer le long de son baston iusques a sa main, & que la resistence ou le mouuement de ces corps, qui est la seule cause des sentimens qu'il en a, n'est rien de semblable aux idées qu'il en conçoit. Et par ce moyen vostre esprit sera deliuré de toutes ces petites images voltigeantes par l'air, nommées des *especes intentionelles*, qui trauaillent tant l'imagination des Philosophes.'

[13] This statement may give rise to misunderstanding, and I therefore wish to make it clear that I share the view that in the history of science there are no absolute beginnings. As will be shown in the two following chapters, some of the important elements of the Cartesian theories of reflection and refraction had existed for a long time before Descartes made use of them. Nevertheless, what Descartes did was more than simply to continue the efforts of his predecessors. By embodying those elements in a new system of ideas he gave them a new meaning and was able to suggest a new set of problems.

[14] Descartes to [Beeckman], 22 August 1634, D, I, pp. 307–8. 'Dixi nuper, cum vna essemus, lumen in instanti non quidem moueri, vt scribis, sed (quod pro eodem habes) à corpore luminoso ad oculum peruenire, addidique etiam hoc mihi esse tam certum, vt si falsitatis argui posset, nil me prorsus scire in Philosophia confiteri paratus sim.' The letter was first published in a French translation from the Latin original in Clerselier's edition of *Lettres de Mr. Descartes*, II, Paris, 1659, pp. 139–45. The edition did not mention the name of Descartes' correspondent,

To this he significantly added that if the finite velocity of light could be proved experimentally (as his correspondent had claimed) he would be prepared to admit that 'the whole of my Philosophy [i.e. physics] was shaken to its foundations'.[15]

This readiness on Descartes' part to stake the whole of his physics on one experiment implies a recognition of the decisive role of experimental evidence. It also reveals, however, a certain rigidity in his system: he is not just willing to give up those parts of his physics which would be directly related to the problem at issue, but finds himself compelled, should the experiments prove him wrong in this case, to renounce the whole of his scientific edifice. The reason is that the doctrine of instantaneous propagation of light happens to be one of these doctrines which Descartes asserts on *a priori* grounds. Consequently, the danger which the Cartesian physics would have to face if that doctrine were to be proved false, is the kind of danger that necessarily threatens a system of ideas which has been conceived *en bloc*.

Descartes distinguishes, in the passage just quoted, between

---

who, in the Adam and Tannery edition of Descartes' works, was conjecturally identified as Beeckman. The same editors later doubted their conjecture when Beeckman's *Journal* had been discovered and nothing in it was found to suggest that the author visited Descartes at any time in 1634 (cf. D, X, pp. 551-4). (The assumption made by J. F. Scott in *The Scientific Work of René Descartes*, London, 1952, pp. 40-41 that Descartes' correspondent was Mersenne is gratuitous.) It is, however, certain from Beeckman's *Journal* that he had adopted the doctrine of finite velocity of light since 1615 or 1616, and that he had imagined various experiments to verify his doctrine. Cf. Cornelis de Waard, *L'expérience barométrique*, Thouars, 1936, p. 86, n. 4; Isaac Beeckman, *Journal*, ed. C. de Waard, I (1939), p. 99, III (1945), pp. 49, 108-9, 112. No experiment in the *Journal* is identical with that which Descartes attributed to his correspondent. (See also Descartes, *Correspondance*, ed. C. Adam and G. Milhaud, I (1936), pp. 267-74, where the conjecture is made that Descartes' letter may have been addressed to Hortensius.)

[15] D, I, p. 308; *Letters*, ed. Clerselier, II, p. 140. Thus it is not an accident that Descartes entitled the treatise which, in his own words, 'contains the whole of my physics': *De la Lumière*; cf. letter to Vatier, 22 February 1638, D, I, p. 562. In the brief account he gives of this treatise at the beginning of Part V of the *Discourse*, the principal components of the cosmos are differentiated according to their optical functions: the sun and fixed stars (first element) emit light, the heavens (second element) transmit it, and the planets (third element) reflect it. Similarly, earthly bodies are distinguished by their properties of luminosity, transparency and opacity; man, as the spectator of all, is a receptor of light (HR, I, p. 107). Adopting a current medieval terminology deriving from Avicenna's *De anima*, III, 1, Descartes called the action of light in the luminous object *lux*, and the action of the subtle matter constituting the second element *lumen* (cf. Letter to Morin, 13 July 1638, D, II, p. 205). Cf. *Principles*, III, 48-52.

instantaneous *movement*, a doctrine which he does not hold, and instantaneous *communication* of movement, which he obviously takes to be a conceivable form of physical action.[16] For, according to him, light does not consist in an actual motion, but rather in a 'tendency to motion' which is transmitted to the eye through a medium. What, then, is this tendency; and what reasons did Descartes have for believing that by its action the light reached the eye in an instant?

In the same letter to X he gives an experimental argument for the instantaneous propagation of light, which is based on observations of the eclipses of the moon. This argument will be discussed later, but first in order to appreciate the extent to which his conception of light was determined by his general physics we have to turn to the *Traité de la Lumière* where the matter is explained in detail.

Descartes presents us in that treatise with a cosmological 'Fable' depicting how the world *might* have come to be as we see it. He claims that he does not propose to talk about the existing world, but to feign another at pleasure which would nevertheless coincide in appearance with our world.[17] There is no doubt that by adopting this mode of exposition he was only hoping to avoid opposition to his cosmological doctrines which were in agreement with the Copernican system.[18]

---

[16] Descartes to Morin, 13 July 1638, D, II, p. 215: 'Et tout ce que vous disputez en suite fait pour moy, excepté seulement ce que vous semblez vouloir dire à la fin, que *si la Lumiere est vn mouuement, elle ne se peut donc transmettre en vn instant.* A quoy ie répons que, bien qu'il soit certain qu'aucun mouument ne se peut faire en vn instant, on peut dire toutefois qu'il se transmet en vn instant, lors que chacune de ses parties est aussi-tost en vn lieu qu'en l'autre, comme lors que les deux bouts d'un baston se meuuent ensemble.'

[17] *Le Monde ou Traité de la Lumière*, D, XI, p. 36: 'Et mon dessein n'est pas d'expliquer comme eux [i.e. 'les Philosophes'] les choses qui sont en effet dans le vray monde; mais seulement d'en feindre vn à plaisir, dans lequel il n'y ait rien que les plus grossiers esprits ne soient capables de concevoir, & qui puissent toutefois estre crée tout de mesme qui je l'auray feint. Cf. ibid., p. 31. The description of *Le Monde* as a 'fable' appears in Descartes' correspondence for the first time in a letter to Mersenne, 25 November 1630 (D, I, p. 179), but must go back to an earlier time (D, XI, p. 699).

[18] In Part V of the *Discourse* Descartes explains that in order to express himself freely in *Le Monde* he decided to leave the existing world to the disputes of the learned 'and to speak only of what would happen in a new world if God now created, somewhere in an imaginary space, matter sufficient wherewith to form it, and if He agitated it in diverse ways, and without any order, the diverse portions of this matter, so that there resulted a chaos as confused as the poets ever feigned, and concluded His work by merely lending His concurrence to Nature in the usual way, leaving her to act in accordance with the laws which He had established' (HR,

We are invited to imagine[19] an indefinite extension of matter in the nature of which there is nothing that cannot be known 'as perfectly as possible';[20] a matter, that is, which has none of the scholastic or even sensible qualities, and whose essence is completely comprised in pure extension. Such a matter, conceived as a perfectly solid body, can be divided into parts of various shapes which can be moved in various ways. Solidity here means nothing but the being at rest of these parts relative to one another together with the fact that there is no void between one part and another.[21] Since extension can be conceived without motion, it is supposed that God, who has created the matter of this new world in the first place, has also actually divided it into parts of diverse shapes and magnitudes (which does not mean creating gaps between them) and set them in motion. Everything that subsequently happens in this imagined world is a necessary consequence of this initial action, in accordance with certain laws also imposed by the Creator.

What are these laws? They are called by Descartes Laws of Nature in as much as they govern changes in the material world which cannot be ascribed to the immediate action of God, since He does not change. They are based, however, on the fact that God continues to conserve matter 'in the same way [*façon*] as he created it'.[22] The first law states 'that every part of matter in particular continues always to be in the same state as long as it is not forced to change it by coming into contact with other parts'.[23] Among the 'states' of matter which are thus conserved Descartes counts motion as well as figure, magnitude and rest. He is concerned to distinguish his conception of motion from that of 'the Philosophers', that is, the Aristotelians. Referring to the Aristotelian doctrine that

---

I, p. 107). In the Preface (signed 'D.R.') to the first edition of *Le Monde*, published posthumously in 1664, we read: 'Il [Descartes] savoit que, si quelque part on defendoit de parler du Systeme de Copernic comme d'une verité, ou encore comme d'une hypothese, on ne deffendoit pas d'en parler comme d'une Fable. Mais c'est une Fable qui, non plus que les autres Apologues ou Profanes ou Sacrés, ne repugne pas aux choses, qui sont par effet' (D, XI, p. ix).

[19] *Le Monde*, VI, D, XI, pp. 31–36.
[20] Ibid., p. 33.
[21] Cf. *Le Monde*, III and IV; *Principles*, II, 54–63.
[22] *Le Monde*, VII, 'Des Loix de la Nature de ce Nouveau Monde', D, XI, p. 37.
[23] Ibid., p. 38.

natural rectilinear motion comes to an end when the moving body reaches its natural place, Descartes remarks that this gives motion an exceptional status as the only mode of being that would seek its own destruction.[24] Furthermore, he finds the resulting definition of motion, as *actus entis in potentia, prout in potentia est,* completely incomprehensible. The only motion he understands is that assumed by Geometers in their definition of lines and surfaces:

the nature of the motion about which I intend to speak here is so easy to understand that even the Geometers who are, of all men, the most careful to conceive very distinctly the objects of their considerations, have found it more simple and more intelligible than their surfaces and lines: as this appears from the fact that they have explained the line by the motion of a point, and the surface by the motion of a line.[25]

That is to say, the only motion which Descartes recognizes in his world is that by which a body passes from one place to another, successively occupying all intermediate positions.[26]

The second law asserts that when two bodies meet, the one loses as much motion as is acquired by the other.[27] These two laws, remarks Descartes, are in agreement with experiment;[28] but they

---

[24] Cf. also *Principles*, II, 37. [25] *Le Monde*, D, XI, p. 39.

[26] Alexandre Koyré has commented on this passage as follows: 'Le mouvement cartésien, ce mouvement qui est la chose la plus claire et la plus aisée à connaître, n'est pas, Descartes nous l'a dit, le mouvement des philosophes. Mais ce n'est pas, non plus, le mouvement des physiciens. Ni même des corps physiques. C'est le mouvement des géomètres. Et des êtres géométriques: le mouvement du point qui trace une ligne droite, le mouvement d'une droite qui décrit un cercle. . . . Mais ces mouvements-là, à l'encontre des mouvements physiques, n'ont pas de vitesse, et ne se font pas dans le temps. La géométrisation à outrance—ce péché originel de la pensée cartésienne—aboutit à l'intemporel: elle garde l'espace, elle élimine le temps. Elle dissout l'être réel dans le géométrique' (*Études galiléennes*, II, 49). The diagnosis that Cartesian physics is ill with *géométrisation à outrance* is penetrating, and I intend to make use of it later, but it seems to me that the interpretation of Descartes' conception of *movement* as something independent of time (or not performed in time) cannot be justified. Time is indeed irrelevant in the definition of line as the movement of a point, etc.; but Descartes could not have intended to exclude time from the movement which he characterized by *successive* change of position. He in fact wrote that the only movement he recognized is that which is 'plus aisé à concevoir que les lignes des Geometres: qui fait que les corps passent d'vn lieu en vn autre, & occupent successivement tous les espaces qui sont entre-deux' (*Le Monde*, D, XI, p. 40). See also passage quoted above, p. 50, n. 16.

[27] *Le Monde*, D, XI, p. 41: '. . . quand vn corps en pousse vn autre, il ne sçauroit luy donner aucun mouvement, qu'il n'en perde en mesme temps autant du sien; ny luy en oster, que le sien ne s'augmente d'autant.'

[28] See above, p. 26, n. 26.

are more firmly grounded in the fact that God is immutable and that He always acts in the same way. The undoubted immutability of God requires that the quantity of motion, deposited by Him in the world at the moment of creation, should remain unaltered—a condition which, in Descartes' view, can be fulfilled only if these two laws are observed.

The third law states that when a body is set in motion it always *tends* to move in a straight line, even though it may be forced to move otherwise. Thus, the 'action' of a moving body, or its 'tendency to move' is different from its actual motion.[29] For example, the action or tendency of a stone in a sling is indicated by the tension of the cord and the fact that the stone begins to move in a straight line as soon as it leaves the sling; the stone is forced to move in a circle, but it is always tending to move in a straight line. Again, this law is supposed to be based on the same metaphysical foundation as the other two: it rests on the fact 'that God conserves every thing by a continuous action, and consequently, that He conserves it, not as it may have been some time before, but precisely as it is at the very moment that He conserves it'.[30] God is therefore the author of all movements in the world in so far as they exist and in so far as they are straight, 'but it is the diverse arrangements of matter which make [these movements] irregular and curved'.[31]

These three laws together with the indubitable truths on which mathematicians found their demonstrations are, in Descartes' view, enough to account for all the visible phenomena of our world.

The formation of the stars and the planets, and the spatial distribution of the elements constituting, respectively, the planets, the heavens and the stars are described as follows.[32] Having supposed that the original matter was actually divided into parts of various magnitudes which have been moved in various ways, and considering that rectilinear movement is impossible in this solid plenum, the parts of the original matter assume a somewhat circular movement, around different centres. In the process of pushing one another some larger parts are separated so as to constitute the bodies of the planets. They are characterized by opacity and are known as the third

---

[29] *Le Monde*, D, XI, p. 44. [30] Ibid. [31] Ibid., p. 46. [32] *Le Monde*, VIII, D, XI, pp. 48–56.

element. Others are crushed and formed into small round particles which make up the second element, a fluid subtle matter which fills the heavens as well as the gaps between the parts of the grosser bodies. Fluidity of the subtle matter simply consists in the fact that its parts are moving in various ways among themselves with great speed. It is characterized by transparency or ability to transmit the action of light. Still smaller parts, forming the first element, are scraped off the subtle matter to fill the interstices between its little globules, and the surplus is pushed to the centres of motion thus forming there the bodies of the sun and the stars. Each of these has a rotational motion in the same direction as its proper heaven which forms a vortex carrying the planets round the centre.

In accordance with the third law, the parts of the circulating matter, and in particular those of the matter of the stars, will tend to move in straight lines. They are, however, prevented from actually so moving by the surrounding matter, and thus they are bound to press against those parts which immediately lie next to them. It is this pressure which constitutes their light; a pressure which spreads throughout the medium formed by the second element along straight lines directed from the centre of the circular movement. In one place Descartes speaks of the particles of the subtle matter as having a 'trembling movement'—a property which he finds 'very suitable for light'.[33] This would make the action of light consist in a succession of shocks received and transmitted by the particles of the second element.

The picture is, as we see, purely mechanical, but why should the action of light be transmitted in an instant? The following is the answer given by Descartes in the *Traité de la Lumière*:

And knowing that the parts of the second Element . . . touch and press one another as much as possible, we cannot doubt that the action by which the first [parts] are pushed, must pass in an instant to the last parts: in the same way as the action by which one end of a stick is pushed, passes to the other end at the same instant.[34]

---

[33] *Le Monde*, D, XI, p. 95.
[34] The analogy with the stick is taken up in the first chapter of the *Dioptric*. Observing how the stick of the blind man serves him as a means of distinguishing the objects around him,

The doctrine of instantaneous propagation is thus a necessary consequence of Descartes' conception of the medium serving as the vehicle of light. The nature of that medium is itself determined by the Cartesian definition of matter. According to Descartes, the nature of corporeal substance consists solely in its being extended, and this extension is the same as that ordinarily attributed to empty space. From this it follows that two equally extended bodies must have the same quantity or substance of matter: 'there cannot be more matter or corporeal substance in a vessel when it is filled with gold or lead, or any other body that is heavy and hard, than when it only contains air and appears to be empty'.[35] It also follows that the same part of matter cannot have variable extension; it may change

---

Descartes continues: 'And to draw an analogy from this, I want you to think that light is, in the bodies which we call luminous, nothing but a certain movement or action that is very quick and very violent which passes to our eyes through the mediation of the air and the other transparent bodies, in the same way as the movement or resistance of bodies, which this blind man encounters, passes to his hand through the mediation of his stick. This will from the very first prevent you from finding it strange that this light could extend its rays in an instant from the sun to us: for you know that the action with which one moves one end of a stick must likewise pass in an instant to the other, and that it should so pass even if the distance between the earth and the heavens were greater than it is' (D, VI, p. 84). The analogy is old. Simplicius in his commentary on Aristotle's *De anima* 'compared the role of the transparent medium to that of a stick transferring the effect of the knock from the hand to the stone' (Sambursky, op. cit., p. 116). We also find it in the *Book of the Ten Treatises on the Eye* attributed to the great ninth-century scholar and translator of Greek medical writings into Arabic, Ḥunayn ibn Isḥāq. In the third treatise (On Vision) Ḥunayn first observes that a man walking in the dark can with the help of a stick in his hand detect the objects he meets with. He then expresses the view that 'sight . . . senses the sense-object which moves it through the mediation of the air just as the blind man feels the object by means of the stick' (*The Book of the Ten Treatises on the Eye Ascribed to Ḥunain ibn Isḥāq*, the Arabic text edited . . . with an English translation . . . by Max Meyerhof, Cairo, 1928, p. 109 (Arabic), pp. 36–37 (English); my translation). According to Ḥunayn vision takes place when the 'luminous spirit', rushing from the brain into the eyes, 'meets the surrounding air and strikes it as in a collision' (ibid., p. 110 of the Arabic text). Yet, it must be noted, the result of this 'collision' is in Ḥunayn's view a *qualitative* change that transforms the air into the nature of the spirit; that is to say, the air itself becomes an organ of vision that is continuous and homogeneous with sight (ibid.). J. Hirschberg has shown (cf. *Sitzungsberichte der Königlich preussischen Akademie der Wissenschaften*, 1903, no, 49, pp. 1080–94) that two medieval Latin versions were made of Ḥunayn's book. The translator of one of these, Constantinus Africanus, ascribed the work to himself, as was his habit, and it was accordingly known as 'Liber de oculis Constantini Africani'. The other translation went under the title, 'Galeni Liber de oculis translatus a Demetrio', and was printed in different Latin editions of Galen's works, including the nine Juntine editions which appeared in Venice between 1541 and 1625 (cf. M. Meyerhof, op. cit., Introduction, especially p. vii). For the passage referred to above see 'Constantini Liber de oculis' in *Omnia opera Ysaac*, Lugduni, 1515, fol. 173ᵛb; and 'Galeni De oculis' in Galeni *Opera omnia*, VII, Venetiis (apud Iuntas), 1609, fol. 188ᵛ.

[35] *Principles*, II, 19, HR, I, p. 264.

its figure, but its volume must remain constant. As Pierre Duhem put it, the Cartesian matter is 'rigorously incompressible'.[36] In such an incompressible and inelastic medium, Descartes considers, pressure must be transmitted instantaneously.

Newton later expressed the objection that the idea of instantaneous propagation of motion would involve a doctrine of infinite force. At first sight this might appear as a criticism of the Cartesian doctrine. A careful reading of Newton's text, however, shows that his objection was directed against an opinion that was not actually held by Descartes. We read in Query 28 of Newton's *Opticks*:

> If Light consisted only in Pression propagated without actual Motion, it would not be able to agitate and heat the Bodies which refract and reflect it. If it consisted in Motion propagated to all distances in an instant, it would require an infinite force every moment, in every shining Particle, to generate that Motion. And if it consisted in Pression or Motion, propagated either in an instant or in time, it would bend into the Shadow.[37]

There are only two objections here against the (Cartesian) doctrine that light consisted in pression propagated in an instant without actual motion: namely that such a pression would fail to account for the observed rectilinear propagation of light and the fact that it heats the bodies on which it falls. On the other hand, Newton remarks that an infinite force would be required in every shining particle, *if light consisted in motion propagated to all distances in an instant*. This last hypothesis was not held by Descartes. It may be noted here that Newton himself adopted the doctrine of instantaneous propagation of pressure through an incompressible medium. Considering, in Bk. II, Prop. XLIII of *Principia*, how pulses generated in a medium by a tremulous body would be propagated, he writes: 'If the medium be not elastic, then, because its parts cannot be condensed by the pressure arising from the vibrating parts of the tremulous body, the motion will be propagated in an instant . . .'[38]

---

[36] P. Duhem, 'Les théories de l'optique', *Revue de Deux Mondes*, CXXIII (1894), pp. 95–96.

[37] Newton, *Opticks*, p. 362. Earlier objections by Newton against the Cartesian view of light as pressure are contained in a passage quoted from Newton's MS. *Quaestiones quaedam dhilosophicae* (c. 1664) by Richard S. Westfall in 'The foundations of Newton's philosophy of nature', *The British Journal for the History of Science*, I (1962), p. 174.

We come now to Descartes' experimental arguments in support of his view. These, as has been remarked before, are contained in his letter to X of 1634. The fact that they do not occur in any of Descartes' formal writings would seem to imply that they had, in Descartes' view, only a secondary importance: they merely confirmed him in a belief which was ultimately based on his primary conception of matter. X, who believed that light had a finite velocity, had suggested the following experiment to decide the issue between him and Descartes. An observer would move a lantern in front of a mirror placed at a certain distance: the interval between moving the lantern and perceiving the reflection of this movement in the mirror would measure the time required by the light from the lantern to cover the distance from the mirror twice.

But, Descartes replied, there was a better experiment, one which had already been made by thousands of 'very exact and very attentive'[39] observers, and it showed that there was no lapse of time between the moment light left the luminous object and the moment it entered the eye. This experiment was provided by the eclipses of the moon.

A   B   C

In the figure, let A, B and C represent the positions of the sun, the earth and the moon respectively; and suppose that from the earth at B the moon is seen eclipsed at C. The eclipse must appear at the moment when the light which has been sent off by the sun at A, and reflected by the moon at C, arrives at B, if it has not been interrupted in its journey from A to C by the interposition of the earth. Assuming that the light takes half an hour to cover the distance BC once, the eclipse will be seen one hour after the light from the sun reaches the earth at B. Moreover, the sun appears at A precisely at the moment when the light coming from A reaches B. Therefore, the moon will not appear eclipsed at C until one hour after the sun is seen at A.

---

[38] Newton, *Principia*, p. 372.
[39] D, I, p. 308; *Lettres*, ed. Clerselier, II, p. 140.

But the unvarying and exact observation of all Astronomers, which is confirmed by many experiments, shows that when the moon is seen from the earth at *B* to be eclipsed at *C*, the sun must not be seen at *A* one hour previously, but at the same instant as the eclipse is seen.[40]

As the lapse of one hour in these observations would be certainly more appreciable than the much shorter interval which would have to be perceived in X's terrestrial experiment, Descartes concluded: 'your experiment is useless, and mine, which is that of all Astronomers, very clearly shows that the light is not perceived after any sensible interval of time.'[41]

In the preceding considerations Descartes was so generous as to assume, for the sake of argument, a velocity of light which was in fact 24 times that envisaged by his correspondent. But he was not

---

[40] D, I, p. 310; *Lettres*, ed. Clerselier, II, p. 142.

[41] D, I, p. 310: 'Ergo & tuum experimentum est inutile, & meum, quod est omnium Astronomorum, longe clarius ostendit, in nullo tempore sensibili lumen videri.' In the French version this was rendered as follows: 'Par consequent, & vostre experience est inutile, & la mienne, qui est celle de tous les Astronomes, monstre clairement, que la lumiere se voit sans aucun interualle de temps sensible, *c'est à dire, comme i'auois soustenu, en vn instant.*' (*Lettres*, ed. Clerselier, II, pp. 142–3.)

The occurrence of the italicized words (added freely by the translator) following the assertion that light is seen 'sans aucun interualle de temps sensible' has led J. F. Scott to suggest (in op. cit., pp. 40–41) that Descartes did not mean the doctrine of instantaneous propagation literally; that by the expression *in an instant* Descartes simply meant, as Scott put it, 'an extremely short interval of time, the twinkling of an eye, the lightning flash!' Scott does not seem to have consulted Descartes' letter in the original Latin where the words on which he bases his interpretation do not occur. He also unjustifiedly identifies Descartes' correspondent as Mersenne (see above, p. 48, n. 14). This interpretation cannot be maintained in the face of the many explicit statements which we find in Descartes' treatises and letters. As an example I quote the following passage from Descartes' letter to Mersenne (27 May 1638), in which Descartes makes quite clear what he means by the expression *in an instant*: 'Et pour la difficulté que vous trouuez en ce qu'elle [i.e. light] se communique en vn instant, il y a de l'équiuoque au mot d'instant; car il semble que vous le considerez comme s'il nioit toute sorte de priorité, en sorte que la lumiere du Soleil pust icy estre produite, sans passer premierement par tout l'espace qui est entre luy & nous; *au lieu que le mot d'instant n'exclud que la priorité du temps, &* n'empesche pas que chacune des parties inferieures du rayon [that is, the parts of the ray farther from the luminous object] ne soit dependante de toutes les superieures, en mesme façon que la fin d'vn mouvement successif depend de toutes ses parties precedentes' (D, II, p. 143; my italics). See also Descartes to Plempius, 3 October 1637 (D, I, pp. 416–17); Descartes to Morin, 13 July 1638 (D, II, p. 215, quoted above, p. 50, n. 16); Descartes to Mersenne, 11 October 1638, with reference to an experiment described by Galileo in the *Dialogues* to measure the speed of light: 'Son experience, pour sçauoir si la lumiere se transmet en vn instant, est inutile: car les Ecclipses de la lune, se rapportant assez exactement au calcul qu'on en fait, le prouuent incomparablement mieux que tout ce qu'on sçauroit esprouuer sur terre' (D, II, p. 384); and *Principles*, III, 64.

generous enough: the first estimation of the velocity of light (by Roemer) gave eleven minutes as the time required for a ray from the sun to arrive at the earth. Using this result Huygens was able to show why the eclipses of the moon were not suitable for discovering the successive movement of light.[42]

It will not be out of place here to consider Descartes' explanation of what Huygens later described as 'one of the most marvellous'[43] properties of light, namely the fact that light rays are not impeded by crossing one another. In the *Dioptric*[44] Descartes compares the light-bearing medium to a vat which is full of half-crushed grapes and which has two apertures at the base. The grapes are compared to the parts of the gross transparent bodies, while the liquid corresponds to the subtle matter which fills the pores of those bodies. The moment the apertures are opened, the parts of the liquid at a given point on the surface simultaneously tend to descend towards *both* apertures in straight lines. Similarly, the parts of the liquid at any other points on the surface simultaneously tend to move towards one aperture and the other 'without any of these actions being impeded by the others, or even by the resistance of the grapes which are in this vat'.[45] Nor are these actions hindered by any movements which the grapes may have. In the same way, the parts of the subtle matter touching the side of the sun facing us, tend to move in straight lines towards our eyes at the same instant as we open them, without the actions along these lines being hindered by one another, or by the stationary or moving parts of the gross transparent bodies, such as the intervening air.

This, in Descartes' view, is possible because light, as it exists in the medium, is not an actual movement, but a tendency to move. For although a body cannot be conceived to move simultaneously in various directions, or even in a straight line when obstacles are placed in its way, it may nevertheless tend to move at the same instant towards different sides, and without this tendency being hindered by obstacles. Considering, then, that it is not so much the movement as the 'action' or tendency to movement of luminous

---

[42] Below, pp. 203ff.
[44] D, VI, pp. 86–88.

[43] Huygens, *Treatise on Light*, pp. 21–22.
[45] Ibid., p. 87.

bodies that should be taken to constitute their light, the rays of light are 'nothing else but the lines along which this action tends'.[46] And, thus, there is an infinite number of such rays proceeding in all directions from each point on the luminous body, without their actions being stifled or hindered when they happen to cross one another in space.

This was perhaps the most unfortunate of Descartes' analogies in the *Dioptric*, but it pointed out a problem which any subsequent wave-theory of light had to reckon with. If, as Huygens later objected, light was a tendency to movement, how could one and the same particle of the medium tend to move in opposite directions, as would be the case when two eyes view each other? To explain this, Huygens was led to introduce elasticity as a property of the medium and, in consequence, renounce the doctrine of instantaneous propagation.[47]

2. Descartes had the idea of writing the *Meteors* long before he conceived the plan of the volume in which it appeared in 1637 together with the *Discourse*, the *Dioptric* and the *Geometry*.[48] The immediate occasion for writing a treatise on the subject of the *Meteors* was a parhelic phenomenon which was observed in Italy in March 1629 and which attracted a great deal of attention. One of Descartes' friends forwarded to him a description of the phenomenon shortly afterwards and asked him how he would account for it.[49]

---

[46] D, VI, p. 88.

[47] Below, pp. 207ff.

[48] In November 1630 Descartes talked about the *Dioptric* as a 'summary' of *Le Monde* which he had started towards the end of 1629 (cf. Letter to Mersenne, 18 December 1629, D, I, pp. 85–86), but he said that the summary would not be ready for a long time; for six months he had been working on a chapter on the nature of colours and light, but even that was 'not yet half finished' (Letter to Mersenne, 25 November 1630, D, I, p. 179; see also D, I, p. 235 and p. 255). It was only in 1635, when the *Dioptric* was ready for printing (D, I, p. 342), that Descartes thought of joining it with the *Meteors* in one volume and of adding a 'preface' to the two treatises (Letter to Huygens, November 1635, D, I, pp. 329–30). This 'preface' later appeared in the 1637 publication as the *Discourse*. Last in the order of composition was the *Geometry* which Descartes wrote while the *Meteors* was being printed in 1636 (Letter to ★★★, October 1637, D, I, p. 458). Cf. Gilson, *Commentaire*, pp. x–xi; L. Roth, op. cit., pp. 13–27.

[49] Cf. D, I, p. 29, editors' note.

His reaction was typical of him:[50] he felt that in order to explain this particular phenomenon he had 'to examine methodically [*par ordre*] all the Meteors'.[51] By October of the same year he believed himself to be ready to give a satisfactory explanation of atmospheric phenomena and had therefore decided to write 'a little Treatise which will contain the explanation of the colours of the rainbow, which have given me more trouble than all the rest, and generally of all the sublunar Phenomena'.[52] He asked his confidant Mersenne not to mention this planned treatise to anyone 'for I have decided to present it to the public as a sample of my Philosophy, and to hide behind the work to hear what will be said about it.'[53]

We have already quoted Descartes' statement of 1638 in which he made it quite clear that when he published his 1637 volume he was not aiming either to teach 'the whole of my method' in the *Discourse* or to show how he actually employed it to arrive at the results contained in the three treatises that followed.[54] At the same time, however, he described his explanation of the rainbow which he presented in the eighth chapter of the *Meteors*, as 'a sample' of the method outlined in the *Discourse*. Indeed, the opening sentence in that chapter contains the only reference to 'the method' in all three treatises: 'The rainbow is a marvel of nature that is so remarkable, and its cause has always been so eagerly sought by men of good sense and is so little understood, that I could not choose a subject better suited to show how, by the method which I employ, we can arrive at knowledge which has not been attained by those whose writings we have.'[55] It will be noted that when, in 1629, Descartes had not yet thought of writing a methodological preface to the

---

[50] Expressing to Mersenne his opinion of Galileo's *Dialogues* Descartes first remarked, rather condescendingly, that Galileo 'philosophe beaucoup mieux que le vulgaire, en ce qu'il quitte le plus qu'il peut les erreurs de l'Eschole, & tasche a examiner les matieres physiques par des raisons mathematiques'. Then he added the following reservation, indicating how in his view one should go about explaining particular phenomena: 'Mais il me semble qu'il manque beaucoup en ce qu'il fait continuellement des digressions & ne s'areste point a expliquer tout a fait vne matiere; *ce qui monstre qu'il ne les a point examinées par ordre, & que, sans auoir consideré les premieres causes de la nature, il a seulement cherché les raisons de quelques effects particuliers, & ainsy qu'il a basti sans fondement*' (Letter to Mersenne, 11 October 1638, D, II, p. 380, my italics; see also similar remarks on Galileo's *Chief Systems*, D, I, pp. 304–5).

[51] Descartes to Mersenne, 8 October 1629, D, I, p. 23.

[52] Ibid.   [53] Ibid.   [54] See above, p. 17, n. 2.   [55] D, VI, p. 325.

Meteors, he described the same explanation as 'a sample of my philosophy'.

The experimental character of Descartes' investigations of colours shows a different aspect of his activities as a physicist from that which the doctrine of instantaneous propagation of light has revealed. For although he argued in support of that doctrine from astronomical observations, his real reasons for holding it were ultimately drawn from another source, namely his *a priori* conception of matter and the cosmological picture in which light occupied a prominent place. When we watch Descartes dealing with the problem of the rainbow and of colours, however, we find him guessing, experimenting, calculating, testing. It would be a mistake to think that by indulging in these things he was sinning against his theory of method. Experimentation and the use of hypotheses are, as I hope the preceding chapter has made clear, integral parts of what the physicist is, in Descartes' view, obliged to do. This is not to say, however, that in his study of the rainbow, Descartes was following certain *rules* which he had already formulated. Scientific results are just not arrived at in such a linear fashion. Nor does it mean that he approached that phenomenon with a mind free from preconceived ideas; he was expressly seeking an explanation in terms of his initial suppositions concerning the nature of light. His attempt is therefore interesting in that it reveals an important aspect of his work that is often passed over in descriptions of his attitude as a practising scientist and as a methodologist of science.

Having observed, like others before him, that rainbows were produced in fountain sprays, and noting that sprays are composed of small drops of water, Descartes obtained a large spherical glass vessel filled with water to facilitate the experimental study of the phenomenon.[56] He stood with his back to the sun and held up the

---

[56] *Meteors*, VIII, D, VI, pp. 325–44. The same experiment, using the spherical glass vessel filled with water as a model of an individual rain drop, was independently performed in the first decade of the fourteenth century by the Persian Kamāl al-Dīn al-Fārisī (d. c. 1320) and the German Dominican Theodoric of Freiberg (d. c. 1311). Kamāl al-Dīn's work was particularly inspired by Ibn al-Haytham's investigations on the burning sphere and also by remarks in Avicenna's *Meteorologica* on the production of rainbows in sprays (Kamāl al-Dīn al-Fārisī, *Tanqīh al-manāzir*, Hyderabad, 1348 H., II, p. 283. Avicenna's observations were reported and discussed by Averroës in his middle commentary on Aristotle's *Meteorologica*, III, 4, which

glass vessel in the sun's light. By moving it up and down he found that a bright red colour appeared at an inferior part of the vessel by rays emerging from it at an angle of approximately 42° with the direction of the incident light from the sun. When he raised the vessel from this position the red disappeared; but as he *lowered* it a little, all the rainbow colours successively appeared. Further, looking at a higher part of the vessel, a fainter red than in the previous case was observed when the rays emerging from that part made an angle of about 52° with the incident light. The other colours successively appeared when he gradually *raised* the vessel through a certain small angle, and then they vanished when that angle was exceeded. No colours appeared at the same part when he lowered the ball from the initial position.

From this Descartes gathered, as he tells us, that in the place where the rainbow appears, there must be seen a bright red point in each of all those drops from which the lines drawn to the eye make an angle of about 42° with the incident light. All these points being viewed together, must appear as continuous circles of a bright red colour. Similarly, continuous circles of other colours must be formed by the points in all those drops from which the lines drawn to the eye make slightly smaller angles with the incident rays. This explains the primary (interior) bow, with the order of the colours from red above to blue below.

The secondary (exterior) bow he similarly accounted for by considering the points from which the lines drawn to the eye make an angle that is either equal to or slightly larger than 52°. Returning to the glass-vessel, Descartes found that the rays emerged in the

---

was translated into Latin in the thirteenth century by Michael Scot). Both Kamāl al-Dīn and Theodoric succeeded in explaining the primary bow by two refractions and one reflection, and the secondary bow by two refractions and two reflections—all of these refractions and reflections being understood as taking place in individual drops. It is not impossible that some of Theodoric's ideas may have reached Descartes, but there is no real evidence that they did. Of all the writers on the rainbow that preceded him, Descartes in the *Meteors* referred only to the sixteenth-century Italian Maurolyco whose work on this subject (contained in his *Diaphaneon* of 1553 and *Problemata ad perspectivam et iridem pertinentia* of 1567) was definitely inferior to his (D, VI, p. 340). For a comprehensive account of Theodoric's theory together with a study of the transmission of ideas on the rainbow to the seventeenth century, see A. C. Crombie, *Grosseteste*; also Carl Boyer, *The Rainbow*. An extensive bibliography will be found in these two books.

first case, corresponding to the primary bow, after two refractions (one on entering the vessel near the top and another on leaving it near the bottom) and one reflection (at the farther side of the vessel). In the second case, corresponding to the secondary bow, the rays emerged after two refractions (one on entering near the bottom and the other on leaving near the top) and two reflections. This explained why the order of the colours of the secondary bow was the reverse of that of the primary bow.

But some difficulties still remained to be tackled. One was to explain the production of colours as such. Descartes' procedure to solve this difficulty recalls to mind Bacon's method of exclusion. '. . . I inquired whether there was another subject [*suiet*] in which [colours] appeared in the same fashion, so that, by comparing one with the other, I might better be able to determine their cause.'[57] Remembering that the rainbow colours could be produced by a triangular glass prism, he turned to the examination of that.

He allowed the sun's rays to fall perpendicularly on one face of the prism so that no appreciable refraction took place at that surface; and he covered the other face through which the light was refracted with an opaque body in which there was a small aperture. The rays emerging through that opening exhibited the rainbow colours on a white sheet of paper.

From this Descartes learnt, first, that the curvature of the surface of the water drop was not necessary for the production of these colours, since both surfaces of the prism were plane. Second, that the angle at which the rays emerged from the prism was irrelevant, for this angle could be altered without changing the colours. Third, that neither reflection nor a multiplicity of refractions were necessary, as here there was only one refraction and no reflection.

But I have judged that at least one [refraction] was necessary, and even one whose effect was not destroyed by a contrary [refraction]; for experience shows that when the surfaces [of the transparent body through which the light passed] . . . were made parallel, the rays, having straightened up at one [of the surfaces] after they have been broken by the other, would not produce these colours.[58]

---

[57] *Meteors*, VIII, D, VI, p. 329.   [58] Ibid., pp. 330-1.

Finally, Descartes observed, the light should be limited by a shadow; for when the opaque body was removed the colours disappeared. Now the problem was to know why red always appeared at one end of the image and blue at the other, even though the rays giving rise to these colours were both refracted once and both terminated by a shadow, and to account for the appearance of the intermediate colours in the observed order.

Here Descartes recalls what he has asserted regarding the nature of light in the *Dioptric*, namely that it is a certain action or movement transmitted through the subtle matter whose parts he imagines to be small globules which can roll through the pores of terrestrial bodies. Before the light is refracted, these globules have only one movement, which is their movement in the direction of propagation. When they obliquely strike a refracting surface they acquire a rotatory motion which, disregarding external influences, would be of the same speed as their movement of translation. The rotatory motion of each globule is, however, affected by the velocity of the surrounding globules. Consider, for example, a globule travelling along the extreme red ray in the prism experiment described above. Such a globule, by pressing against the slower globules on the side of the shadow, and being pressed by those on the other side (whose velocity is greater) will suffer an effect similar to that of rolling a sphere between both hands; thus the rotary velocity of the globule will be increased or diminished depending on the sense of the rotation originally acquired at the refracting surface. Clearly, the effect of the shadowed medium bordering on the globules travelling along the extreme blue (or violet) ray will be contrary to that produced on the other side, since all globules are supposed to rotate in the same sense. Descartes considers that the sense of rotation is such that, whereas the rotary motion of globules along the red ray is accelerated, that of the globules along the blue ray is retarded. This accounts for the appearance of red and blue at the sides of the shadow. The other colours are explained by supposing that the globules along their rays are rotating with intermediate velocities ranging between the greatest rotational velocity (for red) and the smallest (for blue).

In Descartes' view, the preceding explanation was in perfect agreement with our experience of colours. For, he argued, the sensation of light being due to the movement or tendency to movement of the subtle matter touching our eyes, it is certain that the various movements of this matter must give rise to different sensations. Considering that the surfaces of the prism could not affect the movements of the globules in any way other than that described, he concluded that sensations of colours must be attributed to the various rotational velocities of the globules.

He admits that refraction and the termination of the light by a shadow are not always necessary for the production of colours, as for example in the case of opaque bodies. The colours of these, however, must be produced by the effect on the rotational motions of the globules that is due to the 'magnitude, figure, situation and movement of the parts' of these bodies when the light is reflected against their surfaces.[59]

It is these highly speculative considerations which, if we take the autobiographical account in the *Meteors* at its face value, finally led Descartes to his most important discovery in connection with the rainbow. For these speculations suggested a problem which Descartes expresses as follows:

... I doubted at first whether the colours were produced in [the rainbow] in exactly the same way as in the prism ... for I did not observe there any shadow terminating the light, and I did not know why they appeared only at certain angles, until I have taken my pen and calculated in detail all the rays falling on the various points of a drop of water....[60]

His purpose was to know at what angles the rays would come to the eye after two refractions and one or two reflections. By applying the law of refraction which he already possessed he found that, after one reflection and two refractions, many more rays would be seen at an angle of 41° for blue to 42° for red (the angles being made with the incident light) than at any smaller angle; and that no rays would be seen at a greater angle. Also, after two refractions and two

---

[59] *Meteor* VIII, D, VI, p. 335.   [60] Ibid., pp. 335-6.

reflections, the eye would receive many more rays at an angle of 51° (red) to 52° (blue) than at any greater angle; and no rays would proceed to the eye at any smaller angle.

So that there is a shadow bordering on both sides of the light which, after having passed through an infinite number of rain drops illuminated by the sun, comes to the eye at an angle of 42 degrees, or a little less, and gives rise to the first principal rainbow. And there is also a shadow terminating [the light] which comes at an angle of 51 degrees, or a little more, and causes the exterior rainbow; for, not to receive any rays of light in one's eyes, or to receive considerably less of them from one object than from another near it, is to perceive a shadow. This clearly shows that the colours of these arcs are produced by the same cause as those which appear with the aid of the prism. . . .[61]

The calculations involved here constitute Descartes' contribution to the theory of the rainbow.[62] By their means he could determine, for the first time, why the coloured circles appeared at the angles observed, as well as explain the appearance of the secondary bow in a quantitative manner.

His explanation of the formation of colours by a prism, however, was not successful. This task was left to Newton. Nevertheless, Descartes' speculations made a decided advance on previous accounts. Before him writers on the subject were content to explain colours as a result of the mixture of light and darkness, or of a finite number of 'primary' colours, in various proportions. In Descartes' theory the individuality of all colours is strongly suggested by the fact that to each colour on the spectrum there corresponds a definite physical (and, as it happens, periodic) property, the rotational velocity of the corresponding globules.[63] But the weakness lay in the fact that he could not provide a means of measuring or calculating this

---

[61] Ibid., p. 336.

[62] Cf. Carl Boyer, *The Rainbow*, pp. 211–18; J. F. Scott, op. cit., pp. 78–81.

[63] Descartes argued that since the reality of colours consists in their appearing, all colours are equally real: 'Et ie ne sçaurois gouster la distinction des Philosophes, quand ils disent qu'il y a [des couleurs] qui sont vrayes, & d'autres qui ne sont que fausses ou apparentes. Car toute leur vraye nature n'estant que de paroistre, c'est ce me semble, vne contradiction de dire qu'elles sont fausses & qu'elles paroissent' (D, VI, p. 335).

velocity and, to that extent, his explanation of colours remained qualitative, though mechanical. Newton substituted the size of the light corpuscle for the rotational velocity of the globule, but his theory is distinguished by taking into account the experimental fact of unequal refractions of different colours which had escaped the notice of everyone before him.

Chapter Three

DESCARTES' EXPLANATION OF REFLECTION. FERMAT'S OBJECTIONS

1. The first explicit formulation of the law of reflection, stating the equality of the angles of incidence and reflection of sight or visual rays, is to be found in Euclid's *Optics* (Proposition XIX).[1] Euclid here states the law in connection with a problem concerning the determination of heights. A reference to this law also exists in the Peripatetic *Problemata*,[2] which is supposed to contain ideas mainly deriving from Aristotle. The passage in which this reference occurs is interesting from the point of view of subsequent attempts to explain optical reflection in mechanical terms. The author of this passage seems to be concerned to bring out a *contrast*, rather than an analogy, between the appearance of images in mirrors and the rebound of objects. An object thrown against a resisting surface rebounds in virtue of the movement that has been imparted to it by the thrower—its natural movement, if any, having ceased when the body reached its natural place. Thus in preventing the movement in the straight line of incidence, the surface causes the object to change its direction. We are told that the object returns at an angle equal to the angle of incidence, but we are not told *why* this must be so. As opposed to this mechanical situation, we see the image of an object in a mirror at the end of the line along which our sight travels—as if this line, or our sight, were *not* impeded by the mirror. Although it is difficult to ascertain exactly what the author wanted to convey,[3] he did mention the formation of images in the course of a discussion about mechanical reflection.

---

[1] Cf. Euclidis *Optica*, in *Opera omnia*, VII, ed. I. L. Heiberg, Leipzig, 1895, pp. 28–31; Euclide, *L'Optique et la Catoptrique*, tr. Paul Ver Eecke, Paris, 1959, pp. 13–14.

[2] [Aristotle], *Problemata*, XVI, 13.

[3] See the interpretation given by Carl B. Boyer in 'Aristotelian references to the law of reflection', *Isis*, XXXVI (1945–46), pp. 92–95.

In what has come down to us of the *Catoptrics* of Heron of Alexandria (about A.D. 75) we find a brief account of the mechanical conditions for the reflection of visual rays.[4] Heron observes that hard bodies repel the movement of projectiles whereas soft bodies,

FIG. III. 1.

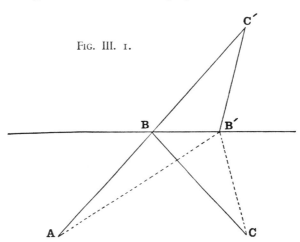

such as wool, arrest it; similarly, visual rays are reflected from polished rather than rough surfaces. For a smooth surface is one whose parts are so compact as not to permit the rays to fall into gaps between them. Glass and water surfaces reflect rays only partially because of the irregularity of these substances: they consist of solid parts which repel the rays falling on them, and of porous parts which allow other rays to pass through. Heron knew the law of the parallelogram of velocities[5] which had been already formulated in the Peripatetic *Mechanica*,[6] but so far as we know he made no attempt to apply it in the derivation of the law of reflection. Instead, he appealed to the widespread dictum that nature does nothing in

---

[4] Cf. Heronis *Catoptrica*, III, in *Herons von Alexandria Mechanik und Katoptrik*, herausgegeben und übersetzt von L. Nix und W. Schmidt (Heronis Alexandrini *Opera quae supersunt omnia*, vol. I, fasc. I, Leipzig, 1900), pp. 322–25 (Latin text with German translation). See English translation of the relevant passage in *A Source Book in Greek Science*, ed. M. R. Cohen and I. E. Drabkin, Cambridge, Mass., 1948, pp. 263–4.

[5] Cf. Heronis *Mechanica*, I, 8, in *Herons von Alexandria Mechanik und Katoptrik* . . ., pp. 18–21 (Arabic text with German translation).

[6] [Aristotle], *Mechanica*, I, 848b.

vain.[7] Interpreting this dictum here as a principle of *minimum path*, he proves that it is presupposed by the equality of the angles of incidence and reflection.[8] For (Fig. III. 1) let AB, BC be the incident and reflected visual rays making equal angles with the mirror BB', and let B' be any point on the surface of the mirror other than B in the plane of incidence. The actual path ABC must be shorter than the hypothetical $AB'C$ which makes unequal angles with the mirror. This is shown by producing AB to C', such that $CB = BC'$, and joining $C'B'$. The triangles CBB' and $C'BB'$ are equal and, therefore, $C'B' = B'C$. Since $AB' + B'C'$ is greater than AC', it follows that $AB' + B'C$ is greater than $AB + BC$. The shortest path, which the ray follows from the eye A to arrive by reflection at the object C, is that for which the angles of incidence and reflection are equal. Heron extends this proof to cover the case of spherical convex mirrors.[9]

In addition to proving the law of optical reflection experimentally, Ptolemy tried in his *Optics* to give a theoretical explanation of this law by comparing the reflection of visual rays to the rebound of projectiles. He observes[10] that when a ball (*spera*) is thrown on to a wall at right angles, its movement in that direction is totally prevented. On the other hand the grip of a bow does not impede the movement of the arrow. Thus while an object will prevent a movement to which it is directly opposed, a tangential movement will not be affected by it. This being true of everything that moves, it applies to visual rays. A ray falling perpendicularly on the surface of a mirror is thrown back in the same line, while a ray travelling tangentially to the surface continues to move forward without being deflected. Between these two extreme cases, a ray that falls obliquely to the surface is reflected in a direction symmetrical with that of incidence, that is, in such a way as to make the angle of reflection equal to the angle of incidence. Ptolemy seems to have had in mind here the parallelogram of displacements, but he makes no explicit use

---

[7] We are told this by Damianus and Olympiodorus who had more information about Heron's *Catoptrica* which has not survived in a complete form. Cf. A. Lejeune, *Catoptrique grecque* (1957), pp. 48–49.

[8] *Heronis Catoptrica*, IV, pp. 324–9 (Latin and German).

[9] *Ibid.*, IV, pp. 328–30; *A Source Book in Greek Science*, pp. 264–5.

[10] Cf. *Ptolemaei Optica*, III, 19–20, ed. A. Lejeune, Louvain, 1956, pp. 98–99.

of it, and his text, which has survived only in a Latin translation made from an Arabic version which has itself been lost, is not quite clear.[11]

The ideas of Heron and Ptolemy were raised to a high level of elaboration by Ibn al-Haytham,[12] whose theory deserves to be presented here in some detail for two reasons: first, because it is the most complete mechanical treatment of reflection that we have up until the publication of Descartes' *Dioptric*; and second, because it is very likely that Descartes was acquainted with it.[13] But without necessarily maintaining that Ibn al-Haytham did in fact influence Descartes, it will be interesting to observe the striking similarities, and also the significant differences, between their theories.

Ibn al-Haytham explains in the fourth book of his *Optics*[14] that

---

[11] I have followed Lejeune's interpretation of this passage in ibid., p. 99, n. 33. See also his *Catoptrique grecque*, pp. 34–35.

[12] Avicenna was familiar with the analogy between optical and mechanical reflections, but he explicitly rejected it. He argued that if light were reflected by repulsion, as in the case of a ball, it would be reflected from all impenetrable bodies, even if they are not smooth. He wrote in *De anima*, III, 6, in *Opera*, Venetiis, 1508, fol. 14ᵛb: 'Si autem causa reverberatione [lucis] est repercussio retro aut tumor, sicut accidit pille, deberet reverberari ab omni corpore, quid non penetrat, quamvis non esset lene.'

[13] Descartes nowhere refers to Ibn al-Haytham (Alhazen) or to his *Optics*. It would, however, be most implausible to suppose that he ignored a work that was well known to Snell (*Janus*, XXXIX (1935), p. 64), Beeckman (*Journal*, ed. C. de Waard, II, p. 405), Mersenne (e.g. *Quaestiones celeberrimae* (1623), pp. 761, 763, 774, 778) and Fermat (D, I, p. 356), to mention only a very few of his contemporaries; a work, moreover, to which he must have seen many allusions in Kepler's *Paralipomena* (1604, *passim*) as well as in works of other writers. The *Optics* of Ibn al-Haytham was available to Descartes in the volume entitled *Opticae thesaurus* which F. Risner edited in 1572 and which also contained Witelo's *Optics*, which Descartes certainly knew (cf. D, I, p. 239; D, II, p. 142; D, III, p. 483; D, XI, p. 646). The fact that Descartes wrote 'Vitellion', the form which we find in the Nuremberg editions of 1535 and 1541 of Witelo's *Optics* (D, I, p. 241) and in Kepler's *Ad Vitellionem Paralipomena*, as distinguished from Risner's 'Vitello', cannot be taken as proof that his knowledge was confined to the Nuremberg editions. Fermat also used the form 'Vitellio' although he was certainly acquainted with Risner's 1572 volume. (D, I, p. 356.)

[14] I have followed in this account the Arabic text (Istanbul MS. Fātiḥ 3215, fols. 66ᵛ9–76ʳ13) which has been somewhat compressed in the Latin translation edited by Risner. Since it is the Latin text that is important for the study of the transmission of Ibn al-Haytham's ideas, I give it here in full. It will be seen that the Latin preserves all the main ideas of the original. Alhazeni *Optica*, IV, 17 and 18, pp. 112–13:

17. *Reflexio lucis & coloris a superficie aspera facta, plerumque fugit visum.*
Amplius, quare ex politis corporibus, non ex asperis fiat reflexio, est: Quoniam lux, ut diximus, non accedit ad corpus, nisi per motum citissimum, et cum pervenerit ad politum, eiicit eam politum a se; corpus vero asperum non potest eam eiicere; quoniam in corpore aspero sunt pori, quos lux subintrat; in politis autem non invenit poros, nec accidit eiectio haec, propter corporis fortitudinem vel duriciem, quia videmus in aqua reflexionem; sed est haec repulsio propria politurae; sicut de natura accidit, quod aliquid ponderosum cadens ab alto super lapidem durum, revertitur in altum; et quanto minor fuerit durities lapidis, in quem

light is reflected because of a property residing in the reflecting body, namely its 'force of repulsion' or 'opposition' (*mudāfaᶜa, mumānaᶜa: eiectio, repulsio, prohibitio*). This force is stronger in polished than in

ceciderit, tanto regressio cadentis debilior erit; et semper regreditur cadens versus partem, a qua processit. Verum in arena propter eius mollitiem non fit regressio, quae accidit in corpore duro. Si autem in poris asperi corporis sit politio, tamen lux intrans poros non reflectitur; et si eam reflecti acciderit, dispergitur, et propter dispersionem a visu non percipitur. Pari modo si in aspero corpore partes elatiores fuerint politae, fiet reflexa dispersio; et ob hoc occultabitur visui. Si vero eminentia partium adeo sit modica, ut eius quasi sit idem situs cum depressis, comprehendetur eius reflexio tanquam in polito, non aspero, licet minus perfecte.

18. *Radii incidentiae & reflexionis, situs similitudine conveniunt. Itaque anguli incidentiae & reflexionis aequantur.*

Quare autem fiat reflexio lucis secundum lineam eiusdem situs cum linea, per quam accedit ad speculum ipsa lux, est: Quoniam lux motu citissimo movetur, et quando cadit in speculum, non recipitur; sed ei fixio in corpore illo negatur; et cum in ea perseveret adhuc prioris motus vis et natura, reflectitur ad partem, a qua processit, et secundum lineas eundem situm cum prioribus habentes. Huius autem rei simile in naturalibus motibus videre possumus, et etiam in accidentalibus. Si corpus sphaericum ponderosum ab aliqua altitudine descendere permittamus perpendiculariter super politum corpus, videbimus ipsum super perpendicularem reflecti, per quam descenderat. In accidentali motu, si elevetur aliquod speculum secundum aliquam altitudinem hominis, et firmiter in pariete figatur, et in acumine sagittae consolidetur corpus sphaericum, et proiiciatur sagitta per arcum in speculum, hoc modo, ut elevatio sagittae sit aequalis elevationi speculi, et sit sagitta aequidistans horizonti; planum, quod super perpendicularem accedit sagitta ad speculum, et videbitur super eandem perpendicularem eius regressus. Si vero motus sagittae fuerit super lineam declinatam in ipsum, videbitur reflecti non per lineam, per quam venerat, sed per lineam aequidistantem horizonti, sicut et alia erat, et eiusdem situs, respectu speculi cum ea, et respectu perpendicularis in speculo. Quod autem ex prohibitione corporis politi accidat luci motus reflexionis, palam: quia cum fortior fuerit repulsio vel prohibitio, fortior erit lucis reflexio. Quare autem accidat idem motus reflexionis et eius accessus, haec est ratio. Cum descendit corpus ponderosum super perpendicularem, repulsio corporis politi, et motus descendentis ponderosi directe sibi sunt oppositi, nec est ibi motus, nisi perpendicularis; et prohibitio fit per perpendicularem, quare repellitur corpus secundum perpendicularem. Unde perpendiculariter regreditur. Cum vero descenderit corpus super lineam declinatam, cadit quidem linea descensus inter perpendicularem superficiei politi, per ipsum politum transeuntem, et lineam superficiei eius orthogonalem super hanc perpendicularem; et si penetraret motus ultra punctum, in quod cadit, ut liberum inveniret transitum, caderet quidem haec linea inter perpendicularem, transeuntem per politum, et lineam superficiei orthogonalem super perpendicularem, et observaret mensuram situs, respectu perpendicularis transeuntis, et respectu lineae alterius, quae orthogonalis est super perpendicularem illam. Compacta est enim mensura situs huius motus ex situ ad perpendicularem et situ ad orthogonalem. Repulsio vero per perpendicularem incedens, cum non possit repellere motum secundum mensuram ad perpendicularem transeuntem per politum, quia nec modicum intrat; repellit ergo secundum mensuram situs ad perpendicularem, quam habet ad orthogonalem. Et quando motus regressio eadem fuerit mensura situs ad orthogonalem, quae fuit prius ad eandem ex alia parte, erit similiter ei eadem mensura situs ad perpendicularem transeuntem, quae fuit prius. Sed ponderosum corpus in regressu, cum finitur repulsionis motus, ex natura sua descendit, et ad centrum tendit. Lux autem eandem habens reflectendi naturam, cum ei naturale non sit ascendere aut descendere, movetur in reflexione secundum lineam incoeptam usque ad obstaculum, quod sistere faciat motum. Et haec est causa reflexionis.

rough bodies because the parts of the former are so closely packed as not to allow the light to get dissipated among them. Thus it is the compactness of the parts of polished bodies, not their hardness, that is responsible for optical reflection; water, for example, reflects light, but it is not hard. Light may, however, be reflected from some rough bodies because they consist of small polished parts; but these parts are variously situated and consequently they scatter the light falling on them. Also, the gaps between the parts of rough bodies allow some of the light to penetrate the body, and the absorbed light may not emerge again even after it strikes other polished parts within. Strong optical reflection takes place, therefore, when the reflecting body has more polished than rough parts, when the polished parts are similarly (or almost similarly) situated, and when the gaps between them are few and narrow.

Like Heron of Alexandria, Ibn al-Haytham observes that a heavy body falling on an extremely hard body, such as rock or iron, is immediately and strongly repelled; on the other hand, soft bodies, such as wool or sand, arrest the movement of the falling body. He further observes that bodies with intermediate degrees of hardness repel the impinging body with intermediate forces: thus the force with which the impinging body returns is dependent on the degree of hardness with which it meets at impact. Hardness and softness correspond to smoothness and roughness in optical reflection.

He then gives an explanation of the fact that light is reflected at equal angles and in the plane determined by the line of incidence and the normal to the reflecting surface at the point of reflection. He is first concerned to show that the force with which the light is reflected depends both on the force of the incident movement and on the repelling force of the reflecting body. He tries to establish this first with reference to natural movements, that is, movements of freely falling bodies. A small sphere, made of iron or copper, is allowed to fall from variable distances on a plane iron mirror placed horizontally on the ground. The sphere is supposed to be so polished as not to touch the plane surface at more than one point. The greater the distance covered by the sphere in the downward movement, the higher will be the point to which it will rebound. This means that 'the movement of return depends on the movement acquired by the heavy body during its descent, not on the natural movement due to its heaviness' (fol. 70ᵛ).

Ibn al-Haytham then turns to similar experimental considerations of 'accidental' or forced movements. This time the plane iron mirror is set up against a vertical wall and the iron sphere is thrown on to the mirror horizontally by means of a bow. When thrown perpendicularly to the mirror, the sphere returns in the same line before it begins to have a downward movement due to its heaviness. Here Ibn al-Haytham states that a projectile rebounds when opposed because it *acquires* from this opposition a movement in the direction of return; consequently, the greater the opposition, the greater the force with which the projectile rebounds. He states further that the force of opposition increases with the force of impact. In perpendicular projection both the incident movement and the opposition are acting in the same line; therefore, the projectile rebounds in the same perpendicular direction.

A different situation exists when the sphere is thrown at another angle in the horizontal plane. Here the incident movement consists of two parts, one perpendicular to the mirror and the other parallel to it. (He describes the direction of the second part as perpendicular to the first perpendicular part; his aim is obviously to include curved as well as plane surfaces, the perpendicular to the first perpendicular being parallel to the tangent to the surface at the point of reflection.) Thus in inclined projection, the incident movement and the resistance of the mirror are not directly opposed. When the sphere impinges on the mirror, the perpendicular part of the incident movement is 'annulled' because the resisting surface is opposed to the movement of the sphere in this direction. From the incident perpendicular movement *and* the perpendicular opposition, there results an equal movement in the opposite sense. The second, parallel part of the incident movement remains unaltered, being unopposed by the surface. The reflected movement, compounded of the reversed perpendicular part and the unchanged parallel part, will thus be in the plane of these two lines; further, its position will be symmetrical with that of the incident movement, that is, it will

75

make with the normal an angle equal to the angle of incidence. The same is true of the reflection of light, but with one difference: the reflected movement of a body, being composed of a movement due to reflection and another due to the heaviness of the body, will not continue in a straight line. Light, not being itself determined to move in one direction rather than another, has no reason to change the direction given to it by reflection.

Ibn al-Haytham explains that the force of repulsion or opposition in hard bodies consists in the fact that these bodies do not allow of being affected by, or yielding to other impinging bodies. From this it would seem that by 'hardness' he meant rigidity. His account of what happens in mechanical reflection, however, forces us to adopt a different interpretation. He makes three assertions: (1) that the incident perpendicular movement is destroyed at impact; (2) that the reversed movement depends on the incident movement that has been destroyed; and (3) that the reversed movement is acquired from the force of repulsion. It would seem that in order to reconcile (1) with (2) one would have to assume that the initial movement is first communicated to the reflecting body which then imparts it again to the projectile, in accordance with (3). That is to say, the reflecting body acts as a spring, and its force of repulsion is the same as its elastic force.

Before turning to Descartes' treatment of reflection it may be well to observe that before the seventeenth century, one part or another of Ibn al-Haytham's theory had appealed to various Latin authors in varying degrees. The cases of Roger Bacon and Kepler are particularly interesting. Bacon invokes the ball analogy to show that only a perpendicular ray returns in the same line because it is totally resisted by the reflecting body.[15] He also remarks that bodies reflect light because of their density, not hardness or solidity;[16] and

---

[15] *De multiplicatione specierum*, pars II, cap. III, *Opus majus*, ed. Bridges, II, p. 468: 'Quod si corpus recipiens rem cadentem perpendiculariter resistit omnino, tunc res cadens perpendiculariter rediret propter incessus fortitudinem in eandem viam per quam incessit, sicut de pila jacta ad parietem vel ad aliud resistens omnino. Et pila cadens ex obliquo labetur ex altera parte incessus perpendicularis secundum casum obliquum, ut patet ad sensum, et non rediret in viam qua venit propter casus debilitatem.'

[16] *Mult. spec.*, pars II, cap. V, ed., cit. II, p. 479: 'Considerandum etiam . . . quod durum et solidum nec faciunt reflexionem nec fractionem, sed solum densum et rarum. Nam crystallus

those which are not perfectly dense refract as well as reflect the light falling on them.[17] Referring to Ibn al-Haytham, he notes that light is best reflected from polished, not rough, bodies, because the polished body repels (*ejicit*) the *species* of light, whereas the rough body cannot, since there are pores in it which allow some of the light to enter.[18] In spite of the verb '*ejicit*' in this sentence Bacon did not in fact conceive of optical reflection as a mechanical process. He clearly states that the *species* of light is reflected simply because the opposing surface offers it an *opportunity* to multiply itself in a direction other than that of incidence.[19] The *species* thus turns away from the surface by a power all its own; its reflection is not to be understood as a case of repulsion but of self generation. Since light is not a body, its reflection cannot be due to the same cause as the rebound of a ball.[20] This simply amounts to a rejection of Ibn

---

est dura res et solida, et vitrum et hujusmodi multa, et tamen quia rara sunt, pertransit species visus et rerum visibilium, et fit bona fractio in eis; quod non contingeret si esset ita densa sicut sunt dura et solida. Densum enim est quod habet partes propinque jacentes, et rarum est quod habet partes distanter jacentes, et ideo vitrum est rarum, et crystallum et hujusmodi non densum perfecte, licet aliquantulum, sed sufficienter sunt rara ut permittant species lucis transire.'

[17] *Ibid.*, p. 478: 'Sunt etiam alia corpora mediocris densitatis, a quibus fit reflexio simul et fractio, ut est aqua. Nam videmus pisces et lapides in ea per fractionem, et videmus solem et lunam per reflexionem, sicut experientia docet. Unde propter densitatem, quae sufficit reflexioni aliquali, radii omnes reflectuntur, sed propter mediocritatem densitatis, quae non impedit transitum lucis, franguntur radii in superficie aquae.'

[18] *Ibid.*, p. 479: 'Et Alhazen dicit in quarto libro, quod ex politis corporibus, non ex asperis, fit bona reflexio, quoniam corpus politum ejicit speciem lucis, sed asperum non potest, quum in corpore aspero sunt pori, quos subintrat species lucis vel alterius.'

[19] *Perspectiva*, pars III, dist. I, cap. I, in *Opus majus*, ed. Bridges, II, p. 130: 'Nam omne densum in quantum densum reflectit speciem, sed non quia fiat violentia speciei, immo quia species sumit occasionem a denso impediente transitum ejus ut per aliam viam se multiplicet ei possibilem.'

Mult. spec., pars II, cap. II, ed. cit., II, p. 463: 'Si vero corpus secundum non differt in diaphaneitate a primo, sed omnino est densum, ita quod potest impedire transitum speciei, tunc species sumens occasionem a denso in partem alteram redit ex propria virtute; ut cum non possit se multiplicare in densum corpus multiplicat se in primo corpore faciens angulum, et dicitur species reflexa proprie, et in communi usu apud omnes; nec tamen repellitur per violentiam, sed solum sumit occasionem a denso impediente transitum, et vadit per aliam viam, ut possibile est ei.'

[20] *Mult. spec.*, pars III, cap. I, ed. cit., II, p. 505: 'Si vero arguitur de reverberatione a corpore, patet ex dictis quod non fit ex violentia, sed generat se in partem sibi possibilem cum prohibetur transire propter densitatem resistentis. Si enim violenter repercuteretur ut pila a pariete, oporteret necessario quod esset corpus. Quod si dicatur, cum facit se iterum per reflexionem in alium locum per suam naturam propriam, medio nec pellente nec movente nec moto, nec aliquo alio juvante nec faciente quod removeat locum, quod non accidit in umbra,

al-Haytham's mechanical model for reflection. Bacon does not make use of Ibn al-Haytham's application of the parallelogram of velocities for demonstrating the law of equal angles. He attempts instead a geometrical 'proof' which is a *petitio principii*.[21]

A clear and concise use of the parallelogram method, as applied to the problem of reflection, is to be found in Kepler's *Paralipomena* (Ch. I, Proposition XIX). Adopting the analogy between the behaviour of light and of physical objects,[22] Kepler observes that a resisting surface is not directly opposed to oblique movements, and consequently such movements must be reflected in a similarly oblique direction. To prove the equality of the angles, he considers the incident movement to be composed of two parts, one perpendicular and the other parallel to the surface. The equality of the angles follows from supposing the surface to be opposed to the first but not to the second component. There can be no doubt that the source of this proof was Ibn al-Haytham's *Optics* which Kepler frequently cited;[23] and as far as reflection is concerned, Kepler's *Paralipomena*, published in 1604, may have been a link between Ibn al-Haytham and Descartes.

2. Descartes' attempt in the *Dioptric* to explain the reflection of light by comparison with the mechanical reflection of bodies is in a long tradition that had been carried down from antiquity to the seventeenth century. Yet that which was for his predecessors merely an analogy, acquires in his system a new significance. For although he

---

quia ad motum corporis renovatur, videtur quod per se locum occupare debeat; dicendum est, quod locum non quaerit ut corpus sed subjectum, nec tamen unum in numero illud quaerit solum sed diversum semper, propter hoc quod species in una parte medii generata potest facere sibi similem in alia. Et ideo non est ibi acquisitio loci ut corpus acquirit, sed est ibi renovatio speciei per generationem in partibus medii pluribus.'

[21] Cf. *Perspectiva*, pars III, dist. I, cap. I, ed. cit., p. 131; also *Mult. spec.*, pars II, cap. VI, ed. cit., II, p. 484. In preferring to give a geometrical 'proof' Bacon was following the example of al-Kindi, *De aspectibus*, 17, ed. Björnbo and Vogl, pp. 29–30.

[22] Cf. *Ad Vitellionem Paralipomena*, Francofurti, 1604, pp. 14–15.

[23] Kepler refers here to Witelo's *Optica*, V, 20, where in fact the parallelogram method is not used. The reference is corrected in Kepler's *Gesammelte Werke*, II, Munich, 1939, p. 25 to Witelo's *Optica*, V, 10. This is an *experimental* demonstration which is derived from Alhazeni *Optica*, IV, 10.

does not conceive of the propagation of light as an actual movement, he still asserts that light is no more than a mechanical property of the medium transmitting it; it is, as we have seen, a static pressure existing simultaneously in all parts of the subtle matter that pervades all space. Furthermore, Descartes put forward a conception of matter which entailed the exclusion of all forces other than movement. From this point of view, to set a body in motion, another body that is already moving has to come into contact with it and convey to it part or all of its motion. Thus the idea of collision acquires in his physics a new status as the basic and only form of action in the material world to which light belongs.

By looking at optical reflection as a collision phenomenon Descartes was faced with a serious difficulty: if, as he asserted, light was a tendency to movement that was propagated instantaneously, how could it be compared to the successive motion of a projectile? He thought he could overcome this by assuming that the tendency to movement, being a potential movement, follows the same laws as motion itself. Thus he implied that in investigating optical reflection and refraction, one may forget about the actual mechanism of light for a while and study the reflection and refraction of actually moving bodies. What can be proved concerning these will be true of light by virtue of that bridging assumption.

In the Cartesian analogy for reflection a tennis ball takes the place of the small iron sphere in Ibn al-Haytham's model. This was misleading since, as we shall see,[24] it was Descartes' intention to eliminate elasticity from his abstract consideration of mechanical collision. He begins[25] by supposing that the surface of the ground, towards which the ball is pushed with a racquet, is perfectly smooth and perfectly hard (i.e. rigid) and, further, that the ball returns after impact with a speed equal to the speed of incidence. Abstraction is also made from such things as weight, size and figure; and the question, 'What power keeps the ball in motion after it is no longer in contact with the racquet?' is here set aside as irrelevant to the action of light. (The answer to this question, as we know, would

---

[24] Below, p. 81f.
[25] *Dioptric*, II, D, VI, pp. 93–95.

be based on Descartes' first law of motion, the law of inertia.) 'Only it must be noted that the power which continues the motion of this ball, whatever it may be, is different from that which determines it to move in one direction rather than another.'[26] The former, he explains depends on how hard we hit the ball, whereas the latter depends on the position of the racquet at the moment of striking. This distinction

already shows that it is not impossible for the ball to be reflected by the collision with the ground, and thus its former determination to tend towards B [the point of reflection] is changed without this resulting in a change of the force of its motion, as these are two different things. Consequently, one must not think it necessary, as many of our Philosophers do, that the ball should stop for a moment at B before turning back . . . For once its motion were interrupted by this pause, there would be no cause to start it again.[27]

Descartes denies here the medieval doctrine of *quies media*,[28] namely the doctrine that there is a moment of rest between two motions of the same body in opposite or different directions. If the body were to have a moment of rest before it resumed its motion in a new direction, where, he asks, would it derive this motion from? As we have seen, Ibn al-Haytham had tried to answer this question by postulating something like an elastic force which allows the reflecting body to *push* the projectile back after it has deprived it of its motion. Such an explanation would not, however, be acceptable to Descartes. He had his own reasons for believing, and indeed insisting, that the projectile should return by the same 'force' that has always been in it and that had never left it. In other words, he regarded the function of the surface as merely consisting in preventing the ball from continuing its motion in the same direction, while it is the ball itself that decides on the basis of its ever inherent resources where it should go. In *this* respect the situation as viewed here by Descartes is not unlike Roger Bacon's

---

[26] *Dioptric*, II, D, VI, p. 94.
[27] Ibid.
[28] See also Descartes to Mersenne, 18 March 1641, D, III, pp. 338–9.

account of how light is reflected: both the light *species* and the ball return by their own power, and for both the surface is no more than an occasion for a change of direction.

That the preceding remarks express Descartes' own meaning may be clearly seen from statements in his correspondence. Thus he wrote to Mersenne in 1640: 'Your saying that the speed of a hammer stroke takes Nature by surprise, so that she has no time to gather her forces in order to resist, is entirely against my opinion; for she has no forces to gather, nor does she need time for that; rather, she acts in everything Mathematically.'[29] The following sentence indicates what this means in the case of the rebound of bodies in collision: 'When two balls collide and, as often happens, one of them rebounds, it does so by the same force that was formerly moving it: for the force of the movement and the direction in which it takes place are entirely different things—as I have said in the Dioptric.'[30]

He later conceded in a letter to Mersenne for Hobbes that when a ball impinges upon the ground, both the surface of the ground and of the ball curve in a little at the point of impact and then they regain their shape; but he affirmed his belief that the subsequent rebound is impeded rather than helped by the compression and elasticity of these bodies.[31] Far from conceding that reflection would be impossible if the colliding bodies were supposed incompressible (a view which he found incredible), he maintained that compressibility only results in reflection not taking place at exactly equal angles.

---

[29] Descartes to Mersenne, 11 March 1640, D, III, p. 37.
[30] Ibid.
[31] Descartes to Mersenne for Hobbes, 21 January 1641, D, III, pp. 289–90: 'Concedo tamen libenter partem terrae, in quam pila impingit, aliquantulum vi cedere, vt etiam partem pilae in terram impingentem non nihil introrsum recuruari, ac deinde, quia terra & pila restituunt se post ictum, ex hoc iuuari resultum pilae; sed affirmo hunc resultum magis semper impediri ab istâ incuruatione pilae & terrae, quam ab eius restitutione iuuetur; atque ex eo posse demonstrari reflexionem pilae, aliorumque eiusmodi corporum non extremè durorum, nunquam fieri ad angulos accuratè aequales. Sed, absque demonstratione, facilè est experiri pilas molliores non tam altè resilire, nec ad tam magnos angulos, quam duriores. Inde patet quam perperam adducat istam terrae mollitiem ad aequalitatem angulorum demonstrandam; praesertim cum ex eâ sequatur, si terra & pila tam durae essent, vt nullo modo cederent, nullam fore reflexionem; quod est incredibile. Patet etiam quam meritò ego & terram & pilam perfecte duras assumpserim, vt res sub examen mathematicum cadere possit.'

He had therefore assumed incompressibility so that the matter of reflection could be treated mathematically.

Coming back to the same subject in another letter to Mersenne for Hobbes, he flatly asserted that experiment refuted Hobbes's opinion that the rebound of bodies was due to repulsion or elasticity; if this were true, he argued, a ball would be made to rebound by merely pressing it against a hard stone.[32]

What all this boils down to is Descartes' firm belief that the behaviour of bodies in collision can be fully explained solely in terms of conservation of motion. The ball rebounds simply because its motion, understood as an absolute quantity, persists; this is nature's mathematical way. To allow elasticity a role in collision would be to abandon the truly mathematical interpretation of nature! Descartes' treatment of reflection is thus one more example of what Alexandre Koyré has called 'géométrisation à outrance'.

To find the direction of reflection Descartes appeals to the parallelogram method which had been applied to the same problem by Ibn al-Haytham and Kepler: 'it must be remarked that the determination to move in a given direction, as well as motion, and generally every other kind of quantity, can be divided into all the parts of which it can be imagined to be composed.'[33] He imagines the 'determination' along AB (Fig. III. 2) to be composed of two others, one perpendicular to the surface and the other parallel to it. At the moment of impact the ground must hinder (empescher) the first component 'because it occupies all the space that is below CE', but not the second, 'since the ground is not at all opposed to [the ball] in that direction'.[34]

---

[32] Descartes to Mersenne, 18 March 1641, D, III, p. 338: 'Vous . . . parlez de l'opinion de l'Anglois [Hobbes] qui veut que la reflexion des cors ne se face qu'a cause qu'ils sont repoussez, comme par vn ressort, par les autres cors qu'ils rencontrent. Mais cela se peut refuter bien aysement par l'experience. Car s'il estoit vray, il faudroit qu'en pressant vne bale contre vne pierre dure, aussy fort qu'elle frape cete mesme pierre, quand elle est ietée decontre, cete seule pression la pust faire bondir aussy haut que lors qu'elle est ietée. Et cete experience est aysée a faire, en tenant la bale du bout des doigts, & la tirant en bas contre vne pierre qui soit si petite qu'elle puisse estre entre la main & la bale, ainsy que la chorde d'vn arc de bois est entre la main & la fleche, quand on la tire du bout des doigts pour la decocher; mais on verra que cete bale ne reiallira aucunement, si ce n'est peut estre fort peu, en cas que la pierre se plie fort sensiblement comme vn arc.'

[33] Dioptric, II, D, VI, pp. 94–95.

[34] Ibid., p. 95.

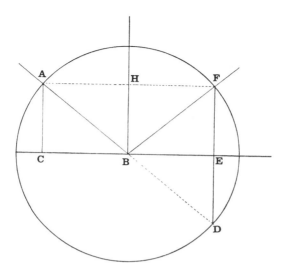

FIG. III. 2.

To find, therefore, exactly in what direction the ball must be reflected, let us describe a circle, passing through *A*, with *B* as centre. And we say that, in an equal time to that which it will have taken to move from *A* to *B*, it must inevitably return from *B* to a point on the circumference of the circle; since all the points that are as distant from *B* as *A*, are to be found on this circumference; and we have assumed the motion of the ball to be always of equal speed.[35]

Now, to know precisely to which of all the points on the circumference it must return: let us draw three straight lines *AC*, *HB* and *FE* perpendicular to *CE*, such that the distance between *AC* and *HB* is neither greater nor smaller than that between *HB* and *FE*. We can then say that in the same time that the ball has taken to advance in the right-hand direction from *A*, one of the points of the line *AC*, to *B*, one of the points of the line *HB*, it must also advance from the line *HB* to some point on the line *FE*. For all the points on the line *FE* are each as distant, in this direction, from *HB* as those on the line *AC*. And the ball is as much determined to advance in this direction as it was before. But it cannot arrive at the same time at a point on *FE*, and also at a point on the circumference of the circle *AFD*, unless this is either *D* or *F*, these being

_____

[35] Ibid., pp. 95–96.

the only two points where the circumference and *FE* intersect. But since the ground prevents the ball from passing through to *D*, it must be concluded that it necessarily goes towards *F*. And thus you easily see how reflection happens, namely at an angle always equal to that which is called the angle of incidence. As when a ray coming from *A* falls at *B* on the surface of the plane mirror *CBE*, it is reflected towards *F*, such that the angle of reflection *FBE* is neither greater nor smaller than the angle of incidence *ABC*.[36]

Descartes distinguishes between what he calls the 'force' of the ball's movement and its 'determination'. His subsequent application of these terms shows that by 'force' he means either the *absolute* quantity of motion or the quantity on which this depends, viz. the *absolute* speed. The term 'determination' proved to be more troublesome. Fermat understood it to mean simply the *direction* in which the ball moved, and this gave rise to difficulties which were not clarified until twenty years after his controversy with Descartes had started, when it was resumed with Clerselier. We need not, however, decide the nature of what Descartes understood by 'determination' in order to follow his proof of the law of reflection. Nor was Fermat's interpretation of it essential to his objections against Descartes' derivation of this law. We shall therefore leave this problem until we come to the discussion of refraction where the mentioned difficulties in fact belong.

In order to deduce the equality of the angles of incidence and of reflection Descartes assumes, first, that the reflecting surface will not affect the 'force' or speed of the ball in any way. That is, if v_i, v_r are the velocities of incidence and reflection, his first assumption is:

(1) $$v_i = v_r.$$

Further, since, as he argues, the surface is not opposed to the parallel motion, the speed in that direction will also be conserved after reflection. His second assumption is:

(2) $$v_i \sin i = v_r \sin r,$$

where *i* and *r* are the angles of incidence and reflection made with the normal.

---

[36] *Dioptric*, II, D, VI, p. 96.

From (1) and (2) it follows that

$$\sin i = \sin r,$$

or, $$i = r.$$

It should be noted that Descartes does not *postulate* in his proof anything about the perpendicular component of the incident velocity. In particular, he does not assume that it will be *reversed* by the reflecting surface. His conclusion is based on two assumptions, of which one is about the actual speeds, and the other about the parallel speeds, before and after reflection. Not to observe this would not only be to miss the whole point in the proof as a preparation for the derivation of the law of refraction, but would also imply a way of thinking that was not Descartes'.[37] When one says 'reversed' one is thinking of something like Newton's law of action and reaction. We have seen, however, that according to Descartes the ball does not act upon the surface, nor does the surface react upon it. It is not, therefore, an accidental feature of his proof that the conclusion is meant to follow from merely supposing the motion to have been *conserved* in two directions. This point is also essential for appreciating Fermat's objections.

3. The importance of the controversy that took place between Descartes and Fermat after the publication of the *Dioptric* can hardly be exaggerated. Leading as it eventually did to Fermat's formulation of the principle of least time, it has been rightly described by Paul Mouy as 'one of the most interesting and most fruitful in the history of science'.[38] Nevertheless, it has not been studied in any sufficient detail. Gaston Milhaud, who devotes a long chapter[39] to the quarrel between Fermat and Descartes over the former's method of deriving tangents, only refers to the dispute about refractions summarily;[40] and his remarks, which were

---

[37] Compare J. F. Scott, op. cit., p. 34.
[38] Paul Mouy, *Le développement de la physique cartésienne, 1646–1712*, Paris, 1934, pp. 60–61.
[39] Gaston Milhaud, *Descartes savant*, pp. 149–75.
[40] Ibid., pp. 110–13.

concerned with Descartes' proof of the law of refraction, were not always correct. The account, by far the longest, given in Mouy's excellent book, is too general although it is quite instructive.[41]

The circumstances of this controversy were as follows. Descartes' 1637 volume did not arrive in France until the end of that year. Before the printing was completed, however, Descartes had sent a copy to Father Mersenne in Paris, who undertook the task of distributing it in parts to various persons. The *Dioptric* was allotted to Fermat and was accordingly sent to him in Toulouse with the request that he give his opinion of it. As remarked by the editors of Fermat's works, it appears from the end of Fermat's letter to Mersenne of (probably) September 1637[42] that neither the *Discourse* nor the two other treatises, the *Meteors* and the *Geometry*, had been sent to him then; nor did he know that they were to appear together in one volume, or that his reply would be communicated to Descartes.[43] But from that time on, Mersenne played the part of intermediary between the two mathematicians who exchanged their letters through him.

Fermat's arguments, in that first letter of his, were directly concerned with Descartes' proof of the law of reflection, for he believed that similar arguments would equally apply to refraction. Descartes answered by a letter to Mersenne dated (probably) October 1637.[44] Fermat's reply to this, in his letter to Mersenne of (probably) December 1637,[45] took up the question of refraction and in it he composed what he intended as a refutation of Descartes' proof of the sine law. Descartes received Fermat's letter when he was about to defend his own criticism of Fermat's tangent method against Roberval. He consigned his reply to a letter written (probably) on 1 March 1638[46] which was addressed to Mydorge who had been

---

[41] Mouy's account (*Physique cartésienne*, pp. 55–61) is given in the course of a summary of all physical questions discussed in Descartes' correspondence as published by Clerselier in the three volumes which appeared successively in 1657, 1659 and 1667.

[42] F, II, pp. 106–12.

[43] Cf. F, II, pp. 106–7, editors' note.

[44] F, II, pp. 112–15.

[45] F, II, pp. 116–25.

[46] F, IV, pp. 93–99.

taking Descartes' side at the discussions in Father Mersenne's circle. This letter did not reach Fermat until about June of the same year when he was preparing to enter the dispute about tangents. He was not satisfied with Descartes' replies and the discussion concerning the *Dioptric* was suspended.[47]

Twenty years later, in the beginning of 1658, the discussion was resumed between Fermat and Descartes' follower, Clerselier. On May 15 Fermat's last letter to Mersenne for Descartes was made the subject of a special refutation by Rohault,[48] author of the famous *Traité de Physique*, which was the generally accepted text-book of physics until the publication of Newton's *Principia*.[49] In what immediately follows we shall be concerned with the part of the controversy dealing with reflection.

Fermat could not accept Descartes' argument for establishing the law of reflection as a 'legitimate proof and demonstration'.[50] To his mind there was something in this argument that was *logically* wrong; and his attack was directed against the method of resolving motions that was adopted by Descartes in his treatment of both reflection and refraction. For Fermat believed that, in resolving the motion of the incident ball into those particular components, the one perpendicular and the other parallel to the reflecting surface, Descartes had chosen but one out of an infinite number of reference systems which were all valid. But since he had chosen the one which could help him to arrive at the desired, and already known result, his procedure was in Fermat's view completely arbitrary. Accordingly Fermat set out to show that, by adopting a different system of axes, a different result from Descartes' would be obtained—and this, he believed, on the same lines as in Descartes' argument:

---

[47] F, II, p. 125, n. 1. The letter addressed to Mydorge is said by the editors of Fermat's works to have been sent to Mersenne on or about 22 February 1638 (cf. F, II, p. 125, n. 1, p. 126, n. 1). This date cannot be correct if the letter was written on 1 March 1638, as indicated on p. 93 of vol. IV of Fermat's works.

[48] Cf. Rohault's 'Réflexions ou projet de réponse à la lettre de M. de Fermat' [i.e. Fermat's letter of December 1637], 15 May 1658, F, II, pp. 391–6.

[49] For letters exchanged during this second phase of the discussion, see next chapter.

[50] F, II, p. 109.

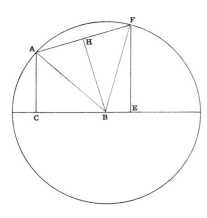

FIG. III. 3

. . . in the attached figure [Fig. III. 3], where *AF* is no longer parallel to
CB, and the angle *CAF* is obtuse, why cannot we imagine that the
determination of the ball moving from *A* to *B* is composed of two others,
of which one makes it descend from the line *AF* towards [*vers*] the line
CE [i.e. in a direction perpendicular to *AF*] and the other makes it advance towards *AF* [i.e. parallel to *AF*]? For it is true to say that, in as
much as the ball descends along the line *AB*, it progresses towards [*vers*]
AF [i.e. parallel to *AF*], and that this progress is to be measured by the
perpendiculars [strictly, the distance between the perpendiculars] drawn
to the line *AF* from the various points that can be taken between *A* and
B. And this is to be understood, however, when *AF* makes an acute
angle with *AB*; otherwise, if [the angle] were right or obtuse, the
ball would not advance towards *AF*, as it is easy to understand.

Having supposed this, we will conclude by the same reasoning of the
author [Descartes], that the smoothed body *CE* only hinders the first
movement [viz. the movement perpendicular to *AF*], being opposed to
it only in that direction; so that, not being in the way of the second
[movement], the perpendicular *BH* having been drawn, and *HF* made
equal to *HA*, it follows that the ball must be reflected to the point *F*, and
thus the angle *FBE* will be greater than *ABC*.

It is therefore evident that, of all the divisions of the determination to
motion, which are infinite, the author has taken only that which can serve
to give him his conclusion, of which we know as little as before. And it
certainly appears that an imaginary division that may be varied in an
infinite number of ways never can be the cause of a real effect.

By the same reasoning, we can refute the proof of his foundations for
Dioptrics, since they are based on a similar discourse.[51]

Fermat's construction needs clarification. *AB* may be taken to
represent the velocity of incidence. From *A* he draws a line *AF* to
meet the circumference in *F*, such that the perpendicular *FE* is
greater than the perpendicular *AC*. He then draws *BH* perpendicular
to *AF* and therefore it bisects *AF* in *H*. *BF* represents the velocity
of reflection. The components of *AB* are *AH* and *HB*; and the
components of *BF* are *BH* and *HF*.

It is clear in what sense Fermat believed that his figure satisfied
Descartes' assumptions for deducing the law of reflection as the latter
had expressed them. For in order to justify his assumption about the
conservation of the horizontal component, Descartes had relied
on the fact that the surface was *not opposed* to the motion of the ball
in that direction. But Fermat could make the same claim for his
oblique component *AH* which is actually going away from the
surface. As for Descartes' other condition, it is fulfilled in Fermat's
figure by the equality of *AB* and *BF*.

On the other hand, Fermat's figure does *not* satisfy Descartes'
two conditions as we have formulated them. For we have assumed
in equation (2) above [52] that *i* and *r* are angles made with the normal
to the surface. This, however, is precisely what Fermat would
denounce as arbitrary: why should an imaginary line, the normal
to the surface, be privileged in the definition of *i* and *r*? If *i* and *r*
were angles made instead with any oblique line, such as *HB* in
Fermat's figure, their equality would indeed follow, but not the
equality of the angles *ABC* and *FBE* which Descartes and Fermat
called the angles of incidence and reflection.

Descartes replied[53] by saying that, when he wrote that the motion
can be divided into all the parts of which it can be imagined to be
composed, he meant that it can be 'really' so divided, and not only
by imagination. Any motion can indeed be divided in imagination

[51] Fermat to Mersenne, September 1637, F, II, pp. 109–10.
[52] Above, p. 84.
[53] Descartes to Mersenne, October 1637, F, II, p. 114.

into an infinite number of different components. But the surface *CBE* being a real surface, and also being opposed to the motion of the ball in the perpendicular direction alone, it actually divides the motion of the ball into a perpendicular and a parallel component. Fermat's mistake therefore consisted in the choice of the direction of the oblique *HB* (in Fermat's figure). It was thus Descartes' turn to impute arbitrariness to Fermat's own demonstration.

What did Descartes mean by this? In particular, what did he mean by saying that the reflecting surface was opposed to the motion only in the perpendicular direction? For it must be remembered that the reason he gave in the *Dioptric* for regarding the surface as hindering the downward motion was that the ground 'occupies all the space that is below'. If, therefore, by *opposition to motion in a given direction* he meant that the surface does not allow the ball to pass through *in that direction,* then the surface should be considered equally opposed to the motion in the direction of the oblique *HB*. Descartes was obliged to answer the following question: How did he know that the opposition existed only in the perpendicular direction?

His answer would seem to be implied in his use of the word *real*: the *real* surface *really* divides the ball's motion precisely into the perpendicular and parallel components *as a matter of fact*; our knowledge of the manner in which this division takes place is ultimately based on experience. That is to say, he would seem to agree with Fermat that, before the ball strikes the surface, its motion can be imagined to be divided in an infinite number of ways, and consequently there is so far no reason why one system of axes should be preferred to another. Experiment shows, however, that the ball rebounds in such a way that the horizontal speed remains constant, while the perpendicular speed is reversed. Experiment is therefore the foundation of the supposition that the surface is opposed to the ball's motion in the normal direction; and it is also the basis for the choice of a system in which one axis is perpendicular and the other parallel to the reflecting surface. This kind of argument would thus imply that the mathematical device adopted by Descartes, far from dictating what should take place in nature, was in fact itself informed by the actual behaviour of bodies.

Now Descartes did not make it absolutely clear that this is what he had in mind. The preceding interpretation of his argument, however, seems to be supported by the way he expressed the difference between his own argument and Fermat's.[54] He drew a triangle which he divided into four equal and four unequal triangles. The difference as he saw it between himself and Fermat consisted in the following: both he and Fermat agreed that the triangle could be divided into all those triangles of which it could be imagined to be composed; both also agreed that the same triangle could be imagined to be composed of the four equal triangles; but whereas he, Descartes, *having drawn* the lines joining the middle points on the sides of the original triangle, said that it was, 'really and truly',[55] divided into those equal triangles and no others, Fermat was saying that the triangle *could* be divided into another set of unequal triangles. In other words, the decomposition effected by the reflecting surface corresponded to the actual division of the triangle into four equal ones. It is not a mathematical, or imaginary decomposition, but a physical operation; and, as such, it can only be ascertained by the observation of what actually takes place in nature.

These remarks had no effect on Fermat and he accordingly wrote to Mersenne his final word on the disputed question:

In four words I shall cut short our dispute on reflection which, however, I could prolong further and prove that the author has accommodated his *medium* to his conclusion, about the truth of which he had already been certain; for if I were to deny him that his division of the determinations to motion is the one that must be taken, since we have an infinite number of them, I would compel him to prove a proposition which he would find very embarrassing.[56]

This is but a restatement of his original objections, from which it appears that Fermat remained convinced to the end of the discussion about reflection that Descartes' proof did not constitute a 'legitimate demonstration'.[57]

---

[54] F, II, pp. 114–15.   [55] F, II, p. 115.
[56] F, II, p. 117.   [57] F, II, p. 109.

In agreement with a certain *a priori* conception of matter, and in accordance with the decision to deal with natural phenomena in a purely mathematical fashion, Descartes tried to deduce the reflection law from merely assuming the impenetrability of matter and the conservation of the absolute quantity of motion. Fermat's objections showed that there existed an infinite number of laws, each of which would satisfy both of these assumptions. Subsequent writers, as we shall see, had to introduce new elements. Huygens' kinematical (and, to that extent, Cartesian) treatment of reflection made use of a new idea embodied in his principle of secondary waves and he admitted elasticity as a property of the medium. Newton retained the parallelogram method, but he operated explicitly with forces.

Chapter Four

DESCARTES' EXPLANATION OF
REFRACTION. FERMAT'S 'REFUTATIONS'

1. Ptolemy, who made the first serious experimental study of refraction, was aware of a connection between the change of direction when light passes from one medium into another and the difference in density between the two media. He observed that in rare-to-dense refraction (as when a beam passes from air into water) the light turns towards the normal, and in the reverse case, away from the normal. The amount of deviation from the original path depended on the degree of density-difference: the greater the difference, the greater the deviation. He also compared optical refraction with the passage of a projectile from one medium into another more or less resisting medium.[1]

These remarks became the basis of an elaborate theory of refraction which Ibn al-Haytham developed nine hundred years after Ptolemy, and in which he attempted to explore mathematically the suggested mechanical analogy for optical refraction.

In Bk. VII of his *Optics*[2] Ibn al-Haytham first explains why light

---

[1] Cf. Ptolemaei *Optica*, V, 19, 31 and 33; A. Lejeune, 'Les tables des réfractions de Ptolémée', *Annales de la Société Scientifiques de Bruxelles, série I (Sciences Mathématiques et Physiques)*, LX (1940), pp. 93–101; *Euclide et Ptolémée*, pp. 73–74; *Catoptrique grecque*, p. 158. Definition VI of the pseudo-Euclidean *Catoptrica* describes the experiment in which a coin being placed at the bottom of an empty vessel becomes visible from a certain point when water is poured into the vessel. But there is no application of this observation in the book, and it may have been derived from a lost work attributed to Archimedes; see Lejeune, *Catoptrique grecque*, p. 153. The experiment is recorded in Ptolemaei *Optica*, V, 5; see translation of relevant passage in Marshall Clagett, *Archimedes in the Middle Ages*, I, Madison, 1964, p. 634.

[2] Alhazeni *Optica*, VII, 8, in *Opticae thesaurus*, ed. Risner, pp. 240–2: 'Quare autem refringatur lux, quando occurrit corpori diaphano diversae diaphanitatis, causa haec est: quia transitus lucis per corpora diaphana fit per motum velocissimum, ut declaravimus in tractatu secundo. Luces ergo, quae extenduntur per corpora diaphana, extenduntur motu veloci, qui non patet sensui propter suam velocitatem. Praeterea motus earum in subtilibus corporibus, scilicet in illis, quae valde sunt diaphana, velocior est motu earum in iis, quae sunt grossiora illis, scilicet quae minus sunt diaphana. Omne enim corpus diaphanum, cum lux transit in ipsum, resistit luci aliquantulum, secundum quod habet de grossitie. Nam in omni corpore

93

is refracted when it strikes the surface of a medium denser than the medium of incidence. Light, he says, moves with very great speed (*per motum velocissimum*) in transparent bodies, and its speed is

naturali necesse est, ut sit aliqua grossities; nam corpus parvae diaphanitatis non habet finem in imaginatione, quae est imaginatio lucidae diaphanitatis; et omnia corpora naturalia perveniunt ad finem, quem non possunt transire. Corpora ergo naturalia diaphana non possunt evadere aliquam grossitiem. Luces ergo cum transeunt per corpora diaphana, transeunt secundum diaphanitatem, quae est in eis, et sic impediunt lucem secundum grossitiem, quae est in eis. Cum ergo lux transiverit per corpus diaphanum, et occurrit alii corpori grossiori primo, tunc corpus grossius resistit luci vehementius, quam primum resistebat; et omne motum cum movetur ad aliquam partem essentialiter aut accidentaliter, si occurrerit resistenti, necesse est, ut motus eius transmutetur; et si resistentia fuerit fortis, tunc motus ille refringetur ad contrariam partem; si vero debilis, non refringetur ad contrariam partem, nec poterit per illam procedere, per quam incoeperat, sed motus eius mutabitur.

Omnium autem motorum naturaliter, quae recte moventur per aliquod corpus passibile, transitus super perpendicularem, quae est in superficie corporis, in quo est transitus, erit facilior. Et hoc videtur in corporibus naturalibus. Si enim aliquis acceperit tabulam subtilem, et paxillaverit illam super aliquod foramen amplum, et steterit in oppositione tabulae, et acceperit pilam ferream, et eiecerit eam super tabulam fortiter, et observaverit, ut motus pilae sit super perpendicularem super superficiem tabulae; tunc tabula cedet pilae aut frangetur, si tabula subtilis fuerit, et vis, qua sphaera movetur, fuerit fortis. Et si steterit in parte obliqua ab oppositione tabulae, et in illa eadem distantia, in qua prius erat, et eiecerit pilam super tabulam illam eandem, in quam prius eiecerat; tunc sphaera labetur de tabula, si tabula non fuerit valde subtilis, nec movebitur ad illam partem, ad quam primo movebatur, sed declinabit ad aliquam partem aliam. Et similiter, si acceperit ensem, et posuerit coram se lignum, et percusserit cum ense, ita ut ensis sit perpendicularis super superficiem ligni, tunc lignum secabitur magis; et si fuerit obliquus, et percusserit oblique lignum, tunc lignum non secabitur omnino, sed forte secabitur in parte, aut forte ensis errabit deviando; et quanto magis fuerit ensis obliquus, tanto minus aget in lignum; et alia multa sunt similia; ex quibus patet, quod motus super perpendicularem est fortior et facilior, et quod de obliquis motibus, ille, qui vicinior est perpendiculari, est facilior remotiore.

Lux ergo, si occurrit corpori diaphano grossiori illo corpore, in quo existit, tunc impedietur ab eo, ita quod non transibit in partem, in quam movebatur, sed quia non fortiter resistit, non redibit in partem, ad quam movebatur. Si ergo motus lucis transiverit super perpendicularem, transibit recte propter fortitudinem motus super perpendicularem; et si motus eius fuerit super lineam obliquam, tunc non poterit transire propter debilitatem motus; accidit ergo, ut declinetur ad partem motus, in quam facilius movebitur, quam in partem, in quam movebatur; sed facilior motuum est super perpendicularem; et quod vicinius est perpendiculari, est facilius remotiore. Et motus in corpore, in quod transit, si fuerit obliquus super superficiem illius corporis, componitur ex motu in parte perpendicularis transeuntis in corpus, in quo est motus, et ex motu in parte lineae, quae est perpendicularis super perpendicularem, quae transit in ipsum.

Cum ergo lux fuerit mota in corpore diaphano grosso super lineam obliquam, tunc transitus eius in illo corpore diaphano erit per motum compositum ex duobus praedictis motibus. Et quia grossities corporis resistit ei ad verticationem, quam intendebat, et resistentia eius non est valde fortis; ex quo sequeretur, quod declinaret ad partem, ad quam facilius transiret; et motus super perpendicularem est facilimus motuum; necesse est ergo, ut lux, quae extenditur super lineam obliquam, moveatur super perpendicularem, exeuntem a puncto, in quo lux occurrit superficiei corporis diaphani grossi. Et quia motus eius est compositus ex duobus motibus, quorum alter est super lineam perpendicularem super superficiem corporis grossi, et reliquus super lineam perpendicularem super perpendicularem hanc; et motus compositus,

greater in a rare body (such as air) than in a dense body (such as water or glass). He accounts for the variable speed of light as follows: all natural bodies, including transparent bodies, share in the property of grossness, density or opacity; any transparent body can thus be imagined to be more transparent than it is; owing to their density, all transparent bodies resist the movement of light; the denser they are, the greater the resistance they offer.

When, therefore, light strikes the surface of a denser body, its movement must be altered (*transmutatur*). But since the resistance is not strong enough to repel the movement altogether (as is the case in reflection), the movement is only weakened.

Now, he observes, a natural body finds it easier to break through 'passive' bodies along the perpendicular to their surfaces than in any other direction. For example a small iron sphere thrown perpendicularly on to a thin plate (*tabula*) covering a wide opening will in most cases break the plate and pass through, whereas if thrown obliquely with the same force and from the same distance

---

qui est in ipso, non omnino dimittitur, sed solummodo impeditur; necesse est, ut lux declinet ad partem faciliorem parte, ad quam prius movebatur, remanente in ipso motu composito; sed pars facilior parte, ad quam movebatur remanente motu in ipso, est illa pars, quae est vicinor perpendiculari. Unde lux, quae extenditur in corpore diaphano, si occurrit corpori diaphano grossiori corpore, in quo existit, refringetur per lineam propinquiorem perpendiculari, exeunti a puncto, in quo occurrit corpori grossiori, quae extenditur in corpore grossiore per aliam lineam quam sit linea, per quam movebatur. Haec ergo causa est refractionis splendoris in corporibus diaphanis, quae sunt grossiora corporibus diaphanis, in quibus existunt; et ideo refractio proprie est inventa in lucibus obliquis. Cum ergo lux extenditur in corpore diaphano, et occurrerit corpori diaphano diversae diaphanitatis a corpore, in quo existit, et grossiori, et fuerit obliqua super superficiem corporis diaphani cui occurrit, refringetur ad partem perpendicularis super superficiem corporis diaphani extensae in corpore grossiore.

Causa autem, quae facit refractionem lucis a corpore grossiore ad corpus subtilius ad partem contrariam parti perpendicularis, est: quia cum lux mota fuerit in corpore diaphano, repellet eam aliqua repulsione, et corpus grossius repellet eam maiore repulsione, sicut lapis, cum movetur in aere, movetur facilius et velocius, quam si moveretur in aqua; eo quod aqua repellit ipsum maiore repulsione, quam aer. Cum ergo lux exierit a corpore grossiore in subtilius, tunc motus eius erit velocior. Et cum lux fuerit obliqua super duas superficies corporis diaphani, quod est differentia communis ambobus corporibus, tunc motus eius erit super lineam existentem inter perpendicularem, exeuntem a principio motus eius, et inter perpendicularem super lineam perpendicularem, exeuntem etiam a principio motus. Resistentia ergo corporis grossioris erit a parte, ad quam exit secunda perpendicularis. Cum ergo lux exiverit a corpore grossiore, et pervenerit ad corpus subtilius, tunc resistentia corporis subtilioris facta luci, quae est in parte, ad quam secunda exit perpendicularis, erit minor prima resistentia; et fit motus lucis ad partem, a qua resistebatur, maior. Et sic est de luce in corpore subtiliore ad partem contrariam parti perpendicularis.'

The Latin closely follows the Arabic text, Istanbul MS. Fātiḥ 3216, fols. 28ʳ9–31ᵛ3.

it will only slide on the surface of the plate without breaking it. Similarly a sword breaks a piece of wood more easily when applied perpendicularly; the more obliquely it strikes the wood the weaker its effect. This helps to establish the general principle 'that movement on the perpendicular is stronger and easier, and of the oblique movements that which is nearer the perpendicular is easier than that which is farther from it'.

Analogically a perpendicular ray enters into a dense body in the same line because of the strength of the movement along this line. The movement of an oblique ray is, however, not strong enough to maintain the same direction. Consequently, the light turns into another direction along which its passage will be easier; that is, it turns towards the normal.

As in his treatment of reflection Ibn al-Haytham considers the incident movement to consist of two perpendicular components; and he makes use of this here to explain why an oblique ray is not always refracted into the perpendicular itself which, according to him, would be the easiest path. He argues that since the compounded (resultant) movement is not completely destroyed at the interface, the light continues to have in the refracting medium both a perpendicular and a parallel component; that is to say it takes a path situated between the original direction and the normal to the surface at the point of incidence.

His application of the parallelogram method to the refraction from a dense into a rare medium is more interesting, though perhaps more problematic. In this case the light meets with less resistance at the common surface, 'just as a stone moves more easily and quickly in air than in water, since the water resists it [repellit ipsum] more than the air'. Here Ibn al-Haytham assumes that the resistance acts particularly in the direction of the component parallel to the surface. Since the resistance in that direction was greater in the denser medium than in the rarer medium of refraction, the light is allowed to turn away from the normal. What is the basis of this assumption? Why should the decrease in resistance, and hence the increase in speed, take place particularly in the parallel direction? As a possible explanation we may note that the observed fact that in the dense-to-rare refraction the light turns away from the normal, and the supposition that the velocity of refraction is in this case greater than the velocity of incidence, together entail the conclusion that the parallel velocity must have increased. It is also interesting to note that he says nothing about what happens in this case to the perpendicular velocity.[3] For (again on the supposition that the actual speed has become greater) the increase in the parallel velocity (when the deflection is farther from the normal) is mathematically compatible with any one of three alternatives: the perpendicular velocity may increase, decrease, or remain constant.

Now let us suppose that Ibn al-Haytham moved one step further and assumed the increase in the parallel velocity to be in a constant ratio. His assumption would have been expressible in this form:

(a) $$v_r \sin r = m \, v_i \sin i,$$

where i = angle of incidence, r = angle of refraction, v_i = velocity of incidence, v_r = velocity of refraction, and m = a constant. Combining this with another assumption that he made, namely that the velocity of light is a property of the medium, or

(b) $$v_r = n \, v_i,$$

where n is a constant, the conclusion follows that

(c) $$\frac{\sin i}{\sin r} = \frac{m}{n} = k, \text{ a constant.}$$

In other words, the sines of the angles of incidence and refraction are in a constant ratio, which is the geometrical statement of the law of refraction. (In the form (c) the refraction index k would not of course depend solely on the constant ratio of the velocities n.)

He did not, however, take that step; but something, I think, may be learnt from our supposition: it was *not impossible* to arrive at the sine law along this path. We shall see that Descartes derived the law from two assumptions, of which one is identical with (b) and the other can be obtained from (a) by putting $m = 1$. This yields the

---

[3] H. J. J. Winter, in 'The optical researches of Ibn al-Haytham', *Centaurus*, III (1954), p. 201, attributes to Ibn al-Haytham the assumption that the velocity along the normal to the refracting surface remains constant. But there is nothing to support this either in the Arabic text or in the Latin translation.

law in the form $\dfrac{\sin i}{\sin r} = \dfrac{v_r}{v_i} = n$, a constant. While this does not explain how in fact he discovered the law, his derivation appears less *ad hoc* in the light of Ibn al-Haytham's treatment than it might without it.[4]

Practically all subsequent explanations of refraction, up until the publication of Descartes' *Dioptric*, were almost entirely dependent upon Ibn al-Haytham; and Descartes' explanation itself was largely based on considerations which he may have derived either directly from Risner's edition of Ibn al-Haytham's *Optics*, or indirectly through Witelo and Kepler.

Roger Bacon, Witelo and Kepler all made the assertion that movement along the normal was stronger than oblique movement, and they all attributed the refraction of oblique rays at an interface to the weakness of oblique incidence.[5]

Again, all three of them explained the rare-to-dense refraction towards the perpendicular by reference to the principle that the nearer the movement is to the perpendicular, the stronger, easier and quicker it is. Witelo cites in this connection the principle '*natura . . . frustra nihil agit*',[6] thus linking ideas that were later explored by Fermat.

Bacon and Witelo considered that all transparent bodies being somewhat gross or dense, they all must resist the movement of light with varying degrees; both adopted the view that transparency (or rarity) has no upper limit.

Bacon ignored the resolution of motion into perpendicular components, but it was adopted by Witelo and Kepler.[7] They both asserted that the compounded movement of an oblique incident ray is not totally abolished, but only impeded; hence the movement of

---

[4] There is no foundation for V. Ronchi's statement that 'Descartes demonstrates the law of refraction by the same reasoning as that of Alhazen' (*Histoire de la lumière*, Paris, 1956, p. 115). It is not the case that for Ibn al-Haytham the parallel velocity remains unchanged in refraction (ibid., p. 44).

[5] Cf. R. Bacon, *De multiplicatione specierum*, II, 3, *Opus majus*, ed. Bridges, II, especially pp. 468–9; Vitellonis *Optica*, II, 47, in *Opticae thesaurus*, ed. Risner, pp. 81–83; Kepler, *Paralipomena* (1604), I, Proposition XX, pp. 15–17, and p. 84.

[6] Vitellonis *Optica*, p. 82, line 21 from bottom.

[7] Vitellonis *Optica*, end of p. 82; Kepler, *Paralipomena*, p. 84.

the ray is merely altered, that is, refracted into a new direction that still consists of a perpendicular and a parallel component.

Light striking the surface of a dense medium was compared by Kepler to the impinging of a small sphere (*sphaerula*) on a water surface: the movement is weakened as a result of being somewhat repelled by the surface.[8] This brings to the fore the idea that refraction is due to a surface action.

Witelo explained refraction into a rare medium in a line going away from the perpendicular by the assumption that the resistance becomes less in the direction parallel to the interface.[9]

It will have been noticed that in all this hardly anything was added to what these authors had already found in the *Optics* of Ibn al-Haytham.

2. The law of refraction was published for the first time by Descartes in the *Dioptric* in 1637—fifteen hundred years after Ptolemy had made an attempt to discover the law experimentally. Ptolemy's initiative was not abandoned during that period; his pioneering

---

[8] *Paralipomena*, p. 16.

[9] Vitellonis *Optica*, II, 47, p. 83: 'Cum vero radius *ac* exiverit a corpore grossiore ad subtilius, tunc quia minus habet resistentiae, erit motus eius velociter et magis sui diffusivus. Et quoniam resistentia medii densioris impellit semper lucem obliquam, ut coadunetur ad perpendicularem lineam a puncto incidentiae super superficiem illius corporis productam, quae est *cg*,

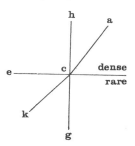

patet, quod in medio rarioris diaphani illa resistentia erit minor quam prima; fit ergo motus lucis ad partem, a qua per resistentiam repellebatur motus maior. Movetur ergo lux in corpore diaphano rariore plus ad partem contrariam parti perpendicularis, ita, quod angulus *gck* sit maior angulo *ach*; fit tamen semper motus lucis *ac* in refractione a corpore secundo rarioris diaphani quam primum, inter lineas *cg* et *ce*; quoniam cum angulus *gce* sit rectus, angulus *gck* nunquam potest fieri rectus.'

investigations were continued by such assiduous students of optics as Ibn al-Haytham, Witelo and Kepler, who tried to bring theoretical considerations to bear upon the problem of refraction. There was, however, no success until, apparently almost simultaneously, Snell and Descartes hit upon the correct law.[10] It is not known for certain when exactly Snell made his discovery, and we have no exact idea about how he made it. His work on refraction, seen in manuscript by Jacobus Golius, Isaac Vossius and Christian Huygens, has since been lost;[11] the autograph of the table of contents, containing Snell's own formulation of the law, has been found and published by C. de Waard, but it bears no date.[12] J. A. Vollgraff has suggested

---

[10] Recent research has indicated an earlier experimental determination of the sine law by Thomas Harriott. So far no connection has been established between Harriott's work and that of Snell or Descartes. See J. W. Shirley, 'An early experimental determination of Snell's law', *American Journal of Physics*, XIX (1951), pp. 507–8; Johs. Lohne, 'Thomas Harriott (1560–1621), the Tycho Brahe of optics', *Centaurus*, VI (1959), pp. 113–21.

The important studies on Snell and on the question of Descartes' possible dependence on his work are the following:

P. Kramer, 'Descartes und das Brechungsgesetz des Licthes', *Abhandlungen zur Geschichte der Mathematik*, IV (1882), pp. 233–78; P. van Geer, 'Notice sur la vie et les travaux de Willebrord Snellius', *Archives néerlandaises des sciences exactes et naturelles*, XVIII (1883), pp. 453–68; D.-J. Korteweg, 'Descartes et les manuscrits de Snellius d'après quelques documents nouveaux', *Revue de métaphysique et de morale*, IV (1896), pp. 489–501; Gaston Milhaud, *Descartes savant*, Paris, 1921, pp. 103–23 (Ch. IV: 'Les travaux d'optique de 1620 à 1629', first published as 'Descartes et la loi des sinus', *Revue générale des sciences*, XVIII, 1907;) J. A. Vollgraff, 'Pierre de la Ramée (1515–1572) et Willebrord Snel van Royen (1580–1626)', *Janus*, XVIII (1913), pp. 515–25; 'Snellius' notes on the reflection and refraction of rays', *Osiris*, I (1936), pp. 718–25; C. de Waard, 'Le manuscrit perdu de Snellius sur la réfraction', *Janus*, XXXIX (1935), pp. 51–73; J. F. Scott, *The Scientific Work of René Descartes (1596–1650)*, London, 1952, pp. 36–39 (a summary of Korteweg's article).

[11] Regarding the nature of Snell's research Huygens has briefly stated that Snell arrived at the correct measure of refractions 'after much effort and many experiments [*multo labore multisque experimentis*] . . . without, however, sufficiently understanding what he had discovered' (H, XIII, p. 7). The last words refer to Snell's incorrect explanation of the apparent raising of objects immersed in water by the contraction of vertical rays. C. de Waard points out that the contraction hypothesis was debated in Snell's time, and he refers to discussions taking place in 1604 and 1607 between Kepler and Brengger who held the same opinion as that of Snell; cf. *Janus*, XXXIX (1935), p. 55, n. 2.

[12] Snell expresses the law in the following words: 'Radius verus ad apparentem in uno eodemque medio diverso eandem habent inter se rationem. Ut secans complementi inclinationis in raro ad secantem [complementi] refracti in denso, ita radio apparens ad verum seu incidentiae radium' (C. de Waard, *Janus*, XXXIX, 1935, p. 64). What he calls 'radius verus' is the refracted ray, and the 'radius apparens' is the prolongation of the incident ray from the point of incidence until it meets the normal drawn from the foot of the refracted ray to the interface. This is equivalent to the proportionality: cosec i : cosec $r=k$, a constant (where i and r are the angles of incidence and refraction made with the normal to the surface at the point of incidence).

that Snell already knew the law in 1621, but this was proposed as a mere conjecture unsupported by positive evidence; the dated text of Snell on which it was based deals with reflection, not refraction.[13]

Snell died in 1626. When Golius found his manuscript in 1632, the law of refraction had already been known to several scholars close to Snell, including Golius himself; they all attributed the law to Descartes. No one seems to have been aware of Snell's result until Golius made his discovery.[14] The first publicly to accuse Descartes of plagiarizing the law from Snell's manuscript was Isaac Vossius, who published his accusation in 1662.[15] Christian Huygens had already expressed certain doubts, however. He wrote in his *Dioptrica* (begun in 1653 and first published posthumously in 1703) that he assumed (*accepimus*) that Descartes had seen Snell's manuscript, adding that 'perhaps' (*fortasse*) it was from this

---

[13] In a note appended to Bk. III (*De visione composita reflexa*) of Risner's *Optica*, Snell wrote on 22 December 1621 that 'the place of the image follows in each case a well-defined perpendicular in such a way that always the incident ray observes to the place of the image from the point of incidence its own perpetual proportion'. ('At locus imaginis certas in singulis perpendiculares ita sequiter ut semper radius incidentiae ad locum imaginis a puncto incidentiae in singulis suam et perpetuam analogiam observet.') Taking this to refer to a constant ratio between the distance of the object to the point of incidence and the distance of the image to the same point, and noting the form in which Snell in fact expressed the refraction law (see preceding note), Vollgraff concludes: 'I do not see that the same formula applies—or could be thought by Snellius to apply—to the case of reflection. Notwithstanding the fact that these words occur in a note on reflection, I venture therefore, not to affirm, but to suggest, that at the same time, December 1621, Snellius had already found the law of refraction' (*Osiris*, I, 1936, p. 724). On the next page he remarks: 'The fact that the law of refraction is not mentioned in the marginal notes belonging to Book IV [*De visione refracta*], may easily be explained by admitting that they were written at an earlier date than December 1621.' He further remarks that Snell lectured on optics at Leiden in 1621, and that Descartes is believed to have stayed at the Hague in winter 1621–2. But he adds: 'Unfortunately it is quite impossible to say in what manner Snellius spoke that winter about reflection and refraction, and what of his sayings, if any, may have reached the ears of Descartes' (ibid., p. 724, n. 14). When Descartes began his next long sojourn at Leiden in 1629 (three years after Snell's death), he had already been acquainted with the law; see Van Geer, op. cit., p. 467.

[14] So far as we know, Snell's work on optics was first mentioned by a friend who was present at his death, André Rivet, in a letter to Mersenne written in 1628. It is doubtful that he was acquainted with the contents of Snell's manuscript. Isaac Beeckman was Rivet's and Snell's friend; he learnt of the sine law from Descartes in 1628; when he later alluded to research on the subject of refraction he could only think of Kepler. See letter of Mersenne to André Rivet, 25 December 1628, *Correspondance du P. Marin Mersenne*, II (1936), pp. 157–8, and 161–2; C. de Waard, *Janus*, XXXIX (1935), p. 53. See also, Korteweg, op cit., pp. 495–9.

[15] Cf. Issac Vossius, *De lucis natura et proprietate*, 1662, p. 36. Vossius may have seen Snell's manuscript in the winter of 1661; cf. C. de Waard, *Janus*, XXXIX (1935), p. 55.

manuscript that Descartes had derived the sine law.[16] Later, in 1693, he wrote that the law was 'not the invention of Mr. des Cartes in all likelihood [*selon toutes les apparences*], for it is certain that he has seen the manuscript book of Snellius, which I have also seen'.[17] It is to be noted that in these two passages Huygens was more sure of Descartes' having seen Snell's manuscript than of his having derived the law from it.

There exists in fact other evidence in support of the assumption that Descartes learnt of Snell's discovery at some time during the period 1632–1637. This appears from the following circumstances. It was in arrangement with Descartes that Golius had planned to test Descartes' law experimentally before he discovered Snell's manuscript in 1632.[18] In November of the same year Golius communicated the news of his finding to Constantin Huygens,[19] whose friendship with Descartes continued until the publication of the *Dioptric* in 1637. As Korteweg has remarked, it does not seem likely that Descartes could not have been informed by either Golius or Constantin Huygens of Snell's work. But there are no texts to support this suspicion.

Nevertheless, the assumption that Descartes deliberately suppressed his knowledge of Snell's discovery after he had learnt about it in or shortly after 1632 does not settle the question of plagiarism. For it can be ascertained from Descartes' correspondence that he already had the sine law in 1626 or 1627, when he persuaded his friend Claude Mydorge to have a hyperbolic glass made to test it.[20] That was five or six years before Golius found Snell's manuscript.

Thus, it is still valid to repeat today the conclusion reached by Korteweg in 1896, namely that neither the question of Descartes'

---

[16] Cf. H, XIII, p. 9. Huygens attributed the law to Descartes until at least 8 March 1662. In January 1665 he wrote of the 'principle which has been employed in Dioptrics since Snellius and Monsieur Desc.' He probably saw Snell's manuscript in 1662 or 1663; ibid., p. 9, n. 1; H, V, p. 188.

[17] Cf. H, X, p. 405.

[18] Cf. Descartes to Golius, 2 February 1632, D, I, pp. 236–40.

[19] Golius' letter to Constantin Huygens, dated 1st November 1632, was discovered and published by Korteweg; see *Revue de métaphysique et de morale*, IV (1896), pp. 491–5.

[20] Cf. Descartes to Golius, 2 February 1632, D, I, p. 239; Descartes to Constantin Huygens, December 1635, D, I, p. 335–6. Cf. G. Milhaud, *Descartes savant*, p. 104.

originality nor that of priority can be settled on the evidence available: he may well have discovered the law of refraction independently of Snell (indeed this is more likely than the contrary supposition), and his discovery may have antedated that of Snell.

If, in the absence of any evidence to the contrary, we have to assume that Descartes made an independent discovery of the sine law, the question now to be asked is: how did he make it? As is often the case with similar questions in the history of science it is not easy to give a sure answer. One thing is certain, however: he did not discover the law 'by experiment'. He himself wrote in 1632 that the only experiment he had ever made was with the glass designed by Mydorge in 1626 or 1627 *for the purpose of verifying* the law he had already arrived at. The result of the experiment agreed with what he had predicted. 'Which assured me either that the Craftsman had fortunately failed, or that my reasoning was not false.'[21] What was the nature of the 'reasoning' that had led him to his prediction? The only argument that we have from Descartes for establishing the law of refraction is that presented in the second chapter of the *Dioptric*. It is, as we shall see, an argument based on comparing the refraction of light to the behaviour of a projectile when passing through a surface offering more or less resistance, and in which he applied the method of resolving motions that had been already applied to the same problem by Ibn al-Haytham, Witelo and Kepler. Had he arrived at the law by a different line of thought, what reason would he have had for suppressing it, especially since he was convinced of its correctness, as the passage from the letter to Golius shows?[22]

---

[21] Descartes to Golius, 2 February 1632, D, I, p. 239: 'Si vous n'auez point encore pensé au moyen de faire cette experience, comme ie sçay que vous auez beaucoup de meilleures occupations, peut-estre que celuy-cy vous semblera bien aussi aisé, que l'instrument que dècrit Vitellion. Toutesfois ie puis bien me tromper, car ie ne me suis point seruy ny de l'vn ny de l'autre, & toute l'experience que i'ay iamais faite en cette matiere, est que ie fis tailler vn Verre, il y a enuiron cinq ans, dont M. Mydorge traça luymesme le modelle; & lorsque qu'il fut fait, tous les rayons du Soleil qui passoient au trauers s'assembloient tous en vn point, iustement à la distance que i'auois predite. Ce qui m'assura, on que l'Ouurier auoit heureusement failly, ou que ma ratiocination n'estoit pas fausse.' Korteweg further points out that, given the technological difficulties involved, an experiment performed with a hyperbolic lens could not be decisive; cf. *Revue de métaphysique et de morale*, IV (1896), p. 500.

[22] In 1882 Kramer (op. cit., pp. 233–78) proposed an alternative explanation of how Descartes might have arrived at the sine law. According to his hypothesis, later endorsed by G.

Referring to the deduction of the sine law in the *Dioptric* Paul Tannery has remarked that Descartes was the first to give an example of what theoretical physics should be like, by showing how mathematics could be applied to physical problems. The ancients, Tannery pointed out, had only provided models for statics, the theory of centres of gravity and the principle of Archimedes; and Galileo's *Dialogues* were not published until 1638, that is, after the *Dioptric*.[23] The particular interest and importance of the Cartesian deduction has been recognized even by unsympathetic readers both in his and in our own time. To take only two examples. Fermat, who never accepted Descartes' reasoning for establishing the law of refraction, wrote that he 'much appreciated the spirit and invention of the author'.[24] And Ernst Mach, who described Descartes' explanation of refraction as 'unintelligible and unscientific', admitted that it 'exerted a very stimulating influence' upon subsequent writers.[25] Nevertheless, the general view of Descartes' proof has been that it is open to serious objections. Fermat first denounced the proof from a mathematical point of view, and his opinion seems to have been shared later by Huygens[26] and Leibniz.[27] This agreement among

Milhaud (op. cit., pp. 103–23), Descartes was led to his discovery by the study of conic sections; and this is confirmed by the fact that the experiment suggested to Mydorge for testing the law was with a hyperbolic lens. (See letter of Mydorge to Mersenne of probably February–March 1626, in *Correspondance du P. Marin Mersenne*, I, pp. 404–15.) While there is nothing to refute this conjecture, it would seem quite removed from the way we know Descartes was disposed to think about the problem of refraction, not only in the *Dioptric* and *Le Monde*, but also earlier in the *Regulae* (where the problem of the anaclastic is viewed as a physico-mathematical problem, not to be solved by mathematical means alone, see above, pp. 29ff), and earlier still in the *Cogitationes privatae* (see below, p. 105f).

[23] Cf. P. Tannery, 'Descartes physicien', *Revue de métaphysique et de morale*, 1896, p. 480; *Mémoires*, VI (1926), pp. 307–8.

[24] Fermat to Mersenne, September 1637, F, II, p. 111. Descartes' first public accuser, Isaac Vossius, thought the style of demonstration was new (J. F. Scott, op. cit., p. 37).

[25] E. Mach, *Principles of Physical Optics*, London, 1926, pp. 33 and 34.

[26] 'It has always seemed to me (and to many others besides me) that even Mr. Des Cartes, whose aim has been to treat all the subjects of Physics intelligibly, and who assuredly has succeeded in this better than any one before him, has said nothing that is not full of difficulties, or even inconceivable, in dealing with Light and its properties' (Huygens, *Treatise on Light*, p. 7). The words in parentheses are missing in the English translation; cf. H, XIX, pp. 465 and 467.

[27] Cf. Leibniz, *Discours de métaphysique*, edited by Henri Lestienne, 2nd edition, Paris, 1952, Article XXII, p. 67: 'And the demonstration of the same theorem [i.e., the sine law] which M. des Cartes wished to offer by way of the efficient [causes], is far from being as good [as Fermat's demonstration of the same law by the final causes, i.e. the principle of least

three of the greatest mathematicians of their time has had one effect that is interesting from our point of view: it strengthened the suspicion that Descartes did not himself discover the law. How could he have arrived at the law deductively, when the only argument he has for establishing it is so faulty? Not, of course, that this is impossible, but it would seem rather improbable. Mach, for example, adopts this kind of argument when he remarks that after reading Descartes' 'unintelligible' deductions in the second chapter of the *Dioptric*, 'it will scarcely be assumed . . . that Descartes discovered the law of refraction. It was easy for him as an applied geometrician to bring Snell's law into a *new* form, and as a pupil of the Jesuits to "establish" this form.'[28] The assumption on which this argument rests is not true. For from a mathematical point of view, Descartes' proof is perfectly correct; indeed, no less a mathematician than Newton thought it 'not inelegant'.[29] Moreover, the suggestion that Descartes artificially constructed an argument to establish the law which he had derived in a different form from other sources seems far-fetched. In any case there is no historical evidence to support it.

3. Descartes' interest in optics, and particularly in the problem of refraction, goes back to the early period of 1619–21. The notebook, known as the *Cogitationes privatae*, in which he recorded his thoughts at that time, has the following passage:

Since light can be produced only in matter, where there is more matter it is produced more easily, other things being equal; therefore it penetrates more easily through a denser than through a rarer medium. Whence it comes about that the refraction is made in the latter away from the perpendicular, in the former towards the perpendicular. . . .[30]

---

time]. At least there is reason to suspect that he would not have found it by those means, if he had not learnt in Holland about Snell's discovery.' It is to be noted that already in Leibniz's time the alleged deficiency in Descartes' proof was taken to confirm the view that he did not discover the sine law independently of Snell.

[28] Mach, op. cit., p. 33. See also Van Geer, op. cit., pp. 466–7.

[29] Newton, *Optical Lectures*, London, 1728, p. 47; below, p. 300.

[30] D, X, pp. 242–3: 'Lux quia non nisi in materia potest generari, vbi plus est materiae, ibi facilius generatur, caeteris paribus; ergo facilius penetrat per medium densius quam per

Two assertions are made here, one after the other. The first states a view which is contrary to what had been universally accepted since Aristotle,[31] namely that 'light penetrates more easily through a denser than through a rarer medium'. Descartes bases this assertion on the particular connection he establishes between light and matter, a connection which gained greater plausibility in Newton's theory of refraction.[32]

The second assertion, beginning with 'whence', in fact records an observation that is completely independent of any view regarding the speed of light in different media. Why, then, does Descartes present this second assertion as a consequence of the first? Now such a deduction can be performed if we combine with the first assertion a further assumption expressed in the *Dioptric*, viz. that the horizontal component of the incident velocity is unaltered by refraction. This combination, however, would necessarily yield the sine law. Did Descartes therefore possess the sine law when he wrote the above passage in 1619–21?[33] Was this law already associated at this time with a proof similar to that published in the *Dioptric*? If not, what were his reasons for regarding the deflection from or towards the normal as a result of the decrease or increase in speed respectively? Why 'whence'?

On the other hand, if we do not think it likely that his reasons were connected with the proof published in 1637, then we must at least grant that Descartes' first assertion (the speed of light is greater

---

rarius. Vnde fit vt refractio fiat in hoc a perpendiculari, in alio ad perpendicularem; omnium autem maxima refractio esset in ipsa perpendiculari, si medium esset densissimum; a quo iterum exiens radius egrederetur per eumdem angulum.'

[31] Cf. Aristotle, *Meteorologica*, I, 5, 342[b] 5.

[32] In Newton's theory the light rays suffer a greater attraction towards the particles of the denser body than towards those of the rarer body; accordingly the speed must be greater in the former than in the latter. See below, pp. 301ff.

[33] According to G. Milhaud (op. cit., p. 109, n. 1) the proof presented in the *Dioptric* was not formulated until after 1628–29. C. de Waard (*Correspondance du P. Marin Mersenne*, I, 1932, p. 426) finds the earliest evidence of Descartes' use of the method employed in that proof in Isaac Beeckman's notes of 1633. It should be noted, however, that already in 1626 when Mydorge explained his propositions on hyperbolic glasses to Mersenne, he illustrated the sine law (which he had learnt from Descartes) with reference to a diagram from which the constancy of the parallel velocity could be deduced, and which would consequently yield the law in the form $\frac{\sin i}{\sin r} = \frac{v_r}{v_i} =$ a constant, that is the form obtained in the *Dioptric*. Cf. ibid., p. 405.

in denser media) was not simply an embarrassing result of an artificially constructed proof, or a price paid for obtaining a desired
physico-mathematical demonstration of the sine law. The grounds
for this assertion would be totally independent of the form this
demonstration took in the *Dioptric*. We now turn to Descartes'
treatment of refraction in that work.

In the Cartesian model for refraction a tennis ball strikes a frail
canvas which takes the place of the breakable plate in Ibn al-
Haytham's corresponding analogy. Arriving from *A* at *B* (Fig. IV.1)
the ball breaks through the canvas 'thus losing only a part of its
speed, say a half'.[34] That the loss relates to the actual speed along
AB is made clear by further steps in the argument.

Having assumed this, let us observe again, in order to know what course
the ball must follow, that its motion is entirely different from its determination to move in one direction rather than another; from which it
follows that their quantities must be examined separately. And let us
also note that of the two parts of which this determination can be imagined
to be composed, only that which makes the ball tend downwards can in
any way be changed by the encounter with the canvas; and that the other

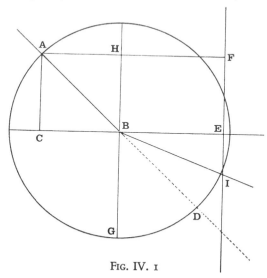

FIG. IV. 1

[34] *Dioptric*, II, D, VI, p. 97.

which makes it tend to the right must always remain the same as it was, because the canvas is not in any way opposed to it in this direction.

Then, having described the circle *AFD* with *B* as centre, and drawn the three straight lines *AC*, *HB*, *FE* at right angles with *CBE*, such that the distance between *FE* and *HB* is twice that between *HB* and *AC*, we shall see that the ball must tend towards the point *I*. For, since the ball loses half of its speed in going through the canvas *CBE*, it must employ twice the time it took above the canvas from *A* to *B*, to travel below from *B* to any point on the circumference of the circle *AFD*. And since it loses nothing whatsoever of its former determination to advance in the right hand direction, in twice the time which it employed to go from the line *AC* to *HB*, it must cover twice the distance in the same direction, and consequently arrive at a point on the straight line *FE* at the same moment as it also reaches a point on the circumference of the circle *ADF*. But this would be impossible if it did not proceed towards *I*, as this is the only point below the canvas *CBE* where the circle *AFD* and the straight line *EF* intersect.[35]

The same considerations apply when, instead of the canvas, the ball strikes a water surface: once the 'force' of the ball is diminished in the same ratio by the opposition of the surface it proceeds in the same straight line:

as to the rest of the water which fills all the space from *B* to *I*, although it resists the ball more or less than did the air which we previously supposed to be there, we should not say for this reason that it deflects it more or less. For the water can open itself up, to make way for the ball, just as easily in one direction as in another, at least if we assume all the time, as we do, that neither the heaviness or lightness of this ball, nor its size, nor figure, nor any other such external cause may change its course.[36]

The more obliquely the ball strikes the surface the more it is deflected towards it, until at a certain inclination it 'must not go through the surface, but rebound . . . just as if it encountered there the surface of the ground. An experiment which was regretfully made sometimes when, firing cannon balls for amusement's sake towards the bottom of the river, one hurt those who were on the other side.'[37]

---

[35] Ibid., pp. 97–98.   [36] Ibid., pp. 98–99.   [37] Ibid., p. 99.

Descartes' figure for this case shows the perpendicular to the surface from *F* outside the circle, thus indicating the impossibility of refraction.[38]

To account for the deflection towards the normal, Descartes supposes that the ball on reaching *B* (Fig. IV. 2)

is pushed once more . . . by the racquet *CBE* which increases the force of its motion, for example by a third, such that it can now travel in two moments a distance which it formerly covered in three. And the same effect would be produced if the ball encountered at *B* a body of such a nature that it would pass through its surface *CBE* a third more easily than through the air.[39]

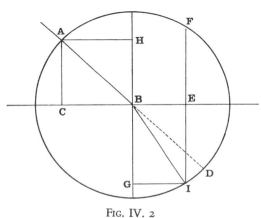

FIG. IV. 2

Accordingly he draws the perpendicular *FE* at a distance *BF*=2/3 *CB*; the direction of refraction is determined by the point *I* at which *FE* cuts the circle.[40]

It is of course assumed throughout that 'the action of light follows in this the same laws as the motion of this ball'.[41] When, therefore,

---

[38] See Fermat's comments, below, pp. 130 ff.

[39] *Dioptric*, II, D, VI, pp. 99–100.

[40] Descartes adds: 'But one may also take the converse of this conclusion and say that, since the ball coming from *A* in straight line to *B* is deflected at *B* and takes its course from there towards *I*, this means that the force or facility with which it enters into the body *CBEI* to that with which it goes out of the body *ACBE*, is as the distance between *AC* and *HB* to that between *HB* and *FI*, i.e. as *CB* to *BE*' (ibid., p. 100).

[41] Ibid., p. 100.

rays of light 'pass obliquely from one transparent body into another which receives them more or less easily than the first, they are deflected in such a way that their inclination to the surface of these bodies is always less on the side of the body which receives them more easily, than on the other side: and this exactly in proportion as it receives them more easily than the other.'[42] The inclinations, Descartes adds, should be measured by lines such as *AH* and *IG*, not by angles such as *ABH* and *GBI*, 'nor even by the magnitudes of angles similar to *DBI* which are called the angles of refraction'.[43]

4. In all the cases considered by Descartes he assumes the incident motion to be increased or decreased at refraction in a given ratio. What he immediately infers from this assumption makes it quite clear that what is so increased or decreased is the actual motion or speed. For suppose, as in the first case, that the canvas deprives the ball of exactly half its speed. To deduce from this, as Descartes does, that the ball will reach a point on the circumference in twice the time it formerly employed to cover the equal distance from *A* to *B*, implies that he is comparing the speeds along the actual paths of the ball.

This point has sometimes been misunderstood by Descartes' readers and commentators in the seventeenth century and in our own day.[44] Since the parallel velocity is supposed to be unchanged by refraction, it easily comes to the mind that what is increased or decreased by a constant ratio is the *perpendicular* component. But this would invalidate the proof, and we should no longer be in a position to see the problems to which it gave rise. The fact is that, whatever be the force responsible for the change suffered by the perpendicular velocity, Descartes does not provide an independent expression for this force which would allow us to construct the

---

[42] *Dioptric*, II, D, VI, pp. 100–101.

[43] Ibid., p. 101.

[44] This misunderstanding is to be found in the following works: E. Mach, op. cit., pp. 32–33; J. F. Scott, op. cit., pp. 34–35; V. Ronchi, op. cit., p. 115; C. Boyer, *The Rainbow*, p. 203. All these writers mistakenly attribute to Descartes the assumption that the perpendicular velocity is altered in a constant ratio. Their version of Descartes' proof is therefore incorrect.

refracted path. As in his proof of the law of reflection, he arrives at the law of refraction from two assumptions: the one is about the actual speeds, and the other is about the horizontal speeds. In this lies the intended symmetry between the two proofs.

Descartes' first assumption is therefore:

(1) $$v_r = n v_i$$

where v_r, v_i are the velocities of refraction and of incidence, and n a constant.

As applied to light, this equation amounts to the assertion that the velocity of light is a property of the medium it is traversing; in other words, the velocity is independent of the angle at which the light enters the refracting medium. The problem of reconciling the physical meaning of this equation with the asserted instantaneous propagation of light will be discussed later.

The second assumption concerning the conservation of speed parallel to the separating surface may be formulated thus:

(2) $$v_i \sin i = v_r \sin r.$$

Combining (1) and (2), we get the law:

$$\sin i = n \sin r.$$

Expressed in terms of v_i and v_r, the law reads:

$$\frac{\sin i}{\sin r} = \frac{v_r}{v_i} = n,$$

the sines are in the inverse ratio of the velocities, a result which the corpuscular theory inherited through Newton's adoption of a proof essentially similar to that of Descartes.

Although Descartes is careful to mark the place for the phenomenon of total reflection, his investigation lacks the systematic approach which characterized Kepler's experimental researches.[45] Descartes observes that at normal incidence no refraction takes place, and further that the incident and refracted rays rotate in the same sense. He then mentions total reflection. This, he says, takes place when the line *FE* falls outside the circle.[46] But he does not consider the intermediate critical case when *FE* would be tangential to the circle, and he thus fails to give an expression for the critical angle

---

[45] See E. Mach, op. cit., pp. 30–32.   [46] See above, pp. 108f.

(i.e. the angle of incidence for which the refracted ray makes 90°
with the normal) for any two given media.

Such an expression, however, can be obtained in his theory. For,
supposing

$$v_i > v_r,$$

there will be an angle of incidence at which the parallel component

$$v_i \sin i = v_r.$$

But this is impossible unless the resultant velocity v_r coincides with
the parallel velocity. Call that angle C; we have:

$$v_i \sin C = v_r,$$

$$\sin C = \frac{v_r}{v_i},$$

$$\sin C = n,$$

or,

$$C = \sin^{-1} n.$$

We come now to the physical interpretation of Descartes' two
assumptions, and first we consider assumption (1).

It is asserted at the beginning of the *Dioptric* that light, in the
luminiferous medium, is a tendency to motion rather than an actual
motion. It is further supposed to be transmitted in an instant. The
analogy between the action of light and the transmission of pressure
through a stick was meant to illustrate and support these assertions.
How, then, could the comparison with the moving ball be expected
to enlighten the reader as to the mechanism of light in reflection and
refraction? Fermat was the first among Descartes' contemporaries
to point out this difficulty; he wrote to Mersenne (September, 1637):

it seems that there is a particular disproportionality in that the motion of
a ball is more or less violent, according as it is pushed with different
forces, whereas light penetrates the diaphanous bodies in an instant and
seems to have nothing successive in it.[47]

In view of this apparent lack of analogy Descartes had assumed in
the *Dioptric* that the tendency to motion follows the same laws as

---

[47] F, II, p. 109.

motion itself.[48] That is to say, the same equations of motion apply to the action of light, in spite of the absence of the element of time from the latter. He had thus believed to have established a bridge between that branch of physics which studies actual motion and the other branch whose subject is light.

Fermat, however, still felt ill at ease; he found no reason to believe that what is true of motion must also be true of the tendency to motion; for, he objected, there is as much difference between them as between what is actual and what is potential.[49] The appeal to these Aristotelian terms was not a happy one, and it allowed Descartes to give a plausible answer. In perfect accord with the Aristotelian doctrine, he said, he was only asserting that the actual must also exist in the potential, and not vice versa.[50]

The problem becomes clearer when we concentrate on Descartes' first equation: How should we interpret v_i and v_r in the equation? What is it in the action of light that corresponds to the speed of the ball? Descartes would reply: 'its force'. But what is this force with which light *passes* more or less easily from one medium into another? How are we to understand this *passing* as a process without introducing the element of time into the picture? It appears that, in order to have any clear idea of what the first assumption means, one is forced to operate explicitly with speeds, and thus dispose of the oppressive assertion of the instantaneous transmission of light. It must be emphasized, however, that Descartes never actually took that step; he never used the word 'speed' in connection with light, although he sometimes used 'force' to mean practically the same thing, for instance, when he spoke of the force of the moving ball.

This only natural step was taken later by Fermat and Huygens; and Descartes' first assumption, thus understood, forms an essential part of their theories of refraction. But already during the discussion with which we are here concerned, Fermat used 'force' and 'speed' synonymously—a practice which at least did not provoke an objection from Descartes and was readily adopted by his defenders, Clerselier and Rohault.

---

48 Cf. D, VI, p. 89; see also pp. 78 ff above.   49 Cf. F, II, pp. 108–9.
50 Descartes to Mersenne, October 1637, F, II, p. 113.

The only physical meaning, therefore, that can be attached to the equation

$$v_r = nv_i$$

is that the velocity of light is characteristic of the medium it is traversing. As we have seen, this idea had been employed by Latin writers since the translation of Ibn al-Haytham's *Optics*, and is already to be found in Ptolemy. When Descartes first formulated it in 1619–21 he departed from the generally accepted view by asserting the speed to be greater in denser media.

In an interesting passage of the *Dioptric*,[51] Descartes attempts to explain why a ray of light passing from air into a denser medium such as water or glass turns towards the normal, whereas a ball falling into water is deflected away from the normal. We know from his proof that this means, in the case of light, that the speed has increased by refraction, while the contrary has taken place in the case of the ball. The problem is to account for the fact that the 'force' or speed of light increases when the medium is denser and consequently offers greater resistance. Descartes first remarks that a ball loses more of its speed when it impinges on a soft body than when it strikes a hard one, and it moves more easily on a polished hard table than on a carpet. The reason, he explains, is that a soft body yields to the shock of the ball and thus deprives it of a part of its speed (or momentum) whereas a hard body offering greater resistance takes away only a little of the momentum. In collision, therefore, the lost force, speed or momentum is less by how much the resistance is greater. Now, Descartes continues, light is 'a certain movement or action in a very subtle matter which fills the pores of other bodies'. As the particles of water or glass are 'harder and firmer' than those of air, they offer greater resistance to the action of the subtle matter, and as a result, allow the light to 'pass more easily' than the ball in water. 'For this light does not have to push from their places any of these particles [and consequently communicate to them at least part of its momentum], as a ball has to push away the particles of water to find a passage among them.'[52]

---

[51] Cf. D, VI, pp. 102–3.   [52] Ibid., p. 103.

These considerations in fact avoid a real problem to which Descartes' mechanical explanation of refraction gives rise. For imagine two rays travelling with the same speed in air. The one strikes a water surface which it penetrates, while the other enters into a denser medium *than water*, say glass. Descartes would inform us that, owing to the greater resistance of the glass, the velocity in glass will be greater than in water. This he would attempt to explain by the fact that the ray which has entered into the glass loses less of its momentum than the one which has passed into water. But he does not explain the fact that the velocity in glass (and in water) will be greater than the velocity of incidence, that is, in air. Such increase, however, as takes place in refraction from a rare into a dense medium is implied by his mathematical assumptions. In other words, whereas his mechanical picture may be taken, as far as it goes, to account for the loss of momentum when the refraction is from a dense into a rare medium, it utterly fails to explain the increase in momentum when the refraction is reversed.

Whatever Descartes' reasons were for asserting the velocity of light to be greater in the denser medium, and however weak was his argument for establishing this assertion in the *Dioptric* we know that he formulated it at a much earlier time, in 1619–21. We are now led to ask: on what grounds did he make the second assumption '$v_i \sin i = v_r \sin r$'? For the view that the velocity increases when the light is deflected towards the normal (as happens when the light passes into a denser medium) does not necessarily imply this assumption although it is compatible with it. We shall see that this problem was in fact brought up during the discussion between Fermat and Clerselier.

But how are we to account for this assumption in Descartes? The question is important, for it is precisely the apparently *ad hoc* character of this assumption which has led several writers to suspect Descartes of having artificially constructed his deductive proof of the sine law after he had obtained this law by different means. If these means were valid, why would he have suppressed them? Ought we therefore to conclude (with Leibniz and Mach) that he must have derived the law in the first place from Snell's manuscript?

It would seem, however, that the question about the origin of Descartes' assumption '$v_i \sin i = v_r \sin r$' is capable of quite a simple and straightforward answer: this equation is a direct consequence of the model employed. Refraction is explained by Descartes with reference to the same collision model which Ibn al-Haytham had used before him for the same purpose. This was no accident in Descartes' treatment of refraction, since in his view all phenomena must be reduced to collision phenomena. Now in every collision between two bodies the velocity component parallel to their common tangent at the point of contact must remain constant. Hence Descartes' assumption, which means nothing more than that refraction is to be treated as a special case of reflection, a case in which the perpendicular speed is altered *at the surface*. It might be objected that if this were as natural as it looks, then why do we not find the same assumption in Ibn al-Haytham? But again the answer is close to hand: to assume the constancy of the parallel velocity would be in conflict with Ibn al-Haytham's belief that the actual velocity decreases in the denser medium where the refracted ray bends towards the normal. Descartes, however, had from the beginning (i.e. in 1619–21) adopted the opposite view which is perfectly compatible with his assumption. It is not therefore unlikely that Descartes' discovery of the sine law may have been the result of bringing two unrelated assumptions together for the first time. That this is in fact how he arrived at the refraction law independently of other scientists or other methods must remain a conjecture, but a conjecture which is not, as has been usually supposed, implausible.

5. In 1664 Fermat wrote a letter to an unknown person[53] describing what appeared to him, in retrospect, as his first reaction to Descartes' *Dioptric*. Having examined Descartes' proportion (that the sines are in constant ratio), he became suspicious of the proof—for the following reasons. First, it was based on a mere analogy, and

---

[53] Cf. Fermat to M. de ***, 1664, F, II, pp. 485-9.

analogies do not found proofs. Second, it presupposed that the passage of light was easier in denser media, a proposition which 'seems shocking to common sense'.[54] And third, it assumed that the horizontal motion was unchanged by refraction—an unjustifiable assumption in Fermat's view.[55]

Apart from the first reason, it would be a mistake to believe that the latter two were really among the reasons for Fermat's rejection of the proof in the first place. The point involved in the second reason was never raised in the correspondence with Descartes; and it is more than probable that Fermat did not formulate this objection until after he had found that a contrary view to that of Descartes (regarding the speed of light in different media) was essential to his own principle of least time. It is significant to observe in this connection that this so-called presupposition was brought into the discussion by Fermat only after he had effected (in 1661–1662) the demonstration of the relation which gives the velocities in direct proportion to the sines. What we learn from Fermat's correspondence about the third reason is that he expressed his objection to Descartes' assumption concerning the horizontal component for the first time in 1658, in a letter to Clerselier,[56] that is, in the second phase of the discussion about the *Dioptric*.

We should not therefore take what Fermat said in the letter to M. de *** of 1664 as a true account of his own views about the *Dioptric* in the years immediately following the publication of that treatise in 1637. The objections he expressed in 1664 were the outcome of a long and winding discussion with Descartes and his defenders. Moreover, they were greatly influenced by a result obtained from the principle of least time about twenty-four years after the discussion started. His first difficulties and, consequently, his first objections were of a completely different kind.

In his letter to Mersenne of December 1637, Fermat undertook to expose what he believed to be the 'paralogisms' of the author of the *Dioptric*. For the sake of argument he accepted Descartes' distinction between the determination and the force of the moving ball, and

---

[54] Cf. Fermat to M. de ***, 1664, F, II, p. 485. [55] Ibid.
[56] Cf. Fermat to Clerselier, 10 March 1658, F, II, p. 371.

set out to show that Descartes was not faithful to his own distinction in his arguments to establish the sine relation.

The way Fermat understood the distinction is clearly revealed in the following words.

if we imagine that the ball is pushed [perpendicularly] from the point H to the point B, it is evident that, since it falls perpendicularly on the canvas CBE, it will traverse it in the line BG [G being on the perpendicular HB extended], and thus its moving force will be weakened, and its motion will be retarded while the determination is unchanged, since... [the ball] continues its movement in the same line HBG.[57]

'Determination' is here used to mean something which remains constant when the ball continues to move in the same line even though its speed has changed. That is, determination is identical with direction. Thus understood, it is not surprising that Fermat could find faults with Descartes' arguments. For Descartes maintained that the perpendicular determination of the falling ball was altered when it pierced the canvas and its speed in that direction was thereby changed. But Fermat naturally objected: what does that mean, if the distinction is precisely between the determination and 'the moving force or speed of the motion'?[58] If the distinction is to be maintained, 'one cannot say that, since the movement of the ball has been weakened, the determination which makes it go from above downwards has changed'.[59] Again, if the determination is to be distinguished from the speed, how could Descartes deduce from his assumption about the conservation (after refraction) of the horizontal 'determination' that the speed of the ball will be the same in that direction as before?[60] Understood in this manner, it is obvious that Descartes' arguments would lead to absurdities.[61]

One might be inclined to say that Fermat's difficulty lay in the fact that he took Descartes' words too literally; that the so-called distinction aside, one can still follow Descartes' deduction in terms of speed and direction alone. For what Descartes really meant was that the speed of the incident ball (or ray) is conserved in the

---

[57] Fermat to Mersenne, December 1637, F, II, pp. 117–18.
[58] Ibid., p. 118.   [59] Ibid.   [60] Ibid., p. 119.   [61] Ibid., pp. 119–20.

horizontal direction after refraction, while the speed along the refracted path maintains a constant ratio to the speed of incidence. From these two assertions the sine relation follows immediately. But this suggestion presupposes that we already understand Descartes' proof. Fermat was not in this happy position; and his difficulty lay precisely in understanding the distinction here in question. Also, it would still remain for us to explain the point in Descartes' differentiation between what he called 'determination' and the speed.

Besides, the view has been expressed that Fermat's difficulty (at the time when he made these objections, i.e. in 1637) lay elsewhere; that he had not only accepted Descartes' distinction but understood it better than Descartes. For example, Gaston Milhaud writes about this point:

we see that Descartes radically distinguishes the motion or quantity of motion and consequently, the speed on which it depends, from the determination or tendency to move in one direction or another. For instance, in the case of the reflection of a ball from a hard body, Descartes saw the determination change, but not the motion or the speed. But it is not this distinction which would be sufficient to trouble us. Fermat, too, will draw it more rigorously than Descartes himself and still find this demonstration of the sine law absolutely incomprehensible.[62]

Paul Mouy also follows Fermat in his interpretation of 'determination' as meaning the direction of motion.[63]

Is direction the only meaning that can be attached to 'determination', as Fermat, Milhaud and Mouy have assumed? Did Fermat really draw the distinction more rigorously than Descartes, when he saw it as between direction and speed? If one answers these questions in the affirmative, one is also forced to accept Fermat's conclusion, namely that Descartes' arguments which were based on this distinction are beyond understanding, that they are in fact merely a confusion of that alleged distinction.

This, however, would be an improbable conclusion. It would seem rather strange that Descartes should not only introduce a

---

[62] Milhaud, op. cit., p. 110.
[63] Cf. Paul Mouy, Le développement de la physique cartésienne, p. 55.

quantity, the determination, that was not at all necessarily required for performing his proofs (as these could be formulated in terms of speed and direction alone), but also take pains to establish a fundamental and seemingly elementary distinction which he so shamefully failed to manage. It would also be strange that, in spite of Fermat's disruptive criticism, which has seemed so convincing to recent commentators, the same Cartesian distinction should appear later at the basis of the rules of motion as formulated in the *Principles* in 1644, that is about six years after Descartes had read and considered Fermat's remarks.[64] The question, therefore, should be asked again: what was Descartes' distinction about?

The answer is in fact contained in a passage by Descartes which appears to have escaped attention. In a letter to Mydorge of (probably) 1 March 1638, Descartes pointed out that Fermat was arguing as if

I had supposed such difference between the determination to move in this or that direction [*ça ou là*] and the speed, that they were not to be found together, nor that they could be diminished by the same cause, namely by the canvas *CBE*. . . : which is against my meaning, and against the truth; seeing that this determination cannot be without some speed, although the same speed can have different determinations, and the same determination can be combined with various speeds.[65]

One thing at least comes out clearly after a first reading of this passage—namely that, for Descartes, the determination to move in this or that direction is *not*, as Fermat understood it, identical with direction ('this determination cannot be without some speed'). This means that when the speed of a moving body is altered, its determination is also altered, even though the body still moves in the same direction. If, for example, the canvas diminishes the speed of the perpendicularly falling ball, as in the case envisaged by Fermat, it thereby diminishes the determination of the ball to move in the perpendicular direction, even though the motion is continued in the same line. We may thus understand Descartes' assertion that the

---

[64] Cf. Descartes, *Principles*, II, 44.   [65] F, IV, pp. 94–95.

speed and the determination can be 'diminished by the same cause'. Also, since determination involves direction, when a moving body changes its direction, while its speed remains unaltered, its determination should be considered to have changed. We may thus understand Descartes' statement that 'the same speed can have different determinations'; a more fortunate rendering of this statement should, however, read: different determinations can have the same speed. As to the last sentence in Descartes' passage, 'the same determination can be combined with various speeds', it should not present any difficulty. For example, in his proof of the sine law, the same horizontal determination is combined, both with the actual speed along the actual path of the incident ball (or ray), and with the speed along the actual path of the refracted ball (or ray); these two actual speeds being different. (It is to be noted that Descartes does not say that the same determination can have different speeds.) Again, if the determination is a quantity depending on both direction and speed, when Descartes infers from the conservation of the horizontal determination that the speed in that direction is unchanged, his inference is of course correct. It becomes inconclusive only if, following Fermat's interpretation, we identify determination with direction.

In the light of the preceding passage we are therefore able to give 'determination' a meaning which fits all of Descartes' sentences and arguments which were expressed in terms of that quantity. This meaning can be defined as follows: two bodies A and B have the same determination if, and only if, they move (or tend to move) in the same direction and with the same speed. Thus understood, Descartes' distinction between the determination of a moving body and its speed should appear to us perfectly valid; it corresponds in fact to the distinction between vector and scalar quantities.

But in order to 'destroy completely'[66] Descartes' law of refraction, Fermat composed in the same letter to Mersenne (of December 1637) a refutation of the proof in the *Dioptric*; he actually deduced from what he believed to be Descartes' assumptions a different sine relation from that of Descartes.[67]

---

[66] F, II, p. 120.   [67] Cf. F, II, pp. 120–4.

Fermat considers for this purpose the case in which the speed is increased by refraction, and he composes the velocity of the refracted ball from the incident velocity and a given perpendicular component received at the surface of separation. His demonstration is essentially as follows:

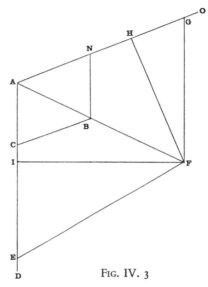

FIG. IV. 3

Suppose that (in Fig. IV. 3)

$$AN = v_i, \text{ the velocity of incidence;}$$

and

$AC = v_p$, the given perpendicular velocity added to the perpendicular component of v_i at the refracting surface.

We thus have the assumption:

(1) $$\frac{AN}{AC} = \frac{v_i}{v_p} = n, \text{ a constant.}$$

If NB and CB are drawn parallel to AC and AN respectively, then

$$AB = v_r, \text{ the velocity of refraction.}$$

The angle DAO is any angle corresponding to the angle of incidence i (the fact that DAO is obtuse in Fermat's figure does not essentially alter the argument). The angle DAB corresponds to the angle of refraction r. It follows that

$$BAO = i - r.$$

F is any point taken on AB extended, from which FG and FE are drawn parallel to BN and BC; and FH, FI are drawn perpendicular to AG, AD, respectively.

From consideration of similar triangles, it is seen that

(2)
$$\frac{FE}{FG} = \frac{BC}{BN},$$

and, the triangles FGH, FIE being similar, we have

(3)
$$\frac{FE}{FG} = \frac{FI}{FH} = \frac{\sin r}{\sin (i-r)}.$$

From (1), (2), and (3), it follows that

$$\frac{\sin r}{\sin (i-r)} = \frac{BC}{BN} = \frac{AN}{AC} = \frac{v_i}{v_p} = n.$$

We see the difference between Fermat's demonstration and that of Descartes: for it is clear from Fermat's figure that AB will vary in length with the angle DAO; in other words, v_r will vary with the angle of incidence i. Fermat's assumption (1) thus contradicts Descartes' requirement that the ratio of v_i and v_r should remain constant.

Are we here faced with a trivial case of misunderstanding, a case of misreading, for example? Hardly; for Fermat saw the contradiction and pointed it out himself in the same letter; though he saw it in a particular way:

the principal reason of the author's [Descartes'] demonstration is founded on his belief that the composite motion on BI [the direction of the refracted ray] is always of equal speed, although the angle GBD [equal to the angle of incidence] that is comprised between the lines of direction of the two moving forces [the one acting in the direction of the *incident* ray and the other in the perpendicular direction] has changed: which is false, as we have already fully demonstrated.[68]

Thus Fermat sees the contradiction as existing, not between two different sets of assumptions, the one belonging to Descartes and the other being his own (which certainly would not continue a refutation of Descartes' proof), but as a contradiction contained in Descartes' theory itself. In other words, he takes Descartes to be

---

[68] F, II, p. 124.

assuming that both the speed along the direction of refraction (v_r) and the perpendicular velocity received at the refracting surface (v_p) are independent of the angle of incidence.

Where did Fermat get the second assumption? How did he understand it from the *Dioptric* where it is not stated? I believe that the answer is to be found in the comparison used by Descartes to illustrate the case which Fermat has chosen for his refutation. Descartes compares the action of the refracting surface in this case with that of a racquet hitting the incident ball perpendicularly, thus increasing its perpendicular velocity. Fermat added the assumption that the racquet always hit the ball with equal force. Consequently, he constructed the velocity of refraction from the incident velocity and the constant perpendicular velocity supplied by the racquet (or refracting surface), and correctly deduced his own sine relation.

In order, therefore, to protect his analogy, Descartes would have to state explicitly that the racquet is supposed to hit the ball perpendicularly with varying degrees of force. But once this implicit supposition is brought to light, the artificial character of the comparison with the racquet becomes manifest. For every time the racquet hits the ball at the point of incidence, the amount of perpendicular speed thus imparted to the ball must be such that v_r (the resultant velocity) bears a constant ratio to v_i. What is this force which acts at the refracting surface and either increases or diminishes the perpendicular component of the incident velocity in such a manner that the value of v_r is always the same? Descartes' theory does not provide an answer to this question. No answer was forthcoming until the publication of Newton's *Principia*. Fermat had thus unintentionally exposed in Descartes' treatment of refraction a serious defect: the failure to provide an independent expression governing the force responsible for refraction.

It is important to realize that Fermat's difficulty in understanding Descartes' proof had nothing to do with the latter's assumption concerning the horizontal velocity. In the letter we have been discussing there is no objection, explicit or implicit, against that assumption. Fermat's arguments have been interpreted differently, however, by Milhaud and the editors of Fermat's works.

Milhaud thought that Fermat's demonstration not only replaces the constancy of v_r by that of v_p, but also fails to satisfy Descartes' condition that the horizontal component of the velocity is conserved after refraction. This remark of Milhaud's is in accord with his view that Fermat's difficulties were, from the beginning, connected with that assumption (and would therefore confirm his interpretation of Fermat's attitude towards Descartes' theory). He writes the following concerning Fermat's demonstration:

Fermat departs . . . from Descartes' hypotheses in that he relates the acceleration or retardation, which are determined by the media, to the normal determination of the motion and not to the direction, which is primarily unknown, of the refracted ray; *and, on the other hand, in that he does not take into account that the determination parallel to the surfaces of separation remains constant.* As he argues with Descartes, and later with Clerselier, he varies his objection; never did he resolve to adopt the postulates of Descartes. It is these postulates *and especially the postulate concerning the parallel determination which he absolutely refuses to accept.*[69]

The first remark in this passage concerning the parallel determination is not correct. For Descartes' condition, expressed in the postulate in question, is satisfied in Fermat's demonstration by the very fact that he composes the resultant velocity of refraction v_r from v_i and a perpendicular component v_p. It follows from this that the component of v_r parallel to the refracting surface is equal to the corresponding component of v_i, that is $v_r \sin r = v_i \sin i$, which is Descartes' postulate.

An opinion similar to Milhaud's had been expressed by the editors of Fermat's works, P. Tannery and C. Henry, in their comment on Fermat's refutation. This comment may have been the origin of Milhaud's remarks. It is as follows:

Fermat concludes that if one should consider, with Descartes, the motion along the refracted ray as the resultant of the motion along the incident ray and an action along the normal, the proportionality must exist not between the sines of the angles of incidence and of refraction, $\sin i$ and $\sin r$, but between $\sin (i - r)$ and $\sin r$. To this effect, he implicitly supposes the normal action to be independent of the incidence. [That is true:

---

[69] Milhaud, op. cit., pp. 111–12; italics added.

v_p is constant in Fermat's demonstration.] The hypothesis of Descartes is, on the contrary, that the component parallel to the surface of refraction keeps the same value after refraction as before. It is clear that one cannot decide *a priori* between these two suppositions.[70]

Thus it is thought here that the constancy of v_p is not compatible with the conservation of the horizontal speed after refraction; that Fermat's refutation ignores Descartes' postulate about that horizontal speed since it postulates the constancy of the normal action; and consequently that the problem between Descartes and Fermat was to decide between these two postulates, which could not be done *a priori*. In view of what has been remarked above, all this must be based on a misunderstanding.

The conclusion that we reached regarding Fermat's first attitude towards Descartes' proof is therefore justified: his difficulties lay outside the assumption concerning the horizontal speed. He misinterpreted the distinction between the determination and the speed and, consequently, could not follow Descartes' application of it; and he was misled by the comparison of the racquet into believing that the increase (or decrease) in the normal speed was supposed constant.

Descartes' reply in the letter to Mydorge of (probably) 1 March 1638 dealt mainly with two points in Fermat's letter (of December 1637): first, with the latter's interpretation of the distinction between the determination and speed; and second, with Fermat's demonstration itself. Fermat's objections to that distinction and Descartes' comments on them have already been discussed. These comments seem to have left no impression on Fermat as it appears from his letter to Clerselier of 10 March 1658. This letter was written shortly after Fermat had received, from Clerselier, another copy of Descartes' letter to Mydorge, which letter had formerly been forwarded to Fermat by Clerselier.[71] The point in Descartes' distinc-

---

[70] F, II (1894), p. 124, editors' note 1.

[71] Cf. F, II, p. 365, note 3. Examples showing Fermat's persistence in his own interpretation of Descartes' distinction are the following phrases from his letter to Clerselier, 10 March 1658: 'One of these aims (*visées*) or determinations [of the ball]'; or, thinking that he was merely expressing Descartes' intentions, 'this determination from left to right remains the same after refraction, that is to say, it conserves the same aim (*visée*) or direction'; or again, 'the determination or direction of the motion differs from its speed'. Ibid., pp. 371 and 373.

tion was not in fact made clear in Fermat's mind until after he had read the explanation offered by Clerselier and Rohault.[72] As to Fermat's demonstration, this appeared to Descartes as nothing more than a series of paralogisms. His answer, however, was insufficient in that it failed to point out clearly the crucial difference between his own demonstration and Fermat's, namely, that in the one an assumption is asserted which contradicts the corresponding assumption in the other. In any case, it was not to be expected that Fermat would get any satisfaction from Descartes' remarks, since these were expressed in terms of that fundamental distinction of which Fermat could not make sense. It was again Rohault who clearly pointed out the misunderstanding in Fermat's refutation. Rohault wrote in his *Projet* of 15 May 1658:

M. de Fermat considers that, on page 20 of the *Dioptric*, the supposition of M. Descartes is that the increase of one third of the motion which the ball suffers is from above downwards or along the [perpendicular] line *BG*, whereas it is measured in the line which the ball actually describes. And this is easy to understand, because, if that [i.e. what Fermat assumed] were the case, M. Descartes would not have supposed, as he did, that the force of the ball's motion is increased by a third, but that the determination from above downwards is increased by a third. One should not therefore say [with Fermat] that, in his [Descartes'] sense, the motion of the ball along *BI* [the direction of refraction] is composed of the motion which it had along *BD* [the direction of incidence], and another along [the perpendicular] *BG* whose quantity one would want him [Descartes] to have supposed to be greater than the motion along *AB* [i.e. the velocity of incidence] by a third. One should rather say that the actual motion of the ball [after refraction] is faster by a third than before, and leave it to calculation to determine what change must thereby result in the determination from above downwards.[73]

6. When the controversy was later resumed between Fermat and Clerselier,[74] the main point at issue between them was Descartes' assumption concerning the conservation of the horizontal speed and whether it was compatible with his other assumption, stating the

---

[72] See below, p. 129, n. 77.　　[73] F, II, p. 395.　　[74] Above, pp. 86f.

actual speeds to be determined by the media. Throughout the dispute with Descartes, Fermat's objections had mainly been due to misunderstandings, though they were interesting misunderstandings which sometimes had their roots in Descartes' theory itself. When, twenty years later, Fermat resumed the discussion with Clerselier, his objections began to take a different line. In order to understand correctly Fermat's arguments, it should be borne in mind that his attitude was always that of a mathematician, not of a physicist. If by his patient and sincere analysis he helped to expose certain physical difficulties, that was only by implication. His objections against Descartes' arguments, and those of his defenders, were always of a mathematical or logical character.

In 1658, Fermat still denied, as he always did before and afterwards, that the argument in the *Dioptric* to establish the refraction law constituted a demonstration or even approached a demonstration.[75] Accordingly, his criticisms were directed against the Cartesian proof in so far as it claimed to be a demonstration. With this attitude Fermat imagined, in his letter to Clerselier of 3 March 1658, a 'scrupulous sceptic' who wants to examine Descartes' reasonings from a new angle. This imaginary sceptic is willing (no doubt for the sake of argument) to grant their conclusiveness as applied to reflection, but he questions the validity of their being extended to refraction. For, the sceptic protests, in reflection the speed of the ball is the same after striking the surface as before; the ball is all the time moving in the same medium; and the surface is totally opposed to the perpendicular determination:

But, in refraction, everything is different. Are we to obtain the consent of our sceptic here without proof? Will the determination from left to right remain the same when the reasons which have persuaded him of that in reflection have all vanished? But this is not all: he has reason to be afraid of ambiguity; and, when he will have accorded that this determination from left to right remains the same, he has reason to suspect that the author will confuse him over the explanation of this term. For, although he [the author] has protested that the determination is different from the

---

[75] Cf. Fermat's letter to Clerselier, 3 March 1658, F, II, p. 366.

moving force, and that their quantity should be examined separately, if our sceptic grants him at this point that this determination from left to right remains the same in refraction, that is to say, that it preserves the same aim or direction, it seems that the author will want to force him afterwards to grant him that the ball, whose determination towards the right has not changed, advances towards the right with the same speed as before, although the speed [i.e. the actual speed] and the medium have changed.[76]

We note that Fermat still identifies the determination with the direction of motion. Yet it now seems that his interpretation of Descartes' distinction is irrelevant to the kind of objection he has in mind. For his argument, as expressed in this passage (and as later developed in another letter to Clerselier of 2 June 1658 which he wrote after reading the explanations offered by Clerselier and Rohault concerning the distinction in question)[77] can be put as follows: Granting that the horizontal determination remains unchanged after refraction, that is (according to his first understanding of that term) granting that the ball (or ray) remains to have a motion in that direction, it does not follow that the speed of that motion will be the same; but if Descartes is simply assuming (as he was informed by Rohault and Clerselier) that the horizontal speed is unaltered by refraction, then the question is: on what grounds should that assumption be accepted?

Not that this proposition cannot be true, but it is so only if the conclusion, which M. Descartes draws from it, is true, that is to say, if the ratio or proportion for measuring refractions had been legitimately and truthfully

---

[76] Ibid., p. 371.

[77] Fermat did not come to apprehend that distinction as Descartes had intended it until after it was explained to him by Clerselier and Rohault in May 1658 (cf. F, II, pp. 383-4, and 392; see also F, II, p. 475). The remarks of Clerselier and Rohault were a development of Descartes' brief comment in his letter to Mydorge (see above, p. 120). In agreement with the definition formulated above (see p. 121) they explained that the determination should be regarded as having changed even when the direction remains the same and only the quantity of the determination measured by the speed has increased or decreased. In his letter to Clerselier of 2 June 1658, Fermat confessed that he had not understood Descartes' distinction in this manner, although he still was not satisfied with it (cf. F, II, p. 397). He did not give reasons for his dissatisfaction.

determined by him. He has therefore only proved it [the assumption] by a proposition [the sine relation] that is so doubtful and so little admissible.[78]

Fermat here rejects the Cartesian proof of the sine law, not any longer because it is not conclusive, as he believed twenty years earlier, but simply because it now appears to him to be founded on an assumption that is 'neither an axiom, nor is . . . legitimately deduced from any primary truth'. The Cartesian proof is therefore not a 'demonstration' since 'demonstrations which do not force belief cannot bear this name'.[79]

There are two distinct problems involved in Fermat's remarks, and it is important to know which one of these he had in mind. First, there is a mathematical question which may be expressed as follows: can the equation

$$v_i \sin i = v_r \sin r$$

be true for all values of i when v_i does not equal v_r? It will be shown presently that this is the kind of question he wanted to ask. Second, there is the question of whether a physical interpretation can be given which would satisfy Descartes' equations for deducing the sine law. It is this second question which constituted a really serious problem for the Cartesian theory. And although it is doubtful that Fermat ever conceived it clearly, his objections and suspicions ultimately led Clerselier to construct a mechanical picture which, he hoped, would accommodate Descartes' assumptions. Whether Clerselier succeeded in this will be examined later.

Concerning the mathematical question, Clerselier replied by simply repeating what Descartes had already remarked in his letter to Mydorge: namely that the same (horizontal) determination can be combined with different speeds (in the actual direction of motion).[80] In reply to this, Fermat proceeded to construct, as a challenge to Clerselier and his friends, a counter-example to which the statement

---

[78] Fermat to Clerselier, 10 March 1658, F, II, p. 373. This passage indicates that Fermat had not yet accepted the sine law when he wrote the present letter to Clerselier, that is twenty years after the publication of the *Dioptric*. (See also in the same letter: 'I maintain that the true ratio or proportion of refractions is not yet known.' Ibid., p. 374.) In fact he did not accept the law until after he had derived it himself from his own principle of least time; see next chapter.

[79] Ibid., p. 373.   [80] Cf. F, II, p. 384.

cannot apply. He introduced an imaginary case,[81] and this already indicates that he was concerned with a purely mathematical problem. He pictured a ball falling obliquely on a resisting surface which the ball cannot penetrate. On reaching the surface, the ball loses part of its actual speed, owing to the interference of an imaginary agent; but the horizontal speed remained the same. There is thus an essential parallelism between this case and what Descartes considered to take place in refraction; except, of course, that in Fermat's case the ball does not go through the surface. (This shows again that the intended parallelism is merely mathematical.) If, therefore, v_i and v_l are the velocities before and after the ball strikes the surface, we have by supposition:

(1) $$\frac{v_i}{v_l} = n, \text{ a constant less than unity;}$$

(2) $$v_i \sin i = v_l \sin l.$$

Suppose now that the ball falls at an angle i greater than the angle whose sine is equal to n. At such an angle,

(3) $$v_i \sin i > v_l.$$

And it follows from (2) and (3) that, at the same angle of incidence,

$$v_l \sin l > v_l,$$

which is impossible, since $\sin l$ cannot be greater than unity. Therefore, Fermat concluded, the ball will not be reflected. But, by supposition, it will not be refracted either. Where will it go? The problem for Clerselier and Descartes' friends was 'to provide the ball with a passport and to mark for it the way out of this fatal point'.[82]

Fermat's deductions are, of course, correct. But what did he want to prove by deriving that impossibility? That on the assumptions made, there is a case in which the direction of v_l cannot be constructed; and that case is realized when the angle of incidence is greater than the angle whose sine equals $\frac{v_l}{v_i}$. What does this mean when it is applied to the actual case of refraction? The same thing of course: namely, if $v_i > v_r$ and $v_i \sin i = v_r \sin r$, there is a case in

---

[81] Cf. Fermat to Clerselier, 2 June 1658, F, II, pp. 399–402.   [82] Ibid., pp. 401–2.

131

which the direction of v_r cannot be constructed; and that case is realized when the angle of incidence is greater than the angle whose sine equals $\frac{v_r}{v_i}$. But why should this constitute an objection against Descartes' theory? Descartes himself was aware of the situation described by Fermat, and he explicitly pointed it out in the *Dioptric*.[83] For the case envisaged by Fermat is precisely the case in which the light is *not* refracted but totally reflected. The fact that, when the refraction is from a dense into a rare medium, there is a case in which the refracted ray cannot be constructed from Descartes' assumptions, should be counted for, not against, Descartes' theory. It means that the theory makes room for an actual property of light.

Fermat, however, would insist on considering his own imaginary case, where the ball was abandoned in its strife to leave the impenetrable surface 'for the honour of M. Descartes'.[84] Descartes could interpret the impossibility of constructing the direction of refraction on the given assumptions, by the fact that the ball (or ray) will in this case be reflected; but the ball, in Fermat's case, is in a different situation, since it cannot go anywhere. How, then, is it going to employ the quantity of motion which it still has? Fermat himself believed that ball will be reflected, and at an angle equal to the angle of incidence.[85] This would of course mean that both the vertical and horizontal components of the ball's motion will be reduced in the same proportion as the actual speed. In other words, Descartes' assumption concerning the conservation of the horizontal speed would have to be abandoned, if the ball were to move at all.

Now Fermat was right in drawing that last conclusion regarding the special situation in his own imaginary case. But, as Clerselier objected in his answer to Fermat,[86] that was of no relevance to Descartes' treatment of refraction. The fact that Descartes' assumption concerning the horizontal speed has to be abandoned in Fermat's imaginary situation does not mean that the same assumption cannot

---

[83] See above, pp. 108f.
[84] Cf. Fermat to Clerselier, 16 June 1658, F, II, p. 408.
[85] Ibid., pp. 409–10.
[86] Cf. Clerselier to Fermat, 21 August 1658, F, II, pp. 414ff.

be maintained in the consideration of refractions. We have seen that, when a similar situation to Fermat's arises in the actual refraction of light, one can conclude that the ray will not penetrate the refracting surface, and this conclusion is confirmed by experiment. But, by incessantly challenging the basis of Descartes' assumptions, Fermat's remarks finally led Clerselier to envisage a mechanical situation which, as a rival to Fermat's imaginary case, would be in agreement with Descartes' equations. The examination of Clerselier's attempt brings us to the physical problem mentioned before.

Clerselier's attempt (contained in his letter to Fermat of 13 May 1662) was no doubt inspired by some of Descartes' remarks in the *Dioptric*.[87] It had the merit, however, of going beyond the analogies with which Descartes had been satisfied; instead of Descartes' frail canvas, we have here a ballistic model.[88]

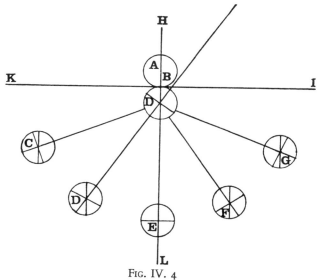

FIG. IV. 4

A is an elastic sphere stationed at *B* (Fig. IV. 4). Relying on experiment, Clerselier observes that if any of the spheres *C, D, E, F* or *G* impinges on *A* at the point *B* (i.e. in such a way that the normal common to *A* and the impinging sphere is perpendicular to

---

KI), A will move in the (perpendicular) direction of BH, whatever be the angle of incidence. This means that the motion (momentum) imparted to A has been taken away from the normal component of the motion of the incident sphere, the horizontal component (parallel to KI) being unaltered. After impact the incident sphere (if it loses only part of its initial momentum) will thus have at B two motions, one parallel to KI and equal to its motion in that direction before impact, and the other perpendicular to KI; and both of these will determine the speed and direction of the sphere at the moment of collision. If now the medium that is supposed on the upper side of KI is such that it will resist the motion of the sphere, that, in Clerselier's view, can only affect the speed of the sphere, and not its direction to which the medium is totally indifferent. According to Clerselier, this explains the refraction away from the normal when the speed is reduced at the refracting surface. Similarly is 'explained' the refraction towards the normal, when the velocity is increased; only in this case A is supposed to yield more easily to the impinging sphere and, 'so to speak, drags it towards H'.[89]

Clerselier's model, in spite of its elaborations, only succeeds in making more manifest the difficulties which it was proposed to remove. It in fact fails to satisfy the main condition which it was required to fulfil: namely, the conservation of the horizontal speed. For although this condition is preserved at the moment of impact, if the further resistance of the medium subsequently changes the actual speed without altering the direction (as is supposed by Clerselier), both the perpendicular and the horizontal components of the motion will be diminished in the same proportion. Moreover, the model fails to explain, even in a general way, how the velocity can be increased by refraction. To suppose that the ball A yields more easily to the impinging ball does not mean that the latter will thereby acquire new momentum. And to say, as Clerselier did, that the incident sphere can be supposed to be 'dragged' into the refracting medium would be to introduce something like an attractive force which would seem completely out of place in this

---

[89] F, II, p. 479.

mechanical picture. (It is interesting to note, however, that Clerselier was led to introduce an idea which Newton later used in his explanation of refraction.)

Clerselier's model thus raises more problems than it solves, and it shows that no solution of the fundamental physical difficulties was forthcoming along the lines suggested by him and earlier by Descartes. Not that Descartes' two fundamental equations contradicted one another; they are both asserted in Newton's theory of refraction. But the dynamical interpretation they received from Newton would be completely repugnant to Descartes. The latter's dream was to build the whole of physics solely on the idea of motion, to the exclusion of all forces. Descartes' favoured idea of collision was not itself to be abandoned altogether in the later development of optics. It is the fundamental idea underlying Huygens' theory of light. But in Huygens' theory there is no place for Descartes' assumption of the conservation of the parallel speed.

There were no comments from Fermat on Clerselier's mechanical considerations. Before he read them he had arrived at Descartes' relation (in the form: $\sin i = n \sin r$) from his own principle of least time. In the face of this unexpected result, he was willing to abandon the battlefield, as he said, leaving to Descartes the glory of having first made the discovery of an important truth, and himself being content to have provided the first real demonstration of it. With this conditional declaration of peace in his last letter to Clerselier of 21 May 1662, the discussion came to an end.[90]

---

[90] Cf. Fermat to La Chambre, 1 January 1662, F, II, p. 462; and Fermat to Clerselier, 21 May 1662, F, II, p. 484.

Chapter Five

FERMAT'S PRINCIPLE OF LEAST TIME

1. The discussion in the preceding chapter of Fermat's controversy with Descartes and Clerselier has revealed a negative aspect of the Cartesian theory of refraction, namely its failure to provide a plausible physical interpretation fitting the mathematical assumptions used by Descartes in his deduction of the sine law. Fermat himself went further than that: he doubted the validity of applying the method of the parallelogram of velocities to the problem of refraction, and this led him to doubt the truth of Descartes' law itself. To discover the true law of refraction, Fermat appealed to his own method of maxima and minima which he had invented about eight years before the beginning of the controversy with Descartes in 1637. In order to bring this method to bear on the problem under investigation, however, he relied on the metaphysical principle that nature performed its actions in the simplest and most economical ways. His law of least time was to him a justifiable specification of this principle. Thus, in the hands of Fermat, geometry and metaphysics joined forces in an attempt to defeat Descartes and his followers[1] by going beyond mere opposition to their arguments and actually producing *the* true law of refraction.

Fermat's attempt might appear preposterous and unscientific. But why? Had not the principle of economy been accepted, in one form or another, by many philosophers and scientists since antiquity? Had not an early specification of this principle, the law of shortest distance, been successfully applied by Heron of Alexandria to some cases of optical reflection?[2] Had not considerations of simplicity

---

[1] Thus Fermat wrote to La Chambre in 1657: '. . . si vous souffrez que je joigne un peu de ma géométrie à votre physique, nous ferons un travail à frais communs qui nous mettra d'abord en défense contre M. Descartes et tous ses amis' (F, II, p. 354). The nature of the 'physics' here referred to is revealed by the immediately following sentence: 'Je reconnois premièrement avec vous la vérité de ce principe, que la nature agit toujours par les voies les plus courtes'.

[2] Above, pp. 70f.

and economy guided the steps of a great seventeenth-century scientist, Galileo, towards the discovery of the important law of freely falling bodies?[3] Why should not Fermat make a similar attack on the problem of refraction when the appropriate mathematical tools were in his hands?[4]

It might be protested that in the case of refraction, a law had already been proposed; why, then, not consult the experiments before embarking on an endeavour that might well prove chimerical? Such a question would imply, however, that experiment enjoys a certain authority with which Fermat did not invest it. For, as we shall see, he was in fact informed, before he performed his calculations, that the sine law had been confirmed experimentally, and he believed his informants. Fortunately, however, this discouraged him only temporarily. He then reasoned that the true ratio for refractions might still not be identical with that proposed by Descartes, though so near to it as to deceive the keenest observer; there was, therefore, room for a fresh attack on the problem *in spite of* the apparent verdict of experiment.

Fermat was disappointed in his expectations in so far as he discovered that the principle of least time leads to the very sine ratio which Descartes had laid down. But this principle also requires the velocity of light to be greater in rarer media, contrary to Descartes' view; and this result has since been supported by experiment. Fermat has been rewarded for his bold attempt by the fact that his principle (in a modified form) has remained to this day an accepted theorem in optics; a theorem which, as Huygens later showed, in fact followed from wave considerations.[5]

2. In 1657, about six months before Fermat resumed the discussion concerning the *Dioptric* with Clerselier, he received a copy of a

---

[3] Below, p. 157, n. 57.

[4] The idea of 'easier' and 'quicker' path was the basis of Ibn al-Haytham's explanation of refraction from a rare into a dense medium, and Witelo, who adopted the same idea, quoted in this connection the principle of economy; see above pp. 95f, and p. 98. Fermat referred to the work of these two writers on refraction; cf. F, II, p. 107.

[5] Below, pp. 218f.

treatise on light that had been published in the same year by a physician called Cureau de la Chambre.[6] The author, who sent the copy to Fermat, held the view that light was a quality, not a substance; that it was capable of a local motion which, nevertheless, took place in an instant; and he offered as the general causes of reflection and refraction the 'animosity' and 'natural antipathy' between light and matter.[7] Fermat, in his letter of acknowledgement to La Chambre (August 1657),[8] does not appear to have been convinced by the author's argument in support of these views, although he described it, presumably out of politeness, as 'very solid and very subtle'.[9] He found in the physician's book, however, one principle which he could accept without hesitation: 'I first recognize with you the truth of this principle, that nature always acts by the shortest courses [*que la nature agit toujours par les voies les plus courtes*].'[10] La Chambre had recalled the successful application of this principle to the reflection of light at plane surfaces, and his book contained a geometrical demonstration of the following theorem: if A and B be any two points on the incident and reflected rays, and C a point on the plane surface where the light is reflected at equal angles, then, if D be any other point on the surface in the plane of incidence, the distance ACB is shorter than ADB.[11] But he mentioned two difficulties in the way of consistently implementing his adopted principle.[12] First, there was the objection that in reflection at concave surfaces, the light sometimes followed a longer path than that required by the principle; this was illustrated by the case in which the two points related as object and image are taken on a spherical concave surface. And second, the principle was not applicable to the behaviour of light in refraction: obviously, if the light always followed the shortest path, it should always go in a

---

[6] *La Lumière a Monseignevr L'Eminentissime Cardinal Mazarin, par Le Sieur De La Chambre, Conseiller du Roy en ses Conseils, & son Médecin ordinaire*, Paris, 1657.

[7] Cf. ibid., pp. 276–81, 296–302 and 335–41.

[8] Cf. F, II, pp. 354–9.

[9] Ibid., p. 354. Later in the same letter (p. 357), however, Fermat poured doubt on the opinion that the movement of light was not successive.

[10] Ibid., p. 354.

[11] La Chambre, op. cit., pp. 312–13.

[12] Ibid., pp. 313–15.

straight line from one medium into another. La Chambre's own answer to these difficulties was that the light was not 'free' to act in these exceptional cases in accordance with its 'natural tendency'.[13] For him, therefore, the principle of shortest course should be understood to govern, not the actual behaviour of light, but rather its hidden tendency which manifested itself only in the case of reflection at plane surfaces!

Looking at these difficulties from a different angle, the mathematician Fermat could not fail to see the possibility of a more satisfactory answer, at least as far as refraction was concerned:[14] if instead of shortest path one postulated *easiest course*, the principle might be found to agree with the behaviour of light when passing from one medium into another. For, assuming that different media offer different resistances, it might be the case that the straight line joining two points in the two media is not the path for which the resistance is a minimum.

For example, suppose that DB (Fig. V.1) separates the medium of incidence below from the medium of refraction above; and let the resistance of the lower medium be less than that of the upper medium, say by a half. The sum of the resistances along the incident ray CB and the refracted ray BA may, according to Fermat, be represented by $CB+2BA$. In the same way, the resistance along the straight line CDA can be represented by $CD+2DA$. Now although $CB+BA$ is greater than CDA, it may be the case that, for a certain position of B, $CB+2BA$ is less than $CD+2DA$.

Assuming, therefore, that light follows the easiest path, the problem of refraction is in this case reduced to the following

---

[13] Ibid. pp. 322–4.

[14] Concerning the difficulty connected with reflection at concave surfaces, Fermat simply suggested that the light should be understood to act, not on the concave surface as such, but on the tangent to that surface at the point of reflection in the plane of incidence. The measurement of the light's path should, therefore, be considered in relation to the tangent and not to the concave surface itself. On this suggestion the problem would be reduced to that of reflection at plane surfaces and Heron's theorem would hold. In Fermat's view this suggestion was justified by the 'physical principle' that 'nature performs its movements by the *simplest courses*' (F, II, pp. 354–5, my italics), since the straight line (the tangent with which the light should be concerned) is simpler than the curved surface. It is interesting to note the transformations that the principle of economy had to undergo in order to suit the various cases.

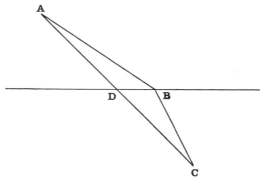

FIG. V. I

mathematical problem: given C and A, to find the point of refraction B such that $CB + 2BA$ is a minimum. Concerning this problem, Fermat wrote to La Chambre in the same letter of 1657:

I confess to you that this problem is not one of the easiest; but, since nature solves it in all refractions so that she may not deviate from her ordinary way of acting, why cannot we undertake the [solution] ?[15]

He ended his letter by promising to supply the solution whenever it would please his correspondent to receive it; and that he would be able to deduce such consequences as would 'firmly establish the truth'[16] of the accepted principle by their exact agreement with all the relevant observations.

That promise remained unfulfilled for more than four years, and it will be interesting to follow the development of Fermat's thought during that period.

He could first easily prove on a numerical example that the straight line was not necessarily the most economical path for refracted light. To show this to La Chambre in 1662,[17] he readily interpreted the principle of easiest course as a principle of *least time*: Let the diameter AB (Fig. V. 2) represent the interface. It is supposed that the light can pass twice as 'easily' in the rare medium above as in the dense medium below:

---

[15] F, II, p. 358.   [16] Ibid., p. 359.
[17] Fermat to La Chambre, 1 January 1662, F, II, pp. 457–63.

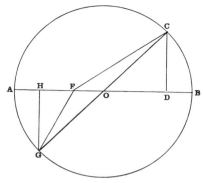

FIG. V. 2

It follows from this supposition that the time employed by the moving thing or the light from C to O is less then the time taken from O to G, and that the time of the movement from C to O in the rarer medium is but half the time of the movement from O to G. And consequently the measure of the total movement along the straight lines CO and OG can be represented by half CO added to OG; similarly, if you take another line such as F, the time of the movement along the straight lines CF and FG can be represented by half CF added to FG.[18]

Taking $CO=OG=10$, $HO=OD=8$, and $OF=1$, he found by calculation that $\frac{1}{2}CF+FG$ was less than $\frac{1}{2}CO+OG$ (the latter sum being equal to 15, and the former less than 59/4, i.e. less than 15). Since these two sums measured the times of the movements through F and O respectively, he concluded that in this case the time taken along the straight line COG was more than that taken along the sides CF and FG:[19]

I arrived at that result without much effort, but the investigation had to be carried farther; for, in order to satisfy my principle, it is not sufficient

---

[18] Ibid., p. 459.

[19] To La Chambre, for whom the movement of light was instantaneous, Fermat wrote: 'If you continue to deny successive movement to light, and to maintain that it is performed in an instant, you need only compare either the facility, or the aversion and resistance which become greater or less according as the media change. For this facility, or this resistance, being more, or less in different media, and this in diverse proportion according as the media differ more, they can be considered to be in a given ratio and, consequently, they fall under the calculation as well as the time of the movement, and my demonstration will apply to them in the same manner' (ibid. p. 463).

to have found a certain point F through which the natural movement is performed more quickly, more easily and in less time than along the straight line COG, but it was necessary to find the point through which the movement would be made in less time than through any other point taken on either side. For this purpose I had to appeal to my method of *maxima* and *minima* which expedites the solution of this sort of problem with much success.[20]

Before he undertook the task of applying his method to the problem, however, a certain obstacle appeared in his way and nearly discouraged him from making the attempt. He had never accepted Descartes' method for establishing the law of refraction and, as a result, he had never believed that Descartes' law was true.[21] He had thus assumed that, by means of his own method of maxima and minima, the principle of easiest course would lead to a different law from the one that had been proposed by Descartes; and, of course, he had no doubts that that 'well established'[22] principle would yield *the* correct law. Before he undertook the calculations, however, he was informed by various persons whom he greatly esteemed that the experiments exactly agreed with the Cartesian ratio of sines. It therefore appeared to him at first a useless task to try to invent a new law that was bound to be born dead, especially as the calculations involved were not easy to make. Fortunately for the history of science, he got over that obstacle by a hopeful resolution:

I disposed of [that] . . . obstacle by my knowledge that there is an infinite number of proportions which, though all different from the true one, approach to it so insensibly that they can deceive the most able and the most exact observers.[23]

---

[20] Fermat to La Chambre, 1 January 1662, F, II, p. 460.

[21] Thus we read in his first letter to La Chambre of August 1657: 'The use of these composed movements is a very delicate matter which must not be handled and employed except with very great precaution. I compare them to some of your medicines which serve as poison if they are not well and duly prepared. It is therefore sufficient for me to say in this place that M. Descartes has proved nothing, and that I share your opinion in that you reject his' (F, II, p. 356). See also his letter to La Chambre 1 January 1662 (F, II, pp. 457–8), and his letter to M. de ★★★, 1664, (F, II, pp. 485–6).

[22] F, II, p. 458.

[23] F, II, p. 461. See also ibid., pp. 486–7.

That is to say, he hoped that the true proportion might be one that was very near to Descartes' though not identical with it. Such a proportion would be as much in agreement with experiment as the one proposed by Descartes, since the difference would be too small to be detected. But, then, how would Fermat know that his own proportion would be 'the true' one? Because 'nothing was so plausible and so obvious'[24] as the principle from which he was going to deduce it, whereas Descartes' proportion was based on a pseudo-demonstration. The question of the *truth* or *falsity* of the law of refraction was thus, in Fermat's view, not to be decided by experiment alone; the law had to be based on a more solid foundation by correctly deducing it from an assumption whose truth was, for him, beyond doubt. This attitude towards establishing an experimental law was not peculiar to Fermat; we shall see[25] that Newton also was not content to accept the truth of the sine law *as far as it appeared from experiments,* but wanted to prove its *accurate truth* by deducing it mathematically from an assumption yielding the exact ratio.

Having got over that obstacle, Fermat then set out to attack the technical difficulties connected with his problem. As he first conceived it, the problem presented four lines by their square roots and thus involved four asymmetries which would have required calculations of great length. After repeated attempts he finally succeeded in reducing the four asymmetries to only two, 'which relieved me considerably'.[26] When he reached the end of his calculations he found himself face to face with Descartes' sine ratio:

the reward for my effort has been the most extraordinary, the most unforeseen and the happiest that ever was. For, after having gone through all the equations, multiplications, antitheses and other operations of my method, and having finally concluded the problem which you will see in a separate paper, I have found that my principle gave exactly and precisely the same proportion for refractions as that which M. Descartes has laid down.

I have been so surprised by this unexpected result that I find it difficult to recover from my astonishment. I have repeated my algebraic calculations several times and the result has always been the same.[27]

---

[24] F, II, p. 460.   [25] Below, p. 299.   [26] F, II, p. 461.   [27] Ibid., pp. 461–2.

3. Before I give an account of Fermat's proof as presented in the work referred to here, it will perhaps be useful to describe briefly his method of maxima and minima.

Suppose[28] that, in a given problem, a is the unknown to be determined by the condition that a certain quantity is maximum or minimum. To find a, Fermat first expresses the maximum or minimum quantity in terms of a—let us call this expression M. He substitutes $a+e$ for a in M (where e is a very small quantity) and thereby obtains another expression M'. The two expressions M and M' may then be compared as if they were equal. To denote this operation Fermat used a term (*adaequare*) meaning approximate equation.[29] The quasi-equation $M=M'$ is then divided by e or by one of its higher powers so as to make e completely disappear from at least one of the terms. Omitting the terms in which e remains after division, the result will be an equation whose solution gives the value of a.[30]

To illustrate this by a simple example given by Fermat, suppose that b is a straight line to be divided into two segments a and $b-a$, such that the product

$$a(b-a)=ba-a^2=M, \text{ a maximum.}$$

Let the first segment equal $a+e$; the second will be equal to $b-a-e$; and their product will be given by:

$$ab-a^2+be-2ae-e^2=M'.$$

Equating M and M', and cancelling the common terms:

$$be=2ae+e^2 \text{ approx.}$$

---

[28] See Fermat's account (written before 1638) entitled '*Methodus ad Disquirendam Maximam et Minimam*', in F, I, pp. 133–6; French translation, F, III, pp. 121–3.

[29] On the relation of Fermat's term to Diophantus' παρισότης, see F, I, p. 140 and p. 133, editors' note 2. Cf. T. L. Heath, *Diophantus of Alexandria*, 2nd ed., Cambridge, 1910, pp. 95–98.

[30] It is seen that Fermat's method contains the fundamental idea of the differential calculus. He principally made use of this method in the construction of tangents to curves. An account of it was published for the first time in 1644 (see Pierre Hérigone, *Cursus mathematicus*, VI (Paris, 1644), pp. 59–69 of the *Supplementum* beginning after p. 466 with separate pagination). We gather from Fermat's correspondence that he invented his method in, or shortly before, 1629; see Paul Tannery, 'Sur la date des principales découvertes de Fermat', in *Bulletin des sciences mathématiques et astronomiques*, 2e série, VII (1883), tome XVIII de la collection, première partie, p. 120. It had not been known for certain whether Newton was acquainted with Fermat's ideas until L. T. More brought attention, in 1934, to a letter of Newton's in which he wrote: 'I had the hint of this method [of fluxions] from Fermat's way of drawing tangents, and by applying it to abstract equations, directly and invertedly, I made it general.' Cf. Louis Trenchard More, *Isaac Newton*, A biography, New York and London, 1934, p. 185, note 35. See also Newton, *Correspondence*, ed. Turnbull, II, p. 167, n. 4; III, pp. 182 and 183.

Dividing by e, we have:
$$b = 2a + e \text{ approx.}$$
Omitting e, we get:
$$b = 2a.$$
That is, on the condition supposed, the line should be divided in the middle.

It took Fermat more than four years and a great deal of effort before he could see his way to applying this method to the problem of refraction. The result was the following demonstration.[31]

In the figure (Fig. V. 3) the diameter AB represents the interface between the rare medium above and the dense medium below. The incident ray CD meets AB at the middle point D; CF is perpendicular to AB; m is a line given outside the circle.

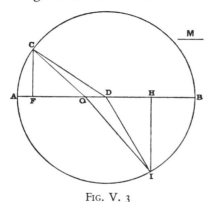

FIG. V. 3

If R_i and R_r be the 'resistances' of the medium of incidence and of refraction respectively, it is assumed that

(1)
$$\frac{R_r}{R_i} = \frac{DF}{m} = K > 1.$$

On the supposition that the light follows the *easiest* path, the problem of constructing the refracted ray consists in finding a point H on the diameter AB such that, having drawn the perpendicular HI and joined ID, the sum
$$CD.m + DI.DF$$

[31] See Fermat's *'Analysis ad Refractiones'*, in F, I, pp, 170–2; French translation, F, III, pp. 149–51.

is a minimum. For this sum may be taken to represent the 'movement' along CDI.

Let $\qquad\qquad n=CD=DI,$

$\qquad\qquad\qquad\quad b=DF,$

and $\qquad\qquad\quad a=DH.$

a is determined by the condition:

(2) $\qquad\qquad\qquad nm+nb=$ a minimum.

To find a, Fermat takes a point O on the diameter AB such that:

$$DO=e=\text{a very small quantity.}$$

Joining CO and OI, we have:

(3) $\qquad\qquad\qquad CO^2=n^2+e^2-2be,$ and,

(4) $\qquad\qquad\qquad OI^2=n^2+e^2+2ae.$

Taking the square roots of (3) and (4); and multiplying (3) by m, and, (4) by b:

(3') $\qquad\qquad\quad CO.m=\sqrt{m^2n^2+m^2e^2-2m^2be},$

(4') $\qquad\qquad\quad IO.b=\sqrt{b^2n^2+b^2e^2+2b^2ae}.$

Now, according to Fermat's method, we may write:

$$CO.m+IO.b=nm+nb.$$

Therefore,

$$\sqrt{m^2n^2+m^2e^2-2m^2be}+\sqrt{b^2n^2+b^2e^2+2b^2ae}=nm+nb.$$

From this equation the following is obtained by repeated squaring and cancelling of common terms:[32]

$8b^2e^2m^2n^2 \quad -8b^3m^2n^2e$

$+2e^4b^2m^2 \quad -4b^3e^3m^2$

$+8b^2m^2n^2ae+4e^3b^2m^2a$

$\qquad\qquad -8b^3e^2m^2a= -4m^3e^2n^2b+8m^3b^2n^2e$

$\qquad\qquad\qquad\qquad -4b^3e^2n^2m-8b^3n^2aem$

$\qquad\qquad\qquad\qquad -4m^4e^3b \quad +4b^4e^3a$

$\qquad\qquad\qquad\qquad\quad +e^4m^4+4m^4b^2e^2$

$\qquad\qquad\qquad\qquad\quad +b^4e^4+4b^4a^2e^2.$

Dividing by e, and omitting the terms in which e (or one of its higher powers) remains, we get:

$$8b^2m^2n^2a-8b^3m^2n^2=8m^3b^2n^2-8b^3n^2am,$$

---

[32] The following deductions are not given by Fermat; he describes, however, the steps leading to conclusion (5).

$$8mb^2n^2(ma-bm)=8mb^2n^2(m^2-ba),$$
$$ma-bm=m^2-ba,$$
$$a(m+b)=m(m+b),$$
$$a=m.$$

Therefore, by (1),

$$\frac{DF}{a}=K,\text{ a constant.}$$

Since

$$\frac{DF}{CD}=\sin i,$$

and

$$\frac{a}{DI}=\frac{DH}{DI}=\sin r$$

(*i* and *r* being, respectively, the angles made by *CD* and *DI* with the normal to *AB* at *D*), it follows that

(5)
$$\frac{\sin i}{\sin r}=K,$$

'which absolutely agrees with the theorem discovered by Descartes; the above analysis, derived from our principle, therefore gives a rigorously exact demonstration of this theorem.'[33]

It will have been observed that in the above demonstration the word *time* does not occur. Perhaps Fermat wanted to formulate his proof in terms that would be acceptable to his friend La Chambre.[34] But suppose now we write—with Descartes:

$$\frac{R_r}{R_i}=\frac{v_r}{v_i},$$

that is, the resistances are *directly* proportional to the velocities. It would then follow, by assumption (1) and conclusion (5) in Fermat's demonstration, that

$$\frac{\sin i}{\sin r}=\frac{v_r}{v_i}=K.$$

This result is identical with that obtained in the Cartesian proof of the sine law; it means that the velocity of light is greater in denser (and more resisting) media. Had Fermat adopted Descartes' opinion concerning the velocity of light in different media, his

---

[33] F, I, p. 172; F, III, p. 151. [34] See above, p. 141, n. 19.

principle of *easiest course* would have been identical with a principle that was proposed by Leibniz in 1682 *against* the principle of least time. Leibniz suggested[35] that light follows the path of least 'resistance', that is, the path for which the sum of the distances covered, each multiplied by the 'resistance' of the medium, is a minimum. In the case of two homogeneous media, if s_i and s_r are the paths covered in the medium of incidence and of refraction, and R_i, R_r the 'resistances' of the media, then, according to him:

$$R_i.s_i + R_r.s_r = \text{a minimum.}$$

If we let R_i and R_r be represented, in Fermat's figure (Fig. V. 3), by m and DF respectively, and let CD and DI represent s_i and s_r, it is seen that Leibniz's principle yields the same condition as Fermat's condition (2) above in accordance with which the latter deduced the sine law. But Leibniz further assumed, however, in further agreement with Descartes, that light travels faster in denser and more resisting media. He argued that as the particles of such media are close together, they prevent the light from being diffused and thus cause its flow to be accelerated, just as a stream of water runs faster as the passage becomes narrower.

This, however, was not Fermat's intention in the preceding *Analysis*. To him, 'resistance' simply meant the reciprocal of velocity. His initial assumption (1) was, therefore, that the velocity of the light in the (rare) medium of incidence was greater than the velocity in the (dense) medium of refraction; and the quantity assumed to be a minimum—see condition (2)—simply measured the sum of the *time* along the incident and refracted rays. Consequently, his surprise at obtaining Descartes' ratio was all the greater since, to his understanding, Descartes had 'supposed' in his deductions that the velocity was greater in denser media.[36]

This was of looking at his own and Descartes' demonstrations had the result of confirming him in his belief that the Cartesian proof was logically incorrect. Thus, at the beginning of his *Synthesis for*

---

[35] Cf. Leibniz, '*Unicum opticae, catoptricae, & dioptricae principium*', in *Acta eruditorum, Leipzig*, 1682, pp. 185–90; R. Dugas, *Histoire de la mécanique*, p. 249.
[36] Fermat to La Chambre, 1 January 1662, F, II, p. 462.

Refractions,[37] after having remarked that he and Descartes had started from contrary suppositions regarding the velocity of light in different media, he asked whether it was possible 'to arrive, without paralogism, at one and the same truth by two diametrically opposed ways'.[38] This question he left in that place for the consideration of the 'more subtle and more rigorous Geometers', so that he might not involve himself in 'vain discussions' and 'useless quarrels'.[39] Later, however, in the letter to M. de *** of 1664, he made known his own answer to his query: after he had arrived at Descartes' ratio (from the principle of least time and consistently with the supposition that the velocity was greater in the rarer medium) and having made sure that there was no mistake in his deductions, he became convinced of two things, 'the one, that the opinion of M. Descartes on the proportion of refractions is very true; and the other, that his demonstration is very faulty and full of paralogisms'.[40]

Fermat was certainly mistaken in drawing the latter conclusion. What he overlooked was, strangely enough, that his principle does *not*, strictly speaking, yield the same law which is obtained in Descartes' proof, though both laws assert the constancy of the ratio of the sines. Thus in his *Synthesis for Refractions*, he attributed to Descartes the theorem which can be expressed as follows:[41]

$$(A) \qquad \frac{\sin i}{\sin r} = \frac{v_i}{v_r} = n.$$

As we have seen in the preceding chapter, Descartes' theorem is on the contrary:

$$(B) \qquad \frac{\sin i}{\sin r} = \frac{v_r}{v_i} = n.[42]$$

---

[37] Cf. Fermat, '*Synthesis ad Refractiones*', in F, I, pp. 173–9; French translation, F, III, pp 151–6. This work was written after the '*Analysis ad Refractiones*', and was sent to La Chambre in February 1662. See Fermat to La Chambre, 1 ᵀanuary 1662, F, II, p. 463 (last sentence in P.S.); and F, I, p. 173, editors' note 1.

[38] F, I, p. 173; F, III, p. 152.

[39] Ibid.

[40] F, II, p. 488.

[41] Cf. F, I, p. 175; F, III, p. 153.

[42] It is curious to note that Fermat thus failed to realize that he had in fact achieved what he had originally hoped for—namely, to deduce a law of refraction different from that of Descartes, though the difference was not of the kind he had expected.

Now (A) is a necessary result of Fermat's principle of least time;[43] and since light in going from a rare into a dense medium is bent towards the normal (the angle of refraction being thereby made smaller than the angle of incidence, and its sine less than the sine of incidence), one has to conclude (rather than assume), in accordance with (A), that the velocity in the rare medium of incidence (v_i) must be greater than the velocity in the dense medium of refraction (v_r). For the same reason the contrary conclusion has to be drawn from (B) with which this conclusion is, therefore, perfectly consistent.

4. The purpose of Fermat's *Synthesis* is to deduce from (A) the proposition that the actual path of light in refraction is that for which the time of the movement is a minimum, while being consistent with the supposition—itself a consequence of (A)—that the velocity is greater in rarer media. The undoubted validity of Fermat's deductions does not, however, imply—as he thought—that Descartes' proof is logically inconclusive. The following is an account of Fermat's *Synthesis*.

The diameter ANB (Fig. V. 4) separates the rare medium of incidence above from the dense medium below; MN is an incident ray that is refracted into NH; MD and HS are perpendiculars.

R is any point (other than N) of the diameter AB—taken, for example, on the radius NB.

---

[43] This is already clear from the preceding demonstration by 'analysis'. Bearing in mind what has been remarked above concerning Fermat's understanding of resistance, his assumption (1), expressed in terms of v_i and v_r, should be written thus:

$$\text{(i)} \quad \frac{v_i}{v_r} = \frac{DF}{m} = n.$$

Joining this with his conclusion (5), we get:

$$\text{(ii)} \quad \frac{\sin i}{\sin r} = \frac{v_i}{v_r} = n.$$

It is to be noted that in deriving this result it is not logically necessary to postulate the condition, stated in Fermat's assumption (1), that n (v_i/v_r) is greater than unity. This condition is in fact obtained as a result of comparing (ii) with the actual behaviour of light in going from a rare into a dense medium.

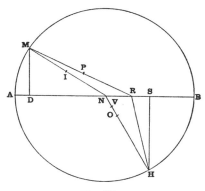

FIG. V. 4

It is assumed that

(1) $$\frac{DN}{NS}=\frac{\sin i}{\sin r}=\frac{v_i}{v_r}=\frac{MN}{NI}=\frac{MR}{RP}=n>1$$

(where i and r are the angles respectively made by MN and NH with the normal to AB at N; and v_i, v_r, the velocities of incidence and of refraction).

It is to be proved that the time along MNH is less than the time along MRH.

Since

$$\frac{\text{time along } MN}{\text{time along } NH}=\frac{MN}{NH}\times\frac{v_r}{v_i}=\frac{MN}{NH}\times\frac{NI}{MN}=\frac{NI}{NH},$$

and

$$\frac{\text{time along } MR}{\text{time along } RH}=\frac{MR}{RH}\times\frac{v_r}{v_i}=\frac{MR}{RH}\times\frac{RP}{MR}=\frac{RP}{RH},$$

therefore,

$$\frac{\text{time along } MNH}{\text{time along } MRH}=\frac{NI+NH}{RP+RH}.$$

It is now to be proved that

$$RP+RH>NI+NH.$$

Let

(2) $$\frac{MN}{DN}=\frac{RN}{NO} \text{ and } \frac{DN}{NS}=\frac{NO}{NV}.$$

Since, by construction,

$$DN< MN \text{ and } NS< DN,$$

we have:

(3) $NO < RN$ and $NV < NO$.

But,

$$MR^2 = MN^2 + RN^2 + 2DN.RN.$$

Therefore, by (2),

$$MR^2 = MN^2 + RN^2 + 2MN.NO.$$

From which it follows, by (3), that

$$MR^2 > MN^2 + NO^2 + 2MN.NO = (MN + NO)^2.$$

Therefore,

(4) $MR > MN + NO.$

But, from (1) and (2),

$$\frac{DN}{NS} = \frac{MN}{NI} = \frac{NO}{NV} = \frac{MN + NO}{NI + NV} = \frac{MR}{RP}.$$

Therefore, by (4),

$$RP > NI + NV.$$

It now remains to be proved that

$$RH > HV,$$

for then it will follow that

$$RP + RH > NI + NV + HV,$$
$$RP + RH > NI + NH.$$

In the triangle NHR,

(5) $RH^2 = NH^2 + NR^2 - 2NS.NR.$

From (2)

$$MN(= NH).NO = DN.NR,$$
$$NS.NO = DN.NV.$$

Therefore,

(6) $\dfrac{NH}{NS} = \dfrac{NR}{NV}.$

From (5) and (6),

$$RH^2 = NH^2 + NR^2 - 2NH.NV$$

But since, by (3),

$$NR > NV, \quad NR^2 > NV^2,$$

it follows that

$$RH^2 > HN^2 + NV^2 - 2NH.NV,$$

and we finally have:

$$RH > HN - NV, \quad RH > HV,$$

which was to be proved.

Fermat provides a similar proof for the case in which R is one of the points on the radius AN.

Having satisfied himself as to the truth of Descartes' ratio, Fermat offered to make peace with the Cartesians on the following terms:[44] Descartes had made an important discovery; this, however, he had achieved 'without the aid of any demonstration'; nature, as it were, had not dared to resist 'this great genius'; as in those battles which were won on the sole strength of the conqueror's reputation, nature had surrendered her secret to him without being forced by demonstration; the glory of victory was Descartes' and Fermat was 'content that M. Clerselier should at least let me enter into the society of the proof of this very important truth'.

Peace under these conditions was not, of course, acceptable to Clerselier.[45] He admitted that Fermat's proof was logically valid; but so, he (rightly) maintained, was Descartes'. The difference between them, in his view, was that whereas Descartes founded his proof on physical considerations, the principle which formed the basis of Fermat's demonstration was 'only a moral and not a physical principle, which is not and cannot be the cause of any natural effect'.[46] To hold this principle was to ascribe knowledge and choice to nature, whereas nature in fact acted by the 'force' residing in all things and the dispositions of bodies to receive the action of this force—in short, by a 'necessary determinism'.[47] Once a body was set in motion, its speed and 'determination' depended solely on the 'force' of its movement and the 'disposition' of that force.[48] Only motion in a straight line was naturally determined (in accordance with the law of inertia formulated by Descartes). Thus a ray of light would always travel in the same direction so long as it remained in the same medium. It would change direction at the meeting of a refracting surface, not for the sake of Fermat's principle (for, then, the ray would have to remember its point of departure, choose a certain destination, and perform the necessary calculations!), but

---

[44] Fermat to La Chambre, 1 January 1662, F, II, p. 462.
[45] Cf. Clerselier's letter to Fermat, 6 May 1662, F, II, pp. 464–72. He wrote this letter after having seen Fermat's letter to La Chambre (1 January 1662) and also Fermat's 'Synthesis for Refractions'.   [46] F, II, p. 465.   [47] Ibid.   [48] Ibid., p. 466.

because the different disposition of the refracting body would of necessity alter the ray's force and determination—in the manner that Descartes had shown. As time was not a cause of movement, the shortness of time along the lines of incidence and of refraction could not be the cause of the light's following those lines. Fermat's principle was, therefore, metaphysical, imaginary and had no foundation in physics. Moreover, his view that light passed more easily through rarer media mistakenly ignored Descartes' physical argument in support of the opposite view. Thus, far from Descartes' having conquered nature without the force of demonstration, it would, according to Clerselier, be more true to say that Fermat had forced geometry to adapt itself to false opinions.

It was in answer to this that Fermat wrote the following passage in his last letter to Clerselier of 21 May 1662:[49]

I believe that I have often said both to M. de la Chambre and to you that I do not pretend, nor have I ever pretended to be in the inner confidence of Nature. She has obscure and hidden ways which I have never undertaken to penetrate. I would have only offered her a little geometrical aid on the subject of refraction, should she have been in need of it. But since you assure me, Sir, that she can manage her affairs without it, and that she is content to follow the way that has been prescribed to her by M. Descartes, I willingly hand over to you my alleged conquest of physics; and I am satisfied that you allow me to keep my geometrical problem— pure and *in abstracto*, by means of which one can find the path of a thing moving through two different media and seeking to complete its movement as soon as it can.[50]

5. It would be a mistake to conclude from the preceding passage that Fermat really looked at his efforts as having resulted merely in the solution of an abstract geometrical problem. The ironical tone of his words is in fact more telling about his real beliefs than what his statements might appear to say. If he expressed his willingness to hand over his conquest of physics to Clerselier, that was only in order to end a controversy which had been getting to be increasingly unpleasant. In fact, he himself indicated immediately after the above

---

[49] Cf. F, II, pp. 482–4. [50] Ibid., p. 483.

passage that he still found it improbable that he could have arrived, so unexpectedly, at Descartes' true ratio from a false principle, while making an assumption that was directly opposed to the corresponding assumption of Descartes. It must also be remembered that Fermat originally set out to discover *the true* law of refraction; he was not concerned to deduce an arbitrary law from an arbitrary assumption. When, to his great surprise, he finally obtained Descartes' law (in the form $\sin i = n \sin r$), he interpreted his calculations as a 'demonstration' of an important truth. As we have seen[51], a demonstration for Fermat was not simply a valid inference from supposed premises, but a deduction from *true* principles. It is very doubtful that he would have embarked on the difficult task of applying his method of maxima and minima to the problem of refraction, had he not been convinced that the general principle of economy, which inspired this application, was a true law of nature. Indeed he was not convinced of the truth of the refraction law itself, even after it had been confirmed by experiments, until he had derived it from his principle of least time. It would not, therefore, be correct to suppose, as his preceding passage might lead us to do, that he performed his deductions in the interests of pure geometry alone. Rather, he undertook the solution of the problem suggested to him by the principle of shortest course as a mathematician whom chance seemed to have presented with an opportunity to render an important service to physics, to found the science of dioptrics on a sound basis, and not merely to provide it with a tool for calculation. In accordance with this aim, he had understood that principle as a *true physical principle*, not as a mathematical hypothesis.

Fermat started from a principle of economy which had had a long history before him. In its most general form, it asserted that nature did nothing in vain. As applied to reflection at plane surfaces it had been interpreted as a principle of *shortest distance*. Since this interpretation, however, could not be made to fit the phenomenon of refraction, Fermat substituted a new specification, namely that of *easiest course* which he understood to mean *least time*. Heron's theorem

---

[51] Above, pp. 129f, 142f.

would then be shown to be only a special case of Fermat's principle and, therefore, in agreement with it. But this was not the only meaning which Fermat attached to his principle. In order to answer the objection that reflection at concave surfaces did not satisfy the law of shortest course, he had to appeal to a different interpretation in which considerations of *simplicity* replaced the shortness of distance and of time.[52] The suggestions he made in this connection could only help to evade the problem which was a real one. In fact, Fermat's principle is now accepted as generally true only if understood as a principle of extremum, that is, of maximum or minimum.[53] He was bound to avoid this formulation as its admission would have conflicted with the metaphysical reasoning which had determined his approach.

Supposing, however, that the principle of economy was generally true, there was still no *a priori* reason why time, rather than any other quantity, should be the minimum. As it happened, however, Huygens later showed in his *Traité de la Lumière* (1690) that the principle of least time was deducible from his own law of secondary waves.[54] Fermat's principle thus received a physical foundation by being shown to follow from wave considerations. Before the appearance of Huygens' *Traité*, Newton had already published in *Principia* a dynamical explanation of refraction which required the velocity of light to be greater in denser media[55]—in contradiction to Huygens' theory and Fermat's principle. In the eighteenth century Newton's explanation was accepted as part of a corpuscular theory of light which had completely overshadowed Huygens' theory; and Fermat's principle was regarded as a detached metaphysical principle to be examined on its own merits, or, rather, demerits. Final causes had not then completely disappeared from physical considerations; but the adherents of Newton's theory could point to an arbitrary character of Fermat's principle: if light could not at once travel in

---

[52] See above, p. 139, n. 14.

[53] There are also cases in which the path of reflected light is neither a minimum ncr a maximum but stationary, as when the reflecting surface is an ellipsoid of revolution and the two points related as object and image are the foci.

[54] Below, pp. 218f.

[55] Below, pp. 301ff.

the shortest time by the shortest path, why should it choose one of these courses rather than the other?—that was Maupertuis' argument in 1744. Instead of the shortness of either distance or time, he proposed that the path really followed by light is that for which the *quantity of action* is a minimum.[56] Thus Maupertuis accepted the principle of economy, but he offered a new interpretation. By *action* he understood a quantity proportional to the sum of the distances covered, each multiplied by the velocity with which it is traversed; and he showed that his principle of least action (as he called it) leads to the Newtonian law of refraction giving the sines of incidence and of refraction in the inverse ratio of the velocities.

Maupertuis' procedure was no less metaphysical than Fermat's. In a sense it was even more arbitrary. For whereas Fermat could have at least argued that time was a natural and basic concept whose intimate relation to motion should recommend it as the minimum quantity,[57] Maupertuis' 'action' was an artificially constructed quantity introduceed to fit the already formulated Newtonian law. Similarly to what had happened with Fermat's principle, however, Euler showed (in 1744) that the principle of least action was applicable in several important cases of particle dynamics, as, for example, when a body moves under the action of a central force.[58] And later,

---

[56] Cf. R. Dugas, *Histoire de la mécanique*, p. 252.

[57] Galileo had made use of such an argument in connection with his law of naturally accelerated motion. Having stated that nature employs in her various processes 'only those means which are most common, simple and easy', he concluded: 'When, therefore I observe a stone initially at rest falling from an elevated position and continually acquiring new increments of speed, why should I not believe that such increases take place in a manner which is exceedingly simple and rather obvious to everybody? If now we examine the matter carefully we find no addition or increment more simple than that which repeats itself always in the same manner. *This we readily understand when we consider the intimate relationship between ime and motion*; forj ust as uniformity of motion is defined by and conceived through equal times and equal spaces . . . so also we may, in a similar manner, through equal time-intervals, conceive additions of speed as taking place without complications . . .' *Dialogues Concerning Two New Sciences*, ed. H. Crew and A. de Salvio, New York, 1914, p. 161; my italics. Fermat himself quoted the example of Galileo twice in support of his principle of least time; cf. Fermat to La Chambre, August 1657, F, II, p. 359; '*Synthesis ad Refractiones*', F, I, p. 173 French translation, F, III, p. 152.

[58] Cf. R. Dugas, *Histoire de la mécanique*, Ch. V, Sec. 11. Euler in fact started from the assertion that 'all the effects of Nature follow some law of maximum or minimum' (ibid., p. 262), in violation of the principle of economy. But although he presented his principle of extremum as a law to be verified *a posteriori*, he still sought for metaphysical justifications (cf. ibid., p. 263).

Lagrange extended Euler's applications of Maupertuis' principle (as a law of extremum) which he regarded, not as a metaphysical explanation, but as a 'simple and general result of the laws of mechanics'.[59]

Thus, as far as optical refraction is concerned, the incompatibility of Fermat's principle with that of Maupertuis became a conflict, not between two interpretations of a metaphysical view of nature, but between the wave and the dynamical (or corpuscular) theories of light in which these two principles were respectively verified. Until 1850 there had been no experiment to decide between the wave and the corpuscular explanations of refraction. When, in that year, Foucault performed his famous experiment, he found that the velocity of light was greater in air than in water—in agreement with Huygens' explanation and against the Newtonian view.

---

[59] Ibid., p. 327.

Chapter Six

HUYGENS' CARTESIANISM AND HIS THEORY OF CONJECTURAL EXPLANATION

1. Huygens' commitment to a Cartesian point of view in physics was most clearly expressed in the course of a controversy which took place at the *Académie Royale des Sciences* in 1669. Although this controversy was concerned with the cause of gravity, not with light, a discussion of Huygens' views on the former subject will be of help towards a better understanding of the statements relating to physical explanation and hypotheses which later appeared in his *Traité de la Lumière.*

The chief opponent of Huygens was the great enemy of Descartes, Roberval. His memoir, which served as the basis of discussion, was delivered on 7 August 1669.[1] It explained that the gravity of a body is 'that which inclines this body to descend towards a centre naturally and without artifice.'[2] According to Roberval one may, in this generalized sense, recognize gravities other than terrestrial, for example, lunar, or solar, or jovial. This does not mean, however, that he conceived the idea of universal gravitation: he did not speak of the earth, the sun, and the other heavenly bodies as gravitating towards one another. Rather, the gravities which he had in mind were between bodies belonging to one whole; that is, terrestrial bodies gravitate towards the earth, solar bodies towards the sun, and so forth.[3]

---

[1] Cf. H, XIX, pp. 628–30.

[2] Ibid., p. 628.

[3] Thus we read on the first page of his *Traité de méchanique* (1636): '. . . the line of direction of a freely falling body is the line drawn from the centre of gravity of the same heavy body to the natural centre of ponderable things which, for terrestrial bodies, is the centre of the earth.' The idea that there is a *natural* centre for heavy bodies which varies according as the body is terrestrial, or jovial, etc., cannot be reconciled with the idea of universal gravitation. For it would imply, for example, that a terrestrial body does not gravitate towards Jupiter or towards the sun. Roberval's concept, which is to be distinguished also from Aristotle's conception of heavy bodies tending towards the *centre of the world*, as a point determined independently of the nature of the body occupying it, is immediately derived from Copernicus.

As Newton later found it necessary to point out in the *Principia*, Roberval remarked that one did not have to attribute a certain virtue to the centre 'which is but a point';[4] it was sufficient to understand that all the parts of a body tended to be united together so as to form a single body. 'For there will result from that a centre of gravity towards which all these parts will be directed with greater or lesser force, according to their proper nature: and it is in this force that gravity consists.'[5]

He then distinguished three views regarding the nature of gravity. According to the first view, gravity resides only in the gravitating body owing to a certain quality which drives it downwards (that is, towards a natural centre). On the second view, gravity is a quality common to all parts of a body, and in virtue of which all those parts attract one another. The third view ascribed gravity to the action of an external agent, a subtle matter, which either causes the heaviness of a body by pushing it downwards, or its lightness by pushing it upwards. The first two opinions agreed in that they made gravity or heaviness the first and independent cause of the movement downwards, and lightness the first and independent cause of the movement upwards. As distinguished from these, the third opinion considered *motion* to be the cause of both heaviness and lightness.

Roberval granted that all three opinions had no foundation other than in the imagination of their authors. Yet, the first two appeared to him more easily tenable, and he himself preferred the second. His main reason was that experiments could be made to test it. For example, if it were true that bodies mutually attracted one another, then it would follow that the same body would weigh less near the centre of the earth than at the circumference (where, according to him, the weight would be greater than at any other point on either side of it).[6] This, he pointed out, could be tested by a spring balance.

Cf. on these distinctions Alexandre Koyré, *La gravitation universelle de Képler à Newton*, Paris, 1951.

[4] H, XIX, p. 628. Compare Newton, *Principia*, Definition VIII, pp. 5–6: 'the reader is not to imagine . . . that I attribute forces, in a true and physical sense, to certain centres (which are only mathematical points); when at any time I happen to speak of centres as attracting or as endowed with attractive powers.'

[5] H, XIX, p. 628.

[6] Cf. ibid., p. 629. Roberval's reason why the weight would decrease as the body approached

It would also follow, in his view, that a huge and very high mountain would deflect a small hanging weight from the vertical direction towards it. But, finding these tests rather difficult to realize, he left the judgement on this matter to the '*spéculatifs*'.

Nevertheless, if one admits occult qualities; that is, qualities for which we have no proper and specific sense, this second opinion seems to me to be the most plausible of the three. But it is also possible that the three opinions are all false, and that the true one is unknown to us.[7]

Roberval then concluded his discourse with the following declaration which bears a certain similarity to Newton's views on the same subject as they were expressed in the General Scholium to the *Principia*:

... I shall always do my best to imitate Archimedes who, on this occasion of gravity, lays down, as a principle or postulate, the invariable fact which has to the present day been verified throughout the past centuries, that there are heavy bodies, which possess the conditions of which he speaks in the beginning of his treatise on this subject; and on this foundation I shall, as he did, establish my reasonings for Mechanics, without bothering to know at bottom the principles and the causes of gravity, waiting to follow the truth, if it suits her to reveal herself one day clearly and distinctly in my mind.[8]

This, Roberval said, was the maxim which he would always follow in uncertain matters, if he was not obliged to take sides in them.

In contrast to Roberval's attitude, the question for Huygens (who

---

the centre from the circumference was, presumably, that the attraction towards the central parts of the earth would be gradually weakened by the opposite attraction towards the parts near the circumference.

[7] Ibid., p. 629.

[8] Ibid., pp. 629–30. Both Roberval and Newton found it sufficient for their limited purposes to consider that gravity was a fact—Newton, asserting in the General Scholium that 'to us it is enough that gravity does really exist' (*Principia*, p. 547) and Roberval, pointing out that 'there are heavy bodies'. Both preferred not to commit themselves to any view regarding the cause of gravity, either for want of a clear and distinct idea as to the nature of that cause (Roberval), or for lack of experiments (Newton). Neither one nor the other denied that it was within the limits of science to search for such a cause. They differed, however, in that Newton extended gravity to the solar system as a whole (and, indeed, to all parts of matter everywhere), and that, unlike Roberval, he explicitly denied that attraction could be a primary quality of matter.

read his discourse on 28 August 1669)[9] was to look for an 'intelligible cause of gravity' without supposing in nature anything other than 'bodies made up of the same matter, in which one does not recognize any quality, or tendency to approach one another'; that is, bodies which differ merely by their 'magnitudes, figures, and movements'.[10] From these components alone, and without resorting to forces or occult qualities, one had to explain how several bodies 'directly tend towards the same centre, and there remain assembled around it, which is the most ordinary and principal phenomenon of what we call gravity'.[11]

Thus Huygens starts from a criterion of intelligibility which leads him to banish tendencies and attractions from physical considerations.[12] He accepts the Cartesian view according to which explanations in physics ought to be in terms of the 'intelligible', geometrical properties: magnitude, figure and motion. In consequence, one has to assume the existence of certain invisible corpuscles which have only those admissible properties, and which in some way cause the gravity of bodies. And the problem to be solved is then the following: On which of these properties does gravity depend, and how? According to Huygens, the simplicity (or, rather, scarcity) of these principles did not leave much room for choice. For, as it did not appear to him that gravity could be due to the magnitude or figures of the corpuscles, he concluded that the phenomenon, 'being a tendency or inclination to movement, must probably [*vraysemblablement*] be produced by a movement'.[13] What kind of movement? There were only two in nature, the straight and the circular.[14] But, as there was nothing in the nature

---

[9] Cf. H, XIX, pp. 631–40.

[10] Ibid., p. 631.

[11] Ibid.

[12] At a later meeting of the *Académie des Sciences* (23 October 1669), Huygens defended his position, against a previous objection from Roberval, in the following words: 'I exclude attractive and repulsive qualities from nature because I am looking for an intelligible cause of gravity'. H, XIX, p. 642.

[13] H, XIX, p. 631.

[14] Huygens' assertion that there existed a circular motion in nature does not mean, as A. E. Bell understood in his *Christian Huygens* (London, 1947, pp. 64 and 164), that he believed (in 1669) this form of motion to be 'fundamental' or 'natural'. The same misunderstanding was implied in an objection of Roberval made during the session of the *Académie* on 4 September,

of the first or in the laws governing its communication or reflection that appeared to determine bodies to move towards a centre, he concluded that the required property must be looked for in the second. And he found it precisely in the inclination of a circulating body to recede from the centre of its motion. For this inclination of the body (its centrifugal force) increases with the speed of the motion. If now it is supposed that a fluid and very subtle matter circulates with great speed around the earth, the gross bodies which do not participate in this motion (or which participate in it to a lesser degree) will be less inclined to recede from the centre of the earth than the surrounding matter, and will thus be continually replaced by the parts of the fluid which lie next to them towards the centre. In this way the gross bodies which happen to be in the region around the earth that is filled with the circulating fluid, will be driven towards the centre; this accounts for their gravity.[15]

Huygens illustrated these ideas by an improved version of an 'experiment' that had been described by Descartes. The improvement is interesting as it shows Huygens trying to be more Cartesian than Descartes himself. A round vessel is filled with water (or some other liquid). A small sphere, of a substance whose density may be greater than the density of the liquid or equal to it, is immersed near the wall of the vessel. The sphere is hindered from moving freely by two stretched strings that allow it to move only along the diameter of the vessel. The vessel is then placed on a round table, which is then made to rotate. The motion will be gradually communicated to the liquid, but the sphere will be prevented by the strings from participating in the circular motion. If now the table is suddenly stopped, the liquid will continue to circulate for a while, but the

---

1669 (cf. H, XIX, p. 641, Art. 3). To this objection Huygens answered on 23 October 1669 (H, XIX, p. 643): '. . . I have not said that circular motion is natural but that such motion exists in the world, which cannot be denied.' The view attributed to Huygens by Bell would not have been reconcilable with his Cartesian belief that matter naturally tended to move only in straight lines. In fact the explanation given by Huygens (in the same discourse of 28 August 1669) of the circular motion of the fluid matter surrounding the earth is in principle identical with that of Descartes: namely, owing to the existence of 'other bodies' beyond it in space, the fluid matter is prevented from pursuing the rectilinear course which it would otherwise take, and, as a consequence, it is *forced* to take a curvilinear course (H, XIX, p. 634). Cf. Descartes, *Principles*, II, 37 and 39.

[15] H, XIX, pp. 632–3.

sphere will move towards the centre and, once there, will come to a stop.

The difference between this experiment and that of Descartes is that the latter had required the vessel to be filled with fine shots of lead (representing the circulating subtle matter), and the immersed body had been supposed to be pieces of a *lighter* material, wood.[16] But, Huygens objected, the motion of the wood towards the centre would in this case be 'the effect of the difference in gravity of the wood and the lead, whereas one should explain gravity without supposing any, and by considering all bodies to be made of one and the same matter'.[17] In Huygens' experiment, on the other hand, the weight (or gravity) of the sphere is immaterial (as it may be of the same density as the liquid) and, therefore, the effect is here produced, according to him, by 'motion alone'.[18] The intended improvement is thus introduced in the name of the Cartesian doctrine of the perfect homogeneity of all matter; and for Huygens himself, the superiority of his own experiment lay in that it provided for an explanation of gravity in terms of motion alone, as should be demanded by a consistent Cartesian.

Huygens expressed these views in 1669, that is about eighteen years before the appearance of Newton's *Principia* in 1687. It is, however, evident from the *Discours de la Cause de la Pesanteur*, which he published in the same volume with his *Traité de la Lumière* in 1690, that Newton's book had not altered his fundamental position. The *Discours* itself was only an amplified version of the memoir of 1669, apart from a final *Addition* which he wrote after he had read Newton's *Principia*.[19] It is true that in this *Addition* Huygens appears to be aware of more difficulties facing the Cartesian vortex theory than he had realized before. For example, having accepted the Newtonian extension of gravity to the whole of the solar system, he now had to take into account such complicated facts as the constant eccentricity of planetary orbits; the constant

---

[16] Cf. Descartes to Mersenne, 16 October 1639, D, II, pp. 593-4.
[17] H, XIX, p. 634.
[18] H, XIX, p. 633.
[19] The *Discours* together with the *Addition* are printed in H, XXI, pp. 445–88.

obliquity of their planes to one another; the fact that the motion of comets is often contrary to that of the planets; and so forth.[20] All this made him renounce the Cartesian vortices in their original form.[21] But it did not change his opinion as to the necessity of explaining gravity by vortex motions. The reason, no doubt, is that he still maintained his original view concerning the nature of physical explanation, which he had inherited from Descartes. Thus we read in a new Preface to the *Discours*:

Mr Des Cartes has recognized better than those who came before him that nothing would be better understood in physics than that which could be related to Principles not exceeding the capacity of our mind, such as those which depend on bodies, considered without qualities, and on their movements. But, as the greatest difficulty consists in showing how such a great variety of things are the result of these Principles alone, he has not greatly succeeded in that [task] when he proposed to treat of several particular subjects: among which, in my opinion, is that of gravity. . . . Nevertheless I confess that his trials, and his views, though false, have served to open the way for me towards what I have found on this same subject.[22]

And again in the same Preface:

I do not offer [this Discourse] as something beyond the reach of doubt, or as something against which one cannot make objections. It is too difficult to go that far in researches of this nature. It is, however, my belief that if the principal hypothesis on which I stand is not the true one, there is little hope that [such a true hypothesis] can be found, while remaining within the limits of the true and sane Philosophy.[23]

---

[20] Cf. H, XXI, pp. 472–3. For Huygens' proposals to meet these difficulties, see Mouy, *Le développement de la physique cartésienne*, pp. 258–63. See also H, XXI, pp. 429–41, editors' *Avertissement*.

[21] Huygens wrote the following note on comets in 1689, after he had made Newton's acquaintance during a visit to England (June-August, 1689): 'I am now almost of the opinion of Mr Newton who holds that the comets turn in very oblong ellipses round the sun which occupies one of the foci. This becomes very probable after he has removed the vortices of des Cartes which, besides, have failed to agree with several phenomena of planetary motions' H, XIX, p. 310). Cf. on Huygens' meeting with Newton: H, IX, p. 333, note 1; H, XXI, p. 435, note 31; David Brewster, *Memoirs of the Life, Writings, and Discoveries of Sir Isaac Newton* Edinburgh, 1885, I, p. 215; J. Edleston, *Correspondence of Sir Isaac Newton and Professor Cotes*, London, 1850, p. xxxi.

[22] H, XXI, p. 446.

[23] Ibid.

The 'principal hypothesis' mentioned here is one in which an invisible subtle matter is supposed to produce the effects of gravity. As to the 'true and sane Philosophy', this is the mechanical philosophy which aims to explain motion by motion alone, without bringing in attractive or other powers.[24] For although Huygens adopted Newtonian gravitation as extended to the solar system,[25] he still could not accept the idea which, as he pointed out, was assumed in some of Newton's calculations, namely that the constituent parts of different bodies attracted one another or tended to approach one another. His reason for rejecting this idea was 'that the cause of such an attraction is not explicable by any principle of Mechanics, or by the laws of motion,'[26] that is, the laws governing the communication of motion when bodies come into contact with one another.

Thus, up to the publication of his *Traité de la Lumière* in 1690, Huygens' position had remained unaltered: gravity and the other natural phenomena had to be explained in purely mechanical terms.[27] This he maintained as a result of his adoption of the Cartesian doctrine according to which physical explanations ought to be formulated with reference to a conceptual system which is determined by a fixed criterion of intelligibility, a system which would be made up of such words as magnitude, figure and motion. For Huygens, as for Descartes, no explanation was intelligible unless it could be completely expressed in these words. This amounts to the Cartesian requirement that all physical explanations should be in terms of push or contact action, a requirement which, in turn,

---

[24] In his *Traité de la Lumière* Huygens speaks of 'the true Philosophy in which the cause of all natural effects is conceived by mechanical reasons' (H, XIX, p. 461).

[25] Cf. *Addition* to the *Discours*, H, XXI, p. 472: 'I have ... nothing against the *Vis Centripeta*, as Mr. Newton calls it, by which he makes the Planets gravitate towards the Sun, and the Moon towards the Earth ... not only because we know from experience that such a manner of attraction or impulsion exists in nature, but also because it is explained by the laws of motion, as has been seen in what I have written above concerning gravity. For nothing prevents the cause of this *Vis Centripeta* towards the Sun from being similar to that which pushes bodies, that are called heavy, towards the Earth.'

[26] H, XXI, p. 471.

[27] It is gathered from Huygens' correspondence that he in fact persisted in this position until his death (in 1695). Cf. Huygens to Leibniz, 24 August 1694, H, X, p. 669; and H, XXI, p. 439, editors' *Avertissement*.

demands the postulation of some hypothetical matter whose motion or mechanical action is responsible for the production of natural phenomena. Hence Huygens' rejection of attraction as existing between the parts of bodies, while, at the same time, he accepted astronomical gravitation. He believed that whereas the latter could be explained by a complicated system of vortex motions, the former was not, in his view, capable of such an explanation.

Huygens' position does not imply, however, that he accepted the *a priori* part of Descartes' physical doctrine. For Descartes, since he starts from the identification of space and matter, the phrase *empty space* is a contradiction in terms; the existence of the void is thus denied in Descartes' physics as a result of an *a priori* definition giving the essence of matter. But this Huygens could not accept. Having expressed in the *Addition* his readiness to accept the astronomical facts as asserted in Newton's *Principia*, he pointed out one 'difficulty'.[28] Newton, he remarked, would only go so far as to allow the celestial space to contain an 'extremely rare matter',[29] so that the planets and the comets might easily move in them. But if that were assumed, Huygens objected, it would be impossible to explain either the action of gravity or that of light, 'at least by the means which I have made use of'.[30] Therefore, according to him, Newton's condition for the possibility of celestial motions had to be reconsidered. And to avoid misunderstandings, he distinguished two meanings of rarity: either the particles of the ethereal matter are far apart from one another 'with much void' between any two of them (as Newton had required), or they 'touch one another, but the tissue of each is rare and inter-mixed with many small empty spaces'.[31] But since he found it 'entirely impossible' to account for the 'prodigious' velocity of light (which Roemer had estimated to be at least six hundred thousand times greater than that of sound) without assuming contact between the ether particles (so that the action of light might be transmitted through them), he concluded by rejecting rarity in Newton's sense:[32]

---

[28] H, XXI, p. 473.   [29] Ibid.   [30] Ibid.   [31] Ibid.
[32] H, XXI, p. 473. In 1694, Huygens still maintained against Newton that 'such a rapid passage of the [light] corpuscles from the Sun or Jupiter to us' was inadmissible. H, X, p. 613.

As to the void, I accept it without difficulty, and I even believe it necessary for the movement of small particles among themselves, not being of the opinion of Mr Descartes, who holds that extension alone makes the essence of body.[33]

This declaration brings Huygens on the side of Democritus and Gassendi, farther from Descartes. It will be seen later that he also endowed his ether particles with a property, namely that of elasticity, which Descartes was prevented from ascribing to his matter on *a priori* grounds. This property allowed Huygens to postulate a finite velocity of light, where Descartes had to assert an instantaneous propagation.

Thus, although Huygens adopted Descartes' criterion of intelligibility as applied to physical explanation, he did not follow what the latter had regarded as a rigorous application of this criterion. This means, however, that he rejected Cartesian rationalism only in so far as it sought to establish certain physical doctrines *a priori*. He nevertheless accepted Descartes' demand, itself a consequence of his rationalism, that only geometrical concepts should be admitted into physics, a demand which implied the doctrine that all physical actions must be of the nature of impact.

Following Descartes, Huygens attached primary importance to causal explanations in physics and, like Descartes, he would only admit explanations in terms of movement. A physical question would not be completely settled until such an explanation could be found. It was not enough to establish the experimental laws governing a certain phenomenon; for while such laws might be useful in practical applications, and although they formed the basis for further research, they were not sufficient by themselves.

This may be illustrated by his attitude towards Newton's inverse square law, and towards Newton's theory of colours. Huygens wrote in the *Addition*:

I had not thought . . . of this regulated diminution of gravity, namely that it was in inverse ratio to the squares of the distances from the centre:

---

[33] H, XXI, p. 473.

which is a new and remarkable property of gravity, *of which the reason is well worth looking for*.[34]

Huygens here accepts Newton's law; but this suggests to him a further problem which he hastens to point out at the same time as he expresses his admiration for the discovery: What is the cause of this diminution? Newton himself certainly recognized the validity of such a question when he attempted to explain gravity by the action of a rare and elastic ethereal medium.[35] But whereas Newton was prepared at least to consider [36] alternative explanations in terms of what he called 'active principles' of a non-mechanical order, there was for Huygens only one possible form of explanation, namely by the mechanical properties of the subtle matter whose existence he never doubted. In this he was in sharp disagreement with Newton's followers who, like Roger Cotes, went so far as to regard attraction as a primary property of matter—a view which implied that a causal explanation of gravity was pointless.[37]

Again Huygens accepted Newton's discovery (published in 1672) that light rays of different colours were not equally refracted by one and the same medium as a fact 'very well proved by experiment'.[38] At the same time, however, he was of the opinion that the question of colours was one of those matters 'in which no one until now [i.e. 1690] can boast of having succeeded'.[39] At one time (1673) Huygens was inclined towards Hooke's view that there were only two principal colours (red and blue) because he thought it would be easier to find 'an Hypothesis by Motion' to explain two colours, than for an infinite variety of them.[40] It would seem from the words just quoted from the Preface to the *Traité* that, by 1690, Huygens had abandoned Hooke's opinion. But they also indicate that he had not completely reconciled himself to Newton's theory.

---

[34] H, XXI, p. 472; italics added.

[35] Cf., for example, Newton, *Opticks*, Query 21, pp. 350–2.

[36] Cf. ibid., Query 31, pp. 401–2.

[37] Cf. Cotes' Preface to the second edition of Newton's *Principia*, pp. xxvi–xxvii.

[38] Huygens, *Treatise*, p. 106.

[39] Ibid., Preface (dated 8 January 1690), p. vii.

[40] Cf. *Phil. Trans.*, No. 96, 21 July 1673, p. 6086. Huygens in fact subscribed to Hooke dualistic theory until at least 1678. Cf. H, XIX, pp. 385–6, *Avertissement*.

No reasons for this are given in the *Traité*, but we know that Huygens' main objection in 1672 against the Newtonian theory was that it had omitted to explain 'by the mechanical physics wherein this diversity of colours consists'.[41] And there is nothing to suggest that he had withdrawn this objection before (or after) he published the *Traité* in 1690. Huygens' attitude greatly contrasts with Newton's view that his theory of colours was not in need of any mechanical or other explanation to support it. And it was this kind of attitude that Newton had in mind when he first raised his objections against the use, or rather (in his view) the abuse, of hypotheses. For it appeared to him that whereas he was propounding a theory of colours wholly derived from experiments, others (including Huygens) were, unjustly, more interested in seeking mechanical hypotheses that had to conform with their own preconceived ideas.[42] Huygens' commitment to the Cartesian view of physical explanation will thus have to be borne in mind when we study his controversy with Newton over the latter's theory of colours. A proper understanding of Newton's views on hypotheses can only be reached by reference to the mechanistic programme to which Huygens, and other adversaries of Newton's theory, had subscribed.

2. Having seen that Huygens always remained faithful to Descartes' views on the aim of physical science and the character of physical explanation, it might now come as a surprise to learn that, both before delivering the 1669 memoir on gravity and after the publication of the *Discours de la Cause de la Pesanteur* in 1690, he praised the excellency of Bacon's views on scientific research.[43] Since we have seen,[44] however, that Descartes himself recommended Bacon's

---

[41] Cf. H, VII, p. 229. See below, pp. 270f.

[42] See below, pp. 287, 293f.

[43] A. E. Bell, for example, finds Huygens' laudatory attitude (in 1668) towards Bacon's teachings 'the more striking when one reflects that Descartes had so long been his model'. Bell then explains: 'The point here is that while both Bacon and Descartes distrusted formal logic, Descartes scorned empiricism [*sic*] while Bacon apprehended its power' (*Christian Huygens*, p. 61).

[44] See above, p. 36.

suggestions regarding the task of experimentation, Huygens' attitude to Bacon's empiricism should not be too surprising. It will be seen from the following discussion that what impressed Huygens in Bacon's writings in no way conflicted with his Cartesian leanings. On the other hand, Huygens' views on the status of scientific explanations and the role of hypotheses will be found to be completely un-Baconian. This will appear from an examination of some important references in Huygens to the author of the *Novum Organum* and, later, from a comparison of Bacon's inductive method with Huygens' statements in the Preface to his *Traité de la Lumière*.

In (probably) 1668,[45] Huygens drew up a plan for the Physical Assembly of the *Académie Royale des Sciences* in which he set forth his views on the proper way of going about research in physics. It begins as follows:

The principal and most useful occupation of this Assembly should be, in my opinion, to work on the Natural History, somewhat according to the plan of Verulam. This History consists in experiments and observations which are the only means for attaining knowledge of the causes of all that is seen in nature.[46]

Later on we read: 'The collecting of all ["particular experiments"] is always a firm foundation for building a natural philosophy in which one must necessarily proceed from the knowledge of the effects to that of the causes.'[47]

There are, in Huygens' view, two aims of the natural history. The first is to obtain knowledge of 'all' physical things and natural effects that have so far been discovered and verified—'as much for the sake of curiosity as to derive from them every possible utility'.[48] To achieve this, one must collect the history of all plants, all animals and all minerals. The second aim is to seek knowledge of the causes. Such knowledge consists in a 'perfect understanding of the conformation

---

[45] Cf. H, XIX, p. 268, editors' note 1.
[46] H, XIX, p. 268.
[47] Ibid.
[48] H, XIX, p. 269.

of all physical bodies and of the causes of their observed effects.[49] This second task will, in Huygens' view, become infinitely useful when 'one day we shall reach its end',[50] and men will be able to employ the things created in nature for the production of their effects with certainty. For this purpose we must first collect 'all observations of the phenomena which seem to be capable of opening the way towards the knowledge of the conformation of physical things and of the causes of the natural effects that appear before our eyes'.[51]

But since natural history should be collected for every branch of physics separately, Huygens finds it necessary to prepare a general and orderly classification of these branches. His plan divides physical science into six branches corresponding to the following subject matters: the 'so-called' four elements, the meteors, the animals, the plants, the fossils, and the natural effects. Each of these is further divided into chapters. The natural effects, for example, include such phenomena as gravity, magnetism, sound, light, colour and so forth.[52]

The function of this plan, when complete, will be to present the the investigator with 'all the material'[53] from which he can select particular items for his consideration, to register the various observations which occasion or chance may bring to notice, and to facilitate the consultation of whatever will have been recorded concerning a given matter.

As a final practical advice Huygens adds that there should be six portfolios corresponding to the six general divisions of physics, and each should contain a loose book bearing the heads of chapters and

---

[49] H, XIX, p. 269. The term 'conformation' appears to be Huygens' translation of Bacon's schematismus by which Bacon means the configuration of the smaller parts of bodies. Cf. Novum Organum, especially Bk. I, 50 and 51; Bk. II, 1 and 7. See Fowler's edition (1889), p. 227, note 83; and p. 354, note 39. According to Bacon (Novum Organum, I, 50) a knowledge of the invisible structure of bodies is a necessary requirement for the knowledge of causes and, consequently, for the artificial reproduction of natural effects. He mentions in this connection (ibid., I, 51) the school of Democritus as an example of those who recognized the true method of penetrating the merely sensible properties of things to their ultimate components.

[50] H, XIX, p. 269.
[51] Ibid.
[52] H, XIX, pp. 270-1
[53] H, XIX, p. 269.

sections included in it. If these sections are separately filed, one will be able to interleave as many of them as will be necessary. There is no evidence from Huygens' papers and writings that he ever followed this advice himself.[54]

Almost all of these suggestions are derived from Bacon. Huygens shares Bacon's optimistic view that the task of physical science is a finite one; he accepts Bacon's opinion that a complete enumeration of the topics of physics, and even of the material required, is both possible and desirable; he attaches great practical value to the classification of data; he emphasizes the importance of experiments and maintains that knowledge of the particular natural effects should be the starting point for the inquiry into their causes. All this, however, does not constitute any serious departure from Descartes' views. Descartes was also impressed by Bacon's idea of enumeration, and the Cartesian method equally requires that when inquiry concerns particular phenomena, one should begin with the effects whose explanation we are then to seek.

It is to be noted that there is no reference in Huygens' suggestions to Baconian induction. When he did refer to Bacon's 'method', he understood by that term something that would have been repudiated by Bacon himself. Thus, in a letter to E. W. von Tschirnhauss (10 March 1687) Huygens says that the difficulties involved in physical research cannot be overcome except by 'starting from experiments . . . and then contriving hypotheses against which the experiments are weighed, in which task the method of Verulam seems to me excellent and deserving of further cultivation'.[55] Huygens here understands Bacon's method as one in which the formation of hypotheses, after the experiments have been made, is a permissible procedure. The same understanding is implied in later correspondence with Leibniz. In a letter to Leibniz (16 November 1691), Huygens complained that too much effort was being spent on pure geometry at the expense of physics. To advance empirical science, he suggested, 'one would have to reason methodically on

---

[54] H, XIX, p. 270, n. 3.
[55] H, IX, p. 124.

experiments, and collect new ones, somewhat according to the plan of Verulam'.[56] In reply, Leibniz agreed that Bacon's plan should be followed—on condition, however, that 'a certain art of guessing, should be adjoined to it.[57] Huygens' answer to this reveals the source of his interpretation of Bacon's method:

It seems to me that Verulam has not omitted this art of guessing in Physics on given experiments, considering the example which he has given on the subject of heat in metallic and other bodies, where he has well succeeded, if only because he has thought of the rapid movement of the very subtle matter which must temporarily maintain the vibration [le bransle] of the particles of bodies.[58]

It should be first observed that what Huygens seems to have particularly liked in Bacon's study of heat was the fact that it had resulted in the kind of mechanical explanation which, as a true Cartesian, he was bound to favour. Consciously or unconsciously, he readily introduced into Bacon's account the expression 'subtle matter' which he borrowed, not from Bacon, but from Descartes. Bacon had in fact simply proposed the following assertion: 'Calor est motus expansivus, cohibitus, et nitens per partes minores.'[59]

Now to come to the question of hypotheses. It is true that Bacon gives the above definition of heat as a conjecture, a tentative hypothesis, or, as he called it, a 'First Vintage'. It would not be correct, however, to consider this example to be characteristic of Bacon's method in general, as Huygens seems to have thought. In fact Huygens' own doctrine of the essential role of hypotheses (as he had expressed it before he wrote the preceding words to Leibniz) is the exact opposite of Bacon's views and cannot be reconciled with Bacon's conception of induction. To show this, a brief account of Bacon's method is needed in order to contrast it afterwards with Huygens' opinions.

---

[56] H, X, p. 190.
[57] Leibniz to Huygens, 8 January 1692, H, X, p. 228: 'Je suis de vôtre sentiment, qu'il faudroit suivre les projects de Verulamius sur la physique en y joignant pourtant un certain art de deviner, car autrement on n'avancera gueres.'
[58] Huygens to Leibniz, 4 February 1692, H, X, 239.
[59] Novum Organum, II, 20; Fowler's edition (1889), p. 412.

Bacon called his task 'interpretation of nature' in contrast to the peripatetic method which he termed 'anticipation of nature'. In the latter, Bacon explains, one hastens, in a premature and precipitate fashion, from a vague and incomplete information of the senses, to the most general principles. The syllogism is then applied to these rashly acquired principles to deduce consequences from them with the help of middle terms.[60] As opposed to this discreditable procedure, the interpretation of nature would consist in laying down 'stages of certainty' [certitudinis gradus] through which the mind would slowly and surely advance from the lowest level generalizations (or axioms, as Bacon called them) through higher and higher ones until the highest principle would be reached in due course.[61] After one or more axioms have been formed, one may start to move in the opposite direction to see whether they point to 'new particulars'.[62] Thus, whereas the greater attention in the method of anticipation is concentrated on deducing what is in agreement with the principles, the primary concern of the interpretation is to discover the principles themselves and to establish them on a firm basis.[63]

---

[60] Cf. Plan of the *Great Instauration* (the work of which the *Novum Organum* was conceived as the second part), B, IV, p. 25. Bacon used the expressions '*anticipatio naturae*' and '*anticipatio mentis*' synonymously; cf. B, I, pp. 154 and 161. For an illuminating analysis of Bacon's concept of *interpretatio*, see Karl R. Popper, *Conjectures and Refutations*, London, 1963, pp. 13–15.

[61] Cf. ibid.; Preface to *Novum Organum*, B, IV, p. 40; *Novum Organum*, I, 104, B, IV, p. 97.

[62] Cf. *Novum Organum*, I, 106 B, IV, p. 98; II, 10 B, IV, pp. 126–7.

[63] Cf. Plan of the *Great Instauration*, B, IV, p. 24, and Preface to *Novum Organum*, B, IV, p. 42.

Bacon's ascending-descending ladder of axioms must not be understood as a hypothetico-deductive scheme. The axioms from which we deduce new 'particulars' (facts, phenomena, experiments) are *not* hypotheses (i.e. conjectures that may turn out to be false), but propositions whose certain truth has already been established on the basis of previously performed observations and experiments. Thus, for example, Bacon writes: '. . . the true method of experience . . . first lights the candle, and then by means of the candle shows the way; commencing as it does with experience duly ordered and digested, not bungling or erratic, and from it educing axioms, and from established axioms [*axiomatibus constitutis*] again new experiments . . .' (*Novum Organum*, I, 82, B, IV, p. 81; B, II, p. 190). Again, in *Novum Organum*, I, 103, Bacon speaks of the 'axioms, which having been educed from those particulars by a certain method and rule [*certa via et regula*] shall in their turn point out the way again to new particulars . . .' (B, IV, p. 96; B, I, p. 204). Propositions derived 'by a certain method and rule' cannot be called hypotheses. Accordingly, Bacon does not descend down the ladder of axioms in order to *test* them, i.e. to see whether they are true or false—he already knows they are true. His only aim is to find out whether or not they point to new phenomena. If they do, then they are fruitful; if they do not, then they are trivial but still true. He does not envisage the possibility of counter instances. Cf. *Novum Organum*, I, 106: 'But in establishing axioms

In order to achieve this Bacon proposes a new *form of demonstration* corresponding to the syllogistic form in the old method. This new form he calls *induction*. It is the method which allows one to move from lower to higher axioms on the ladder of generalizations—with certainty.

Although therefore I leave to the syllogism and these famous and boasted modes of demonstration their jurisdiction over popular arts and such as are matter of opinion (in which department I leave all as it is), yet in dealing with the nature of things I use induction throughout, and that in the minor propositions as well as in the major. For I consider induction to be that form of demonstration which upholds the sense, and closes with nature, and comes to the very brink of operation, if it does not actually deal with it.[64]

That the contrast here is between *probable* opinion and *certain* knowledge is made clear by Bacon's distinction of his form of induction from Aristotelian induction:

But the greatest change I introduce is in the form itself of induction and the judgment made thereby. For the induction of which the logicians speak, which proceeds by simple enumeration, is a puerile thing; concludes at hazard [*precario concludit*]; is always liable to be upset by a contradictory instance; takes into account only what is known and ordinary; and leads to no result.

Now what the sciences stand in need of is a form of induction which shall analyse experience [*experientiam solvat*] and take it to pieces, and by a due process of exclusion and rejection lead to an inevitable conclusion [*necessario concludat*].[65]

---

by this kind of induction, we must also examine and try whether the axiom so established be framed to the measure of those particulars only from which it is derived, or whether it be larger and wider. And if it be larger and wider, we must observe whether by indicating to us new particulars it confirm that wideness and largeness as by a collateral security; that we may not either stick fast in things already known, or loosely grasp at shadows and abstract forms; not at things solid and realised in matter' (B, IV, p. 98). The only possibilities contemplated here by Bacon are the following: (1) the axiom is made to the measure of particulars from which it was derived; (2) the axiom is wider in a real sense, i.e. it points to new particulars actually realized in matter; (3) the axiom is wider in an illusory sense, i.e. it proposes only shadows and abstract forms and therefore has no bearing on the empirical world.

[64] Plan of the *Great Instauration*, B, IV, pp. 24–5.
[65] Ibid., B ,IV, p. 25; B, I, p. 137.

The certainty of inductive knowledge is thus derived from two sources. First, from the solid basis of experience on which it is founded as on a rock bottom;[66] this, in Bacon's view, distinguishes his induction from the syllogism whose ultimate components, the terms, are often only signs of 'notions' that are 'improperly and over-hastily abstracted from facts' that are vague and not sufficiently defined.[67] And second, from the sure method of exclusion which distinguishes Baconian induction from the Aristotelian induction by simple enumeration. In view of the first source it naturally appeared to Bacon that an experimental history of phenomena should con-stitute the foundation of interpretation.[68] In this primary stage observations and experiments are collected, verified and recorded in a somewhat passive manner without interference from the mind, that is, without allowing the mind to anticipate or indulge in its natural weakness for hasty generalizations.

But this is only a preparatory stage which, strictly, does not form part of the inductive procedure. For, according to Bacon, induction (being a method of demonstration) does not begin with natural history, nor even with the classification of what has been collected into tables of presence, of absence and of comparison. The function of these tables merely consists in presenting the collected material to the mind in an orderly form.[69] Induction proper begins when the mind starts to act upon these tables, that is, when the method of exclusion begins to operate.

What, then, is the method of exclusion? Suppose that heat is the phenomenon or, in Bacon's language, the nature whose form, cause or law (these words being used by him as equivalents) is to be discovered. The Table of Presence should contain all instances

---

[66] *Novum Organum*, I, 70: 'But the best demonstration by far is experience, if it go not beyond the actual experiment' (B, IV, p. 70).

[67] Cf. Plan of the *Great Instauration*, B, IV, p. 24.

[68] *Novum Organum*, II, 10: 'For first of all we must prepare a *Natural and Experimental History*, sufficient and good; and this is the foundation of all; for we are not to imagine or suppose, but to discover, what nature does or may be made to do [neque enim fingendum aut excogitandum sed inveniendum, quid natura faciat aut ferat]' (B, IV, p. 127; B, I, p. 236).

[69] *Novum Organum*, II, 15: 'The work and office of these three tables I call the Presentation of Instances to the Understanding. Which presentation having been made, Induction itself must be set at work' (B, IV, p. 145).

(that is, things, conditions and situations) in which heat occurs. The Table of Absence should include instances in which heat would be expected to occur although this is not in fact the case. The Table of Comparison includes instances in which some other nature suffers an increase or decrease when the same happens to the nature under consideration. Induction then begins by forming the Table of Exclusion in which are recorded all the natures which should be rejected from the form of heat by a comparative examination of every item in each of the first three tables individually. For example, from the information (recorded in the Table of Presence) that heat is produced by the sun's rays, we exclude elementary nature (earth, common fire, etc.). And on account of subterranean fire, we reject celestial nature. And so forth.[70]

There are other aids that come to the help of the mind during the inductive procedure. Such, for example, are the twenty-seven Prerogative Instances which occupy the greater part of the second book of the *Novum Organum*. They are distinguished for the extraordinary help which, according to Bacon, they can offer to the mind on different levels of the investigation. Outstanding among the Prerogative Instances are the *instantiae crucis*. The particularly important role which these have in the inductive process is apparent from the various names which Bacon has given them: Decisive Instances, Judicial Instances, Instances of the Oracle, Instances of Command.[71] These instances may be readily available in nature and, perhaps, already noted in the Tables of Presentation, 'but for the most part they are new, and are expressly and designedly sought for and applied, and discovered only by earnest and active diligence'.[72] Their function is to decide between two or more opinions as to the cause or form of a certain nature on account of its ordinary occurrence with two or more other natures. An *instantia crucis*, exhibiting the nature whose form is to be discovered together with only one of the other concurrent natures, will, according to Bacon, decide which of these natures should be rejected and which should be included in

---

[70] *Novum Organum*, II, 18, B, IV, pp. 147-9.
[71] *Novum Organum*, II, 36, B, IV, p. 180.
[72] Ibid.

the form sought. And so, instances of this kind, unlike any of the other Prerogative Instances, 'afford very great light, and are of high authority, the course of interpretation sometimes ending in them and being completed'.[73]

The method of exclusion in general and the *instantiae crucis* in particular are thus assigned a role similar to that of the indirect proof in mathematics.[74] For Bacon believed that a complete enumeration of the particulars of nature could eventually be achieved.[75] Assuming, therefore, that the Tables of Presentation (relating to the investigation of a particular nature) have, at one stage or another, been perfected, one may, after a sufficient number of rejections, conclude in the affirmative regarding the form of the nature in question. If the process of elimination has been properly conducted, and the various aids of induction duly applied, the conclusion reached must, in Bacon's view, be necessarily true. This, indeed, is the aim of the Baconian science of induction as a '*forma demonstrativa*', that is a form that leads from certain premises derived from experience to certain conclusions necessarily entailed by them.

But, then, what place does the First Vintage have in this general scheme? This brings us to Bacon's study of heat to which Huygens referred. Having performed fourteen rejections in the Table of Exclusion for heat, Bacon writes: 'There are other natures besides these; for these tables are not perfect, but only meant for examples'.[76] Moreover, Bacon continues, some of the natures rejected in that

---

[73] Ibid.

[74] This has been noted by Pierre Duhem; see his *Théorie physique, son objet, sa structure*, Paris, 1914, p. 286.

[75] *Novum Organum*, I, 112:' . . . let no man be alarmed at the multitude of particulars, but let this rather encourage him to hope. For the particular phenomena of art and nature are but a handful to the inventions of the wit, when disjoined and separated from the evidence of things. Moreover this road has an issue in the open ground and not far off; the other has no issue at all, but endless entanglement. For men hitherto have made but short stay with experience, but passing her lightly by, have wasted an infinity of time on meditations and glosses of the wit. But if some one were by that could answer our questions and tell us in each case what the fact in nature is, the discovery of all causes and sciences would be but the work of a few years' (B, IV, pp. 101–2).
See also *Novum Organum*, II, 15 and 16, where the exclusion of negative instances is viewed as a finite operation; and ibid., II, 21, where Bacon indicates the possibility of making a 'Synopsis of all Natures in the Universe' (B, IV, p. 155).

[76] *Novum Organum*, II, 18, B, IV, p. 148.

table, as the notion of elementary and celestial nature, are 'vague and ill-defined'.[77] The matter must therefore be pushed further and 'more powerful aids'[78] (such as the Prerogative Instances) must come to the help of the understanding:

And assuredly in the Interpretation of Nature the mind should by all means be so prepared and disposed, that while it rests and finds footing in due stages and degrees of certainty, it may remember withal (especially at the beginning) that what it has before it depends in great measure upon what remains behind.[79]

Then, Bacon adds,

And yet since truth will sooner come out from error than from confusion, I think it expedient that the understanding should have permission after the three Tables of First Presentation (such as I have exhibited) have been made and weighed, to make an essay of the Interpretation of Nature in the affirmative way; on the strength both of the instances given in the tables, and of any others it may meet with elsewhere. Which kind of essay I call the *Indulgence of the Understanding* [*permissionem intellectus*], or the *Commencement of Interpretation*, or the *First Vintage*.[80]

From this it is clear that the First Vintage is attempted by Bacon only *faute de mieux* ('truth', he says, 'will sooner come out from error than from confusion'). He gives his mind permission to venture a tentative definition of the form of heat simply because, at this stage of inquiry, when the table of exclusion is not yet completed and the natures mentioned in it not yet clearly defined, nothing better can be offered to complete his example. But when the natural history of heat is completed and the various aids of induction duly applied to a perfected table of exclusion, and when the real task of interpretation comes to an end, all hypotheses will have disappeared. Only certain and necessary knowledge will remain. As R. L. Ellis has pointed out,

---

[77] *Novum Organum*, II, 19, B, IV, p. 149.
[78] Ibid.
[79] Ibid., II, 20, B, IV, p. 149.
[80] Ibid.

the Vindemiatio prima, though it is the closing member of the example which Bacon makes use of, is not to be taken as the type of the final conclusion of any investigation which he would recognise as just and legitimate. It is only a parenthesis in the general method, whereas the Exclusiva, given the eighteenth aphorism of the second book [of the Novum Organum], is a type or paradigm of the process on which every true induction (inductio vera) must in all cases depend.[81]

The influence of Bacon's illustrative study of heat can be seen in the views on hypothesis generally held by seventeenth-century members of the Royal Society. Taking advantage of Bacon's permissio intellectus, while at the same time remaining faithful to his general method, they were willing to allow the use of hypotheses in the course of inquiry—subject to the following conditions: (1) that experiments have to be made first; (2) that if one has to invent hypotheses they should be either fitted to explain the already discovered facts or temporarily used to predict new facts; (3) that hypotheses formed for these purposes should be proposed as conjectures, queries or problems, not as asserted doctrines or theories; (4) that the ultimate aim should be to deduce from a sufficient number of experiments a theory or theories in which hypothetical elements no longer exist. Boyle, for example, quoted Bacon's sentence (that truth may be more easily extricated from error than confusion) to justify the use of hypotheses for making new experimental discoveries while agreeing with him that all hypotheses, as such, will have been discarded at the end of investigation.[82] And Newton's views on this question were not essentially different from Boyle's, as will be seen below.[83]

How does Bacon's method, and the views adopted by his followers, compare with Huygens' doctrine of hypotheses? The following is what Huygens wrote on 8 January 1690 in the Preface to his Traité de la Lumière:

There will be seen in it [the Treatise] demonstrations of those kinds which do not produce as great a certitude as those of Geometry, and which even

---

[81] B, I, p. 365. Quoted by Fowler in his edition of Novum Organum (1889), p. 404, note 96.
[82] See below, p. 322; see also Hooke's passage on p. 187 below.
[83] See also above, p. 31.

differ much therefrom, since whereas the Geometers prove their Propositions by fixed [*certains*] and incontestable Principles, here the Principles are verified by the conclusions to be drawn from them; the nature of these things not allowing of this being done otherwise. It is always possible to attain thereby to a degree of probability [*un degré de vraisemblance*] which very often is scarcely less than complete proof [*qui bien souvent ne cède guère à une évidence entière*]. To wit, when things which have been demonstrated by the Principles that have been assumed correspond perfectly to the phenomena which experiment has brought under observation; especially when there are a great number of them, and further, principally, when one can imagine and foresee new phenomena which ought to follow from the hypotheses which one employs, and when one finds that therein the fact corresponds to our prevision. But if all these proofs of probability [*preuves de vraisemblance*] are met with in that which I propose to discuss, as it seems to me they are, this ought to be a very strong confirmation of the success of my inquiry; and it must be ill if the facts are not pretty much [*à peu pres*] as I represent them.[84]

The following may be gathered from this passage. First, there is no question here of an inductive method in the proper Baconian sense. Huygens does not claim that his 'principles' or theories are *deduced* from the experimental propositions which they propose to explain (as Newton, for example, claimed for his own optical theories). Huygens' principles, therefore, do not share the certainty which he might wish to attach to the experimental propositions.[85] Since the direction in the kind of 'demonstrations' he wants to offer is from the principles to the experimental laws and not *vice versa*, the truth of the latter is not thereby transmitted to the former. This is to be contrasted with the Baconian 'form of demonstration' which seeks to establish the truth of the axioms or principles by a deductive movement (effected by the method of exclusion) in the opposite direction.

Second, Huygens does not propose his hypothetico-deductive

---

[84] Huygens, *Treatise*, pp. vi-vii; H, XIX, pp. 454-5.

[85] Huygens, *Treatise*, p. 1: 'As happens in all the sciences in which Geometry is applied to matter, the demonstrations concerning Optics are founded on truths drawn from experience. Such are that the rays of light are propagated in straight lines; that the angles of reflexion and of incidence are equal; and that in refraction the ray is bent according to the law of sines, now so well known, and which is no less certain than the preceding laws.'

method for the same reasons which Bacon adduced in justification of his *permissio intellectus* or the First Vintage. Here the mind is 'permitted' to form hypotheses right from the beginning, not because nothing better can be done at a given moment, or at a certain stage of inquiry, but simply because the 'nature' of the subject matter *does not allow of this being done otherwise*. In other words, what is now a hypothesis will always remain so, however strong is the evidence which has been or will be collected in its favour.

Third, it is true that Huygens maintains that his proofs can attain '*un degré de vraisemblance*' which very often is scarcely less than '*une évidence entière*', namely, when the number of facts in agreement with the theory is very large and, especially, when the predictions made on the basis of the supposed hypotheses are later confirmed by experiments. But it is important to note that we are always concerned here with '*preuves de vraisemblance*', that is, proofs in which we may approach closer and closer to certitude (as the confirming experiments accumulate) without ever attaining complete proofs. The '*évidence entière*' of which Huygens speaks is a limiting state of knowledge that is never achieved.

It is thus seen that, for all the naïve views which he communicated to the *Académie Royale des Sciences* in 1668, Huygens was in fact (at least in his more mature years) completely free from Bacon's naïve empiricism. In spite of his 'religious respect for the facts' (as Mouy has described his attitude),[86] he did not assign to them the determinative role which they had in Bacon's method.

Does the passage quoted above also imply that he equally freed himself from Descartes' position?

Descartes, it will be remembered, expressed views similar to those contained in Huygens' passage on more than one occasion.[87] As in Huygens' *Traité de la Lumière*, the explanations given in Descartes' *Dioptric* are presented as 'suppositions' to be verified by their experimental consequences. But whereas Descartes simultaneously believed his suppositions to be deducible from certain *a priori* principles, no such belief is to be found in Huygens' writings. In

---

[86] Cf. P. Mouy, *Développement de la physique cartésienne*, p. 186.
[87] See above, pp. 18ff, 23, 38ff.

fact his main criticism of Descartes was that he should have presented his system of physics as a system of plausible conjectures, not of verities.[88] The implicit assumption in this criticism is no doubt Huygens' belief (expressed at the beginning of his passage above) that in physics no propositions can be established by deducing them from *a priori* truths, that no physical theory (nor any part thereof) can be developed *ordine geometrico*.

And yet Huygens' aim in the *Traité* is explicitly stated as an attempt to explain the properties of light 'in accordance with the principles accepted in the Philosophy of the present day'.[89] This Philosophy he also describes as 'the true Philosophy in which one conceives the causes of all natural effects in terms of mechanical motions [*par des raisons de mécanique*]. This, in my opinion, we must necessarily do, or else renounce all hopes of ever comprehending anything in Physics'.[90] Thus, together with Huygens' assertion that physical explanations should always be regarded as conjectures or hypotheses, we find the simultaneous belief that they can be of only one possible type, namely, that they should be mechanical explanations. A renunciation of mechanism would be, for Huygens, a renunciation of the task of physical science itself, since nothing else would be *intelligible*. This firm belief in a fixed framework within which alone all physical hypotheses have to be formulated is a result of Huygens' adoption of the Cartesian *programme* after it has been detached from the part that is asserted by Descartes on *a priori* grounds.[91]

---

[88] In 1693 Huygens wrote the following in his annotations on Baillet's *Vie de Monsieur Descartes* which appeared in 1691: 'Descartes, who seemed to me to be jealous of the fame of Galileo, had the ambition to be regarded as the author of a new philosophy, to be taught in academies in place of Aristotelianism. He put forward his conjectures [and fictions] as verities, almost as if they could be proved by his affirming them on oath. He ought to have presented his system of physics as an attempt to show what might be anticipated as probable in this science, when no principles but those of mechanics were admitted: this would indeed have been praiseworthy; but he went further, and claimed to have revealed the precise truth, thereby greatly impeding the discovery of genuine knowledge.' H, X, p. 404; quoted and translated by Whittaker in *History of the Theories of Aether and Electricity*, the classical theories, Edinburgh, 1951, pp. 7–8. Cf. also Huygens to Leibniz, 4 February 1692, H, X, p. 239.

[89] Huygens, *Treatise*, p. 2.

[90] Huygens, *Treatise*, p. 3; H, XIX, p. 461.

[91] Above, pp. 24ff.

Chapter Seven

TWO PRECURSORS OF HUYGENS'
WAVE THEORY: HOOKE AND PARDIES

1. Huygens first communicated his *Traité de la Lumière* to the *Académie Royale des Sciences* in 1679.[1] Before that date some progress in optical theory had already been achieved in addition to the discovery of the sine law and of Fermat's least-time principle. An elaborate account of the colours of thin transparent bodies was given by Hooke in his *Micrographia* which appeared in 1665.[2] In the same year Grimaldi's *Physico-mathesis*[3] was posthumously published, and this book contained an elaborate description of some diffraction phenomena. Four years later Erasmus Bartholinus published his new observations on double refraction.[4] In 1672 an account of Newton's theory of prismatic colours appeared in the *Philosophical Transactions*,[5] and this publication was followed by a controversy in which Huygens himself took part. And, finally, in 1676, Roemer communicated to the *Académie des Sciences* his astronomical 'demonstration' that light travelled with a finite speed, and gave his estimation of that speed.[6]

None of these achievements, however, can be said to have contributed to the formation of Huygens' wave theory. Nowhere in his *Traité* does Huygens treat of any colour phenomena; and we have seen that even in 1690 he was still of the opinion that no acceptable physical explanation of colours was forthcoming. Nor

---

[1] The date given by Huygens in the Preface to his *Traité* is 1678. But according to the registers of the *Académie des Sciences* the reading did not take place until 1679. The year 1678 is therefore taken to be that in which the *Traité* was, most probably, completed. Cf. H, VIII, p. 214 (editors' note 3); H, XIX, p. 453 (editors' note 1) and p. 439.

[2] Robert Hooke, *Micrographia*, London, 1665.

[3] Francesco Maria Grimaldi, *Physico-mathesis de lumine, coloribus et iride*, Bononiae, 1665.

[4] Erasmus Bartholinus, *Experimenta crystalli Islandici disdiaclastici, quibus mira & insolita refractio detegitur*, Hafniae, 1669.

[5] *Philosophical Transactions*, No. 80, 19 February 1671-2, pp. 3075-87.

[6] *Mémoires de l'Académie Royale des Sciences, depuis 1666 jusqu' à 1699*, X (Paris, 1730), pp 575-7.

does he mention Grimaldi's name, or his book, or the phenomena of diffraction anywhere in his writings.[7] The *Traité* does contain an explanation of double refraction; but this was a later application of Huygens' theory after its fundamental ideas had already been developed.[8] As to Roemer's discovery, it will be seen that Huygens had adopted the finite velocity of light as a *hypothesis* several years before Roemer announced his results. The fact that Huygens gives an account of Roemer's proof in the beginning of his *Traité* does not mean that his theory was inspired by it. Huygens originally devised his theory to account for precisely those phenomena which Descartes' theory had proposed to explain: namely, rectilinear propagation, the fact that rays of light may cross one another without hindering or impeding one another, reflection, and ordinary refraction in accordance with the sine law. His aim was to give a clearer and more plausible explanation than the unsatisfactory comparisons proposed in Descartes' *Dioptric*; and his starting point was exactly those physical problems which the Cartesian theory had left unsolved.[9]

In his attempt to reform the Cartesian theory Huygens certainly benefited from ideas introduced by previous writers. He specifically mentions in the *Traité* Robert Hooke and the Jesuit Father Ignatius Pardies as two of those who had 'begun to consider the waves of light'.[10] His dependence on these two writers was not accidental. Both Hooke and Pardies had followed Descartes in attempting to explain the properties of light by the action of a subtle matter that fills all space and permeates all matter. Hooke, in particular, had arrived at his ideas through a close examination of Descartes' assumptions, and his work had thus been a natural preparation for

---

[7] It is, however, known for certain that Huygens possessed a copy of Grimaldi's *Physico-mathesis* before he died in 1695, cf. H, XIX, p. 389 (*Avertissement*); XIII, *fasc.* I, p. CII, editors' note 4. It may also be noted that a description and an attempted explanation of some diffraction phenomena were given (under the name 'inflexion') by Newton in his *Principia* (1687).

[8] See below, pp. 221f.

[9] Compare the account in A. Wolf, *A History of Science, Technology, and Philosophy in the 16th and 17th centuries* (London, 1950, p. 260) of how Huygens' theory came to be elaborated out of preceding ideas 'established' or 'suggested' by observation and experiment.

[10] Huygens, *Treatise*, p. 20.

Huygens' attempt. It will therefore be instructive to look at Hooke's and Pardies' investigations before we approach Huygens' theory.

2. The principal aim of Hooke's optical investigations in the *Micro-graphia* was to give an explanation of his observations on the colours of thin transparent bodies. His attempt must have been one of those *excesses* to which he refers in the following address to the Royal Society which we read at the beginning of his book:

The Rules You have prescrib'd Your selves in YOUR Philosophical Progress do seem the best that have ever been practis'd. And particularly that of avoiding *Dogmatising*, and the *espousal* of any Hypothesis not sufficiently grounded and confirm'd by *Experiments*. This way seems the most excellent and may preserve both *Philosophy* and *Natural History* from its former corruptions. In saying which, I may seem to condemn my own Course in this Treatise; in which there may perhaps be some Expressions, which may seem more *positive* then YOUR Prescriptions will permit; And though I desire to have them understood only as *Conjectures* and *Quaeries* (which YOUR Method does not altogether disallow) yet if even in those I have exceeded, 'tis fit that I should declare, that it was not done by YOUR Directions.[11]

Hooke in fact broke the 'Rules' of the Society by *committing* himself to nothing less than the Cartesian hypothesis of an ethereal medium serving as the vehicle of light. This is not altogether to be regretted. For he was in fact able to make proper and fruitful use of his observations by confronting them with already-formulated hypotheses and bringing them to bear upon already existing problems. In this way he succeeded in exposing certain difficulties in Descartes' assumptions, and, by proposing more plausible conjectures, he pushed the Cartesian theory a step forward. Hooke looked at the colour phenomena exhibited by thin transparent bodies as providing an *experimentum crucis* that falsified Descartes' explanation of colours.[12] While this may have been the starting point of his own investigations in this field, much more common observations seem

---

[11] Hooke, *Micrographia*, 'TO THE ROYAL SOCIETY' (page not numbered).
[12] See above, pp. 65f.

to have been more decisive in the process of building up his fundamental ideas. The following account will be concerned with his ideas only in so far as they may have contributed to Huygens' theory.

Hooke begins the exposition of his theory by asserting that 'it seems very manifest, that there is no luminous Body but has the parts of it in motion more or less'.[13] Whittaker has interpreted this statement as an attack on 'Descartes' proposition, that light is a tendency to motion rather than an actual motion'.[14] Actually Descartes had distinguished in the *Dioptric* between what constitutes light in the luminous body and in the medium: '. . . light, in the bodies which are called luminous, is nothing but a certain movement, or a very prompt and very violent [viue] action . . . .'[15] The distinction was not, however, clearly stated in the *Dioptric*, as the correspondence between Descartes and Morin indicates.[16] But it was later made clear in the *Principles* where Descartes spoke explicitly of a circular motion of the parts of the sun and the stars, while the spreading of light in straight lines was attributed to the pressure exerted by those parts on the neighbouring medium. It appears therefore that the disagreement between Hooke and Descartes was rather on the *kind* of motion that should constitute light in the luminous body:

for though it be a motion, yet 'tis not every motion that produces it, since we find there are many bodies very violently mov'd, which yet afford not such an effect; and there are other bodies, which to our other senses, seem not mov'd so much, which yet shine.[17]

Descartes' theory could not plausibly apply to a wide range of circumstances in which light was produced. He had constructed his theory mainly to account for the light proceeding from the stars. But what about flames and the shining of a diamond in the dark

---

[13] *Micrographia*, p. 54.
[14] Whittaker, op. cit., p. 14.
[15] D, VI, p. 84. Also, *Le Monde*, D, XI, p. 8.
[16] Cf. Descartes to Morin, 13 July 1638 (D, II, p. 204), where Descartes makes the distinction more explicit by calling the actual motion of light in the luminous body *lux*, and the tendency to motion in the medium *lumen*.
[17] *Micrographia*, p. 55.

when it is rubbed? It was natural for Hooke to ask such questions. The example of the diamond appeared to him particularly instructive: it provided him with an argument against Descartes' attribution of light to a circular motion of the parts of the luminous object, and, having eliminated other hypotheses, he was finally led to propose a vibrating movement. Hooke's reasoning to establish this conclusion was as follows:

. . . the newly mention'd *Diamond* affords us a good argument: since if the motion of the parts did not return, the Diamond must after many rubbings decay and be wasted: but we have no reason to suspect the latter, especially if we consider the exceeding difficulty that is found in cutting or wearing away a Diamond. And a Circular motion of the parts is much more improbable, since, if that were granted, and they be suppos'd irregular and Angular parts, I see not how the parts of the Diamond should hold so firmly together, or remain in the same sensible dimensions, which yet they do. Next, if they be *Globular*, and mov'd only with a *turbinated* motion, I know not any cause that can impress that motion upon the *pellucid medium*, which yet is done. Thirdly, any other *irregular* motion of the parts one amongst another, must necessarily make the body of a fluid consistence, from which it is far enough. It must therefore be a *Vibrating* motion.[18]

Moreover, a diamond being one of the hardest bodies and one of the least to yield to pressure, he concludes that the vibrations of its parts must be 'exceeding short', that is, of a very small amplitude.[19]

Hooke then goes on to consider how the motion of light is propagated through the interposed medium.

First, the medium 'must be a body *susceptible* and *impartible* of this motion that will deserve the name of a Transparent'.[20] He does not explain in physical terms what this 'susceptibility' consists in; it remained for Huygens to introduce elasticity as the requisite property. Hooke in fact preserved Descartes' conception of the light-bearing medium as a perfectly dense and incompressible body until at least 1680-2. In his lectures on optics dating from that period he defines light as

---

[18] Ibid., pp. 55–56.   [19] Ibid., p. 56   [20] Ibid.

nothing else but a peculiar Motion of the parts of the Luminous Body, which does affect a fluid Body that incompasses the Luminous Body, which is perfectly fluid and perfectly Dense, so as not to admit of any farther Condensation; but that the Parts next the Luminous Body being moved, the whole Expansum of that fluid is moved likewise.[21]

Second, the parts of the medium must be 'Homogeneous, or of the same kind'.[22] This was also a property of the Cartesian heaven, but Hooke makes use of it in arriving at an important result of his own conceptions, to be mentioned presently in the fifth remark.

Third,

the constitution and motion of the parts must be such, that the appulse of the luminous body may be communicated or propagated through it to the greatest imaginable distance in the least imaginable time; though I see no reason to affirm, that it must be an instant.[23]

Hooke here questions Descartes' hypothesis of the instantaneous propagation of light. He does not actually assert that the velocity of light must be finite. But that he favoured such a view (at the time of writing the *Micrographia*) may be gathered from the following discussion of Descartes' arguments from the eclipses of the moon:

I know not any one Experiment or observation that does prove it [viz. instantaneous propagation]. And, whereas it may be objected, That we see the Sun risen at the very instant when it is above the sensible Horizon,[24]

---

[21] Hooke, *Posthumous Works* (1705), p. 113. (The whole passage is italicized in the text.) Quoted by A. Wolf, *op. cit.*, p. 258. Consistent with this conception of the medium, some passages of Hooke's lectures suggest that the propagation of light is instantaneous (see, for example, *Posthumous Works*, p. 77). It is strange that Hooke should revert to this Cartesian idea in 1680–2 after he had rejected in *Micrographia* (1665) Descartes' astronomical arguments to establish it (as will be seen shortly). Roemer's estimation of the velocity of light had been published before the date of the above-mentioned lectures. But Hooke, instead of accepting Roemer's calculations as a hypothesis, in fact maintained that Roemer's argument was not conclusive (cf. *Posthumous Works*, pp. 77–78, 130). It must be mentioned, however, that the passages relating to the velocity of light in those lectures are not always consistent (compare pp. 74, 130 with pp. 77–78 in *Posthumous Works*).

[22] *Micrographia*, p. 56.

[23] Ibid.

[24] This is not Descartes' argument yet. It seems to be one that was used by supporters of instantaneous propagation in general. In objecting against *this* argument in the above passage, Hooke was in fact repeating what had already been expressed by Galileo. Cf. Galileo, *Two New Sciences*, p. 42.

and that we see a Star hidden by the body of the Moon at the same instant, when the Star, the Moon, and our Eye are all in the same line; and the like Observations, or rather suppositions, may be urg'd. I have this to answer, That I can as easily deny as they affirm; for I would fain know by what means any one can be assured any more of the Affirmative, then I of the Negative. If indeed the propagation were very slow, 'tis possible something might be discovered by Eclypses of the Moon; but though we should grant the progress of the light from the Earth to the Moon, and from the Moon back to the Earth again to be full two Minutes in performing, I know not any possible means to discover it; nay, there may be some instances perhaps of Horizontal Eclypses that may seem very much to favour this supposition of the slower progression of Light than most imagine. And the like may be said of the Eclypses of the Sun, &c.[25]

Hooke remarks that the arguments from the eclipses presuppose what they propose to prove. He points out their inconclusiveness as they assume a sufficiently small velocity that would easily be detected by the observations described. He does not himself produce any positive arguments, experimental or theoretical, to support successive propagation (though he suggests that 'there may be some instances' in favour of non-instantaneous progression). But the *picture* which he gives in the fifth remark (below) clearly depicts the propagation of light as a process taking place at a finite speed.

Fourth, 'the motion is propagated every way through an *Homogeneous medium* by *direct* or *straight* lines extended every way like Rays from the center of a Sphere'.[26]

And fifth, the important result that

in an *Homogeneous medium* this motion is propagated every way with *equal velocity*, whence necessarily every *pulse* or *vibration* of the luminous body will generate a Sphere, which will continually increase, and grow bigger, just after the same manner (though indefinitely swifter) as the waves or rings on the surface of the water do swell into bigger and bigger circles about a point of it, where by the sinking of a Stone the motion was begun, whence it necessarily follows, that all the parts of these spheres undulated through an *Homogeneous medium* cut the Rays at right angles.[27]

---

[25] *Micrographia*, p. 56.
[26] Ibid, pp. 56–57. [27] *Micrographia*, p. 57.

These ideas represent a definite advance towards a wave theory. Hooke makes use here of the concept of wave-front which he illustrates by the propagation of water-waves. And he correctly remarks that in a 'homogeneous' (we would say *isotropic*) medium, the wave-front describes a sphere which, at every point of its surface, is perpendicular to the ray or direction of propagation from the centre of disturbance. But, in spite of the analogy with water-waves, there is no reason to suppose that he necessarily understood the vibrations in the light-bearing medium to be transverse, that is, at right angles to the direction of propagation. Nor does he explicitly say that his pulses or waves follow one another at regular intervals. Not that he was aware of any reasons for excluding one of these concepts. But, rather, he was not in a position to make specific use of them, and, in consequence, he left out the whole question of what type of waves should correspond to light. It will be seen later that Huygens went further than Hooke (but not forward) by expressly denying the periodicity of light waves.

We come now to Hooke's application of the preceding ideas in his treatment of refraction. This is of importance since he devised a construction for the refracted ray which has been described as a 'rather crude anticipation of that of Huygens'[28] and it will be worthwhile to try to define Hooke's contribution here. The following is his account of what happens to a 'pulse' or wave-front when it passes from one medium into another:

But because all transparent *mediums* are not *Homogeneous* to one another, therefore we will next examine how this pulse or motion will be propagated through differingly transparent *mediums*. And here, according to the most acute and excellent Philosopher *Des Cartes*, I suppose the sign [i.e. sine] of the angle of inclination in the first *medium* to be to the sign of refraction in the second, As the density of the first, to the density of the second, By density, I mean not the density in respect of gravity (with which the refractions or transparency of *mediums* hold no proportion) but in respect only to the *trajection* of the Rays of light, in which respect they only differ in this; that the one propagates the pulse more easily and weakly, the other more slowly, but more strongly. But as for the pulses

---

[28] Cf. A. Wolf, op. cit., p. 258.

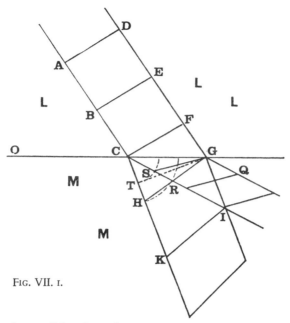

FIG. VII. I.

themselves, they will by the refraction acquire another propriety, which we shall now endeavour to explicate.

We will suppose therefore in the first Figure [Fig. VII. I] *ACFD* to be a physical Ray, or *ABC* and *DEF* to be two Mathematical Rays, *trajected* from a very remote point of a luminous body through an *Homogeneous* transparent *medium LLL*, and *DA, EB, FC*, to be small portions of the orbicular impulses which must therefore cut the Rays at right angles; these Rays meeting with the plain surface *NO* of a *medium* that yields an easier *transitus* to the propagation of light, and falling *obliquely* on it, they will in the medium *MMM* be refracted towards the perpendicular of the surface. And because this *medium* is more easily *trajected* then the former by a third, therefore the point *C* of the orbicular pulse *FC* will be mov'd to *H* four spaces in the same time that *F* the other end of it is mov'd to *G* three spaces, therefore the whole refracted pulse *GH* shall be *oblique* to the refracted Rays *CHK* and *GI*; and the angle *GHC* shall be an acute, and so much the more acute by how much the greater the refraction be, then which nothing is more evident, for the sign of the inclination is to be the sign of refraction as *GF* to *TC* the distance between the point *C* and the perpendicular from *G* to *CK*, which being as four to three, *HC* being longer then *GF* is longer also then *TC*, therefore the angle *GHC* is less than *GTC*. So that henceforth the parts of the pulses *GH* and *IK* are mov'd ascew, or cut the Rays at *oblique* angles.[29]

A clearer idea of how Hooke arrives at these results can be gathered from the dotted lines in his figure. Let the distance *FG* be equal to $v_i t$, where v_i is the velocity of incidence and *t* the time required for the side of the wave-front at *F* to cover that distance. It is supposed by Hooke that in the same time *t*, the side of the wave-front at *C* will have travelled in the refracting medium a distance $v_r t$ equal to $\frac{4}{3}FG$ (v_r being the velocity of refraction).

Accordingly, the larger dotted semi-circle in the figure is described with *C* as centre and a radius equal to $\frac{4}{3}FG$: the side of the wave-front at *C* will have reached some point on this semi-circle when the side at *F* arrives at *G*.

To find the *direction* of the refracted ray Hooke *assumes* with Descartes that

$$\frac{\sin i}{\sin r} = \frac{v_r}{v_i} = n = \frac{4}{3}.$$

Accordingly, with *C* as centre and a radius equal to $\frac{3}{4}FG$, he describes the smaller arc in the figure. He then draws the tangent to this arc from *G*; the line joining *C* and the point of tangency *T* gives the direction of refraction. For, *FCG* being equal to the angle of incidence and *CGT* being equal to the angle of refraction, we have

$$\frac{FG}{CT} = \frac{\sin i}{\sin r} = \frac{4}{3} = \frac{v_r}{v_i}.$$

To find the position of the wave-front after refraction, *CT* is extended to meet the larger arc at *H*. *GH* therefore represents the wave-front; it is oblique to the direction of propagation *CH* since, in the triangle *GTH*, the angle *GTH* is a right angle.

It is clear that according to Hooke's construction the velocity of light must be greater in denser media, since it is based on the Cartesian relation giving the sines in inverse ratio to the velocities.

We shall see that in Huygens' construction for refraction the wave-front must be perpendicular to the direction of propagation after

---

[29] *Micrographia*, p. 57.

refraction, and that this construction yields a law according to which one must adopt the opinion opposite to that of Descartes regarding the velocity of light in different media.[30] The crucial considerations on which Huygens relied in arriving at these results are lacking in Hooke's treatment. But, as Whittaker has remarked,[31] it was Hooke's merit to have introduced the concept of wave-front; and, by considering what the wave-front undergoes in passing from one medium into another, he has replaced Descartes' comparisons with a clear mechanical picture that was later more successfully used by Huygens.

Hooke attempted to explain the generation of colours by refraction as being due to the deflection of the wave-front. His explanation will be discussed later.[32]

3. Pardies' speculations on light were contained in an unfinished treatise on refraction which Huygens saw in manuscript before 24 June 1673.[33] This treatise has been lost;[34] but we can form some idea of its contents from Pardies' own reference to it in his published work, and from a book on optics published in 1682 by the Jesuit Father Pierre Ango who had also seen Pardies' manuscript and adopted some of its ideas.[35] As in the preceding discussion of Hooke we shall here concentrate on those conceptions which may have played a role in Huygens' theory.

Pardies intended his treatise to form part of a sixth discourse in a complete system of mechanics. Only the first two discourses have

---

[30] Had Hooke represented the wave-front by the perpendicular GT instead of the oblique GH, he would have obtained the following:

$$\frac{FG}{CT} = \frac{\sin i}{\sin r} = \frac{v_i t}{v_r t} = \frac{v i}{v_r} = \frac{4}{3},$$

which is in accordance with Fermat's and Huygens' law. But this would of course imply that the velocity of light is *less* in denser media, and he would also have to give up the idea that the wave-front is deflected by refraction, that is, renounce the foundation of his theory of colours.

[31] Cf. Whittaker op. cit., pp. 15–16.

[32] See below, pp. 254 ff.

[33] Cf. Huygens to Oldenburg, 24 June 1673, H, VII, p. 316.

[34] Cf. H, XIX, p. 393 (*Avertissement*).

[35] Cf. Pierre Ango, *L'optique*, Paris, 1682.

been published (in 1670 and 1673 respectively).[36] We learn from the Preface to the second discourse that the sixth was to be devoted to wave motion 'on the example of these circles which are formed in the surface of water when a stone is dropped into it'.[37] The author added that he would consider how similar circles are formed, propagated, reflected and refracted—in air as well as in 'other more subtle substances'. He would also explain by considerations of wave motion 'all that concerns sounds';

and making a conjecture on the propagation of light, we examine if one could also suppose, that the vehicle of light were a similar movement in a more subtle air; and we show that in this hypothesis one would in fact explain all the properties of light and of colours in a very natural manner.

Pardies also promised that he would provide a demonstration of the law of refraction from his hypothesis. This in itself would constitute an advance over Hooke's treatment which, as we have seen, simply takes Descartes' formula for granted. We learn that Pardies did in fact attempt such a demonstration in his unpublished treatise from Huygens' testimony in the *Traité*.[38] But in order to get an idea of this demonstration we have to turn to Ango's *L'optique*.

Ango provides a construction for refraction which is not unlike that of Hooke[39]. Like Hooke, he considers what happens to an incident wave-front that is perpendicular to the direction of propagation when it obliquely strikes a refracting surface. The side of the wave-front which first meets the surface proceeds with the velocity proper to the refracting body while the other side travels with the velocity of the medium of incidence. But he departs from Hooke's construction in two important respects. First, he represents the wave-front as perpendicular to the direction of propagation *after refraction*. Second, he considers the velocity of light to be greater in rarer media. On these two points Ango's construction perfectly agrees with Huygens' theory. But we would search in vain for a

---

[36] Ignace Gaston Pardies, *Discours du mouvement local*, Paris, 1670; *La statique ou la science des forces mouvantes*, Paris, 1673.

[37] This and other quotations in the same paragraph are taken from the Preface to Pardies *La statique*. The pages of this Preface are not numbered.

[38] Cf. Huygens, *Treatise*, p. 20.   [39] Cf. Ango, op. cit., figure on p. 64; and pp. 59–67

satisfactory proof of the sine law in Ango's book. As Leibniz observed, he practically presupposes what is to be proved.[40] In view of Ango's opinion concerning the velocity of light in different media, the law which he adopts is the following

$$\frac{\sin i}{\sin r} = \frac{v_i}{v_r} = n.$$

This is the same as Huygens' (and Fermat's) law, as opposed to the law (giving the velocities in inverse ratio to the sines) proposed by Descartes and adopted by Hooke.

We may safely assume with Leibniz[41] that Ango's construction had been taken from Pardies' manuscript. Apart from Ango's own confession of his indebtedness to Pardies,[42] there is in his book a remark which may support this assumption. He informs us that Pardies had performed a demonstration of the principle of least time as applied to optical refraction and that Pardies had sent his demonstration to Fermat.[43] Neither Fermat nor Huygens mentions this demonstration. But, if correct, it would presuppose a law of refraction identical with that of Fermat and Huygens, and also the view (adopted by Ango and assumed in his construction) that the velocity of light is less in denser media.

We cannot of course be certain as to whether Pardies had provided in his manuscript a more satisfactory proof of the sine law than the one given in Ango's *L'optique*. At any rate, Huygens, who readily expressed his admiration for Pardies' treatise,[44] has stated in the *Traité* that the main foundation of his own theory (and of his deduction of the sine law) was lacking in Pardies' work.[45] And there is no reason to discredit this statement which is in fact confirmed by Ango's account. This foundation consists in the idea of secondary waves which Huygens made use of to explain the fact that the wave-front remains perpendicular to the direction of propagation after refraction. As it would seem from Ango's treatment, this fact Pardies had either simply assumed or attempted to explain in a different way from Huygens.

---

[40] Cf. Leibniz to Huygens, October 1690, H, IX, pp. 522–3. [41] Cf. ibid.
[42] Cf. Ango, op. cit., p. 14. [43] Cf. ibid., pp. 92–94.
[44] Cf. Huygens to Oldenburg, 24 June 1673, H, VII, p. 316.
[45] Cf. Huygens, *Treatise*, p. 20.

Chapter Eight

HUYGENS' WAVE THEORY

1. The fact that Huygens, like Hooke, occupied himself with problems in the Cartesian theory is clear enough from his *Traité de la Lumière*. Indeed, when he communicated this *Traité* to the *Académie des Sciences* in 1679, his task was understood as an attempt to solve 'difficulties' in Descartes' theory. The account of Huygens' communication, published in the *Histoire de l'Académie Royale des Sciences* in 1733, begins as follows:

The inadequacies [*inconvenients*] of M. Descartes' system of light obliged M. Huygens to endeavour to conceive another more suitable for avoiding or resolving the difficulties. Such are the errors of M. Descartes that he often illuminates the other philosophers, either because, where he erred, he has not moved far from the goal and that the mistake can be easily corrected, or because he expresses deep views and produces ingenious ideas, even when he is mostly mistaken.[1]

There is in fact evidence to show that Huygens first arrived at his views regarding the nature of light and the mode of its propagation through an examination of Descartes' ideas.

Huygens started his work on dioptrics in 1652 when he was twenty-three years old[2] (about the same age as Newton when, in 1666, he arrived at his definitive theory of colours). He first conceived his wave theory in about 1672–3[3] (about three years after Newton had started lecturing on his theory of light in Cambridge). In (probably) 1673 Huygens was already planning a work under the title *Dioptrique* which was to contain his wave theory together with questions of dioptrics proper. We have in the *Projet*, which he wrote probably in that year, a brief but valuable indication of the problems

---

[1] Cited by Mouy in *Développement de la physique cartésienne*, p. 204. Cf. *Histoire de l'Académie Royale des Sciences*, I, *depuis son établissement en 1666 jusqu'à 1686*, Paris, 1733, pp. 283–93. This account was written in 1679 by Fontenelle in his capacity as secretary of the *Académie*.

[2] Cf. H, XIII, *fasc*. I, pp. v–x.

[3] Cf. ibid., pp. ix–x.

and applications which occupied Huygens' thought at that early stage in the formation of his theory. It will therefore be interesting first to examine this *Projet*, and to see the extent to which he was still under the influence of some of Descartes' views, while at the same time he realized, and tried to tackle, difficulties in the Cartesian theory. It was in this context that Huygens' wave theory was first conceived.

Owing to the particular character of the *Projet*, consisting mainly of phrases and incomplete sentences, I have adjoined the French original to my translations and, in some cases, inserted complementary words in brackets. To facilitate reference in my subsequent remarks I have provided Huygens' notes with numbers without changing their order in the published text.

From Huygens' *'Projet du Contenu de la Dioptrique'* (1673)[4]
  (1) *Refraction comment expliquee par Pardies.*
    How refraction is explained by Pardies.
  (2) *Comparée au son.*
    [Light] compared with sound.[5]
  (3) *ondes en l'air.*
    waves in air.
  (4) *comparées à celles de l'eau.*
    [Waves in air] compared to those of water.
  (5) *la pesanteur est cause de celles cy comme le ressort des autres.*
    weight is the cause of these [water waves] as elasticity is the cause of the others.
  (6) *transparence sans penetration.*
    transparency without penetration [of rays].[6]
  (7) *corps capable de ce mouvement successif.*
    a body [or medium] capable of this successive movement [of light].
  (8) *Propagation perpendiculaire aux cercles.*
    Propagation perpendicular to the circles [described by the expanding waves].
  (9) *difficultez contre des Cartes.*
    difficulties against Descartes.

---

[4] H, XIII, *fasc.* II, p. 742.
[5] For the insertion here compare the following line from the same *Projet*: *'lumière comparée au son'*, ibid., p. 739.
[6] Compare: *'transparence sans penetration de rayons'*, ibid.

(10) *d'ou viendrait l'acceleration.*
whence would the acceleration come.

(11) *il fait la lumiere un conatus movendi, selon quoy il est malaisè d'entendre la refraction comme il l'explique, a mon avis au moins.*
he [Descartes] takes light to be a *conatus movendi* [or tendency to motion], in consequence of which it is difficult to understand refraction as he explains it, in my opinion at least.

(12) *Cause de la reflexion a angles egaux.*
Cause of reflection at equal angles.

(13) *lumiere s'estend circulairement et non dans l'instant, au moins dans les corps icy bas.*
light spreads in circles and not instantaneously, at least in the bodies here below.

(14) *car pour la lumiere des astres il n'est pas sans difficultè de dire qu'elle ne seroit pas instantanee.*
for as to the light from the stars, it is not without difficulty to say that it would not be instantaneous.

(15) *Cette explication convient avec les Experiences.*
This explanation agrees with the Experiments.

(16) *pour les sinus.*
for the sines.

(17) *pour le rayon entrant et sortant.*
for the ray passing into and out of [a medium].

(18) *pour celuy qui ne peut penetrer.*
for that [ray] which cannot penetrate [the interface].

(19) *pour le verre.*
for glass.

(20) *dans l'eau.*
in water.

(21) *maniere de Rohaut de faire voir les conveniences.*
the manner that Rohaut[7] shows the agreements.

(1) indicates that Huygens' projected work was to include an account of Pardies' explanation of refraction. The *Traité de la Lumière* does not give any such account. The analogy between light and sound, referred to in (2) must have been already developed by Pardies to some extent, as it appears from the discussion of his

---

[7] Reference to Jacques Rohault, author of *Traité de physique* which was first published in 1671. I have not been able to find the passage to which Huygens refers.

Statique in the previous chapter.[8] The comparison with water-waves did not lead Huygens to adopt transverse motion for light. Light waves are conceived in the *Traité* rather on the analogy of sound waves; that is, they are longitudinal. Consequently, elasticity of the ethereal matter, the vehicle of light, is assumed in accordance with the remark in (5). That Huygens was also thinking about Hooke's explanations at the time of writing the *Projet* is indicated by the following words which he wrote in the margin of the manuscript: 'vid. micrograph. Hookij'.[9]

(15–20) indicate applications of the theory. (16) refers to the sine law. (17) refers to the reciprocality law for refraction, namely the law stating that when a refracted ray is reversed, it retraces its original path in incidence after its emergence from the refracting body.[10] (18) refers to total reflection which takes place when a ray, falling at a sufficiently great angle of incidence on a separating surface from the side of the denser medium, does not penetrate the surface.[11]

(9–11), (13) and (14) directly deal with Descartes' theory. (10) points out the difficulty (noted in Chapter IV above) that is involved in Descartes' explanation of the increase in speed which, in his view, would take place when light passes from a rare into a dense body. We have seen that Descartes' model does not adequately provide for a plausible physical explanation of this hypothesis.[12] According to Huygens' theory the velocity of light must be less in denser media. On the assumption that light consists in waves in the ethereal

---

[8] Judging from Ango's *L'optique* which, as we have remarked, embodies Pardies' ideas, it would seem that Pardies had not developed the analogy between light and sound far enough. Ango observes (op. cit., pp. 38–39) that the loudness and pitch of sound respectively depend on the amplitude and the frequency of vibrations. But he does not attempt to relate the intensity and colour of light to corresponding properties of the light waves.

[9] H, XIII, *fasc.* II, p. 742, editors' note 1.

[10] Cf. Huygens, *Treatise*, pp. 35–39. Some historians have credited Ibn al-Haytham with the discovery of this law. He himself attributed it to Ptolemy, *Optics*, Bk. V. Cf. J. Baarmann, '*Abhandlung über das Licht von Ibn al-Haitam*', *Zeitschrift der Deutschen Morgenländischen Gesellschaft*, XXXVI (1882) pp. 225–6 (Arabic text with German translation); M. Nazif, *al-Hasan ibn al-Haytham' buhūthuhu wa-kushūfuhu al-basariyya*, I (Cairo, 1942), pp. 72–73. See Ptolemaei *Optica* (ed. Lejeune), V, 31–32, pp. 242–3 and editor's note 31.

[11] Cf. Huygens, *Treatise*, p. 39.

[12] See above, pp. 114 f, 133 ff.

matter which fills the spaces between the particles of transparent bodies, Huygens later suggested in the *Traité* that 'the progression of these waves ought to be a little slower in the interior of bodies, by reason of the small detours which the same particles cause'.[13]

(11) repeats the objection which had been raised by Fermat: how could light be a tendency to motion (rather than an actual motion) if, in the explanation of refraction, one has to argue (as Descartes did) in terms of greater and smaller velocities? The dilemma which Huygens seems to point out in Descartes' theory may be expressed thus: either light is an actual motion, or it is a tendency to motion existing simultaneously in the parts of the subtle matter. On the first assumption, the propagation of light must be successive and not instantaneous. On the second, it is 'difficult' to explain refraction. In (13) Huygens chooses the first alternative: 'light spreads in circles and not instantaneously. . . .'

At the same time (14) asserts that 'as to the light from the stars, it is not without difficulty to say that it would not be instantaneous'. (14) thus shows that Huygens had not completely shaken himself free from Descartes' eclipses arguments (which had been published in the second volume of Clerselier's edition of Descartes' letters in 1659). In contrast to Hooke, who questioned the conclusiveness of Descartes' arguments, Huygens thought (in 1673) that it would not be easy to assert the successive propagation of light in interplanetary space.[14]

But, at least 'in the bodies here below'—see (13)—the spreading of light must not be instantaneous; for here below, on earth, light is refracted by its passage through the atmosphere and the other transparent bodies; and to explain refraction, mechanically, one has to understand it as a process taking place in time.

Huygens therefore first adopted the finite velocity of light (in the bodies here below) about three years before Roemer's discovery,

---

[13] Huygens, *Treatise*, p. 32.
[14] In the communication of 1679 Huygens was still of the opinion that Descartes' belief in the instantaneous propagation of light as based on the arguments from the eclipses was 'not without reason', thus admitting their validity though, by that time, he was fully aware of their inconclusiveness and convinced of the contrary opinion to Descartes'. Cf. Huygens' *Treatise*, p. 5.

not because any terrestrial experiment had forced him to do so,[15] but simply because this hypothesis was required for a clear understanding of the properties of light, and particularly, of refraction. It is implied in the *Traité* that Huygens had changed his mind also about Descartes' eclipses arguments before Roemer announced his results. One of the reasons given by Huygens confirms the preceding account of the development of his thought:

I have then made no difficulty, in meditating on these things [Descartes' eclipses arguments], in supposing that the emanation of light is accomplished with time, *seeing that in this way all its phenomena can be explained, and that in following the contrary opinion everything is incomprehensible.* For it has always seemed to me that even Mr Des Cartes, whose aim has been to treat all the subjects of Physics intelligibly, and who assuredly has succeeded in this better than any one before him, has said nothing that is not full of difficulties, or even inconceivable, in dealing with Light and its properties.

But that which I employed only as a hypothesis, has recently received great seemingness [*vraisemblance*] as an established truth by the ingenious proof of Mr Römer . . . .[16]

We thus see what exactly Roemer's contribution was to Huygens' attitude towards Descartes' eclipses arguments. As Roemer had estimated that light would take eleven minutes to reach the earth from the sun, Huygens could now see precisely why the eclipses of the moon did not provide a sufficient argument for deciding the

---

[15] Galileo described in the *Two New Sciences* a terrestrial experiment designed to decide the question of the velocity of light. Two observers sent light messages to each other by uncovering a lantern; as soon as the second observer perceives the light sent off by the first, he uncovers his own lantern which is then seen by the first observer; the interval between sending a message by one observer and receiving an answer from the other would be the measure of the time required for the light to travel the distance between them twice. But, we are told by Salvatio, the result was negative: 'In fact I have tried the experiment only at a short distance, less than a mile, from which I have not been able to ascertain with certainty whether the appearance of the opposite light was instantaneous or not; but if not instantaneous it is extraordinarily rapid—I shall call it momentary.' Galileo's real reason for not accepting instantaneous propagation was theoretical, not experimental: 'What a sea we are gradually slipping into without knowing it! With vacua and infinities and indivisibles and instantaneous motions, shall we ever be able, even by means of a thousand discussions, to reach dry land?' *Two New Sciences*, pp. 43–44.
[16] *Treatise*, p. 7; italics added.

question of the velocity of light. This is Huygens' re-formulation of Descartes arguments:[17]

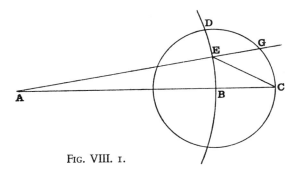

FIG. VIII. 1.

In the figure (Fig. VIII. 1) *A* is the place of the sun, supposed in the argument to be at rest. *BD* is part of the annual path of the earth round the sun, and the circle *CD*, the orbit of the moon. *AB* is a beam of light interrupted by the earth arriving at *B*. Assuming that light takes one hour to travel the distance *BC* (*AB* extended), a shadow will be cast on the moon if the moon happens to be at *C* one hour after the earth was at *B*. The reflection of the shadow will reach the earth at *E* another hour later, *BE* being the arc described by the earth in two hours. Therefore, two hours after the earth was at *B*, the moon will be seen from *E* eclipsed at *C* while the sun is still at *A*. According to Huygens' computations, the angle *GEC* (the supplementary of *AEC*) will be 'very sensible, and about 33 degrees'.[18] This was contrary to astronomical observations according to which this angle was unappreciable.

But it must be noted that the speed of light in this argument has been assumed such that it takes a time of one hour to make the passage from here to the Moon. If one supposes that for this it requires only one minute of time, then it is manifest that the angle *CEG* will only be 33 minutes; and if it requires only ten seconds of time, the angle will be less than six minutes. And then it will not be easy to perceive anything of it in

[17] Cf. ibid., pp. 5–6.
[18] Ibid., p. 6.

observations of the Eclipses; nor, consequently, will it be permissible to deduce from it that the movement of light is instantaneous.[19]

In the last supposition the velocity of light would be according to Huygens a hundred thousand times greater than that of sound. But as Roemer had in fact estimated the velocity of light to be 'at least six times greater'[20] than in this supposition, it was now understandable why the eclipses of the moon could not reveal the successive movement of light.

But it should now be observed that Roemer's discovery itself was not commonly accepted as definitive in Roemer's time. Roemer proposed the hypothesis that light travels with a finite velocity in connection with observations on the eclipses of the first (innermost) satellite of Jupiter which he had been making for several years with Cassini and other members of the *Académie des Sciences* in Paris. It was observed that the periods of revolutions of this satellite round Jupiter exhibited certain inequalities which were found to be related to the orbital motion of the earth: the eclipses of the satellite were delayed when the earth was farthest from Jupiter, and accelerated when the earth was in the contrary position. Roemer attributed these irregularities to the fact that the light had to travel a longer distance in the former case than in the latter and, on the basis of this hypothesis, he calculated the velocity of light to be such as to require eleven minutes to travel a distance equal to the radius of the earth's orbit.[21]

Roemer was not the first to propose the hypothesis of finite velocity of light to account for these observations. Cassini put forward the same hypothesis in August 1675 but withdrew it shortly afterwards.[22] Roemer adopted it and showed that it was in agree-

---

[19] Ibid., pp. 6–7

[20] Ibid., p. 7.

[21] Cf. 'Démonstration touchant le Mouvement de la Lumière trouvé Par M. Roemer' in *Mémoires de l'Académie Royale des Sciences, depuis 1666 jusqu'à 1699*, X (Paris, 1730), pp. 575–7.

[22] This fact is generally ignored in recent histories of the subject. Cf. the account oɪ Maraldi's communication to the *Académie des Sciences* on 9 February 1707 (entitled 'Sur la seconde inégalité des satellites de Jupiter') in *Histoire de l'Académie Royale des Sciences, année 1707. Avec les Mémoires de mathématique & de physique pour la même année. Tirés des Registres de cette Académie.* Paris, 1708, p. 78, Cf. also J.-E. Montucla, *Histoire des mathématiques, nouvelle édition*, II, Paris, AN VII, p. 579.

ment with all the observations on Jupiter's first satellite which had been recorded at the *Académie* for eight years. He also predicted that the emergence of the satellite from Jupiter's shadow which was to occur on 16 November 1676 (Roemer announced his hypothesis to the *Académie* in September 1676) should be later than would be expected on the ordinary calculations; and his prediction was confirmed. Nevertheless, Cassini 'who was better informed than any one else'[23] about the world of Jupiter, could not accept Roemer's explanation; and in this he was not alone. In fact there were serious difficulties. It was argued, for example, that if the hypothesis were true, then the periods of the other three satellites of Jupiter would exhibit the same inequalities as those of the first; but this was not observed.[24] We are told in the *compte-rendu* of Roemer's communication in the *Histoire de l'Académie des Sciences* that another astronomical hypothesis was put forward which would take 'all the Observations' into account without assuming the finite velocity of light, but that that hypothesis lacked the '*vrai-semblance*' which Roemer's hypothesis seemed to have.[25] '*Il falut donc admettre le Retardement de la Lumiere, si vrai-semblable selon la Physique, quand il ne seroit pas prouvé par l'Astronomie.*'[26] It would seem from the text of the *Histoire* that the discussion between members of the *Académie des Sciences* concerning Roemer's hypothesis gradually shifted from the purely astronomical arguments (which, to some of them, appeared inconclusive) to turn round the question whether that hypothesis was acceptable from a *physical* point of view. There is no doubt that Huygens would be foremost among those who answered this question in the affirmative. But, even after the publication of Huygens' *Traité de la Lumière* in 1690, Roemer's hypothesis was not universally accepted by members of the *Académie des Sciences*. Some of them still believed that the observed inequalities of periods might be due to the eccentricity of the satellite or to the irregularity of its

---

[23] Cf. *Histoire de l'Académie Royale des Sciences*, I, *depuis son établissement en 1666 jusqu'à 1686*, Paris, 1733, p. 214.

[24] On this and other difficulties, see Montucla, op. cit., II, pp. 580–1.

[25] Cf. *Histoire de l'Académie Royale des Sciences*, I, *depuis son établissement en 1666, jusqu'à 1686*, Paris, 1733, p. 214.

[26] Ibid., p. 215.

motion 'or to some other cause which may be revealed in time'.[27] In view of all this one is inclined to conclude that Huygens accepted Roemer's 'demonstration' not so much because he saw in it an 'impressive revelation of facts'[28] but, rather, because it was in agreement with what he had adopted as a physical hypothesis which, as we have seen, he had required for a clear explanation of the properties of light.

Among the properties which Huygens proposed to explain in the *Traité* is the fact that rays of light are not interrupted by crossing one another.[29] His explanation was an attempt to solve another difficulty arising from the Cartesian conception of light and the nature of the light-bearing medium. To sharpen the difficulty Huygens considers the special case in which the rays are opposite and in the same line, as when two torches illuminate each other or when two eyes view one another: if, as Descartes supposes, light is a tendency to movement and not a successive motion, how could one and the same particle tend to move in two opposite directions at the same instant? To overcome this difficulty Huygens finds it necessary to endow the ethereal matter with the property of elasticity and, consequently, he rejects the doctrine of instantaneous propagation. This he illustrates by reference to the following experiment.

Imagine a row of contiguous spheres of equal size. If two similar spheres strike the ends of the row in opposite directions, they will both rebound with their velocity before impact, while the rest of the spheres remain motionless. This indicates to Huygens that the movements have passed through the length of the row in both directions. 'And if these contrary movements happen to meet one

---

[27] Cf. the text quoted by the editors of Huygens' works from *Recueil d'Observations faites en plusieurs voyages par ordre de Sa Majesté, pour perfectionner l'astronomie et la geographie, avec divers traitez astronomiques, par Messieurs de l'Académie Royale des Sciences*, Paris, 1693, H, XIX, pp. 400–1, *Avertissement*. For a detailed discussion of Roemer's investigations on the velocity of light and a bibliography on this subject, see I. Bernard Cohen, 'Roemer and the first determination of the velocity of light (1676)', *Isis*, XXXI (1940), pp. 327–9.

[28] Cf. Mouy, *Développement de la physique cartésienne*, p. 201.

[29] Cf. *Treatise*, pp. 21–22. Ibn al-Haytham described an experiment (the well-known *camera obscura* experiment) to show that beams of coloured light do not mix, and therefore do not affect one another, when they meet in space (at the opening of 'the dark place'). Alhazeni *Optica*, I, 29, in *Opticae thesaurus*, p. 17: 'Et significatio, quod luces et colores non permisceantur in aere, neque in corporibus diaphanis, est: quod quando in uno loco fuerint

another at the middle sphere . . . that sphere will yield and act as a spring at both sides, and so will serve at the same instant to transmit these two movements.'[30] To understand the corresponding effects of light one must therefore suppose the ether particles to be capable of contraction and expansion, which must require time.

But in my judgement . . . [these effects] are not at all easy to explain according to the views of Mr Des Cartes, who makes Light to consist in a continuous pressure merely tending to movement. For this pressure not being able to act from two opposite sides at the same time, against bodies which have no inclination to approach one another, it is impossible so to understand what I have been saying about two persons mutually seeing one another's eyes, or how two torches can illuminate one another.[31]

On account of the extremely high velocity of light the particles of the ether are supposed to have perfect hardness and elasticity. Huygens is not willing to explain in detail in what the elasticity of the ether consists. But the explanation which he gives 'in passing' is interesting from the point of view of the present discussion.

. . . we may conceive that the particles of the ether, notwithstanding their smallness, are in turn composed of other parts and that their springiness

---

multae candelae in locis diversis et distinctis, et fuerint omnes oppositae uni foramin pertranseunti ad locum obscurum, et fuerit in oppositione illius foraminis in obscuro loco paries, aut corpus non diaphanum, luces illarum candelarum apparent super corpus vel super illum parietem, distinctae secundum numerum candelarum illarum, et quaelibet illarum apparet opposita uni candelae secundum lineam transeuntem per foramen. Et si cooperiatur una candela, destruetur lux opposita uni candelae tantum; et si auferatur coopertorium revertetur lux. Et hoc poterit omni hora probari: quod si luces admiscerentur cum aere admiscerentur cum aere foraminis, et deberent transire admixtae, et non distinguerentur postea. Et nos non invenimus ita. Luces ergo non admiscentur in aere, sed quaelibet illarum extenditur super verticationes rectas; et illae verticationes sunt aequidistantes, et secantes se, et diversi situs. Et forma cuiuslibet lucis extenditur super omnes verticationes, quae possunt extendi in illo aere ab illa hora; neque tamen admiscentur in aere, nec aer tingitur per eas, sed pertranseunt per ipsius diaphanitatem tantum, et aer non amittit suam formam. Et quod diximus de luce, et colore, et aere, intelligendum est de omnibus corporibus diaphanis, et tunicis visus diaphanis.' The sentence 'Et nos non invenimus ita.' has been wrongly interpreted to mean that Ibn al-Haytham had not himself discovered this (S. L. Polyak, *The Retina*, Chicago, 1941, p. 133; Colin Murray Turbayne, *The Myth of Metaphor*, Yale University Press, 1963, p. 155). In fact he is simply saying that we do not observe (find) what would have resulted had the lights been mixed at the opening; therefore, etc. Ibn al-Haytham did not attempt a mechanical explanation of the property he asserts here.

[30] *Treatise*, p. 18.   [31] Ibid, p. 22.

consists in the very rapid movement of a subtle matter which penetrates them from every side and constrains their structure to assume such a disposition as to give to this fluid matter the most overt and easy passage possible. This accords with the explanation which Mr Des Cartes gives for the spring [*ressort*: elasticity], though I do not, like him, suppose the pores to be in the form of round hollow canals. And it must not be thought that in this there is anything absurd or impossible, it being on the contrary quite credible that it is this infinite series of different sizes of corpuscles, having different degrees of velocity, of which Nature makes use to produce so many marvellous effects.[32]

Descartes had tried to explain the elasticity which 'generally exists in all the bodies whose parts are joined by the perfect contact of their small superficies' by the fluid matter which, being itself incapable of reduction in volume, was not elastic.[33] He assumed those bodies to have pores through which the subtle matter incessantly streams. The pores are normally disposed in such a way as to give the subtle matter the most free and easy passage and therefore are in the form of circular canals to accommodate the spherical shape of the parts of the streaming matter. When the body is deformed its pores take a different shape, and the subtle matter must consequently exert some pressure on the walls of the canals, thus endeavouring to make the body regain its original form. In Descartes' system the incompressibility of the fluid matter was suited to the supposed instantaneous transmission of light. Huygens, on the other hand, requires the elasticity of ether for the successive propagation of light. Proceeding on Cartesian lines he explains the elasticity of the ethereal particles by the action of smaller particles and these, in turn, he supposes to be penetrated by still smaller particles, and so on to infinity.

2. Huygens agreed with Descartes (against the views of Gassendi and Newton) that the motion of light cannot consist in the transport of bodies from the luminous object to the eye. Like Descartes, he

---

[32] Ibid., p. 14.
[33] Descartes, *Principles*, IV, 132.

thought it inconceivable that a body, however small, could travel with such a great velocity as that of light, and found the corpuscular conception of rays unsuited to the fact that light rays meet in space without affecting one another. But whereas Descartes thought the action of light in the intervening medium to be instantaneous, Huygens was led, through an examination of the various difficulties involved in Descartes' hypotheses, to adopt the view that light must be a process taking place at a finite rate. This in turn led him to introduce elasticity as a property of the light-bearing medium. Huygens thus replaced the Cartesian conception of light rays as mere geometrical lines whose points are all simultaneous with one another[34] by another picture, already developed by Hooke and Pardies, in which the straight lines are cut by spherical surfaces representing successive loci of a central disturbance. The reform thus introduced by seventeenth-century wave theorists consisted in replacing Descartes' geometristically static picture by another that was truly capable of clear mathematical treatment.[35] To Huygens belongs the merit of having taken the first step in the successful application of mathematics to it. This may be illustrated by Huygens' explanations of rectilinear propagation, ordinary and double refractions.

Like Pardies, Huygens draws the analogy between light and sound: both are propagated by spherical surfaces or waves. But Huygens does not extend the analogy any further than that. He first remarks that their modes of production are different: whereas sound is produced by the agitation of the sounding body as a whole, or of a considerable part of it, light originates 'as from each point of the luminous object'.[36] More important is the difference in their manner of transmission. For the medium serving for the transmission of sound is air; air can be very much compressed and reduced

---

[34] See above, p. 60.

[35] Descartes' conception of the transmission of light, and of light rays as 'nothing more' than geometrical lines, is another example of what Alexandre Koyré would have called 'géométrisation à outrance'; it was indeed geometrical, but, paradoxically, too geometrical to allow of anything much being done with it mathematically. To develop it mathematically the points on the rectilinear rays had to be made successive, not simultaneous.

[36] Huygens, Treatise, p. 10. Cf. Alhazeni Optica, I, 15, in Opticae thesaurus, p. 8.

in volume, and the more it is compressed the more it exerts an effort to regain its original volume. This proves to Huygens that air is made up of small bodies which are agitated by the smaller particles of the ethereal matter, and that sound spreads by the effort of the air particles to escape from the place where they are squeezed together at the regions of compression along the propagating waves. 'But the extreme velocity of Light, and other properties which it has, cannot admit of such a propagation of motion . . . .'[37] The picture which Huygens imagines for the propagation of light bears certain traces of the Cartesian picture. The particles of ether are supposed to act like the row of contiguous and equal spheres mentioned before. If a similar sphere strikes against one end of the row, it will communicate the whole of its motion to the sphere at the other end, while the rest of the spheres remain motionless. This shows that the movement has passed from one end to the other 'as in an instant',[38] but not instantaneously. For if the movement 'or the disposition to movement, if you will have it so',[39] were not transmitted successively, the spheres would all move together at the same time, which does not happen. The ether particles must touch one another in order to be able to transmit the action of light in the same way. This is to be contrasted with the picture which Newton envisaged and in which he supposed the ether to be 'exceedingly more rare . . . than Air'.[40] Huygens, unlike Descartes, sees no reason why the particles should be spherical in shape. But in order to render the propagation easier and to avoid considerable reflection of movement backwards, he finds it desirable that they should be of equal size.[41] Following Descartes, he also remarks that the various motions of the ether particles among themselves cannot hinder the movement of light, as the latter is not effected by the transport of these particles themselves. As has been noted before, every particle of

---

[37] *Treatise*, p. 12.

[38] Ibid., p. 13.

[39] Ibid., p. 13. These words do not occur in the 1678 version of the *Traité* but were added by Huygens in the edition of 1690. Their addition makes the picture even more Cartesian. Cf. H, XIX, p. 383 (*Avertissement*).

[40] Newton, *Opticks*, Query 18, p. 349.

[41] *Treatise*, p. 16.

the luminous body must be regarded as the centre of its own spherical wave. 'But', and this is where Huygens explicitly rejects the periodicity of light, 'as the percussions at the centres of these waves possess no regular succession, it must not be supposed that the waves themselves follow one another at equal distances'.[42] Thus, Huygens' 'waves' are in fact isolated pulses that are generated in the ether by a succession of impacts which follow one another at irregular intervals.

Into the midst of this picture Huygens introduces the idea of secondary waves which, in fact, forms the basis of his explanations of the properties of light. The first consideration in the principle governing these waves consists in the remark that

each particle of matter in which a wave spreads, ought not to communicate its motion only to the next particle which is in the straight line drawn from the luminous point, but that it also imparts some of it necessarily to all the others which touch it and which oppose themselves to its movement. So it arises that around each particle there is made a wave of which that particle is the centre.[43]

This may be stated briefly thus: on any wave surface, each point may be regarded as centre of a particular or secondary wave travelling with the same velocity as the initial principal wave. The condition about the velocity is implied in Huygens' exposition of the principle.

Thus if *DCF* [Fig. VIII. 2] is a wave emanating from the luminous point *A*, which is its centre, the particle *B*, one of those comprised within the sphere *DCF*, will have made its particular or partial wave, *KCL*, which will touch the wave *DCF* at *C* at the same moment that the principal wave emanating from the point *A* has arrived at *DCF*; and it is clear that it will be only the region *C* of the wave *KCL* which will touch the wave *DCF*, to wit, that which is in the straight line drawn through *AB*. Similarly the other particles of the sphere *DCF*, such as *bb*, *dd*, etc., will each make its own wave. But each of these waves can be infinitely feeble only as compared with the wave *DCF*, to the composition of which all the others contribute by the part of their surface which is most distant from the centre *A*.[44]

---

[42] *Treatise*, p. 17.   [43] Ibid., p. 19.   [44] Ibid.

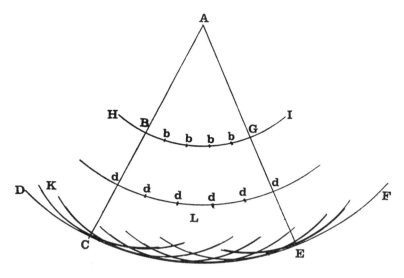

FIG. VIII. 2.

These remarks contain Huygens' fundamental contribution to the wave theory of light. They are not to be found in Hooke's treatment of the subject, and Huygens tells us that they were also lacking in Pardies' manuscript.[45]

To explain rectilinear propagation Huygens adds a further assumption: the particular waves are not effective except where they concur at the same instant, i.e. at their point of tangency with a principal wave. Thus, in Fig. VIII. 2, let BG be an opening limited by opaque bodies BH and GI. The portion BG of a principal wave-front emanating from A will in a certain time t spread out into the arc CE, where C and E are, respectively, in the lines AB and AG extended, and the distance $BC = GE = vt$ (v being the velocity of propagation). In the same time, the secondary waves which have originated (for example) at bb will have travelled, all in *forward* directions, a distance equal to vt.[46] Their common tangent (or

---

[45] See above, p. 197.
[46] Huygens excludes the possibility of back waves travelling towards the centre of disturbance A by supposing the ether particles to be equal. Accordingly, he does not consider the other envelope which can be obtained by completing the small circles in his figure. The mathematical construction is here limited by a physical condition.

envelope) will be the wave-front *CE*. And since it is assumed that the secondary waves are not effective except where they simultaneously concur to make up a single wave, it is concluded that their effect will be sensible only within the space *BGCE*; that is, the illuminated area will be limited by the straight lines *AC* and *AE*.

As opposed to the preceding explanation, Newton had maintained in the *Principia* (which appeared before the publication of Huygens' *Traité*) that any disturbance propagated in a fluid must diverge from a rectilinear progress.[47] On the basis of dynamical considerations he showed that when waves are partially allowed to pass through an opening in a barrier, their progress will not be terminated by straight lines drawn from the centre of disturbance, but will diverge beyond those lines and spread throughout the shaded portion of the medium. This was confirmed by familiar observations on the propagation of water waves and by the fact that sound can be heard round obstacles. As will be seen later,[48] these considerations led Newton to reject the wave hypothesis as applied to light, since in his view this hypothesis was founded on a false analogy between light and sound.

Huygens tried to answer Newton's objections in the *Addition* to his *Discours de la Cause de la Pesanteur* (published in the same volume with the *Traité* in 1690).[49] He recognized the lateral communication of movement into the geometrical shadow; but repeated his remark in the *Traité* that the secondary waves which do cross into that region are too feeble to produce any sensible effect, the reason being that they arrive there individually and not concurrently and, therefore, fail to strengthen one another. Newton was not convinced by this argument,[50] and quite understandably, since it was not clear why the same considerations could not apply to sound. In fact no satisfactory explanation of rectilinear propagation from the wave-theory point of view was given until the beginning of the nineteenth century. It was Fresnel who first showed that in places well beyond

---

[47] Newton, *Principia*, Bk. II, Sec. VIII, Prop. XLII, Theor. XXXIII, pp. 369–71.

[48] See below, pp. 282f.

[49] Cf. H, XXI, pp. 474–5.

[50] This we gather from the fact that he repeated the same objections in the *Opticks*. Cf. Query 28 (pp. 362–3) which first appeared as Query 20 in the Latin edition of 1706.

the limits of the geometrical shadow the secondary waves (which are, in Fresnel's theory, proper wave-trains) arrive with phase relations such that they neutralize one another to produce darkness. Fresnel's theory *simultaneously* explained the slight bending of light which does take place in the immediate vicinity of those limits. Some of the fundamental ideas on which Fresnel relied in his explanations were available neither to Huygens nor to Newton.

Ernst Mach in his *Principles of Physical Optics* considers the question of how Huygens arrived at the ideas involved in his principle of secondary waves and in his explanation of rectilinear propagation. He suggests that Huygens' ideas, in their essentials, 'evidently have a two-fold origin, his natural experience and his particular line of thought'.[51] That particular line of thought, according to Mach, derives from Huygens' earlier work on the percussion of elastic spheres which he took as a model for the transmission of light through ether. Regarding the contribution of Huygens' 'natural experience', Mach suggests the following:

It would be quite natural for the son of a seafaring people and the inhabitant of a town intersected by canals to make observations upon water waves. As a boy, no doubt, he would have thrown pebbles into water and observed the interaction of ripples generated simultaneously or successively at two different points. He could not fail to have observed the wedge-shaped waves produced by moving a stick rapidly through water in one direction, or the waves from the bow of a moving boat, and must have recognized that practically the *same* effect is produced by dropping several pebbles into the water in succession at intervals along a straight line. These observations contain the nucleus of his most important discoveries.[52]

The origin of these remarks is evidently Mach's particular line of thought, and they are in accordance with his view of scientific theories as being ultimately derived from observation and experiment. He actually deduces the sine relation from a situation similar to that in which waves are produced on a water surface by successively dropping pebbles into it along a straight line. But he assumes in his deduction that the velocity of the waves is different on either

---

[51] Mach, op. cit., p. 257.   [52] Ibid.

side of the line joining their centres. This surely was not *observed* by Huygens in the canals of Amsterdam. It would be nearer to the truth to present Mach's deduction as an *application* of some already developed ideas to a hypothetical situation. In the absence of any evidence to the contrary, Mach's deduction cannot be regarded as indicating the 'origin' of Huygens' own discoveries. Indeed, as Newton pointed out, more obvious and less complex observations than those described by Mach clearly pronounced against Huygens' ideas as applied to rectilinear propagation.[53]

In any case Huygens himself does not cite observations in support of his principle of secondary waves. On the contrary, he was aware of its unfamiliar character. After the exposition of that principle he wrote: 'And all this ought not to seem fraught with too much minuteness or subtlety, since we shall see in the sequel that all the properties of Light, and everything pertaining to its reflexion and its refraction, can be explained in principle by this means.'[54] The only justification given here by Huygens for his new ideas is the fact that he could explain the properties of light by their means. Had he been familiar with observations supporting his principle, would he not have cited them instead of admitting that it might seem 'fraught with too much minuteness or subtlety'?

3. Huygens' construction for ordinary refraction may be obtained by application of his principle of secondary waves as follows.[55] In the figure (Fig. VIII. 3) let AC be a plane wave-front which obliquely strikes the separating surface AB at A. AC is perpendicular to the direction of incidence DA. Let the distance CB (parallel to DA) be equal to $v_i t$, where v_i is the velocity of the medium above and t the time required for C to arrive at B. In the same time, the secondary

---

[53] Historically more interesting than Mach's remarks is the similarity, noted by Dijksterhuis (*The Mechanization of the World Picture*, translated by C. Dikshoorn, Oxford, 1961, p. 149), between Huygens' principle and the medieval doctrine of the multiplication of species as applied to the propagation of light, in particular the idea which this doctrine entailed that every illuminated point becomes itself a further source of illumination by virtue of a certain agency being conferred upon it.

[54] Huygens, *Treatise*, p. 20.

[55] Cf. *Treatise*, pp. 35–39.

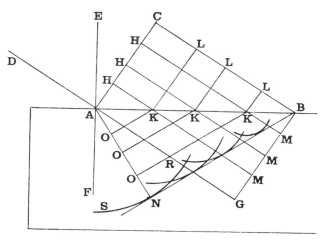

FIG. VIII, 3.

wave generated at A will have travelled in the medium of refraction
a distance equal to $v_r t$, where v_r is the velocity in this medium.

Supposing, then, that

$$\frac{v_i}{v_r} = n,$$ a constant *greater or less* than unity,

the circumference SNR, having A as centre and a radius equal to
$\frac{1}{n}CB$, will give the position of the secondary wave at the time
when the part of the incident wave-front at C arrives at B. The
other arcs in the figure are similarly drawn (with points K as centres
and radii that are equal to the distances LB each divided by n) by
considering the wave-fronts KL in order. All these arcs will have as
a common tangent the straight line BN which is the same as the
tangent from B to the arc SNR. BN therefore gives the position
which the wave-front has reached successively by taking the
positions LKO in order. And the direction of propagation after
refraction is represented by the perpendicular AN.

From this the sine relation is readily obtained. For since the angle
of incidence EAD is equal to the angle CAB, and the angle of
refraction FAN is equal to ABN, it follows that

$$\frac{\sin i}{\sin r} = \frac{CB}{AB} \times \frac{AB}{AN} = \frac{CB}{AN} = \frac{v_i t}{v_r t} = \frac{v_i}{v_r} = n.$$

This law implies that when the angle of refraction is smaller than the corresponding angle of incidence, the velocity must have been diminished by refraction. And since light in passing from a rare into a dense medium is deflected towards the normal, it must be concluded that the velocity of light is greater in rarer media. Huygens' law is the same as that deduced by Fermat (from the least-time principle) and maintained by Pardies and Ango. But whereas Ango and (perhaps) Pardies simply assumed the wavefront to be perpendicular to the direction of propagation after refraction, this is presented by Huygens as a *consequence* of regarding the wave-front as a resultant wave composed from the secondary waves generated successively at the surface of the refracting medium. Fermat's principle of least time then follows as a result of Huygens' law. Although this is already clear from Fermat's proof by synthesis (given in Chapter V above),[56] Huygens' simpler and shorter deduction may be summarized here.

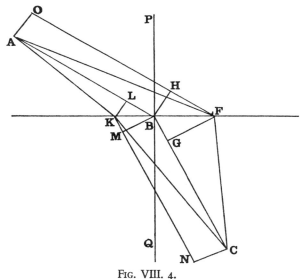

Fig. VIII. 4.

Let *A*, *C* (Fig. VIII. 4) be any two points on the incident and refracted rays *AB*, *BC* respectively—the direction of refraction being

---

[56] Above, pp. 150ff.

determined by the law stated above.[57] It is to be proved that the actual path ABC is that for which the time employed is a minimum. Let AFC be any other path on the right-hand side of B. Huygens proves first that the time along AFC is longer than the time along ABC, as follows.

He draws OA perpendicular to AB, FG perpendicular to BC, OF parallel to AB, and BH perpendicular to OF. BH may therefore represent an incident wave-front which takes the position FG after refraction, and we thus have:

$$\frac{\sin i}{\sin r} = \frac{HF}{BG} = \frac{v_i}{v_r} = n.$$

This means that the time along HF is equal to that along BG: from which it follows that the time along OF is equal to the time along ABG. But, AF being greater than OF, and FC greater than GC, it follows that the time along the hypothetical path AFC would be longer than that required along ABC. (In this case BM may be taken to represent the incident wave-front which occupies the position KL after refraction.) ABC is therefore the path for which the time required is a minimum.

The construction which Huygens gives for the reflection of light is obtained by a similar application of the principle of secondary waves as in the case of refraction.[58] On the supposition that the velocity is unaltered by reflection, he draws the arcs representing the secondary waves that are successively generated (by the incident wave-front) at the reflecting surface in the medium of incidence; their common tangent is drawn, and the direction of the resultant wave is then found to make an angle with the normal equal to the angle of incidence.

Huygens also shows[59] that when the light falls on a separating surface from the side of the denser medium (that is, the medium in which the velocity is less) at an angle whose sine is greater than the refractive index $n \left(\dfrac{v_i}{v_r} \right)$, no tangent can be found common to all the secondary waves which are supposed to be excited in the rarer

---

[57] Huygens, *Treatise*, pp. 42–45. [58] Ibid., pp. 23–25.

[59] Ibid., pp. 39–41.

medium on the other side of the interface. This means that no resultant wave can be constructed in the medium of refraction, and it is therefore inferred that, in this case, the refracted light will not be perceived. At the same time a common envelope can be found for the secondary waves in the medium of incidence. Huygens' principle is thus shown to be in agreement with the phenomenon of total reflection. At the critical angle of incidence whose sine is exactly equal to n, the secondary waves strengthen one another in the direction of the separating surface; that is, the refracted ray will travel along the surface, also in accordance with observation.

It is known from experience that, in general, light is *partially* reflected at refracting surfaces. For example, a beam of light travelling through a block of glass is in general split up into two beams upon meeting the surface of the glass: the one beam is refracted into the outer medium (say air) while the other is internally reflected within the block. From a geometrical point of view this raises no difficulties for Huygens' theory: the refracted beam is determined by the construction for ordinary refraction, and the reflected beam is determined by the construction for reflection. But how should we understand this phenomenon mechanically; how does one and the same surface reflect some of the incident light and refract the rest? Huygens' suggestion was that (in this case) the interior reflection is produced by the particles of the air outside, while the refracted light is transmitted through the ethereal matter. But he himself realized the 'difficulty' involved in such an explanation: 'It is true that there remains here some difficulty in those experiments in which this interior reflection occurs without the particles of air being able to contribute to it, as in vessels or tubes from which the air has been extracted.'[60]

---

[60] *Treatise*, p. 42. The 14th-century Persian scholar Kamāl al-Dīn noted the problem of partial reflection in the following comment on Ibn al-Haytham's explanation of reflection by analogy with the mechanical reflection of bodies from smooth surfaces: 'This is questionable. For if smoothness prevents the transmission of light and forces it to be reflected, then how is it refracted into bodies whose transparency differs from that of the bodies in which it exists; and if smoothness does not prevent its transmission, then how is light reflected from the surfaces of liquids while it still goes through them? And it cannot be said that one and the same light is both transmitted and reflected, the one thus becoming two.' Kamāl al-Dīn concluded by rejecting the analogy with moving spheres and preferred a wave interpretation

Newton interpreted these experiments (and other related experiments which he described in the *Opticks*)[61] to indicate that a purely mechanical picture of reflection was fundamentally unsuitable for explaining the observed behaviour of light. In this he has been confirmed by the later development of optics. Thus, while Huygens' geometrical construction remains classical, the mechanical picture which he used has long been discarded. Duhem would find in this an illustration of his view that only the representative (geometrical or experimental) parts of scientific theories are to be counted as valuable, since the explanatory parts (such as the mechanical considerations involved in Huygens' theory) are always doomed to be abandoned in time.[62] Yet it is the ephemeral nature itself of explanatory theories that indicates their important, indeed essential role in the development of science. For it is only in the light of previous theories that certain experiments, which might otherwise be taken for granted, acquire a problematic character which calls for new and more adequate explanations. For example, to account for the experiments referred to by Huygens above, Newton appealed to his theory of fits which simultaneously served him as an explanation of the colours of thin transparent bodies. Newton's theory itself was not free from difficulties, but it brought out the significance of new experiments which, in their turn, called for new theories. As Popper has insisted, it is through the falsification of preceding conjectural explanatory theories that important progress is often made in science.

4. Huygens was already aware of the phenomenon of double refraction when, in 1673, he drafted the *Projet du Contenu de la Dioptrique*. We learn in fact from the *Projet* that he intended to include a chapter in his *Dioptrique* on 'Cristal d'Island' which exhibited that phenomenon. But, as the editors of Huygens' works observe, this chapter would have contained only a description of

---

of light; he suggested that the movement of light 'is like the movement of sounds, not the movement of bodies, and therefore the repulsion mentioned by [Ibn al-Haytham] cannot be conceived in it [the movement of light]' (*Tanqīḥ al-manāzir*, I, 1928, p. 374). Quoted by M. Nazif, *al-Ḥasan ibn al-Haytham*, I (Cairo, 1942), pp. 136–37. See above, pp. 72ff.

[61] See below, pp. 319f. [62] Cf. P. Duhem, *Théorie physique*, Pt. I, Ch. III, Sec. I.

Iceland crystal and its properties;[63] the only words relating to that subject in the *Projet* are the following: '*difficultè du cristal ou talc de Islande.sa description. figure. proprietez.*'[64] Huygens first succeeded in explaining some of the phenomena connected with double refraction in 1677;[65] hence his idea of writing the *Traité de la Lumière* as a book wholly devoted to the wave theory and its applications without going into the questions of dioptrics which he had planned to include in the *Dioptrique*. Huygens' explanations of the phenomena of double refraction were thus the result of an extended application of a theory which he had previously devised mainly to account for ordinary refraction. He himself has made this quite clear in the fifth chapter of his *Traité*: 'It was after having explained the refraction of ordinary transparent bodies by means of the spherical emanations of light, as above, that I resumed my examination of the nature of this Crystal, wherein I had previously been unable to discover anything.'[66] This resumed examination did not result in deducing the anomalous phenomena of the crystal from his already formed theory as it stood. In fact they persistently appeared to threaten the validity of its basic assumptions. But in this lay their chief interest. They constituted a challenge which could not be ignored by Huygens; and to solve the difficulties he had to invent new hypotheses. He was not completely successful in his attempt. But some of the principles which he introduced are still valid; and he was certainly entitled to regard his partial success as a confirmation of his fundamental principle of secondary waves.

As has been remarked above, a description of Iceland crystal and of its chief phenomena with respect to optical refraction was first given by Erasmus Bartholinus in 1669. Pieces of that crystal were found in the shape of an oblique parallelepiped; each of its faces being a parallelogram. It was observed by Bartholinus that when a small

---

[63] Cf. H, XIII, *fasc.* II, p. 743, note 7.

[64] Cf. H, XIII, *fasc.* II, p. 739.

[65] Cf. Huygens to Colbert, 14 October 1677, H, VIII, pp. 36 and 37.

[66] *Treatise*, p. 61. On 22 November 1679 (the year in which Huygens communicated his theory to the *Académie des Sciences*) he wrote to Leibniz: 'I worked a great deal all last summer on my refractions, especially regarding the Iceland Crystal, which has very strange phenomena the reasons of all of which I have not yet unravelled. But what I have found of them greatly confirms my theory of light and of ordinary refractions' (H, VIII, p. 244).

object was viewed through two opposite faces it appeared double. He attributed this to the fact that when the incident ray entered the crystal it was divided into two refracted rays. One of these (called the *ordinary* ray) followed the usual rules of refraction while the other (called the *extraordinary* ray) did not. For example, a ray falling perpendicularly on one of the parallelogram faces was split up at the point of incidence into two: the one continued in the normal direction, as would be expected, while the other proceeded at an angle with the first. Also (and this was observed by Huygens) there was a certain angle of incidence at which the ray falling obliquely on the surface of the crystal would partially continue in the same oblique direction (thus giving rise to an extraordinary ray), while its other part would be deflected at an angle of refraction bearing a certain constant ratio of the sines to the angle of incidence.[67]

How did Huygens attempt to explain these phenomena on the basis of his original ideas?

As there were two different refractions, I conceived that there were also two different emanations of waves of light, and that one could occur in the ethereal matter extending through the body of the Crystal. Which matter, being present in much larger quantity than is that of the particles which compose it, was alone capable of causing transparency . . . I attributed to this emanation of waves the regular refraction which is observed in this stone, by supposing these waves to be ordinarily of spherical form, and having a slower progression within the Crystal than they have outside it; whence proceeds refraction as I have demonstrated.[68]

This accounts for the ordinary ray. But what about the extraordinary ray? What form of waves correspond to it, and how are we to picture the manner of propagation of these waves in the same crystal while the other, ordinary ray is proceeding by spherical surfaces as was assumed in the explanation of ordinary refraction?

As to the other emanation which should produce the irregular refraction, I wished to try what Elliptical waves, or rather spheroidal waves, would

---

[67] Cf. Huygens, *Treatise*, pp. 56–57. The two refracted rays would continue to be in the plane of incidence only if that plane was parallel to a certain plane of the crystal called by Huygens the *principal section*.

[68] Ibid., p. 61.

do; and these I supposed would spread indifferently both in the ethereal matter diffused throughout the crystal and in the particles of which it is composed, according to the last mode in which I have explained transparency. It seemed to me that the disposition or regular arrangement of these particles could contribute to form spheroidal waves (nothing more being required for this than that the successive movement of light should spread a little more quickly in one direction than in the other) and I scarcely doubted that there were in this crystal such an arrangement of equal and similar particles, because of its figure and of its angles with their determinate and invariable measure.[69]

Thus, according to Huygens, when a wave-front impinges on the surface of Iceland crystal it generates two series of waves which simultaneously traverse the crystal. The waves of the first series are carried through the particles of the ethereal matter alone, and they proceed by spherical surfaces. The waves of the second series travel through both the ether particles and the particles of the crystal, and they are transmitted by spheroidal surfaces with different velocities in different directions. From these assumptions the directions of refractions within the crystal could be determined by application of the principle of secondary waves. The direction of the ordinary ray is determined by the construction for ordinary refraction; and the direction of the extraordinary ray is found by a similar construction in which spheroidal secondary waves take the place of the spherical secondary waves in the ordinary construction.

It is to be noted that Huygens does not tell us that his choice of the spheroidal shape, rather than any other, was determined by a prior quantitative analysis of the phenomena in question. Rather, he adopted the assumption that the extraordinary ray was produced by *spheroidal* waves as a hypothesis which he later set out to examine experimentally. Thus he writes: 'Supposing then these spheroidal waves besides the spherical ones, I began to examine whether they could serve to explain the phenomena of the irregular refraction, and how by these same phenomena I could determine the figure and position of the spheroids . . . .'[70]

---

[69] Cf. Huygens, *Treatise*, pp. 56–57.
[70] Ibid., p. 63.

Huygens' analysis of the wave surface for the extraordinary ray as a spheroid still stands in geometrical optics.[71] But there were certain phenomena which he could not explain by his theory. He discovered these phenomena himself after he had written the greater portion of the *Traité* and of the chapter on Iceland crystal.

Before finishing the treatise on this Crystal, I will add one more mar-vellous phenomenon which I discovered after having written all the foregoing. For though I have not been able till now to find its cause, I do not for that reason wish to desist from describing it, in order to give opportunity to others to investigate it. It seems that it will be necessary to make still further suppositions besides those which I have made; but these will not for all that cease to keep their probability [*vraisemblance*] after having been confirmed by so many tests.[72]

The phenomenon discovered by Huygens was an unexpected one. For he expected a ray emerging from a piece of Iceland crystal to behave in relation to a second piece as the light coming directly from the light source had behaved in relation to the first. But he found that this was not so. He first placed two crystals at a distance above one another such that the faces of the one crystal were parallel to those of the other. A beam of light was allowed to fall per-pendicularly on the surface of the first (higher) crystal. This gave rise to two rays within the crystal, the one continuing perpen-dicularly in the line of incidence (the ordinary ray); and the other (extraordinary) ray, being deflected from the normal direction. At their emergence from the first crystal, the ordinary ray persisted in the same perpendicular direction; and the extraordinary ray was again deflected in such a way as to be parallel to the ordinary ray but displaced from it. Upon their entrance into the second crystal none of the two rays was divided; the ordinary ray gave rise to one or-dinary ray (thus again continuing in the same line), and the extra-ordinary ray was refracted into an extraordinary ray. Naturally, Huygens found it strange that the rays incident on the lower crystal

---

[71] For a detailed account of Huygens' analysis, see Mach, *Principles*, pp. 260–4; Bell, *Christian Huygens*, pp. 186–9.

[72] *Treatise*, p. 92 (H, XIX, p. 517).

should not behave in the same way as the original beam did through the higher one. Could that mean, he asked, that the ordinary ray emerging from the first crystal has lost something which is necessary to move the matter that serves for the transmission of extraordinary refraction; and that likewise the extraordinary ray has lost that which is necessary to move the matter that serves for the transmission of ordinary refraction?[73] If that hypothesis were true, then, it would seem, the ordinary ray would in all circumstances excite only one ordinary ray in the second crystal, and the extraordinary ray would always give rise to only one extraordinary ray. But this was not the case.

When he rotated the lower crystal about the original beam as axis through an angle equal to 90°, the two rays incident on that crystal were still not divided by refraction; but the ordinary ray gave rise to an extraordinary ray, and vice versa. When the lower crystal was held in an intermediate position between the last position and the first, *each* of the two rays incident on it gave rise to *two* rays, one ordinary and the other extraordinary.

When one considers here how, while the rays CE, DG [these are the rays incident on the second crystal], remain the same, it depends on the position that one gives to the lower piece, whether it divides them both in two, or whether it does not divide them, and yet how the ray AB above [this is the original beam incident on the higher crystal] is always divided, it seems that one is obliged to conclude that the waves of light, after having passed through the first crystal, acquire a certain form or disposition in virtue of which, when meeting the texture of the second crystal, in certain positions, they can move the two different kinds of matter which serve for the two species of refraction; and when meeting the second crystal in another position are able to move only one of these kinds of matter. But to tell how this occurs, I have hitherto found nothing which satisfies me.[74]

The problem was taken up by Newton in Queries 17, 18, 20, and 21 of the Latin edition (1706) of the *Opticks*.[75] To him, Huygens'

---

[73] Cf. *Treatise*, pp. 93–4.   [74] Ibid., p. 94.
[75] These re-appeared in the English edition of 1718, and in all subsequent editions, as Queries 25, 26, 28 and 29 respectively.

confession of failure to explain the experiment just described was a confirming sign of defeat of the wave hypothesis itself.[76] He argued[77] that if light consisted in a motion propagated through a uniform medium its properties would be the same in all directions, and the two beams emerging from the first crystal would not change their behaviour with respect to the position of the second. The real explanation must, therefore, be sought not in some 'new modifications'[78] which the rays might undergo in their passage through the first crystal (as Huygens had thought), but rather in the fact that they have certain *original* and *unchangeable* properties on which their fortunes through each one of the crystals depend. Accordingly, he suggested that a ray of light should be conceived as having two opposite 'sides' endowed with an original property on which the extraordinary refraction depends, and two other opposite sides which do not possess this property. Whether or not the ray will be refracted according to the ordinary rules will depend on the position of these sides in relation to the crystal or, rather, to its principal plane.

Thus Newton interprets Huygens' two-crystal experiment in the following manner.[79] The rays contained in the beam of ordinary light that is incident on the surface of the first crystal arrive there with their sides in various (random) positions relative to the principal plane of the crystal. The exact position of the sides of each ray determines whether it will be refracted according to the ordinary rules, or whether it will take the direction of the extraordinary beam. Two beams will thus traverse the first crystal, all the rays contained in the one beam having their sides oriented in a contrary way to those of the rays contained in the other.

Suppose now that the principal plane of the second crystal is parallel to that of the first. Then, since the sides of *all* rays contained in the *two* beams that are incident on the second crystal have the same position with respect to its principal plane as they had with

---

[76] Cf. *Opticks*, Query 28, p. 364.
[77] Cf. ibid., Query 25, p. 358; Query 28, p. 363.
[78] Cf. ibid., Query 28, p. 363.
[79] Cf. ibid., Query 26.

respect to the principal plane of the first, the ordinary beam will again be refracted as an ordinary beam and the extraordinary beam will give rise to one extraordinary beam. If the second crystal is rotated through a right angle, then the sides of the rays in the *ordinary* beam will have the same position to its principal plane as the sides of the rays in the *extraordinary* beam had with respect to the principal plane of the *first* crystal. Consequently, the ordinary beam will in this case traverse the second crystal as an extraordinary beam and, for the same reasons, the extraordinary beam will be refracted as an ordinary beam. By holding the second crystal in an intermediate position we are, according to Newton, back to the case of the ordinary light falling on the first crystal; each beam will therefore give rise to two beams, one ordinary and the other extraordinary.

The basic intuition in these explanations, namely Newton's realization that the rays emerging from the first crystal behave in such a way as to indicate that they do not have the same properties with respect to all directions perpendicular to their direction of propagation, contains in fact the discovery of what is known as the *polarization* of light.[80] This discovery could not be expressed in terms of the wave picture used by Huygens, and to that extent Newton was justified in regarding the two-crystal experiment as a stumbling block to Huygens' wave hypothesis. But he was mistaken in regarding it as a crucial test against the wave hypothesis as such. The idea of the *sidedness* of rays was in fact assimilated into the wave theory when, at the beginning of the nineteenth century, transverse wave motion was adopted for light. It was then shown by Fresnel that ordinary (unpolarized) light could be represented by a transverse wave motion in which the particles of the medium vibrate in all conceivable planes that are perpendicular to the direction of propagation. And polarized light (such as that which has passed through a crystal of the Iceland spar) was characterized by the

---

[80] Cf. Whittaker's Introduction to Newton's *Opticks*, p. lxxvi. The term *polarization* is derived from Newton's reference in this connection to the 'Poles of two Magnets' which, he suggests, act on one another as the crystal acts on the sides of the ray through a 'virtue' which he does not consider to be magnetic. Cf. *Opticks*, Query 29. pp. 373-4.

fact that the vibrations occur in precisely one of these planes. On this representation it could be significantly asserted in wave language that the two rays emerging from the first crystal in Huygens' experiment are polarized, and that their difference consists in the fact that their planes of polarization are perpendicular to one another.

5. Huygens' investigations in his *Traité de la Lumière* do not show any influence of those Baconian suggestions which he submitted to the *Académie des Sciences* in 1668 regarding the proper method of conducting physical research. Unlike Boyle who, as a follower of the Baconian programme, devoted his work on colours to collecting a natural history of those phenomena, Huygens does not attempt to make a complete enumeration of the properties of light, nor does he seem to think that such an enumeration would be necessary for his purpose. His only concern is to give a clear mechanical explanation of a few properties which, he believed, other philosophers had failed to explain before him. True, what he attempts to explain are 'facts of experience' which he takes for granted. But he nowhere claims to *argue from* these facts to the theory which he puts forward. Rather, his arguments consist in showing how these facts agree better with his conceptions than with those which had been proposed by other writers before him. And thus his starting point was the *problems* arising from previous theories rather than the facts themselves. By examining the difficulties involved in already existing hypotheses he was led to modify those hypotheses or to suggest new ones; he then set out to show how they could account for the experiments. His procedure was always from the hypothesis to the experiment, not vice versa, and accordingly, he did not claim for his explanations more than a certain degree of '*vraisemblance*'. In this the character of Huygens' *Traité* greatly contrasts with Newton's *Opticks*. Newton, in faithful observance of Baconian teaching, always sets out the Observations and Experiments before the Propositions which are claimed to have been simply derived from what precedes. The 'hypotheses', those fictions which we might be tempted to invent in the absence of sufficient experiments, are relegated to the end of the *Opticks* where they appear as problems or Queries. Underlying this mode of exposition there is a radical distinction between discoveries or theories on the one hand, and hypotheses on the other. Such a distinction does not exist for Huygens. Newton would explain this by the fact that Huygens was committed to a mechanistic view of nature which forced him to formulate his explanations in terms of hypothetical entities such as the ether. This of course is true and Huygens would readily admit it. But does this mean that by innocent and careful observation of what nature does or may be made to do by experimentation, one would be able to arrive at theories that are free from all hypothetical elements? Newton thought that would be possible and he actually claimed that there was nothing in his *asserted* theories which had not been deduced from the experiments. An examination of that claim will constitute an important part of the chapters that follow.

Chapter Nine

NEWTON'S THEORY OF LIGHT AND COLOURS, 1672

1. Newton first declared his views on scientific method during the famous controversy which took place immediately after the publication of his theory of light and colours in 1672. As is well known, the prominent and most important scientists against whose objections Newton had to defend his theory were Robert Hooke, Ignatius Pardies, and Christian Huygens.[1] All three of them were Cartesians of sorts and all had been engaged in developing a wave theory of light. Perceiving an atomistic tendency in Newton's ideas, they regarded his theory as a hypothesis which indeed agreed with the experiments, but which was no more than one among several possible interpretations of them. Newton rejected this characterization of his doctrine, claiming that there was nothing in the propounded properties of light that was not positively and directly concluded from the experiments. Therefore, in his view, to propose alternative hypotheses about the nature of light was beside the business at hand, which was to deduce the properties of light from the observed facts. This he defended as the proper method of scientific inquiry as opposed to the method of his critics—which, it appeared to him, sought to predetermine the properties of things from the mere possibility of hypotheses. Not that, according to Newton, hypotheses had no function whatsoever in natural philosophy; he expressly allowed that hypotheses might be employed, tentatively, to explain the phenomena after they had been discovered

---

[1] The far less important and not very revealing discussion which started later (in 1674) between Newton and Francis Hall (or Linus), S. J., professor of mathematics at the English Jesuit College at Liège, and which was continued after Hall's death in 1675 by his student Gascoigne and afterwards by Anthony Lucas, will not be of interest to us here. For a bibliography and analysis of this discussion, see: L. Rosenfeld, 'La théorie des couleurs de Newton et ses adversaires,' *Isis*, IX (1927), pp. 47–51. See also: Michael Roberts and E. R. Thomas, *Newton and the Origin of Colours*, London, 1934, Ch. XIII; David Brewster, *Memoirs of the Life, Writings and Discoveries of Sir Isaac Newton*, Edinburgh, 1855, vol. I, Ch. IV.

and ascertained, and even that they might be used to suggest new experiments that had not yet been performed. But he advised that they should not be held against the evidence of experiments; and he believed that when inquiry regarding a certain matter has been successfully accomplished, all hypotheses will have completely vanished. That is to say, hypotheses may be employed in the course of scientific inquiry, but they may not form part of asserted scientific doctrine.

It is a notorious fact that Newton's declarations about hypotheses are often torn out of their context and given a meaning that was never intended by their author. It is, therefore, not a misplaced hope to try first, as is partly the aim of this and the two following chapters, to understand his methodological views in the context in which they were first expressed and argued; this will prepare the way for a discussion of further examples in Chapters XII and XIII.

For this purpose it will be first necessary to analyse Newton's theory of colours as it was presented to the scientific world in 1672. I shall try to show, in terms as close as possible to Newton's, what his theory propounded, and which if any of his expressions justified the corpuscular interpretation which his contemporaries readily placed upon it. It will be also necessary, in Chapter X, to examine closely the objections raised by Newton's critics and see whether they took the experimental results into account, and to what extent they were determined by theoretical preferences. A sufficient understanding of the standpoint of Newton's opponents should naturally help in appreciating his reaction. Finally, in Chapter XI, an examination of Newton's answers will involve further analysis of his theory, and an assessment of his position will be attempted.

Various aspects of this controversy have been studied more than once, sometimes even with a view to clarifying Newton's methodological position. The judgement generally has been that Newton's critics failed to understand his theory; their fault was that while they were faced with an experimental discovery, they preferred to wrangle over hypotheses.[2] Now it is certainly true, particularly

---

[2] R. S. Westfall in an interesting recent article, 'Newton and his critics on the nature of colors', *Archives internationales d'histoire des sciences*, XV (1962), pp. 47–58, put forward the view

at the beginning of the discussion, that the opponents of Newton's theory did not fully appreciate the experimental facts with which they were presented; this is an important factor which will have to be borne in mind in trying to understand Newton's reaction. But we should not be too much influenced by Newton's own view of himself as the man who had been grossly misunderstood. Not only was he partly responsible for the initial misunderstanding, but he also completely and consistently failed to distinguish in his doctrine of colours between the strictly experimental propositions and the particular interpretation of white light which he attached to them. This interpretation, which the experiments certainly did not prove, was to the effect that white light should be viewed as a mixture of differentiated elements. The most important among Newton's critics, viz. Hooke, Pardies and Huygens, eventually conceded the only thing that Newton could have justifiably claimed to have proved experimentally, namely the fact that to every colour there is attached a constant of refrangibility which is not the same for any other colour. But they correctly refused to grant an equal status to Newton's doctrine of white light as a heterogeneous aggregate. Hooke in particular envisaged a new formulation of his pulse hypothesis which would have fully taken the experimental results into account without conceding the original heterogeneity of white light. According to this formulation the pulse of white light could be imagined as the resultant of a large number of 'vibrations' each of which when differentiated would produce a given colour.

---

that the basis of the controversy between Newton and his critics was an ironical misunderstanding: while Newton presented his discovery as further support of the mechanical philosophy, his critics interpreted his position as a reversion to the rejected peripatetic philosophy. Thus he writes: 'Not the nature of light but the nature of qualities, not undulatory vs. corpuscular but mechanical vs. peripatetic – these were the primary concerns of the critics' (ibid., p. 47). This seems to me to lay the emphasis on the wrong place. The suspicion of peripatetic conceptions in Newton's doctrine of colours was only a false start, one, moreover, for which Newton himself was partly responsible. The discussion was not, even from the beginning, solely concerned with this initial misunderstanding, nor did it come to a stop when Newton reassured Hooke on this score. Professor Westfall states that 'Like Hooke, Huygens saw in Newton's theory something that appeared incompatible with mechanical philosophy' (ibid., p. 54). The passages quoted from Huygens, however, show no more than a reserved attitude. He believed that colours should be explained mechanically, but that Newton had not yet provided such an explanation. As we have seen, Huygens himself later advanced a mechanical wave-theory of light which admitted its incapability of explaining colours.

This would imply that white light is compounded only in a mathematical sense, and prismatic analysis would be understood as a process in which colours are manufactured out of the physically simple and undifferentiated pulse. For reasons which will be discussed in the two following chapters Newton rejected this suggestion as unintelligible. And historians of science, confusing a generalized concept of composition with Newton's narrower interpretation, have continued to view this controversy with his own eyes. In this, however, they forget that Hooke's idea was reintroduced in the nineteenth century in a mathematically developed form as a plausible representation of white light from the wave-theory point of view.

2. Newton's first published account of his theory of the prismatic colours was contained in a letter to the Secretary of the Royal Society, Henry Oldenburg, dated 6 February 1671/2. The letter was read before the Society (in Newton's absence) on the eighth of the same month[3] and subsequently printed in No. 80 of the *Philosophical Transactions* of 19 February 1671/2.[4] Newton seems to imply in his letter that his experimental research on the prismatic colours dated from the beginning of 1666 when he applied himself to the grinding of lenses of non-spherical shapes.[5] It was generally believed at that time that the perfection of telescopes, and in particular, the elimination of chromatic aberration, would depend on the shape in

---

[3] Cf. Thomas Birch, *The History of the Royal Society of London*, London, 1756-7, III, p. 9.

[4] Cf. *Correspondence of Isaac Newton*, ed. Turnbull, I (1959), pp. 92-102.

[5] '. . . in the beginning of the Year 1666 (at which time I applyed my self to the grinding of Optick glasses of other figures than *Spherical*,) I procured me a Triangular glass-Prisme, to try therewith the celebrated *Phaenomena of Colours*' (*Correspondence*, I, p. 92). A. R. Hall has pointed out reasons 'for thinking that, in his letter, Newton wrote "1666" for 1665, and that his note of 1699 (verified with his own records by himself) is more accurate, the definitive theory of colours being obtained in January 1666, as a result of experiments on the refraction of a beam of light, carried out either with a new prism or one bought in 1664' ('Sir Isaac Newton's Note-Book, 1661-65', *Cambridge Historical Journal*, IX (1948), p. 246). For Newton's note of 1699 referred to here, see ibid., p. 240, note 6. For the 'period about the middle of 1665' as the more plausible date at which 'Newton's interest in Descartes's suggestion for the use of lenses of non-spherical curvatures was greatest', see Hall, 'Further optical experiments of Isaac Newton', *Annals of Science*, XI (1955), p. 36. Turnbull pushes the date back to 1664 (*Correspondence*, I, p. 59, note 11). But 1665 seems to be the more cautious date.

in which the lenses were formed. In particular, it was hoped that lenses having one of the shapes of the conic sections might serve the purpose. Newton had himself embarked on that task when, as he tells us, he obtained a triangular glass prism to experiment on the phenomena of colours. Having darkened his chamber and made a small (circular) hole in the window-shutters,[6] to let in the sun's light, he placed the prism close to the hole so that the light might be refracted to the opposite wall. 'It was at first a very pleasing divertisement, to view the vivid and intense colours produced thereby....'[7] But that was only a passing divertisement. The thing that Newton found puzzling was the shape rather than the colours of the solar spectrum on the wall: 'I became surprised to see them in an *oblong* form; which, according to the received laws of Refraction, I expected should have been *circular*.'[8] The colours were terminated at the sides with straight lines but faded gradually at the ends in semicircular shapes. But why did Newton find the oblong shape surprising? For, in fact, except for one definite position of the prism, namely that of minimum deviation, a certain elongation of the image should have been expected. As we go on reading Newton's paper, however, we soon discover that the prism was fixed at precisely that position. We are therefore here presented with a carefully planned experiment and not, as the opening sentence of Newton's paper might convey,[9] a chance observation. Newton's expectation that the image should be circular rather than oblong was

---

[6] Newton does not state in his paper that the hole was circular. This, however, is understood from his subsequent reasonings. The shape of the hole is essential for appreciating the problematic character of the image projected on the opposite wall. Compare Newton's *Opticks*, Bk. I, Pt. I, Prop. II, Theor. II, p. 26. See below, n. 9.

[7] *Correspondence*, I, p. 92.

[8] Ibid.

[9] 'The original letter in Newton's handwriting has not been found, but a transcript, written by his copyist Wickins and bearing a few verbal corrections in Newton's own hand, is preserved in the Portsmouth Collection . . .' (*Correspondence*, I, p. 102, editor's note 1). Variants between the two versions are recorded in the *Correspondence* and will be indicated here when relevant. The letter seems, in certain respects, to have been written rather informally and even without much care. It lacked the detailed clarifications and illustrations that were necessary for securing a full appreciation of his new and revolutionary discovery. Newton was thus, to a certain extent, responsible for his paper being misunderstood by his contemporaries. He did not make it sufficiently clear and explicit that he was considering a special case in which the image should be circular; and Pardies' first objections were based on a misunder-

based on calculations involving a great deal of information drawn from geometrical optics.[10]

Comparing the dimensions of the image, Newton found that its length was about five times greater than its breadth, 'a disproportion so extravagant, that it excited me to a more then ordinary curiosity of examining, from whence it might proceed'.[11] To determine the cause of this disproportion, he began to consider several hypotheses or, as he called them, suspicions which suggested themselves to his mind. These were all hypotheses conceived on the implicit assumption that the sine law, in its then accepted form, was not to be modified. Could the shape of the spectrum be due, for example, to the thickness of the prism, or the bigness of the hole in the window-shutters? But observing that, by allowing the light to pass through different parts of the prism, or by varying the magnitude of the hole, the oblong shape was always the same. Or, perhaps, it was caused by some unevenness or another irregularity in the glass? To examine this possibility he placed a second prism in a contrary position behind the first. In this arrangement the second prism should destroy the regular effects of the first and, at the same time, augment the supposed irregular ones. He found, however, that the image became round, as if the light had not been refracted at all. Newton then concluded that the cause of the phenomenon could not be 'any contingent irregularity'[12] of the prism.

A third hypothesis was that the shape might be explained by the different inclinations to the prism of rays coming from different

---

standing of this point. The *experimentum crucis* (which will be soon described) was not illustrated with diagrams; and both Pardies and Huygens could not at first understand it. As we shall see, Newton later admitted that if he had meant his letter for publication, some additions would have been introduced (see below, p. 267, n. 44). In fact, it was not without reluctance that he allowed its publication in the first place (cf. Brewster, *Memoirs*, I, pp. 72–73). Had he adopted in that letter the strictly geometrical and systematic approach which is to be found in his *Optical Lectures* (which had been written, but not published, before his letter appeared in the *Philosophical Transactions*) a considerable part of the controversies with his adversaries would no doubt have been spared. It is partly to these controversies, however, that we should be grateful for the wealth of beautiful experiments and illustrations which Newton adduced in later papers and in the *Opticks* to avoid further misunderstandings.

[10] Cf. Newton, *Optical Lectures*, London, 1728, Sec. I, Arts. 4 and 5, pp. 8–11. See below, p. 237, n. 14.

[11] *Correspondence*, I, p. 92.   [12] *Correspondence*, I, p. 93.

parts of the sun. To decide whether this was the case, Newton made the following measurements and calculations. The diameter of the hole was $\frac{1}{4}$ of an inch, its distance from the image 22 feet, the length of the image was $13\frac{1}{4}$ inches, its breadth $2\frac{5}{8}$ inches; and 'the angle, which the Rays, tending towards the middle of the image, made with those lines, in which they would have proceeded without refraction, 44 deg. 56'. And the vertical Angle of the Prisme, 63 deg. 12'. Also the Refractions on both sides the Prisme, that is, of the Incident, and Emergent Rays, were as near, as I could make them, equal, and consequently about 54 deg. 4''.[13]

The preceding statements imply that the prism was set in the position of minimum deviation for the middle colour of the spectrum. Newton was thus simply assuming it to be known that the equality of the refractions on both sides of the prism (i.e. the symmetrical arrangement of the incident and emergent rays with respect to those sides) is a condition for that position in which the image should be circular and not oblong. By not providing any explicit geometrical explanation of this assumption he was certainly expecting too much from his readers.[14]

Having subtracted the diameter of the hole from the breadth and from the length of the image, its breadth was found to subtend an angle of 31 minutes, corresponding to the diameter of the sun,

---

[13] Correspondence, I, p. 93. An earlier description of this experiment occurs in a Note-Book which Newton probably began in 1665–6; see A. R. Hall, 'Further optical experiments of Isaac Newton', Annals of Science, XI (1955), pp. 28–29. Some of the measurements in this description approach those of the 1672 paper: diameter of the hole = $\frac{1}{8}$ of an inch [?]; distance of wall from prism = 260 inches; breadth of image = $2\frac{1}{4}$ inches; vertical angle of prism = 'about 60^{gr}'. But the length of the image is much smaller than that reported to the Royal Society, 'about 7 or 8 inches' (ibid.).

[14] For the necessary geometrical demonstrations relating to this case, see Optical Lectures, London, 1728, Sec. I, Art. 10 pp. 19–20; Sec. III, Prop. 25, pp. 164–6. Compare Opticks, Bk. I, Pt. I, Prop. II, Theor. II, p. 28. The Optical Lectures were not published until 1728. These were a translation of Pars I of the Latin original (Lectiones opticae) which appeared in the following year. The title-page of this edition stated that the Lectiones were delivered at Cambridge in the years 1669–71. According to W. W. Rouse Ball, An Essay on Newton's Principia, London, 1893, pp. 27–28, Newton started his lectures in the Lent Term 1670 and continued them in Michaelmas 1670, 1671 and 1672 (referred to by A. R. Hall, 'Newton's First Book (I)', Archives internationales d'histoire des sciences, XIII (1960), p. 44 and note 23). Hall notes that Part I of the manuscript of the Lectiones in the Cambridge University Library bears the date 'Jan. 1669'. See Correspondence, I, p. 103, note 1. The Opticks (1704) does not include the demonstrations in question.

whereas its length subtended an angle equal to 2°49'. Newton then computed the refractive index of the glass (obtaining the ratio of sines 20 : 31) and, using this result, he computed the refractions of two rays coming from opposite parts of the sun so as to subtend 31' between them. He found that the emergent rays should have subtended about the same angle. Therefore, he had to account for a difference of 2°18'. 'But because this computation was founded on the Hypothesis of the proportionality of the *sines* of Incidence, and Refraction, which though by my own & others Experience I could not imagine to be so erroneous, as to make that Angle but 31', which in reality was 2 deg. 49'; yet my curiosity caused me again to take my Prisme.'[15]

By rotating the prism about its axis to and fro through a large angle (more than 4 or 5 degrees), the colours were not sensibly displaced from their place on the wall. This further confirmed that a difference in incidence of such a small angle as 31' could not be responsible for the large angle between the emergent rays.

The next hypothesis to be examined by Newton is vividly reminiscent of Descartes' explanation of the prismatic colours. It will be remembered that Descartes ascribed those colours to the rotary motion acquired by the globules of the subtle matter when they obliquely strike the side of the prism.[16] Now Newton suspected that the rays might move in curved lines after their emergence—for the following reason:

it increased my suspition, when I remembred that I had often seen a Tennis-ball, struck with an oblique Racket, describe such a curve line. For, a circular as well as a progressive motion being communicated to it by that stroak, its parts on that side, where the motions conspire, must press and beat the contiguous Air more violently than on the other, and there excite a reluctancy and reaction of the Air proportionably greater. And for the same reason, if the Rays of light should possibly be globular bodies, and by their oblique passage out of one medium into another acquire a circulating motion, they ought to feel the greater resistance

---

[15] *Correspondence*, I, p. 93; '& others' omitted in the text of the *Transactions*.
[16] See above, pp. 64ff.

from the ambient Æther, on that side, where the motions conspire, and thence be continually bowed to the other.[17]

The hypothesis involved in this passage differs from the other 'suspicions' in that it assumes the idea of a hypothetical entity, the ether. It should therefore be observed that Newton was not reluctant to *examine* a hypothesis of the Cartesian type in the course of arriving at his theory.[18] On the contrary, by drawing the analogy between the light corpuscle and the tennis ball, he was trying to relate that hypothesis to observation in order to see whether it could stand the experimental test. The analogy suggested to him that the rays would travel in curved lines after their emergence from the prism. But by receiving the image on a board at various distances from the prism, he found that the variation of the magnitude of the image with the distance was as it should be on the assumption that the rays proceeded in straight lines after refraction.[19] If, therefore, the considered hypothesis was finally rejected, that was not because, *being a hypothesis*, it was unworthy of serious examination, but because it was found to be false. That was in fact Newton's consistent attitude to rival hypotheses which he could not accept.

Having removed all these 'suspicions', Newton was finally led to devise what he called an *experimentum crucis*. That was an arrangement involving two prisms.[20] The first was placed, as before, near the hole in the window-shutter; the emerging rays passed through a small opening in a board set up close behind the prism. At a distance of about 12 feet, he fixed the second prism behind another board with a small hole in it to allow only some of the incident light

---

[17] *Correspondence*, I, p. 94. While Descartes also allowed the 'ambient ether' to play a part in the production of the rotary motion, he did not envisage any curvature of the rays' path. Newton seems to have been the first to explain a ball's swerve correctly; see ibid., pp. 103–4, editor's note 8.

[18] Compare Cajori's remarks to the same effect in the Appendix to his edition of Newton's *Principia*, note 55, pp. 671–2.

[19] *Correspondence*, I, p. 94.

[20] Note that it is only in the course of Newton's 'historicall narration' (*Correspondence*, I, p. 97) that we learn that he had *two* prisms, not one, at his disposal. The narration starts: '. . . I procured me a Triangular glass-Prisme . . .' (ibid., p. 92). A second prism was already required to remove the suspicion that the colours might have been produced by the unevenness in the glass of the first. See above, p. 237, n. 13.

to reach the prism. By rotating the first prism about its axis, the colours cast on the second board were made to pass successively through the opening in it. In this manner he could observe the several positions on the wall where the various colours were refracted by the second prism. Noting that the lower colours of the image projected on the second board were more refracted by the second prism than the higher ones, he arrived at the following conclusion: that

... The true cause of the length of that Image was detected to be no other, then that *Light* consists of *Rays differently refrangible* which, without any respect to a difference in their incidence, were, according to their degrees of refrangibility, transmitted towards divers parts of the wall.[21]

The import of this experiment and the significance which Newton attributed to it will be examined later. But it must be noted here that the fundamental proposition which Newton immediately based on his *experimentum crucis* concerns the refrangibility of the rays rather than their colour. For, in fact, the real problem from which he started in this account was a problem of refraction rather than colour. The appearance of colours by the refraction of light through a prism had been observed long before Newton. Several explanations of these colours had been proposed. But these explanations were mainly concerned with the qualitative aspect of the phenomenon, that is, the appearance of the colours as such. That was one reason why they all missed the problem which engaged Newton's attention. Descartes, for example, was content to ascribe the prismatic colours to the rotation of the ethereal globules; the ratio of the velocity of rotation to the velocity of the globules in the direction of propagation determined the colour. Alternatively, Hooke would explain the same phenomenon by the obliquation of

---

[21] *Correspondence*, I, p. 95. Newton then tells us that it was this discovery, namely his realization that 'Light it self is a *Heterogeneous mixture of differently refrangible Rays*', that made him despair of perfecting refracting telescopes. It appeared to him that however exactly figured the lenses might be, and whatever the shape given them, they would not collect the rays of white light in one focus. This led him to the consideration which finally resulted in the construction of his reflecting telescope. Cf. A. R. Hall, *Annals of Science*, XI (1955), p. 37.

the ethereal pulse to the direction of propagation: the manner in which this oblique pulse struck the eye determined the colour.

But neither Descartes nor Hooke (nor, indeed, anyone before Newton) had paid attention to the particular *geometrical problem* of refraction that was involved in Newton's experiment. To Newton, the appearance of colours on the wall was, as we have seen, more of a 'divertisement' than a problem. The real problem was one of refraction; it consisted in explaining the *shape* of the spectrum *for a given position of the prism*, and this on the supposition that the rays from the sun were all equally refrangible. That supposition was *implicitly* accepted by all writers on optics, or, at least, it had not been challenged by anyone. It was on the basis of that supposition that Newton had expected to see the solar image in a round, and not as he found, in an oblong shape. After having dismissed some of the most obvious hypotheses that might be thought to account for the elongation of the image, he performed the *experimentum crucis*. This experiment showed him that the rays were more or less refracted through the second prism, according as they were more or less refracted by the first. He was thus led to discard the initial supposition itself and to declare that the sun's light is 'not similar, or homogeneal, but consists of *difform* Rays, some of which are more refrangible than others'.[22]

But the same experiment showed that the rays preserved their colours as well as their degrees of refrangibility upon their being refracted through the second prism; the same index of refraction was attached to the same colour. It was thus apparent that with the difference in refrangibility of the rays went the difference 'in their disposition to exhibit this or that particular colour'.[23] Therefore, Newton concluded, colours were not 'qualifications', or modifications suffered by light upon reflection or refraction, as it was generally assumed; they were '*Original* and *connate properties*' of the rays just as their respective degrees of refrangibility were.[24]

Newton's doctrine of colour further stated the unalterability of the rays' colours (and, of course, the degrees of refrangibility associated

---

[22] *Correspondence*, I, p. 96.   [23] Ibid., p. 97.   [24] Ibid.

with them) either by reflection, or refraction, or by any other circumstance that he had tried. Seeming alterations of colours might take place when several sorts of rays were mixed together. But the component colours could be made to reappear when the difform rays were separated by refraction. There are thus two sorts of colours: 'The one original and simple, the other compounded of these.'[25] The original or 'primary' ones are all those that are exhibited in the 'indefinite variety' of colours of the solar spectrum.[26] White is the most compounded of all composite colours since its analysis gives all the spectrum colours, and for its composition all the primary colours should be mixed in due proportion. To illustrate the latter point Newton described an experiment in which the rays of the sun's light were made to converge after they had been dispersed, and a white light just like the light coming directly from the sun was thereby produced. Interpreting this experiment Newton asserted that white light is 'a confused aggregate of Rays indued with all sorts of Colors, as they are promiscuously darted from the various parts of luminous bodies'.[27]

As every sort of ray has a different degree of refrangibility, the production of colours from white light by the prism was thus understood in the following way. The rays which are all originally endowed with colour are merely 'severed and dispersed'[28] by the prism according to their various degrees of refrangibility and consequently the primary colours are distinguished.

It was this interpretation of the constitution of white light and the role which Newton assigned to the prism in the production of colours that occupied the greatest and most important part of the controversy between Newton and the critics of his theory, Hooke, Pardies and Huygens. They all suspected from Newton's expressions that he was inclined towards an atomistic interpretation of light which they found disagreeable. Their feeling was certainly justified by Newton's stand in the same paper on a scholastic issue concerning whether light was a substance or quality. Newton explicitly subscribed (though with some caution) to the view that light was a

---

[25] *Correspondence*, I, p. 98.   [26] Ibid.   [27] Ibid.   [28] Ibid., p. 99.

substance. This opinion he maintained in connection with his explanation of the colours of natural bodies. Those colours, he asserted, have their origin in the fact that opaque bodies reflect one sort of rays in greater quantity than others. He observed that in the dark any body appeared with any colour with which it was illuminated, though in various degrees of vividness. When natural bodies are exposed to the sun's light they put on the colour which they reflect most copiously. Then he wrote:

These things being so, it can be no longer disputed, whether there be colours in the dark, nor whether they be the qualities of the objects we see, no nor perhaps, whether Light be a Body. For, since Colours are the *qualities* of Light, having its Rays for their intire and immediate subject, how can we think those Rays *qualities* also, unless one quality may be the subject of and sustain another; which in effect is to call it *substance*. We should not know Bodies for substances, were it not for their sensible qualities, and the Principal of those being now found due to something else, we have as good reason to believe that to be a substance also.[29]

Newton later drew attention to the word 'perhaps' in the preceding passage when he tried to point out that his doctrine was not necessarily committed to a substantial view of light. But we read, immediately after that passage, the following emphatic words at the head of a new paragraph: 'Besides, whoever thought any quality to be a *heterogeneous* aggregate, such as Light is discovered to be.'[30] That white light is a heterogeneous mixture is a thesis which Newton never abandoned; it was for him an experimental fact proved beyond any possible doubt. But since he expressed himself in terms of this dichotomy, substance or quality, was it not only natural for his readers to assume that he favoured a corpuscular hypothesis about light? Nevertheless, we read again in Newton's paper: 'But, to determine more absolutely, what Light is, after what manner refracted, and by what modes or actions it produceth in our minds the Phantasms of Colours, is not so easie. And I shall not mingle conjectures with certainties.'[31] What was certain for Newton?

---

[29] Ibid., p. 100. [30] Ibid. [31] Ibid.

That light is a heterogeneous aggregate. But if, as he himself argued, it was not possible to conceive of quality as such an aggregate, did he leave much doubt as to the conclusion he wanted to draw?

3. In a later printed version[32] of the 1672 paper Newton tried to extricate himself from the position he appeared to be taking in the passage suggesting the corporeal nature of light. He wrote in a footnote to this passage:

Through an improper distinction which some make of mechanical Hypotheses, into those where light is put a body and those where it is put the action of a body, understanding the first of bodies trajected through a medium, the last of motion or pression propagated through it, this place may be by some unwarily understood of the former: Whereas light is equally a body or the action of a body in both cases. If you call its rays the bodies trajected in the former case, then in the latter case they are the bodies which propagate motion from one to another in right lines till the last strike the sense. The only difference is, that in one case a ray is but one body, in the other many. So in the latter case, if you call the rays motion propagated through bodies, in the former it will be motion continued in the same bodies. The bodies in both cases must cause vision by their motion.[33]

Newton seems to be equivocating here. Is it not odd that he should describe the distinction between the corpuscular and wave views of light as an 'improper distinction which some make of mechanical Hypotheses'? Should we take this to be a sincere judgement when we realize (as we shall see) that he always considered all forms of the wave hypothesis to be false, and that he had already decided in favour of the corpuscular interpretation?
The footnote continues:

---

[32] Only four sheets (pp. 9–16) of this version have survived in two copies. Discovered in a decayed binding by Derek J. de Solla Price, these Waste Sheets (as A. R. Hall calls them) were first published in facsimile and analysed by I. Bernard Cohen, 'Versions of Isaac Newton's first published paper', *Archives internationales d'histoire des sciences*, XI, (1958), pp. 357–75. The circumstances surrounding their first abortive publication (which may have taken place in 1676–7) are not known. See A. R. Hall, 'Newton's First Book (I)', ibid., XIII (1960), pp. 51–54; *Correspondence*, I, pp. 105–7, where variants of the Waste Sheets (here called 'the Print') with the 1672 version are recorded.

[33] *Correspondence*, I, pp. 105–6.

Now in this place my design being to touch upon the notion of the Peripateticks, I took not body in opposition to motion as in the said distinction, but in opposition to a Peripatetick quality, stating the question between the Peripateticks and Mechanick Philosophy by inquiring whether light be a quality or body. Which that it was my meaning may appear by my joyning this question with others hitherto disputed between the two Philosophies; and using in respect of the one side the Peripatetick terms *Quality, Subject, Substance, Sensible qualities*; in respect of the other the Mechanick ones *Body, Modes, Actions*; and leaving undetermined the kinds of those actions (suppose whether they be pressions, strokes, or other dashings,) by which light may produce in our minds the phantasms of colours.[34]

This is not quite exact; for Newton did *not* draw the line of demarcation where he claims here to have drawn it. By arguing that light was a body on the basis of having shown it to be a substance of which colours were qualities, he was in fact arguing *in* peripatetic terms for his own mechanical view. Again one is impelled to ask: Was it really his intention to argue for a generalized mechanical hypothesis which did not distinguish between the transport of body and the transmission of motion? Could he really have expected a man like Hooke (whom he certainly had in mind when he wrote his first paper)[35] to hear the description of light as a substance and still consider the new doctrine as compatible with his own wave-like interpretation?

The first part of Newton's paper, moving with increasing suspense to the final denouement in the crucial experiment, reads like a narrative of events which took place in a rather quick and logical succession over a short period of time: '. . . having darkened my chamber, and made a small hole in my window-shuts, . . . It was at first a very pleasing divertisement, . . . but after a while . . . I became surprised . . . Then I suspected . . . I then proceeded to examine more critically . . . Then I began to suspect . . . The gradual removal of these suspitions at length led me to the *Experimentum Crucis*. . . .' As

---

[34] Ibid., p. 106.

[35] Cf. R S. Westfall, 'The development of Newton's theory of color', *Isis*, LIII (1962), p. 354. Newton's arguments in the Waste Sheets are in fact in contradiction with what he stated in his reply to Hooke's 'Considerations'; see below, p. 276, n. 6.

a compelling tale of discovery, it has captured the imagination of readers since its first publication in the *Philosophical Transactions*. As history, however, it has the mark of implausibility. The progression is sustained throughout; there are no obstacles or hesitations; suspicions are formulated to be immediately removed; the final result is clear and definitive. Not even the 'fortunate Newton'[36] could have been fortunate enough to have achieved this result in such a smooth manner.

Recent studies of Newton's manuscripts have provided a more plausible picture of how he arrived at the position expressed in 1672.[37] In the earliest Note-Book of Newton, one which he started as an undergraduate at Cambridge in 1661 and continued until at least 1665, he asserts the varying refrangibility of different colours, with reference to an experiment which he later incorporated in his published work:

That ye rays which make blew are refracted more y^n ye rays which make red appears from this experiment. If one halfe of ye thred *abc* be blew & ye other red & a shade or black body be put behind it then looking on ye thred through a prism one halfe of ye thred shall appear higher y^n ye other, not both in one direct line, by reason of unequal refractions in ye differing colours.[38]

All experiments in the 1661–5 Note-Book are, like this one, performed with light reflected from coloured objects. No experi-

---

[36] 'Fortunate Newton, happy childhood of science! . . . Nature to him was an open book, whose letters he could read without effort. The conceptions which he used to reduce the material of experience to order seemed to flow spontaneously from experience itself, from the beautiful experiments which he ranged in order like playthings and describes with an affectionate wealth of detail.' Albert Einstein, Foreword to the 1931 edition of Newton's *Opticks*. Einstein is not of course suggesting that the conceptions did in fact flow spontaneously from experience. But that Newton thought they did is quite certain.

[37] Cf. A. R. Hall, *Cambridge Historical Journal*, IX (1948), pp. 239–50; *Annals of science*, XI (1955), pp. 27–43; and Richard S. Westfall, *Isis*, LIII (1962), pp. 339–58; 'The foundations of Newton's philosophy of nature', *The British Journal for the History of Science*, I (1962), pp. 171–82. For a different view of the evidence discussed by Hall, see T. S. Kuhn, 'Newton's optical papers', in *Isaac Newton's Papers & Letters* (ed. I. Bernard Cohen), Cambridge, Mass., 1958, pp. 27–45.

[38] Quoted by A. R. Hall, *Cambridge Historical Journal*, IX (1948), pp. 247–8. In a later Note-Book Newton described a similar experiment in which he viewed through the prism a parti-coloured line drawn on a black piece of paper. Here he also mentioned the experiment with the parti-coloured thread. See A. R. Hall, *Annals of Science*, XI (1955), p. 28.

ment is described in which, as in the 1672 paper, a direct beam from the sun is refracted through the prism. Each colour is further associated with a physical property, the speed of the ray producing that colour in the sensorium. Thus he suggests that the red-end colours are produced by more swiftly moving rays, and the blue-end colours are produced by more slowly moving rays.[39] But the speeds with which the rays reach the sensorium depend on the particular effect they receive from the reflecting body:

Hence redness, yellowness &c are made in bodys by stoping ye slowly moved rays w^{th}out much hindering of ye motion of ye swifter rays, & blew, greene & purple by diminishing ye motion of ye swifter rays & not of ye slower.[40]

But this means that there is no one speed-value that is always associated with the ray, right from the beginning. In other words, the physical property responsible for producing a given colour is not original or connate with the ray, as was insisted upon in the 1672 doctrine (already stated in the *Optical Lectures*). Thus Newton had not, at the time of the Note-Book, clearly abandoned the modification theory which he positively renounced in his paper to the Royal Society. It should be pointed out that already in this early Note-Book Newton readily operated with the notion of the rays as 'globules' which may vary in size as well as in speed.[41] His preference

---

[39] Newton also considers that 'slowly moved rays are refracted more then swift ones' (*Cambridge Historical Journal*, IX, 1948, p. 247).

[40] Ibid., p. 248.

[41] For example: 'Though 2 rays be equally swift yet if one ray be lesse y^n ye other that ray shall have so much lesse effect on ye sensorium as it has lesse motion y^n ye others &c.

Whence supposing y^t there are loose particles in ye pores of a body bearing proportion to ye greater rays, as 9:12 & ye less globules is in proportion to y^e greater as 2:9, y^e greater globulus by impinging on such a particle will loose 6/7 parts of its motion y^e less glob. will loose 2/7 parts of its motion & y^e remaining motion of y^e glob. will have almost such a proportion to one another as their quantity have viz. 5/7: 1/7:: 9: $1\frac{4}{7}$ wch is almost 2 y^e lesse glob. & such a body may produce blews and purples. But if y^e particles on wch y^e globuli reflect are equal to y^e lesse globulus it shall loose its motion & y^e greater glob. shall loose 2/11 parts of its motion and such a body may be red or yellow' (A. R. Hall, *Cambridge Historical Journal*, IX, 1948, p. 248). On one page of the Note-Book Newton drew a sketch of the 'Globulus of light' surrounded by 'a cone of subtile matter wch it carrys before it the better to cut ye ether, wch serves also to reflect it from other bodys' (Cambridge University Library MS, Add. 3996, fol. 104^v).

was, right from the start, for a corpuscular interpretation of light.

As was first suggested by A. R. Hall, it would thus appear that the theory of colours, announced to the world in 1672, was not completed until winter 1666 after an extended investigation which had occupied Newton's mind for about one year and a half. In spite of its autobiographical character, what the 1672 paper presents us with is the final result of a long series of inquiries which had passed through several stages, rather than the actual way in which that result had been achieved. More positively and more exactly, it presents us with an *argument* designed to establish the final doctrine beyond all possible objections. The form of this argument was clearly indicated by Newton himself in the same paper:

A naturalist would scearce expect to see ye science of those [colours] become mathematicall, & yet I dare affirm that there is as much certainty in it as in any other part of Opticks. For what I shall tell concerning them is not an Hypothesis but most rigid consequence, not conjectured by barely inferring 'tis thus because not otherwise or because it satisfies all phaenomena (the Philosophers universall Topick,) but evinced by ye mediation of experiments concluding directly & wthout any suspicion of doubt.[42]

This passage is of great importance for understanding the controversy which followed the publication of Newton's paper. He already repudiates a method of hypothetico-deductive explanation which he finds to be common among philosophers ('the Philosophers universall Topick'), a method in which hypotheses are merely conjectured to account for all the relevant phenomena. In contrast to this objectionable method, he claims to have directly deduced his theory of colours from experiments; in other words, his theory is a (proved) conclusion, not a (conjectured) assumption. Now all this sounds very Baconian. Newton proceeds in his paper as Bacon and

---

[42] *Correspondence*, I, pp. 96–97. This passage was omitted in the text of the *Philosophical Transactions*; it was first published by I. Bernard Cohen, *Archives internationales d'histoire des sciences*, XI (1958), p. 367. Both Newton and Hooke alluded to the suppressed passage in the course of their discussion; cf. *Correspondence*, I, p. 105, editor's note 19.

members of the Royal Society would have required him to do,[43] from the experiments through a series of negatives—but only to reach finally an affirmative proposition.[44] This end is achieved with the aid of an *experimentum crucis* which has in Newton's paper exactly the same role as the *instantiae crucis* of the *Novum Organum*: namely, it does not only refute the false doctrine but also positively establishes the true one. Newton's argument may thus be summarized as follows: the appearance of colours when a beam of the sun's light passes through a prism must be due to one of two and only two causes; the colours are either manufactured by the prism, or they have been with the rays from their origin; on the first supposition white light would be simple or homogeneous and colours would be modifications or confusions or disturbances of white light; on the second, white light would be a heterogeneous aggregate of difform rays which the prism would merely separate in accordance with their original degrees of refrangibility; experiment proves that an isolated coloured beam does not suffer any modification in respect of either colour or refrangibility on being refracted through a second prism; therefore, white light is demonstrated to be, not simple or homogeneous, but a heterogeneous aggregate of difform rays.

The effect of this 'demonstration' is, it must be admitted, almost hypnotic. Nevertheless, it is certainly inconclusive. Why should the

---

[43] See passage quoted above from Hook's *Micrographia*, p. 187.

[44] Bacon's advice was not to venture anything in the affirmative (conjectures, hypotheses) but to work for eliciting the affirmative from the experiments. This eliciting consisted in rejections which finally gave way to affirmatives necessarily implied by the experiments. Thus he maintained that to man 'it is granted only to proceed at first by negatives, and at last to end in affirmatives after exclusion has been exhausted' (*Novum Organum*, II, 15). In the Plan of the *Great Instauration* he described induction as a method which will 'analyse experience and take it to pieces, and by a due process of exclusion and rejection lead to an inevitable conclusion [*necessario concludat*]' (B, IV, p. 25). And again: 'But the induction which is to be available for the discovery and demonstration of sciences and arts, must analyse nature by proper rejections and exclusions; and then, after a sufficient number of negatives, come to a conclusion on the affirmative instances . . .' (*Novum Organum*, I, 105). In an exactly parallel fashion Newton first describes an experiment revealing a certain anomaly (the length of the image) which is to be accounted for. Various possibilities (suspicions) are then successively considered; they suggest new experiments by which they are, in turn, rejected. Finally a doctrine of light and colours is asserted, not simply because other doctrines have been proved false ('inferring 'tis thus because not otherwise'), but because it is *necessarily entailed* by affirmative instances, in particular the *experimentum crucis*, itself representing a decisive stage in the Baconian scheme.

second prism have the same effect on a *coloured* beam as the first had on a *white* beam? And why should not a property acquired by white light through a first refraction remain unaltered on undergoing further refractions?

Some of Newton's contemporaries saw the inconclusiveness of his argument; it is therefore curious that most historians of science have fallen under its spell.[45]

Chapter Ten

THREE CRITICS OF NEWTON'S THEORY: HOOKE, PARDIES, HUYGENS

1. Hooke was present at the meeting of the Royal Society when Newton's letter was read. As requested by the Society he formulated what came to be known as his Considerations upon Newton's theory and he read them before the Society on 15 February 1671/2, that is, only seven days after Newton's paper had been delivered. Hooke was thus the first to raise objections against Newton's doctrine. His Considerations were not published in the *Philosophical Transactions*; only Newton's Answer to them was printed (in No. 88, 18 November 1672) without revealing the identity of the considerer to whom the Answer was addressed. They did not appear in print until 1757 when Thomas Birch published them in his *History of the Royal Society*.[1]

In general, Hooke's attitude to Newton's theory was the following: he was willing to grant the experimental results reported by Newton, but was unable to accept the 'hypothesis' which the latter had proposed to explain them;[2] he further expressed his

---

[1] Birch, op. cit., III (1757), pp. 10–15; references will be to the later edition from Hooke's autograph, in *Correspondence of Isaac Newton*, I, pp. 110–14.

The immediate effect of Newton's letter on the Society and the manner in which it was received by those of its members who were present (who included Hooke) is described by Oldenburg in the opening passage of a letter to Newton, dated 8 February 1671/2: 'The effect of your promise came to my hands this day, just as I was going to attend the publick meeting of the R. Society, where the reading of your discourse concerning Light and Colours was almost their only entertainment for that time. I can assure you, Sir, that it there mett both with a singular attention and an uncommon applause, insomuch that after they had order'd me to returne you very solemne and ample thanks in their name (which herewith I doe most cheerfully) they voted unanimously, that if you contradicted it not, this discourse should without delay be printed, there being cause to apprehend that the ingenuous & surprising notion therein contain'd (for such they were taken to be) may easily be snatched from you, and the Honor of it be assumed by forainers, some of them, as I formerly told you being apt enough to make shew of and to vend, what is not of the growth of their Country' (*Correspondence*, I, pp. 107–8).

[2] *Correspondence*, I, pp. 110–11.

belief that all of Newton's experiments, including the *experimentum crucis*, could be equally well explained by his own hypothesis about the nature of light and colours.

In order to be able to appreciate Newton's reaction to Hooke's objections, it will be necessary to understand the way Hooke interpreted Newton's position and the extent to which he really understood the import of his experiments. In the course of the following analysis of Hooke's objections, it will also be of interest to watch his attempts to envisage possibilities of adjusting his own conception of light, as he had already formulated it in the *Micrographia* (1665), with a view to accommodating Newton's observations. These attempts constitute the first trial to translate the Newtonian account of dispersion, which appeared to Hooke fundamentally (and undesirably) atomistic, into wave terms. The obvious limitations of Hooke's ideas seem to have discouraged historians from paying enough attention to his attempts. For the purpose of the present discussion, however, they will be of importance in bringing out the real point of difference between Hooke and Newton over the proper representation of white light. It will be seen[3] that Hooke's ideas, in a polished and mathematical form developed, no doubt, beyond Hooke's own expectations, were later introduced into optics to replace the Newtonian conception of white light.

Hooke understood Newton's 'first supposition' to be a corpuscular hypothesis about the nature of light, namely,

that light is a body, and that as many colours or degrees thereof as there may be, soe many severall sorts of bodys there may be, all wch compounded together would make white, and . . . further, that all luminous bodys are compounded of such substances condensed, and that, whilst they shine, they do continually send out an indefinite quantity thereof, every way *in orbem*, which in a moment of time doth disperse itself to the outmost and most indefinite bounds of the universe.[4]

The rest of Newton's 'curious Theory', Hooke readily granted, could be demonstrated from this supposition without any difficulty.[5]

---

[3] See below, pp. 280ff.
[4] *Correspondence*, I, pp. 113–14.   [5] *Correspondence*, I, p. 114.

He objected to this fundamental hypothesis, however, on the grounds that 'all the coloured bodies in the world compounded together should not make a white body; and I should be glad to see an expt of the kind'.[6]

Whittaker has rightly observed[7] that, in making this and similar remarks, Newton's opponents were confusing the physiological or subjective aspect of colours with the physical problem with which alone Newton's experiments were concerned. But Newton himself had spoken of light as a substance, and of colours as *qualities* of light existing, as it were, without us. This ambiguous way of speaking was at least partly responsible for the misunderstanding of which his adversaries were victims. It was only natural, in the absence of any explicit remarks to the contrary, that they should understand the *heterogeneous aggregate*, supposed by Newton to constitute white light, on the analogy of the mixture of variously coloured powders. We shall come back to this important point when Newton's answers to Huygens are discussed.[8]

Hooke called Newton's theory a *hypothesis* because he believed that the same phenomena of colours would equally agree with various other views on the nature of light.[9] To him, Newton's supposition was by no means the only possible one. In his Considerations, therefore, he proposed his own hypothesis and tried to show that it would achieve the same purpose. This hypothesis expounded the view, just opposite to Newton's, about the constitution of white light and of colour; it declared that

---

[6] Ibid.

[7] Cf. Whittaker's Introduction to Newton's *Opticks*, New York, 1952, p. lxix.

[8] See below, pp. 290ff.

[9] 'I doe not therefore see any absolute necessity to beleive his theory demonstrated, since I can assure Mr. Newton, I cannot only salve all the Phænomena of Light and colours by the Hypothesis, I have formerly printed and now explicate yt by, but by two or three other, very differing from it, and from this, which he hath described in his Ingenious Discourse. Nor would I be understood to have said all this against his theory as it is an hypothesis, for I doe most Readily agree wth him in every part thereof, and esteem it very subtill and ingenious, and capable of salving all the phænomena of colours; but I cannot think it to be the only hypothesis; not soe certain as mathematicall Demonstrations' (*Correspondence*, I, p. 113). Hooke added in a following paragraph: 'If Mr Newton hath any argument, that he supposeth an absolute Demonstration of his theory, I should by very glad to be convinced by it . . .' (ibid., p. 114).

light is nothing but a pulse or motion propagated through an homogeneous, uniform and transparent medium: And that Colour is nothing but the Disturbance of yt light by the communication of that pulse to other transparent mediums, that is by the refraction thereof: that whiteness and blackness are nothing but the plenty or scarcity of the undisturbd Rayes of light; and that the two colours [blue and red] (then which there are noe more uncompounded in Nature) are nothing but the effects of a compounded pulse or disturbed propagation of motion caused by Refraction.[10]

It appears from the preceding passage that, for Hooke, white is the effect of an undisturbed and uncompounded motion or pulse; and that all colours are the result of the disturbance of light by refraction. In spite of the clause between parentheses, Hooke should not be understood to regard the colours blue and red as simple or primary in Newton's sense. They are themselves 'the effects of a compounded . . . motion caused by refraction' and not *original* as Newton had asserted of all colours. According to Hooke, however, red and blue are simple or uncompounded relative to the other colours, since he regarded the latter as due to the composition in different variations of these two. In order to make these ideas of Hooke clear, we should first look at his explanation of colours in the *Micrographia* where it is given in more detail, and then come back to his new suggestions which Newton's theory had provoked.

In the *Micrographia*,[11] Hooke considers a 'physical ray' falling obliquely on a refracting surface. What he calls physical ray is a portion of the ever expanding sphere described by the propagating pulse or wave-front. In the simpler case of a plane pulse, as in the figure (Fig. X. 1), the physical ray, incident on the refracting surface, is defined, for example, by the parallel lines *EB*, *FA*, which he calls 'mathematical rays', while the perpendiculars *EF*, and *BL*, represent the pulse itself in two successive positions. The mathematical rays thus represent the direction of propagation and they are made

---

[10] *Correspondence*, I, p. 110. The text published by Birch from the Register book of the Royal Society substitutes 'white' for 'light' in its first occurrence at the beginning of this quotation. See Birch, *History*, III, p. 11; *Correspondence*, I, p. 115, editor's note 3.

[11] Cf. *Micrographia*, Observation IX, especially pp. 62–64.

parallel on the assumption that the centre of propagation is infinitely remote.

According to Hooke, when the pulse is perpendicular to the direction of propagation, as in the ray *EFLB*, the light is said to be simple, uniform and undisturbed; it generates the sensation of white. Colours appear when the uniform (or undifferentiated) pulse is confused by refraction—in the following way. Since the ray is falling obliquely on the surface of separation, the side of the pulse

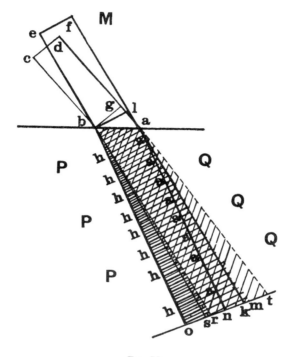

FIG. X.I

at *B* arrives at the surface and starts penetrating into the refracting medium while the other side is still travelling in the medium of incidence. We have seen[12] how Hooke, using Descartes' formula, arrives at the result that, in the medium of refraction, the pulse becomes oblique, instead of perpendicular, to the direction of

---

[12] See above, pp. 192ff.

propagation. This obliquity of the pulse to the mathematical rays constitutes the disturbance or confusion which Hooke asserts to be responsible for the appearance of colours. The refracted mathematical rays *BO, AN* remain parallel; and, of course, the sides of the refracted pulse, at *H* and at *A*, proceed with the same speed. (Otherwise, the inclination of the pulse to the direction of propagation would be continually changing while the ray is travelling in one and the same medium, contrary to what the theory assumes.)

But how are the colours produced as a result of the obliqueness of the pulse? Hooke considers that the preceding part of the pulse which first strikes the refracting surface 'must necessarily be somewhat *obtunded*, or *impeded* by the resistance of the transparent medium'.[13] When the second end of the pulse arrives at the surface, the way will have been, as it were, prepared for it by the first, and will accordingly meet with less resistance from the medium. There will thus proceed in the refracting medium a pulse whose weaker part precedes and whose stronger part follows. The dark or undisturbed medium *P* will further have a 'deadening'[14] effect on the part of the pulse that is adjacent to it and which has already been weakened at the surface; and this effect will penetrate deeper and deeper into the ray as it goes away from the surface. 'Whence all the parts of the triangle, *RBHO* will be of a dead *Blue* colour, and so much the deeper, by how much the nearer they lie to the line *BHH*, which is most deaded or impeded, and so much the more *dilute*, by how much the nearer it approaches the line *BR*.'[15]

To account for the generation of red, Hooke explains that the other side of the pulse at *AA*, being stronger than the part at *HH*, will induce a faint motion into the dark medium *Q*. As the ray goes forward this faint motion will be propagated farther and farther into the medium, that is, as far as the line *AM*, '. . . whence all the triangle *MAN* will be ting'd with a *Red*, and that *Red* will be the deeper the nearer it approaches the line *MA*, and the *paler* or *yellower* the nearer it is the line *NA*'.[16] Thus, on this account, while blue is due

---

[13] *Micrographia*, pp. 62–63.
[14] Ibid., p. 63.
[15] Ibid.
[16] Ibid.

to the deadening effect of the medium P on the weak side of the pulse at HH, red is the result of the disturbing effect of the strong side of the pulse at AA on the medium Q.

Though Hooke does not explicitly mention the spreading out of light by refraction in the *Micrographia*, it should be noted that his preceding explanation implicitly takes that fact into account, at least in a qualitative manner. For the refracted ray is limited in his figure by the *diverging* lines BO and AM. That is, one can infer from his figure that the incident ray, defined by the parallel lines EB and FA, has been dilated, or dispersed by refraction. It should be further noted that his figure represents blue as the most refracted, and red as the least refracted, these two colours being defined respectively by the lines BO and AM.

These observations may enable us to understand why Hooke did not feel that there was anything new in Newton's experiments.[17]

Hooke goes on to explain the appearance of the other colours: As the refracted ray continues, the lines BR and AN, representing the innermost bounds of the diluted blue and red (that is, pale blue and yellow), will intersect; beyond that intersection 'all kinds of Green' will be generated, owing to the overlapping of the regions occupied by blue and yellow.[18] If we further imagine another incident ray like $BCDA$, its corresponding refracted ray will be confined between the lines BS and AT. Again the blue will be adjacent to BS, and the red on the side of AT. All the rays falling between $BCDA$ and $BEFA$ will be refracted between BO and AT, and will be partially superimposed on one another. The disturbance at any point in the medium, say on the line OT, will thus depend on the resultant effect of the various pulses at that point; and every point in the disturbed medium will give rise to a particular colour according to its state of motion.

---

[17] Hooke in fact readily wrote in his Considerations: 'That the Ray of Light is as twere split or Rarifyd by Refraction, is most certaine' (*Correspondence*, I, p. 111); but he insisted that that splitting of light can be *explained* by what the pulse, in his theory, undergoes in refraction: 'But why there is a necessity, that all these motions, or whatever els it be that makes colours, should be originally in the simple rayes of light, I doe not yet understand the necessity . . .' (ibid.). Newton, on the other hand, was convinced that dispersion should be interpreted as the separation of heterogeneous elements.

[18] *Micrographia*, p. 63.

To complete Hooke's account, it will be sufficient to explain how, in his view, the two extreme colours, blue and red, are produced in vision. He imagines two rays falling at different inclinations on the cornea. The rays are focused by the eye-lens on two points on the retina. He shows that, at one of these points, the weaker side of the pulses will strike the retina before the stronger part—which excites the sensation of blue; whereas, at the other point, the stronger part precedes the weaker, and a sensation of red is generated. Thus, he concludes, 'That *Blue is an impression on the Retina of an oblique and confus'd pulse of light, whose weakest part precedes, and whose strongest follows.* And, that *Red is an impression on the Retina of an oblique and confus'd pulse of light, whose strongest part precedes, and whose weakest follows.*'[19] The other colours will be generated as a result of the combined effect on the retina of the various pulses that are focused between the extreme points of blue and red.

That Hooke's explanations are unsatisfactory is only too obvious. Yet his theory is much more subtle than might appear at first consideration. In particular, the sense in which it is dualistic, since it admits only two principal colours, is very sophisticated. For though Hooke repeatedly asserts that all colours are but the various mixtures or dilutions of blue and red, his meaning can only be appreciated by reference to his explanation of what the refracting medium undergoes when a refracted pulse passes through. From this explanation it appears that there corresponds to every colour a certain *physical* property of the medium depending on the degree of 'strength' or 'weakness' of the pulses at any given point. The real deficiency in Hooke's theory, however, lies in the fact that this physical property is not clearly defined: it is not easy to understand what the relative strength or weakness of the various parts of the pulse consist in, since, as has been remarked before, those parts proceed with the same speed. Nevertheless, had Hooke tried to develop long enough the analogy between sound and light that was current in his time, he might have said, for example, that the strength of the pulse at any given point in the medium will depend on the degree of promptness of the vibration at that point. *Promptness* is in

---

[19] *Micrographia*, p. 64.

fact the word that was used by Malebranche about eighteen years later (i.e. in 1699) to denote frequency.[20] It will be seen later that Newton also suggested to Hooke a similar idea in order to bring their respective theories closer together.

We may now proceed to examine Hooke's approach to Newton's experiments and doctrine from the point of view of the theory expounded in the *Micrographia*. He felt there was no difficulty in accounting for the Newtonian experiment in which white light was obtained by allowing the colours to be refracted through a second prism in the opposite direction. Before light suffers any refraction at all, he explained, it consists in a simple and undifferentiated motion; at the first refraction by the first prism, a multiplicity of motions or vibrations are generated and colours appear; when these are refracted again in the opposite direction, the acquired vibrations are destroyed and the motion of light is restored to its original simplicity. There was thus, for Hooke, no need to postulate the original heterogeneity of white light.[21]

From Hooke's point of view, to assert the doctrine of original heterogeneity would mean that the motions (which according to him are created by refraction) 'should be originally in the simple rayes of [white] light'.[22] But he found that as unnecessary to maintain as to say that sound exists in a string before it is plucked. Nevertheless, he himself proceeded to develop further this analogy:

which string (by the way) is a pretty representation of the shape of a refracted ray to ye eye; and the manner of it may be somewt imagined by the similitude there; for the ray is like the string, strained between the luminous object & the eye, & the stop or finger is like the refracting surface, on ye one side of wch the string hath noe motion; on the other, a vibrating one. Now we may say indeed or imagine that the rest or streightness of the string is caused by the cessation of motions or coalition of all vibrations, and that all the vibrations are dormant in it.[23]

---

[20] Cf. P. Duhem, 'L'optique de Malebranche', in *Revue de métaphysique et de morale*, 23ᵉ année (1916), pp. 37ff.

[21] *Correspondence*, I, pp. 111, 112–13.

[22] Ibid., p. 111.

[23] Ibid. The text continues: 'but yet it seems more naturall to me, to imagine it the other way.' And yet Hooke returns to this idea no less than four times in the same letter containing

That is to say, we may imagine that the various vibrations (into which the simple motion of white light is differentiated by a first refraction) are made to coalesce or add up together, and in so doing destroy each other. But, again, Hooke saw no need to adopt this suggestion. This was unfortunate. For the preceding remarks contain in fact an expression of the idea that was later known as the principle of the superposition of waves. Hooke, it seems, was the first to conceive of this idea as applied to light. His gropings are the more interesting for the fact that he went as far as to consider the application of that idea to the problem of representing white light from the point of view of the wave theory. In doing this he was envisaging a possibility that was only realized by M. Gouy in 1886.[24] The degree of clarity with which Hooke conceived that interesting idea is revealed in the following words which come at the end of his Considerations:

Tis true I can in my supposition conceive the white or uniforme motion of light to be compounded of the compound motions of all the other

---

his Considerations. Thus he wrote: 'the motion of Light in an uniform medium, in wch it is generated, is propagated by simple & uniform pulses or waves, which are at Right angles with the line of Direction; but falling obliquely on the Refracting medium, it Receives an other impression or motion, which disturbes the former motion:—somewt like the vibration of a string; and that, which was before a line, now becomes a triangular superficies, in which the pulse is not propagated at Right angles with its line of Direction, but askew; as I have more at large explained in my *micrographia*' (ibid., p. 112). Note the expression 'pulses or waves' and the recognition of dispersion in the consideration that 'that, which was before a line, now becomes a triangular superficies'. Again: '. . . the compound motions are made to coalesse into one simple, where they meet, but keep their disturbd and compounded [motions], when they begin againe to Diverge and Separate . . .' (ibid., p. 113). And again, with reference to superposition of water waves: 'How the split Ray by being made to coalesse does produce a cleer or uniforme light, I have before shewd, that is, by being united thereby from a super-ficiall motion, which is susceptible of two, to a lineary, which is susceptible of one only motion: And tis as easy to conceive, how all these motions again appear after ye Rayes are again split or Rarifyd: He that shall but a little consider the undulations on the surface of a small rill of water in a gutter, or the like, will easily see the whole manner curiously exem-pliffyd' (ibid., p. 113). The fourth return, with reference to Descartes' use of the composition and resolution of linear motion, is quoted above. Can it be doubted that Hooke was attracted to this idea, even though he obviously conceived it under pressure of Newton's experiments? As will be seen, Newton certainly understood him to be proposing the coalescence of pulses (or vibrations or waves) as a possible representation that would not concede the conception of white light as a heterogeneous mixture, and he consequently rejected it. See below, pp. 281f.

[24] See below, pp. 280f.

colours, as any one strait and uniform motion may be compounded of thousands of compound motions, in the same manner as Descartes explicates the Reason of the Refraction, but I see noe necessity of it.[25]

Here Hooke is pointing out that the idea of the composition of motion that was applied by Descartes in the *Dioptric*[26] to linear motion *could* also be applied to the vibrating motion (or waves) which, according to him, constitutes light. If this *were* to be done, the simple, uniform (that is, undifferentiated) *pulse* which constitutes white light would be conceived as the resultant of all the various vibrations corresponding to the various colours. On this supposition, the motion of white light would be compounded in the sense that the variety of vibrations *potentially* exist in it before the pulse is decomposed by refraction. This was fundamentally Gouy's suggestion at the end of the nineteenth century. Unfortunately Hooke saw no necessity for it.

In any case, no theory of light could have profitably digested that suggestion before the analogy between light and sound was fully developed and the necessary mathematical apparatus (i.e. Fourier's theorem) for carrying out that suggestion was available. The important thing to notice, however, is that Hooke was able to conceive of a plausible (though qualitative) representation of white light which, had it been properly developed, would have taken Newton's experiments into full account. He was hindered from developing his ideas because he was content with his dualistic theory in its vague form. It was Newton, an enemy of the wave theory of light, who first clearly saw the necessity of introducing new elements into Hooke's wave picture if it were to give a proper representation of the discovered properties of colours. But we shall see that Newton determinedly rejected Hooke's idea of the 'coalition' or composition of vibrations for the reason that it would do away with his (Newton's) doctrine of the original heterogeneity of white light as he understood it.

It was remarked at the beginning of this account that Hooke

---

[25] *Correspondence*, I, p. 114.
[26] See also: Descartes, *Principles*, II, 32.

claimed to accept the experimental propositions contained in Newton's paper as long as they did not go beyond the actual observations. But since he maintained throughout that there were no more than two principal colours, he could not in fact do justice to Newton's experiments. To support his view, Hooke recalled an experiment, which had been related in the *Micrographia*[27], in which one of two wedge-like glass boxes was filled with a red tincture of aloes and the other with a blue copper solution. The first box exhibited all degrees of colours from deep red near the base to pale yellow near the edge. The colours exhibited by the other box varied from indigo to pale blue. All the other colours were produced by viewing the two boxes together through various thicknesses. Pale green, for example, was produced by passing white light through the boxes near the edges; and so on.

Newton objected in his Answer[28] to Hooke's Considerations that in the production of colours other than those exhibited by the boxes individually, more than two colours were in fact made use of, since neither of the boxes was of one uniform colour. To produce different sorts of green, for example, various degrees of yellow and blue were necessary. And to say, as Hooke had asserted, that yellow was only a diluted red was simply begging the question. But Hooke had already argued in the *Micrographia* that since red and yellow are produced by the same solution according to the various thicknesses of the box, they must be degrees of the same colour; or, in other words, yellow is a diluted red, and red is a deepened yellow. The difficulty, as Michael Roberts and E. R. Thomas have observed, is a real one; and to meet this difficulty, Newton himself was led to propose a theory of selective absorption:[29]

The Tincture of *Aloes* is qualified to transmit most easily the rays indued with red, most difficultly the rays indued with Violet, & with intermediate degrees of facility the rays indued with intermediate colours. So that

---

[27] *Micrographia*, Observation X, pp. 73–75.
[28] Cf. *Philosophical Transactions*, No. 88, 18 November 1672, pp. 5093–7; *Correspondence*, I, pp. 171–88.
[29] Cf. Michael Roberts and E. R. Thomas, *Newton and the Origin of Colours*, London, 1934, pp. 99–100.

where the liquor is very thin it may suffice to intercept most of the Violet, & yet transmit most of the other colours; all wch together must compound a middle colour, that is, a faint Yellow. And where it is so much thicker as also to intercept most of the Blew & Green, the remaining Green Yellow & Red must compound an Orang. And where the thicknesse is so great that scarce any rays can passe through it besides those indued with Red, it must appeare of that colour, & yt so much ye deeper & obscurer by how much ye liquor is thicker.[30]

There is also a certain difficulty involved in interpreting the term 'dilution' in Hooke's account. For he had radically distinguished in the *Micrographia* between diluting and deepening a colour on the one hand, and whitening and darkening it on the other.[31] The second operation consists in varying the intensity of the colour by increasing or decreasing the quantity of light. But '*diluting* a colour, is to make the colour'd parts more thin, so that the ting'd light, which is made by trajecting those ting'd bodies, does not receive so deep a tincture'; and 'deepning a colour, is to make the light pass through a greater quantity of the same tinging body'.[32] From this it appears that Hooke does not want to assert that the difference between yellow and red, for example, is simply a difference in intensity. His remarks in fact cannot be understood without reference to his elaborate theory of the colours of thin plates where there is an imaginative attempt to explain how colour may depend on the thickness of the body through which the light has been trajected. Hooke's attempt will be discussed in Chapter XIII.

In spite of all these subtleties and elaborations, there is one thing which did escape Hooke's careful appreciation when he wrote his Considerations upon Newton's theory. That was the fact, discovered by Newton and of essential importance in his doctrine, that a middle colour, like orange or green, can be produced either from several primary colours or from only one such colour. In the first case the colour can be resolved into its components; whereas, in the second, the colour cannot be altered. This is what Hooke failed to make

---

[30] *Correspondence*, I, p. 180.
[31] Cf. *Micrographia*, Observation X, p. 75.
[32] Ibid.

room for in his dualistic theory. We should not therefore expect Newton to be satisfied with Hooke's claim that he granted the totality of Newton's experimental propositions. It also naturally appeared to Newton that Hooke's inability to appreciate the full import of the experiments was due to his (Hooke's) inclination towards a particular hypothesis about the nature of light. It will be shown later how this interpretation of Hooke's attitude, and the attitude of Newton's adversaries in general, influenced Newton's views on hypotheses.

2. It is clear from Pardies' first two letters[33] to Oldenburg concerning Newton's theory of colours that, like Hooke, he understood Newton's fundamental assertion of the unequal refrangibility of rays to be essentially bound up with a corpuscular view about the nature of light. This view, this 'very ingenious hypothesis', as he referred to it in the opening sentence of his first letter, he found 'very extraordinary' in that it viewed (white) light as an aggregate of an 'almost infinite' number of rays originally endowed with different colours and different degrees of refrangibility.[34] Pardies was naturally alarmed at a theory which obviously upset the very foundations of dioptrics as they were then universally accepted. He applied the word 'hypothesis' to Newton's theory, however, in all innocence; he did not mean that word to carry with it any derogatory implications. Thus, when he found that Newton had taken offence at this term,[35] he hastened to apologize, explaining that he had only used

---

[33] Dated, respectively, 30 March 1672, and 11 May 1672. Cf. *Philosophical Transactions*, No. 84, 17 June 1672, pp. 4087–90; and No. 85, 15 July 1672, pp. 5012–3. Re-edited in *Correspondence*, I, pp. 130–3, 156–8. English translation reproduced from *Phil. Trans., Abridged* (London, 1809) in *Isaac Newton's Papers & Letters on Natural Philosophy*, ed. I Bernard Cohen, Cambridge, Mass., 1958., pp 86–89, 104–5. The dates given in *Phil. Trans.* (viz. 9 April 1672 and 21 May 1672) are those at which Oldenburg forwarded the letters to Newton. The original Latin texts are followed in Turnbull's edition of the *Correspondence* with English paraphrases.

[34] *Isaac Newton's Papers & Letters*, p. 87.

[35] In his reply to Pardies' first letter Newton wrote to Oldenburg (13 April 1672): 'I do not take it amiss that the Rev. Father calls my theory an hypothesis, inasmuch as he was not acquainted with it [*siquidem ipsi nondum constet*]. But my design was quite different, for it seems to contain only certain properties of light, which, now discovered, I think easy to be proved, and which if I had not considered them as true, I would rather have them rejected

the word which first came to his mind.[36]   And we find him, in his second letter, equally applying it with the same readiness to alternative views which he himself favoured about the nature of light. The fact that he referred to Newton's view of the original compositeness of white light as a hypothesis only reflected his understanding that this view was the fundamental postulate of Newton's doctrine, believing of course at the same time that there was no compelling reason for maintaining it.

But his reasons for this belief were not altogether fortunate. Thus he thought, for instance, that the elongated shape of the solar spectrum could be explained by the accepted rules of refraction.[37] To demonstrate this he considered a particular case in which two rays coming from opposite parts of the sun fell at one point on the side of the triangular glass prism whose refracting angle was 60°. The two rays had angles of incidence equal to 30° and 29°30' respectively, and, therefore, their inclination to one another, measuring the apparent diameter of the sun, was 30'. Assuming the same refractive index for all incident rays, he found by calculation that the emerging rays from the other side of the prism subtended an angle of 2°23' (the ray incident on the prism at 30° emerging at an angle of 76°22' with the normal, while the other emerged at an angle of 78°49'). Observing that the angle contained between the emergent rays in his case was smaller by only 26' than Newton's estimation of the corresponding angle, Pardies concluded that there was no need to postulate the varying refrangibility of rays: the slight discrepancy could have been due to an error of observation.

Pardies had of course overlooked in these calculations that his prism was placed in a different position from that required in Newton's experiment. He had obviously overlooked the sentence in Newton's paper, stating that the refractions were made equal on both sides of the prism.[38] Not, however, because he was prejudiced

---

as vain and empty speculation, than acknowledged even as an hypothesis' (*Isaac Newton's Papers & Letters*, p. 92; cf. *Correspondence*, I, pp. 142, 144).

[36] *Isaac Newton's Papers & Letters*, p. 105: 'And as to my calling the author's theory an hypothesis, that was done without any design, having only used that word as first occured to me; and therefore request it may not be thought as done out of any disrespect.'

[37] *Isaac Newton's Papers & Letters*, pp. 87–88.

[38] See above, p. 237.

against Newton's theory: Pardies' sincerity and his readiness to understand are clearly apparent in his second letter to Oldenburg. After having received Newton's further explanations,[39] he recognized that, in the particular case considered by Newton, the image should be circular, not oblong; and, therefore, that was no 'difficulty' (objection) left for him regarding that point.[40]

But only regarding that point. For Pardies still could not accept the varying refrangibility of rays, although he admitted that the oblong shape of the spectrum was something problematic. It was here that he appealed to the hypotheses of Grimaldi and Hooke in order to account for the observed elongation. In Grimaldi's hypothesis light was conceived as a fluid substance capable of a very rapid motion. And Pardies briefly suggested that, on this supposition, dispersion could be attributed to a certain 'diffusion'[41] of the light at the farther side of the hole through which it passed (that is, at the light's entrance into the prism). Alternatively, Pardies went on, Hooke's hypothesis asserted that light was propagated by means of undulatory motion taking place in a very subtle matter. On this hypothesis, dispersion would be attributed to a certain 'diffusion' or

---

[39] For Newton's reply to Pardies' first letter, see *Phil. Trans.*, No. 84, 17 June 1672, pp. 4091–3; *Correspondence*, I, pp. 140–2; English translation, *Isaac Newton's Papers & Letters*, pp. 90–92. Oldenburg was not at all fair in what he wrote to Newton (9 April 1672) referring to Pardies' first letter: 'You see by the enclosed written to me by the Jesuite Pardies . . . how nimble yt sort of men is to animadvert upon new Theories' (*Correspondence*, I, p. 135). As we shall see, Huygens equally failed at first to see the essential point in Newton's experiment. To avoid these misunderstandings, something like the full explanations already elaborated in the *Lectiones Opticae* should have been provided in the first place. See above, p. 235, n. 9.

[40] Pardies wrote in his second letter to Oldenburg (11 May 1672): '. . . with respect to that experiment of the greater breadth of the colours than what is required by the common theory of refractions; I confess that I supposed the refractions at the opposite sides of the prism unequal, till informed by the letter[s] [*in leteris*] in the Transactions, that the greater breadth was observed by Newton in that case in which the refractions are supposed reciprocally equal, in the manner mentioned in these observations [Sed nec ab eo tempore in iisdem *Transactionibus* videre licuit cum eas non potuerim recuperare]. But since I now see that it was in that case that the greater breadth of the colours was observed, on that head I find no difficulty' (*Isaac Newton's Papers & Letters*, p. 104; cf. *Phil. Trans.*, No. 85, 15 July 1672, p. 5012; *Correspondence*, I, pp. 156–7). The 'letters' here referred to are (1) Newton's first letter to the Royal Society on light and colours, and (2) his reply to some experimental proposals (offered by Sir Robert Moray). The latter contained no clarifications concerning the position of the prism. Cf. *Phil. Trans.*, No. 83, 20 May 1672, pp. 4059–62: Correspondence, I, pp. 136–9 and note 3.

[41] *Isaac Newton's Papers & Letters*, p. 104.

'expansion' of the undulations at the farther side of the hole 'by virtue of the very continguity and simple continuity of matter'.[42] Pardies then declared that he had himself adopted the latter hypothesis in a treatise which he had written on undulatory motion, in which colours were explained by lateral spreading of the motion propagated in straight lines.[43]

Besides these brief suggestions, Pardies expressed his feeling of certain difficulties in the Newtonian account of colours, especially in connection with the *experimentum crucis*. He thought that by rotating the first prism near the window in order to allow the colours to fall successively on the second prism, the incidence of the rays on the second prism was thereby continually changed. If this were the case, then obviously Newton's experiment would appear to be inconclusive: the unequal refractions of the various colours by the second prism might be due to their unequal incidence. But, again, Pardies had overlooked the fact that the incidence on the second prism was kept constant by the fixity of the two boards set up between the two prisms at a sufficiently large distance from one another.[44] Pardies was willing to assume that the 'sagacious Newton' had taken all necessary precautions to ensure that the experiment was properly performed.[45] But a second reply from Newton,[46] containing a sufficient clarification of the difficulty in question and

---

[42] '*quae [undulationes] fiat ad latera radiorum ultra foramen, ipsa contagio ipsàque materiae continuatione*' (*Correspondence*, I, p. 157).

[43] See above, pp. 195f.

[44] Newton had written in his first paper: 'I took two boards, and placed one of them close behind the Prisme at the window, so that the light might pass through a small hole, made in it for that purpose, and fall on the other board, which I placed at about 12 foot distance, having first made a small hole in it also, for some of that Incident light to pass through. Then I placed another Prisme behind this second board . . .' (*Correspondence*, I, p. 94; compare the drawing opposite p. 107). Pardies' difficulty in understanding Newton's arrangement for the *experimentum crucis* should not be surprising. Huygens also found it difficult to understand, simply 'because it is somewhat obscurely written' (see Huygens' letter to Oldenburg, 1 July 1672, H, VII, p. 186; quoted by Oldenburg in letter to Newton, 2 July 1672, *Correspondence*, I, p. 207). Newton himself wrote the following in reply to Huygens' complaint: 'As to ye Theory of Light and Colors, I am apt to believe that some of the experiments may seem obscure by reason of the brevity wherewith I writ them wch should have been described more largely & explained with schemes if they had been intended for the publick' (Newton to Oldenburg, 8 July 1672, *Correspondence*, I, p. 212; cf. H, VII, p. 207).

[45] *Isaac Newton's Papers & Letters*, p. 105.

[46] Cf. *Correspondence*, I, pp. 163–8; *Phil. Trans.*, No. 85, 15 July 1672, especially pp. 5016–17.

providing for the first time a diagram of the *experimentum crucis*, stimulated Pardies to write a last and highly appreciative and extremely courteous letter in which he declared that he was 'entirely satisfied'.[47]

3. On 11 March 1672, Oldenburg sent to Huygens a copy of No. 80 (19 February 1671/2) of the *Philosophical Transactions* which contained Newton's first paper to the Royal Society on light and colours. In a covering letter,[48] Oldenburg particularly referred to Newton's paper and requested Huygens to give his opinion of it. Strangely enough, it would seem from Huygens' reply (9 April 1672)[49] that he completely missed the point in Newton's discovery; and this, in spite of the fact that Oldenburg had explicitly referred to Newton's doctrine as a '*theorie nouuelle*' in which the author '*maintient, que la lumiere n'est pas vne chose similaire, mais vn meslange de rayons refrangibles differemment*',[50] thus directing Huygens' attention to the fundamental thesis of Newton's doctrine. The following is what Huygens wrote in answer to Oldenburg's request:

I was pleased to find in the last [*Transactions*] what Monsieur Newton has written regarding the effect of glasses and mirrors in the matter of telescopes, *where I see that he has noticed, like myself, the defect of refraction of convex object glasses due to the inclination of their surfaces.* As for his new Theory about colours, it appears to me very ingenious; but it will be necessary to see whether it agrees with all the experiments.[51]

Now Newton had indeed pointed out the defectiveness of refraction in the construction of telescopes. But he had not ascribed that

---

[47] Pardies to Oldenburg, 30 June 1672: 'Je suis tres satisfait de la réponse que M. Newton a bien voulu faire à mes instances le dernier scrupule qui me restoit touchant *l'experience de la croix*, a esté parfaitement levé. Et je conçois tres-bien par sa figure ce que je n'avois pas compris auparavant. L'experience ayant esté faite de cette façon je n'ay rien á dire' (*Correspondence*, I, pp. 205–6). A Latin translation was published in the *Philosophical Transactions*, No. 85, p. 5018, following Newton's reply.

[48] Cf. H, VII, p. 156; *Correspondence*, I, p. 117.

[49] H, VII, pp. 165–7.

[50] *Correspondence*, I, p. 117.

[51] H, VII, p. 165; italics added. Compare the extract in Oldenburg's Letter to Newton, 9 April 1672, *Correspondence*, I, p. 135.

defectiveness, as Huygens wrote, to anything regarding the shapes of lenses. On the contrary, Newton's point was that the fault lay in the constitution of light itself, namely the varying refrangibility of its rays.[52] The italicized words in Huygens' passage thus show that he still viewed the problem of perfecting telescopes as if Newton's paper had not thrown any new light on it. There is no mention in Huygens' letter of the doctrine of the unequal refrangibility of rays. He obviously understood Newton's contribution to constitute a new theory about *colours* rather than *refractions*.

After a repeated request from Oldenburg, [53] Huygens returned to Newton's doctrine of colours, referring to it as a *hypothesis*:

So far, I find the hypothesis of Monsieur Newton about colours very probable [*fort probable*]. The *experimentum crucis* is presented a little obscurely, but if I understand it well it very much confirms his new opinion . . . As to his new hypothesis about colours . . . I confess that, so far, it appears to me very plausible [*tres vraysemblable*], and the *experimentum crucis* (if I understand it well, for it is written somewhat obscurely) very much confirms it.[54]

Again, we find no mention of the different refrangibility of rays with which Newton's *experimentum crucis* was in fact directly concerned.

On 8 July 1672, Oldenburg forwarded to Huygens a copy of the *Transactions* No. 84 (17 June 1672) which contained Pardies' first letter and Newton's answer to it.[55] And on 29 July 1672, he sent him a copy of No. 85 (15 July 1672).[56] This contained the remaining letters exchanged through Oldenburg between Newton and Pardies, and a further article by Newton on his theory of colours.[57]

---

[52] See above, p. 240.
[53] Cf. Oldenburg to Huygens, 8 April 1672, H, VII, p. 168.
[54] Huygens to Oldenburg, 1 July, 1672, H, VII, pp. 185 and 186. Compare extract in Oldenburg's letter to Newton, 2 July 1672, in *Correspondence*, I, p. 207. Newton's reply has been quoted, above, p. 267, n. 44.
[55] Cf. Oldenburg to Huygens, 8 July 1672, H, VII, p. 196; *Correspondence*, I, p. 213–14.
[56] Cf. Oldenburg to Huygens, 29 July 1672, H, VII, p. 215; *Correspondence*, I, p. 220.
[57] Cf. *Phil. Trans.*, No. 85, 15 July 1672, pp. 5004–5. Newton's article had the following title: 'A Serie's of Quere's propounded by Mr. Isaac Newton, to be determin'd by Experiments, positively and directly concluding his new Theory of Light and Colours; and recommended to the Industry of the Lovers of Experimental Philosophy, as they were generously imparted to the Publisher in a Letter of the said Mr. Newtons of July 8. 1672.' The

We may therefore assume that Huygens was (or should have been) sufficiently informed about the Newtonian theory when, on 27 September 1672, he wrote the following to Oldenburg:

What you have presented of Monsieur Newton's in one of your last journals [i.e. No. 85 of the *Transactions*] confirms even more his doctrine of colours. Nevertheless, the matter could well be otherwise; and it seems to me that he should be content to propose it [i.e. Newton's doctrine] as a very plausible [*fort vrai semblable*] hypothesis. Besides, if it were true that the rays of light were, from their origin, some red, some blue etc., there would still remain the great difficulty of explaining by the mechanical physics wherein this diversity of colours consists.[58]

Still Huygens does not pronounce a word about the unequal refrangibility of rays. Instead, he expresses his concern about a mechanical explanation of colours. As a mechanist and a Cartesian, he was not satisfied with Newton's doctrine as long as it did not make it clear in what sense colours are original properties of the rays. His remark that Newton should be content to propose his theory of colours only as a very plausible hypothesis was no doubt an answer to Newton's claim, in the article published in No. 85 of the *Transactions*, that the experiments *positively* and *directly* concluded his theory.

The sense in which Huygens demanded a mechanical explanation of colours, and the extent to which this primary requirement influenced his understanding of and attitude towards Newton's theory, are clearly revealed in a letter to Oldenburg of 14 January 1672/3.[59] He wrote this letter after he had read Newton's Answer[60] to Hooke's

---

original bears the date 6 July 1672; cf. *Correspondence*, I, pp. 208–11. Although the title was apparently provided by Oldenburg, the claim that the experiments 'positively and directly' concluded Newton's theory was made by Newton in the article itself. This claim will be examined in the following chapter.

[58] H, VII, pp. 228–9; cf. extract from this letter in *Correspondence*, I, pp. 235–6.

[59] Cf. H, VII, pp. 242–4; quoted in Oldenburg to] Newton, 18 January 1672/3, *Correspondence*, I, pp. 255–6 (see p. 257, editor's note 2). Part of this letter was translated from French into English by Oldenburg and published in the *Philosophical Transactions* (No. 96, 21 July 1673, pp. 6086–7) under the following title: 'An Extract of a Letter lately written by an ingenious person from Paris, containing some Considerations upon Mr. Newtons doctrine of Colors, as also upon the effects of the different Refractions of the Rays in Telescopical Glasses.' Quotations from this letter will be taken from Oldenburg's translation.

[60] Cf. *Phil. Trans.*, No. 88, 18 November 1672, pp. 5084–5103; *Correspondence*, I, pp. 171–88.

Considerations. Following Hooke's suggestion, Huygens wrote that 'the most important Objection, which is made against him [Newton] by way of *Quaere*, is that, Whether there be more than two sorts of Colours'.[61] He believed that 'an *Hypothesis*, that should explain mechanically and by the nature of motion the Colors *Yellow* and *Blew*, would be sufficient for all the rest'.[62] But why should Huygens prefer to allow no more than two primary colors: 'because it will be much more easy to find an *Hypothesis* by Motion, that may explicate these two differences, than for so many diversities as there are of other Colors?'[63] Then at last we read the following sentence in which Huygens, for the first time, recognized the unequal refrangibility of rays:

And till he hath found this *Hypothesis*, he hath not taught us, what it is wherein consists the nature and difference of Colours, but only this accident (which certainly is very considerable,) of their *different Refrangibility*.[64]

As to the composition of white, he further suggests, in spite of Newton's detailed explanations to Hooke,[65] that 'it may possibly be, that *Yellow* and *Blew* might also be sufficient for that [difference in refrangibility]'.[66]

Finally this discussion ended in an unfortunate misunderstanding over Huygens' last suggestions. In his answer to Huygens, Newton wrote the following sentence:

If therefore M Hugens would conclude any thing, he must show how white may be produced out of two uncompounded colours; wch when he hath done, I will further tell him, why he can conclude nothing from that.[67]

---

[61] *Phil. Trans.*, No. 96, 21 July 1673, p. 6086.
[32] Ibid.
[63] Ibid.
[64] Ibid.
[65] Cf. *Phil. Trans.*, No. 88 (1672), pp. 5097–5102; *Correspondence*, I, pp. 181–6.
[66] *Phil. Trans.*, No. 96 (1673), p. 6086.
[67] Newton to Oldenburg, 3 April 1673, *Correspondence*, I, p. 265; in the *Philosophical Transactions* (No. 97, 6 October 1673, p. 6110) Huygens' name was replaced by 'N'.

What Newton meant by this sentence was that a white compounded from two primary colours, if it could be produced, would not have the same (physical) properties as the white light of the sun. For the analysis of the former would yield only the two component colours, whereas the analysis of the sun's light gives all the colours of the spectrum.[68] But Huygens misinterpreted Newton's sentence which seems to have sounded rather unreasonable to him. He wrote back in a letter to Oldenburg (10 June 1673, N.S.):

... seeing that he [Newton] maintains his opinion with so much concern [*avec tant de chaleur*] I list not to dispute. But what means it, I pray, that he saith; *Though I should shew him, that the White could be produced of only two Un-compounded colors, yet I could conclude nothing from that.* And yet he hath affirm'd in p. 3083, of the *Transactions* [i.e. No. 80, 19 February 1671/2,] that to compose the White, all primitive colors are necessary.[69]

This caused Newton to write a further letter to Oldenburg in which he clearly explained his meaning and, at the same time, expressed his impatience with the Dutch physicist: 'As for M. Hugens [his] expression, that I maintain my doctrine wth some concern, I confess it was a little ungrateful to me to meet wth objections wch had been answered before, without having the least reason given me why those answers were insufficient.'[70]

To think that a discussion on light and colours between the two greatest writers on optics in the seventeenth century should end in such an anticlimax!

---

[68] Cf. *Phil. Trans.*, No. 96, 21 July 1673, pp. 6087–92; *Correspondence*, I, pp. 291–5.

[69] *Phil. Trans.*, No. 97, 6 October 1673, p. 6112; H, VII, p. 302; quoted in Oldenburg to Newton, 7 June 1673, *Correspondence*, I, p. 285. The translation is Oldenburg's; in the quotation sent to Newton he altered '*tant de chaleur*' to '*quelque chaleur*'.

[70] Newton to Oldenburg, 23 June 1673, *Correspondence*, I, p. 292; cf. *Phil. Trans.*, No. 96, 21 July 1673, p. 6089. It should be noted that Newton's letter printed in No. 96 of the *Transactions* was a reply to Huygens' letter (10 June 1673 N.S.) which was published *afterwards* in No. 97; see *Phil. Trans.*, No. 97, 6 October 1673, p. 6112, editor's note at bottom of page.

Chapter Eleven

NEWTON'S DOGMATISM AND THE REPRESENTATION OF WHITE LIGHT

1. We are now, I hope, in a position to appreciate Newton's reaction to the critics of his theory. It will have been noticed that the objections of Hooke, Pardies and Huygens exhibited somewhat the same pattern. They all understood Newton to be propounding a corpuscular view of light from which, they all granted, the rest of Newton's doctrine of colours could be deduced. They referred to Newton's theory as a hypothesis, thereby implying that the experiments could be interpreted in other ways. Being themselves inclined towards a view according to which light consisted in the transmission of motion through a medium rather than the transport of body, they either proposed alternative hypotheses (Hooke and Pardies) or expressed reservations regarding the Newtonian theory (Huygens). At the same time their proposals failed to show a sufficient appreciation of Newton's experimental findings. Thus Hooke held to his dualistic theory of colours; whether or not his theory was capable of successful development, he appeared to be satisfied with it as it stood (at least in his first reaction to Newton's first paper).[1] Pardies thought that the shape of the solar image could be explained by the diffusion of light on its passing through the hole near the face of the prism. But this opinion was contradicted by the fact that difference between the diameter of the hole and the *breadth* of the image was proportioned to the distance between the hole and the opposite wall; no spreading of the light was observed along the axis of the prism. Pardies' suggestion was more suited to the phenomenon for which it had in fact been originally proposed by Grimaldi, namely diffraction.[2] Huygens expressed the view that two primary colours might be sufficient for mechanically explaining

---

[1] See below, pp. 327f.
[2] Cf. Brewster, *Memoirs*, I, p. 78.

all the others together with their various degrees of refrangibility. This could in no way be reconciled with the experimental results as Newton had reported them.

In the face of such opposition, Newton adopted the following strategy. Seeing that his experimental propositions were being confused with his suggested hypothesis about the corporeity of light, he hastened to deny that this hypothesis was an essential part of his theory. On the other hand he tried to convince his critics (Hooke, in particular) that their own (wave) hypothesis was in no way opposed to his fundamental doctrine of the original heterogeneity of light. Further, suspecting that understanding of his experiments had been hampered by preconceived ideas, he appealed for the separation of the experimental propositions from the task of explaining them by hypotheses; he advised that the properties of light should be investigated independently of any view about its nature. Finally, he claimed that it was not at all necessary to explain his doctrine of colours by any hypothesis regarding the nature of light; that his doctrine, being sufficiently and firmly founded on the experiments, was absolutely infallible. It was in connection with this claim that Newton made his first pronouncements on the proper method of scientific procedure. According to him, this method consisted in deducing the properties of things from experiments; not in arguing from hypotheses.

Before the controversy about colours, Newton had applied the term 'hypothesis' to propositions which were only *sufficiently* but not *accurately true*.[3] For example, the proposition adopted before the discovery of the sine law that for sufficiently small incidence the angles of incidence and of refraction were in a given ratio, was, for Newton, a hypothesis; it was only an approximately true proposition that was not well established by experiments. In this sense he also applied the word 'hypothesis' (in his first paper to the Royal Society

---

[3] Cf. Newton, *Optical Lectures*, Sec. II, 25, pp. 46–47. For detailed studies of the historical development of Newton's views on hypotheses, see: I. Bernard Cohen, *Franklin and Newton* (1956), pp. 129ff and Appendix I, pp. 575ff; 'The first English version of Newton's *Hypotheses non fingo*', *Isis*, LII (1962), pp. 379–88; A Koyré, 'L'hypothèse et l'expérience chez Newton', *Bulletin de la Société Française de la Philosophie*, L (1956), pp. 59–89; 'Les *Regulae philosophandi*', *Archives internationales d'histoire des sciences*, XIII (1960), pp. 3–14.

on colours) to the sine law itself as it had been accepted before his discovery of dispersion.[4] For, disregarding the qualification which he introduced in the same paper (namely that the index of refraction varies with colour), the sine law could only have been an approximation. As he explained in other places,[5] the successful application of the law before he had made his discovery, must have been due to the tacit assumption that, in the determination of refractive indices, the *middle* colour determined the position of *the* refracted ray. Thus, as the old law of refraction was not accurately true for all angles of incidence, the sine law in its unqualified form was not accurately true for all colours. But a proposition (or hypothesis) that is only approximately true, is, strictly speaking, false. This is not altered by the fact that the old law *worked* for small angles of incidence, or that the first formulation of the sine law served some practical purposes. They were sufficiently accurate for the purpose for which they were intended by their authors, but not to serve as a foundation for the science of dioptrics. The fact that Newton has used the word 'hypothesis' in this sense may help to explain his resentment at this word being applied to his theory of colours by his critics.

In any case, Newton was already using the term 'hypothesis' in the 1672 paper itself, and during the discussion about colours, in the sense adopted by all his opponents. According to this usage, a hypothesis is a proposition involving an entity (like the ether) which cannot be perceived. Since a proposition of this kind could not be directly related to observation, it was generally recognized that a hypothesis could be false even if the consequences derived from it agreed with the observations. Only a greater or smaller degree of practical certainty (Descartes) or verisimilitude (Huygens) could be claimed for it. Never after the controversy about colours did Newton apply the word 'hypothesis' to a proposition of the same level as, for example, the sine law. This word came to mean a proposition (concerning a hidden entity) that was only *probably* true, in contrast to a verified experimental law that was *certainly*

---

[4] See above, p. 238.
[5] Cf. Newton, *Optical Lectures*, Sec. II, Art. 27, pp. 50–51; *Opticks*, Bk. I, Pt. I, Prop. VI, Theor. V, p. 76.

true. The probability or lack of certainty of a hypothesis was, according to Newton, due to the fact that, instead of being *deduced* from experiments, it was simply *supposed* in order to *explain* experiments.

Judging from his own experience with his Cartesian opponents, Newton felt that a preconceived supposition had prejudiced their attitude towards his new discoveries. His advice to abstain from contemplating hypotheses, in this context, therefore meant that all views about the nature of light should be suspended until all the relevant experiments had been examined and ascertained. After this difficult task had been fulfilled, hypotheses might be considered to explain the experimentally established facts; but that latter task was, for Newton, a relatively easy matter. In all these comments, Newton took it for granted that his own doctrine of the heterogeneity of white light in respect of both refrangibility and colour was one of these experimentally established facts. On this understanding, he ascribed to his *experimentum crucis* a role which was not accepted by his opponents. They rightly perceived that what he presented as a neutral doctrine was, even after withdrawing his suggestions as to the corporeity of light, identifiable with a corpuscular view and, therefore, no more than a plausible interpretation of the experiments.

In what follows I shall try to illustrate and develop these remarks with a view to clarifying Newton's specific representations of white light as well as his methodological position in this controversy.

2. In his Answer to Hooke's Considerations, Newton denied that the corporeal nature of light was part of his doctrine:

Tis true that from my Theory I argue the corporeity of light, but I doe it without any absolute positiveness, as the word *perhaps* intimates, & make it at most but a very plausible consequence of the Doctrine, and not a fundamentall supposition, nor so much as any part of it.[6]

---

[6] *Correspondence*, I, p. 173. See above, p. 243.
As we have seen, Newton stated in the Waste Sheets that by suggesting the corporeity of light in the 1672 paper his intention had been to exclude the peripatetic conception of light as a quality, but not the mechanical conception of light as a motion transmitted through a corporeal medium (see above, pp. 244f). In other words, he had meant his suggestion to be

The whole of the doctrine of colours, Newton maintained, was contained in the experimental propositions.

He then went on to indicate that the same doctrine could be explained *to a certain extent* by various other hypotheses:

> Had I intended any such Hypothesis [as that of the corporeity of light] I should somewhere have explained it. But I knew that the Properties, wch I declared of light were in some measure capable of being explicated not onely by that, but by many other Mechanicall Hypotheses.[7]

Similar remarks were made by Newton in his reply to Pardies' suggestions.[8] But the qualification in the above passage 'in some measure' is indicative of his real attitude. Newton in fact never admitted the possibility of giving an adequate explanation of the properties of light in terms of the wave picture alone. This belief was partly due to his realization of the inherent difficulties which the wave theory had to face and which at that time had not been solved. These difficulties, which he believed to be insurmountable, he himself pointed out at the same time as he offered his suggestions to reconcile his doctrine of colours with Hooke's hypothesis. Newton further maintained that the wave theory could not explain the rectilinear propagation of light; that is to say, it seemed to him to be falsified by experiment. His only purpose in making these

---

in opposition to *peripateticism*, not to *mechanism*. Here, in his Answer to Hooke, Newton states that the doctrine expounded in the 1672 paper did not commit him to a corporeal view of light—this view being only a very plausible consequence of the doctrine. This statement, if taken in conjunction with what is said in the Waste Sheets, would mean that the doctrine was open to a peripatetic interpretation! I would suggest that Newton's real position is expressed in his Answer to Hooke, and not in what he said later in the Waste Sheets. What he wished to argue 'without any absolute positiveness' could not have been a generalized mechanical view of light, but a specific view within mechanism—namely the view that light consisted of corpuscles.

[7] Ibid., p. 174.

[8] Newton wrote in reply to Pardies' second letter: 'F. Pardies says, that the length of the coloured image can be explained, without having recourse to the divers refrangibility of the rays of light; as supposed by the hypothesis of F. Grimaldi, viz. by a diffusion of light . . . or by Mr. Hooke's hypothesis [*ex Hypothesi Hookij nostri*] . . . . To which may be added the hypothesis of Descartes, in which a similar diffusion of *conatus*, or pression of the globules, may be conceived, like as is supposed in accounting for the tails of comets. And the same diffusion or expansion may be devised according to any other hypotheses, in which light is supposed to be a power, action, quality, or certain substance emitted every way from luminous bodies' (*Isaac Newton's Papers & Letters*, p. 106; see *Correspondence*, I, p. 164).

suggestions, therefore, was to show that Hooke (and the others) had no reason to reject his doctrine because of their theoretical commitments.

Newton's attempt to develop Hooke's concepts, however, is very interesting and should be quoted in full:

> ... the most free & naturall application of this Hypothesis [of Hooke] to the Solution of *Phænomena* I take to be this: That the agitated parts of the bodies according to their severall sizes, figures, & motions, excite vibrations in the Æther of various depths or bignesses, wch being promiscuously propagated through that Medium to our eyes, effect in us a sensation of light of a white colour; but if by any meanes those of unequall bignesses be separated from one another, the largest beget a sensation of a Red colour, ye least or shortest of a deep Violet, & the intermediate ones of intermediate colors: Much after the manner that bodies according to their severall sizes shapes & motions, excite vibrations in the air of various bignesses, wch according to those bignesses make severall tones in sound. That the largest Vibrations are best able to overcome the resistance of refracting superficies, & so break through it with least refraction: Whence ye vibrations of severall bignesses, that is, the rays of severall colors, wch are blended together in light, must be parted from one another by refraction, & so cause the Phœnomena of Prisms & other refracting substances.[9]

Newton introduced in this passage a new idea which marked a great improvement upon Hooke's treatment of light. Led by the analogy between light and sound, he realized that in an account of the properties of light in wave terms, the vibrations (or waves) corresponding to the various colours must differ from one another in some definite property, their bigness or wave-length. The heterogeneity of white light would then consist in the infinite plurality of the wave-forms corresponding to the component colours. But it must be realized that, for Newton, the component wave-forms (the 'unequal vibrations') must exist with their respective characteristic regularities *before* they are separated by refraction. In other words, the *original* compositeness of white light (whatever be

---

[9] *Correspondence*, I, p. 175. I have argued elsewhere that by 'bignesses of vibrations' Newton meant wave-lengths; see *Isis*, LIV (1963), pp. 267-8.

the terms, wave or otherwise, in which it is conceived) must have a definite *physical* meaning. The blending of the various vibrations to compose white light did not mean, in Newton's suggestion, that the waves would lose their individual characteristics in such a mixture; these waves, as they are sent out by the various parts of the luminous body (which according to their different sizes, figures and motions excite different vibrations in the ether) might *cross* one another, but they might not combine, or alter one another;[10] they must exist as differentiated elements of a *heterogeneous* mixture.

That this was for Newton a condition that would have to be satisfied in any wave picture is manifest from the following words which come shortly after the preceding passage in his Answer to Hooke:

But yet if any man can think it possible [to maintain that a pressure or motion in a medium may be propagated in straight lines], he must at least allow that those motions or endeavours to motion caused in ye Æther by the severall parts of any lucid body wch differ in size figure & agitation, must necessarily be unequall. Which is enough to denominate light an aggregate of difform rays according to any of those Hypotheses. And if those originall inequalities may suffice to difference the rays in colour & refrangibility, I see no reason why they that adhere to any of those Hypotheses, should seek for other causes of these effects, unlesse (to use Mr Hooks' argument) they will multiply entities without necessity.[11]

Thus, for Newton, the original difformity of white light should be preserved in any case. Hooke, on the other hand, was inclined towards a different view. Being convinced, as we have seen, of the

---

[10] See Newton's passage quoted below, p. 281.

[11] *Correspondence*, I, p. 176. The last sentence in this quotation is a reference to a passage in Hooke's Considerations (ibid., p. 113) where Newton was accused of multiplying entities without necessity, for admitting an indefinite number of colours when two were sufficient. Newton here repays the compliment by accusing Hooke of committing the same error, by seeking superfluous hypotheses. It would seem from this exchange that such tools (so-called methodological rules) as Occam's razor only serve as *machines de guerre* which one can always direct against the adherents of rival theories. Occam's razor does not inform us, for example, when and under what circumstances it is *not necessary* to multiply entities. Such a question is always left to the choice of the scientist who bases his decision on the requirements of his own theory. These requirements are not themselves methodological rules. The problem under discussion between Newton and Hooke, for example, could be formulated, investigated and solved without reference to any methodological rules.

uniformity (homogeneity, simplicity) of white light, he would rather have the various waves unite and compose one undifferentiated motion, a pulse.[12] The regularities suggested by Newton as necessary characteristics of the waves corresponding to the various colours would, according to Hooke's conception, disappear in the compounded white light. Hooke's reference to Descartes in this connection makes it clear that the compoundedness of white light would only have a mathematical sense, in contrast to Newton's conception. Hooke would thus argue, somewhat like Descartes, in the following manner: the motion constituting white light can be *imagined* to be composed of an infinite number of component motions; when the light passes through a prism, the motion is resolved into those components of which it is imagined to be composed. There would be no meaning in ascribing a *real* compositeness to the initial motion; and the prism could then be said to *manufacture* the colours from the simple motion of white light.

Now Hooke did not in 1672 endow his vibrations or waves with the property of periodicity. Nevertheless, his fundamental idea of the 'coalescence' or composition of vibrations which he envisaged in his Considerations upon Newton's theory came very near to M. Gouy's representation of white light in wave terms. Gouy showed[13] that the motion of white light can be represented as the sum or superposition of an infinite number of waves each corresponding to one of the spectrum colours. As it happens, the composed motion in this representation turns out to be a single *pulse*, such as that produced by a pistol shot or an electric spark. Using Fourier's theorem it could be shown that the Fourier analysis of such a pulse yields a continuous spectrum such as that produced by a dispersive apparatus. *Fourier analysis* is, of course, a mathematical concept; and the regularities produced by the dispersive apparatus (for example, the prism) would not exist in a real or physical sense in white light. What would exist in that sense in white light would be the pulses

---

[12] See above, pp. 255ff.
[13] Cf. M. Gouy, 'Sur le mouvement lumineux', *Journal de physique*, 2ᵉ série, V (1886), pp. 354–62; R. W. Wood, *Physical Optics*, New York, 1911 (second edition), Ch. XXIII: 'The Nature of White Light'. This chapter is not reprinted in the third edition.

sent out by the luminous source at irregular intervals.[14] The point in common between Gouy's interpretation and Hooke's idea is that, in both, the colours are considered to be generated by the prism; and in both, Newton's doctrine of the original difformity of white light has no place.

But as Hooke dismissed his own idea as 'unnecessary', Newton rejected it as 'unintelligible'; he wrote:

. . . though I can easily imagin how unlike motions may crosse one another, yet I cannot well conceive how they should coalesce into one *uniforme* motion [the pulse], & then part again [by refraction] & recover their former unlikenesse; notwithstanding that I conjecture the ways by wch Mr Hook may endeavour to explain it.[15]

This passage should leave no doubt as to Newton's conception of white light: even if it were possible to explain the properties of light in wave terms (as he was willing to assume for a while), it must be

---

[14] R. W. Wood (op. cit., p. 649) writes: 'A pulse or single irregular wave can be represented by Fourier's theorem, as the resultant of a large number of sine waves which extend to infinity on either side of the pulse. The spectroscope will spread this disturbance out into a spectrum, and at every point of the spectrum we shall have a periodic disturbance. In other words, the spectroscope will sort out the Fourier components into periodic trains of waves, just as if these wave-trains were really present in the incident light.'

See also F. A. Jenkins and H. E. White, *Fundamentals of Optics*, 2nd edition, London, 1951, pp. 214–16. Following the publication of Gouy's paper the scientific world witnessed a curious re-enactment of the dispute between Newton and his critics. Poincaré maintained that a high degree of regularity must be attributed to white light, while Schuster and Lord Rayleigh argued in support of Gouy's representation. (See R. W. Wood, op cit., p. 650.) Needless to say, this repetition of the seventeenth-century controversy occurred on a definitely higher level of mathematical and experimental sophistication. It should, however, indicate that Newton's opponents were not simply motivated by their pigheadedness or their addiction to hypotheses. And, in any case, it clearly shows that Newton's experiments had not been sufficient to 'prove' his doctrine of white light. A parallel study of these two disputes, with due attention to their different contexts, would be illuminating.

[15] *Correspondence*, I, p. 177; see p. 176. The text continues: "So that the direct uniform & undisturbed pulses should be split & disturbed by refraction, & yet the oblique & disturbed pulses persist without splitting or further disturbance by following refractions, is as unintelligible.' This objection derives its apparent plausibility only from interpreting the change produced by refraction as a disturbance (or confusion) rather than a *regularization*. But Newton was himself proposing to Hooke a hypothesis according to which the vibrations corresponding to the various colours were distinguished by a *definite* property, their 'bigness'. It should be mentioned here that, according to Newton's testimony, Hooke eventually (i.e before December 1675 and possibly in March of the same year) adopted Newton's suggestion —thereby abandoning both his dualistic theory of colours and the idea that the effect of the prism was of the nature of a 'disturbance' or 'confusion'. See below, pp. 327f.

allowed that the unlike motions, the waves corresponding to the various colours, should keep their individual characteristics unaltered when they mix and compose white light. The function of the prism then consisted in simply *separating* what was already differentiated though blended, not in *generating* new characteristics.

Whittaker has remarked that the word 'mixture', in Newton's assertion that white light is a mixture of rays of every variety of colour,

must not be taken to imply that the rays of different colours, when compounded together, preserve their separate existence and identity unaltered within the compound, like the constituents of a mechanical mixture. On the contrary, as was shown by Gouy in 1886 (*Journal de Physique*,[2] V, p. 354), natural white light is to be pictured, in the undulatory representation, as a succession of short *pulses*, out of which any spectroscopic apparatus such as a prism *manufactures* the different monochromatic rays, by a process which is physically equivalent to the mathematical resolution of an arbitrary function into periodic terms by Fourier's integral theorem.[16]

Since it is my purpose to differentiate between Gouy's interpretation (qualitatively conjectured in Hooke's idea of the coalescence of vibrations) and Newton's conception of white light, it must be observed that, from Newton's last passage just quoted, it is quite clear that he understood white light as a mixture in which the rays of various colours preserve, in Whittaker's words, 'their separate existence and identity unaltered within the compound'. Not to appreciate this would be to miss the point at issue between Newton and Hooke. To adopt Gouy's representation implies a rejection of Newton's particular understanding of the compositeness of white light.

Apart from his formal reservations, Newton further expressed the opinion that Hooke's hypothesis, and indeed any other hypothesis proposing to explain the properties of light by the propagation of pressure or motion in a medium, is fundamentally 'impossible'.[17]

---

[16] E. W. Whittaker, *A History of the Theories of Æther and Electricity, the classical theories*, Edinburgh, 1951, p. 17, note 1.

[17] *Correspondence*, I, p. 176.

In his view, both '*Experiment & Demonstration*' proved that pressures, waves or vibrations in any fluid bend round obstacles into the geometrical shadow.[18] Consequently, a theory of the same type as Descartes' or Hooke's was proved false by the rectilinear propagation of light, that is, by the formation of shadows in the ordinary way. By '*Experiment*' he was referring to observations on the propagation of water waves and the fact that sound is heard round corners; the '*Demonstration*', which was to the effect that the motion will be diffused throughout the space behind the obstacle, came later in the *Principia*.[19] These objections were perfectly valid in Newton's time; and it is not quite fair to answer them bluntly, as Duhem did,[20] by saying that light does in fact bend into the geometrical shadow (as Grimaldi's experiments on diffraction had shown). For Newton maintained that any wave motion will be diffused *throughout* the whole region that is screened off by the obstacle, and he was therefore asking how any shadow at all could be formed. In fact no satisfactory explanation of rectilinear propagation in wave terms was offered until Fresnel supplied such an explanation in the beginning of the nineteenth century. Only then was it shown that *both* diffraction *and* the apparent rectilinear propagation can be understood on the same principles. Using Young's law of superposition and Huygens' principle of secondary waves Fresnel could show that whether or not the light will be completely diffused throughout the space behind a screen (as required by Newton's demonstration) will depend on the dimensions of the aperture and the relation of these to the wave-length. The formation of shadows in the ordinary way (when the aperture is sufficiently large) was then explained as a result of the destructive interference of the secondary waves pre-

---

[18] Ibid., p. 175.

[19] Cf. Newton, *Principia*, Bk. II, Section VIII (the motion propagated through fluids); especially Prop. XLII. Theor. XXXIII, asserting that 'All motion propagated through a fluid diverges from a rectilinear progress into the unmoved spaces.' Newton's demonstration covers three cases: first, he is concerned with the motion of 'waves in the surface of standing water', in which case the motion is transverse; second, he considers pulses 'propagated by successive condensations and rarefactions of the [elastic] medium', as in the propagation of sound; and last, the proposition is asserted of 'motion of any kind'.

[20] Cf. P. Duhem, 'L'optique de Malebranche', in *Revue de métaphysique et de morale*, 23 e année (1916), p. 71.

sumed to proceed from every point at the aperture in *all* directions.[21] All these explanations involved ideas that were either unknown or not sufficiently developed in Newton's time.

3. So far we have witnessed Newton repudiating his initial corporeal hypothesis as a part of his doctrine of light; and we have acquainted ourselves with his suggestion that the rival hypotheses favoured by his opponents were not against his theory. We have also seen with what conditions this suggestion was qualified; these were to the effect that the original heterogeneity of light had to be preserved. At this point it might seem as if Newton would have accepted a wave picture of light, had it not been for his belief that such a picture would not make room for rectilinear propagation. It will, however, be shown in what follows that, owing to his conception of what constituted a ray of light, Newton was in fact committed to a corpuscular view. This Newton was not aware of, since he presented his conception as a doctrine completely neutral to any possible explanatory hypothesis regarding the nature of light.

That Newton made the contention that his *theory* of light was free from hypothetical elements is perfectly clear from his first paper, from his replies to his critics, from his letter to Oldenburg on the experimental method (which was published during the controversy about colours),[22] and from his later writings on optics. His declarations on the role of hypotheses, in this context, were not only connected with that contention but obviously assumed it: it was only because he believed that his own doctrine of light and colours did not go beyond a description of the experimental facts that he would not allow hypotheses more than a secondary role, namely that of *explaining* what has already been *discovered*.

Let us look into some examples. Newton wrote in his reply to Pardies' first letter:

I do not take it amiss that the Rev. Father calls my theory an hypothesis, inasmuch as he was not acquainted with it [*siquidem ipsi nondum constet*].

---

[21] Cf. E. Mach, *Principles of Physical Optics*, pp. 276–7.
[22] Cf. *Phil. Trans.*, No. 85, 15 July 1672, (English text) pp. 5004–5, (Latin translation) pp. 5006–7; *Correspondence*, I, pp. 208–11.

But my design was quite different, for it seems to contain only certain properties of light, which, now discovered, I think easy to be proved, and which if I had not considered them as true, I would rather have them rejected as vain and empty speculation, than acknowledged even as an hypothesis.[23]

This passage is of special importance because it contains Newton's first public reaction to the application of the word 'hypothesis' to his theory. It not only expresses Newton's belief that his doctrine was but a statement of some experimental facts, but also his attitude to hypotheses in general which we find developed in his later writings without fundamental alterations. The key to this attitude is clearly in the contrast which Newton draws between a hypothesis, a conjecture which can be at most probable, and truth, a property of propositions which are directly derived from experiments.[24] This was made even more clear in the following passage from his answer to Pardies' second letter; it is one of the longest and most important statements that Newton made on hypotheses.

In order to reply to these [Pardies' suggestions that Newton's experiments could be explained by the hypotheses of either Hooke or Grimaldi, without assuming the unequal refrangibilities of rays], it is to be noted that the Doctrine which I have expounded about Refraction and colours consists only in certain *Properties of Light* without considering *Hypotheses* by which these *Properties* should be explained. For the best and safest method of philosophizing seems to be, first diligently to investigate the properties of things and establish them by experiment, and then to proceed more slowly to hypotheses to explain them. For hypotheses ought to be fitted [*accomodari*] merely to explain the properties of things and not attempt to predetermine [*determinare*] them except in so far as they can be an aid to experiments [*nisi quatenus experimenta subministrare possint*]. If any one offers conjectures about the truth of things from the mere possibility of hypotheses, I do not see how anything certain can be determined in any science; for it is always possible to contrive [*excogitare*]

---

[23] *Isaac Newton's Papers & Letters*, p. 92; cf. *Correspondence*, I, p. 142.

[24] In the letter to Oldenburg of 6 July 1672, Newton wrote: 'You know the proper Method for inquiring after the properties of things is to deduce them from Experiments. And I told you that the Theory wch I propounded was evinced to me, *not by inferring tis thus because not otherwise*, that is not by deducing it onely from a confutation of contrary suppositions, but *by deriving it from Experiments concluding positively & directly*' (*Correspondence*, I, p. 209).

hypotheses, one after another, which are found to lead to new difficulties [*quæ novas difficultates suppeditare videbuntur*]. Wherefore I judged that one should abstain from considering hypotheses as from a fallacious argument [*tanquam improprio argumentandi Loco*], and that the force of their opposition must be removed, that one may arrive at a maturer and more general explanation.[25]

Apart from the assertion that the propounded doctrine did not involve any hypotheses, the following points emerge from the preceding passage which expounds in fact almost the whole of Newton's methodological position. It is first clear that he does not wish to confine the task of scientific inquiry to ascertaining the properties of things by observation and experiment; he allows for the task of explanation by means of hypotheses; he allows, that is, that one may attempt to explain the discovered properties by hypotheses. Nor does he wish to restrict the use of hypotheses to a stage in which they are merely fitted to explain the experimental facts and, so to speak, made to their measure. For he recognized that hypotheses may help to supply (*subministrare*) experiments that have not yet been performed. From this it appears that, according to Newton, hypotheses are not allowed in only one case: namely, when they are unjustifiably made to predetermine the properties of things. In other words hypotheses should not be maintained *against* what has been (or will be) experimentally established. Thus understood, Newton's advice presupposed two things. First, it presupposed his own interpretation of his experiments on dispersion, and in particular the *experimentum crucis*; this interpretation was to the effect that they *proved* the expounded doctrine of colours. Second, it presupposed the particular attitude taken by his critics towards his doctrine, especially their failure to grasp the full significance of the experimental results. That particular attitude itself presupposed (or was at least connected with) the Cartesian doctrine of hypotheses and, together with this, the Cartesian manner of attempting physical

---

[25] *Correspondence*, I, p. 164. Except for the first sentence and a few alterations the translation given here from the Latin original is that by Florian Cajori in the Appendix to his edition of Newton's *Principia*, p. 673. Compare the English translation in *Isaac Newton's Papers & Letters*, p. 106.

explanation. The latter, as we have seen, consisted in conjecturing hypotheses in terms of motion about the mode of production of natural phenomena, and then showing how they agreed with the observed facts. But then, Newton objects at the end of the passage, how can anything *certain* be determined in science? The Cartesian procedure appears to him to be an improper way of discovering truth; for the initial hypotheses will always remain in the realm of possibility even though their consequences may be shown to be true. Against this 'improper' method Newton therefore proposes what he believes to be the proper method, namely that in which the properties of things are derived with certainty from the observed facts of nature.

It is now clear that in order to declare the innocence of his theory of colours, Newton believed it was sufficient to divest it of the hypothesis regarding the corporeal nature of light. If we are still in any doubt about this, we need only look at his replies to Huygens. There we find him asserting that it was beside his purpose to explain colours hypothetically and that he

never intended to show wherein consists the nature and difference of colours, but onely to show that *de facto* they are originall & immutable qualities of the rays wch exhibit them, & to leave it to others to explicate by Mechanicall Hypotheses the nature & difference of those qualities; wch I take to be no very difficult matter.[26]

Less than three months afterwards, Newton presented a new formulation of his doctrine in which he described the proposition 'The Sun's light consists of rays differing by indefinite degrees of refrangibility' as a 'matter of fact'.[27] If we were now to agree that only statements expressly stating the corporeal (or wave) character of light are to be called 'hypotheses', then we should accept Newton's claim that his doctrine was indeed free from hypothetical elements. Such an agreement, however, would not be useful. It would turn us into victims of the illusion that by formulating his theory in terms of *rays* instead of *corpuscles*, Newton successfully made it neutral to

---

[26] Newton to Oldenburg, 3 April 1673, *Correspondence*, I, p. 264.
[27] Newton to Oldenburg, 23 June 1673, ibid., p. 293.

both corpuscular and wave interpretations. As will be seen presently, Newton's rays were always those of the corpuscular theory and were explicitly denied the meaning they would have in a wave theory. They were, in particular, conceived as discrete entities that could, in principle, be isolated from one another. In consequence, Newton's doctrine of the original heterogeneity of light as expressed in terms of such rays was denied, *a priori*, a wave interpretation. Huygens was therefore right in the reservations he expressed against Newton's doctrine: he was right in regarding it as a hypothesis that was greatly confirmed by the experiments without thereby reaching the factual status assigned to it by Newton.

Newton produced the following as a neutral definition of rays of light in his second reply to Pardies:

By light [*Lumen*] therefore I understand, any being or power of a being, whether a substance or any power, action, or quality of it, which proceeding directly from a lucid body, is apt to excite vision. And by the rays of light I understand its least or indefinitely small parts [*et per radios Luminis intelligo minimas vel quaslibet indefinitè parva sejus partes*], which are independent of each other; such as are all those rays which lucid bodies emit in right lines, either successively or all together. For the collateral as well as the successive parts of light are independent; since some of the parts may be intercepted without the others, and be separately reflected or refracted towards different sides.[28]

We find the same definition, in slightly different and clearer terms, in the beginning of the *Opticks* (1704). There, too, it is immediately preceded by the declaration that the design of the author 'is not to explain the Properties of Light by Hypotheses, but to propose and prove them by Reason and Experiments'.[29] It is as follows:

By the Rays of Light I understand its least Parts, and those as well Successive in the same Lines, as Contemporary in several Lines. For it is manifest that Light consists of Parts, both Successive and Contemporary ; because in the same place you may stop that which comes one moment, and let pass

---

[28] *Isaac Newton's Papers & Letters*, pp. 106–7; cf. *Correspondence*, I, p. 164.
[29] Newton, *Opticks*, p. 1.

that which comes presently after ; and in the same time you may stop it in any one place, and let it pass in any other. For that part of Light which is stopp'd cannot be the same with that which is let pass. The least Light or part of Light, which may be stopp'd alone without the rest of the Light, or propagated alone, or do or suffer any thing alone, which the rest of the Light doth not or suffers not, I call a Ray of Light.[30]

Newton is here thinking of something like the following situation. A beam of light is let through a small hole. By making the hole narrower and narrower, more and more of the light arriving simultaneously at the hole is intercepted and only some of it is allowed to pass. At the same time a cogwheel (say) rotates in front of the hole. The light which arrives at a moment when the hole is closed is reflected backwards, whereas that which has just escaped proceeds forward. So far there seems to be no reason why Newton should not interpret this experiment to indicate that light has 'parts', without thereby necessarily prejudicing his conception of light towards one theory or another. But what does he mean by the 'least' or 'indefinitely small' parts of the light? For what is being made indefinitely smaller and smaller is, in the first operation, a region of space and, in the second, an interval of time. Newton is obviously making the assumption that this double process by which the beam is being chopped both spatially and temporally may be imagined to come to an end before the hole is completely closed. Thus by making the hole narrow enough only those rays coming successively in the same line will be let through. And, further, by making the interval during which the hole is open sufficiently small, only one of these rays will escape. It was this assumption which made Newton's critics suspect that his rays (of which the passage from the reply to Pardies said that they are entities independent of one another and which the doctrine endowed with various original colours and degrees of refrangibility) were simply the corpuscles, in spite of Newton's refusal to attach the proper label upon them.

The preceding interpretation of Newton's rays is confirmed by the

---

[30] Ibid., pp. 1–2.

explicit statement in the *Opticks* that they were not the straight lines of geometrical (and wave) optics,[31] and further by the fact that in his free speculations on the nature of light in the Queries at the end of that book, Newton never permits that light may consist of waves. At most, he allows that vibrations in an ethereal medium may play a complementary part—for example by putting the rays into 'fits'—but they never constitute light. As to the rays themselves, they understandably turned out in the Queries to be the corpuscles. We are led to discuss the nature of these next.

4. In what sense were colours asserted by Newton to be original *qualities* of the rays? Huygens, it will be remembered, remarked that even if the rays were from their origin endowed with colours, it would still be necessary to explain in mechanical terms wherein the diversity of colours consists. Newton on the other hand, realizing the uncertain and unstable character of hypotheses, had preferred to speak of light in general terms:

And for the same reason I chose to speake of colours according to the information of our senses, as if they were qualities of light without us. Whereas by that Hypothesis [of the corporeity of light which Hooke and the others attributed to him] I must have considered them rather as modes of sensation excited in the mind by various motions figures or sizes of the corpuscles of light making various Mechanicall impressions on the Organ of Sense. . . .[32]

Although Newton does not actually assert here that colours are in fact qualities of light existing outside our minds, his words must have sounded sinfully un-Cartesian to Huygens: how could anyone speak of colours as if they were qualities without us? Had not

---

[31] Newton, *Opticks*, p. 2: 'Mathematicians usually consider the Rays of Light to be Lines reaching from the luminous Body to the Body illuminated, and the refraction of those Rays to be the bending or breaking of those lines in their passing out of one Medium into another. And thus may Rays and Refractions be considered, *if Light be propagated in an instant.*' Newton remarked, however, that the last condition (my italics) had been proved false by Roemer. Cf. ibid., p. 2 and p. 277.

[32] *Correspondence*, I, p. 174 (Answer to Hooke's Considerations).

qualities been completely exorcised from matter once and for all? Had they not been very strictly confined to the mind? And, further, what does it mean that colours are to be understood as qualities of the rays 'according to the information of our Senses'? For our senses inform us that colours are qualities of things, not of light. But this is precisely what Newton's doctrine denies; since natural bodies appear in the dark in any colour which they happen to be illuminated with, it is concluded that these bodies are only variously disposed to reflect one sort of rays rather than another. Are colours then qualities of the rays in the same sense in which they *appear* to be qualities of natural objects?

Some writers have answered this question for Newton in the affirmative. M. Roberts and E. R. Thomas, for example, have explained Newton's preceding passage in the following words: 'That is, he has spoken of colours as if they were qualities of light independent of any observer—that is to say, he has regarded light as a primary property, not a secondary property which must be explained as a sensation produced by the action of the primary matter on the sense organs.'[33] And, as if trying to convince the reader that Newton had himself made up for his blunder, the same authors have added: 'His own work had, of course, made it possible to replace a description of colour by a numerical statement of refrangibility.'[34]

Émile Meyerson has also expressed the opinion, to which he was presumably led by similar statements to the one just quoted from Newton, that there is an obvious affinity between Newton's light corpuscles and the qualitative atoms of the seventeenth-century philosopher, Claude G. Berigard.[35] Meyerson[36] describes Berigard's doctrine as a legitimate development of peripatetic philosophy though it was also atomistic; it hypostatized qualities and conceived

---

[33] M. Roberts and E. R. Thomas, *Newton and the Origin of Colours*, p. 97, note 1.

[34] Ibid.

[35] Émile Meyerson, *Identity and Reality*, translated by Kate Loewenberg, London and New York, 1930, p. 334: 'The "caloric", semi-material fluid, bearer of a quality, belongs to the same family as phlogiston, and the relation of Newton's luminous corpuscles to the qualitative atoms of Berigard is equally obvious.'

[36] Cf. ibid., p. 329.

them as atoms. To explain the infinite diversity of the perceptible world, Berigard supposed an infinite variety of elements which he understood as spherical corpuscles each representing an elementary quality. These corpuscles were thus atom-qualities or corporeal qualities (*qualitates corporatae*) which conferred upon bodies their properties as for example (we may add) Newton's rays conferred colour upon them.

Now although Newton's position as he expressed it in 1672 was certainly ambiguous, Meyerson's interpretation of it is no doubt exaggerated.[37] A clearer statement of what Newton in fact wanted to maintain is to be found in the *Opticks*. There he makes it clear that the rays are not bearers of colours (coloriferous), as Berigard's corpuscles would be, but rather makers or producers of colour (colorific) by their action on the sensorium. Properly speaking, colours are, in the rays, *dispositions* to excite this or that sensation.[38] Newton's assertion that the rays are endowed with colour should

---

[37] Gaston Bachelard has passed this judgement on Meyerson's opinion. Cf. *L'activité rationaliste de la physique contemporaine*, Paris, 1951, p. 33. See also Léon Bloch, *La philosophie de Newton*, Paris, 1908, pp. 359–60.

[38] Newton, *Opticks*, Bk. I, Pt. I, Definition, pp. 124–5: 'The homogeneal Light and Rays which appear red, or rather make Objects appear so, I call Rubrifick or Red-making; those which make Objects appear yellow, green, blue, and violet, I call Yellow-making, Green-making, Blue-making, Violet-making, and so of the rest. . . . For the rays to speak properly are not coloured. In them there is nothing else than a certain Power and Disposition to stir up a Sensation of this or that Colour. For as Sound in a Bell or musical String, or other sounding Body, is nothing but a trembling Motion, and in the Air nothing but that Motion propagated from the Object, and in the Sensorium 'tis a Sense of that Motion under the Form of Sound; so Colours in the Object are nothing but a Disposition to reflect this or that sort of Rays more copiously than the rest; in the Rays they are nothing but their Dispositions to propagate this or that Motion into the Sensorium, and in the Sensorium they are Sensations of those Motions under the Forms of Colours.' See also ibid., Bk. I, Pt. II, Prop. V, Theor. IV, Exper. 12, p. 146. In the Waste Sheets, of probably 1676–7 (see above, p. 244, n. 32), Newton wrote: 'Understand therefore these expressions [i.e. substance, qualities, etc.] to be used here in respect of the Peripatetick Philosophy. For I do not my self esteem colours the qualities of light, or of anything else without us, but modes of sensation excited in our minds by light. Yet because they are generally attributed to things without us, to comply in some measure with this notion, I have in other places of these letters, attributed them to the rays rather than to bodies, calling the rays from their effect on the sense, red, yellow, &c. whereas they might be more properly called rubriform, flaviform, &c.' (*Correspondence*, I, p. 106). In the Note-Book of 1661–5 he already spoke of the rays as colour-making rather than colour-bearing, and he was already associating colours with mechanical properties of the light globules (cf. A. R. Hall, *Cambridge Historical Journal*, IX, 1948, p. 247; above, p. 247, and n. 41). Similarly, in the 1665–93 Note-Book, Newton wrote: 'I call those blew or red rays &c, wch make ye Phantome of such colours' (quoted by A. R. Hall, *Annals of Science*, XI, 1955, p. 28).

not, therefore, be taken literally; when he makes this assertion he is speaking roughly, not properly: 'And if at any time I speak of Light and Rays as coloured or endued with Colours, I would be understood to speak not philosophically and properly, but grossly, and accordingly to such Conceptions as vulgar People in seeing all these Experiments would be apt to frame.'[39]

At the same time it would not be a correct description of Newton's position to say that he was completely satisfied with replacing colours by their measurable degrees of refrangibility; that colours were sufficiently *explained* by substituting the difference in refrangibility for the difference in colour. He himself explicitly denied this in one of his replies to Huygens:

But I would not be understood, as if their difference [i.e. the difference of colours] consisted in the different refrangibility of those rays. For that different refrangibility conduces to their production no otherwise than by separating the rays whose qualities they are.[40]

That is to say, the difference in refrangibility only explains the *position* of the colour on the spectrum; it helps in the production of colours only by sorting out the rays which already possess those qualities, or rather the dispositions to excite the corresponding sensations in the sensorium. But this means that Huygens' demand for a physical explanation of colours still remains unsatisfied. Had Newton's intention in regarding colours as qualities of the rays been clarified to him, he would have still asked what those *dispositions* of the rays to produce the various colours consisted in. This question would have been the same as the question in which, as we have seen, he was asking for a theory in which a definite physical (or mechanical) property would represent the various colours and, if possible, would explain that 'accident', their degrees of refrangibility.[41]

Newton, however, always refrained from offering a direct and definite answer to Huygens' question. Just as he wished to speak

---

[39] *Opticks*, p. 124.
[40] *Correspondence*, I, pp. 264–5.
[41] See above, p. 271.

of colours in 1672 'according to the information of our senses', he also preferred to speak in the *Opticks* (1704) 'not philosophically and properly' but as the 'vulgar' would speak. He knew that speaking philosophically would inevitably be in terms of a particular view about the nature of light. But as this would explicitly tie up his theory with a *contestable hypothesis*, he preferred to expound the allegedly *experimentally proved* properties of light in dispositional terms. Nevertheless, he indulged in an attempt to answer Huygens' question—by way of a 'query'—at the end of the *Opticks*, thus admitting at least the validity of Huygens' demand, and making explicit the physical nature of his rays:

Nothing more is requisite for producing all the variety of Colours, and degrees of Refrangibility, than that the Rays of Light be Bodies of different Sizes, the least of which may take violet the weakest and darkest of the Colours, and be more easily diverted by refracting Surfaces from the right Course; and the rest as they are bigger and bigger, may make the stronger and more lucid Colours, blue, green, yellow, and red, and be more and more difficultly diverted.[42]

Physiologically, the light corpuscles produce the various colour sensations by exciting in the optic nerves vibrations of various bignesses according to their different sizes. The smallest and most refrangible corpuscles (for violet) excite the shortest vibrations; the largest and least refrangible (for red) excite the largest vibrations; and the corpuscles of intermediate sizes and degrees of refrangibility excite vibrations of intermediate bignesses to produce the intermediate colours.[43]

5. Having seen that Newton's conception of rays was, from the beginning, that of the corpuscular theory, we can now understand his interpretation of the *experimentum crucis*. It had been generally assumed before Newton that colours are created as a result of light

---

[42] Newton, *Opticks*, Query 29, p. 372.
[43] Cf. ibid., Queries 12 and 13, pp. 345–6. These two Queries are formulated in terms of rays, not of corpuscles; but they have to be understood in the light of Query 29 which was added in the second edition of the *Opticks* (1706).

coming into contact with reflecting or refracting bodies. Thus Descartes explained the generation of colours by the rotatory motion which the ethereal globules acquire when, under certain conditions, they obliquely strike a refracting surface. Grimaldi, for whom light was a fluid substance, made colours depend on the undulatory motions which are excited in the fluid when it meets with obstacles. Hooke attributed colours to the disturbing influence of refraction on the pulses which are originally simple and uniform. Newton argued that if colours were modifications of light due to the action of the reflecting or refracting bodies, then these bodies should produce the same effects whether the light falling on them has been already disturbed or not. But this consequence was proved false by the *experimentum crucis*: the rays emerging from the first prism preserved their respective colours and degrees of refrangibility upon their refraction through the second prism. Therefore, Newton concluded, colours must be unalterable properties of the rays and, consequently, white light must be an aggregate of rays that already possess those properties.

This conclusion, however, does not follow from the experiment. What the experiment does prove is that the light emerging from the first prism behaves differently from the light coming directly from the sun. But it does not prove that the properties of the refracted light exist primarily and unaltered in white light. It might well be that those properties are manufactured out of white light by the first prism but, once generated, they are not alterable by further refractions. The problem of how to represent white light thus remains open; it cannot be solved solely on the basis of Newton's experiment. In Gouy's interpretation, for example, white light is conceived as a succession of isolated pulses which do not possess the regularities characteristic of monochromatic light. Anticipating Gouy's interpretation, Hooke suggested that the composition of white light might be the kind of composition in which the component elements neutralize one another. But this suggestion Newton found 'unintelligible'; indeed, to him, any interpretation of light in wave terms was 'impossible'.

Newton was perhaps justified in his view of Hooke's suggestion by the backward state of the wave theory of his time. This only explains, however, his rejection of Hooke's idea; it does not account for his inclination towards a corpuscular interpretation of light in which the colours are original properties of the rays. Why, then, did Newton prefer such an interpretation?

Newton was an atomist who believed that matter is composed of hard and permanent particles which are endowed with various properties from the beginning of creation. The properties of natural things, on this conception, depend on the connate properties of the ultimate particles which go into their constitution. Natural changes consist, not in the creation or annulment of properties, but in the separating and combining of the particles.[44] These operations merely result in making manifest or concealing the original properties. From this point of view the dispersion of light by a prism could be readily explained: the prism simply *separates* the mixed corpuscles and, as a result, colours appear. Since the colours and their degrees of refrangibility are not altered by further refractions, no further separations seem to be possible and it is inferred that the colours on the spectrum and their degrees of refrangibility are connate properties of the corpuscles. The function of the prism thus consists in sorting out the corpuscles with respect to two of their original properties, colour and refrangibility.

---

[44] Newton, *Opticks*, Query 31, p. 400: '. . . it seems probable to me, that God in the beginning form'd Matter in solid, massy, hard, impenetrable, moveable Particles, of such Sizes and Figures, and with such other Properties, and in such Proportion to Space, as most conduced to the End for which he form'd them . . . While the Particles continue entire, they may compose Bodies of one and the same Nature and Texture in all Ages: But should they wear away, or break in pieces, the Nature of Things depending on them, would be changed . . . And therefore, that Nature may be lasting, the Changes of corporeal Things are to be placed only in the various Separations and new Associations and Motions of these permanent Particles.' Newton's belief in atomism has been generally recognized for a long time. His early attraction to this doctrine—as is shown by his first Note-Book of 1661–5—has been pointed out, first by A. R. Hall (*Cambridge Historical Journal*, IX, 1948, pp. 243–4) and more recently by R. S. Westfall (*British Journal for the History of Science*, I, 1962, pp. 171ff). What is not generally realized is that Newton's specific doctrine of white light cannot be deduced from the *experimentum crucis* without adding his belief in atomism as a necessary premise. It should be noted, moreover, that not only refrangibility and colour, but also reflexibility, polarity and (as we shall see in Ch. XIII) the 'fits' of easy reflection and of easy transmission are viewed as *original* properties of the rays. Thus Newton's explanations of all light phenomena exhibit one invariable pattern which is perfectly in keeping with the kind of atomism outlined in the passage just quoted from Query 31.

The history of science has shown that this is not the only possible interpretation of the experiment, but it should be remembered that, in Newton's time, atomism provided the picture in terms of which the clearest representation of white light could be most easily conceived without running into serious difficulties.

Chapter Twelve

THE TWO LEVELS OF EXPLANATION: NEWTON'S THEORY OF REFRACTION

In this and the following chapter two more examples from Newton's researches in optics are discussed in turn. These are his theory of refraction and his theory of the colours of thin transparent plates. It will be shown that, apart from determining the experimental laws governing the phenomena in question, Newton proposed two kinds of explanation occurring on two different levels which he carefully distinguished from one another. According to him, the explanations of the first level are *theories* propounding only certain properties of light which have been deduced from the phenomena; that is, they are positive discoveries which are to be accepted irrespective of whatever opinion one might have concerning the nature of light; these theories therefore have the same value as that which he attributed to his doctrine of the original heterogeneity of light. Such is his explanation of the experimental law of refraction by the existence of a force acting perpendicularly at the refracting surface, and his explanation of the colours of thin bodies in terms of certain states or dispositions of the rays which he called their 'fits' of easy reflection and easy transmission.

The explanations proposed on the second, higher, level constitute merely an attempt to show how the refracting force and the fits themselves, whose existence is taken for granted, could possibly be accounted for. They are avowedly tentative explanations, or *hypotheses*, whose truth or falsity is regarded as irrelevant to the truth of the theories asserted on the first, lower, level.

Newton's radical distinction between these two levels of explanation is interesting in that it clearly reveals the logical status which he conferred upon his theories, and it helps towards an understanding of his view that scientific theories should be deduced from experiments rather than assumed or conjectured. It also provides an instructive illustration of his simultaneous appreciation of what role or roles hypotheses might possibly have in scientific procedure. Our main purpose will be to examine Newton's explanations of refraction and of the colours of thin plates, and to see whether the theories proposed on the first level were in fact obtained by a method such as that advocated by him, that is, whether they were purely experimental discoveries.

1. The law of refraction first appears at the beginning of Newton's *Opticks* as one of the eight Axioms or propositions giving 'the sum of what hath hitherto been treated of in Opticks. For what hath been generally agreed on I content my self to assume under the notion of Principles, in order to what I have farther to write'.[1] The form of the law as given in that place is the following: '*The Sine of Incidence is either accurately or very nearly in a given Ratio to the Sine of Refraction.*'[2] One might think that the cautious qualification 'either accurately or very nearly' is merely due to the fact that the law is stated here without reference to the unequal refrangibilities of differently coloured rays. But Newton later formulates the law in such a way as to take that fact into account: Proposition VI of Bk. I, Pt. I in fact reads '*The Sine of Incidence of every Ray considered apart, is to its Sine of Refraction in a given Ratio*'.[3] Nevertheless, and although he describes an 'experimental Proof'[4] of the sine law in this qualified and correct form, he is still not willing to accept the truth of the law 'as far as appears by Experiment', but wants to 'demonstrate' that it is 'accurately true'.[5] In other words, he wants to provide a demonstration in which the law is *rigorously* deduced from some assumption, as distinguished from a table of experimental readings which, alone, do not warrant the establishment of a *mathematical* ratio. This demonstration he bases on the following 'supposition': '*That Bodies refract Light by acting upon its Rays in Lines perpendicular to their Surfaces.*'[6] Obviously, this assertion involves an *explanation* of refraction in terms of a perpendicular force.

---

[1] Newton, *Opticks*, Bk. I, Pt. I, pp. 19–20.   [2] Ibid., Bk. I, Pt. I, Axiom V, p. 5.
[3] Ibid., p. 75.   [4] Ibid., pp. 76–79.   [5] Ibid., p. 79.   [6] Ibid.

There is a definite and interesting relation between the Newtonian explanation of refraction and Descartes' proof of the sine law; a relation which Newton was aware of but which has not been adequately defined.[7] Let us first quote what Newton himself had to say about the Cartesian proof in the *Optical Lectures* of 1669–71:[8]

The Ancients determined Refractions by the Means of the Angles, which the Incident and refracted Rays made with the Perpendicular of the refracting Plane, as if those Angles had a given Ratio . . . the Ancients supposed, that the Angle of Incidence . . ., the Angle of Refraction . . ., and the refracted Angle . . . are always in a certain given Ratio, or they rather believed it was a sufficiently accurate Hypothesis, when the Rays did not much divaricate from the Perpendicular . . . . But this estimating of the Refractions was found not to be sufficiently accurate, to be made a Fundamental of Dioptricks. And *Cartes* was the first, that thought of another Rule, whereby it might be more exactly determined, by making the Sines of the said Angles to be in a giving Ratio . . . The Truth whereof the Author had demonstrated not inelegantly, provided he had left no room to doubt of the Physical Causes, which he assumed.[9]

The last sentence in this passage in fact foreshadows the kind of relationship that was going to hold between the Cartesian proof and Newton's explanation as he published it, first in the *Principia* (about eighteen years after this passage had been written), and later in the *Opticks*. Newton, in strong contrast to Fermat, has no objections against Descartes' demonstration; indeed he finds it 'not inelegant'. Quite naturally, however, he displays a reserved attitude towards the 'physical Causes', that is, the mechanical considerations that were

---

[7] E. W. Whittaker has the following remark on the relation between Descartes' and Newton's demonstrations of the law of refraction: 'Newton's proof of the law of refraction, in *Opticks*, i, prop. 6, does not differ greatly in principle from Descartes' proof' (*A History of The Theories of Æther and Electricity*, the classical theories, Edinburgh, 1951, p. 20, note 1).

[8] See above, p. 237, n. 14.

[9] Newton, *Optical Lectures*, London, 1728, Sec. II, pp. 46–47. It is seen from this passage that in 1669–71 (see above, p. 37, n. 14) Newton attributed the discovery of the sine law to Descartes. He also attributed the demonstration of the law to Descartes in 1675 (see letter to Oldenburg, 7 December 1676, in *Correspondence of Isaac Newton*, ed. Turnbull, I, p. 371). When the *Principia* was published (in 1687) he had adopted the view, first expressed in print by Isaac Vossius in 1662, that Descartes had got the law from Snell and merely exhibited it in a different form. Cf., on Vossius, J. F. Scott, *The Scientific Work of René Descartes*, pp. 36–37. See below, p. 304.

involved in it. What Newton showed later was that if refraction is given a dynamical interpretation, then the mathematical assumptions in Descartes' proof and the conclusion to which they lead (i.e. the law giving the sines in inverse ratio to the velocities) become perfectly acceptable.

For let us look at refraction from a dynamical point of view and assume that the ray of light is something or other which obeys Newton's second law of motion. The fact that the ray changes direction in passing from one medium into another will mean, according to that law, that there is a force acting at the surface of separation. Further, since a ray falling perpendicularly on a refracting surface passes through in the same line without suffering any deflection, we will conclude that the force acts only in the direction of the normal to the surface—it has no components in any other direction. Therefore, when the ray falls obliquely, only the perpendicular component of its velocity will be accelerated or retarded according as the perpendicular force is directed towards or away from the refracting medium; and thus Descartes' assumption asserting the conservation of the parallel component of the ray's velocity is preserved. Whether the refracting force is directed towards the medium of refraction or away from it will be indicated by the manner in which the ray is deflected: if the deflection is towards the normal, the perpendicular force must be acting towards the refracting body and consequently the velocity must have been increased; and if the deflection is away from the normal, the force must be acting in the opposite sense, and the velocity must have been diminished. Finally, since we observe that light passing from a rare medium like air into a denser medium such as water or glass is deflected towards the normal, we will conclude that the velocity of light in water or glass is greater than in air, also in accordance with Descartes' proof. Thus the proposition that the velocity of light is greater in denser media is seen to be an *inevitable* result of the supposition that refraction is caused by a *perpendicular* force.

But, so far, we have not established that the velocity in the refracting medium will be to the velocity of incidence in a *constant* ratio. Had Newton simply *assumed* that proposition (as Descartes did), his demonstration of the sine law would have run as follows: Having considered that the refracting force acts only in the direction of the normal to the surface, the following proposition is to be asserted, namely, that

(1) $$v_i \sin i = v_r \sin r,$$

where i, r are the angles of incidence and of refraction; and v_i, v_r the velocities of incidence and of refraction respectively.

Further, *assuming* that

(2) $$v_r = n \, v_i$$

(where n is a constant), it follows:

(3) $$\frac{\sin i}{\sin r} = \frac{v_r}{v_i} = n.$$

It is seen that this demonstration exactly coincides with the Cartesian deduction of the same conclusion (3),[10] with the one difference that here the word *force* is explicitly introduced in virtue of the initial supposition that the ray follows the laws of dynamics. This would not have constituted a significant advance on the Cartesian treatment. But the important merit of Newton's demonstration, as will be seen presently, is that, by providing an *independent* expression E for the refracting force, that is, an expression which does not presuppose equation (2) above, it established for the first time a connection between equations (1) and (2) which were in the Cartesian theory entirely unrelated. On the basis of E and assumption (1), Newton deduces the sine law in the form 'sin $i = n$ sin r'; and this result, again in conjunction with (1), allows him to obtain Descartes' law (3) as well as equation (2). One more advantage gained by introducing the expression E is that it further allows Newton to calculate the refractive power of a given medium,[11] such a calculation being impossible to perform in the Cartesian theory.

Before giving a detailed account of Newton's demonstration in the *Opticks*, it will be instructive to look at the character of that demonstration as it was first published in the *Principia*. At the end of Bk. I, in Section XIV (dealing with '*The motion of very small bodies*

---

[10] See above, p. 111.   [11] See Newton, *Opticks*, Bk. II, Pt. III, Prop. X, pp. 270–6.

when agitated by centripetal forces tending to the several parts of any great body'),[12] Newton considers (in Prop. XCIV) an imaginary situation in which a moving particle passes through a region of space that is terminated by two parallel planes. When the particle arrives at the first plane, it is assumed to be 'attracted or impelled'[13] by a perpendicular force whose action is the same at equal distances from either plane (referring always to the same one). The influence of this force does not extend outside the terminated region and the particle is not disturbed at any point of its journey by any other force. Since the acting force is, like that of gravity, a constant one, the particle will describe a parabola composed of the unaltered parallel component of the incident velocity and the accelerated or retarded motion in the perpendicular direction. The particle will emerge through the second plane tangentially to the element of the parabola at that plane. Newton demonstrates that the direction of emergence out of the terminated region will make with the normal an angle whose sine is to the sine of incidence on the first plane in a given ratio.

The next Proposition (Prop. XCV) further proves that, the same things being supposed, *the velocity of the particle after emergence will be to the velocity of incidence* (before the particle enters the region) *as the sine of incidence to the sine of emergence*. But since the preceding Proposition asserts that the sines will be in a given ratio, it follows that the ratio of the velocities will also be constant.

Suppose now (as is considered in Prop. XCVI) that the velocity of emergence is less than the velocity of incidence; this means that the perpendicular force is directed from the second plane towards the first and that the parabola described by the particle is convex towards the second. As soon as the particle enters the region, the perpendicular component of its motion will be gradually retarded until (if at all) the farther plane is reached and the particle emerges with a velocity composed of the original parallel velocity and what is left of the original normal component. Newton shows that if the angle of incidence is continually increased, the particle will be finally

---

[12] Newton, *Principia*, p. 226.   [13] Ibid.

reflected at an angle equal to the angle of incidence. This will happen when the perpendicular component of the incident velocity is so small that it will be completely lost before the particle escapes from the region of the force's influence. At the point where the normal velocity is lost, the particle will momentarily move in a direction parallel to either plane but will immediately be forced to move symmetrically backwards to the first plane, through which it will emerge with a velocity composed of the original parallel component and a perpendicular component that is equal in magnitude but opposite in direction to the corresponding component in incidence.

Nothing is said about light in particular in any of Newton's demonstrations of the preceding Propositions; but, as he himself remarks in the Scholium to Prop. XCVI,

These attractions bear a great resemblance to the reflections and re-fractions of light made in a given ratio of the secants, as was discovered by *Snell*; and consequently in a given ratio of the sines, as was exhibited by Descartes.[14]

Thus, although Propositions XCIV–XCVI do not refer to any particular real situation, we may assume that they have been developed with the purpose that they may be of help in the investigation of the properties of light.

How then are these Propositions applied in the explanation of optical refraction?

In the *Principia*, the terminated region is supposed to lie in the midst of one and the same medium, and the distance between the two parallel planes may be of any finite magnitude. If now we assume that the interface separating two dissimilar media (e.g. air

---

[14] Newton, *Principia*, p. 229. If the angles of incidence and of refraction are taken to be the angles made with the normal to the refracting surface, then the given ratio must be between the cosecants (not the secants) of those angles. If therefore Snell's law, as here expressed by Newton, is to be correct at all, the angles whose *secants* are in a constant ratio must be measured by the inclinations of the incident and refracted rays to the interface, that is by the angles $(90° - i)$ and $(90° - r)$, where i and r are the angles made with the normal. See Snell's formulation of the law above, p. 100, n. 12.

and glass) lies somewhere between two *very near* parallel planes, and that a ray of light passing through the terminating planes suffers the same action as the particle (and no other action), we will come to the same conclusions about the ray as we have about the particle. Hence, in the *Opticks*, Newton lays down the following proposition concerning the motion of a ray of light falling on any refracting surface:

If any Motion or moving thing whatsoever be incident with any Velocity on any broad and thin space terminated on both sides by two parallel Planes, and in its Passage through that space be urged perpendicularly towards the farther Plane by any force which at given distances from the Plane is of given Quantities; the perpendicular velocity of that Motion or Thing, at its emerging out of that space, shall be always equal to the square Root of the sum of the square of the perpendicular velocity of that Motion or Thing at its Incidence on that space; and of the square of the perpendicular velocity which that Motion or Thing would have at its Emergence, if at its Incidence its perpendicular velocity was infinitely little.[15]

This obviously reduces optical refraction to the imaginary situation examined in *Principia*; except that the thinness of the terminated space is here assumed owing to the fact that no *sensible* curvature of the rays' path is normally observed near refracting surfaces.

The equation stated in the above passage (expression *E* referred to before) is the familiar law for constant acceleration:

$$v = \sqrt{u^2 + 2gs},$$

where *v* is the final velocity (i.e. the *perpendicular* velocity at the emergence from the farther plane), *u* the initial velocity (i.e. the *perpendicular* velocity at the incidence on the first plane), *s* the distance covered (between the two planes), and *g* is a constant.

Putting $s = 1$ and equating $2g$ with some constant *f*, we get the following by squaring the two sides of the equation:

$$(1) \qquad\qquad v^2 = u^2 + f.$$

---

[15] Newton, *Opticks*, Bk. I, Pt. I, pp. 79–80. As Newton immediately adds, if the motion is retarded, then the difference of the squares should be taken instead of their sum.

To determine f, Newton considers a case in which u is nearly equal to zero. For such a case, when the incident ray is almost parallel to the refracting surface, we have:

(2) $$v^2 = f,$$

where v is the perpendicular velocity of the refracted ray.

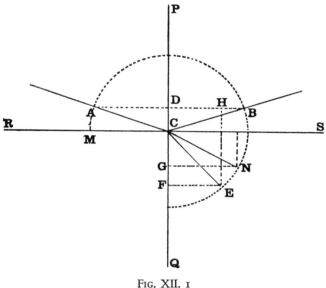

FIG. XII. 1

Suppose then[16] that a ray falling along the line MC (Fig. XII. 1) impinges on the refracting surface RS at C making an angle with the normal PQ almost equal to 90°, and is refracted into the line CN. QCN is thus a *given* angle.

The refracted ray along CN will have a horizontal velocity equal to the velocity of incidence, the latter being unaffected (or very little affected) in this case by the action of the refracting force. It will also have a perpendicular velocity v given by:

(3) $$v = \frac{MC}{GN} \times CG$$

---

[16] Newton, *Opticks*, Bk. I, Pt. I, pp. 80–81.

(on the assumption that MC represents the velocity of incidence and that this is equal to the horizontal component, along GN, of the refracted velocity along CN).

Therefore, from (3) and (2), we obtain:

(4) $$v^2 = \frac{MC^2}{GN^2} \times CG^2 = f.$$

Now if AC is any other incident ray, the problem is to find the line CE into which it will be refracted.

The perpendicular velocity of the refracted ray will be equal to

$$\frac{AD}{FE} \times CF$$

(again on the assumption that the parallel component AD of the incident velocity AC is unchanged by refraction). Putting $u = CD$ in (1), it follows from (1) and (4) that the perpendicular velocity

$$\frac{AD}{FE} \times CF = \sqrt{CD^2 + \frac{MC^2}{NG^2} \times CG^2},$$

i.e.

$$\frac{AD^2}{FE^2} \times CF^2 = CD^2 + \frac{MC^2}{NG^2} \times CG^2.$$

Adding the equals AD^2 and $(MC^2 - CD^2)$, we obtain:

$$AD^2 + \frac{AD^2}{EF^2} \times CF^2 = MC^2 - CD^2 + CD^2 + \frac{MC^2}{NG^2} \times CG^2,$$

so that

$$\frac{(EF^2 \times AD^2) + (AD^2 \times CF^2)}{EF^2} = \frac{(NG^2 \times MC^2) + (MC^2 \times CG^2)}{NG^2},$$

that is,

$$\frac{AD^2}{EF^2}(EF^2 + CF^2) = \frac{MC^2}{NG^2}(NG^2 + CG^2).$$

But since

$$EF^2 + CF^2 = NG^2 + CG^2,$$

therefore,

$$\frac{AD^2}{EF^2} = \frac{MC^2}{NG^2} = \frac{CN^2}{NG^2}$$

(CN being equal to MC).

But, since AD represents sin i, EF represents sin r, and $\dfrac{CN}{NG}$ is the cosecant of the *given* angle NCG, it follows that

$$\frac{\sin i}{\sin r} = \frac{CN}{NG} = n, \text{ a constant.}$$

Or,

$$\sin i = n \sin r,$$

the result obtained by Newton. He does not derive in the *Opticks* a relation of the sines in terms of the velocities. But such a relation can be deduced by combining the last result with the assumption which we have been making throughout, namely, that

$$v_i \sin i = v_r \sin r,$$

and we finally get:

$$\frac{\sin i}{\sin r} = \frac{v_r}{v_i} = n,$$

as in Descartes' proof.

2. At the end of the preceding demonstration Newton writes:

And this Demonstration being general, without determining what Light is, or by what kind of Force it is refracted, or assuming any thing farther than that the refracting Body acts upon the Rays in Lines perpendicular to its Surface; I take it to be a very convincing Argument of the full truth of this Proposition.[17]

This comment has to be understood in conjunction with the declaration at the beginning of Book I (where the demonstration in question occurs):

My Design in this Book is not to explain the Properties of Light by Hypotheses, but to propose and prove them by Reason and Experiment.[18]

We may thus gather that, for Newton, the 'supposition' or 'assumption' on which his demonstration (or, as we have regarded it,

---

[17] Newton, *Opticks*, Bk. I, Pt. I, pp. 81–82. The expression 'this proposition' refers to the sine law in the form 'sin $i = n$ sin r'.
[18] Ibid., p. 1.

explanation) rests, is not a hypothesis. It is not a hypothesis because it does not determine what the *nature* of light is or by what *kind* of force it is refracted. The phenomenon of refraction indicates to him the existence of *a* perpendicular force acting at the refracting surface. From the force as assumption he deduces the sine law whose 'full truth' is thereby established. This ends, as far as refraction is concerned, the double process of 'analysis' and 'synthesis' of which Newton speaks in the *Opticks* as the proper method of investigating natural phenomena.[19] But to determine *a priori*, and without sufficient evidence from experiments, what the nature of the refracting force is—*that* would be a hypothesis.[20]

Although Newton was convinced that his demonstration of the law of refraction did not need a hypothesis to explain it, he in fact indulged in what he himself regarded as hypothetical explanations of refraction. These were of two opposite types, the one being in terms of an *impulsive* force due to the action of an ethereal medium and the other involving the idea of action at a distance.

An explanation of refraction of the former type was first proposed by Newton in a paper presented to the Royal Society on 9 December 1675 containing 'An Hypothesis Explaining the Properties of Light'.[21] In this hypothesis Newton imagines an ethereal medium similar to air, but far rarer, subtler and much more elastic than air. He still does not determine what light itself is, believing that if he abstains from pronouncing on this point, his hypothesis 'will become so generall & comprehensive of other Hypotheses as to leave little room for new ones to be invented'.[22] In any case, light is asserted to be 'neither this Æther not its vibrating motion, but something of a different kind propagated from lucid bodies'.[23] It might be an aggregate of peripatetic qualities, or a multitude of very small and swift corpuscles, or the motion of some other medium permeating the main body of ether—'let every man here take his fancy'.[24] But

---

[19] Cf. Newton, *Opticks*, Query 31, p. 404–5.

[20] It should be noted in this connection that the demonstration of the sine law in the *Principia* (like that in the *Opticks*) is meant to be generally valid, that is, regardless of whether the acting force is impulsive or attractive. See above, p. 303.

[21] Cf. Birch, *History*, III, pp. 248–60; *Correspondence*, I, pp. 362–86.

[22] *Correspondence*, I, p. 363. [23] Ibid., p. 370. [24] Ibid.

whatever light may be, one thing is requisite in order to explain its properties: It should be capable of interacting with the ether. Light acts on the ether by warming it, or by exciting in it swift vibrations (to explain, as will be seen below, the 'fits' of easy transmission and of easy reflection). Refraction is a case in which the ether acts upon light.

To explain this Newton supposes the density of ether within opaque and transparent bodies to be inversely proportional to the density of the body, and that it is greatest in free space. He then imagines at the surface separating any two dissimilar media a very thin region (call it the refracting region) in which the ether grows rarer from one side to the other—its density being the same along lines parallel to the surface of separation, but uneven along the perpendiculars to that surface. Beyond the region of refraction the ether is uniformly distributed on both sides. It is further supposed that the denser the ether is, the stronger is its action on light. When, therefore, an oblique ray penetrates the refracting region in its passage from one medium into another, it will be continually *impelled* perpendicularly from the side where the ether is denser (and, therefore, where the body is rarer) and be forced to recede to the other side, and thus its passage within the refracting region will be curved:

Now if ye motion of the ray be supposed in this passage to be increased or diminished in a certaine proportion according to the difference of the densities of the æthereall Mediums, & the addition or detraction of the motion be reckoned in the perpendicular from ye refracting Superficies, as it ought to be, the Sines of incidence & refraction will be proportionall according to what Des Cartes has demonstrated.[25]

---

[25] *Correspondence*, I, p. 371. The picture is that of atmospheric refraction; Newton imagines at the surfaces of refracting bodies a thin ethereal atmosphere which refracts light by the continuous variation in density of its layers. He made use of the same picture in 1675 (see *Correspondence*, I, pp. 383–84) in his hypothetical explanation of the diffraction phenomena (such as the bending of light around the sharp edge of a shadow-forming body) that had been noted and so named by Grimaldi (see Grimaldi, *Physico-mathesis*, Prop. I). By calling these phenomena by the name *inflection* (see Newton, *Principia*, p. 230; *Opticks*, Bk. III), Newton was using a term that had been introduced into optics by Hooke to denote a situation similar to that of atmospheric refraction, as when a beam of light passes through a solution of varying

These considerations were proposed by Newton about eleven years before his own demonstration of the sine law appeared in the *Principia* and, presumably, some time before this demonstration was formulated. But although they were briefly referred to again, after the publication of the *Principia*, by way of a question in the second English edition of the *Opticks* (1718), [26] the Queries of the *Opticks* simultaneously suggested the possibility of explaining refraction by supposing the refracting body to act upon the light ray at a distance.[27] We read in Query 29:

---

density (Hooke, *Micrographia*, p. 220: 'This *inflection* (if I may so call it) I imagine to be nothing else, but a *multiplicate refraction*, caused by the unequal *density* of the constituent parts of the *medium*, whereby the motion, action or progress of the Ray of light is hindered from proceeding in a straight line, and *inflected* or *deflected* by a curve.' See also Hooke's *Posthumous Works*, p. 81). Hooke had also applied that term, in discourses to the Royal Society, to the phenomena of diffraction which he discovered independently of Grimaldi though after the publication, in 1665, of Grimaldi's *Physico-mathesis* (see Birch, op. cit., III, pp. 54, 63, 69, 194–5, 268–9; also Hooke's *Posthumous Works*, 186–90). It was mainly Hooke's discourses (the first of which was delivered on 19 June 1672) that drew Newton's attention seriously to the investigation of diffraction (see Newton's statement in *Correspondence*, I, p. 383). Not only did Newton borrow the term *inflection* from Hooke, but he also inherited from him the particular interpretation of the phenomena denoted by that term, that is, diffraction was only a special kind of refraction. Thus Newton explained in the 1675 Hypothesis referred to above that the bending of light observed in the formation of shadow by a sharp-edged body was due to the varying density of the ethereal atmosphere surrounding the body. Since it was assumed that the ether grew rarer towards the body, the light should be inflected *into* the geometrical shadow. This explanation may therefore be taken, as far as it goes, to account for the inner fringes that appeared *inside* the shadow. But it fails to explain both the appearance of the outside fringes and the fact that the shadow was bigger than it should been have, had the light proceeded in straight lines. In the *Opticks* Newton proposed an alternative explanation of diffraction (or inflection) by the action – at a distance – of the opaque body upon the light rays (see *Opticks*, Queries 1–3). Here (in the experiments related in Bk. III) we find him concerned with the outer fringes and, consequently, the action of the body should be understood as repulsive, not attractive. But, then, what about the *inner* fringes? Mach has understandably found it strange that they are neither mentioned nor illustrated in the *Opticks* (see Mach, *Principles*, p. 143). Newton's investigations of diffraction phenomena were not completed to his own satisfaction (see *Opticks*, pp. 338–9). It would seem that, in order to explain the six coloured fringes (three inside the shadow and three outside it), which are indicated in the figure accompanying his 1675 discourse (see *Correspondence*, I, p. 384), he would have to assume that while some of the rays are attracted towards the body to form the inner fringes, others are repelled by it and thereby give rise to the outside fringes. To allow for this assumption, he would have to appeal to something like his theory of fits which he formulated to explain another class of what is now recognized as interference phenomena. Newton's undoubted merit in this field lies in the detailed experimental analysis and remarkably accurate measurements which he made.

[26] Cf. Newton, *Opticks*, Queries 19 and 20, pp. 349–50.

[27] The Queries exhibited this dual character of hypothetical explanations (sometimes mechanical, sometimes attractionist) with regard to most properties of light and to gravity.

Are not the Rays of Light very small Bodies emitted from shining Substances? . . . Pellucid Substances act upon the Rays of Light at a distance in refracting, reflecting, and inflecting them, and the Rays mutually agitate the Parts of those Substances at a distance for heating them; and this Action and Re-action at a distance very much resembles an attractive Force between Bodies. If Refraction be perform'd by Attraction of the Rays, the Sines of Incidence must be to the Sines of Refraction in a given Proportion, as we shew'd in our Principles of Philosophy: And this Rule is true by Experience.[28]

On this interpretation the particles of the refracting body are supposed to be endowed with attractive powers. The resultant force of all the attractions from the particles at the surface of the body will be perpendicular to that surface. And, as is always necessary to assume, the influence of the force must not extend beyond the very near neighbourhood of the refracting surface. When the light particle falls into the region of influence of the refracting force, it is attracted perpendicularly towards the surface. But once the particle is totally immersed in the refracting body, the attractions will be equal on all sides and thus neutralize one another. The particle will then proceed in a straight line with its velocity at emergence from the refracting region.

That refraction is caused by an ethereal medium acting on the ray, or by an attractive power residing in the particles of the refracting body, these are *hypotheses* advanced by Newton without consideration of their truth or falsity. The fact that they appear in the *Opticks* as Queries and not as Propositions means that they do not form part of the *asserted* doctrine of light and of refraction. The propositions them-selves, and in particular those of Bk. I, have a different status: they stand on a lower level where they are firmly supported by 'Reason and Experiment'.[29] So far as the sine law is concerned this means that the experiments show the law to be 'either accurately or very nearly' true, while a demonstration based on the assumption of a

---

[28] Newton, *Opticks*, Query 29, pp. 370–1. This Query was originally published in the first Latin edition of *Opticks* (1706) as Query 21. It later appeared in the second English edition of 1718 (and in all subsequent English editions) as Query 29, and a final paragraph was added.
[29] See above, p. 308.

perpendicular force proves it to be 'accurately' true. [30] For Newton, this demonstration constitutes 'a very convincing Argument of the full truth'[31] of the law, not only because it leads to a conclusion that is found to agree with the experiments, but also, and more important, because in his view it is so general as to leave open all questions regarding the nature of the refracting force.

But why should there be a *perpendicular* force at all?—Because, as we have seen, this must be supposed if the ray is to behave in accordance with the laws of dynamics. What Newton, therefore, takes for granted throughout is a dynamical interpretation of refraction. This, of course, was not the only possible interpretation in his time, and it was not general enough to allow for all views regarding the nature of light. For it presupposed a conception of the ray as something that could be acted upon by a force and it thereby excluded the wave conception that was advanced, for example, by Huygens.

Newton had reason to believe that his was the true interpretation. For if he was asked to justify it against Huygens' geometrical principle (which equally leads to the sine ratio though it is not compatible with the assumption of a perpendicular force since they give contradictory results about the velocity of light in different media), he would simply cite his objections against the wave theory itself which embodied Huygens' principle. One of these objections was that it could not explain rectilinear propagation. As has been remarked before, he was justified in this objection.[32]

Newton was mistaken, however, in believing that the difficulties facing the wave theory in his time were insurmountable.[33] All these difficulties have been overcome after Young and Fresnel had enriched the wave hypothesis with new ideas. Moreover, his own dynamical theory of refraction had to be abandoned after Foucault's 1850 experiment had decided against it and in favour of the wave explanation.

An examination of the role of this experiment will help to make clear the logical status of Newton's explanation of refraction.

During the eighteenth century Newton was generally understood

---

[30] See above, p. 299. [31] See above, p. 308. [32] See above, pp. 282ff. [33] See above, p. 282.

as having propounded a corpuscular view of light. This understanding was justified not only by his repeated denunciations of the wave hypothesis, but also because it was the only natural interpretation that could be attached to his conception of light rays, in spite of his deliberate abstaining from explicitly declaring their real nature. It was particularly obvious from his explanation of refraction that he was relying on a corpuscular view, since this explanation (especially as it appeared in *Principia*) clearly presupposed the assumption that the rays obeyed the laws of *particle* dynamics.[34] The rigorous deduction of the sine law on the basis of that assumption provided further evidence of the fruitfulness of Newtonian mechanics, showing as it did that the idea of attraction could be successfully extended to the domain of optics. It was therefore natural for the adherents of Newton's system to subscribe to his corpuscular view of light; and Huygens' theory was almost completely forgotten until it was revived and improved by Young and Fresnel in the beginning of the nineteenth century. It was then shown that all kinds of optical phenomena known at the time could be adequately explained by wave considerations making use of Huygens' principle of secondary wavelets, Young's principle of superposition and the idea of the transversality of light waves introduced by Fresnel to account for the phenomena of polarization. Newton's corpuscular theory was thus pushed aside, having failed to offer any explanations of diffraction, interference or polarization phenomena that could be compared with the convincing mathematical representations of Fresnel. But some Newtonians were not convinced, and, perhaps, understandably; the impressive success of one theory does not by itself constitute a refutation of a rival theory. After all, the corpuscular theory could reasonably claim to have succeeded just as well in explaining at least some of the properties of light (reflection and ordinary refraction); and only a few years before Fresnel entered the scene, Laplace was trying to formulate an explanation of double refraction in terms of forces acting at a distance and in accordance with Maupertuis'

---

[34] See the title of the section in *Principia*, which contained the demonstration of the sine law—quoted on pp. 308f.

principle of least action.[35] There was thus no compelling reason to abandon the corpuscular view until Foucault performed his experiment in 1850.

The purpose of the experiment was to decide between the corpuscular and wave theories by testing their respective explanations of refraction. As we have seen, the corpuscular theory demanded, *as a necessary result of its initial dynamical point of view*, that light should travel faster in denser media; whereas Huygens' principle required that the contrary should be the case. When Foucault finally succeeded in devising an apparatus by which he could compare the velocities of light in air and in water, he found that the light travelled more slowly in the latter, denser medium.

When this result was announced it was generally accepted as a definitive refutation of Newton's explanation of refraction; and Foucault's experiment was regarded as a *crucial experiment* deciding against the corpuscular view and supporting the wave hypothesis. The impact of this experiment on the minds of nineteenth century physicists was such that attempts to develop the corpuscular hypothesis were generally abandoned until Einstein advanced his photon theory in 1905. But, shortly before Einstein published his theory, Pierre Duhem had formulated his well-known view that crucial experiments are not possible in physics and, therefore, that Foucault's 1850 experiment cannot properly have the role which had been assigned to it.[36] This view has recently gained many followers, especially after quantum optics established itself as a universally accepted theory. It is now sometimes argued that since the corpuscles have returned in the form of photons, Foucault's experiment was not crucial after all. But this argument should not be confused with Duhem's own views.

Duhem asserted two theses which should be distinguished from one another. First, he pointed out that a physical experiment cannot,

---

[35] Cf. P. S. de Laplace, 'Sur la loi de la réfraction extraordinaire de la lumière dans les cristaux diaphanes,' in *Journal de physique*, LXVIII (1809), pp. 107–11.

[36] Cf. P. Duhem, *La théorie physique, son objet, sa structure*, 2nd ed., Paris, 1914, Pt. II, Ch. VI, Secs. II & III. The first edition appeared in 1906, but the chapters of the book had been published successively (in the *Revue de philosophie*) in 1904–5; see Preface to the second edition.

logically, refute an isolated hypothesis, but only a whole system of hypotheses taken together. For in deducing a certain prediction from a given hypothesis, in setting up the experimental apparatus, and in interpreting the experimental result, the physicist has to make use of a whole body of propositions which he takes for granted. If, therefore, the result is not in agreement with his prediction, this only tells him that there is something wrong *somewhere* in his system, but the experiment itself does not help him to locate the error. Applying these considerations to Foucault's experiment Duhem concluded that it had not logically refuted the corpuscular *hypothesis* (that the rays of light are small bodies emitted by luminous objects), but had only shown that the corpuscular *theory* (embodying all the propositions that had been admitted by Newton and his successors) was not compatible with the facts.

Duhem's second thesis was that physical experiments cannot, as Bacon had believed, be assigned a role similar to that of the indirect proof in mathematics. That is to say, when an experiment shows that a conclusion obtained in a given theory is not in agreement with the facts, it does not thereby *establish* the truth of any other theory which leads to the contradictory conclusion. It is in this *positive* sense that Duhem asserted the impossibility of crucial experiments in physics. In his view, no experiment is able to prove in this indirect way any given theory or hypothesis, because (contrary to what Bacon had assumed) there can never be a complete enumeration of all possible theories or hypotheses that might successfully fit the facts. If some of Foucault's contemporaries assigned a positive role to his experiment, that was only because they had not conceived the possibility of a different conception of light other than those of Newton and Huygens. Before the end of the century, however, Maxwell had already developed such a different conception in his electromagnetic theory.

These two theses of Duhem should, of course, be granted.[37] But

---

[37] With regard to the first thesis, it is not quite clear whether Duhem would go so far as to maintain that the argument in an experimental refutation necessarily involves the whole of knowledge as the ultimate background of any particular theory. If he does, then, Popper has pointed out, his criticism 'overlooks the fact that if we take each of the two theories (between which the crucial experiment is to decide) *together* with all this background knowledge, as

he also advanced the view that had the nineteenth century physicists wished to preserve the corpuscular *hypothesis*, 'they would no doubt have succeeded in founding on this supposition an optical system that would have been in agreement with Foucault's experiment'.[38] In this he has been followed by more recent writers. Alexander Wood, for example, suggested[39] that the adherents of the corpuscular view could have assumed that when the ray (the corpuscle) passes from a rare into a dense medium, *the perpendicular component of its velocity remains constant* while the component parallel to the refracting surface is diminished by (say) action of a frictional kind. Since this assumption leads to the conclusion that the actual velocity in the dense medium of refraction will be less than in the rare medium of incidence, the corpuscular hypothesis would thus have been brought into agreement with the facts and Foucault's experiment would have ceased to be crucial. Since the appearance of Wood's book his suggestion has been endorsed by Florian Cajori in the Appendix which he wrote to his edition of Newton's *Principia*.[40]

This kind of suggestion might appear to be justified by the power of mathematics to adapt itself to new situations and its capacity to assimilate new facts. Its advocates, however, seem to presuppose that this process of assimilation which has indeed continued throughout the history of science can always be carried out—even in an arbitrary and *ad hoc* fashion. This presupposition is mistaken. It is

---

indeed we must, then we decide between two systems which differ *only* over the two theories which are at stake. It further overlooks the fact that we do not assert the refutation of the theory as such, but of the theory *together* with that background knowledge; parts of which, if other crucial experiments can be designed, may indeed one day be rejected as responsible for the failure. (Thus we may even characterize a *theory under investigation* as that part of a vast system for which we have, if vaguely, an alternative in mind, and for which we try to design crucial tests.)' (Karl R. Popper, *Conjectures and Refutations*, p. 112.)

[38] *Théorie physique*, ed. cit., p. 284.

[39] Cf. A. Wood, *In Pursuit of Truth*, London, 1927, pp. 47-48.

[40] Cf. Newton, *Principia*, Appendix, note 26, pp. 651-2. It may be remarked that Wood's particular suggestion happens to lead to at least one result, namely a *false* law of refraction, which would have been sufficient to dismiss it at once. For his assumption concerning the perpendicular velocity can be expressed thus:

$v_i \cos i = v_r \cos r$.

Combining this with the definition of the refractive index n,

$v_r = n\, v_i$,

a cosine law of refraction is obtained:

$\cos i = n \cos r$.

not, for example, easy to see how the nineteenth century physicists could have effected the desired modification of the corpuscular theory without doing violence to the accepted Newtonian physics.[41] For we have seen[42] that the result refuted by Foucault's experiment is a *necessary* consequence of Newton's second law of motion. It is true, as the current argument runs, that a synthesis has been made (first by L. de Broglie) between particle dynamics and wave optics. But this has been achieved within the framework of a *new* mechanics making use of the relativistic relation $E = mc^2$ and Planck's quantum of action, that is, two concepts completely foreign to Newtonian mechanics.[43]

---

[41] See G. Bachelard's remarks in *L'activité rationaliste*, pp. 46–8.

[42] See above, p. 301.

[43] A. I. Sabra, 'A note on a suggested modification of Newton's corpuscular theory of light to reconcile it with Foucault's experiment of 1850,' *British Journal for the Philosophy of Science*, V (1954), pp. 149–51.

Chapter Thirteen

THE TWO LEVELS OF EXPLANATION: NEWTON'S THEORY OF THE COLOURS OF THIN PLATES

Newton rejected the explanation of reflection by the impinging of light rays on the solid parts of bodies.[1] Three of his reasons for abandoning this idea may be mentioned here. First, he pointed out that when light passed from a dense medium like glass into a rarer medium like air, some of it was reflected at the separating surface, even when the adjacent air was drawn away. This, clearly, could not be ascribed to the impinging of the light rays on something outside the glass.[2] Second, it was known that at a sufficiently great angle of incidence, the whole of the incident light was reflected back into the glass. He naturally found it difficult to imagine that at a certain inclination the light should find enough pores to let it through while these pores should not be available at another inclination, especially considering that when the passage was from air into glass some of the light was always transmitted regardless of the degree of incidence. Third, he noticed that if the coloured rays emerging from a prism were successively cast at the same angle of incidence on a second prism, the latter could be so inclined as to totally reflect the blue rays while rays of other colours (red, for example) were copiously transmitted.[3] 'Now if the Reflexion be caused by

---

[1] Newton, *Opticks*, Bk. II, Pt. III, Prop. VIII: 'The Cause of Reflexion is not the impinging of Light on the solid or impervious parts of Bodies, as is commonly believed.' Cf. pp. 262–9.

[2] This objection was first publicly stated by Newton in 1675; see *Correspondence*, I, p. 360: 'I remember, in some discourse with Mr Hook, I happened to say, yt I thought light was reflected, not by ye parts of glas, water, air, or other sensible bodies....' (7 December 1675). Regarding Newton's possible meeting with Hooke in October 1675, see Birch, *History*, III, p. 228, and *Correspondence*, I, p. 417, editor's note (3).

[3] See *Opticks*, Bk. I, Pt. I, Expers. 9 and 10, pp. 54–63. These experiments led Newton to postulate a new original property of the rays, their 'reflexibility' (cf. ibid., Definition III and Bk. I, Pt. I, Prop III). He measured that property by the critical angle for a certain colour and a given pair of media; he found that it was smallest for the most refrangible rays (blue) and greatest for the least refrangible rays (red).

the parts of Air or Glass, I would ask, why at the same Obliquity of Incidence the blue should wholly impinge on those parts, so as to be all reflected, and yet the red find Pores enough to be in a great measure transmitted.'[4]

The simple picture of mechanical collision was thus found to be incapable of accounting for some of the relevant facts. Newton succeeded in providing an adequate explanation of total reflection by ascribing it to the action of the same force which he supposed to be responsible for refraction:[5] Whether or not a beam of a certain colour (passing from a dense into a rare medium) will be *wholly* reflected can be determined from knowledge of the degree of incidence; the beam will be totally reflected when the angle of incidence is greater than the critical angle for that colour. But the problem of *partial reflection* remains, so far, unsolved: how does one and the same force that is acting at the separating surface refract some of the incident light and reflect the rest when rays of the same colour are passing from the rare into the dense medium at any angle of incidence?[6]

Newton's answer to this question is to be found in his theory of fits.

But although that theory was called upon to solve the problem of partial reflection, it was primarily designed to explain the colours of thin transparent bodies; and it is this explanation which will concern us in the present chapter. The preceding remarks may be taken to illustrate the interesting fact that a seemingly simple phenomenon does not sometimes receive an adequate explanation in a given theory until after a relatively more sophisticated hypothesis has been formulated to account for more complicated phenomena that fall within the scope of the theory. A striking example from the history of optics is the apparent rectilinear propagation of light (i.e. the formation of shadows in the ordinary way) which was not satisfactorily explained from the wave-theory point of view until after Young and Fresnel had developed a complicated system

---

[4] See *Opticks*, Bk. II., p. 264.
[5] See above, pp. 303f.
[6] See formulation of the problem in Kamāl al-Dīn and in Huygens, above, pp. 220f.

designed mainly to account for diffraction and interference phenomena.

Newton was not the first to make a careful study of the colours of thin transparent bodies. And although the principal ones among those phenomena have traditionally borne the name 'Newton's rings,' it will be seen that Robert Hooke had gone a long way in investigating them, thus preparing the road on which Newton followed.

1. About the time that Hooke's *Micrographia* appeared,[7] Robert Boyle published his *Experiments and Considerations touching Colours* as the first part of an experimental history of colours.[8] Both books contained observations on the colours exhibited by thin bodies; but the degree to which these observations were developed in Boyle's treatise was far below that reached in Hooke's book, and the aims of the two authors were different.

Boyle cited his observations as negative instances refuting the view, held by the 'Chymists', that the generation of colours was due to the presence of the sulphurious or the saline or the mercurial element in bodies.[9] He remarked that when essential oils or spirit of wine, for example, are shaken until they form bubbles, 'those bubbles will (if attentively consider'd) appear adorn'd with various and lovely colours'. He drew attention to the fact that both colourless bodies (water) and coloured ones (turpentine) exhibit, when made thin, colours which they do not normally possess. The colours which appear on the surface of bubbles, he further remarked, are 'not always the same Parts of them, but vary'd according to the Incidence of the Light, and the Position of the Eye'.[10] Thin-blown glass exhibited the same rainbow colours 'which were exceedingly vivid'. (Expressing this fact in general terms, Hooke—and after him

---

[7] The date of publication of Hooke's *Micrographia* is 1665, but the *imprimatur* (of Brouncker president of the Royal Society) is dated 23 November 1664.

[8] The full title ran as follows: *Experiments and Considerations touching Colours. First occasionally Written, among some other Essays, to a Friend; and now suffer'd to come abroad as the Beginning of an Experimental History of Colours*, London, 1664.

[9] Cf. Boyle, op. cit., pp. 85 and 242-5.

[10] Newton gave Hooke the credit for having first made this important observation. See below, pp. 329ff.

Newton—asserted that the intensity of the colours depends on the refractive power of the body—see below.) Finally, holding a feather before his eye against the sun when it was near the horizon, 'me thought there appear'd to me a Variety of little Rain-bows, with differing and very vivid Colours, of which none was constantly to be seen in the Feather'. This last observation (being one of diffraction) does not in fact belong to the same class as the preceding ones.[11] It did not matter to Boyle to make the differentiation (if he noticed it, that is) since all he was concerned to conclude from these experiments was that the appearance of colours could not be uniquely determined by the constant presence of any or all of the constituting elements mentioned before.

Both Boyle and Hooke were greatly influenced by Bacon's teaching; both were ardent seekers after new and extraordinary phenomena. But whereas Boyle confined his work on colours to fulfilling the first part of the Baconian programme, that is the recording of instances,[12] Hooke was primarily interested in finding an explanation of the phenomena of colours in general and those of thin bodies in particular. In fact the whole of Hooke's theory of colours was devised ultimately to account for the latter phenomena.

Hooke made most of his experiments concerning the colours of thin bodies on plates of muscovy glass (mica), liquids of various kinds pressed between two plates of ordinary glass, liquids and glass blown into bubbles, and the surfaces of metals.[13] By splitting the

---

[11] Cf. Newton, *Opticks*, Bk. III, Pt. I, Obs. 2, p. 322.

[12] This is already indicated by the title of Boyle's book. The rule under which the book was written is manifest from the following sentence of Bacon's which figures as a motto on the title-page: 'Non fingendum, aut excogitandum, sed inveniendum, quid Natura faciat, aut ferat.' It comes from *Novum Organum*, II, 10, where it occurs in the following context: 'Primo enim paranda est *Historia Naturalis et Experimentalis*, sufficiens et bona; quod fundamentum rei est: neque enim fingendum, aut excogitandum, sed inveniendum, quid natura faciat aut ferat—For first of all we must prepare a Natural and Experimental History, sufficient and good; and this is the foundation of all; for we are not to imagine or suppose, but to discover, what nature does or may be made to do' (B, I, p. 236 and IV, p. 127). The motto 'Non fingendum, aut excogitandum, . . .' is not unlike Newton's 'Hypotheses non fingo'. Newton also opposed *discovery* (or finding what really exists) on the one hand to what is merely *imagined* or *supposed* or *feigned* on the other, and claimed for his theories the status of the former. It is interesting to note, however, that works claiming to follow the Baconian method may vary as much as the difference between Boyle's *Considerations* and Newton's *Opticks*.   [13] Cf. Hooke, *Micrographia*, pp. 48–53.

muscovy glass with a needle into thin flakes he observed that there were several white specks or flaws in some parts of the flake, while other parts appeared tinged with all the rainbow colours. These colours appeared under the microscope to be arranged in rings, circular or irregular according to the shape of the spot which they terminated. The order of the colours was, from the middle, as follows: blue, purple, scarlet, yellow, green; and this series repeated itself around every spot from six to nine times. He called these systems of colours *rings*, *lines* and *irises*—counting all the gradations between the ends of each series for one. (They were later called 'Newton's Rings'!)

He also observed that the rings varied in brightness and breadth with the distance from the centre—being dimmer and narrower as they were farther from it. The spot in the middle was 'for the most part all of one colour'. Another thing which he found 'very observable' was that the colours could be made to change places by pressing the glass where they originally appeared.

Plates which were equally thick in all parts were seen under the microscope to be all over tinged with one determinate colour depending on the plate's thickness. It was necessary for the appearance of any colour at all that the thickness of the plate should lie within two definite limits; when the plates were too thick or too thin the colours disappeared. Two inclined plates (in the shape of a wedge) with some transparent medium interposed between them exhibited the rainbow colours arranged according to the various thicknesses of the medium.

Hooke then observed that when a transparent medium (air or liquid) was pressed between two glass plates, the same coloured rings were visible. He found that the colours could be changed by increasing or relaxing the pressure. The colours were the more vivid the greater the difference was in the refractive power between the glass and the interposed medium.

When the plates of muscovy glass, for example, were formed in the shape of a double-convex lens, the order of the colours was—from the middle: red, yellow, green, blue. This order was reversed when the plates had the shape of a double-concave lens.

He proposed to explain the preceding observations by the following consideration which expressed, in his own terms, the *material cause* of the phenomena in question:

it is manifest . . . that the material cause of the *apparition* of these several Colours, is some *Lamina* or Plate of a transparent or pellucid body of a thickness very determinate and proportioned according to the greater or less refractive power of the *pellucid* body.[14]

The same phenomena were produced by liquid and glass bubbles. Hooke found the appearance of the rings on the surfaces of the glass bubbles surprising 'having never heard or seen any thing of it before'.[15] (As we have seen, the same observation was made by Boyle.)

In accordance with the explanation just stated, he ascribed the appearance of colours on a polished surface of hardened steel when softened by heat to the fact that heating causes the metal to form on its surface a lamina of the requisite thinness and transparency for the production of the colours. It was not, therefore, necessary for producing the colours that the lamina should be terminated on both sides by one and the same medium.

To Hooke, the interest of all these observations consisted in that they supplied him with a *crucial experiment* against the Cartesian theory of colours; and, therefore, they called for a new theory. For if, as Descartes had maintained, the production of colours by refraction was due to the rotary motion which the ethereal globules acquired at their impact on a refracting surface, it would follow—as Descartes himself had pointed out[16]—that no colours would appear if the light passed through two *parallel* surfaces. For the rotation acquired at the first surface should be counteracted by the second (the refraction there being in the opposite sense); and since the two surfaces are parallel, the effect of the second surface should be to restore the globules to exactly their original state before meeting the

---

[14] Cf. Hooke, *Micrographia*, p. 50.
[15] Ibid.
[16] Cf. Descartes, *Meteors*, D, VI, pp. 330-1.

first. But, as Hooke observed, colours did appear by viewing the source of light through laminae of *uniform* thickness:

This Experiment therefore will prove such a one as our *thrice excellent Verulam* calls *Experimentum Crucis*, serving as a Guide or Land-mark, by which to direct our course in the search after the true cause of Colours. Affording us this particular negative Information, that for the production of Colours there is not necessary either a great refraction, as in the Prisme; nor Secondly, a determination of Light and shadow, such as is both in the Prisme and Glass-ball. Now that we may see likewise what affirmative and positive Instruction it yields, it will be necessary, to examine it a little more particularly and strictly; which that we may the better do, it will be requisite to premise somewhat in general concerning the nature of Light and Refraction.[17]

Then follows in the *Micrographia* the theory of light and colours which has been discussed on two previous occasions. The fundamentals of that theory, we have seen, are: that light consists in a succession of pulses generated in the ether by a vibrating movement of the luminous body; that colours are produced when the pulses (or wave-fronts) are made, by refraction, oblique to the direction of propagation; that blue is the effect on the retina of an oblique pulse whose weaker part or side precedes and whose stronger part follows; that red is the effect of an oblique pulse whose stronger side precedes and whose weaker side follows; and that all the intermediate colours on the spectrum are either different degrees of blue or red, or the intermixture of these degrees in various proportions.

How does Hooke explain the colours of thin plates on these principles?

He imagines[18] a pulse impinging in an oblique direction on the first surface of a lamina having the minimum requisite thickness. Some of the light is reflected by that surface while the rest is transmitted into the lamina. When the refracted light reaches the second surface, some of it will be reflected back to the first where it will be again transmitted out of the lamina. Two pulses will thus proceed from the first surface: a pulse that has been reflected at that surface, followed by another which has undergone one reflection at the

---

[17] Hooke, *Micrographia*, p. 54.   [18] Cf. ibid., pp. 65–66.

second surface and two refractions at the first. Owing to these two refractions and the time spent in traversing the thickness of the lamina twice, the succeeding pulse will—according to Hooke—be weaker than the one preceding it. But as the distance between the surfaces of the lamina is very small, the impression of these two pulses on the eye will be rather that of *one* pulse whose stronger part precedes and whose weaker part follows. This generates the sensation of yellow.

If a slightly thicker lamina is used, the distance between the leading strong pulse and the succeeding weak pulse will naturally increase, and, therefore, the action of the latter on the retina will be more retarded than in the first case. This gives the sensation of red.

When the thickness of the lamina is such that the weak part of a first original (i.e. incident) pulse lies exactly in the middle between its preceding strong part and the strong part of a second pulse (i.e. the part that has just been reflected at the first surface), a sensation of purple is generated. Purple is therefore an impression on the retina of a succession of strong and weak pulses, alternating at equal intervals.

By further increasing the thickness of the plate, the weak part of a first pulse will be nearer to the strong part of the immediately following pulse with which it will tend to be associated in the eye, rather than with the strong part that precedes. The order of the pulses with respect to their weakness and strength will thus be reversed; the impression on the eye will be that of a pulse whose weaker part precedes and whose stronger part follows. This gives the sensation of blue.

As the weaker pulse gradually approaches the stronger pulse behind, the blue turns into green, until such thickness of the plate is reached that the weaker pulse coincides with the following stronger pulse. With further increase in the thickness of the plate, the order of the pulses and, consequently, the order of the colours, will be repeated:

if these surfaces [of the plate] . . . are further remov'd asunder, the weaker pulse will yet lagg behind [the stronger] much further, and not onely be *coincident* with the second [pulse] . . . but lagg behind that also, and that so much the more, by how much the thicker the Plate be; so that by degrees it will be *coincident* with the third . . . backward also, and by degrees, as the Plate grows thicker with a fourth, and so onward to a fifth, sixth, seventh, or eighth; so that if there be a thin transparent body, that from the greatest thinness requisite to produce colours, does, in the manner of a Wedge, by degrees grow to the greatest thickness that a Plate can be of, to exhibit a colour by the reflection of Light from such a body, there shall be generated several consecutions of colours, whose order from the thin end towards the thick, shall be Yellow, Red, Purple, Blue, Green; . . . and these so often repeated, as the weaker pulse does lose paces with its Primary, or first pulse, and is *coincident* with a second, third, fourth, fifth, sixth, &c. pulse behind the first.[19]

It is clear from the preceding account that Hooke ascribed the colours of thin plates to the manner in which the pulses reflected at the first surface are associated with those reflected at the second. Fundamentally the same idea underlies the wave-theory explanation of these colours. It is not therefore surprising that the originator of that explanation, Thomas Young, has said that had he not independently satisfied himself regarding these phenomena, Hooke's explanations 'might have led me earlier to a similar opinion'.[20] Following another remark by Young in which he pointed out potentialities in Hooke's theory, David Brewster wrote:

had Hooke adopted Newton's views of the different refrangibility of light, and applied them to his own theory of the coincidence of pulses, he would have left his rival behind in this branch of discovery.[21]

It should be noted in this connection that Newton asserted—in the discourse on colours produced before the Royal Society on 9 December 1675—that Hooke *had* in fact abandoned his dualistic view of colours:

---

[19] Ibid., pp. 66–67.
[20] Cf. Thomas Young, 'On the theory of light and colours'. Paper read before the Royal Society on 12 November 1801. Printed in his *A Course of Lectures on Natural Philosophy*, II, London, 1807, pp. 613–31. The quotation is from p. 627.
[21] Brewster, *Memoirs*, I, p. 160.

I was glad to understand, as I apprehended, from Mr Hooks discourse at my last being at one of your Assemblies, that he had changed his former notion of all colours being compounded of only two Originall ones, made by the two sides of an oblique pulse, & accomodated his Hypothesis to this my suggestion of colours, like sounds, being various, according to the various bignesse of the Pulses.[22]

And yet, there is no evidence that Hooke ever applied Newton's ideas to his own explanation of the colours of thin plates. Had he done so, Young has remarked, 'he could not but have discovered a striking coincidence with the measures laid down by Newton from experiment'.[23]

In any case, Hooke himself felt at the time of writing the *Micrographia* that he had not carried his investigations as far as he would have liked. We read towards the end of his account of the colours of thin plates:

One thing which seems of the greatest concern in this *Hypothesis*, is to determine the greatest or least thickness requisite for these effects, yet so exceeding thin are these coloured Plates, and so imperfect our Microscope, that I have not been hitherto successful.[24]

That important task was first undertaken by Newton.

Hooke's experiments on the colours of thin plates were instructive and his explanation of those colours was far from being absurd. He was the first to make a serious investigation of those phenomena,

---

[22] *Correspondence*, I, pp. 362–3. Newton's allusion is (probably) to the remarks made by Hooke during a meeting of the Royal Society (11 March 1674/5) which are rendered in Birch's *History* (III, p. 194) in the following words: 'as there are produced in sounds several harmonies by proportionate vibrations, so there are produced in light several curious and pleasant colours, by the proportionate and harmonious motions of vibrations intermingled; and, those of the one are sensated by the ear, so those of the other are by the eye.' Thus, as far as dispersion was concerned, Hooke finally conceded all the modifications that his theory would have to undergo in order to accommodate Newton's experiments from the wave-theory point of view. We do not know whether he wished to maintain in 1675 the possibility (first suggested by him in 1672) of representing white light by the coalescence or superposition of the waves associated with the different colours. But there was nothing in these experiments that would have forced him to give up the possibility of that representation. See above, pp. 259ff, 278ff.

[23] Thomas Young, op. cit., II, p. 628.

[24] *Micrographia*, p. 67.

and his study of them was quite elaborate. Many of his experiments were later repeated by Newton, and the problems which he left unsolved constituted the starting point of Newton's own researches in this field.

Newton himself expressed his debt to Hooke on more than one occasion. Thus, in a letter to Oldenburg dated 21 December 1675,[25] Newton credited Hooke with having preceded him in observing and attempting an explanation of the colours of thin plates. And we are further informed by Brewster that there accompanied that letter an unpublished paper, entitled 'Observations', in which Newton said that Hooke in the *Micrographia* 'had delivered many very excellent things concerning the colours of thin plates, and other natural bodies, which he [Newton] had not scrupled to make use of as far as they were for his purpose'.[26]

Later in a letter to Hooke of 5 February 1675/6, Newton wrote:

What Des-cartes did [that is, in optics] was a good step. You have added much several ways, & especially in taking ye colours of thin plates into philosophical consideration. If I have seen further it is by standing on ye sholders of Giants. But I make no question but you have divers very considerable experiments beside those you have published, & some it's very probable the same wth some of those in my late papers.[27] Two at least there are wch I know you have observed, ye dilatation of ye coloured rings by the obliquation of ye eye, & ye apparition of a black spot at ye contact of two convex glasses & at the top of a water bubble; and it's probable there may be more, besides others wch I have not made: so yt I have reason to defer as much, or more, in this respect to you as you would to me . . . .[28]

---

[25] Cf. Isaaci Newtoni *Opera*, IV (London, 1782), pp. 378–81; also printed (in part) in Birch, *History*, III, pp. 278–9; *Correspondence*, I, p. 406.

[26] Brewster, *Memoirs*, I, p. 139, note 2.

[27] These are the papers read before the Royal Society (in Newton's absence) on the following dates: 9 December 1675 (Birch, *History*, III, pp. 248–60), 16 December 1675 (ibid., pp. 262–9), 30 December 1675 (ibid., p. 270), 20 January 1676 (ibid., pp. 272–8), 3 February 1676 (ibid., pp. 280–95), 10 February 1676 (ibid., pp. 296–305). These comprised the 'Hypothesis Explaining the Properties of Light' and the 'Discourse on Observations' which accompanied Newton's letter to Oldenburg, 7 December 1675; see *Correspondence*, I, pp. 362–92.

[28] *Correspondence*, I, p. 416. Turnbull remarks that 'No reply to this letter has been found' (p. 417, note 4). The passage was quoted with some variations by David Brewster, *Memoirs*, I, pp. 142–3.

Newton here credits Hooke with two important observations which, as Brewster has noted, are not to be found in the *Micrographia*. Both observations are, however, described in a paper by Hooke which he read in a meeting of the Royal Society on 19 June 1672.[29] He reported that by pressing 'two thinn pieces of glass'[30] (not two convex glasses) together, a red spot first appeared in the middle. When he increased the pressure, he saw several rainbow colours encompassing the middle point,

& continuing to presse the same closer and closer, at last all the colours would disappear out of the middle of the circles or Rainebows, and the middle would appear white; and if yet I continued to press the said plates together, *the white would in severall places thereof turne into black.*[31]

Concerning the second observation, Hooke wrote:

all the said Rings, or Rainbows would vary their places by varying the position of the eye by wch they were observed; and not only their position but their colours . . . .[32]

This observation was later made the subject of a detailed quantitative examination by Newton. In the *Opticks*, Bk. II, Pt. I, Obs. 7, he determined the rule according to which the diameters of the rings vary with the obliqueness of the line of vision.

In the same discourse of 19 June 1672, Hooke mentioned another observation (also lacking in the *Micrographia*) which later received attention from Newton. Hooke wrote:

Moreover that [part of the plate] wch gives one colour by reflection [that is, when viewed from the side of the source of illumination], gives another by trajection [when viewed from the other side].[33]

---

[29] Cf. Birch, op. cit., III, pp. 52–54; *Correspondence*, I, pp. 195–7.

[30] *Correspondence*, I, p. 196.

[31] Ibid.; italics added. A previous paper of Hooke's on the colours of soap bubbles (read to the Royal Society on 28 March 1672), does not contain the observation of a black spot on top of the bubble (Cf. Birch, op. cit., III, p. 29).

[32] *Correspondence*, I, p. 197.

[33] Ibid. Compare with Newton, *Opticks*, Bk. II, Pt. I Obs. 9, pp. 206–7, where it is remarked that the order of the colours appearing by reflection is the reverse of that of the colours appearing by trajection or refraction.

This observation revealed one of the fundamental features to be accounted for by Newton's theory of fits.

The sentences quoted above from Newton's letters to Oldenburg and to Hooke greatly contrast with the fact that when Newton published his *Opticks* in 1704, after Hooke had died, he failed even to mention Hooke's name in connection with the subject of the colours of thin plates. Newton's account of those colours simply begins with the following:

It has been observed *by others*, that transparent Substances, as Glass, Water, Air, &c. when made very thin by being blown into Bubbles, or otherwise formed into Plates, *do exhibit various Colours according to their various thinness*, altho' at a greater thickness they appear very clear and colourless.[34]

The attribution of this observation to 'others' is surprisingly inadequate; for the discovery of what is asserted here, namely that the appearance of a particular colour depends on a particular thickness of the plate, was due to Hooke and to no one else.

2. Newton's interest in the colours of thin plates dates from a period before 1672. This we gather from his reference to those phenomena in his Answer to Hooke's Considerations which was written in that year.[35] There he pointed out what had been observed by Hooke in the *Micrographia*—namely, that those colours depended for their production on the thickness of the plate; and further proposed the *hypothetical* explanation (to which he did not then nor ever afterwards commit himself) which was developed in his later publications. The first detailed account of those colours by Newton was contained in the discourses produced before the Royal Society in 1675–6.[36] We learn from two letters of Newton to Oldenburg (dated, respectively, 13 November 1675 and 30 November 1675)

---

[34] Newton, *Opticks*, Bk. II, Pt. I, p. 193; my italics.
[35] Cf. *Philosophical Transactions*, No. 88, 18 November 1672, pp. 5088–9; *Correspondence*, I, pp. 179–80.
[36] See above, p. 329, n. 27.

that he had written those discourses—apart from a 'little scrible', namely his 'hypothesis' for explaining the properties of light—before he sent his first letter on colours to the Royal Society in 1672.[37] But this should be understood as only generally true; his interest in diffraction phenomena which he also considered in the same discourses did not in fact begin until at least the middle of 1672.[38] In any case it is clear from his Answer to Hooke that he had in 1672 the leading idea in his explanation of the colours of thin plates which is contained in the revised discourses of 1675. The part of these discourses dealing with those phenomena was later reproduced, with additions, in the *Opticks* (1704). The following analysis will be based on the final account given in the *Opticks*.[39] My aim will be to give a description of some of the fundamental experiments with a view to understanding Newton's explanations which will be the subject of the subsequent discussion.

As we have seen, the experimental problem before which Hooke's investigations came to a stop was the determination of the requisite thickness in a plate of a given medium for the production of a particular colour. Hooke ascribed his failure to solve this problem to the defectiveness of his microscope. Newton, however, overcame the difficulties involved, not by using a better microscope, but because he struck upon a happy experimental device—a lens combination which allowed him to make the necessary measurements and calculations. His study was also facilitated and made more effective by using monochromatic light. This had not been attempted by Hooke.

In open air, Newton placed upon a double-convex lens of a large radius of curvature another plano-convex lens with its plane side downwards.[40] There was thus between the lenses a thin film of air, bounded by a plane and a spherical surface, which increased in

---

[37] Cf. Brewster, *Memoirs*, I, pp. 131–2; *Correspondence*, I, p. 358 and note 8, p. 359.

[38] See above, p. 310, n. 25; also A. R. Hall, 'Further optical experiments of Isaac Newton', *Annals of Science*, XI (1955), pp. 27–43; 'Newton's First Book (I)', *Archives internationales d'histoire des sciences*, XIII (1960), p. 48; Richard S. Westfall, 'Newton's reply to Hooke and the theory of colors', *Isis* LIV (1963), pp. 88–89 and notes 27 and 30.

[39] It would be interesting to study in detail the development of Newton's ideas on this subject, but this will not be attempted here.

[40] Cf. Newton, *Opticks*, Bk. II, Pt. I, Obs. 4.

thickness from the point of contact. Viewing the lenses by reflection and slowly pressing them together he saw coloured circles successively emerging from the central point and being formed in multicoloured rings; the last to appear was a black spot in the middle. He observed that while the diameters of the rings were gradually becoming larger (by increasing the pressure), the breadths of their orbits decreased. When he slowly released the pressure the circles gradually approached the central spot and disappeared in it one after the other. This indicated (what had been concluded by Hooke) that the particular colours were related to the air thicknesses at which they appeared.

Illuminating the lenses in a dark room with the prismatic colours one after the other he noticed that the rings were more distinct and greater in number than when white light was used.[41] The largest rings were formed by red light, the smallest by violet, and the other colours occupied places between these two extremities according to their order in the spectrum.[42] In each of these cases the phenomenon simply consisted in a series of alternating dark and bright rings, with the dark spot in the middle, and the bright rings all exhibiting the same colour with which the lenses were illuminated. It was therefore apparent that the multi-coloured rings—when white light was used—were the combined effect of an indefinite number of monochromatic rings. Newton remarked that when the lenses were viewed from the side of the illuminating source the bright rings indicated the places where the light was reflected, while the dark ones indicated the places where it was transmitted. Thus, the light was transmitted at the point of contact—hence the black spot, reflected at the place where the first bright ring appeared, transmitted again, and so forth. When viewed by transmission, the rings were exactly complementary to those perceived by reflection and the central point appeared bright.

Viewing the rings perpendicularly, or almost perpendicularly, by reflection (other specifications need not be mentioned here but are

---

[41] Cf. ibid., Bk. II, Pt. I, Obs. 12 and 13.
[42] Cf. ibid., Bk. II, Pt. I. Obs. 14.

carefully stated by Newton), he measured their diameters with a pair of compasses. He found that while the squares of the diameters of the dark rings were in the arithmetic progression of the even numbers, 0, 2, 4, etc. (0 being the central point), the squares of the diameters of the bright rings were in the progression of the odd numbers 1, 3, 5, etc.[43] From this he concluded that the air thicknesses (or intervals) corresponding to the dark rings were in the progression of the first sequence, whereas the intervals corresponding to the bright rings were in the progression of the second.

Having determined the refractive index of the double-convex lens and its focal length he calculated its radius of curvature. Using this result he computed the air interval corresponding to a sufficiently large ring (of, say, the colour in the confines of yellow and orange) whose diameter he had already measured. Finally he calculated the air interval corresponding to the first (innermost) bright ring produced by this colour. That was the $\dfrac{1}{178000}$th part of an inch. It follows that the thicknesses corresponding to the remaining bright rings of the same colour were given by $\dfrac{3}{178000}$, $\dfrac{5}{178000}$, etc.; and the thickness of the dark rings, by 0, $\dfrac{2}{178000}$, $\dfrac{4}{178000}$, etc. [44]

He also observed that the absolute values of the intervals corresponding to rings of a certain colour changed with the density (and, consequently, with the refractive index) of the enclosed medium. Thus, by allowing a drop of water to creep slowly into the air gap, the rings gradually contracted until the gap was full.[45]

Newton's investigations of these phenomena did not come to an end with the determination of the experimental laws governing them. Such, for example, was the law expressing the thicknesses in terms of the angles of incidence and of refraction,[46] or the law stating that the rings made, successively, by the limits of the seven colours—

---

[43] Cf. Newton, *Opticks*, Bk. II, Pt. I, Obs. 5.
[44] Cf. ibid., Bk. II, Pt. I, Obs. 6.
[45] Cf. ibid., Bk. II, Pt. I, Obs. 10.
[46] Cf. ibid., Bk. II, Pt. I, Obs. 7, p. 205.

red, orange, yellow, green, blue, indigo and violet—were to one another as the cube roots of the squares of a certain musical sequence.[47] He offered an explanation: his theory of fits.

His observations showed that the appearance of the rings was independent of the degree of convexity of the lenses,[48] and the nature of the material used. From this he concluded (like Hooke) that their appearance solely depended on the film surfaces and the distances between those surfaces.[49] By wetting either face of a muscovy-glass plate the colours grew faint. This indicated to him that both faces played a role in the production of the phenomenon. What, then, are the roles he assigned to the surfaces? The following is Newton's answer:

Every Ray of Light in its passage through any refracting Surface is put into a certain transient Constitution or State, which in the progress of the Ray returns at equal Intervals, and disposes the Ray at every return to be easily transmitted through the next refracting Surface, and between the returns to be easily reflected by it.[50]

That is to say, *assuming* that the ray has been transmitted by a refracting surface, it will always[51] be alternately disposed to be easily transmitted or easily reflected by a second surface—at equal intervals between every two dispositions. Newton called the returns of the state which disposed the ray to be easily transmitted its *fits of easy transmission*, and the returns of the state disposing it to be easily reflected its *fits of easy reflection*. He defined the 'interval of fits' as 'the space [which the ray traverses] . . . between every return and the next return', that is the *distance* covered by the ray between any two consecutive and similar fits.[52]

---

[47] Cf. ibid., Bk. II, Pt. I, Obs. 14, p. 212; Bk. II, Pt. III, Prop. XVI, p. 284.
[48] Cf. ibid., Bk. II, Pt. I, Obs. 6, pp. 200 and 202.
[49] Cf. ibid., Bk. II, Pt. III, p. 279.
[50] Ibid., Bk. II, Pt. III, Prop. XII.
[51] Cf. ibid., Bk. II, Pt. III, p. 279: 'this alternation seems to be propagated from every refracting Surface to all distances without end or limitation.'
[52] Ibid., Bk. II, Pt. III, p. 281.

Suppose then that a ray of a particular colour has been transmitted by the surface of the air film considered in the two-lens experiment. The ray will, after a whole interval, be in a fit of easy transmission. Therefore, if the thickness of the film happens to be equal to the interval of fits, the ray will be transmitted by the second surface. And the same will take place where the thicknesses are 2, 3, 4, . . . times a whole interval. This, according to Newton, explains the dark rings: they appear where the light is transmitted by the second surface.

But if the ray meets the second surface after a half interval, then, being in a fit of easy reflection, it will be reflected back towards the first. When it arrives there it will have completed a whole interval and will consequently be transmitted to the eye. The same of course will happen where the thicknesses are 2, 3, 4, . . . times a half-interval. This explains the bright rings: they are visible where the light is reflected by the second surface.

It is clear that the interval of fits (for a given colour and a given medium) can be calculated from the thickness at the first (innermost) bright ring produced by that colour and medium. For, by supposition, the interval must be twice that thickness. For example, having determined that thickness—for the colour in the confines of yellow and orange and for the medium air—to be the $\frac{1}{178000}$th part of an inch, the interval of fits of easy reflection must be $\frac{2}{178000} = \frac{1}{89000}$ parts of an inch.[53] The same number also measures the interval of fits of easy transmission for the same colour and medium.

It should be noticed that the interval of fits depends not only on the colour but also on the nature of the medium used. This is evident from the fact—observed by Newton—that the rings produced by a given colour were displaced when the air gap was filled with water, thus changing their diameters and the corresponding thicknesses.

So far we have neglected the *reflection* which takes place at the *first* surface of the transparent plate. According to Newton, the light

---

[53] Cf. Newton, *Opticks*, Bk. II, Pt. III, Prop. XVIII.

reflected at that surface does not play any part in the production of the rings. But the problem of partial reflection, which applies to both thick and thin transparent bodies, still remains. Newton's answer to that problem is contained in the following formulation of his theory of fits:

The reason why the Surfaces of all thick transparent Bodies reflect part of the Light incident on them, and refract the rest, is, that some Rays at their Incidence are in Fits of easy Reflexion, and others in Fits of easy Transmission.[54]

And hence Light is in Fits of easy Reflexion and easy Transmission, before its Incidence on transparent Bodies. And probably it is put into such fits at its first emission from luminous Bodies, and continues in them during all its progress.[55]

According to this formulation the fits are ('probably') with the rays from their origin. When the rays meet a refracting surface, those in a fit of easy reflection will be reflected and those in a fit of easy transmission will be refracted. Neglecting the former rays and following the subsequent course of the latter, the phenomena of thin transparent bodies are explained by Newton in the manner described before.

We are now in a position to discuss the logical status which Newton assigned to his theory. The following is what he wrote regarding the fits in a sequel to Prop. XII of Bk. II, Pt. III:

---

[54] Ibid., Bk. II, Pt. III, Prop. XIII, p. 281. That Newton did not mean to restrict this proposition to the partial reflection made at the surfaces of *considerably* thick bodies is clear from the sentence immediately following the statement of the proposition, and in which he mentions as an example the light 'reflected by thin Plates of Air and Glass' (ibid., p. 281) and also from the following comment: 'In this Proposition I suppose the transparent Bodies to be thick; because if the thickness of the Body be much less than the Interval [exactly, less than half the interval] of the Fits of easy Reflexion and Transmission of the Rays, the Body loseth its reflecting power. For if the Rays, which at their entering into the Body are put into Fits of easy Transmission, arrive at the farthest Surface of the Body before they be out of those Fits, they must be transmitted. And this is the reason why Bubbles of Water lose their reflecting power when they grow very thin; and why all opake Bodies, when reduced into very small parts, because transparent' (ibid., p. 282). Therefore, by the phrase *thick transparent bodies* Newton meant here bodies thicker than half an interval.

[55] Ibid., p. 282.

What kind of action or disposition this is: Whether it consists in a circulating or a vibrating motion of the Ray, or of the Medium, or something else, I do not here enquire. Those that are averse from assenting to any new Discoveries, but such as they can explain by an Hypothesis, may for the present suppose. . . .[56]

The proposed supposition or hypothesis will be quoted later. Having stated it, Newton concluded his sequel thus:

But whether this Hypothesis be true or false I do not here consider. I content my self with the bare Discovery, that the Rays of Light are by some cause or other alternately disposed to be reflected or refracted for many vicissitudes.[57]

From this the following points clearly emerge:

First, so long as he did not assert what kind of action or disposition the fits were, or assign their cause, the theory of fits was not—for Newton—a hypothesis; it constituted a positive contribution, a 'bare Discovery' borne out solely by the experiments. It therefore had to be accepted regardless of all hypotheses about the nature of light.

Second, only an attempt to explain the fits themselves, that is, an attempt to state their cause or nature or mode of production, would constitute a hypothesis—as long as there were no *new* experiments to support it.

Third, Newton himself proposed such a hypothesis, though rather unwillingly, and definitely without committing himself to it.

In this hypothesis the reader is invited to suppose:

that as Stones by falling upon Water put the Water into an undulating Motion, and all Bodies by percussion excite vibrations in the Air; so the Rays of Light, by impinging on any refracting or reflecting Surface, excite vibrations in the refracting or reflecting Medium or Substance, and by exciting them agitate the solid parts of the refracting or reflecting

---

[56] Newton, *Opticks*, Bk. II, Pt. III, Prop. XIII, p. 280.
[57] Ibid., pp. 280–1.

Body, and by agitating them cause the Body to grow warm or hot; that the vibrations thus excited are propagated in the refracting or reflecting Medium or Substance, much after the manner that vibrations are propagated in the Air for causing Sound, and move faster than the Rays so as to overtake them; and that when any Ray is in that part of the vibration which conspires with its Motion, it easily breaks through a refracting Surface, but when it is in the contrary part of the vibration which impedes its Motion, it is easily reflected; and by consequence, that every Ray is successively disposed to be easily reflected, or easily transmitted, by every vibration which overtakes it.[58]

Since it is here supposed that the rays are put into fits by the waves excited *in the reflecting or refracting medium*, it is clear that this hypothesis does not suit the formulation according to which the fits exist in the rays *before* their incidence on the surfaces of transparent bodies. In Query 18[59] it is alternatively suggested that a medium 'exceedingly more rare and subtile than the Air, and exceedingly more elastick and active' might be responsible for putting the rays into fits of easy reflection and easy transmission. Since this ethereal medium is also supposed to expand 'through all the heavens' the rays would excite vibrations in it at their emission from luminous objects, and would thus be put into fits before they encounter any reflecting or refracting media.

Led by Newton's reference—as for example in the above passage (see also Query 17)—to water waves, I. B. Cohen has remarked[60] that 'the disturbance [in the refracting medium, or in the ether] would be transverse'. But it is equally justifiable to argue—as Cohen also observed—that the analogy with sound waves suggests that the disturbance would be longitudinal. The question can perhaps be decided by considering the function assigned to these vibrations by Newton. For since they are supposed to accelerate the ray or retard

---

[58] Ibid., p. 280. 'And do they [the vibrations excited in the refracting or reflecting medium] not overtake the Rays of Light, and by overtaking them successively do they not put them into the Fits of easy Reflexion and easy Transmission described above? For if the Rays endeavour to recede from the densest part of the Vibration, they may be alternately accelerated and retarded by the Vibrations overtaking them' (ibid., Query 17, p. 348).

[59] Cf. ibid., p. 349.

[60] Cf. I. B. Cohen, Preface to the New York edition of Newton's *Opticks*, 1952, note 32, p. iv.

it according as their motion conspires with the motion of the ray or impedes it, the movement to and fro of the ether particles ought to be in the line of direction of the ray; i.e. it is longitudinal. References to water waves are found in the works of many seventeenth-century writers on optics other than Newton (as we have seen, in those of Hooke, Pardies, Huygens, Ango); but none of them—including Newton—tried to make use of transverse vibrations as such in their theories.

The preceding explanation of the fits is mechanical, that is, conceived in terms of mutual action by contact between the rays and the particles of ether or other bodies. But, as in the case of refraction, the Queries of the *Opticks* propose another kind of explanation—in terms of an attractive power:

Nothing more is requisite for putting the Rays of Light into Fits of easy Reflexion and easy Transmission, than that they be small Bodies which by their attractive Powers, or some other Force, stir up Vibrations in what they act upon, which Vibrations being swifter than the Rays, overtake them successively, and agitate them so as by turns to increase and decrease their Velocities, and thereby put them into those Fits.[61]

Of the colours of thin plates Newton therefore offered an explanation, his theory of fits, which in his view was safely based on the experimental results which he obtained. Of the fits themselves he offered an explanation in terms of ether waves excited either by the impinging of the light rays on the ether particles, or by means of an attractive power with which the rays are endowed. This higher level explanation was proposed by him as a hypothesis whose truth or falsity he did not consider, a query to be examined in the light of new experiments; it did not form part of his doctrine of light and colours. Whether the experiments would pronounce for or against it, the fits would, according to him, remain as real properties of light.

The question must now be asked whether the fits had this status. To answer this question it is not necessary to enumerate inherent

---

[61] Newton, *Opticks*, Query 29, pp. 372–3.

difficulties; it is sufficient to point out what has been recognized since Young and Fresnel—namely, that the phenomena which Newton tried to explain by his theory of fits are wave phenomena. In the wave interpretation the rings are fully explained by the interference of the rays reflected at both surfaces of the film. This explanation is therefore nearer to the one proposed by Hooke than to Newton's; since in Hooke's explanation—as distinguished from Newton's—the light reflected at the first surface plays an essential part in the production of the phenomena in question.

The experiments may have *suggested* to Newton a certain periodicity in light; that was revealed in the regular succession of the dark and bright rings in the progression of the natural numbers. But he had to *interpret* this periodicity in accordance with an already formed conception of the rays as discrete entities or corpuscles. This *a priori* conception prevented him from envisaging the possibility of an undulatory interpretation in which the ray, as something distinguished from the waves, would be redundant. Indeed he found in the fits an argument against an independent wave theory of light. For, he argued, [62] if light consisted of waves in an ethereal medium, it would be necessary to postulate the existence of a second ethereal medium whose swifter waves would put those of the first into fits. 'But how two Æthers can be diffused through all Space, one of which acts upon the other, and by consequence is re-acted upon, without retarding, shattering, dispersing and confounding one anothers Motions, is inconceivable.'[63] In this argument Newton was obviously taking for granted what the nineteenth-century wave theory had no need of in order to explain the colours of thin plates—namely, the fits themselves. This can be explained only by his unshakable belief in their existence.

Newton's theory of fits was forced to pass into oblivion after the impressive success of the wave theory during the last century. Since the invention of wave mechanics, however, interest has been renewed—from a historical point of view—in Newton's speculations concerning the origins of the fits. His attempt to combine corpuscular

---

[62] Cf. ibid., Query 28, p. 364.

and wave conceptions has been described as constituting 'a kind of presentiment of wave mechanics'.[64] It is odd (but perhaps understandable) that Newton should now be praised for a hypothetical explanation which he proposed, condescendingly, only for the sake of those who 'are averse from assenting to any new Discoveries, but such as they can explain by an Hypothesis'.[65] Fortunately, his fertile imagination was not hampered by his low opinion of imaginative products.

---

[64] L. de Broglie, *Ondes, corpuscules, mécanique ondulatoire*, Paris, 1945, p. 50. Whittaker has also remarked that Newton's theory of fits was 'a remarkable anticipation of the twentieth-century quantum-theory explanation: the "fits of easy transmission and easy reflection" correspond to the transition probabilities of the quantum theory.'

[65] *Opticks*, p. 280.

Bibliography

(A: 17th-century and earlier works. B: Later works and studies*.)

A

ACADÉMIE ROYALE DES SCIENCES, *Histoire de l'Académie Royale des Sciences,* I, *depuis son établissement en 1666 jusqu'à 1686* [i.e. to the end of 1685], Paris, 1733

ACADÉMIE ROYALE DES SCIENCES, *Mémoires de l'Académie Royale des Sciences, depuis 1666 jusqu'à 1699,* X, Paris, 1730

ACADÉMIE ROYALE DES SCIENCES, *Histoire de l'Académie Royale des Sciences, année 1707, avec les Mémoires de mathématique et de physique pour la même année, tirés des Registres de cette Académie,* Paris, 1708

ALHAZEN, see Ibn al-Haytham

ANGO, PIERRE, *L'optique divisée en trois livres, où l'on démontre d'une manière aisée tout ce qui regarde: 1. La propagation et les proprietez de la lumière, 2. La vision, 3. La figure et la disposition des verres,* Paris, 1682

ARISTOTLE, *De anima; Mechanica; Meteorologica; Problemata; De sensu*

AVERROËS, *In Aristotelis de anima,* Venetiis, 1562. [Facsimile reproduction in *Aristotelis Opera cum Averrois Commentariis,* Frankfurt am Main, 1962, Suppl. II]

AVERROËS, *In libros meteorologicorum expositio media,* in *Aristotelis Opera cum Averrois Commentariis,* Venetiis, 1562, fols. 400^r–487^v. [Facsimile reproduction, Frankfurt am Main, 1962, Vol. V]

AVERROËS, *Kitāb al-nafs* [i.e. Epitome of *De anima,* Arabic text], in *Rasā'il Ibn Rushd,* Hyderabad, 1947

AVICENNA, *De anima,* in *Opera philosophica,* Venetiis, 1508. [Facsimile reproduction, Louvain, 1961]

BACON, FRANCIS, *Novum Organum,* edited with introduction, notes, etc., by Thomas Fowler, 2nd edition corrected and revised, Oxford, 1889

BACON, FRANCIS, *The Works of,* collected and edited by James Spedding, R. L. Ellis and D. D. Heath, 14 vols, London, 1857–74

BACON, ROGER, *The 'Opus Majus' of,* edited with introduction and analytical table by John Henry Bridges, 2 vols, Oxford, 1897; Supplementary Volume, London, 1900

BARTHOLINUS, ERASMUS, *Experimenta crystalli Islandici disdiaclastici, quibus mira & insolita refractio detegitur,* Hafniae, 1669

BEECKMAN, ISAAC, *Journal tenu par Isaac Beeckman de 1604 à 1634,* edited by C. de Waard, 4 vols, La Haye, 1939–53

BIRCH, THOMAS, *The History of the Royal Society of London for improving of Natural Knowledge, from its first Rise, in which the most considerable of those Papers communicated to the Society, which have hitherto not been published, are inserted in their proper order, as a supplement to the Philosophical Transactions,* 4 vols, London, 1756–7

BOYLE, ROBERT, *Experiments and Considerations Touching Colours. First occasionally written, among some other Essays to a Friend; and now suffer'd to come abroad as the Beginning of an Experimental History of Colours,* London, 1664

---

*The two following lists include, in addition to works cited in this book, only a small selection of works that have a bearing on the problems discussed in it.

BOYLE, ROBERT, *The Works of the Honourable Robert Boyle, to which is prefixed The Life of the Author* [by Thomas Birch], a new edition, 6 vols, London, 1772

CLAGETT, MARSHALL, *Archimedes in the Middle Ages*, I (The Arabo-Latin Tradition), Madison, Wisconsin, 1964

CLAGETT, MARSHALL, *The Science of Mechanics in the Middle Ages*, Madison, Wisconsin, 1959

COHEN, MORRIS R. and I. E. DRABKIN (editors), *A Source Book in Greek Science*, Cambridge, Mass., 1948

'CONSTANTINI AFRICANI Liber de oculis' [which is a translation of Ḥunayn ibn Isḥāq's *Book of the Ten Treatises on the Eye*, q.v.], in *Omnia opera Ysaac*, Lugduni, 1515

DE LA CHAMBRE, *see* La Chambre

DESCARTES, RENÉ, *Correspondance*, edited by C. Adam and G. Milhaud, 7 vols, Paris, 1936–60

DESCARTES, RENÉ, *Lettres de Mr Descartes*, edited by C. Clerselier, 3 vols, Paris, 1657, 1659, 1667

DESCARTES, RENÉ, *Œuvres de*, edited by Charles Adam and Paul Tannery, 12 vols and *Supplément*, Paris, 1897–1913

DESCARTES, RENÉ, *Œuvres inédites de*, precédées d'une introduction sur la méthode, par Foucher de Careil, 2 vols, Paris, 1859–60

DESCARTES, RENÉ, *The Philosophical Works of*, translated by Elizabeth Haldane and G. R. T. Ross, 2 vols, 2nd edition, Cambridge, 1931, 1934

DRABKIN, I. E., *see* Cohen, Morris R.

EDLESTON, J., *Correspondence of Sir Isaac Newton and Professor Cotes, including Letters of Other Eminent Men, now first published from the originals in the Library of Trinity College, Cambridge; together with An Appendix containing other unpublished letters and papers by Newton; with notes, synoptical view of the philoso-pher's life and a variety of details illustrative of his history*, London, 1850

EUCLIDE, *L'Optique et la Catoptrique*, oeuvres traduites pour la première fois du grec en français, avec une introduction et des notes par Paul Ver Eecke, nouveau tirage, Paris, 1959. [First published in 1938]

EUCLIDIS *Optica, Opticorum recensio Theonis, Catoptrica, cum Scholiis anti-quis*, ed. I. L. Heiberg (Euclidis *Opera omnia*, ed. I. L. Heiberg & H. Menge, VII), Leipzig, 1895

FERMAT, PIERRE DE, *Œuvres de*, edited by Paul Tannery and Charles Henry, 4 vols, Paris, 1891–1912; *Supplément*, edited by C. de Waard, Paris, 1922

'GALENI Liber de oculis' [which is a translation of Ḥunayn ibn Isḥāq's *Book of the Ten Treatises on the Eye*, q.v.], in Galeni *Opera omnia*, VII, Venetiis, apud Iuntas, 1609

GALILEI, GALILEO, *Dialogues Concerning Two New Sciences*, translated from the Italian and Latin by Henry Crew and Alfonso de Salvio, New York, 1914

GRIMALDI, FRANCESCO MARIA, *Physico-mathesis de lumine, coloribus et iride, aliisque annexis libri II*, Bononiae, 1665

GROSSETESTE, ROBERT, *De luce*, in *Die philosophischen Werke des Robert Grosseteste*, ed. Ludwig Baur, Mün-ster i. W., 1912

HEATH, THOMAS L., *Diophantus of Alexandria*, a study in the history of Greek algebra, 2nd edition, Cambridge, 1910. Republished, New York, 1964

HERIGONE, PIERRE, *Cursus mathematicus*, VI, Paris, 1664 [This volume con-tains the first published account of Fermat's method of maxima and minima in a *Supplementum* beginning with separate pagination after p. 466]

HERONS VON ALEXANDRIA *Mechanik und Katoptrik*, herausgegeben und übersetzt von L. Nix und W. Schmidt: Heronis Alexandrini *Opera quae supersunt omnia*, vol II, fasc. I, Leipzig, 1900

HOBBES, THOMAS, 'Tractatus opticus, prima editione integrale a cura di Franco Alessio', *Rivista critica di storia della filosofia*, anno XVIII, fasc. II, 1963, pp. 147–288

HOOKE, ROBERT, *Micrographia, or some physiological descriptions of minute bodies made by magnifying glasses, with observations and inquiries thereupon*, London, 1665

HOOKE, ROBERT, *The Posthumous Works of*, edited by Richard Waller, London, 1705

ḤUNAYN IBN ISḤĀQ, *The Book of the Ten Treatises on the Eye Ascribed to Ḥunain ibn Isḥāq (809–877 A.D.)*, the earliest existing systematic text-book of ophthalmology. The Arabic text edited from the only two known manuscripts with an English translation and glossary by Max Meyerhof, Cairo, 1928. [See 'Constantini Africani *Liber de oculis*', and 'Galeni *Liber de oculis*', which are medieval translations of this work]

HUYGENS, CHRISTIAN, *Œuvres complètes de*, published by the Société Hollandaise des Sciences, 22 vols, La Haye, 1888–1950

HUYGENS, CHRISTIAN, *Treatise on Light, in which are explained the causes of that which occurs in reflexion, & in refraction, and particularly in the strange refraction of Iceland crystal*, rendered into English by Silvanus P. Thompson, London, 1912

IBN AL-HAYTHAM (ALHAZEN), 'Abhandlung über das Licht von Ibn al-Haitam', *Zeitschrift der Deutschen Morgenländischen Gesellschaft*, XXXVI (1882), pp. 195–237. [Edition of the Arabic text of Ibn al-Haytham's *Discourse on Light* (*Qawl* or *Maqāla fi'l-ḍawʾ*) with German translation by J. Baarmann]

IBN AL-HAYTHAM, Alhazeni *Optica*, in *Opticae thesaurus*, ed. F. Risner, Basel, 1572

KAMĀL AL-DĪN AL-FĀRISĪ, *Tanqīḥ al-manāẓir li-dhawi 'l-abṣār wa'l-baṣāʾir*, 2 vols, Hyderabad, 1347–8 H (1928–30) [A commentary in Arabic on Ibn al-Haytham's *Optics*, i.e. al-*Manāẓir*]

KEPLER, JOHANNES, *Ad Vitellionem paralipomena*, Francofurti, 1604. Re-edited in J. K., *Gesammelte Werke*, II (ed. Franz Hammer), Munich, 1939

KEPLER, JOHANNES, *Dioptrice*, Augustae Videlicorum, 1611. Re-edited in J. K., *Gesammelte Werke*, IV (ed. Max Caspar and Franz Hammer), Munich, 1941

AL-KINDĪ, *De aspectibus*, in *Alkindi, Tideus und pseudo-Euklid, drei optische Werke*, herausgegeben und erklärt von Axel Anthon Björnbo und Seb. Vogl, Leipzig und Berlin, 1912. (Abhandlungen zur Geschichte der mathematischen Wissenschaften mit Einschluss ihrer Anwendungen. Heft XXVI.3)

LA CHAMBRE, MARIN CUREAU DE, *La Lumière à Monseignevr l'Éminentissime Cardinal Mazarin*, par le sieur De la Chambre, conseiller du Roy en ses Conseils et son Médecin ordinaire, Paris, 1657

LEIBNIZ, G. W., *Discours de métaphysique*, édition collationnée avec le texte autographe, présentée et annotée par Henri Lestienne, 2nd edition, Paris, 1952. [First published at Hanover in 1846]

LEIBNIZ, G. W., 'Unicum opticae, catoptricae, & dioptricae principium', in *Acta eruditorum*, Leipzig, 1682, pp. 185–90

MAUROLYCUS, FRANCISCUS, *Photismi de lumine et umbra ad perspectivam et radiorum incidentiam facientes. Diaphanorum partes, seu libri tres, in quorum primo de perspicuis corporibus, in secundo de iride, in tertio de organi visualis structura et conspiciliorum formis agitur. problemata ad perspectivam et iridem pertinentia*, Neapoli, 1611

MERSENNE, P. MARIN, *Correspondance du*, publiée par Mme. Paul Tannery, éditée et annotée par Cornelis de Waard avec la collaboration de René Pintard, 9 vols, Paris, 1932–1965

MERSENNE, P. MARIN, *Quaestiones celeberrimae...*, Lutetiae Parisiorum, 1623

NEWTON, ISAAC, *The Correspondence of*, ed. H. W. Turnbull, 3 vols, Cambridge, 1959, 1960, 1961. Vol I (1661–75), vol II (1676–87), vol III (1688–94), continuing

NEWTON, ISAAC, *Lectiones opticae, annis 1669, 1670, et 1671 in scholis publicis habitae; et nunc primum ex MSS. in lucem editae*, Londini, 1729

NEWTON, ISAAC, *Sir Isaac Newton's Mathematical Principles of Natural Philosophy and his system of the World.* Motte's translation (of 1729) revised and supplied with an historical appendix by Florian Cajori, Berkeley, California, 1934. [First edition as *Philosophiae Naturalis Principia Mathematica*, Londini, 1687]

NEWTON, ISAAC, *Isaaci Newtoni Opera quae extant omnia*, commentariis illustrabat Samuel Horsley, 5 vols, London, 1779–85

NEWTON, ISAAC, *Optical Lectures, Read in the Publick Schools of the University of Cambridge, Anno Domini 1669, never before printed. Translated into English out of the Original Latin*, London, 1728

NEWTON, ISAAC, *Opticks: or a Treatise of the Reflections, Refractions, Inflections and Colours of Light.* Reprinted from the 4th edition (London, 1730) with a Foreword by Albert Einstein and an Introduction by E. T. Whittaker, London, 1931

NEWTON, ISAAC, *Opticks*, etc., New York, 1952. Reprint of the London edition of 1931 with an additional Preface by I. Bernard Cohen and an Analytical Table of Contents by Duane H. D. Roller

NEWTON, ISAAC, *Isaac Newton's Papers and Letters on Natural Philosophy and Related Documents*, edited with a General Introduction by I. Bernard Cohen, assisted by Robert E. Schofield, Cambridge, Mass., 1958

NEWTON, ISAAC, *Unpublished Scientific Papers of Isaac Newton*, edited by A. Rupert Hall and Marie Boas Hall, Cambridge, 1962

PARDIES, IGNACE GASTON, *Discours sur le mouvement local, avec des remarques sur le mouvement de la lumière*, Paris, 1670

PARDIES, IGNACE GASTON, *La statique ou la science des forces mouvantes*, Paris, 1673

PTOLEMAEI *Optica: L'Optique de Claude Ptolémée*, dans la version latine d'après l'arabe de l'émir Eugène de Sicile, édition critique et exégétique par Albert Lejeune, Louvain, 1956

RÉGIS, PIERRE-SILVAIN, *Cours entier de philosophie, ou système général selon les principes de M. Descartes*, etc., 3 vols, Amsterdam, 1691

RIGAUD, STEPHAN JORDAN, *Correspondence of Scientific Men of the Seventeenth Century, including Letters of Barrow, Flamsteed, Wallis, and Newton*, printed from the originals in the collection of the Right Honourable the Earl of Macclesfield, 2 vols, Oxford, 1841

RISNERUS, FRIDERICUS, *Opticae libri quatuor*, ex voto P. Rami novissimo per F. Risnerum... in usum et lucem publicam producti, Cassellis, 1606

RISNERUS, FRIDERICUS, Risneri *Optica cum annotationibus Willebrordi Snellii*, ed. J. A. Vollgraff, Gandavi, 1918

ROBERVAL, G. PERS. DE, *Traité de méchanique*, in Marin Mersenne, *Harmonie universelle*, Paris, 1636 [The pages are not consecutively numbered throughout this volume. Roberval's *Traité*, which comprises 36 pages, begins after the first three treatises in the volume]

ROHAULT, JACQUES, *Traité de physique*, Paris, 1671

ROYAL SOCIETY OF LONDON, *Philosophical Transactions*, London, 1671/2–1675

ROYAL SOCIETY OF LONDON, *The Philosophical Transactions . . . abridged*, with notes . . . by C. Hutton, G. Shaw, R. Pearson, 18 vols, London, 1809

SPRAT, THOMAS, *The History of the Royal Society of London for the Improving of Natural Knowledge*, 4th edition, London, 1734. [First published in 1667]

VITELLONIS *Optica*, in *Opticae thesaurus*, ed. F. Risner, Basel, 1572

VOSSIUS, ISAAC, *De lucis natura et proprietate*, Amstelodami, 1662

VOSSIUS, ISAAC, *Isaaci Vossii Responsum ad objecta J. de Bruyn*, in J. de Bruyn, *Epistola ad clariss. virum D.D. Isaacum Vossium*, Amstelodami, 1663

B

ALQUIÉ, FERDINAND, *La découverte métaphysique de l'homme chez Descartes*, Paris, 1950. [Includes interesting discussions of Descartes' *Le Monde* and his theory of the creation of eternal truths]

BAARMANN, J., *see* Ibn al-Haytham in Bibl. A.

BACHELARD, GASTON, *L'activité rationaliste de la physique contemporaine*, Paris, 1951

BACHELARD, SUSANNE, 'Maupertuis et le principe de la moindre action', *Thalès*, année 1958, pp. 3–36

BADCOCK, A. W., 'Physical optics at the Royal Society, 1660–1800', *British Journal for the History of Science*, I (1962), pp. 99–116

BEARE, JOHN I., *Greek Theories of Elementary Cognition, from Alcmaeon to Aristotle*, Oxford, 1906

BECK, L. J., *The Method of Descartes*, a study of the *Regulae*, Oxford, 1952

BELL, A. E., *Christian Huygens and the Development of Science in the Seventeenth Century*, London, 1947

BLOCH, LÉON, *La philosophie de Newton*, Paris, 1908

BOAS, MARIE, 'The establishment of the mechanical philosophy', *Osiris*, X (1952), pp. 412–541

BOAS, MARIE, 'La méthode scientifique de Robert Boyle', *Revue d'histoire des sciences*, IX (1956), pp. 105–25

BOEGEHOLD, H., 'Einiges aus der Geschichte des Brechungsgesetzes', *Zentral-Zeitung für Optik und Mechanik, Elektro-Technik und verwandte Berufszweige*, XL (1919), pp. 94–97, 103–5, 113–16, 121–41

BOEGEHOLD, H., 'Keplers Gedanken über das Brechungsgesetz und ihre Einwirkung auf Snell und Descartes', *Kepler-Festschrift*, Teil I, ed. Karl Stöckl, Regensburg, 1930, pp. 150–67

BOUASSE, HENRI, *Introduction à l'étude des théories de la mécanique*, Paris, 1895. [Contains an illuminating discussion of Descartes' laws of motion; cf. Ch. X: 'Des lois du choc dans Descartes']

BOYER, CARL B., 'Aristotelian references to the law of reflection', *Isis*, XXXVI (1945–1946), pp. 92–95

BOYER, CARL B., 'Descartes and the radius of the rainbow', *Isis*, XLIII (1952), pp. 95–98

BOYER, CARL B., 'Early estimates of the velocity of light', *Isis*, XXXIII (1941), pp. 24–40

BOYER, CARL B., *The Rainbow, from Myth to Mathematics*, New York & London, 1959

BREWSTER, DAVID, *Memoirs of the Life, Writings and Discoveries of Sir Isaac Newton*, 2 vols, Edinburgh, 1855

BROAD, C. D., *The Philosophy of*

Francis Bacon, an address delivered at Cambridge on the occasion of the Bacon tercentenary, 5 October 1926, Cambridge, 1926

BROGLIE, LOUIS DE, *Matière et lumière*, Paris, 1948. [An instructive account of the development of optics (Ch. III), and a discussion of the problem of representing white light from the points of view of the wave and quantum theories, Ch. V, Sec. 4]

BROGLIE, LOUIS DE, *Ondes, corpuscules, mécanique ondulatoire*, Paris, 1949

BROGLIE, LOUIS DE, 'On the parallelism between the dynamics of a material particle and geometrical optics', in *Selected Papers on Wave Mechanics* by Louis de Broglie and Léon Brillouin, authorized translation by Winifred M. Deans, London and Glasgow, 1929

BRUNET, P., *Étude historique sur le principe de la moindre action* (Actualités scientifiques et industrielles, No. 693), Paris, 1938

BRUNSCHVICG, LÉON, *L'expérience humaine et la causalité physique*, 3rd edition, Paris, 1949

BRUNSCHVICG, LÉON, 'La révolution cartésienne et la notion spinoziste de la substance', *Revue de métaphysique et de morale*, 12ᵉ année (1904), pp. 755–98. [Remarks on the place of the doctrine of instantaneous propagation of light in Descartes' physics]

BUCHDAHL, GERD, 'Descartes' anticipation of a "logic of scientific discovery"', *Scientific Change* (ed. A. C. Crombie), London, 1963

BUCHDAHL, GERD, 'The relevance of Descartes' philosophy for modern philosophy of science', *The British Journal for the History of Science*, I (1963), pp. 227–49

BURTT, EDWIN ARTHUR, *The Metaphysical Foundations of Modern Physical Science*, a historical and critical essay, revised edition, London, 1950

CAJORI, F., *History of Physics*, 2nd edition, New York, 1929

CLAGETT, MARSHALL, ed., *Critical Problems in the History of Science* (Proceedings of the Institute for the History of Science at the University of Wisconsin, September 1–11, 1957), Madison, Wisconsin, 1959

COHEN, I. BERNARD, 'The first English version of Newton's *Hypotheses non fingo*', *Isis*, LII (1962), pp. 379–88

COHEN, I. BERNARD, 'The first explanation of interference', *The American Journal of Physics*, VIII (1940), pp. 99–106

COHEN, I. BERNARD, *Franklin and Newton*, an inquiry into speculative Newtonian experimental science and Franklin's work in electricity as an example thereof, Philadelphia, 1956

COHEN, I. BERNARD, 'Newton in the light of recent scholarship', *Isis*, LI (1960), pp. 489–514

COHEN, I. BERNARD, 'Roemer and the first determination of the velocity of light (1676)', *Isis*, XXXI (1940), pp. 327–79

COHEN, I. BERNARD, 'Versions of Isaac Newton's first published paper', *Archives internationales d'histoire des sciences*, XI (1958), pp. 357–75

CROMBIE, A. C., *Augustine to Galileo: I* (*Science in the Middle Ages, 5th–13th Centuries*), II (*Science in the Later Middle Ages and Early Modern Times, 13th–17th Centuries*), 2nd edition, London, 1961. [First edition published in 1952]

CROMBIE, A. C., *Robert Grosseteste and the Origins of Experimental Science, 1100–1700*, 2nd impression, Oxford, 1962. [First published in 1953]

DIJKSTERHUIS, E. J., *The Mechanization of the World Picture*, translated by C. Dikshoorn, Oxford, 1961. [Dutch original first published in 1950]

DIJKSTERHUIS, E. J., 'La méthode et les *Essais* de Descartes', in *Descartes et le cartésianisme hollandais*, études et documents, par E. J. Dijksterhuis *et al.* Paris and Amsterdam, 1950, pp. 21–44

DONDER, TH. DE, and J. PELSENEER, 'La vitesse de propagation de la lumière selon Descartes', *Académie Royale de Belgique, Bulletin de la classe des sciences*, XXIII (1937), pp. 689–92

DUGAS, RENÉ, *De Descartes à Newton par l'école anglaise* (Conférences du Palais de la Découverte, série D, No. 16), Paris, 1953

DUGAS, RENÉ, *Histoire de la mécanique*, Neuchâtel, 1950

DUGAS, RENÉ, *La mécanique au xviie siècle, des antécédents scolastiques à la pensée classique*, Neuchâtel, 1954

DUGAS, RENÉ, 'Sur le cartésianisme de Hugens', *Revue d'histoire des sciences*, VII (1954), pp. 22–23

DUHEM, PIERRE, '*Σῴζειν τὰ φαινόμενα*. Essai sur la notion de théorie physique de Platon à Galilée', *Annales de philosophie chrétienne*, 4e série, VI (1908), pp. 113–39, 277–302, 352–77, 482–514, 561–92

DUHEM, PIERRE, 'L'optique de Malebranche', *Revue de métaphysique et de morale*, 23e année (1916), pp. 37–91

DUHEM, PIERRE, 'Les théories de l'optique', *Revue des deux mondes*, CXXIII (1894), pp. 94–125

DUHEM, PIERRE, *La théorie physique, son objet, sa structure*, 2nd edition, Paris, 1914

FABRY, C., 'Histoire de la physique' [i.e. in France in the 17th century], in G. Hanotaux, *Histoire de la nation française*, XIV, Paris, 1924

FEDERICI VESCOVINI, GRAZIELLA, 'Le questioni di "perspectiva" di Biagio Pelacani da Parma', *Rinascimento*, XII (1961), pp. 163–243

FREDERICI VESCOVINI, GRAZIELLA, *Studi sulla prospettiva medievale*, Torino, 1965

GILSON, É., *Discours de la méthode, texte et commentaire*, Paris, 1930

GILSON, E., 'Météores cartésiens et météores scolastiques', *Études de philosophie médiévale*, Strasbourg, 1921, pp. 247–86

GOUY, M., 'Sur le mouvement lumineux', *Journal de physique théorique et appliquée*, 2e série, V (1886), pp. 354–62

HALBERTSMA, K. T. A., *A History of the Theory of Colour*, Amsterdam, 1949

HALL, A. RUPERT, *From Galileo to Newton, 1630–1720* (The Rise of Modern Science, 3), London, 1963

HALL, A. RUPERT, 'Further optical experiments of Isaac Newton', *Annals of Science*, II (1955), pp. 27–43

HALL, A. RUPERT, 'Newton's First Book (I)', *Archives internationales d'histoire des sciences*, XIII (1960), pp. 39–61

HALL, A. RUPERT, 'Sir Isaac Newton's Note-book, 1661–65', *The Cambridge Historical Journal*, IX (1948), pp. 239–50

HALL, A. RUPERT, *The Scientific Revolution, 1500–1800, the formation of the modern scientific attitude*, 2nd edition, London, 1962. [First published in 1954]

HIRSCHBERG, J., 'Über das älteste arabische Lehrbuch der Augenheilkunde', *Sitzungsberichte der Königlich Preussischen Akademie der Wissenschaften* (1903, XLIX, 26 November. Sitzung der philosophisch-historischen Classe), pp. 1080–94

HORTEN, M., 'Avicenna's Lehre vom Regenbogen nach seinem Werk al Schifāʾ', *Meteorologische Zeitschrift*, XXX (1913), pp. 533–44

HOSKIN, M. A., 'Clarke's notes to Rohault's *Traité de physique*', *The Thomist*, XXIV (1961), pp. 353–63

JENKINS, FRANCIS A., and HARVEY E. WHITE, *Fundamentals of Optics*, 2nd edition, London, 1951

KEELING, S. V., *Descartes*, London, 1934

KNESER, A., *Das Prinzip der kleinsten Wirkung von Leibniz bis zur Zeit der Gegenwart* (Wissenschaftliche Grundfragen, herausgegeben von R. Hönigswald, Nr. IX), Leipzig, 1928

KORTEWEG, D.-J., 'Descartes et les manuscrits de Snellius d'après quelques documents nouveaux', *Revue de métaphysique et de morale*, 4ᵉ année (1896), pp. 489–501

KOYRÉ, ALEXANDRE, *Études galiléennes: I. À l'aube de la science classique; II. La loi de la chute des corps, Descartes et Galilée; III. Galilée et la loi d'inertie* (Actualités scientifiques et industrielles, Nos. 852–4), Paris, 1939

KOYRÉ, ALEXANDRE, 'La gravitation universelle de Képler à Newton', *Archives internationales d'histoire des sciences*, IV (1951), pp. 638–53 (Conférence du Palais de la Découverte, Paris, 1951)

KOYRÉ, ALEXANDRE, 'L'hypothèse et l'expérience chez Newton', *Bulletin de la Société Française de la Philosophie*, L (1956), pp. 59–89

KOYRÉ, ALEXANDRE, 'The origins of modern science, a new interpretation', *Diogenes*, No. 16, Winter 1956, pp. 1–22. [Review of A. C. Crombie, *Robert Grosseteste*]

KOYRÉ, ALEXANDRE, 'Les Queries de l'Optique', *Archives internationales d'histoire des sciences*, XIII (1960), pp. 15–29

KOYRÉ, ALEXANDRE, 'Les Regulae philosophandi', *Archives internationales d'histoire des sciences*, XIII (1960), pp. 3–14

KRAMER, P., 'Descartes und das Brechungsgesetz des Lichtes', *Abhandlungen zur Geschichte der Mathematik*, IV (1882), pp. 233–78

KUHN, THOMAS S., 'Newton's optical papers', in I. Bernard Cohen (ed.), *Isaac Newton's Papers and Letters on Natural Philosophy*, Cambridge, Mass., 1958, pp. 27–45

LALANDE, ANDRÉ, L' '*interprétation*' *de la nature dans le* '*Valerius terminus*' *de Bacon*, Mâcon, 1901

LALANDE, ANDRÉ, 'Quelques textes de Bacon et de Descartes', *Revue de métaphysique et de morale*, 19ᵉ année (1911), pp. 296–311

LALANDE, ANDRÉ, *Les théories de l'induction et l'expérimentation*, Paris, 1929

LAPLACE, PIERRE SIMON DE, 'Sur la double réfraction de la lumière dans les cristaux diaphanes', *Bulletin de la Société Philomatique*, I (1807), pp. 303–10. Reproduced in *Œuvres complètes de Laplace*, XIV, Paris, 1912, pp. 278–87

LAPLACE, PIERRE SIMON DE, 'Sur la loi de la réfraction extraordinaire de la lumière dans les cristaux diaphanes', *Journal de physique*, LXVIII (1809), pp. 107–11. Reproduced in *Œuvres complètes de Laplace*, XIV, Paris, 1912, pp. 254–8

LAPORTE, JEAN, *Le rationalisme de Descartes*, Paris, 1945

LEJEUNE, ALBERT, 'Archimède et la loi de la réflexion', *Isis*, XXXVIII (1947), pp. 51–53

LEJEUNE, ALBERT, *Euclide et Ptolémée, deux stades de l'optique géométrique grecque*, Louvain, 1948

LEJEUNE, ALBERT, 'Les lois de la réflexion dans l'*Optique* de Ptolémée', *L'antiquité classique*, XV (1946), pp. 241–56

LEJEUNE, ALBERT, *Recherches sur la catoptrique grecque d'après les sources antiques et médiévales*, Bruxelles, 1957

LEJEUNE, ALBERT, 'Les tables de réfractions de Ptolémée', *Annales de la Société Scientifique de Bruxelles*, série I (Sciences mathématiques et physiques), LX (1940), pp. 93–101

LE LIONNAIS, F., 'Descartes et Einstein', *Revue d'histoire des sciences et de leurs applications*, V (1952), pp. 139–54

LOHNE, JOHANNES, 'Zur Geschichte des Brechungsgesetzes', *Sudhoffs Archiv*, Band 47, Heft 2, Juni 1963, pp. 152–72

LOHNE, JOHANNES, 'Newton's "proof" of the sine law and his mathematical principles of colours', *Archive for History of Exact Sciences*, vol 1, No. 4 (1961), pp. 389–405

LOHNE, JOHANNES, 'Thomas Harriott (1560–1621), the Tycho Brahe of optics', *Centaurus*, VI (1959), pp. 113–21

MACH, ERNST, *The Principles of Physical Optics*, an historical and philosophical treatment, translated by John S. Anderson and A. F. A. Young, London, 1926. [German original first published in 1921]

MEYERSON, ÉMILE, *Identity and Reality*, translated by Kate Loewenberg, London, 1930

MILHAUD, GASTON, *Descartes savant*, Paris, 1921

MILHAUD, GASTON, *Nouvelles études sur l'histoire de la pensée scientifique*, Paris, 1911. [A chapter on 'Descartes et Newton', pp. 219–35]

MONTUCLA, JEAN-ÉTIENNE, *Histoire des mathématiques*, nouvelle édition, considérablement augmentée, et prolongée jusque vers l'époque actuelle, 4 vols, Paris, 1799–1802 (Vols III and IV edited and published by Jérome de La Lande)

MORE, LOUIS TRENCHARD, *Isaac Newton*, a biography, New York and London, 1934

MOUY, PAUL, *Le dévelopment de la physique cartésienne, 1646–1712*, Paris, 1934

MOUY, PAUL, *Les lois du choc des corps d'après Malebranche*, Paris, 1927

NAPIER, MACVEY, 'Remarks, illustrative of the scope and influence of the philosophical writings of Lord Bacon', *Transactions of the Royal Society of Edinburgh*, VIII (1818), pp. 373–425

NAZĪF, MUṢṬAFĀ, *al-Ḥasan ibn al-Haytham, buḥūthuhu wa-kushūfuhu al-baṣariyya*, 2 vols, Cairo, 1942–43. [A study in Arabic of the *Optics* of Ibn al-Haytham, based on the extant MSS]

PAPANASTASSIOU, CH.-E., *Les théories sur la nature de la lumière de Descartes à nos jours et l'évolution de la théorie physique*, Paris, 1935

PELSENEER, JEAN, 'Gilbert, Bacon, Galileo, Kepler, Harvey et Descartes—leurs relations', *Isis*, XVII (1932), pp. 171–208

PELSENEER, JEAN, see Th. de Donder and J. Pelseneer.

POGGENDORFF, J. C., *Geschichte der Physik*, Vorlesungen gehalten an der Universität zu Berlin, Leipzig, 1879

POLYAK, S. L., *The Retina*, Chicago, 1941

POPPER, KARL R., *Conjectures and Refutations, the growth of scientific knowledge*, London, 1963

POPPER, KARL R., *The Logic of Scientific Discovery*, London, 1959

PRIESTLEY, JOSEPH, *The History and Present State of Discoveries Relating to Vision, Light and Colours*, London, 1722

REILLY, CONOR, 'Francis Line, peripatetic (1595–1675)', *Osiris*, XIV (1962), pp. 222–53

ROBERTS, MICHAEL and E. R. THOMAS, *Newton and the Origin of Colours*, a study of the earliest examples of scientific method, London, 1934

ROBINSON, BRYAN, *A Dissertation on the Æther of Sir Isaac Newton*, Dublin, 1743

ROBINSON, BRYAN, *Sir Isaac Newton's Account of the Æther*, Dublin, 1745

RONCHI, VASCO, *Histoire de la lumière*, translated by Juliette Taton, Paris, 1956. [First published as *Storia della luce*, Bologna, 1939]

ROSENBERGER, F., *Newton und seine physikalischen Prinzipien*, Leipzig, 1895

ROSENFELD, L., 'Marcus Marcis Untersuchungen über das Prisma und ihr Verhältnis zu Newton's Farbentheorie', *Isis*, XVII (1932), pp. 325–30

ROSENFELD, L., 'Le premier conflit entre la théorie ondulatoire et la théorie corpusculaire de la lumière,' *Isis*, XI (1928), pp. 111–22

ROSENFELD, L., 'La théorie des couleurs de Newton et ses adversaires', *Isis*, IX (1927), pp. 44–65

ROTH, LEON, *Descartes' Discourse on Method*, Oxford, 1948

ROUSE BALL, W. W., *An Essay on Newton's Principia*, London, 1893

SABRA, A. I., 'Explanation of optical reflection and refraction: Ibn al-Haytham, Descartes, Newton', *Actes du dixième congrès international d'histoire des sciences* (1962), Paris, 1964, I, pp. 551–4

SABRA, A. I., 'Newton and the "bigness" of vibrations', *Isis*, LIV (1963), pp. 267–8

SABRA, A. I., 'A note on a suggested modification of Newton's corpuscular theory of light to reconcile it with Foucault's experiment of 1850', *The British Journal for the Philosophy of Science*, V (1954), pp. 149–51

SAMBURSKY, S., 'Philoponus' interpretation of Aristotle's theory of light', *Osiris*, XIII (1958), pp. 114–126

SARTON, G., 'Discovery of the dispersion of light and of the nature of colour (1672)', *Isis*, XIV (1930), pp. 326–41

SCHRAMM, MATTHIAS, *Ibn al-Haythams Weg zur Physik*, Wiesbaden, 1963

SCHRECKER, P., 'Bibliographie de Descartes savant', *Thalès*, 3ᵉ année (1936, published 1938), pp. 145–54

SCHRECKER, P. 'Notes sur l'évolution du principe de la moindre action', *Isis*, XXXIII (1941), pp. 329–334

SCOTT, J. F., *The Scientific Work of René Descartes (1596–1650)*, London, 1952

SHIRLEY, J. W., 'An early experimental determination of Snell's law', *American Journal of Physics*, XIX (1951), pp. 507–8

SIRVEN, J., *Les années d'apprentissage de Descartes (1596–1628)*, Paris, 1930

SMITH, NORMAN KEMP, *New Studies in the Philosophy of Descartes*, London, 1952

SNOW, A. J., *Matter and Gravity in Newton's Physical Philosophy*, a study in the natural philosophy of Newton's time, London, 1926

STOCK, HYMAN, *The Method of Descartes in the Natural Sciences*, New York, 1931

STRONG, E. W., 'Newton's "mathematical way" ', *Journal of the History of Ideas*, XII (1951), pp. 90–110

STRONG, E. W., *Procedure and Metaphysics*, a study in the philosophy of mathematical-physical science in the sixteenth and seventeenth centuries, Berkeley, California, 1936

SUPPES, PATRICK, 'Descartes and the problem of action at a distance', *Journal of the History of Ideas*, XV (1954), pp. 146–152

TANNERY, PAUL, 'Sur la date des principales découvertes de Fermat', *Bulletin des sciences mathématiques et astronomiques*, 2ᵉ série, VII (1883), première partie, pp. 116–128

TANNERY, PAUL, 'Descartes physicien', *Revue de métaphysique et de morale*, 4ᵉ année (1896), pp. 478–88

TANNERY, PAUL, *Mémoires scientifiques*, publiés par J. L. Heiberg et H.-G. Zeuthen, 17 vols, Toulouse-Paris, 1912–1950

THOMAS, E. R., see Michael Roberts and E. R. Thomas

TOULMIN, STEPHEN, *The Philosophy of Science*, London, 1953

TURBAYNE, COLIN MURRAY, *The Myth of Metaphor*, New Haven, Conn., 1962

VAN GEER, P., 'Notice sur la vie et les travaux de Willebrord Snellius', *Archives néerlandaises des sciences exactes et naturelles* (published by: La Société Hollandaise des Sciences), XVIII (1883), pp. 453–68

VAVILOV, S. I., 'Newton and the atomic theory', in *Newton Tercentenary Celebrations*, Cambridge, 1947, pp. 43–55

VOLLGRAFF, J. A., 'Pierre de la Ramée (1515–1572) et Willebrord Snel van Royen (1580–1626)', *Janus*, 18ᵉ année (1913), pp. 595–625

VOLLGRAFF, J. A., 'Snellius' notes on the reflections and refractions of rays', *Osiris*, I (1936), pp. 718–25

WAARD, C. DE, *L'expérience barométrique, ses antécédents et ses explications*, étude historique, Thouars, 1936

WAARD, C. DE, 'Le manuscrit perdu de Snellius sur la réfraction', *Janus*, 39ᵉ année (1935), pp. 51–73

WAHL, JEAN, *Du rôle de l'idée de l'instant dans la philosophie de Descartes*, 2nd edition, Paris, 1953

WESTFALL, RICHARD S., 'The development of Newton's theory of color', *Isis*, LIII (1962), pp. 339–58

WESTFALL, RICHARD S., 'The foundations of Newton's philosophy of nature', *The British Journal for the History of Science*, I (1962), pp. 171–82

WESTFALL, RICHARD S., 'Newton and his critics on the nature of colours', *Archives internationales d'histoire des sciences*, 15ᵉ année (1962), pp. 47–58

WESTFALL, RICHARD S., 'Newton's reply to Hooke and the theory of colours', *Isis*, LIV (1963), pp. 82–96

WHEWELL, WILLIAM, *History of the Inductive Sciences, from the Earliest to the Present Times*, new and revised edition, 3 vols, London, 1847

WHEWELL, WILLIAM, *The Philosophy of the Inductive Sciences*, London, 1840

WHITE, HARVEY E., see Francis A. Jenkins and Harvey E. White

WHITTAKER, EDMUND T., *A History of Æther and Electricity*, the classical theories, 2nd edition, Edinburgh, 1951

WILDE, EMIL, *Geschichte der Optik*, 2 vols, Berlin, 1838–43

WINTER, H. J. J., 'The optical researches of Ibn al-Haitham', *Centaurus*, III (1954), pp. 190–210

WOLF, A., *A History of Science, Technology, and Philosophy in the 16th & 17th Centuries*, 2nd edition prepared by Douglas McKie, 1950

WOOD, ALEXANDER, *In Pursuit of Truth*, a comparative study in science and religion, London, 1927

WOOD, ROBERT W., *Physical Optics*, 2nd edition, New York, 1911

WÜRSCHMIDT, JOSEPH, 'Die Theorie des Regenbogens und des Halo bei Ibn al-Haitam und bei Dietrich von Freiberg', *Meteorologische Zeitschrift*, XXXI (1914), pp. 484–87

YOUNG, THOMAS, 'On the theory of light and colours', in *A Course of Lectures on Natural Philosophy*, II, London, 1807, pp. 613–31

ZOUBOV, V., 'Une théorie aristotélicienne de la lumière du xviiᵉ siècle', *Isis*, XXIV (1936), pp. 341–60

Additional Bibliography 1966–1980

As in the original bibliography, only works closely related to the questions discussed in this book are included.

BECHLER, ZEV, 'Newton's search for a mechanistic model of colour dispersion: a suggested interpretation', *Archive for History of Exact Sciences*, XI (1973), pp. 1–37.

BECHLER, ZEV, 'Newton's law of forces which are inversely as the mass: a suggested interpretation of his later efforts to normalise a mechanistic model of optical dispersion', *Centaurus*, XVIII (1974), pp. 184–222.

BECHLER, ZEV, 'Newton's 1672 optical controversies: a study in the grammar of scientific dissent', in Y. Elkana, ed., *The Interaction Between Science and Philosophy*, Atlantic Highlands, N.J., 1974, pp.115 – 42.

BECHLER, ZEV, 'A less agreeable matter: the disagreeable case of Newton and achromatic refraction', *British Journal for the History of Science*, VIII (1975), pp.101 – 26.

BIERNSON, GEORGE, 'Why did Newton see indigo in the spectrum?', *American Journal of Physics*, XL (1972), pp. 526 – 33.

BOS, H. J. M., et al., eds., *Studies on Christiaan Huygens*, Lisse, 1980.

BUCHDAHL, GERD, *Metaphysics and the Philosophy of Science: the classical origins, Descartes to Kant*, Oxford, 1969.

BUCHDAHL, GERD, 'Methodological aspects of Kepler's theory of refraction', *Studies in History and Philosophy of Science*, III (1972), pp.265 – 98.

DESCARTES, RENÉ, *Discourse on Method, Optics, and Meteorology*. Translated by Paul J. Olscamp, Indianapolis, 1965.

GRUNER, S. M., 'Defending Father Lucas, a consideration of the Newton–Lucas dispute on the nature of the spectrum', *Centaurus*, XVII (1973), pp.315 – 29.

HOLTZMARK, TORGER, 'Newton's *Experimentum crucis* reconsidered', *American Journal of Physics*, XXXIX (1970), pp.1229 – 35.

KNUDSEN, OLE and KURT M. PEDERSEN, 'The link between "determination" and conservation of motion in Descartes' dynamics', *Centaurus*, XIII (1968), pp. 183 – 6.

LAYMON, RONALD, 'Newton's advertised precision and his refutation of the received laws of refraction', in Peter K. Machamer and Robert G.

Turnbull, eds., *Studies in Perception: interrelations in the history of philosophy and science*, Columbus, Ohio, 1978, pp.231 – 58.

LAYMON, RONALD, 'Newton's *Experimentum crucis* and the logic of idealization and theory refutation', *Studies in History and Philosophy of Science*, IX (1978), pp.51 – 77.

LOHNE, J. A., 'Isaac Newton: the rise of a scientist 1661 – 1671', *Notes and Records of the Royal Society of London*, XX (1965), pp. 125 – 39.

LOHNE, J. A., 'The increasing corruption of Newton's diagrams', *History of Science*, VI (1967), pp.69–89.

LOHNE, J. A., 'Experimentum Crucis', *Notes and Records of the Royal Society of London*, XXIII (1968), pp.169 – 99.

LOHNE, J. A. and BERNHARD STICKER, *Newtons Theorie der Prismenfarben, mit Übersetzung und Erläuterung der Abhandlung von 1672*, Munich, 1969.

LOHNE, J. A., 'Newton's table of refractive powers: origins, accuracy, and influence', *Sudhoffs Archiv für Geschichte der Medizin und Naturwissenschaften*, LXI (1977), pp.229 – 47.

MAHONEY, M. S., *The Mathematical Career of Pierre de Fermat (1601 – 1665)*, Princeton, 1973.

MAMIANI, MAURIZIO, *Isaac Newton filosofo della natura: le lezioni giovanili di ottica e la genesi del metodo Newtoniano*, Florence, 1976.

NEWTON, ISAAC, *The Mathematical Papers of I.N.*, ed. D. T. Whiteside, I (1664 – 1666), III (1670 – 1673), Cambridge, 1967, 1969. [Sections on optics with notes by the editor.]

NEWTON, ISAAC, *The Unpublished First Version of Isaac Newton's Cambridge Lectures on Optics 1670 – 1672: a facsimile of the autograph, now Cambridge University Library MS. Add. 4002*, with an introduction by

D. T. Whiteside, Cambridge, 1973.

SHAPIRO, ALAN E., 'Kinematic optics: a study of the wave theory of light in the seventeenth century', *Archive for History of Exact Sciences*, XI (1973), pp.134 – 266.

SHAPIRO, ALAN E., 'Light, pressure, and rectilinear propagation: Descartes' celestial optics and Newton's hydrostatics', *Studies in History and Philosophy of Science*, V (1974), pp.239 – 96.

SHAPIRO, ALAN E., 'Newton's definition of a light ray and the diffusion theories of chromatic dispersion', *Isis*, LXVI (1975), pp.194 – 210.

SHAPIRO, ALAN E., 'Newton's "achromatic" dispersion law: theoretical background and experimental evidence', *Archive for History of Exact Sciences*, XXI (1979), pp.91 – 128.

SHAPIRO, ALAN E., 'The evolving structure of Newton's theory of white light and color', *Isis*, LXXI (1980), pp.211 – 35.

STRAKER, S. M., *Kepler's Optical Studies: a study in the development of seventeenth-century natural philosophy*, Ph.D. dissertation, Indiana University, 1971. Available from University Microfilms, Ann Arbor, Michigan.

STUEWER, ROGER H., 'A critical analysis of Newton's work on diffraction', in *Isis*, LXI (1970), pp.188 – 205.

TATON, RENÉ, ed., *Roemer et la vitesse de la lumière*, Paris, 1978.

WESTFALL, RICHARD S., 'Isaac Newton's coloured circles twixt two contiguous glasses', *Archive for History of Exact Sciences*, II (1965), pp.181 – 96.

WESTFALL, RICHARD S., 'Newton defends his first publication: the Newton-Lucas correspondence', *Isis*, LVII (1966), pp.299 – 314.

WESTFALL, RICHARD S., 'Uneasily fitful reflections on fits of easy transmission', *The Texas Quarterly*, X (1967), pp.86 – 102. Also in *The Annus Mirabilis of Sir Isaac Newton, 1666 – 1966*, ed. Robert Palter, Cambridge, MA, and London, 1970, pp.88 – 104.

WESTFALL, RICHARD S., 'Huygens' rings and Newton's rings: periodicity and seventeenth-century optics', *Ratio*, X (1968), pp.64 – 77.

WESTFALL, RICHARD S., 'Newton and the fudge factor', *Science*, CLXXIX (1973), pp.751 – 8.

ZIGGELAAR, AUGUST, *Le physicien Iqnace Gaston Pardies S. J. (1636 – 1673). Acta historica scientiarum naturalium, edidit Bibliotheca Universitatis Hauniensis*, vol. 26, Odense, 1971.

Corrections

p.7, l.14: *for* 212 *read* 209

p.30, l.1: realize

p.31, l.32: straightway

p.38, l.25: realized

p.46, n.4, l.5: *for* 55ff *read* 57f

p.55, n.34, l.22: Arabic text

p.97, l.21: $\frac{n}{m}$

p.100, n.10, l.8: *Lichts*

p.123, l.29: *for* continue *read* constitute

p.148, l.30: This way

p.243, l.22: who ever

p.244, n.22, l.8: *for* with *read* from

p.275, l.17: *for* has *read* had

p.300, n.9, l.2: *for* 37 *read* 237

p.311, n.25, l.4: streight

p.311, n.25, l.19: *for* been have *read* have been

p.314, n.34, l.2: *for* 308f *read* 302f

p.347, col.A, l.40: Suzanne

p.353, col.B, l.2: *Sciences,* 2 vols.

p.355, col.A, l.33: Suzanne

p.360, col.B, l.32: *Principia* (Newton)

p.361, col.A, l.36: *for* 113 – 16 *read* 131 – 2

Index